FIFTH BOOK OF
Junior Authors
& Illustrators

EDITED BY SALLY HOLMES HOLTZE

THE H. W. WILSON COMPANY • NEW YORK 1983

Library of Congress Cataloging in Publication Data

Main entry under title:

Fifth book of junior authors & illustrators.

   Continues: Fourth book of junior authors &
illustrators.
   Includes index.
   1. Children's literature—Bio-bibliography.
2. Illustrated books, Children's—Bio-bibliography.
I. Holtze, Sally Holmes.   II. Fourth book of junior
authors & illustrators.
PN1009.A1F47   1983   809.89282   83-21828
ISBN 0-8242-0694-0

FIFTH BOOK OF

Junior Authors
& Illustrators

The Junior Book of Authors
More Junior Authors
Third Book of Junior Authors
Fourth Book of Junior Authors & Illustrators
Fifth Book of Junior Authors & Illustrators

Preface

THE FIRST VOLUME in the Junior Authors and Illustrators series was published in 1935, and in her introduction to it Effie L. Power, Director of Work with Children for the Cleveland Public Library, wrote, "The expansion of children's literature into a broader field, progress in socialized methods in teaching and the continuing influence of school and public libraries have brought about an added zest for books and reading among our young people."

Now, nearly fifty years later, interest in children's literature continues stronger than ever, with college courses offered by departments of psychology, education, and English. Thousands of students are learning about the history of books for children, the influence of and trends in publishing for children, and such issues as censorship and the representation of members of minority groups in children's books. The Junior Authors and Illustrators series is a useful tool to scholars, but, as always, its most important service is to children. Like Effie Power's patrons, today's young readers want to know more about authors and illustrators than can be written on a book jacket. They can discover in the present volume, for instance, that science writer D. S. Halacy has a solar-powered pocket calculator, or that novelist Diana Wynne Jones likes to tell fortunes, or that Helen M. Hoover absent-mindedly put a coffeepot in the freezer while plotting a novel. Some authors and illustrators chose to reveal more serious thoughts. Mildred Ames writes that in life, "the drones are the heroes"; David Kherdian states simply, "a poet cannot make a living in America"; and Robert Westall tells a moving, direct tale of love and loss. Abounding with anecdote and personal observation, the volumes in the Junior Author and Illustrators Series provide young readers with a direct way of learning more about their favorite authors and books. At the same time, the Series provides librarians and teachers with access to information that will help pique the interest of children in reading.

The Series. As already noted, *The Junior Book of Authors*, edited by Stanley J. Kunitz and Howard Haycraft, was first published in 1935. A revised edition was published in 1951. *More Junior Authors*, edited by Muriel Fuller, was published in 1963. The *Third Book of Junior Authors*, edited by Doris de Montreville and Donna Hill and published in 1972, introduced to the series the lists of selected works and of references to other biographical material that appear at the end of each sketch. The *Third Book* was also the first to contain a cumulative index to the entire series, a feature that has been continued in subsequent volumes. While the first three volumes included many sketches of illustrators, it was not until the publication in 1978 of the *Fourth Book of Junior Authors and Illustrators*, edited by Doris de Montreville and Elizabeth D. Crawford, that the word "Illustrators" was incorporated into its title, reflecting recognition of the contribution of artwork to children's literature.

The *Fifth Book of Junior Authors and Illustrators* comprises 239 sketches of authors and illustrators who have come to prominence since the publication of the previous volume. From a file of several thousand names, the editor compiled a preliminary list of 750 authors and illustrators. As the basis for selection to this list, several aspects of a candidate's work were considered: awards and honors won; the recommendations of reviews and criticism and the appearance of titles on recommended lists; and popularity. An advisory committee of children's and young adult literature specialists was chosen to vote on names from the preliminary list and was invited to suggest additional names. The committee and the editor voted for approximately 250 names, and at least four votes were required in order for a name to be included on the final list. The committee consisted of Jane Botham, Coordinator of Children's Services, Milwaukee Public Library; Mary Mehlman Burns, Coordinator, Curriculum Library and Children's Literature Specialist, Framingham (Massachusetts) State College; Margaret N. Coughlan, Reference Specialist in Children's Literature, Library of Congress; Caroline W. Field, Coordinator, Office of Work with Children, The Free Library of Philadelphia; Barbara H. Fischer, Coordinator of Children's Services, Wichita (Kansas) Public Library; Jack Forman, Reference/Bibliographic Services, Mesa College Library, San Diego, California; and M. Jean Greenlaw, Associate Professor, College of Education, North Texas State University.

Sketches are arranged in alphabetical order by that version of an author's or illustrator's name appearing most often on title pages. The index provides cross references for all names and pen names, not only in this volume but in the earlier volumes of the Series as well. Phonetic pronunciations of names are given whenever necessary. When authors and illustrators have omitted from their sketches important information about themselves, such as awards or degrees, editorial additions follow their autobiographical sketches. When biographical sources disclosed contradictory information, every possible attempt was made to obtain the correct information, including checking with the biographee. As in previous volumes, most sketches include a photograph. Many authors and illustrators were willing to permit their signature to appear.

There are so many awards and prizes given to children's books and their creators that editorial decisions had to be made to include only those that would be of greatest interest to readers. In particular, awards voted upon by children from selected lists of books were omitted—not because the popularity of the books with their intended audience is not valued or considered, but because of the unusual rules of eligibility for most of these awards.

Because of space limitations, the SELECTED WORKS sections may not be a complete list of all of the books produced by a writer or artist; we have tried to include those books that have received particularly favorable attention or that are representative of an author's or illustrator's work, even if a title is out of print. Books published for adults and books not published in the U.S. are not listed in SELECTED WORKS. The ABOUT sections provide biographical references to books and articles that are likely to be generally available and that are in English. For the most part, articles that are strictly critical have not been included.

When it has been impossible to obtain autobiographical material, biographical sketches have been supplied. When a sketch has been written by someone who knew the subject personally or who is an authority on his or her work, credit is given the writer in the heading of the sketch. Otherwise, sketches were written anonymously by the editor and by Sharon Ann Bart, Linda C. Falken, Joan L. Frongello, Betsy Groban, Dorcas Hand, Karen Jameyson, Jean E. Karl, Karen M. Klockner, Patricia

McMahon, Amy Meeker, Karen Gray Miller, Hazel Rochman, Amy Rolnick, Nancy Sheridan, Anita Lynne Silvey, and Roger Sutton.

Lastly, the editor would like to acknowledge the many people who have helped in the preparation of the book. These include the editors, library promotion departments, and publicity departments of many publishing companies; Linda Essig and the staff of the Denver Public Library Central Children's Room, where much of the research was done; the staff of the Children's Book Council; the staff of the reference collection of the Horn Book, Inc.; and the staff of the Beatley Library of Simmons College, Boston. The editor is also grateful to Mary Mehlman Burns, to Pamela D. Pollack, and to Kate Waters for their judgment and advice; Beryl B. Beatley, Ann A. Flowers, and Sarah L. Rueter for their helpful suggestions of additions to the preliminary list of names; to the members of the advisory committee for their hard work and careful consideration; to the staff of The H. W. Wilson Company, especially Bruce R. Carrick, Editor of General Publications.

Above all, the editor appreciates the contributions of the authors and illustrators who took the time from their work to compose sketches and who, gratifyingly often, expressed their pleasure in being able to write a few words directly to their readers.

SALLY HOLMES HOLTZE
September 1, 1983

Contents

Fifth Book of Junior Authors and Illustrators

VERNA AARDEMA

June 6, 1911–

AUTHOR OF *Why Mosquitoes Buzz in People's Ears,* etc.

Autobiographical sketch of Verna Aardema Vugteveen:

I GOT TO BE a writer by default—the fault being that I was a born bookworm in a household that desperately needed Mother's Little Helpers. I was third among the nine children of Alfred and Dora Norberg, in the little town of New Era, Michigan. It was such a big family that, to our mother, help with the housework was a matter of survival. But in order to get me to do anything in the house, she first had to get me away from my book.

What made matters worse was that my younger sister, Sally, was such a good worker! When I was eleven and Sally was nine, we had to do the supper dishes every night. Sally would get the dishes all washed and be gone from the kitchen before I had made an impression on the pile on the drainboard.

With Sally gone, I'd finish at my own speed. I'd take a dish, cross over to the kitchen stool, sit down and wipe and wipe until evaporation took over. Sometimes I'd hear my father say, "Where's Verna?" And Sally would answer, "She's still drying the dishes." Then I'd cringe with embarrassment and drag myself off the stool to go get another dish.

I felt that I was a great disappointment to my parents. That was my status in the family when I got an *A* on a poem I had written

Verna Aardema

at school. When Mama read it, she said, "Why, Verna! You're going to be a writer, just like my grandfather!"

That was the first time I can recall being noticed for any good reason. Mama made such a wonderful fuss that I decided to make a career of being like my great-grandfather.

Mama understood about writers needing time and a quiet place in which to think. There wasn't a quiet corner in our house. It seems Great-grandfather had had the same problem. He had done his thinking while walking through the country. That didn't appeal to me. But it didn't take me long to discover that a visit to the cedar swamp, which we could see from our kitchen window, could be passed off as practicing to become a writer.

I found that, at dishwashing time, I could get away with taking a couple of dishes from the dining table out to the kitchen, and then flying out the back door. I would hear Mama say, "Let her go. She's going to the swamp." Mama knew that I sometimes told stories to the neighborhood kids back there in the swamp, and she thought the swamp was a good place for a bookworm to hatch into a writer.

It really was in a dark secret room of that swamp that I made up my first stories. I would sit on a log, dig my heels into the spongy black earth and think and think, until I'd think my sisters must be finished with the dishes. Soon I began writing down the stories I thought of in the swamp, and asking God to help me become as good a writer as Gene Stratton-Porter.

At Michigan State College, I won three writing contests during my senior year. After college, I taught school for twenty-four years, and was a staff correspondent for *The Muskegon Chronicle* for twenty-one years—concurrently. In 1973, I retired from teaching and from the newspaper, and now I have become just the writer and storyteller I hoped to become when I was eleven.

In 1936, I married Albert Aardema. He died in 1974, and the next year, I married Dr. Joel Vugteveen. He also had grown up in our little town of New Era. I have two children, Dr. Austin Aardema and Paula Dufford, and four grandchildren.

———

Verna Aardema's interest in Africa has led her to specialize in writing tales set in that continent. *Why Mosquitoes Buzz in People's Ears,* illustrated by Leo and Diane Dillon, won the 1976 Randolph Caldecott Medal and the Brooklyn Art Books for Children award in 1977. Several of her works have beeen designated Notable Books by the American Library Association, and *Who's in Rabbit's House* was placed on the 1978 list of the Lewis Carroll Shelf Awards. Aardema also recieved the Children's Reading Round Table Award in 1981. Her books have been published in Japan, France, England, and South Africa, and a number have been adapted for television, recordings, and filmstrips.

SELECTED WORKS: Tales from the Story Hat, 1960; More Tales from the Story Hat, 1966; Tales for the Third Ear from Equatorial Africa, 1969; Behind the Back of the Mountain: Black Folktales from Southern Africa, 1973; Why Mosquitoes Buzz in People's Ears: A West African Tale, 1975; Who's in Rabbit's House?, 1977; Ji-Nongo-Nongo Means Riddles, 1978; The Riddle of the Drum, 1979; Half-a-Ball-of-Kenki, 1979; Bringing the Rain to Kapiti Plain, 1981; What's So Funny, Ketu?: A Nuer Tale, 1982.

ABOUT: Contemporary Authors, Vol. 7-8; (First Revision), Vol. 5-8; Something About the Author, Vol. 4; Ward, Martha E. and Dorothy A. Marquardt. Authors of Books for Young People, 2nd edition (Supplement); Who's Who of American Women; The Writers Directory 1982–84; Junior Libraries November 1960; Language Arts February 1969; (as Verna Aardema Vugteveen) Contemporary Authors (New Revision Series), Vol. 3.

JAN ADKINS

November 7, 1944–

AUTHOR AND ILLUSTRATOR of *The Art and Industry of Sandcastles,* etc.

Biographical sketch of Jan Adkins:

JAN ADKINS was born in Gallipolis, Ohio. He grew up in Ohio, attending public schools and graduating from high school in 1961. For the next eight-and-a-half years he studied architecture and literature at Ohio State University, graduating in 1969. During his college years he worked as an architectural designer for a firm in Columbus. Adkins describes his main college activities, however, as "roistering, gamboling, [and] feckless and madcap antics."

Following college, Adkins moved east and taught fifth-grade math and science for a year in Mattapoisett, Massachusetts. Subsequently, from 1974 to 1976, he was the art director and vice president of Buzzard, Inc., an advertising agency in Cambridge,

Massachusetts. Eventually, he settled in Marion, Massachusetts, doing free-lance work from a studio in his home, and frequently sailing his boat out of Marion Harbor into Buzzard's Bay. Over the years, Adkins has done a variety of work—including construction, sheet metal shopwork, sign painting, guiding, and radio commercials—but the focus of his career has been writing and illustrating, lecturing, and consulting as a graphic designer.

Describing himself as a "professional looker and learner," a "professional explainer," and a "catcher-in-the-rye by vocation," Adkins has made a career of learning about the things that fascinate him and then presenting the information to his readers in clear and intricate detail.

He is perhaps best known for his picture books, which he writes, designs, and illustrates. The publisher says on the jacket flap of *The Art and Industry of Sandcastles:* "[Jan Adkins] drew and lettered *everything* in this book. Except he was nice enough to let us have this part of the book to write on." In his picture books, Adkins has explored such subjects as symbols, sailing, woodworking, lettering, building houses, and sandcastles. Zena Sutherland, of *The Bulletin of the Cen-*

ter for Children's Books, has described *Toolchest* as "a fine piece of craftsmanship, both in example and execution" and *The Craft of Sail* as "an excellent book on sailing . . . packed with information."

Most of Adkins's work has been nonfiction, but *Wooden Ship,* an account of the building and design of a nineteenth-century whaling ship, interweaves a story with nonfiction events. His first full-length work of fiction, *A Storm Without Rain*—which is the story of a boy growing up in Marion, Massachusetts, who travels back in time to share his grandfather's boyhood—was published in 1983. The *Horn Book* calls it "remarkable," to be considered "fantasy, an excursion into history, or a moving study of the relationship between generations."

Adkins has won many awards for his work, including the Brooklyn Museum art citations three times, in 1972, 1973, and 1974. *The Art and Industry of Sandcastles* was a National Book Award nominee in 1972 and earned a Lewis Carroll Shelf Award in 1973. His work was included in the Children's Book Showcase exhibit, in 1974 for *Toolchest* and in 1976 for *Inside;* and *Moving Heavy Things* received a New York Academy of Sciences Children's Science Book Award in 1981.

Adkins's books for adults also cover an impressive range of subjects: winemaking, wood stoves, energy conservation, wood, and more. He has written articles for *Harper's, The Smithsonian, Woodenboat, Sail, Cricket,* and *The Mother Earth News.*

Adkins has a daughter Sally, from his marriage to Deborah Kiernan, who died in 1976. He married Dorcas Sheldon Peirce, a carpenter and a potter, in 1977. With her son, Robbie, and the child they had together, Samuel Ulysses, they are the parents of three children. Jan Adkins and his family currently live in Washington, D.C., where Adkins is the assistant art director of *National Geographic* magazine.

Selected Works Written and Illustrated: The Art and Industry of Sandcastles, 1971; How a House

Happens, 1972; The Craft of Sail, 1973; Toolchest: A Primer of Woodcraft, 1973; The Bakers: On Making Bread, 1975; Inside: Seeing Beneath the Surface, 1975; Luther Tarbox, 1977; Moving on: Stories of Four Travelers, 1978; Symbols: A Silent Language, 1978; Wooden Ship, 1978; Heavy Equipment, 1980; Moving Heavy Things, 1980; Letterbox: The Art and History of Letters, 1981; A Storm Without Rain, 1983.

SELECTED WORKS ILLUSTRATED: Chains, Webs and Pyramids: The Flow of Energy in Nature, by Laurence Pringle, 1975.

ABOUT: Contemporary Authors, Vol. 33–36; Kingman, Lee and others, comps. Illustrators of Children's Books: 1967–1976; Something About the Author, Vol. 8; Ward, Martha E. and Dorothy A. Marquardt. Authors of Books for Young People, 2nd edition (Supplement); Who's Who in the East, 1977–1978; Language Arts May 1980.

ALLAN AHLBERG

ALLAN AHLBERG

June 5, 1938–

and

JANET AHLBERG

October 21, 1944–

AUTHORS AND ILLUSTRATORS OF *Each Peach Pear Plum,* etc.

Biographical sketch of Allan and Janet Ahlberg:

JANET AND ALLAN Ahlberg were born and raised in England. They met at the Sunderland College of Education near Newcastle, Northumberland, where both were studying to become teachers—a career Janet never pursued. Instead she went on to study graphic design and became an illustrator. Allan has had a variety of occupations in addition to teacher, including mailman, grave-digger, soldier, plumber's helper, and, now, full-time writer—"the best job I have so far come upon!" he says.

The Ahlbergs devote most of their time

JANET AHLBERG

to creating books, Allan writing the text and Janet doing the illustrations. "The tale is not in the typescript or the pictures but in the way the two go together . . . a marriage of words and pictures." This is how they describe their vision of the process that has made their books remarkably successful since their first collaboration, *The Brick Street Boys,* published in England in 1975.

They see their work as inseparable, and speak of themselves as picture book "makers" rather than as an independent author and artist. They continually talk out and modify ideas together, and concern themselves equally and meticulously with each detail of the book, from the text and illustrations themselves to things like type size, margins, and jacket copy. As critic Aidan Chambers wrote in the *Horn Book*, " . . . their books certainly possess that integrated relationship between words and pictures usually achieved only when writer and illustrator are the same—one person."

Janet and Allan Ahlberg live in Leicester, England, with their young daughter Jessica, who is already providing them with ideas for books. One of their most recent picture book collaborations, *The Baby's Catalogue,* was inspired by the observation that, like many babies, Jessica's preferred reading material was mail-order catalogues advertising anything from motorcycles to gardening equipment. Why not a catalogue especially for young children, they reasoned, and went on to produce a collection of the familiar people, objects, and activities that make up a baby's world. It was a bestseller in England.

The Ahlbergs' special ability to create books for the very young child has also resulted in *Peek-A-Boo! (Peepo!* in England), based on the classic game babies love, and in the highly acclaimed *Each Peach Pear Plum: An "I-Spy" Story* in which the reader, searching for clues in the pictures, helps create the story as he reads. *Peek-A-Boo!* and *Each Peach Pear Plum* were chosen American Library Association Notable Books in the U.S., and in England *Each Peach Pear Plum* won the Kate Greenaway Medal in 1978. *Mrs. Plug the Plumber,* in the Wacky Families series, won the Other Award in 1980.

SELECTED WORKS WRITTEN BY ALLAN AHLBERG AND ILLUSTRATED BY JANET AHLBERG: Burglar Bill, 1977; Cops and Robbers, 1979; Funnybones, 1981; Mr. Biff the Boxer, 1982; Mrs. Wobble the Waitress, 1982.

SELECTED WORKS WRITTEN AND ILLUSTRATED BY JANET AND ALLAN AHLBERG: The Brick Street Boys, 1975; The Old Joke Book, 1977; Jeremiah in the Dark Woods, 1978; Each Peach Pear Plum: An I-Spy Story, 1979; Peek-a-Boo!, 1981; The Baby's Catalogue, 1983.

SELECTED WORKS WRITTEN AND ILLUSTRATED BY JANET AHLBERG: The Vanishment of Thomas Tull, 1977.

WORKS WRITTEN BY ALLAN AHLBERG: Master Salt the Sailor's Son, 1982; Mrs. Lather's Laundry, 1982; Miss Brick the Builder's Baby, 1982; Mr. and Mrs. Hay the Horse, 1982; Mr. Buzz the Beeman, 1982; Mrs. Plug the Plumber, 1982.

ABOUT: (Janet Ahlberg) Graphis No. 200, 1979.

HARRY ALLARD

January 27, 1928–

AUTHOR OF *The Stupids Die,* etc.

Biographical sketch of Harry Allard:

HARRY ALLARD was born in Evanston, Illinois, on January 27—the same birthday, he is fond of pointing out, as Mozart and Lewis Carroll. After growing up in California, Long Island, and Chicago, Allard graduated from Northwestern College in 1948. After college he entered the Signal Corps of the U.S. Army and was sent to Korea. On his release from active duty, he lived and worked in Paris for three years before returning to the United States, where he earned his master's degree in French from Middlebury College in 1960. After another year in France, Allard came back to teach, first in Virginia, then in Texas. From 1965 to 1968 he attended Yale on a fellowship, then moved to Massachusetts, where he has lived ever since. Allard received his Ph.D. in French from Yale in 1973, and is currently a member of the Foreign Language Department at Salem State College in Massachusetts.

After his move to Charlestown, Massachusetts, Harry Allard met James Marshall, author and illustrator of the "George and

Martha" books. It was Marshall's art that was the inspiration for Harry Allard's first book, *The Stupids Step Out.* James Marshall provided the illustrations as well as the inspiration for this book, of which critic Gene Shalit of NBC's "Today Show" said, "Of course, kids will adore it; this is one of those special books that could become a cult book."

Aside from James Marshall's art, Allard says there has been no special influence on his work. In fact, he says, "Except for a German edition of Grimms' Tales, I barely read children's books at all. I think it's better not to because if you know too much about someone else's work you might begin to copy without even realizing it."

The Stupids Step Out was followed in 1977 by *Miss Nelson Is Missing,* which was highly praised. *Booklist* said of it: "Rarely has the golden rule been so effectively interpreted for children." The book was a runner-up for a 1977 Edgar Allan Poe Award.

In the same year as *Miss Nelson Is Missing,* Allard's own favorite, *It's So Nice to Have a Wolf Around the House,* was published. Eventually, this book was made into a full-length cartoon feature for television. Three of the books on which Allard and Marshall collaborated have been recognized with honors. *The Stupids Step Out* was included on the *School Library Journal* "Best of the Best 1966–1978" list (December 1979); *I Will Not Go to Market Today* was exhibited in the 1980 American Institute of Graphic Arts show; and *The Tutti-Frutti Case* was named a *New York Times* Best Illustrated Children's Book of the Year 1975.

A lover of animals, Harry Allard has one blind French bulldog named Olga and five cats, including Uncle Boris who is about eighteen years old. Allard enjoys drawing, reading, listening to classical music, and learning languages. He speaks French fluently and reads Spanish and German, and can translate Latin. At present he is learning ancient Greek and working on a horror novel for adults.

SELECTED WORKS: The Stupids Step Out, 1974; The Tutti-Frutti Case, 1975; It's So Nice to Have a Wolf Around the House, 1977; Miss Nelson Is Missing, 1977; The Stupids Have a Ball, 1978; Bumps in the Night, 1979; I Will Not Go to Market Today, 1979; The Stupids Die, 1981; There's a Party at Mona's Tonight, 1981; Miss Nelson Is Back, 1982.

ABOUT: Ward, Martha E. and Dorothy A. Marquardt. Authors of Books for Young People, 2nd edition (Supplement).

MILDRED AMES

November 2, 1919–

AUTHOR OF *Anna to the Infinite Power,* etc.

Autobiographical sketch of Mildred Ames:

FROM THE New Haven railroad one can look down upon the section of Bridgeport, Connecticut, where I grew up. It appears all concrete now with tired old houses and grimy factories. Although never the most beautiful of cities, the place had other riches: a few fine parks, some majestic trees, and streets where old and new Yankees lived side by side, hating, loving, and sometimes learning from each other.

All in all, New England was a good place to grow up. One never forgets the vitality of changing seasons and the awesomeness of weather. I still have that part of my life tucked carefully away in a sturdy trunk in my mind's attic.

I lived in and went through secondary school in Bridgeport during the Great Depression. For my book *The Dancing Madness,* set in 1932, I searched the old trunk and found more than enough memories to evoke the period.

I married during World War II. My husband, Bill, was in the Air Force, so I joined him in Wichita Falls, Texas, where we lived until the war was over. Finally, we settled in the Los Angeles area of California and have been here so many years now that we consider ourselves westerners.

Mildred Ames

Most of my working life was spent in offices, big and small, private and government, tediously keeping the records that allowed the country to get on with its business. If I learned anything from that experience, it's that the drones are the heroes.

When I was a schoolgirl in Connecticut I was an avid reader and, like so many avid readers, thought I'd like to become a writer, but it wasn't until I was forty years old that I decided to seriously give it a try. After the standard mountain of rejection slips for my literary and slick stories, I began to sell confessions. From that apprenticeship, I went on to write a couple of gothic novels, which were published by Thomas Bouregy and Company. By trying a little of everything, I finally found a field I loved, juvenile literature.

People often ask, "How can you write for children when you have no children of your own?" The one fact seems to have nothing to do with the other. My sturdy trunk holds not only pictures from the place where I grew up, but all the emotions, all the joys and sorrows I experienced there. Places may change; the conditions under which we live may change, but emotions never change.

Also, I feel that I just might have something to say to young people. After all, I've lived longer than they have and I've seen more. I would hope that I had learned something of worth to pass on to them.

In a letter, one little girl asked me, "How do you know how children feel?" I was tempted to answer, "Because adults are only big children," but of course I didn't. We grown-ups hate to admit that.

As for what I hope to achieve in my books, I remember a quote from some long ago editor that said: "Make 'em laugh. Make 'em cry. Make 'em wait." I try very hard to follow that advice with yet another requisite of my own: Make 'em think.

———

Two of Mildred Ames's books, *What Are Friends For?* and *Anna to the Infinite Power*, have been adapted for television.

SELECTED WORKS: Is There Life on a Plastic Planet?, 1975; Without Hats, Who Can Tell the Good Guys?, 1976; The Wonderful Box, 1977; What Are Friends For?, 1978; Nicky and the Joyous Noise, 1980; The Dancing Madness, 1980; Anna to the Infinite Power, 1981; Philo Potts, or The Helping Hand Strikes Again, 1982.

ABOUT: Contemporary Authors, Vol. 69-72; Something About the Author, Vol. 22.

MARGARET J. ANDERSON

December 24, 1931–

AUTHOR OF *The Journey of the Shadow Bairns*, etc.

Autobiographical sketch of Margaret Jean Anderson:

I was born in Gorebridge, Scotland, and spent my childhood in Lockerbie where my father was a Presbyterian minister. We lived in a stone house surrounded by a big garden. Beyond the garden were fields and woods. I was the middle child in the family, and we used to go exploring and had many

Margaret J. Anderson

adventures—some real, some imaginary—in the countryside around our home.

I grew up during World II, yet my memories of those years are not unhappy. We became accustomed to the blackout, rationing, army convoys, and evacuees who stayed for a while and then left. We worried as much about homework, teachers, and friends as about the war. I tried to capture some of this feeling in *Searching for Shona*. Writing it was like a journey back to my childhood.

I have always loved reading. There wasn't any children's library in Lockerbie, but we did have lots of books of our own. I read them over and over until the people in those books became my friends. Getting to know the characters better in that second, third, or fourth reading made up for the fact that there were no longer any surprises in the plot! Reading the same book over is a good habit to develop if you're going to be an author. You can learn something about writing that way. I rewrite each of my books several times. While I'm doing this, I get to know the characters better and they become quite real to me. Elspeth and Robbie in *The Journey of the Shadow Bairns* gave me a lot of trouble while I was writing

the book but I missed having them on my mind when the book was finished.

I had always wanted to write, but thought I first needed to see far away and exotic places to write about. So I set off to see the world. In 1955 I emigrated to Canada. But it has turned out that some of the far away and exotic places I have written about have been the part of Scotland I started from!

I worked as a statistician, mostly in biology labs. In 1956 I married Norman Anderson. He is now an entomology professor at Oregon State University in Corvallis. We have four children, Richard, Judy, Susan, and Karen. We all share Norm's interest in insects and the outdoors. This led to my first book, *Exploring the Insect World*.

Even though I now mostly write fiction, my interest in biology and the outdoors is still reflected in my books. Even my interest in insects is useful. In my book *In the Circle of Time* some of the brown people (who live in the future) have insects' Latin names. *Lara avara* is really a small black beetle, but I think the name suits my ten-year-old heroine better.

I've been fortunate to be able to travel with my family, and this has given me some far away and exotic places to write about. *Light in the Mountain* is set on the west coast of New Zealand where the rain forests are beautiful and magical. I find it easier to write about places when I am no longer there. Maybe that's why I live in Oregon but have written several books set in Scotland. Writing a book is like visiting the place you're writing about—but cheaper.

Margaret J. Anderson graduated from the University of Edinburgh with honors in biology and genetics. She wrote articles for *Nature and Science* before writing her first book, *Exploring the Insect World,* which was named an outstanding science book for children by the National Science Teachers Association and the Children's Book Council in 1974. She has also written science articles for such magazines as *Ranger Rick's*

Nature Magazine. Two of her fiction titles, *In the Keep of Time* and *In the Circle of Time,* are two parts of a trilogy, and at this writing she is working on the conclusion.

SELECTED WORKS: Exploring the Insect World, 1974; To Nowhere and Back, 1975; Exploring City Trees and the Need for Urban Forests, 1976; In the Keep of Time, 1977; Searching for Shona, 1978; In the Circle of Time, 1979; The Journey of the Shadow Bairns, 1980; The Brain on Quartz Mountain, 1982; Light in the Mountain, 1982.

ABOUT: Contemporary Authors, Vol. 69-72; Something About the Author, Vol. 27.

JULES ARCHER

January 27, 1915–

AUTHOR OF *You Can't Do That to Me!,* etc.

Autobiographical sketch of Jules Archer:

BORN in New York City, I've been writing since I was six. My father was a printing foreman. I loved the smell of printer's ink and the sight of huge whirring presses. At school teachers used to call me up to tell stories—made up at the spur of the moment—to the class, while they corrected papers. My Dad proudly printed copies of poems I wrote (the first at age six). At thirteen I wrote long letters to the New York *World-Telegram,* which were featured with big headlines on the editorial page. (The editors didn't know I was just a kid with a compulsion to write.)

At DeWitt Clinton High School I was feature editor of the school magazine and newspaper. Graduating at sixteen during the Depression, I went to work as an office boy while attending night college and writing stories half the night. I finally got jobs writing advertising copy, and publicity for Universal Pictures. At twenty-three I quit work, took all my savings and spent a summer biking around Europe, staying at youth hostels.

I sold a number of stories in my spare time, which was also devoted to skiing and shooting rapids. When Pearl Harbor launched us into the Second World War, I spent four years in Australia, New Guinea, and the Philippines as an Air Corps Master Sergeant and war correspondent. I married an Australian girl, who died in 1975. We had three sons—a paleontologist, a professor of social psychology, and a doctor.

After the war I worked in Hollywood for six months, then went back to Australia to write for a similar period. For the next thirty years I wrote over a thousand stories and articles for magazines, and over sixty books, from my home in upstate New York. Many of the books were for young adults. I began writing in this field because I was unhappy with the books given to my sons to read in school. Many were shallow, only partially true, and left out many facts to conceal the sins of our government, such as our shameful treatment of the Indians (see my book *Indian Foe, Indian Friend*).

Because I never write down to young people in my books, many of them are also read by adults. I pull no punches, tell both sides of controversial subjects, and let readers make up their own minds. I do not believe, "My country, right or wrong." I believe in the truth. Concealment of the truth made possible the dreadful war in Vietnam.

After my wife died I moved to Santa Cruz, California, trading my skiing for roller-skating along the Pacific. When I'm not writing or playing chess, I teach a course called "Writing for Publication" at the University of California, Santa Cruz Extension. I also continue to take trips around the world to seek out the unusual and interesting, which sooner or later I get around to writing about.

On a recent trip to the Pacific I explored the sensations of flying in a glider over Oahu, sailing in a two-master at sunset in Maui, observing the murder trial of an Aborigine in Australia, boating in a glowworm cave in New Zealand, and snorkeling the coral reefs in Tahiti and Moorea. On a previous trip to Rumania and the Soviet Union, I was arrested in Bucharest for "fraternizing."

All is grist for the writer's mill.

At present I'm working on a new book, *Jungle Fighters: The New Guinea Campaign,* about the campaign I fought in, which was the turning point of the Second World War in the Pacific. Writing it is like vividly reliving the experiences of forty years ago.

———

Biographer and historian Archer studied advertising at the College of the City of New York (now called the City College of the City University of New York). His interest in biographical subjects such as Roy Chapman Andrews has led him to write from unpublished, original records. His stories and articles have appeared in *Esquire, Family Circle, Redbook, Playboy, Cosmopolitan, The New Republic,* and other magazines, and many have been translated into other languages. Some of his work has been reprinted by the U.S. Department of State for distribution overseas. With the late editor of *Variety,* Abel Green, he wrote *Show Biz,* a book for adults. *Epidemic!* received honorable mention in the Children's Science Book Awards of the New York Academy of Sciences, in 1977.

SELECTED WORKS: Indian Foe, Indian Friend: The Story of William S. Harney, 1970; The Philippines' Fight for Freedom, 1970; Ho Chi Minh: The Legend of Hanoi, 1971; China in the Twentieth Century, 1974; Washington vs. Main Street: The Struggle Between Federal and Local Power, 1975; Watergate: America in Crisis, 1975; From Whales to Dinosaurs: The Story of Roy Chapman Andrews, 1976; Epidemic!: The Story of the Disease Detectives, 1977; Police State: Could It Happen Here?, 1977; Superspies: The Secret Side of the Government, 1977; You and the Law, 1978; Who's Running Your Life?: A Look at Young People's Rights, 1979; You Can't Do That to Me: Famous Fights for Human Rights, 1980.

ABOUT: Contemporary Authors (First Revision), Vol. 9-12; International Authors and Writers Who's Who, 1977; Something About the Author, Vol. 4; Ward, Martha E. and Dorothy A. Marquardt. Authors of Books for Young People, 2nd edition; The Writers Directory 1982-84; Library Journal May 15, 1970; June 15, 1970; September 1970; New York Times Book Review November 3, 1968.

RICHARD ARMOUR

July 15, 1906–

AUTHOR OF *A Dozen Dinosaurs,* etc.

Autobiographical sketch of Richard Willard Armour:

I SOMETIMES say I wear two costumes: cap-and-gown and cap-and-bells. Wearing cap-and-gown (figuratively), I took a Ph.D. in English Philology at Harvard, was a professor of English at several colleges and universities, did research in England and France on various fellowships, and wrote the necessary number of scholarly publish-or-perish books. Also I had the unusual experiences of being on the faculty of the University of Freiburg in Germany during Hitler's first year in power, being a member of the War Department General Staff in World War II, and later lecturing in twenty countries of Europe and Asia for the State Department.

Still wearing cap-and-gown, or being a

scrambled egghead, I have written a couple of shelves of books of humor and satire on a wide variety of subjects in prose and light verse. Combining lightness and enlightenment, books such as *It All Started with Columbus, Twisted Tales from Shakespeare,* and *The Classics Reclassified* have been popular with high school and college students. Three of my books of prose humor-satire have been aimed at education, and I bit the hand that for forty years fed me.

I began writing books for young readers (which I hope are also read by old or older readers) rather late in life. It was not until I had completed my graduate work at Harvard, married a girl with whom I had gone through school from first grade through college, returned to Southern California, where I was born, to continue college teaching, and written numerous books and several thousand magazine pieces of humor and satire—only then, that I wrote my first book for children.

Reading books to my children before they were old enough to read, and enjoying the books they enjoyed, made me wish I could write books for young readers.

My first book for children, *The Year Santa Went Modern,* was written as a Christmas feature for *Family Circle* and then revised and published as a book. It was illustrated by the talented Paul Galdone, who has done the beautiful and appropriate drawings for ten of my fourteen junior books.

And yet we have never met. He and I live across the country from one another. He lives part of the year on his farm in New Hampshire and part of the year on his farm in upstate New York, while I live in the six-college town of Claremont in Southern California. Our editor, in New York City, is our intermediary.

My earliest books for children, such as *The Adventures of Egbert the Easter Egg,* were fanciful narratives—in verse and with a touch of humor. Later I began what was to become my specialty: playful-factual books, again in verse, in such fields as paleontology, biology, marine biology, cetology, and entomology, from *A Dozen Dinosaurs* to *Insects All Around Us.*

To make sure of the correctness of facts, I used general and special libraries and picked the brains of specialists in the various fields. These scientists suggested the many books I should read, answered my questions about what I did not understand, and checked every word to catch any errors. For some years now, I have entered field after field with an empty mind and emerged as an amateur expert.

I try to do several things at once in these factual books: select what I think will be of most interest, introduce some humor into what is usually presented seriously, and write in verse. Young readers, I have found, like lilting meter and unusual rhymes. They also like an occasional big-funny word. I hope I send children, and even their parents, to the dictionary now and then.

With my fourteen books for children and fifty-eight books in all, I may have more quantity than quality. But I try my best every time, with much adding, cutting, and rewriting. I owe a great debt to writers of the classic books for children, books I read, enjoy, and envy. I am also indebted to my wife (my severest critic), my children, and my grandchildren, with whom I check for favorable or unfavorable response. If they like what I write, perhaps others will too. But I can never be sure.

———

Richard Armour has been a Professor of English and Dean of the Faculty at Scripps College and Claremont Graduate School in California, as well as a Trustee of Claremont Men's College. He is on the editorial board of the *The Writer* and is a member of P.E.N., the Modern Language Association, and the American Association of University Professors. In addition to the titles he mentions in his sketch, some of his other books for adults that adolescents enjoy are *Punctured Poems, American Lit Relit, English Lit Relit,* and *Through Darkest Adolescence, with Tongue in Cheek and Pen in* Checkbook.

SELECTED WORKS: Our Presidents, 1964; The Year Santa Went Modern, 1964; The Adventures of Egbert the Easter Egg, 1965; Animals on the Ceiling, 1966; A Dozen Dinosaurs, 1967; Odd Old Mammals, 1968; On Your Marks: A Package of Punctuation, 1969; All Sizes and Shapes of Monkeys and Apes, 1970; Who's in Holes?, 1971; The Strange Dreams of Rover Jones, 1973; Sea Full of Whales, 1974; Strange Monsters of the Sea, 1979; Insects All Around Us, 1981.

ABOUT: Allen, Everett S. Famous American Humorous Poets; Author's and Writer's Who's Who, 1971; Burke, W. J. and Will D. Howe. American Authors and Books, 1640 to the Present Day, 3rd edition; Contemporary Authors (First Revision), Vol. 1-4; (New Revision Series), Vol. 4; Current Biography, 1958; Directory of American Scholars, 11th edition, Vol. 2; Encyclopedia Americana; Herzberg, Max J. The Reader's Encyclopedia of American Literature; International Authors and Writers Who's Who, 1977; Kirkpatrick, D. L. Twentieth-Century Children's Writers; Something About the Author, Vol. 14; Ward, Martha E. and Dorothy A. Marquardt. Authors of Books for Young People, 2nd edition; Who's Who, 1978; Who's Who in America, 1982; Who's Who in the World, 1978; The Writers Directory 1982-84; Library Journal November 1, 1964.

JIM ARNOSKY

September 1, 1946–

AUTHOR AND ILLUSTRATOR OF *Drawing from Nature,* etc.

Autobiographical sketch of Jim Arnosky:

I HAD no formal art training but learned a great deal from my father, a skilled patent draftsman. I started work in the printing field as a mail boy, worked to trainee in the art department and then up to layout designer. After a hitch in the United States Navy I returned to printing for a while to support my family while I built a modest free-lance art business. In 1972 I left the printing company and began a full-time free-lance business. I began illustrating stories for *Jack & Jill, Ranger Rick,* and *Cricket* magazines. After five years I broke into the children's literature field as an artist and soon was writing and illustrating my own books for children. All of my books stem from my personal experience and observation. I consider myself a naturalist first, an artist second, and a writer third. As Ernest Thompson Seton did before me, I am now encouraging youngsters who will become the future naturalists, outdoorsmen, artists, writers, engineers, and poets. All of which will better the world they live in.

I live in northern Vermont. My wife Deanna and I have two daughters, Michelle and Amber. We grow all our own food, keep bees for honey, and raise sheep for wool, which Deanna spins into yarn for sweaters, hats, and gloves. We also eat lamb and mutton from our own efforts.

I am an avid fisherman. I enjoy walking, gardening, farming, and canoeing. We have a team of Newfoundland dogs that I have trained to pull a sledge. I hope to use them to haul some firewood.

I spend all of my time at home with my family, and around home in the fields and woods. I do much of my writing in our living room and I do my drawing in a room set aside for drawing in the center of our home.

———

Crinkleroot's Animal Tracks and Wildlife Signs and *Moose Baby* were both named outstanding science books of 1979 by a joint committee of the National Science Teachers Association and the Children's Book Council, and *Swim, Little Duck* was a Junior Literary Guild selection.

Drawing from Nature won a Christopher Award in 1983 and was given honorable mention in the older category of the New York Academy of Sciences Children's Science Book Awards. The book was named a Notable Book of 1982 by the American Library Association, and Arnosky will appear in a WGBH (Boston) television series based on the book.

SELECTED WORKS WRITTEN AND ILLUSTRATED: I was Born in a Tree and Raised by Bees, 1977; Nathaniel, 1978; Outdoors on Foot, 1978; Crinkleroot's Animal Tracks and Wildlife Signs, 1979; A Kettle of Hawks and Other Wildlife Groups, 1979; Mudtime and More Nathaniel Stories, 1979; Drawing from Nature, 1982; Freshwater Fish and Fishing, 1982; Mouse Numbers and Letters, 1982; Secrets of a Wildlife Watcher, 1983.

SELECTED WORKS ILLUSTRATED: Fitting In: Animals in Their Habitats, by Melvin and Gilda Berger, 1976; Swim, Little Duck, by Miska Miles, 1976; Small Rabbit, by Miska Miles, 1977; Look!: How Your Eyes See, by Marcel Sislowitz, 1977; Porcupine Baby, by Ber-

niece Freschet, 1978; Possum Baby, by Berniece Freschet, 1978; Moose Baby, by Berniece Freschet, 1979; Joel and the Great Merlini, by Eloise Jarvis McGraw, 1979; Raindrop Stories, by Margaret Bartlett and Preston Bassett, 1981; Up a Tall Tree, by Anne Rockwell, 1981; Shadow Bear, by Joan Marlow, 1981; Chipper's Choices, by Betty Boegehold, 1981; Rocky the Cat, by A. R. Swinnerton, 1981; Wood Duck Baby, by Berniece Freschet, 1983.

ABOUT: Contemporary Authors, Vol. 69-72; Kingman, Lee and others, comps. Illustrators of Children's Books: 1967-1976; Something About the Author. Vol. 22.

RUTH M. ARTHUR

May 26, 1905–March 6, 1979

AUTHOR OF *Requiem for a Princess,* etc.

Biographical sketch of Ruth Mabel Arthur:

BORN in Glasgow, Scotland, Ruth M. Arthur began writing at boarding school. She won first prize for a poem in honor of World War I, and though her family was skeptical of her writing abilities (with the exception of a grandmother who wrote and illustrated privately) she continued to write. Her first publication, in 1923, came when a Glasgow publisher included three of her stories in one of his collections.

Arthur trained as a teacher at the Froebel Training College in London, receiving her diploma in 1926. Returning to Glasgow, she worked in a kindergarten for three years, and continued writing. Her work at this time included both fiction and poetry, which she occasionally presented on radio broadcasts.

Ruth Arthur left Scotland to teach in Essex, England until 1932, when she married a lawyer, Fredrick N. Huggins. She then interrupted her career to raise six children.

When the youngest child was six, Ruth Arthur began to write again, this time for children. Her earliest stories were aimed at children as young as her six-year-old daughter. As her daughter grew older, the

RUTH M. ARTHUR

age group that her books were aimed at progressed as well, until she found her niche in the young adult group. She continued producing these books at the rate of one every year or so until her death in 1979.

Ruth Arthur's books reflect her abiding interest in young adults and the serious problems that face them. She confronted the problem of adoption (*Requiem for a Princess*), new stepparents (*The Little Dark Thorn* and *The Whistling Boy*), interracial families (*Portrait of Margarita*), serious illness (*The Saracen Lamp*), and the death of parents (*My Daughter Nicola* and *Portrait of Margarita*). Her books, however, are not merely "problem" novels.

"I have always been interested in the supernatural," Arthur said, and in her writing she drew upon this interest. In her later novels, for young adults, her female protagonists, who are most often visiting or relocated to a strange environment, become aware of and intertwined with the "living" past around them. Through local legend or a handed-down object such as a doll, a medallion, a portrait, or even through a local song, the characters find themselves involved in the history surrounding them. In her young adult fiction, Arthur tied this su-

pernatural element to the question of young adult problems, in such a way that the knowledge her heroines gain from their encounters with the past usually allows them to see their difficulties in a new light and leads them to the necessary resolution.

Ruth Arthur's love of the country (she once listed country living as one of her avocations), historic homes, and traveling are also reflected in her books. She chose isolated, rural locales such as the coasts of Dorset, Cornwall, and Norfolk, a small island off the coast of Scotland, and the countries of Italy, Malaysia, and Norway as the settings for her books. She liked to choose real, ancient houses as the center of her novels. Margery Gill, who illustrated all of Arthur's later books, would then journey to and sketch the house in order to insure authenticity.

Ruth M. Arthur lived her life surrounded by children: those she taught, her own six children, and finally her numerous grandchildren. She combined her feelings for and interest in them with her belief that "there is magic to be found by those who seek it" to produce over twenty-five books for children and young adults.

A Candle in Her Room and *Requiem for a Princess* were both included on the American Library Association's list, "Notable Children's Books 1940–1970." *Requiem* was also a Junior Literary Guild selection.

SELECTED WORKS: Dragon Summer, 1963; My Daughter Nicola, 1965; A Candle in Her Room, 1966; Requiem for a Princess, 1967; Portrait of Margarita, 1968; The Whistling Boy, 1969; The Saracen Lamp, 1970; The Little Dark Thorn, 1971; The Autumn People, 1973; On the Wasteland, 1975; Miss Ghost, 1979.

ABOUT: Contemporary Authors, Vol. 85–88; (First Revision), Vol. 11–12; (New Revision Series), Vol. 4; The International Authors and Writers Who's Who, 1977; Jones, Cornelia and Olivia R. Way. British Children's Authors: Interviews at Home; Kirkpatrick, D. L. Twentieth-Century Children's Writers; Something About the Author, Vol. 7; Vol. 26; Ward, Martha E. and Dorothy A. Marquardt. Authors of Books for Young People, 2nd edition (Supplement); The Writers Directory 1980–1982; Publishers Weekly March 19, 1979.

AVI

December 23, 1937-

AUTHOR OF *Encounter at Easton,* etc.

Autobiographical sketch of Avi Wortis:

I WAS BORN in the city of New York, upon the island of Manhattan, in 1937. I was a twin. During my first year my family moved to Brooklyn and it was there that I was raised. It was there too that I began school. With a very bright older brother (he started college at the age of fifteen) and an equally bright twin sister (high honors in college) I seemed at best to slog along. Still, at my graduation from elementary school I won the science award.

High school was quite another matter. I virtually flunked out of high school during the first term, not getting a passing grade anywhere, not even for shop. I had many problems too in the private school to which I was hastily sent. Simply put, I could neither write, nor spell. What little grammar I knew I learned, not from school, but from books I had read.

For fortunately I had always been a voracious reader, reading everything and anything. It was important that I lived in a house full of books, and that reading was encouraged. I read comic books, of course, and popular science magazines by the volume. Above all I read books, adventure stories, histories, novels, classics, and plays. There were things I did not completely understand, but I read them all the same.

I had friends, good ones; but I spent a great deal of time by myself, doing things alone, like taking long nighttime walks through the city streets (I don't think I'd do it now). All in all I was caught up in a great deal of thinking, wondering, daydreaming.

Third year in high school marked the turning point. It was then that my English teacher threw up his hands in despair about my writing skills. He insisted I go to a tutor that summer or flunk the course, which meant dismissal from the school. I spent the summer learning to write. Or rather, I

learned to want to write. Perhaps it was stubbornness, but from that time forward I wanted to write in some way, some form. It was the one thing everybody said I could not do.

In the main I taught myself to write, avoiding every English class I could. I hated my low grades, the red-penciled corrections that looked like splattered blood (*my* blood), the frustration of *never* getting anyone to pay attention to what I was trying to say. (In all fairness it *was* hard to see through the mess.) Sometimes I would show people things I wrote, but insisted I had copied them from a book. They paid attention then. Interestingly, when I did get encouragement, and I did, it was from established writers. They never held back their criticism, but they always urged me on.

I didn't really start to write for young people until my own children were born. The two boys loved to hear stories. We played a game in which they would give me a subject ("a glass of water") and I would have to make up the story right then. Out of that game came my first children's book, *Things That Sometimes Happen.*

Once the notion of writing for young people came into my head I never let it go. I

Avi: *AH vee*

loved to do it. I seemed to do it well. I could write about everything I wanted. The books were published. Young people cared for them.

I do believe that young people are special, as fascinating, as complex and compelling as any other person, no matter what age. To make contact with them is a special sort of grace. Young people don't easily take adults into their private world or trust. To be welcomed there is a gift.

Not that it's simple for me to write the books. In fact, though I write a lot, and love to write, it never seems to come with ease. There is always a way to make things better. But when, as a young fellow once wrote to me: "Thank you for putting another book in the world," that kind of thanks makes it all so worthwhile.

———

Avi attended the University of Wisconsin and received a master's degree in Library Science from Columbia University, in 1964. He has been librarian for the Theater Collection of the New York Public Library and a librarian at Trenton State College. He teaches college courses in children's literature and is a member of the Authors Guild and the Mystery Writers of America.

Snail Tale was named one of the Best Books of the Year by the British Book Council in 1973, and *Encounter at Easton* won a 1980 Christopher Award. Two of Avi's books have been runners-up for the Edgar Award of the Mystery Writers of America, *No More Magic* in 1975 and *Emily Upham's Revenge* in 1978.

SELECTED WORKS: Things That Sometimes Happen, 1970; Snail Tale: The Adventures of a Rather Small Snail, 1972; No More Magic, 1975; Captain Grey, 1977; Emily Upham's Revenge or How Deadwood Dick Saved the Banker's Niece: A Massachusetts Adventure, 1978; Night Journeys, 1979; Encounter at Easton, 1980; The History of Helpless Harry: To Which Is Added a Variety of Amusing and Entertaining Adventures, 1980; Man from the Sky, 1980; A Place Called Ugly, 1981; Who Stole the Wizard of Oz?, 1981; Sometimes I Think I Hear My Name, 1982; Shadrach's Crossing, 1983.

ABOUT: (as Avi Wortis) Contemporary Authors, Vol. 69-72; Something About the Author, Vol. 14.

ALICE BACH

April 6, 1942–

AUTHOR OF *The Meat in the Sandwich,* etc.

Biographical sketch of Alice Hendricks Bach:

ALICE BACH was born in New York City and grew up there and in Princeton, New Jersey. She describes herself as a former "preppie"; she attended Dana Hall in Wellesley, Massachusetts, where she set her first novel, *They'll Never Make a Movie Starring Me.* She writes that she is concerned with what happens to teenagers and that she bases her feelings and emotions about adolescence on her own teenage years. "I had a sad adolescence, although most folks didn't know that. I was the class clown, but underneath my wit and fast moves, I was sad with perennial feelings of inadequacy."

In 1963 she graduated from Barnard College, where she changed her major "every few months," finally choosing medieval studies, concentrating on French and Middle English. She worked in book publishing for ten years, at Random House and Harper & Row, before becoming senior editor of books for young readers at Dial Press. In 1972 she left publishing for writing and free-lance editing.

Bach has also been a consultant to the Bedford-Stuyvesant Writers Workshop in Brooklyn from 1973 to 1976 and Adjunct Professor of Creative Writing in New York University's School for Continuing Education from 1977 to 1979. She is a member of the Authors Guild and the C. G. Jung Foundation for Analytical Psychology.

Alice Bach works with teenagers at Riverside Church in New York City, teaching Sunday School and running a college-bound support program for students who

Alice Bach

are usually the first in their families to attend college. She is concerned with many of the interests of her readers, and writes, "I envy kids coming of age in the computer era, and am scheming ways to be able to afford an IBM computer myself. So many of the tedious things we had to learn how to do—arithmetic computation stands out in my mind as a horror—they will be able to shortcut and spend their time and creativity on more challenging projects. Video games bore me, but that may be because I am a lousy player. I look forward to the day when the super computer graphics are linked to more interesting stories. I think the computer-game world is now at the stage of silent movies in the early part of the century."

The sometimes unusual topics of her books frequently reflect her interests or work. The women's movement and its affect on families led her to write *The Meat in the Sandwich*. The insecurity of children in the face of divorce is treated in *A Father Every Few Years. Waiting for Johnny Miracle* was the result of several years of Bach's work with teenage cancer patients at the Sloan-Kettering Institute for Cancer Research in New York City.

Alice Bach has also written books for younger children, including a series about twin bears. She uses a more complex vocabulary than most picture book authors because she wants children to encounter the richness of language and to learn by trying to understand unfamiliar words.

She has received several awards and honors for her writing. The *New York Times* named *Mollie Make-Believe* one of the best books of the year 1974, and *Waiting for Johnny Miracle* was named an American Library Association Notable Book for 1980. Bach received fellowships to attend the MacDowell Colony in 1976 and 1977. She writes book reviews and articles for periodicals like the *New York Times*, the *Village Voice*, the *Christian Science Monitor*, and *Publishers Weekly*.

Alice Bach lives in New York City with her three cats.

SELECTED WORKS: They'll Never Make a Movie Starring Me, 1973; Mollie Make-Believe, 1974; The Meat in the Sandwich, 1975; The Smartest Bear and His Brother Oliver, 1975; The Most Delicious Camping Trip Ever, 1976; A Father Every Few Years, 1977; Grouchy Uncle Otto, 1977; Millicent the Magnificent, 1978; Waiting for Johnny Miracle, 1980; Warren Weasle's Worse Than Measles, 1980; The Grouter Connection, 1983.

ABOUT: Contemporary Authors, Vol. 101; Foremost Women in Communications, 1970; Something About the Author, Vol. 27; Vol. 30; Ward, Martha E. and Dorothy A. Marquardt. Authors of Books for Young People, 2nd edition (Supplement); Publishers Weekly February 24, 1975.

LORNA BALIAN

December 14, 1929-

AUTHOR AND ILLUSTRATOR OF *The Sweet Touch*, etc.

Autobiographical sketch of Lorna Balian:

I WAS BORN in Milwaukee, Wisconsin. My father worked for the telephone compa-

Balian: *BAL yun*

Lorna Balian

ny there so we lived in Milwaukee, and had all of the cultural advantages of a large city. But my father owned a farm his grandfather had homesteaded, located about 100 miles north of Milwaukee. The farm was worked by one or another of my eight uncles, and throughout our childhood my younger sister and I spent weekends and summers there. We were free to roam 360 acres of woods, fields, and a swamp, and mingle with horses, cows, pigs, sheep, chickens, dogs, and cats. Most of the neighbors were relatives, and there was a secure sense of family with many aunts, uncles, and cousins to visit. I enjoyed the best of both worlds—city and country.

My mother died when I was three years old, but I do not remember it being a traumatic occurrence. As a substitute a great-aunt moved in and took over, and my sister and I both adored her. We had an undisciplined childhood, which I think probably fosters creativity.

After graduation from high school in 1948, I attended the Layton School of Art in Milwaukee. After completion of one year there I got a summer job in the art department of a paper products company. I loved the job and it was so educational I decided to stay on, and not return to school.

I met John in art school and we were married in 1950. We bought and renovated an old red brick schoolhouse in the country, and raised six children, four girls and two boys, who are now all grown.

I have loved to draw ever since I can remember, and I did commercial artwork at home to supplement our income. I became interested in children's books when my children were small. We would get stacks of books from the library, and I read to the children every night at bedtime. After reading hundreds of books aloud, I learned the difference between a good book and an indifferent one, and the children's reaction to both was enlightening. My initial interest was in illustrating, but you need a story to illustrate. Since I didn't know anyone who could write the stories, I decided to do it myself, and have been happily doing both ever since. I've concentrated on books for young children because they have more illustrations, and it's an age I have a good rapport with.

I believe books for young children should be entertaining, and not didactic. Children should discover at an early age that reading is fun, if we expect them to be eager readers later in their life.

I remember very clearly my interests and emotions as a young child and the ideas for my stories and illustrations are primarily accumulated bits and pieces of things I recall from my own youth. The experiences I've had with six children have heightened this recall. It is very exciting to create a children's book, and it is essential that the author/illustrator be emotionally involved because that excitement somehow communicates itself to the reader. I can't imagine a more enjoyable occupation. It's been a career that combined easily with being a wife and mother, so I have had the best of those two worlds too.

———

Three of Lorna Balian's books have been Junior Literary Guild selections: *Humbug Rabbit, Humbug Witch,* and *I Love You, Mary Jane. The Sweet Touch* has won three

awards: the Georgia Children's Picture Storybook Award, in 1978; the Colorado Children's Book Award, in 1978; and the University of Wisconsin's Little Archer Award, in 1979.

SELECTED WORKS: Humbug Witch, 1965; I love You, Mary Jane, 1967; The Animal, 1972; Where in the World Is Henry, 1972; Sometimes It's Turkey—Sometimes It's Feathers, 1973; Humbug Rabbit, 1974; The Sweet Touch, 1976; Bah! Humbug?, 1977; A Sweetheart for Valentine, 1979; Leprechauns Never Lie, 1980; Mother's Mother's Day, 1982.

ABOUT: Contemporary Authors, Vol. 53-56; (New Revision Series), Vol. 4; Something About the Author, Vol. 9; Ward, Martha E. and Dorothy A. Marquardt. Authors of Books for Young People, 2nd edition (Supplement); The Writers Dictionary 1982-84.

BETSY GARRETT BANG

July 9, 1912–

TRANSLATOR AND ADAPTER OF *The Old Woman and the Red Pumpkin: A Bengali Folk Tale,* etc.

Biographical sketch of Betsy Garrett Bang:

BETSY BANG was born in South Carolina. After graduating from George Washington University with a B.A. degree in 1933, she attended Johns Hopkins University. In 1937 she received a diploma in Art as Applied to Medicine at Johns Hopkins University School of Medicine. From 1937 to 1940, she was a free-lance surgical illustrator and an illustrator in comparative anatomy at the American Museum of Natural History in New York. In 1940 she married Frederik Barry Bang, a physician. She writes, "We became interested in effects of malnutrition on respiratory infections and worked on these interactions in a program in India directed by my physician husband." The work was done at the Center for Medical Research in Calcutta from 1962 to 1974.

Since 1958, Bang has been a research associate in pathobiology at the School of Hygiene and Public Health at Johns Hopkins

University. She has also been a summer investigator at the Station Biologique at Roscoff in Brittany and the Marine Biological Laboratory at Woods Hole. She has contributed about fifty articles to scientific journals as well as textbook chapters on respiratory anatomy and pathology. She is a member of the American Association for the Advancement of Science and the Marine Biological Association.

Bang is also a past president of Maryland Prisoners Aid Association, and was a member of the police commissioner's advisory panel of the Baltimore Criminal Justice Commission and of the Health and Welfare Council.

Betsy Bang has three children: Kelly, born in 1941; Axel, born in 1946; and Molly, the Molly Garrett Bang who is the author and illustrator of children's books and illustrator of several of Betsy Bang's books. Betsy Bang has translated and adapted tales from Bengali folklore; she writes, "Bengali is one of the most beautiful, expressive and musical of languages and, like all non-mother-tongue languages, is best learned by nursery rhymes and folktales. At first I translated them for sheer fun, and later as vehicles for Molly's sketches of Bengal village life in all its age-old talent for making simple tasks graceful and common implements beautiful." Her daughter Molly visited her parents in Calcutta, and Betsy Bang comments, "We all responded to the magic of story time at dusk when lamps are lit and shadows cloak innumerable beings that are perfectly believable."

School Library Journal calls *The Old Woman and the Rice Thief* an "amusing and beguiling cumulative tale, simply and dramatically told." In a review of *Tuntuni*, which is written in the easy-to-read format, the *Horn Book* calls the humorous tales "Excellent traditional material to enrich the bland reading diet of young readers."

SELECTED WORKS TRANSLATED AND ADAPTED: The Old Woman and the Red Pumpkin: A Bengali Folk Tale, 1975; Tuntuni, the Tailor Bird: Adapted from a Bengali Folktale, 1978; The Demons of Rajpur: Five Tales from Bengal, 1980.

SELECTED WORKS ADAPTED: The Cucumber Stem: Adapted from a Bengali Folktale, 1980.

SELECTED WORKS TRANSLATED: The Old Woman and the Rice Thief, 1978.

ABOUT: Contemporary Authors, Vol. 102.

MOLLY GARRETT BANG

December 29, 1943–

AUTHOR AND ILLUSTRATOR OF *The Grey Lady and the Strawberry Snatcher*, etc.

Biographical sketch of Molly Garrett Bang-Campbell, who writes under the pen names "Garrett Bang" and "Molly Bang":

MOLLY GARRETT BANG was born in Princeton, New Jersey, and spent her childhood in Baltimore, Maryland. Her father was a research physician and her mother, Betsy Bang, is a medical researcher, a translator, and the author of several books that her daughter illustrated. As a child, Molly Bang remembers discovering and loving the Arthur Rackham books in her parents'

collection and, after that, always wanting to illustrate children's books.

Molly Bang brings a varied educational and cultural background to her work as a reteller, translator, and illustrator. She graduated from Wellesley College in 1965 with a degree in French, but not wanting to be a French teacher, she went to Japan to live for eighteen months to teach English at Doshisha University in Kyoto. Bang chose Japan because of her knowledge of Japanese art. Wanting to further her study in this area, she returned to the United States to study at the University of Arizona and Harvard University for master's degrees in Oriental Studies.

Next, she lived in Calcutta and Bangladesh for ten months, illustrating health manuals for rural health projects for both UNICEF and the Johns Hopkins Center for Medical Research and Training. Then, after spending a year in Mali, working as a civil servant, she went back again to illustrating manuals for village health workers and midwives, using local folktales as a basis for instruction.

Bang's picture books have been well received; *Wiley and the Hairy Man* was named a Notable Book by the American Library Association in 1976, and *The Grey Lady and the Strawberry Snatcher* was a Caldecott Honor Book in 1981. It was also a Boston Globe-Horn Book Award Honor Book and it was included in the 1980 American Institute of Graphic Arts show. Despite eventual recognition of her work, Bang had a difficult time breaking into book illustration, having first been told that there was no market for her work. The reasons she was given was that no one wrote the way she illustrated—that her work was too scary, and too much in the Japanese manner. Bang then compiled her own collection of scary stories that would suit her style of illustration, which became her first published work, *The Goblins Giggle and Other Stories.* It was followed by a second book, *Men from the Village Deep in the Mountains,* a translation of stories she knew from her time in Japan, and which she illustrated in the Japanese Sumi style.

Bang continued to concentrate on illustrating a variety of folktales mostly derived from her experiences in Asia, and collaborated on four books with her mother, who translated and adapted the Indian and Bengali tales. With the exception of *Tye May and the Magic Brush,* which is set in China, Molly Bang has visited all the places from which her stories are drawn. Her strong sense of geographical place and of the culture and the art of each country brings an authenticity to her retellings as well as her illustrations.

For *Wiley and the Hairy Man,* a conjure tale that she adapted from a black American folktale, Bang spent three months riding around the South on a motorcycle in order to understand the area and the people from which the story grew. *The Grey Lady and the Strawberry Snatcher* is a wordless picture book in which the principal characters engage in a game of chase and hide, often eluding the reader, who must decipher where the figures are in the landscape that continually envelops them. Although it is an original tale, the book echoes the folk motifs of her earlier work.

Ten Nine Eight, a warm, comfortable counting book that ends with a child safe in bed, is a departure from her previous work, but *Dawn* represents a return to Bang's interest in folktales. An adaptation of a Japanese tale, "The Crane Wife," is retold and set in 1850s America and the crane is replaced by a Canadian goose.

Bang lives in Woods Hole on Cape Cod in Massachusetts with her husband Richard Campbell, an acoustical engineer, and her daughter Monika.

SELECTED WORKS WRITTEN AND ILLUSTRATED (AS MOLLY BANG): The Grey Lady and the Strawberry Snatcher, 1980; Ten Nine Eight, 1983.

SELECTED WORKS ADAPTED AND ILLUSTRATED: Wiley and the Hairy Man: Adapted from an American Folktale, 1976; Tye May and the Magic Brush: Adapted from the Chinese, 1981; Dawn, 1983.

SELECTED WORKS TRANSLATED AND ILLUSTRATED (AS GARRETT BANG): Men from the Village Deep in the Mountains and Other Japanese Folk Tales, 1977.

SELECTED WORKS ILLUSTRATED: The Goblins Giggle and Other Stories, 1973; The Buried Moon and Other Stories, 1977.

SELECTED WORKS ILLUSTRATED (TRANSLATED AND ADAPTED BY BETSY BANG): The Old Woman and the Red Pumpkin: A Bengali Folk Tale, 1975; The Old Woman and the Rice Thief, 1978; Tuntuni, the Tailor Bird: Adapted from a Bengali Folktale, 1978; The Demons of Rajpur: Five Tales from Bengal, 1980.

ABOUT: Contemporary Authors, Vol. 102; Something About the Author, Vol. 24.

BYRON BARTON

September 8, 1930–

AUTHOR AND ILLUSTRATOR of *Building a House,* etc.

Autobiographical sketch of Byron Theodore Vartanian Barton:

I WAS BORN in Pawtucket, Rhode Island. I had three brothers and one sister. My mother and father emigrated to this country from Armenia. We lived in a small house with a large barn in the backyard. My father sold coal, wood, and ice, and all year round wood was stacked high in the yard and inside the barn, where there was also machinery for chopping and sawing wood; a big room for storing ice; an attic loft for storing things; and a place to park the truck. When I was nine years old, our family left Pawtucket and moved to Los Angeles.

In grammar school I liked all the subjects, particularly drawing and painting, and I liked sports. In junior high school and high school, however, I got a little lost. After high school, without a definite course in mind, I went to Los Angeles City College. In about the third semester I decided on art, and I took all drawing and painting classes. I liked to draw, and I liked to look at other people's drawings; so, during the three

Byron Barton

years I was at City College, I also spent much time looking at reproductions in art books in the Los Angeles Library. From City College I went to Chouinard Art Institute.

In my first semester, the army drafted me and sent me to Korea and Japan for two years. After the army, I worked for about a year in a stamp and coin business and then went back to art school for three more years. In 1957 or 1958, I came to New York City and worked in a couple of art studios doing design and illustration; then I went to work at CBS Television in the graphic arts department. At CBS I designed short films for titles and promotions. This involved making designs, photographs, and drawings and putting them together with sound and music. Among the many artists whose paintings I admired at the time were Stuart Davis and Jean Dubuffet. Later I became interested in children's art, native art, and folk art. In 1963 I met Harriett Wyatt and we were later married for three years. Harriett designed children's books and her interest rubbed off on me. The first illustrations I did for a children's book were for Constance C. Greene's *A Girl Called Al.*

Later, I tried doing some picture books of my own. Now I am doing picture books all of the time and am hardly ever too far away from the drawing board.

I like making picture books for children who are just learning to read. I try to make the words and pictures combine so the children can read the story by themselves. In most of my pictures, I like to use intense colors in flat shapes that at the same time suggest space; however, in a book that I'm working on now I am drawing more solid forms in space and using some more muted colors.

Of the books that I've read, *The Wind in the Willows* is one of my favorites. I like fantastic stories; I like stories about plain everyday things. Among illustrators, I like Lois Lenski, whose books about working people always appeal to me.

Although picture-making is what I like to do and there are many things about picture books that I want to find out and try, some day I would like to try a book without pictures.

———

Several of Barton's books have received honors and awards. *The Paper Airplane Book,* which was written by Seymour Simon, was in the Children's Books Showcase in 1972. *Where's Al?* was also in the Showcase for 1973 and on the *New York Times* list of Best Illustrated Books of the Year in 1972. *Harry Is a Scaredy-Cat* was included in the American Institute of Graphic Arts Book Show in 1973-1974. *Buzz, Buzz, Buzz* and *Hester* were both Junior Literary Guild selections, and Constance Greene's *A Girl Called Al,* which Barton illustrated, was chosen as an American Library Association Notable Book for the years 1940–1970. Both *Building a House* and *Airport* were named ALA Notable Books in their years of publication.

SELECTED WORKS WRITTEN AND ILLUSTRATED: Elephant, 1971; Where's Al?, 1972; Applebet Story, 1973; Buzz, Buzz, Buzz, 1973; Harry Is a Scaredy-Cat, 1974; Jack and Fred, 1974; Hester, 1975; Building a House, 1981; Airport, 1982.

SELECTED WORKS ILLUSTRATED: A Girl Called Al, by Constance C. Greene, 1969; The Paper Airplane Book, by Seymour Simon, 1971; Bullfrog Grows Up, by Rosamond Dauer, 1976; Good Morning, Chick, by Mirra Ginsburg, 1980; The Tamarindo Puppy and Other Poems, by Charlotte Pomerantz, 1980; Jump, Frog, Jump!, by Robert Kalan, 1981; My Dog and the Key Mystery, by David A. Adler, 1982.

ABOUT: Contemporary Authors, Vol. 57-60; Kingman, Lee, and others, comps. Illustrators of Children's Books: 1967-1976; Something About the Author, Vol. 9; Ward, Martha E. and Dorothy A. Marquardt. Authors of Books for Young People, 2nd edition (Supplement).

LEONARD BASKIN

August 15, 1922–

ILLUSTRATOR OF *Hosie's Alphabet*, etc.

Biographical sketch of Leonard Baskin:

LEONARD BASKIN was born in New Brunswick, New Jersey, the son of an orthodox rabbi. The year he was seven, the family moved to Brooklyn, New York, where he began Talmudic studies that were supposed to lead to his becoming a rabbi. Everything changed, however, when he was fourteen and attended a craft demonstration at Macy's department store and saw a sculptor molding a head—"the capital event of my life," he has called it. He watched her all day and into the evening, and when he left he took five pounds of clay with him. The next year, he began to study sculpture at the private studio of Maurice Glickman, and his first exhibition of sculpture was held at the Glickman Studio Gallery in 1939. From 1939 to 1941, he studied at the New York University School of Architecture and Allied Arts and from 1941 to 1943 at the Yale University School of Fine Arts. During World War II, he served in the Navy and the Merchant Marine from 1943 to 1946, and resumed his education immediately upon his return. He was married in 1946 and had one son. The marriage ended in divorce.

In 1947, he received a Louis Comfort Tiffany Foundation Fellowship for Sculpture and in 1949 he received his B.A. from the New School for Social Research. He continued his education in Paris in 1950 at the Académie de la Grande Chaumière and in Florence in 1951 at the Accademia di Belle Arte. In 1952, he accepted a position as an instructor in printmaking at the Worcester Art Museum in Massachusetts. His work in that medium won him a Guggenheim Fellowship in Creative Printmaking in 1953. That same year he joined the faculty of Smith College in Northampton, Massachusetts, first as an instructor, and eventually as a full professor of sculpture and graphic arts.

During the 1950s, Baskin exhibited regularly in New York City, around the country, and overseas. In 1954, he received the O'Hara Museum Prize from the Japanese National Museum of Tokyo.

In 1962, Baskin founded Gehenna Press in Northampton, a small publisher of rare books in limited editions, many of which are now collector's items. His interest in books extends beyond illustration to all aspects of book design: the integration of type, paper, illustrations, and binding to form an aesthetic object. He said, "Book illustration is meaningful, splendid, useful, apt, and bright when it performs as a partner, paralleling the text; the illustration should extend implications, deepen tragedy, heighten insights. The illustrations should stand as works, without the text; they should comment on the text, argue with it, elevate it, and ultimately be an extension of it." *Newsweek* proclaimed Baskin to be " . . . the literary man's visual artist, . . . close to succeeding [Ben] Shahn as the godlike poet laureate, in essence, of the visual arts."

During the 1960s, Baskin's work continued to be widely exhibited. In 1961, he won a grant from the National Institute of Arts and Letters and in 1962 the prize for Best Foreign Engraver at the São Paulo Biennale. In 1965, he won a Special Medal of Merit from the American Institute of Graphic Arts and in 1969 he won the Gold Medal from the National Institute of Arts and Letters. In 1967 Baskin remarried, and became the father of two more children.

In addition to being a sculptor, Baskin is a watercolorist, a designer, a calligrapher, an engraver, an essayist, an illustrator, and a poet. He became a success at illustrating children's books with his first attempt, *Hosie's Alphabet,* published in 1972. The book was created when his three-year-old son, Hosie, asked him to draw an alphabet for him. The result was a Baskin family project that marked a new beginning for the well-established multi-media artist. Hosie helped choose the creatures to represent each letter in the book, and his brother and mother helped him with the "big words." *Hosie's Alphabet* was a Caldecott Honor Book in 1973; an American Institute of Graphic Arts Children's Book Show selection in 1971–1972 and a Fifty Books of the Year selection in 1972; one of ten of the *New York Times* choice of Best Illustrated Children's Books of the Year 1972; and a Brooklyn Art Books for Children selection of the Brooklyn Museum and the Brooklyn Public Library in 1975. The Baskin family followed up with *Hosie's Aviary* and *Hosie's Zoo.* In between, Baskin illustrated several books of poetry for children written by his close friend, Ted Hughes. One of them, *Season Songs,* was included in the 1976 Children's Book Showcase.

Baskin retired from Smith College in 1973 and moved with his family to Devon, England. Summers are spent on Little Deer Isle, Maine. Baskin's work is represented in the permanent collection of many museums around the world, including the Museum of Modern Art in New York; the Museum of Fine Arts in Boston; the National Gallery of Art in Washington, D.C.; the Bezalel National Museum in Jerusalem; and Kunst Pä Arbeidsplassen in Oslo, Norway. He is a member of the National Institute of Arts and Letters and the American Institute of Graphic Arts, and has received honorary degrees from Clark University and the University of Massachusetts.

SELECTED WORKS WRITTEN AND ILLUSTRATED: Leonard Baskin's Miniature Natural History, 1983.

SELECTED WORKS ILLUSTRATED: Hosie's Alphabet, by Hosea, Tobias, and Lisa Baskin, 1972; Season Songs, by Ted Hughes, 1975; Moon-Whales and Other Moon Poems, by Ted Hughes, 1976; Hosie's Aviary, by Tobias, Lucretia, Hosie, and Lisa Baskin, 1979; Hosie's Zoo, by Tobias, Hosea, Lucretia, and Lisa Baskin, 1981.

ABOUT: Baskin, Leonard. Baskin: Sculpture, Drawings and Prints, 1970; The Britannica Encyclopedia of American Art; Current Biography Yearbook, 1964; Jaffe, Irma B. The Sculpture of Leonard Baskin, 1980; Kingman, Lee and others, comps. Illustrators of Children's Books: 1967–1976; Something About the Author, Vol. 27; Vol. 30; Who's Who in America, 1980–1981; Who's Who in American Art, 1982; Who's Who in Graphic Art, 1982; Who's Who in the World, 1974–1975; Art and Artists October 1976; Atlantic Monthly September 1964; Newsweek June 29, 1970.

MARION DANE BAUER

November 20, 1938–

AUTHOR OF *Tangled Butterfly,* etc.

Autobiographical sketch of Marion Dane Bauer:

I GREW up in the shadow of a cement mill on the edge of a small, Illinois prairie town called Oglesby. My family moved once, and that was from the tiny house where I had been born on one side of a dusty corn field, to a larger house just the other side of the field. My childhood was circumscribed by the woods that grew up to the edge of our yard, the dust-colored mill, the corn field, and just beyond that, a highway. The highway went places—I knew that—and I occasionally walked the quarter mile of red-slag road to that highway with my most precious belongings slung on a stick, hobo style. Arriving there, I always peered down the highway and then went back home. The dreaming and the doing were so different.

I knew where the highway went. It went to my school, to the town library and the post office with its wonderfully terrifying mural of an Indian war, to the indoor municipal pool, an echoing concrete cavern, sharp with the aroma of chlorine, and to the drugstore where, if the owner's wife was on duty behind the ice cream counter, we could get two scoops of ice cream on a cone for a nickel. It also went to ballet lessons, to the homes of friends, and to the little Episcopal Church on the other side of the Illinois River, but I knew there had to be something more out there. There was always something more in my dreams, the stories I made up to live by.

I was a teenager before I began to write the stories down, though I had always known I would write them one day, but the stories I wrote never seemed to match the dreams I had lived. I was an adult, a graduate of the University of Oklahoma, the wife of an Episcopal priest, and the mother of two children, Peter and Beth Alison, before I discovered that it was my real life I needed for writing, not my dreams. Maybe the dreams have to come first, though, to give the stories color and drama.

All of my novels are based in places I have lived or visited frequently, the Oklahoma Panhandle; a small town in Missouri—Hannibal, really, though my story doesn't call it that; the Apostle Islands in Lake Superior. I am completing one now, set in the cement-mill housing of a small Illinois prairie town. The places are real. Only the people and the events are dreamed. Sometimes that dream touches my real life (we own a white German shepherd named Nimue who had two litters of puppies in her younger days, and my husband I have been foster parents for a number of children) and sometimes the dream reaches so deeply into my real life that it discovers what never was but always could be (like Michelle's illusions in *Tangled Butterfly*).

How fortunate I feel that the most important dream of all has become reality. I write stories. People read them. I mine nuggets from my past, special only to me, and other people treasure them. In my memory, I walk, again, along that red-slag road beneath the poplar trees and arrive at the highway. The highway stretches into places I have yet to travel, but standing there, gazing down it, I am recording the pressure of the sunlight against my skin, the slim length of the stick that supports my bundle, the ache to be home again, and I turn back, content. Tomorrow I will travel. Today I will record the walk.

———

Marion Dane Bauer has been a high school English teacher in Waukesha, Wisconsin, and has taught creative writing to adults. She is a member of the Authors Guild and the Society of Children's Book Writers.

SELECTED WORKS: Shelter from the Wind, 1976; Foster Child, 1977; Tangled Butterfly, 1980.

ABOUT: Contemporary Authors, Vol. 69–72; Something About the Author, Vol. 20.

JOHN BELLAIRS

January 17, 1938-

AUTHOR OF *The House with a Clock in Its Walls,* etc.

Autobiographical sketch of John Bellairs:

I'VE WRITTEN seven books, five of which are currently in print. The last four are all children's books, and they've turned out to be very popular. I have received fan letters from kids in forty states and Canada, and two of my books have been made into TV specials, *The House With a Clock in Its Walls* and *The Treasure of Alpheus Winterborn.* All four of my children's books are autobiographical. They're a combination of the everyday and the fantastic, like the books of my favorite author, Charles Dickens. The common ordinary stuff—the bullies, the scaredy-cat kid Lewis, the grown-ups, the everyday incidents—all come from my own experience. I grew up in a beautiful small town in Michigan. Marshall is full of strange and enormous old houses, and the place must have worked on my imagination, because I turned it into New Zebedee, the town in my trilogy about Lewis and Rose Rita. I've written about other places I've lived in, like Winona, Minnesota,

which becomes Hoosac in *The Treasure of Alpheus Winterborn.* Gradually, I seem to be working in all the details of my childhood, my dad's saloon, my mom's money worries, and so on. Writing seems to be (for me) a way of memorializing and transforming my own past. I write about the things I wish had happened to me when I was a kid.

My first career was college teaching. After getting an A.B. at Notre Dame and an M.A. in English at the University of Chicago, I taught for seven years. But when my first book was a success, I threw over teaching and tried to become a full-time writer. Later I had to return to teaching to live, but the success of my children's books enabled me to become a full-time writer finally. I'm separated and have one child, named Frank, who is twelve. I'm crazy about baseball, architecture, pinball machines, history, archeology, and chocolate-chip ice cream. Also I do community theatre acting (foreign accents and character parts) and walk a lot in good weather. I read and reread Dickens, Henry James, history by C. V. Wedgwood and Garrett Mattingly, and the ghost stories of M. R. James. And I love the fan letters I get: some are decorated, some have drawings of scenes from my books. Recently I've been sent such things as a piece of mica, a sports quiz game, and a purple wooden fish. And I'm opinionated and my mind drifts off when people are talking to me, but I don't take myself seriously. And I like looking myself up in reference books.

———

John Bellairs has taught English in colleges in Minnesota and Massachusetts and was a member of the humanities faculty at Shimer College in Mount Carmel, Illinois. He is a member of the Authors League and the Authors Guild.

SELECTED WORKS: The Face in the Frost, 1969; The House With a Clock in Its Walls, 1973; The Figure in the Shadows, 1975; The Letter, the Witch, and the Ring, 1976; The Treasure of Alpheus Winterborn, 1978.

ABOUT: Contemporary Authors (First Revision), Vol. 23–24; Something About the Author, Vol. 2; Who's Who in the East, 1974; The Writers Directory 1982–84.

JAN BERENSTAIN

JAN BERENSTAIN

July 26, 1923–

and

STAN BERENSTAIN

September 29, 1923–

STAN BERENSTAIN

AUTHORS AND ILLUSTRATORS OF the Berenstain Bears series, etc.

Autobiographical sketch of Janice Berenstain:

CHILD of the Great Depression sounds depressing, doesn't it? Although it must have been for my parents (their new building business in the suburbs of Philadelphia, Pennsylvania, "went under" when the banks closed), it was a wonderful time in my memory. My unemployed dad, who was a trained artist as well as a carpenter, was always at work at his drawing board or workbench and extremely available to his three children. My brothers followed their mechanical inclinations under his guidance and I my artistic ones. Both parents and a grandfather who lived with us were also very generous guides into the world of books. Besides my favorite illustrated editions of *A Child's Garden of Verses, The World Book of Nursery Tales* and *Alice's Adventures in Wonderland,* I adored the daily and Sunday funnies—especially the ones I considered well-drawn. Every day, some neat new facile penwork challenged me to reproduce it—and the materials I needed were right on my father's shelves. Later, as a parent, I knew how important it was to have books and supplies related to a child's special interests handy at the times those interests blossom.

It was with amusement that I learned that the student behind the charcoal applying "tone" to the drawing I had picked out as the best in my first class at the Philadelphia College of Art had similarly picked out mine. But it was with astonishment that I learned he also had shared an early enthusiasm for the work of the same comics artists as well as the same illustrators. With it all, we were both serious art students with the same current interest in the work of the old masters, French Impressionists, American Realists, etc. and classical music—although he knew a lot more about painters and composers than I did—and still does. We did, however, develop individual painting styles. When Stan's army service during World War II separated us for four long years, I opted for some civilian service as an aircraft riveter and draftsman before returning to my art training. Then, when Stan returned to civilian life—having already made inroads into the magazine cartoon market when off duty—I happily teamed up with him. His discharge was on April Fools' Day and we were married on the thirteenth, two very lucky days in our lives, funnily enough. We pooled our talents to create cartoons and covers for magazines and books, raise a family, and continue to explore all the challenging areas of visual and written humor. It was while observing our children's speech development and early reading patterns—children first "read" pictures—that we got interested in creating

stories for Beginner Books at Random House edited by Ted Geisel (Dr. Seuss). Our funny furry bear family now have a couple of logos of their own (Bear Facts Library and First Time Books) as well, and those books continue to hold the interest of children beyond the beginner stage. To reinforce that interest the bears now have adventures on prime-time TV, a medium that involves not only pictures and words, but music as well. So, it seems we've come full circle—back to the enthusiasms of our childhood—could this be what is meant by "discovering the fountain of youth?"

Autobiographical sketch of Stanley Berenstain:

AS A BOY, in the late twenties, I didn't see much of my father. He worked long hours six days a week in the Army & Navy Store business in Philadelphia, and slept all day Sunday. My mother belonged to a bridge club that played for modest prizes and placed modest bets. She was an excellent card player and gave me her winnings each Sunday to buy books at the second-hand bookstore. I became a precocious reader and a precocious young artist as well, because among my selections were some fascinating how-to-paint-and-draw books. My first masterpiece—a huge boxing mural painted right on the dining room wall—wasn't appreciated, however, so I worked on the laundry cardboard that came in my father's shirts. I soon mastered the drawing of my favorite comics, too—I can still draw Popeye on demand.

When the Depression hit, we moved around a lot. For a short period, I lived only blocks away from Janice Grant (my future collaborator in cartooning, writing, and illustration, as well as in marriage and parenting), although I never met her until I entered the Philadelphia College of Art years later.

It was the start of World War II, and within a year, the U.S. Army sent me to the Midwest as a medical artist. My duties involved making detailed drawings of the new procedures used by plastic surgeons doing reconstructive surgery on facial wounds. While in the army, cartooning seemed to me to be a way to earn extra money, since all transactions could be conducted by mail. I came across *The Saturday Review of Literature,* a magazine then unfamiliar to me, but that used cartoons dealing with subjects on which I felt I had something to say. I sent four cartoons to the editor, Norman Cousins, whom I had also not heard of before. When all four were accepted I was sure I had hit on the field in which an artist could make a living. I didn't sell another for a year.

After the war, I got married, returned to art school on the G.I. Bill (this time, the Academy of Fine Arts) and began collaborating with Jan (who had switched from student to assistant teacher at our old Alma Mater, P.C.A.) on the cartoons. They were appearing in the *Saturday Evening Post, This Week, Better Homes & Gardens,* and *Collier's* (including a series of covers) when our first child, Leo, was born. The work caught the attention of book publishers, and a parallel career as authors and illustrators ensued. We were a real Mom and Pop operation by this time, and even became Mom and Pop in actual fact a second time with the birth of our second son, Michael. Although the free-lance life is one that tends to keep the pressure on to produce or else, we began to feel a sense of security when *McCall's* asked us to create a feature for them. "It's All In The Family" first appeared in 1956 and moved to *Good Housekeeping* in 1970.

The first of our bumptious bear family books was published in 1962—as a result of our becoming interested in the books our young sons were reading. While they enjoyed many types of books, they were also attracted by humor and cartoons, and at that time, except for Dr. Seuss, no one was creating robust, falling-down, laugh-out-loud funny books for kids. We felt, too, we could bring our own specialty, family humor, to children. The books are a source,

now, for television—the first animated special based on the characters appeared Christmas, 1979.

Our sons are now grown. Leo, married to an early education specialist, is a primatologist with published studies in scientific journals, and Michael is an author/illustrator with several published children's books of his own.

———

In addition to the great popular success of the Berenstains's cartoons, magazine work, and books, they have won many honors and awards for their work. They received the School Bell Award of the National Education Association in 1960 for an article, "How to Undermine Junior's Teacher," and the Drexel Citation in 1982 for contributions to children's literature, from the Drexel University School of Library and Information Science. Five of their Berenstain Bear books have been named Honor Books by the Philadelphia Library Children's Reading Round Table; the Child Study Association has also honored five Bears books as Children's Books of the Year, one in 1977 and four in 1982.

The Bear Scouts was an American Institute of Graphic Arts Best Book in 1970, and *Bears in the Night* won a Michigan Council of Teachers of English Young Readers' Award in 1981. The International Reading Association's Children's Choices of 1982 include *The Berenstain Bears Go to the Doctor* and *The Berenstain Bears Visit the Dentist. The Berenstain Bears and the Spooky Old Tree* won the Ohio State Library Association, Teachers of English, and International Reading Association Buckeye Award in 1982.

Two awards have been presented to the TV show "The Berenstain Bears' Christmas Tree" in 1980: the Mifed Silver Diploma, presented at the International Film and TV Festival of Naples, Italy, and the International Film and TV Festival of New York Silver Award.

Their work was also represented in a Metropolitan Museum of Art exhibition of cartoons, and has been exhibited in London. A manuscript collection of their work has been established at Syracuse University.

SELECTED WORKS WRITTEN AND ILLUSTRATED: The Big Honey Hunt, 1962; The Bears' Picnic, 1966; The Bear Scouts, 1967; Inside, Outside, Upside Down, 1968; Bears on Wheels, 1969; The Bears' Christmas, 1970; Old Hat, New Hat, 1970; Bears in the Night, 1971; He Bear, She Bear, 1974; The Bear Detectives, 1975; The Berenstain Bears and the Spooky Old Tree, 1978; The Berenstain Bears' Christmas Tree, 1980; The Berenstain Bears and the Sitter, 1981; The Berenstain Bears Go to the Doctor, 1981; The Berenstain Bears Visit the Dentist, 1981; The Berenstain Bears in the Dark, 1982.

ABOUT: Burke, W. J. and Will D. Howe. American Authors and Books, 1640 to the Present Day, 3rd edition; Something About the Author, Vol. 12; Ward, Martha E. and Dorothy A. Marquardt. Authors of Books for Young People, 2nd edition; People January 22, 1979.

MELVIN BERGER

August 23, 1927–

AUTHOR OF *The New Earth Book: Our Changing Planet,* etc.

Autobiographical sketch of Melvin Berger:

I WAS BORN and grew up in Brooklyn, New York. During those years, I had two main interests—science and music. In school, I took as many science courses as I could. After hours, I studied and practiced the viola, and played in local orchestras. While I started preparing for a degree in electrical engineering at City University, I dropped out after two years, to join the New Orleans Philharmonic and later the Pittsburgh Symphony, to pursue the life of an orchestra musician. After a few years, I returned to school, earning degrees from the University of Rochester and Columbia University.

Although I had always done my own writing for fun, I never seriously considered a career as writer until around 1960. At that time, I met an editor at a party who asked me if I would be interested in developing my twin interests in science and music in a book for children. The result was *Science and Music,* published by McGraw-Hill in 1961, which explores the interrelationships between the two fields. One book led to another, and by now I have over eighty publications, almost all on one or the other or my two preoccupations.

I feel very fortunate to have devoted so many years to producing books for children. My books have earned many special honors from the National Science Teachers Association, the National Council for Social Studies, the Child Study Association, and the Library of Congress. They have been translated into sixteen foreign languages, including Urdu, Telugu, and Vietnamese. I am especially proud of the science books, because I agree with those who say that science is much too important to be left to the scientists. In my books, I try to provide the reader with a depth of understanding that will make him or her scientifically aware, better able to participate as an informed citizen.

When I am not writing—or practicing the viola—I enjoy traveling. Often, I try to combine travel with research on some book project. I have had the good opportunity to meet with scientists at the nuclear energy lab at Harwell in England, at Woods Hole in Massachusetts, at Cornell University in New York, and at numerous other places in the United States and Europe. Wherever I go, I keep a sharp eye out for antique scientific instruments, which I love to collect, as well as stereograph cards from the nineteenth century.

Currently I live in Great Neck, New York, a suburb of New York City. My wife Gilda and I share a large writing studio. She is also a writer of books for children, and most recently we have had the pleasure of co-authoring several books.

In 1957, Melvin Berger was married to Gilda Shulman and they have two daughters. He attended the City College of the City University of New York, and also studied at the Eastman School of Music and at Columbia University. He has since lectured at City College and has taught music to high school students.

Berger's Scientists at Work Series has investigated such topics as pollution, cancer, crime detection, oceanography, weather, and medical research. Many of his books have won honors and have been placed on lists of recommended books. *The New Water Book, Disease Detectives,* and *The Stereo-Hi Fi Handbook* were all named Outstanding Science Trade Books for Children by the Joint Committee of the National Science Teachers Association and the Children's Book Council. *Consumer Protection Labs* was named a 1975 Notable Trade Book in the Field of Social Studies by the National Council for the Social Studies. *Quasars, Pulsars, and Black Holes in Space* was named a Library of Congress Best Children's Book, 1964–1978, and was also a Child Study Association Children's Book of the Year. Several other books named Child Study Association Children's Books of the year are *The Stereo-Hi Fi Handbook, Consumer Protection Labs,* and *Disease Detectives.*

SELECTED WORKS: Consumer Protection Labs, 1975; Quasars, Pulsars, and Black Holes in Space, 1977; Disease Detectives, 1978; The Stereo-Hi Fi Handbook, 1979; Computers in Your Life, 1980; Mad Scientists in Fact and Fiction, 1980; The New Earth Book: Our Changing Planet, 1980; Comets, Meteors and Asteroids, 1981; Censorship, 1982.

SELECTED WORKS WRITTEN WITH FRANK CLARK: Science and Music, 1961.

SELECTED WORKS WRITTEN WITH GILDA BERGER: Fitting In: Animals in Their Habitat, 1976; Test and Improve, 1982 (Wendy Barish, editor).

ABOUT: Contemporary Authors (First Revision), Vol. 4; Something About the Author, Vol. 5; Ward, Martha E. and Dorothy A. Marquardt. Authors of Books for Young People, 2nd edition.

T. ERNESTO BETHANCOURT

October 2, 1932-

AUTHOR OF *New York City Too Far from Tampa Blues,* etc.

Autobiographical sketch of Tomas Ernesto Bethancourt, who also uses the pseudonym "Tom Paisley":

I NEVER expected to be a novelist. There's nothing in my family background that would have led to it, either. My father, a truck driver from Puerto Rico, was illiterate in English. My mother graduated from elementary school. But I was blessed by receiving a top-flight education from the New York City public school system. My teachers instilled in me a love for learning. They also taught me how to use a library. I owe my career as a writer to my teachers and the Brooklyn Public Library.

I enlisted in the U.S. Navy on graduating from high school. I served with a singular lack of distinction, during the Korean War. I attended City College of New York on the G.I. Bill. In the late 1950s the Folk Music boom began. As I already played the guitar and had a repertoire of such material, I began working in coffee houses in Greenwich Village. It became a career. I recorded for

Bethancourt: *BAYTH en cort*

ABC Paramount Records, toured internationally, and performed for two presidents of the United States. My songs, primarily social satire, were performed on TV and on the off-Broadway stage, and were recorded. It led to a stint as a staff lyricist for the publishing company of Cy Coleman, the Broadway producer/composer. Also during this time, I was a critic for *High Fidelity* magazine. This, in turn, led to my becoming biographer of principal artists for RCA and CBS Records.

In 1970, I married Nancy Soyeshima, a lovely lady of Japanese-American descent. Our first daughter Kimi, was born in 1974. At the time, I was performing at the New York Hilton hotel. I began writing a memoir for Kimi to read one day, all about my childhood in Brooklyn. A patron of the Hilton saw me working on my longhand manuscript and asked to see it. It turned out she was an acquisitions editor for Holiday House, a small but prestigious publisher of juvenile literature. I was offered a contract to finish my memoir. It became *New York City Too Far from Tampa Blues,* my first novel for young adults. Now, thirteen novels later, I have a new career as an author. And all by accident. I sometimes wonder how far along I'd be, had I begun before I was forty years of age.

Because I realize I owe my career to teachers and librarians, I maintain a heavy schedule of lectures and talks at inner-city schools and libraries. I encourage disadvantaged kids to read, and perhaps become writers, themselves.

I now live in Huntington Beach, California, and our second daughter Thea was born in 1975. Kimi has already begun her career as a writer. She won a story contest for grades K-3 at her elementary school. Thea is undecided as to whether she wants to be an acrobat or a tap dancer. We have two cats, Boris Badenov, a Russian Blue, and Dandy, who is made up of spare parts from other cats. I work at home, and no longer perform as an entertainer. I prefer the more rewarding work of entertaining young people with my books.

New York City Too Far from Tampa Blues was made into a one-hour TV special that was nominated for an Emmy Award for best script (the screenplay was written by Ed Pomerantz). Bethancourt's *The Mortal Instruments* won an Irvine Fol Author Award in 1978 from the University of California.

Bethancourt was a child actor in radio under the name "Tom Paisley." He is a member of the American Federation of Musicians and the American Society of Composers, Authors, and Publishers, and has won their 1969–1970 Popular Division Award. In addition to his satirical songs for adults, he has also written songs for children.

SELECTED WORKS: New York City Too Far from Tampa Blues, 1975; The Dog Days of Arthur Cane, 1975; The Mortal Instruments, 1977; Tune In Yesterday, 1978; Dr. Doom: Superstar, 1978; Instruments of Darkness, 1979; Doris Fein: Superspy, 1980; Doris Fein: Quartz Boyar, 1980; Doris Fein: Phantom of the Casino, 1981; Doris Fein: Murder Is No Joke, 1982.

ABOUT: Something About the Author, Vol. 11; (as Tom Paisley) Contemporary Authors, Vol. 61–64.

JOHN BIERHORST

September 2, 1936–

EDITOR AND TRANSLATOR OF *In the Trail of the Wind, etc.*

Autobiographical sketch of John William Bierhorst:

SOMETIMES I receive letters from children asking, "Where do you get your ideas?" or "Did you enjoy writing these stories?" Well, I wish I *could* have written them. The stories, poems, and songs in my books are American Indian compositions that I have edited or translated. I am always careful to explain this. But it gives me pleasure, nevertheless, to think that a few of my readers are carried away by the story itself and forget that it wasn't written in the usual manner.

What I want, most of all, is to present stories and poems that children can enjoy without having to remind themselves that they are reading in order to learn about Indians. This is because I want them to respect Indian culture and Indian abilities. I want them to discover that the great works of Indian verbal art can be as beautiful, as mysterious, or as amusing as the stories and songs of Europe and modern America.

My interest in Indian literature did not begin early. As a child I was not exposed to Indian legends or Indian music and do not recall being aware that such things existed. I was born in Boston in the mid 1930s and grew up in Greenhills, Ohio, one of the three "greenbelt" villages built by the government during the Depression. In those days the American Indian had been all but banished from textbooks (not reappearing until the 1960s). Ethnic diversity was supposed to have been lost, or eliminated, in something called the melting pot. I know now that a few children's books on Indian themes were published in the 1930s and 1940s, but they did not find their way to Greenhills.

The subject I loved was botany. While other children were leading more or less normal lives, I was spending thousands of hours classifying the plants that grew in the greenbelt around my village. Somewhere along the way, I had heard that there were many botanists at Cornell University, and I thought that if I could only get there I might become one of them. As it happened, I did go to Cornell. But I studied physics and English literature instead. At Cornell I discovered that I could become a writer. As soon as I graduated, I went to New York and began supporting myself as a writer of advertisements, saving enough after three or four years to take my first trip abroad.

The trip was to Peru, and in the mountain villages north of Lima I heard the Quechua language and was struck by the beauty of American Indian life. It was as a result of this trip that I eventually decided to become what is known as an Americanist, a person who studies the native cultures of the New World.

In 1965 I married Jane Byers, a children's book designer. With her encouragement, I began editing my first collection of Indian stories, *The Fire Plume*. Jane was the designer of *The Fire Plume*, and we worked together on my books from that time on.

Since 1974 we have lived in a small village in the Catskills with our daughter, Alice. Each morning shortly before dawn, the dog scratches at the kitchen door, and I come down to let her out. Soon Jane is up, too, and as the day begins, Jane is in her studio and I am in mine, both of us working on books.

———

John Bierhorst, a folklorist and a translator and adapter of Native American literature, has edited material collected by Henry Rowe Schoolcraft (*The Fire Plume* and *The Ring in the Prairie*) and by Edward Curtis (*The Girl Who Married a Ghost . . .*). A former concert pianist, he wrote a study of American Indian music, *A Cry from the Earth,* and edited a recording of the same name that was issued in 1979. His translation of eight tales by Perrault in *The Glass Slipper* was made from the 1697 text, and he has won praise from critics on the accuracy of this translation as well as for his research in and documentation of folklore in the body of his work. *In the Trail of the Wind, Black Rainbow, The Girl Who Married a Ghost . . . , The Whistling Skeleton,* and *A Cry from the Earth* were designated Notable Books by the American Library Association; and *In the Trail of the Wind* was among the books chosen to represent the United States at the Moscow Book Fair in 1979. A member of the American Folklore Society and the American Anthropological Association, Bierhorst has published articles in the *Bulletin of Research in the Humanities* ("The Concept of Childhood in American Indian Lore," Winter 1978), in the *Journal of American Folklore* ("American Indian Verbal Art and the Role of the Literary Critic," 1975, No. 350), and in several Children's Book Council publications. He has received grants from the Center for Inter-American Relations, the Columbia Translation Center, and the National Endowment for the Humanities.

SELECTED WORKS EDITED: The Fire Plume: Legends of the American Indians, 1969; The Ring in the Prairie: A Shawnee Legend, 1970; In the Trail of the Wind: American Indian Poems and Ritual Orations, 1971; Four Masterworks of American Indian Literature: Quetzalcoatl, The Ritual of Condolence, Cuceb, The Night Chant, 1974; Songs of the Chippewa, 1974; Black Rainbow: Legends of the Incas and Myths of Ancient Peru, 1976; The Red Swan: Myths and Tales of the American Indians, 1976; The Girl Who Married a Ghost and Other Tales from the North American Indian, 1978; A Cry from the Earth: Music of the North American Indians, 1979; The Whistling Skeleton: American Indian Tales of the Supernatural, 1982; The Sacred Path: Spells, Prayers, and Power Songs of the American Indians, 1983.

SELECTED WORKS TRANSLATED: The Glass Slipper: Charles Perrault's Tales from Times Past, 1981.

ABOUT: Contemporary Authors (First Revision), Vol. 33-36; The International Author's and Writer's Who's Who, 1977; Something About the Author, Vol. 6; Ward, Martha E. and Dorothy A. Marquardt. Authors of Books for Young People, 2nd edition (Supplement); The Writers Directory 1984–86.

QUENTIN BLAKE

December 16, 1932–

ILLUSTRATOR OF *How Tom Beat Captain Najork and His Hired Sportsmen,* etc.

Autobiographical sketch of Quentin Blake:

A BOOK ILLUSTRATOR is a peculiar kind of hybrid person. My own interest in children's book illustration is made up of a number of things: they include an interest in drawing, an interest in reading, an interest in humour, an interest in drama, and an interest in design.

My first published drawings were for the humorous weekly magazine *Punch*—a few at first when I was still at school, and frequently later, when I stopped being a student. Doing that kind of drawing was exciting to begin with, but after a while I felt I wanted to work on a larger scale. I did this partly by starting to do oil painting, and partly (this is the aspect of my work that developed most strongly) by illustrating books. To get into illustrating books (I didn't really know how you began), I asked my friend John Yeoman to write a book for me: this was *A Drink of Water,* published in England in 1960. Later on I wanted to do a picture-story book and so I wrote *Patrick,* published in 1969. Since then I have written half a dozen other texts for my own picture books. This isn't, however, the main interest for me in illustration, as it is for some artists. What really interests me, and what I find steadily more interesting as time goes on, is the diversity of authors and their writings: to be presented with the problems involved in illustrating, designing and interpreting a new manuscript. To give only one example: each book of Roald Dahl that I have illustrated (there are six so far) has a different mood and presents different problems. So my illustration autobiography is in terms of books: I suppose there must be about a hundred and fifty of them so far.

There is nothing extraordinary about my everyday life. I live in London, in a big apartment that looks out over a garden with trees in it. In the summer I spend a lot of time in an old house (five hundred years old!) in Hastings, where I keep on drawing. The other important part of my life is running the Illustration Department of the Royal College of Art. It's exciting and stimulating to be involved with many of the best and most interesting young illustrators: in fact the only disadvantage is that it leaves so little time to talk to children about books and pictures.

Quentin Blake was born in Sidcup, Kent, a suburb of London, where he attended the local grammar school. After two years' national service in the Army Education Corps, he studied English at Cambridge under F. R. Leavis, and took a teacher's diploma at London University. Subsequently, he attended life classes at Chelsea School of Art.

He began drawing for *Punch* in 1948. In 1957, after leaving Cambridge, he became a regular illustrator for the literary and political weekly the *Spectator.* In 1965 he became a part-time tutor in the Illustration Department at the Royal College of Art, and he has been head of the department since 1978. In 1980 he was elected to the honor of RDI (Royal Designer for Industry).

Quentin Blake has received several important awards for his work, including the 1980 Kate Greenaway Medal, for *Mister Magnolia.* His *How Tom Beat Captain Najork and His Hired Sportsmen* was named a Notable Book of 1974 by the American Library Association and a Hans Christian Andersen Honor Book for illustration. It also won a Whitbread Literary Award in 1974. *A Near Thing for Captain Najork* was a *New York Times* Choice of Best Illustrated Children's Books of the Year 1976.

SELECTED WORKS WRITTEN AND ILLUSTRATED: Patrick, 1969; Snuff, 1973; (with John Yeoman) The Improbable Book of Records, 1976; Mister Magnolia, 1980.

SELECTED WORKS ILLUSTRATED: Riddles, Riddles Everywhere, by Ennis Rees, 1964; The Bear's Water Picnic, by John Yeoman, 1970; Mouse Trouble, by John Yeoman, 1973; Tales of Arabel's Raven, by Joan Aiken, 1974; How Tom Beat Captain Najork and His Hired Sportsmen, by Russell Hoban, 1974; Beatrice and Vanessa, by John Yeoman, 1975; A Near Thing for Captain Najork, by Russell Hoban, 1976; Wouldn't You Like to Know?, by Michael Rosen, 1979; The BFG, by Roald Dahl, 1982; You Can't Catch Me. by Michael Rosen, 1982; The Witches, by Roald Dahl, 1983.

ABOUT: Contemporary Authors (First Revision), Vol. 25–28; Kingman, Lee and others, comps. Illustrators of Children's Books: 1957–1966; 1967–1976; Something About the Author, Vol. 9; Ward, Martha E. and Dorothy A. Marquardt. Illustrators of Books for Young People; Graphis No. 131, 1967; Punch December 15, 1965.

JOAN W. BLOS

December 9, 1928–

AUTHOR OF *A Gathering of Days: A New England Girl's Journal, 1830–32,* etc.

Autobiographical sketch of Joan Winsor Blos:

Blos: *BLOSE*

Joan W. Blos.

THREE THINGS which matter a lot to me are language, truth, and children. When I say *language* I mean words themselves: their nuances and derivations, their sounds and their implicit rhythms, the ways they are put together in poetry or speech. When I say *truth* I mean trying to find it out, especially the simplest and least explanations for the most events. (The ways and nature of human life are central to my interests. I majored in physiology as an undergraduate and have a master's degree in psychology.) And, finally, my concern for children refers to children in general, not just to our son and daughter although I love them dearly.

Knowing this it is not so surprising that when the compass of my life came to rest it pointed at children's books. For more than twenty years I was principally occupied as a teacher, teaching children's literature to those who planned to teach. Then the balance shifted. Once a teacher who sometimes wrote, I would now describe myself as a writer who sometimes teaches.

People seem to like to know that I often wear an apron when I write, and that our cat lies near my desk, asleep on an old blue sweater, folded to her size. I must like to tell about these things, else others would not know them. Between us we build an agreeable image, cozy and eccentric. The Lady Author at work. But is the picture a truthful one? And does it matter that the apron is there because I want to spare my clothes and have come from household chores? That the cat lies equally often in the exact, mathematical center of my work, and sometimes crosses the typewriter keyboard, depressing random keys?

It is hard to find and hold to the truth when reporting on one's self: why did you become a writer? Where do you get the ideas for your books? Are your characters based on people you know? Do your own kids like your books? More pertinent than the answers to these questions may be what Paul Klee said about art ("Art does not reproduce the visible, it renders it visible."), and to ask if art is closer to science than the twentieth century thinks. Writer Grace Paley once said in an interview, "To be an artist is to have an absolute compulsion to tell the truth." Art may itself by a way of finding out, of stating what is known.

My early life and the school I attended started me thinking in these ways. And, as my mother was a teacher at that school, the two had much in common. It was a very unusual place—decades ahead of its times. Words that later became clichés—innovative, unique, creative—apply without stint to a school of the 1930s where boys learned to cook and girls worked electric printing presses and academic skills were learned within the dynamic context of the whole curriculum. Standards were extremely high; the maximum discipline, seldom evoked: stay home from school for a day. We did not marvel at any of this (nor at our teachers' dedication) but took it all for granted which, to us, it was. Similarly blithe was our response to the very city of New York, our access to it all. A five-cent fare was standard then, and one could pretty much travel in safety as far as that fare allowed.

In a 1980 *Horn Book* article my friend, Betty Miles, described me as a *caring* person, going on in particular to recall that "[She] cares about the color of wooden beads against a dress or of a picnic cloth spread out on a meadow grass." I had not thought of it that way before. When *she* did, it made me so happy.

Recently I told a fifth grade class that they might think of writing as caring: caring about the things which surround you in your daily life, caring about the words you use, caring about the people for whom you write the words. I wish I had gone on to add that writing for me, and for many other writers, is a matter of very hard work.

"Do you enjoy writing?" someone asked me once. To which my spontaneous answer was: only when I stop.

———

Joan W. Blos was raised in New York City and received her B.A. degree from Vassar College in 1950 and her M.A. from the City College of New York in 1957. She is married to a psychoanalyst and has two children, born in 1955 and 1958. She lives in Ann Arbor, Michigan.

Blos was an associate member of the Publications Division of the Bank Street College of Education from 1959 to 1966 and an associate editor of the Bank Street-Macmillan Readers from 1962 to 1966. For eleven years she was an Instructor at the Teacher Education Division of the Bank Street College of Education in New York. From 1970 to 1972 she was Research Assistant and Specialist in Children's Literature at the Department of Psychiatry, University of Michigan Medical Center, and Lecturer at the Teacher Education Division of the School of Education at the University of Michigan.

Joan W. Blos was the U.S. editor of *Children's Literature in Education,* a critical journal on children's literature, from 1977 to 1982. She has published articles about children's literature and education in such magazines as *Saturday Review, Reading and Child Development,* and *School Library Journal.*

A Gathering of Days, Blos's first novel, is a fictional journal of a girl's life on a New England farm. It won the 1980 Newbery Medal and a 1980 American Book Award for hardcover fiction. It was also named a Notable Children's Trade Book in the Field of Social Studies by the joint committee of the National Council for the Social Studies and the Children's Book Council.

SELECTED WORKS: "It's Spring," She Said, 1967; (with Betty Miles) Just Think!, 1971; A Gathering of Days: A New England Girl's Journal, 1830–32, 1979.

ABOUT: Contemporary Authors, Vol. 101; Something About the Author, Vol. 27; Ward, Martha E. and Dorothy A. Marquardt. Authors of Books for Young People, 2nd edition (Supplement); Horn Book August 1980.

CECIL BØDKER

March 27, 1927–

AUTHOR OF *Silas and the Black Mare,* etc.

Biographical sketch of Cecil Bødker:

CECIL BØDKER was born in Fredericia, Denmark. She grew up with five brothers in an area surrounding the town. Her father H. P. Jacobsen was an author and artist, although he also worked as a silversmith for many years. Because it was a long, cold bicycle ride to school, her mother clothed Cecil as she did her brothers—warmth being more important than femininity. She spent her childhood rambling over the countryside with her brothers and their friends; she enjoyed reading what were considered "boys' books" because they were more exciting to her, she says, than books of the period written for girls.

At seventeen she became a silversmith apprentice in the factory where her father worked; she was the only girl among fifty apprentices. She received her silversmith's certificate four years later, and moved to Copenhagen where she worked at Georg Jensen from 1948 to 1951. In 1951 and

Bødker: *BOD ker*

1952, she was employed by Markstroem's, another silversmith shop, in Stockholm, Sweden.

Bødker thinks she was about ten when she wrote her first poem. She wrote constantly all through adolescence, but none was published until she was twenty-eight. In 1955, two books of her poems, *Luseblomster* (which means "Lice Flowers") and *Fygenda Heste* (which means "drifting horses") were published in Europe, and, in 1956, she received the Edith Rodes grant of five hundred Danish crowns for her efforts. She used the money to buy a typewriter and to leave her job so that she could continue to write. Between 1956 and 1966 she won several prizes and awards for excellent writing. She has published many poetry collections, adult prose, and radio plays in Danish.

In 1966, Bødker's local post office received by accident two copies of the Danish Author's Union magazine, one without an address, and the postmaster insisted on giving it to her. This curious twist of fate led her to read the announcement of the Danish Academy's first and only (to date) juvenile book competition. She entered the competition with *Silas og den Sorte Hoppe* (*Silas and the Black Mare* in the U.S.), and won. The book was also named Best Children's Book of the Year by the Danish Ministry of Cultural Affairs in 1968.

In 1969, Bødker and her husband were invited to live in Ethiopia. They found Ethiopians interested in children's books about Ethiopian life, for the country at that time had no children's literature of its own. *Leoparden* (*The Leopard* in the U.S.) was the first book Bødker wrote as a result of this experience and also her first book published in the United States. It was generally well received as depicting graphically and authentically life in a small rural Ethiopian village.

In 1970, Bødker was nominated for the Hans Christian Andersen Medal, and finally received it in 1976 for her works for children. In 1972, she was awarded the Silver Pencil Award in the Netherlands for *The Leopard*; in 1975, she won the Mildred L. Batchelder Award presented by the American Library Association for the same title. *Silas and Ben-Godik* was a 1979 Boston Globe-Horn Book Honor Book.

In 1978, when *Silas and the Black Mare* and two sequels were published in the U.S., Lucia Binder commented in *Bookbird* that "It is a general characteristic of Cecil Bødker's human portrayals that there are no black-white depictions. Her narratives always remain grounded in reality and show how an unmerciful environment can produce unscrupulous people."

Bødker attributes her frequent choice of boys as main characters to her childhood associations. However, she hopes both boys and girls will read her books with interest. Lucia Binder also wrote in *Bookbird* that she believes Bødker's "outstanding ability to understand young people, their behavior and their problems, comes from the fact that she had contact with a great many other young people in her childhood . . . and that she now has four teenage daughters."

She and her husband live on a farm in Jutland with four daughters, Dorete, Mette, Tadjure, and Madena. Two of them were adopted during their stay in Ethiopia.

SELECTED WORKS: The Leopard, translated from Danish by Gunnar Poulsen and Solomon Deressa, 1975; Silas and the Black Mare, translated from Danish by Sheila La Farge, 1978; Silas and Ben-Godik, translated from Danish by Sheila La Farge, 1978; Silas and the Runaway Coach, translated from Danish by Sheila La Farge, 1978.

ABOUT: Contemporary Authors, Vol. 73–76; Cassell's Encyclopedia of World Literature; The International Authors and Writers Who's Who, 1982; Something About the Author, Vol. 14.

NANCY BOND

January 8, 1945–

AUTHOR OF *A String in the Harp,* etc.

Naucey Bond

Autobiographical sketch of Nancy Barbara Bond:

I WAS BORN in the Bethesda Naval Hospital in Maryland, near the end of World War II; I don't remember it and I've never been back. I consider myself a New Englander and I think of Concord, Massachusetts, as home. I've lived in Concord off and on for about thirty years; I've gone away to other parts of the state and to Britain to live, work, and study at various times, but I always come back. I like living in a small town where I recognize people and know my way around and where there is countryside to walk in. Natural history has been one of my greatest interests ever since I can remember, and it finds its way in some form or another in my books. When you begin to look—really look—for one thing: birds, flowers, geology, you begin to see lots of other things as well that you may never have noticed before.

I went to public school in Concord, then to Mount Holyoke College where I got a B.A. in English Composition, which meant that I could take lots of writing courses and get credit for them, something my puritan conscience used to give me twinges over. I had no thought of being a writer then, I simply enjoyed writing and it seemed almost cheating to get credit for it, just as it seemed cheating to get credit for taking a course in children's literature when I was in library school. Reading children's fiction is another one of the things I enjoyed most.

In 1971–72 I spent a year in Wales studying librarianship, and the experience of living in a small town in the Welsh countryside meant so much to me that when I came home I began to write about it. Eventually, with my new degree, I got a job in a public library, but I kept writing although more slowly. By that time I was too involved with the characters and the story I was creating to abandon them. Two years later, when I finished, I had a huge stack of manuscript pages. Until then I hadn't really thought much about what I was going to do with it, but I had put so much time and energy into writing the story that I decided to send it to a publisher. I was afraid it was so long that no one would consider reading it! To my great good fortune, my present editor at Atheneum not only read the manuscript, she accepted it, and in 1976 she published *A String in the Harp*. It was very exciting to see my tattered, corrected pages appear as a genuine book, but then it came as something of a shock to me to realize that wasn't the end of being a writer, it was only the beginning.

I was twenty-eight when I started to write *A String in the Harp*. Until then, everything I had written had been for fun, to amuse myself and a few other people. It was all good experience. I'm convinced that if you really want to write, nothing you put on paper is wasted: poems, stories, letters, journal entries. It teaches you how to put words together to make them mean what you want—or as nearly as possible—and that is surprisingly hard. I will go on learning as long as I go on writing.

Each book I have written has been a mixture of my own real experiences, my observations of places and people, my memories, things I have been told about, and a good deal of imagination to fill in the gaps and provide me with a plot. Although I write about real places—Wales, Concord, Northumberland, Cape Cod—I don't use real people. When I make up characters I use pieces of people I know and pieces of myself at different ages. Getting to know these characters as I write about them is often hard and frustrating because when I begin it's like meeting a roomful of strangers. But as I get acquainted with them it can be very exciting, and they become the most important part of my books. I invariably end up changing my original story because it doesn't seem right for the characters—it doesn't work for me to change the characters to suit the story.

I don't know whether I will always write books about children. Right now I am especially interested in younger characters, but I also feel that the adult characters in my books are extremely important. I suppose there may come a time when the balance shifts and I may write primarily about adults. But the world is made up of such a fascinating mixture, and I am interested in relationships among people of all ages.

———

Nancy Bond's first novel, *A String in the Harp,* concerns a contemporary boy spending a holiday in Wales with his family. The boy finds an ancient key that allows him to look into the past, where he sees people and events from *The Mabinogion,* a collection of Medieval Welsh tales. The novel, lengthy by 1976 standards, won several major awards.

A 1977 Newbery Honor Book, it also won the 1977 International Reading Association Children's Book Award and was named a Boston Globe-Horn Book Honor Book and an American Library Association Notable Book. Both *A String in the Harp* and *The Best of Enemies* were Junior Literary Guild selections.

A String in the Harp was set near Aberystwyth, Wales, where in 1971-72 Bond attended the College of Librarianship. She has worked in England for the Oxford University Press and has been a children's librarian in the Lincoln, Massachusetts, public library and Director of the Gardner Public Library in that state. She has been active in the Massachusetts Audubon Society, the National Audubon Society, and the Jersey Wildlife Preservation Trust. She has also taught at Simmons College in Boston.

SELECTED WORKS: A String in the Harp, 1976; The Best of Enemies, 1978; Country of Broken Stone, 1980; The Voyage Begun, 1981.

ABOUT: Contemporary Authors, Vol. 65–68; Something About the Author, Vol. 22; Ward, Martha E. and Dorothy A. Marquardt. Authors of Books for Young People, 2nd edition (Supplement).

MALCOLM J. BOSSE

May 6, 1933–

AUTHOR OF *The 79 Squares,* etc.

Biographical sketch of Malcolm Joseph Bosse:

MALCOLM BOSSE was born in Detroit and graduated from high school in Moline, Illinois. In 1950, he received his B.A. degree from Yale University, where he won the Masefield Award for Poetry and served as Class Poet. He received his M.A. from the University of Michigan, where he won two Hopwood Awards for Poetry and Fiction. He earned a Ph.D. in 1969 from New York University, where he won a University Scholar Award. He also served in the Navy from 1950 to 1954.

Bosse was granted a Creative Writing Fellowship from the National Endowment for the Arts and was the first American novelist invited to lecture by the People's Republic of China. He has written criticism of eighteenth-century literature and is co-editor of three series of academic publications of eighteenth-century English novels. In addition to poetry and criticism, Bosse writes novels for both adults and young adults.

Bosse: *BAHS ee*

Bosse spent two years as a Fulbright Scholar in India, and several of his books—*Ganesh, The 79 Squares, Journey of Tao Kim Nam, The Incident at Naha,* and *The Warlord*—have Asian settings or themes drawn from Eastern mysticism. Bosse told *Publishers Weekly* that the Far East seemed "comfortable to me in a way that Europe is not. In the Far East I feel at home, for some reason. The Hindus would say that in other lives I was an Oriental. It's something I've been told several times." The *New York Times* said of *The Warlord,* "Not since *Shogun* has a western novelist so succeeded in capturing the essence of Asia." Two of his adult books have been nominated for Edgar Allan Poe Awards.

While *Ganesh* and *The 79 Squares,* two of Bosse's novels for young adults, are set in the United States, each relies on techniques of Eastern meditation as a major element of the story. In *Ganesh,* the hero (an American boy who grew up in India) convinces his friends to join him in a Gandhi-like demonstration of passive resistance and fasting to save his aunt's house from government demolition. Eric, in *The 79 Squares,* realizes his own strength as well as his unity with nature by sitting for long periods of time in the marked-off squares of a garden. The book was named a Notable Book of 1979 by the American Library Association.

Bosse's two other novels for teenagers, *Cave Beyond Time* and *The Barracuda Gang,* are both stories about growing up, about adolescents who find through trial and struggle a path toward maturity. *Cave Beyond Time* concerns Ben, who is bitten by a rattlesnake and experiences visions of living in a prehistoric society, hunting and battling animals. Twelve bright high school students come together in *The Barracuda Gang,* competing for a scholarship in a national essay contest. They learn about themselves from each other, as well as from nature, when three of them are trapped in a coral reef, threatened by a barracuda and the rising tide. Both *Cave Beyond Time* and *Ganesh* were named Notable Children's Trade Books in the Field of Social Studies by the joint committee of the National Council for the Social Studies and the Children's Book Council.

Malcolm Bosse shows the same respect for both the teenage and the adult audiences he writes for: "I consider any reader above 10 or 12 years old (depending on the rate of maturation) to be an adult. I write for a young person as I would for someone my own age, but perhaps leave out long-winded reflections, which, of course, is better for us all."

Malcolm Bosse is married to Marie-Claude Aullas, a translator, and has one son. He lives in New York and is a professor of English at City College of the City University of New York. He is a member of the Authors Guild, the Society of Eighteenth Century Studies and Scholars in England, the Modern Language Association of America, Phi Gamma Delta, and Phi Beta Kappa. His avocational interests include Yoga and Tai Chi Chuan, jogging, swimming, and the practice of classical ballet. In conformance with this physical discipline, Bosse even writes standing up. He told *Publishers Weekly,* "It helps keep me awake, and I see writing as a physical activity. My body is involved in the act of writing."

SELECTED WORKS: The 79 Squares, 1979; Cave Beyond Time, 1980; Ganesh, 1981; The Barracuda Gang, 1982.

ABOUT: Contemporary Authors, Vol. 106; Publishers Weekly May 20, 1983.

BEN BOVA

November 8, 1932–

AUTHOR OF *Exiled from Earth,* etc.

Biographical sketch of Benjamin William Bova:

BORN AND RAISED in Philadelphia, Ben Bova first became interested in science as a schoolboy while visiting the Franklin Institute and Fels Planetarium.

After graduating from Temple University in 1954 with a B.S. degree in journalism, he attended Georgetown University School of Foreign Service in Washington, D.C. He then worked for a few years on a newspaper, and then in a variety of fields combining science and writing. He was a technical editor for Project Vanguard of the Martin Aircraft Company from 1956 to 1958. At the Massachusetts Institute of Technology he wrote movie scripts for high school physics instruction. For eleven years he was a science writer and marketing manager with an industrial research laboratory in Massachusetts, working closely with scientists and engineers in such fields as lasers, magnetohydrodynamics, and artificial hearts.

Bova is a member of the National Space Institute and was its director in 1981, a Fellow of the British Interplanetary Society, and a member of the American Association for the Advancement of Science. He draws on his technical experience and scientific background in his many books, articles, and short stories, whether he is writing fact or fiction.

Many of his nonfiction books have been about lasers, magnetism, space, and weather. "The writing style is brisk and informal, the organization of material logical, and the

BEN BOVA

information authoritative and interesting," children's literature critic Zena Sutherland said.

Bova insists that good science fiction also requires careful attention to scientific fact. "If you're going to write science fiction, you will have to know what science is doing," he says in his practical guide, *Notes to a Science Fiction Writer.* "Poets who sing about the beauty of the stars, without understanding what makes them shine and how they were created, are missing more than half of the real splendor of the heavens."

Bova's work in the aerospace industry and his detailed knowledge of the space program have helped him with the scientific background for his fiction. His first book, *The Star Conquerors,* was published in 1959. In his dramatic *Exiles* trilogy, two thousand leading scientists and their families are exiled by government leaders from an overpopulated and barbaric Earth; they travel in a spaceship-cryogenics laboratory; and a young man, born and brought up on the spaceship that is slowly deteriorating, discovers its secrets and the way to get the survivors to their ultimate destination. Overpopulation is a theme in much of Bova's fiction. In *City of Darkness* (which was named a Notable Children's Book in 1976 by the American Library Association), young people who are forced to live in overcrowded conditions rebel violently and try to escape.

Bova rejects the stereotypical science fiction hero who is "unruffled, supercool." In *The Dueling Machine* the hero is a gangling, bumbling young man, who nevertheless has sincerity, honesty, and a dogged kind of persistence. In novels like *The Weathermakers,* Bova's typical hero is a leader who struggles to defy bureaucracy and who sees that man can use scientific technology to benefit himself. "At the core of all good SF," Bova says, "is the very fundamental faith that we can use our intelligence to understand the world and solve our problems."

This faith in their craft of science fiction is shared by Isaac Asimov, Bova's close friend and colleague. Asimov says that even though he and Bova might be competitors, "the 'competition,' however it turns out, can only help science fiction and it is science fiction that is our life and brotherhood." In his editor's introduction to Asimov's novella, *Profession,* Bova acknowledges his debt to Asimov, and says: "I have known Isaac Asimov for just about twenty years. . . . We have shared many trials, and millions of laughs."

From his first marriage, which ended in divorce, Bova has two children, Michael and Regina. In 1974 he married Barbara Berson Rose. Besides science and writing, Bova is interested in fencing (he is a member of the Amateur Fencer's League of America), history, and anthropology.

Starflight and Other Improbabilities was a Junior Literary Guild selection. In 1974 Bova received the E.S. Smith Memorial Award for imaginative fiction from the New England Science Fiction Society. He also had a distinguished career as an editor, both of anthologies and of magazines. In 1971 he became editor of *Analog Science Fiction and Science Fact,* a widely read and influential magazine; and while there, he received the prestigious science fiction achievement award, the Hugo, for Best Editor, every year from 1973 to 1979. Then he moved to *Omni* magazine, which under his editorship received the Balrog award for Best Professional Publication in 1980 and 1982. Since September 1981 he has been free-lancing and he is a special contributor to *Science Digest.*

Bova's readers have given him the highest recognition for his whole body of work. He received the 1983 Balrog award for Outstanding Professional Achievement, an award which is decided by the votes of fans. The citation states simply: "To Ben Bova, for writing fiction and nonfiction, and for editing *Omni* and *Analog.*"

SELECTED WORKS: The Star Conquerors, 1959; The Weathermakers, 1969; The Dueling Machine, 1969; Escape! 1970; Exiled from Earth, 1970; The Amazing Laser, 1971; Flight of Exiles, 1972; Man Changes the Weather, 1973; Starflight and Other Improbabilities, 1973; The Winds of Altair, 1973; (with Gordon R. Dickson) Gremlins, Go Home!, 1974; Workshops in Space, 1974; End of Exile, 1975; Notes to a Science Fiction Writer, 1975; City of Darkness, 1976; The Seeds of Tomorrow, 1977.

ABOUT: Who's Who in Science Fiction; Contemporary Authors (First Revision), Vol. 7–8; The International Authors and Writers Who's Who, 1972; Nicholls, Peter, ed. The Science Fiction Encyclopedia; Reginald, R. Science Fiction and Fantasy Literature: A Checklist, 1700–1974 with Contemporary Science Fiction Authors II, Vol. 2; Reginald, R. Science Fiction and Fantasy Awards 1981; Smith, Curtis C., ed. Twentieth Century Science-Fiction Writers; Something About the Author, Vol. 6; Ward, Martha E. and Dorothy A. Marquardt. Authors of Books for Young People (Supplement); Who's Who in America, 1982–1983; Who's Who in the East, 1977–1978; The Writers Directory 1982–84.

ROBIN F. BRANCATO

March 19, 1936–

AUTHOR OF *Blinded by the Light,* etc.

Autobiographical sketch of Robin Fidler Brancato:

Robin F. Brancato

I HAVE ALWAYS wanted to be a writer. When I was in the first grade, I used to come home from school, lie on my bed, and write stories that I illustrated. The illustrations were never any good, and I soon gave them up, but I kept on being fascinated with words. I enjoyed growing up in Wyomissing, Pennsylvania, where I spent a lot of time at the local swimming pool, at the creek that ran through town, and at the public library. Part of the time, in those days, I was the organizer of games and sports in the neighborhood and at school, and part of the time I was the quiet, introspective, rather shy reader and writer. Many of my memories of my childhood found a place in my first novel, *Don't Sit Under the Apple Tree.*

In junior high my three best friends and I liked to write skits, imitate our teachers, and devise a whole string of private jokes about our classmates and our school subjects. This comfortable situation was disturbed when I was fifteen and learned that my father was being transferred to a Pennsylvania coal-mining town. Although at the time I didn't see how I was going to survive the separation, I did adjust, and in the long run I was stretched by the experience of living in a new place. One thing I learned in these years was that when you are separated from friends, books and writing become even more important to you.

In high school and later at the University of Pennsylvania I was active in sports and other activities and I majored in creative writing. The biggest benefits of this major were my learning to discipline myself to write and my learning to accept criticism of my work. As it turned out, I didn't begin writing for publication for another fifteen years, but I see now that everything I did in the in-between period contributed to my writing. The experiences of those years included: working as a waitress, traveling with a friend to Europe for three months, working as a textbook editor (which I didn't like very much), teaching high school English (which I loved), marrying and raising two sons, and living, with my husband John and my sons, Chris and Greg, in Modena, Italy, for two years.

My recent novels have all come about because I have been deeply affected by some cluster of events or ideas. I wrote *Winning,* the story of a boy who suffers paralytic injury in a football accident, partly because such an accident happened at my school and partly because I was concerned about the safety of my sons, who played football. I had always been interested in religious cults, so when I read about a young man in my town who was rescued from a cult, I decided to write a novel on that subject, (*Blinded by the Light*). My long-time fascination with radio resulted in my writing *Come Alive at 505,* about a high school senior who wants a career in radio. Usually as I'm working on a book I formulate a question that I'm trying to answer for myself. (One of those questions, in *Sweet Bells Jangled Out of Tune,* was What is your responsibility toward a once-loved relative who loses touch with reality as she grows old?) I always hope that the question that intrigued me enough to write the book will intrigue my readers to think and talk about the book after they finish reading it.

I work full-time at writing now. I also teach a few courses. I swim, bicycle, jog, and cook, but my favorite pastime is still reading. Some of my favorite books in my adolescence were *The Grapes of Wrath, Rebecca, Gone with the Wind,* and the humor of James Thurber. Now I read a lot of fiction by contemporary women. My favorite is the Canadian writer Alice Munro.

Robin F. Brancato was born in Reading, Pennsylvania. She received her B.A. degree from the University of Pennsylvania in 1958 and her M.A. from the City College of the City University of New York in 1976. She has two sons and lives with her family in Teaneck, New Jersey.

Three of her books were named Best Books for Young Adults by the American Library Association: *Winning,* in 1977; *Come Alive at 505,* in 1980; and *Sweet Bells Jangled Out of Tune,* in 1982. Both *Winning* and *Blinded by the Light* were adult Literary Guild selections, and *Blinded by the Light* was made into a TV movie for CBS in 1980.

SELECTED WORKS: Don't Sit Under the Apple Tree, 1975; Something Left to Lose, 1976; Winning, 1977; Blinded by the Light, 1978; Come Alive at 505, 1980; Sweet Bells Jangled Out of Tune, 1982.

ABOUT: Contemporary Authors, Vol. 69–72; Something About the Author, Vol. 23.

FRANZ BRANDENBERG

February 10, 1932–

AUTHOR OF *A Secret for Grandmother's Birthday,* etc.

Autobiographical sketch of Franz Brandenberg:

LOOKING THROUGH the fifteen books I have written so far, I found that they are full of circuses, plays, magic shows, and competitions of all sorts. Moving house, making new friends, catching and missing

trains, visiting friends and relatives are themes that run through many of them. I'd like to think that they are a reflection of my own, very happy childhood, and of the ones of our children.

I was born and grew up in Switzerland, the eldest of five boys. By the time I was seven we had moved four times, the last time from a small town to a tiny village, where "nothing was going on." Of course, I wasn't accepted for several reasons: I was a town boy, spoke differently (although the town of 5,000 inhabitants from where we had come was only ten miles away), and was doing much better in school than the other village children in the two-room schoolhouse.

To make myself popular, I organized all sorts of activities the village children had never heard of before: sweepstakes, sporting competitions, circuses, magic shows, plays. All these events took place either in our carless garage, in my father's bakery, or in front of our house. The prizes for the competitions, usually stale pastry, were donated by my parents.

The plays we performed were my adaptations of fairy tales and historical events. I always reserved the principal roles for myself. And since I was the only one who re-membered the unwritten lines, I usually spoke them for the other actors as well. My parents helped us make the costumes and props and saw to it that things didn't get out of hand.

We constantly imitated the adult world. We were forever selling and trading things. There were processions with banners up and down the village, elaborate funerals for pets in our garden. When the village was constructing a sewage system we took ad-vantage of the freshly-dug trenches to sim-ulate the war that was going on a few miles away, across the border.

An important influence on me was our Aunt Nina. She took me to the theater, the circus, swimming, fishing, to the moun-tains, everywhere. She always brought pres-ents when she came to see us. And I loved visiting her and Grandmother in their house in a big garden, by a large lake.

When I was thirteen I went to boarding school. My mother settled me on the train, with my suitcases, then went to buy the tickets. She didn't come back on time, and the train left without her. This incident in-spired my story *Everyone Ready?*

At seventeen I started an apprenticeship with a bookseller and publisher. At twenty I went to work in a bookstore in London. From there I went to Paris for two years. My French employer was the model for my first story, *I Once Knew a Man*. From Paris I went to Florence. There, one Saturday morning, an American girl came into the bookshop and asked for a guide to Florence. I offered to guide her through the city my-self, and she took me up on it. She was Aliki Liacouras, an artist. We were married in 1957, in Berne, Switzerland.

In 1960 we moved to New York. Aliki be-gan to write and illustrate children's books. I started a literary agency, representing Eu-ropean authors.

In 1964 our son, Jason, was born. In 1966 we had our daughter, Alexa. I hope their childhoods were as happy as mine. In any case, they were the inspiration for several of our stories.

In the course of my activity as a literary agent I had the good fortune of meeting Su-san Hirschman, who was then the children's book editor at Macmillan. She encouraged me to write, and has been my editor ever since.

I am very fortunate to have my books il-lustrated by my wife. Illustrating is much harder work than writing.

Aliki and Susan made it possible for me to prolong my childhood indefinitely. I am very indebted to them, and consider myself a lucky man.

———

SELECTED WORKS: I Once Knew a Man, 1970; A Se-cret for Grandmother's Birthday, 1975; I Wish I Was Sick, Too!, 1976; A Robber! A Robber!, 1976; What Can You Make of It?, 1977; Everyone Ready?, 1979; It's Not My Fault, 1980; Leo and Emily, 1981; Leo and Emily's Big Ideas, 1982.

ABOUT: Contemporary Authors (First Revision), Vol. 29–32; International Authors and Writers Who's Who, 1977; Something About the Author, Vol. 8; The Writers Directory 1982–84.

ROBBIE BRANSCUM

June 17, 1937–

AUTHOR OF *Johnny May,* etc.

Biographical sketch of Robbie Branscum:

BORN ON a hot summer night in 1937 on the outskirts of Big Flat, Arkansas, Robbie Branscum had an unusual childhood. Her father, Donnie H. Tilley, a farmer, died when she was four years old, and her moth-er Blanch sent the five children into the hills to live with their grandparents on a small sharecropper's farm. The family was poor and lived without modern conve-niences such as indoor toilets or electricity, but the days were busy and filled with all kinds of activities.

The walls of their home were papered with newspaper, and the words fascinated the girl so much that she read every wall in every room. She went to school in a one-room schoolhouse, and it was there that she developed a love of books. She writes, "The only book in our home was the Bible and anything else was a sin and a waste of time and money. I only saw other books in school and loved them." This passion for books proved to be a strong influence on her writing. "I had such a hunger for books when I was a child, that I grew up wanting to give other people the joy that books gave me."

When Robbie was thirteen, her mother reclaimed the children and took them to Colorado, literally stealing them from their one-room school since the grandparents opposed the move. Robbie Branscum remembers the episode as a great adventure. In Colorado, she again had access to many books. Never going beyond seventh grade in school, she nevertheless started writing songs and poetry as a teenager. A marriage at fifteen to Duane Branscum ended in divorce in 1969.

Branscum's firsthand knowledge of the people of the rural Arkansas hills lends authenticity to her books, all of which draw in some way from her own childhood experiences. She says she still dreams "of a small farm, a creek, a moon as big as a summer sky, the far-off bay of hounds, running fox and coon, and my Arkansas hills that never quite leave one's blood."

Her book *Johnny May,* the story of a young girl living with her grandparents on a farm in the hills, is similar to her own story. It was included in the *School Library Journal* "Best of the Best 1966–1978" list (December 1979), and a review of it in *The Horn Book Magazine* says: "With humor, a fine sense of description, and well-shaped dialect, the author has re-created the feeling and ambience of the hill country and has set in that distinct landscape a vivid and indomitable heroine." Two of Robbie Branscum's books were named outstanding books of the year by the *New York Times*— *The Saving of P.S.,* in 1977, and *To the Tune of a Hickory Stick* in 1978. In 1976 Doubleday published a book about a spunky char-

acter named Toby. *Toby, Granny and George* was the winner of the 1977 Friends of American Writers Award. In 1979 two sequels to it were published: *Toby Alone* and *Toby and Johnny Joe* continue the story of a girl's life in rural Arkansas.

In 1975, Robbie Branscum married a second time, but was divorced. After living in California for a while, she now makes her home on a small farm in Eufaula, Oklahoma, where she raises calves and chickens and tends a garden. She enjoys being with children and spends as much time as possible with them. Her daughter, Deborah, enjoys reading and writing. too.

SELECTED WORKS: Me and Jim Luke, 1971; Johnny May, 1975; The Three Wars of Billy Joe Treat, 1975; Toby, Granny and George, 1976; The Saving of P.S., 1977; To the Tune of a Hickory Stick, 1978; Three Buckets of Daylight, 1978; The Ugliest Boy, 1978; Toby Alone, 1979; Toby and Johnny Joe, 1979; The Murder of Hound Dog Bates, 1982; Spud Tackett and the Angel of Doom, 1983.

ABOUT: Contemporary Authors, Vol. 61–64; (New Revision Series), Vol. 8; Something About the Author, Vol. 23.

SUE ELLEN BRIDGERS

September 20, 1942–

AUTHOR OF *Home Before Dark,* etc.

Autobiographical sketch of Sue Ellen Bridgers:

I LIVE in the mountains of western North Carolina although I was born and grew up in the eastern part of the state. So far, my stories and books have been set in that area which, until recently, was mostly small towns and farmland. I have an older sister and younger brother. My sister and I were avid readers. Luckily for us, our mother thought reading was an important endeavor, so we had an excuse not to clean up the house, do the dishes, or help freeze the vegetables.

I graduated from the local school and

Sue Ellen Bridgers

went to East Carolina University, where I worked for the literary magazine and met my husband, an English instructor. After we were married, we lived in Mississippi and South Dakota while he served in the Air Force. In 1967 we moved to Chapel Hill, where my husband studied law and I took care of three very small children. From there, we came to Sylva, and I finally graduated from college with a B.A. degree in English from Western Carolina University. During our last year in Chapel Hill I had begun writing, a pleasure neglected during the baby period, and having renewed my interest and revived what little ability I had stored up, I began writing a short story about a migrant family. This story became my first novel, *Home Before Dark*.

Following the publication of *Home Before Dark*, my husband suggested I write about a retarded man he had known when he was a boy in Arkansas. His memories of this man interested me, but I was concerned about an accurate picture of him. His relationship with Casey, a girl who pretends to be a boy, was just the situation I needed to show Dwayne at his best. Like *Home Before Dark*, *All Together Now* is set in a small southern town, but it is less rural in its em-

phasis. I like to think it is a book about community, about the extended family that includes our friends and neighbors.

My third book *Notes For Another Life* is perhaps more personal than the other two, since I know something of the problem of a family faced with mental illness. Although it is not autobiographical, I think I drew more directly on my own emotional life than I ever have before. A major part of all writing is empathizing with the characters. The writer is like an actor in that way. She takes her emotional response to a real situation and adapts it to a fictitious one.

My personal life is typical of small town existence. I am a lay reader in the Episcopal Church. I belong to a book club that has as its one goal not studying anything. I serve on the board of directors of an organization whose aim is the preservation and improvement of the quality of life in our mountain area. I take what is probably minimal care of a husband, two daughters, one son, and a dog. We all enjoy going to the theater, music, books, public television, old movies, basketball, and ethnic food. My favorite writers are Eudora Welty, Anne Tyler, and Virginia Woolf. My favorite music is Baroque.

Because the children are teenagers, I think I should have more concentrated time for writing, but so far that hasn't been the case. I spend an enjoyable amount of time traveling and speaking to teachers and librarians. I like hearing from readers and try to answer their letters. All in all, I stay busy without writing, and so I sometimes need an extra nudge and several days clear of outside obligations to get any work done on a manuscript.

I always wanted to be a writer and I am very grateful that my first book had such good luck as to make a career in writing possible for me. I just hope my luck holds out.

———

All Together Now was a finalist in the paperback fiction reprint category of the American Book Awards in 1980 and also received a 1979 Christopher Award. *Notes for Another Life* was nominated for a 1983 American Book Award in the children's paperback fiction category and was named a 1981 Best Book for Young Adults by the American Library Association. Bridgers's stories have appeared in *Ingenue* and *Redbook.*

SELECTED WORKS: Home Before Dark, 1976; All Together Now, 1979; Notes for Another Life, 1981.

ABOUT: Contemporary Authors, Vol. 65–68; Something About the Author, Vol. 22.

K. M. BRIGGS

K. M. BRIGGS

November 8, 1898–October 15, 1980

AUTHOR OF *Hobberdy Dick,* etc.

Biographical sketch of Katharine Mary Briggs:

K. M. BRIGGS was born in London, one of three daughters of watercolorist Ernest Briggs. She studied English literature at Lady Margaret Hall, Oxford, earning a B.A. in 1922, an M.A. in 1926, and a Ph.D. in 1952, having written her thesis on folklore in seventeenth-century literature.

An internationally acclaimed English folklorist, scholar, literary critic, and author, Briggs's many books on the subject of folklore have been hailed universally for their detail, scholarship, and charm. In 1953, she published the first part of her historic survey of English folklore, *The Personnel of Fairyland: A Short Account of the Fairy People of Great Britain for Those Who Tell Stories to Children.* In 1959, she followed up with *The Anatomy of Puck: An Examination of Fairy Beliefs Among Shakespeare's Contemporaries and Successors.* In 1965, she published *The Folktales of England. The Fairies in English Tradition and Literature* was published in 1967, and referred to by reviewer B. A. Botkin as " . . . a contribu-

tion to folklore, written with the love, learning, and imaginative and social insight that make the English such good social historians and folklorists." The reviewer from the *Times Literary Supplement* was impressed by the "wonderful harvest" of facts garnered by Briggs and quoted from her preface: "This is not an attempt . . . to prove that fairies are real. . . . I am agnostic on the subject." In 1970 and 1971, she published her definitive, four-volume *A Dictionary of British Folktales in the English Language.* The *Times Literary Supplement* wrote: "This enormous, fascinating collection will appeal as much to browsers delighted to find out why the Owl was a Baker's daughter and the Grey Mare the better Horse, as to scholars." *Library Journal* wrote in kind: "Briggs . . . has performed a yeoman service. . . . Professional and student folklorists, children's and school librarians, and anyone interested in the English folktale tradition will find this work essential." In 1976, Briggs published *A Dictionary of Fairies* and *An Encyclopedia of Fairies: Hobgoblins, Brownies, Bogies, and Other Supernatural Creatures*; and *British Folktales* came out in 1977; in 1978, she published *The Vanishing People*; in 1979,

Abbey Lubbers, Banshees and Boggarts: An Illustrated Encyclopedia of Fairies; and in 1980, *Nine Lives: The Folklore of Cats.*

In between researching and producing this enormous body of work on folklore, Briggs wrote two very highly acclaimed novels for young readers. *Hobberdy Dick,* published in 1977, is the fascinating story of a hobgoblin in mid-seventeenth century England and the people whose lives he both guards and governs. *School Library Journal* said of *Hobberdy Dick*: "Briggs' finely crafted story—a microcosm of Cromwellian England in which Puritan morality battles ancient folkways—is so steeped in traditional lore that it rivals Kipling's *Puck of Pook's Hill* in its evocation of the spirits that guard British hearth and hillside." In 1980, Briggs published *Kate Crackernuts,* a moving and dramatic story of two young women, both "Kates," steeped in the folklore and politics of seventeenth-century Scotland amid witch hunts, religious argument, inter-family disputes, and the wars between Royalists and Parliamentarians. *Horn Book* said that in it "History and folklore are melded into a strong, anguished story of evil incarnate pitted against compassion and love."

Briggs lived almost all her life in England, but lectured widely in American universities and spent one year each as a visiting professor at the University of Pennsylvania in 1970 and the University of California at Berkeley in 1973. In addition to her scholarly and literary accomplishments, Briggs headed an amateur touring company for about fifteen years, produced plays in the Air Force, and wrote and produced plays locally in Perthshire and Oxford.

She was a member of the Folklore Society (and its president in 1967), an honorary life member of the American Folklore Society, and held memberships in the Bibliographical Society, the Historical Association, and the English Folk Dance and Song Society. In 1969, she was presented with an honorary D. Litt. from her alma mater, Oxford University.

SELECTED WORKS: Hobberdy Dick, 1977; Kate Crackernuts, 1980.

ABOUT: Contemporary Authors, Vol. 102; (First Revision), Vol. 9–10; The International Authors and Writers Who's Who, 1982; Something About the Author, Vol. 25; Who's Who in the World, 1978–1979; Ward, Martha E. and Dorothy A. Marquardt. Authors of Books for Young People, 2nd edition (Supplement); The Writers Directory 1982–84.

BILL BRITTAIN

December 16, 1930–

AUTHOR OF *Devil's Donkey,* etc.

Autobiographical sketch of William Brittain, who also writes under the pseudonym "James Knox":

IT'S kind of hard for me to think of myself as a writer because I am, by profession, a full-time schoolteacher. My writing is all done on weekends, summer vacations, and whenever I can steal the time from other activities.

Born in 1930, I grew up in Spencerport, a small village in upstate New York. Early memories include accompanying my dad—he was a doctor—on his house calls, hunting woodchucks and pheasants, working most of every summer on my uncle's farm, and losing about every fistfight I got into. Typical small town stuff, and I look back on it with a good deal of nostalgia.

After graduating from Brockport State Teachers College in 1952, I went right into teaching, and I've been doing it ever since. The first two years I was in LeRoy, New York. Then I moved to Long Island, where I've been teaching junior high school in the same district for twenty-nine years now. During that time my wife Ginny and I managed to raise two kids, Jim and Sue.

My writing attempts began in 1958, but I wasn't to get anything published for another six years. Finally, in 1964, I had a short mystery story accepted. The big break, however, came a year later, when

William (Bill) Brittain

another mystery story found its way into *Ellery Queen's Mystery Magazine*. This put me in contact with Frederic Dannay—Ellery Queen himself—who freely offered countless tips about how to improve my material. The result has been that some seventy-five of my stories have appeared in *EQMM*, and my series character, Mr. Strang, is still seen there from time to time. My gratitude to Fred for his help knows no bounds. Generous with his time and expertise, he was a gentleman in the finest sense of the word.

In 1978, William Brittain the mystery writer became Bill Brittain, when I wrote my first children's book, *All the Money in the World*. It's still hard for me to believe that my publisher, Harper & Row, was willing to take a chance on an unsolicited manuscript by an unknown author. *ATMITW* was followed in 1981 by *Devil's Donkey*, and in 1983 by *The Wish-Giver*.

Observations on writing? The first draft is fun to write, but going through the editorial process is pure drudgery. Techniques? Rule One is to finagle time for writing whenever possible. Then I try to tell a story that intrigues *me*. I rarely change or adapt my language because of the young age of

my readers. Kids are sharp. They know when they're being patronized and written down to.

Many of the best-selling juvenile books today seem to have teenage (and younger) people involved in the serious problems of growing up and discovering the inadequacies of an imperfect world. I have nothing against this kind of thing, but I can't write it myself—I've tried. Still, the success of my books makes me believe there are many kids who want a sense of wonder and magic in an age when, on TV and in the newspapers, mayhem and marital infidelity abound, and the Grim Reaper holds sway over all. I want such wonder and magic, and for everybody to "live happily ever after" when the magic is done. Call me a case of arrested development, but there it is.

———

Bill Brittain's character, the detective Mr. Strang, is a high school science teacher. Brittain is a member of the Mystery Writers of America, and his stories have also appeared in *Alfred Hitchcock's Mystery Magazine*.

All the Money in the World has been adapted for an ABC children's weekend special in 1983 and was named a Children's Choice book in 1980 by the joint committee of the Children's Book Council and the International Reading Association. *Devil's Donkey* was named a 1981 Notable Book by the American Library Association and was nominated for a William Allen White Award. Brittain's latest book, *The Wish Giver*, is about some of the same characters in the same locale as *Devil's Donkey*.

SELECTED WORKS: All the Money in the World, 1979; Devil's Donkey, 1981; The Wish Giver: Three Tales of Coven Tree, 1983.

ABOUT: Contemporary Authors, Vol. 77–80; Reilly, John M. Twentieth-Century Crime and Mystery Writers.

BEVERLY BRODSKY

August 16, 1941–

AUTHOR AND ILLUSTRATOR OF *The Golem,* etc.

Autobiographical sketch of Beverly Brodsky, whose first books appear under the name Beverly Brodsky McDermott:

CREATING is a vital matter to me. Every once in a while I ask myself what I would do if I did not have paintings to paint or words to write or books to illustrate. The answer comes to me. I have no choice but to be a creator, to transform the world around me into my own personal vision and order. This is a necessary undertaking that is a lifetime commitment. I have been a maker of images since I was old enough to hold a crayon. As a child I used to transform my world of tenements into the world of the theater. I spent most of my time sitting in front of a slate board in our kitchen while I listened to the radio. Day after day I drew the dancers, the scenery, and the costumes that I imagined while I heard the operatic performances my mother loved so much. She enjoyed translating the librettos of Puccini's most famous romantic arias while tears flowed from her eyes. This romantic and dramatic vision of life had a tremendous impact on me. The ballet was important to me as well; perhaps more so. *The Red Shoes* and *Tales of Hoffman* were my favorite films, for they contained images of dancers in imaginary places. I loved to dream and imagine just like the character Marusha in my book *The Crystal Apple.* This was my very first attempt to illustrate a folk tale. Folk tales, fairy tales, and legends were always a source of great delight to me as a child and fed my imagination. My father read to me almost every night just before I went to sleep. I remember how frightened I was when he told me the tale of the three billy goats gruff and the troll underneath the bridge. I remember how comforted and safe I felt afterwards when I heard my father's deep voice tell me everything was all right as he tucked me in for the night. These were important years, the years that influenced my entire life. *Secret Places* is the book wherein I am able to reconstruct those Brooklyn days, the scenes and sensory memories of my childhood. In this dreamlike fantasy world of mine, there really existed a garden full of roses and irises, cats and birds, and laundry lines, as well as dark and frightening shadows that looked like bogey men and lurked in hallways. I chose to work in watercolors in order to make those fluid bright images look as if they were dream-like.

As a painter, I am largely self-taught. I had brief training at the Brooklyn Museum. I majored in painting, however, at Brooklyn College with Ad Reinhardt, who was a prime influence in my development. Abstraction gave me the most freedom to work with color, so I began to develop a free and fluid style. At that time I was not interested in figurative work, although I had basic courses in drawing. I spent several years during the sixties working on large canvasses creating color field paintings. I earned my living teaching art to children, and then, later, I worked as a textile colorist and designer. But the textile designing bored me. It was too repetitive and I became interested in illustrating books for children. I applied my knowledge of painting and combined it with my knowledge of design and my love for children and their art. The child's directness and sensitivity to color and bold design impressed and delighted me.

My former husband, who is a graphic designer and illustrator, encouraged me at that time. It was when we moved to the south of France that I discovered the story of *The Golem*, which was to be my most important and successful work, earning me a Caldecott Honor Medal in 1977. *Der Golem* was a German film that was made in the 1920s. The story haunted me as well as the expressionistic images on the television screen. When we returned to the United States and settled in the Hudson River Valley, I began my intense research into this Jewish legend. It was then that I examined my Jewish heritage. I was rewarded by its richness. Mysticism, cabbalism, mysteries of the legend of Prague, the powerful Rabbi Lowe and the clay automoton called *the golem* became a part of my life for several years. How fascinated I was, and how engrossed in the subject matter! I never visited Prague, but I embellished on the photographs I saw and the stories I read in order to re-create the sixteenth-century golem of Prague. I also began to read history and holocaust material, Elie Wiesel in particular. I began to understand how deeply the story of the golem is a metaphor for the history of prejudice and senseless hatred toward Jews. In my story good triumphs over evil, and order is restored by the Rabbi with the assistance of God. The golem, the antidote for evil and prejudice, is put to rest. The enigmatic ending is a reflection of the contradiction of the powers of *the golem*, to destroy and protect.

In 1980 I began further investigation into my own history and ancestry. Many questions arose in my mind. Where did my mother and father come from, and why are they here? I wanted to know more about them. As I spoke to my mother I could feel a new story incubating. The more questions I asked, the more fascinated I became with the universal story of immigration. In Russia where my father was born, there were pogroms. Inside the Austro-Hungarian Empire was a little village called Rohatyn where my mother was born. Here the inhabitants suffered from disease and starvation. During this period of the 1920s, Eastern European Jews fled to America; my parents were among them. The story about my mother in particular grew into an illustrated book for children called *Gooseberries to Oranges*, my most recent book and first collaborative work. Gooseberries are a symbol of the "old country," and my mother picked them from the bushes when she had nothing to eat. The orange is a symbol of the "new country," America, and the crossing on the stormy sea to Ellis Island.

The journey of my mother and father is my journey as well. It is my metaphor, much like *Jonah,* for transformation, growth, and restoration. For I have taken the voyage, and traveled from the "old country." And I have entered the "Isle of Tears." The storm has passed and there is a fertile field to plant new hopes and dream new dreams. Now, before me, stands a great mountain to climb.

———

Besides being named a 1977 Caldecott Honor Book, *The Golem* was adapted into a filmstrip in 1979 (as was *The Crystal Apple* in 1974), and it was made into a multimedia dance and theater production in collaboration with the M.I.T. Center for Advanced Visual Studies. It was also presented by the Phoenix Dance Theatre at the Cambridge River Festival in 1978. *Gooseberries to Oranges* was named a Notable Book of 1982 by the American Library Association.

Brodsky, a Professor at the Adelphi University Art Department and at Parsons School of Design, has been commissioned to create posters for the New York City Opera at Lincoln Center ("The Love for Three Oranges") and for the National Fine Arts Commission of the Olympic Winter Games in Lake Placid, New York (Olympic Medal and Certificate for Olympic Arts Poster, 1980).

A member of the Author's Guild, Brodsky attended the School of Visual Arts in 1969–70 and received a fellowship from the Connecticut Commission on the Arts, for painting, in 1979. She has lectured at numerous institutions, including the University of California at Berkeley, the University of North Carolina at Chapel Hill, the New York Public Library, and at a New England Library Association Conference. Her work has been exhibited at the State University of New York at Plattsburgh, the Washington Art Association, Oliver Wolcott Library in Litchfield, Connecticut, and the Wilson Arts Center at the Harley School in Rochester, New York. Her work has appeared in *Print* magazine and on the cover of the *Wilson Library Bulletin* (January 1976).

Selected Works Written and Illustrated as Beverly Brodsky McDermott: The Crystal Apple: A Russian Tale, 1974; Sedna: An Eskimo Myth, 1975; The Golem: A Jewish Legend, 1967.

Selected Works Written and Illustrated as Beverly Brodsky: Jonah: An Old Testament Story, 1977; Secret Places, 1979.

Selected Works Illustrated as Beverly Brodsky McDermott: Forest of the Night, by John Rowe Townsend, 1975.

Selected Works Illustrated as Beverly Brodsky: Gooseberries to Oranges, by Barbara Cohen, 1982.

About: Kingman, Lee and others, comps. Illustrators of Children's Books: 1967–76; (as Beverly Brodsky McDermott) Contemporary Authors, Vol. 65–68; Something About the Author, Vol. 11; Ward, Martha E. and Dorothy A. Marquardt. Authors of Books for Young People, 2nd edition (Supplement).

MARC BROWN

November 25, 1946–

Author and Illustrator of *Arthur's Nose,* etc.

Autobiographical sketch of Marc Tolon Brown:

I'VE HAD many jobs before writing and illustrating books, such as truck driver, short-order cook, soda jerk, television art director, actor, costume and set designer, college professor, and gentleman farmer; and there is a funny story that goes with each job. All have helped my books directly or indirectly.

All the characters I write about are people I know. Arthur is part me and part my sons, Tolon and Tucker. Francine is a combination of two sisters, Bonnie and Colleen. Mr. Ratburn is modeled after a former teacher of mine who does look like a rat.

I went to college and art school for five years and had a scholarship for graduate school in 1970, but decided to enter the real world instead. That was the year I illustrated my first book, *What Makes the Sun Shine,* by Isaac Asimov. Not long after that I discovered I could tell stories to amuse my son at bedtime. That's how Arthur happened.

The Arthur books are always the most fun to work on, and with each new book I come to know Arthur and his friends a little better. To me Arthur is real.

I believe that all experiences are more meaningful when you reflect on them and for me writing and illustrating is a good way to gather insight and solve problems. And books are my way to celebrate what is wonderful!

When I develop books I'm careful that the words and pictures are balanced. I think the best children's books work well for adults too. If there isn't a good story line and some strong psychological ballast, it probably won't have much to offer children either.

My work habits vary. I like to rise early, watch the sun rise over Hingham Harbor,

Goes Feathertop! by Norma Farber was selected for the 1980 American Institute of
Graphic Arts Book Show. Several of his
books have been shown in the Society of Illustrators annual exhibit. *Dinosaurs Beware*
was named a Notable Book of 1982 by the
American Library Association.

SELECTED WORKS WRITTEN AND ILLUSTRATED: Arthur's Nose, 1976; One Two Three: An Animal Counting Book, 1976; Marc Brown's Full House, 1977;
Arthur's Valentine, 1980; Your First Garden Book,
1981; Arthur's Halloween, 1982; (with Stephen Kren-
sky) Dinosaurs Beware: A Safety Guide, 1982; The
True Francine, 1982.

SELECTED WORKS ILLUSTRATED: The Four Corners
of the Sky, selected by Theodore Clymer, 1975; How
the Rabbit Stole the Moon, by Louise Moeri, 1977;
There Goes Feathertop!, by Norma Farber, 1979; The
Banza: A Haitian Story, by Diane Wolkstein, 1981.

ABOUT: Contemporary Authors, Vol. 69–72; Something About the Author, Vol., 10; Graphis No. 156,
1979.

and work. Occasionally, I go through periods where I work at night and sleep beneath
my desk. I always know when a book is going well because I forget to eat. I keep myself busy working on more than one project
at the same time. And each day I dream
and fantasize—if I don't I become very
grouchy.

Each year I set aside what amounts to
several weeks to travel around the country
and talk with children about Arthur and
how my books are made. Sometimes Arthur
comes along, but usually he has school.

I feel fortunate making my living doing
what I love most: writing and illustrating
children's books. Children must sense the
great respect I have for them; that's how I
explain the success of my books.

———

Marc Brown was born in Erie, Pennsylvania and graduated from the Cleveland Institute of Art in 1968. His marriage ended
in divorce in 1977. Brown has been an art
educator, a college professor, and a guest
lecturer at colleges and universities. *There*

PALMER BROWN

May 10, 1919–

AUTHOR AND ILLUSTRATOR OF *Beyond the
Pawpaw Trees,* etc.

Biographical sketch of Palmer Brown:

PALMER BROWN was born in Chicago
and grew up in nearby Evanston and in ru-
ral Pennsylvania. He graduated from
Swarthmore College and has an M.A. from
the University of Pennsylvania. During
World War II, he was a major in the Air
Force and served for three years in North
Africa and Europe.

In 1954 he published his first book,
Beyond the Pawpaw Trees, which recounted
the remarkable adventures of a young girl,
Anna Lavinia. Asked how he came to write
it, Brown replied, "I should like to say that
the story of Anna Lavinia was written in invisible ink and mailed at sea in a ginger-
beer bottle to beguile the convalescence of
two little second cousins—but it wouldn't

be so. In sober truth, the story was written to amuse, and to provide its readers with something which would be neither the history of the man who invented shoelaces nor an explanation of how to build a birch-bark box kite or raise electric eels in the bathtub. If it has any moral at all, it is hoped that it will always be a deep secret between the author and those of his readers who still know that believing is seeing." The critics reacted favorably to *Beyond the Pawpaw Trees.* Louise Seaman Bechtel, writing in the *New York Herald Tribune,* wrote, " . . . a brilliant bit of imaginative nonsense. It has that rare combination of wit, pathos, poetry, and continuously surprising invention that holds the listening child and delights the adult who reads it." Jennie D. Lingquist, writing in *Horn Book,* called it "An imaginative story by a promising new author who writes with freshness and charm, and leaves the reader hoping for more books." *Cheerful,* published in 1957, was exhibited in the 1958 American Institute of Graphic Arts show. *Hickory,* published in 1978, was also received well by the critics. *Language Arts* said, "Rhymes, songs, and lilting conversation, plus a bittersweet message demand that this be read aloud and shared." *School Library Journal* said, "There is a gentle humor, love, and sweetness in this satisfying story." *Hickory* was selected by the *American Library Association* as a Notable Book for 1978.

Palmer Brown's drawings appeared in many magazines, both for adults and children, including *Gourmet, Woman's Day, Story Parade,* and *Jack and Jill.* He lives on a one-acre farm in Bareville, Pennsylvania.

SELECTED WORKS WRITTEN AND ILLUSTRATED: Beyond the Pawpaw Trees: The Story of Anna Lavinia, 1954; The Silver Nutmeg, 1956; Cheerful: A Picture Story, 1957; Something for Christmas, 1958; Hickory, 1978.

ABOUT: Bader, Barbara. American Picturebooks from Noah's Ark to the Beast Within; Kingman, Lee and others, comps. Illustrators of Children's Books: 1957–1966; Ward, Martha E. and Dorothy A. Marquardt. Illustrators of Books for Young People, 2nd edition; Viguers, Ruth Hill and others, comps. Illustrators of Children's Books: 1946–1956.

DICK BRUNA

1927–

AUTHOR AND ILLUSTRATOR OF *Miffy,* etc.

Biographical sketch of Dick Bruna:

DICK BRUNA was born in the Netherlands to a family that had directed the publishing firm of A.W. Bruna since its founding by his great-grandfather in 1869. He drew a great deal during his childhood and produced the first of his many book jackets for A.W. Bruna when he was only sixteen. After World War II, Bruna left school without taking his final exams; he then held three year-long apprenticeships with booksellers and publishers in Utrecht, London, and Paris. However, instead of becoming a publisher himself, he decided to pursue graphic arts, and for a short time attended the Art Academy in Amsterdam.

Bruna's first children's book, created in 1952 and published by the family's firm, sold few copies and was not a success. He continued to write and illustrate books for children, but it was not until his own children were old enough to be read to that he became truly successful in the field. His wife, Irene, also plays a vital role in the creation of his books, providing critical commentary on his concepts and designs. Today Bruna is the author and illustrator of more than forty-five books for children, with a total of over thirteen million copies in print. His books have been translated into Afrikaans, Danish, English, Finnish, French, German, Hebrew, Italian, Japanese, Norwegian, Portuguese, Serbo-Croat, Spanish, and Swedish.

Writing of the extraordinary success of Dick Bruna's books, developmental psychologist Dolf Kohnstamm proclaims, "The first and by far the most important thing that must be said about Dick Bruna's pic-

DickBruna

up. . . . It always comes down to directness, to get as direct an effect as possible."

Dick Bruna now lives in Utrecht and divides his time evenly between writing and
illustrating children's books and working on
a variety of other graphics projects. He has
designed over eighteen hundred book jackets, as well as posters, a series of children's
postal stamps, murals, postcards, and greeting cards. In 1977 the Gemeente-museum
in Arnhem hosted an exhibition based on
his popular character Miffy.

SELECTED WORKS WRITTEN AND ILLUSTRATED BY
DICK BRUNA: Snuffy, 1969; The Apple, 1975; I Can
Read, 1975; I Can Count, 1975; Miffy, 1975; My Shirt
Is White, 1975; A Story to Tell, 1975; I Can Count
More, 1976; Another Story to Tell, 1978; I Can Dress
Myself, 1978; Miffy in the Hospital, 1978; Miffy at the
Beach, 1979.

ABOUT: Hürlimann, Bettina. Picture-Book World;
Kingman, Lee and others, comps. Illustrators of Chil-
dren's Books: 1967–1976; Kirkpatrick, D. L., ed.
Twentieth-Century Children's Writers; Something
About the Author, Vol. 30.

tures is that so little appears in them."
Bruna, who is said to admire Matisse and
Picasso for their flattening of perspective,
depicts his strong, simple, representational
figures in bold, often primary colors set
strongly against one another with no shad-
ing. "It begins with the drawings," Bruna
said. "I already have the plot in my head by
then. While I am working on the drawings,
texts occur to me. I make the first draft of
a book like this; then I look into the other
possibilities of almost all the drawings to see
if I can't find something better. So for a
book of twelve pictures I make at least a
hundred. The funny thing is that even after
all this endless trying out, I frequently come
back to the first draft after all."

Another striking and distinguishing characteristic of Bruna's books is that the characters, no matter what action they are
engaged in on the page, are never looking
at other objects or even at one another, but
are always gazing out at the reader—a trait
that reflects the philosophy behind his
work, the prime importance of immediacy
Bruna comments, "I have often tried to
draw a face from the side. I thought it
would be fun to have a nose and all the other things you can see. But I always gave it

ASHLEY BRYAN

July 13, 1923–

SELECTOR AND ILLUSTRATOR OF *Walk Together Children: Black American Spirituals,* etc.

Biographical sketch of Ashley F. Bryan:

ASHLEY BRYAN is a highly respected reteller and illustrator of African folk tales
and American spirituals. He was born and
spent his childhood with his three brothers
and two sisters in the Bronx, New York, and
attended New York City public schools. In
Illustrators of Children's Books: 1967–1976,
he said of his early years, "I grew up in
tough New York City neighborhoods. I
learned from kindergarten that drawing
and painting were the toughest assets I had
to offer to my community, and I have developed them ever since. My book is a natural outgrowth of my love of drawing and

painting." He was graduated from the Cooper Union Art School and from Columbia Art School and from Columbia University, where he majored in philosophy.

The idea of retelling and illustrating African folktales came to Bryan as a young man in the late 1940s, but did not become a reality for almost twenty-five years. The first book he illustrated was *Fabliaux,* in 1964. Next, he illustrated *Moon, for What Do You Wait?,* one-line poems of the Indian poet Sir Rabindranath Tagore. This was the first book he did for Jean Karl, at Atheneum, who has been his editor ever since. At that time, Bryan was living in the same Bronx neighborhood in which he had grown up and was teaching drawing and painting at Queens College. The experience of giving a course in black American poetry at Lafayette College had a strong influence on his later work, but it is the teaching of children—which he has done at the Dalton School, the Brooklyn Museum, and other institutions in and around New York—that is special to him: "I love to teach children, especially those under twelve, and participate in their development both as artists and as people." He was also very involved in community activities, such as the local Head-

start program and church-sponsored educational and social programs. After a one-term stint as artist-in-residence at Dartmouth College in Hanover, New Hampshire, in 1973, Bryan accepted a permanent position on the faculty there and has lived in Hanover during the school year ever since. He has spent his summers on an island in Maine for over thirty years.

Bryan's first book was *The Ox of the Wonderful Horns and Other African Folktales,* five stories. Bryan said in *Illustrators of Children's Books* that in retelling the African folktales he tries to approach the spirit of the black oral tradition: "I play with sounds and I encourage others to read my stories aloud for best effect. I take the skeletal story motifs from the scholarly collections and use every resource of my background and experience to flesh them out and bring them alive. Despite extensive research, when necessary, I forgo literal authenticity to achieve this. This means that my storytelling and my illustrations combine my African heritage with all the world cultural influences to which any contemporary artist falls heir."

The Ox of the Wonderful Horns was well received by the critics. *The Horn Book Magazine* called it "attractively printed and boldly interpreted . . . the tellable tales will reach a wider audience than most of the other recent volumes containing African lore."

Bryan began serious work on his next book, *Walk Together Children: Black American Spirituals,* when he received a proverb in the mail from a friend, librarian Dolores Koenig, who had been encouraging him for many years. The proverb said: "God admires me when I work, but He loves me when I sing." One of Bryan's great regrets is that she did not live to see the book completed. Black American spirituals, the religious songs of an enslaved African people in the United States, inspired Bryan because of their special appeal and beauty and because of his early exposure to them at family music fests. Among his earliest childhood recollections is one of his mother singing "from one end of the day to the other." He remembers his father saying, "Son, your mother must think she's a bird."

For *Walk Together Children,* and whenever he illustrates black themes, it is often the blacks he has known in his New York City community and in the Caribbean islands that he is picturing. He is especially familiar with the island of Antigua, in the West Indies, where his parents had lived before coming to New York after World War I and where they returned in the late 1960s. For *Walk Together Children,* he also did woodcuts for the titles of the songs and worked out a system for cutting and printing the music to give the book the visual unity he sought. *School Library Journal* said of the collection of over 20 black American spirituals, "A well-chosen selection, attractively assembled." It was chosen as an American Library Association Notable Book in 1974. *The Dancing Granny,* a West Indian folktale, received high praise from the critics as well; *Booklist* called it "rich for reading aloud."

Critics responded in kind to *Beat the Story-Drum, Pum-Pum,* another collection of African folktales, five from Nigeria. The *Horn Book* said it was "a collection as pleasing to the eye as it is to the ear," ideal for story telling or reading aloud." *Booklist* said, "Bryan's retellings make graceful dips into modern slang, giving the stories a faint American bouquet without compromising their ethnicity." It was selected as an ALA Notable Book in 1980 and won the 1981 Coretta Scott King Illustrator's Award. It was also named a Notable Children's Trade Book in the Field of Social Studies by the joint committee of the National Council for the Social Studies and the Children's Book Council.

In 1982, eight years after the publication of *Walk Together Children,* Bryan published a companion volume, *I'm Going to Sing: Black American Spirituals, Volume Two,* containing twenty-five spirituals. Again, the critics were enthusiastic, and it was selected as an ALA Notable Book in 1982.

Ashley Bryan is a tall, kindly, and soft-spoken man who, when he reads his work aloud, as he often does, electrifies his audiences with his grand gestures, wide range of voices, and total immerson in what he is doing. He has spoken of his desire to bring life to the printed word, and in his readings he does exactly that. In the summers in Maine he combs the beaches searching for sea glass, shells, bones, and driftwood with which he creates puppets. He has used these puppets as the actors in his African tales, but only on the Maine island. Bryan lived in France and Germany and has traveled to many countries, including Kenya, Uganda, Italy, England, Spain, Yugoslavia, Greece, and Israel. He had many one-man shows for his paintings, and he has lectured all over the country on his own work and on black American poets. He likes to quote a line from a poem by the Senegalese poet Leopold Sedar Senghor in which he united past and present, childhood and Eden, with one line, "Un pont de douceur les relie" (a tender bridge connects them). It is this tender bridge between the African past and the American present that Ashley Bryan tries to build for children, both black and white, today.

SELECTED WORKS SELECTED AND ILLUSTRATED: Walk Together Children: Black American Spirituals, 1974; I'm Going to Sing: Black American Spirituals, Volume Two, 1982.

SELECTED WORKS RETOLD AND ILLUSTRATED: The Ox of the Wonderful Horns and Other African Folktales, 1971; The Adventures of Aku, 1976; The Dancing Granny, 1977; Beat the Story-Drum, Pum-Pum, 1980.

SELECTED WORKS EDITED AND ILLUSTRATED: I Greet the Dawn: Poems of Paul Laurence Dunbar, 1978.

SELECTED WORKS ILLUSTRATED: Fabliaux, translated by Robert Hellman and Richard O'Gorman, 1964; Moon, for What Do You Wait?, by Sir Rabindranath Tagore, compiled by Richard Lewis, 1967; Jethro and the Jumbie, by Susan Cooper, 1979; Jim Flying High, by Mari Evans, 1979.

ABOUT: Kingman, Lee and others, comps. Illustrators of Children's Books: 1967–1976.

"EVE BUNTING"

December 19, 1928–

AUTHOR OF *The Cloverdale Switch,* etc.

Autobiographical sketch of Anne Evelyn Bunting, who writes under the pen names "Evelyn Bolton," "A. E. Bunting," and "Eve Bunting":

I USED TO BE embarrassed by the fact that I did not always "want to be an author!" Sitting on writers' panels, I'd listen as guest after guest proclaimed: "I don't ever remember a time when I didn't want to write." Or, "I had my first story published in our church magazine when I was seven years old." When my turn came I'd mumble and stammer.

I don't mumble and stammer any longer. Because I've found that "wanting to be a writer" is something that can happen at any time in one's life. And in my own way, I am an inspiration to other women who are middle-aged and "starting over."

The truth is, it never occurred to me that I could be a writer or ever would be one. I was forty years old. One day I looked around me and realized that I didn't know what I was going to do with the rest of my life. My husband, a professional man, was busy with his own career. My three children were growing rapidly and no longer really needed mother. I had dropped out of college to marry at an early age so there I was, unfocused and unqualified. What to do?

My local junior college offered several classes through adult extension courses. There was sewing. And painting. And photography. And . . . WRITING FOR PUBLICATION.

Writing for publication? I remembered how I'd loved to write essays in school. How I'd joyfully embarked on short story assignments. I decided I'd just check out this Writing for Publication class. What could I lose?

It was undoubtedly one of the major and most meaningful decisions of my life. Twelve years later I have more than 130 published children's books, numerous articles, and short stories. I have taught my own classes on writing for publication at the University of California, the kind of class I attended all those years ago at Pasadena City College.

I hasten to say that it is my belief that no one can be "taught to write." The talent is there, latent or awake. It is a gift, like naturally curly hair or a great sense of humor. What can be taught is how to structure a story. How to plot. How to create characters that are real, not cardboard. What to do with your book or story once you've written it. Those are the things I try to teach.

My first love is still writing. Many of my books are set in Ireland because that is where I came from and where I lived for the first thirty years of my life. Christine, Sloan, and Glenn, our three grown-up children, were all born there. It still holds a part of my heart.

I seem to write a lot about birds. Eagles, hawks, blackbirds, owls, cormorants, parrots . . . all of them used in fiction as symbols of freedom and the unfettering power of love. I have done science fiction, romances, and a few factual nonfiction books on subjects that really interest me.

I don't force myself to write every day. I don't have to. Every spare minute finds me at my typewriter because creating stories is the thing I enjoy most in the whole world. So I'm doing what I like to do best. I found it. I pursued it. I prospered. Which makes me one of the world's most fortunate of women.

———

Born in Maghera, Ireland, Anne Evelyn Bunting graduated from Methodist College, and Belfast Queen's University in 1945. She married Edward Davison Bunting in 1951 and came to the U.S. in 1958. She was naturalized in 1969.

She has written many series for children, including, as Evelyn Bolton, a series of horse stories like *Stable of Fear*; and, as Eve Bunting, a science fiction series. She has had stories published in *Cricket* and *Jack & Jill* magazines. Bunting is active in many writers' organizations, such as P.E.N., the Authors Guild, the California Writer's Guild, and the Society of Children's Books Writers.

In 1976 *One More Flight* won a Golden Kite Award and was named an outstanding science book for children and an outstanding social science book for children by the National Science Teachers Association and the Children's Book Council.

Ghost of Summer won the Southern California Council on Literature for Children and Young People Award for fiction in 1978, and *Winter's Coming* was named one of the ten best books of 1977 by the *New York Times*.

SELECTED WORKS AS EVE BUNTING: Barney the Beard, 1975; One More Flight, 1976; Ghost of Summer, 1977; The Big Cheese, 1977; The Haunting of Kildoran Abbey, 1978; The Cloverdale Switch, 1979; The Robot Birthday, 1979; Demetrius and the Golden Goblet, 1980.

SELECTED WORKS AS A.E. BUNTING: High Tide for Labrador, 1975; Springboard to Summer, 1975.

SELECTED WORKS AS EVELYN BOLTON: Stable of Fear, 1974; Goodbye Charlie, 1974; Dream Dancer, 1974.

SELECTED WORKS AS EVE BUNTING WITH GLENN BUNTING: Skateboards: How to Make Them, How to Ride Them, 1977.

ABOUT: (as Anne Evelyn Bunting) Contemporary Authors, Vol. 53–56; (New Revised Series), Vol. 5; Something About the Author, Vol. 18; Ward, Martha E. and Dorothy A. Marquardt. Authors of Books for Young People, 2nd edition (Supplement); Who's Who in America, 1978.

W. E. BUTTERWORTH

November 10, 1929–

AUTHOR OF *Leroy and the Old Man,* etc.

Autobiographical sketch of William Edmund Butterworth III, who also writes under a number of pseudonyms, including "Webb Beach," "Walker E. Blake," "James McM. Douglas," "Eden Hughes," "Edmund O. Scholefield," and "Patrick J. Williams":

I WAS BORN in New Jersey and raised there, in Boston, in Philadelphia, and in Manhattan, but after more than a quarter century in Alabama, I think of myself as a Southerner.

I was educated as a political scientist, but after service as a sergeant combat correspondent during the Korean War, decided to become a writer. I've published well over a hundred books, under my own and a dozen pen names.

I've been married since 1950 to the former Emma Macalik, who was a dancer in the Corps de Ballet of the Vienna State Opera when we met. Her autobiographical novel, *As the Waltz Was Ending,* was published in October of 1982. It was recommended for Christmas giving by the New York Public Library, and was selected as a "Best Book of 1982" by the American Library Association. She is also the author of *The Complete Book of Calligraphy.*

On my release from military service, I became a civilian information officer for the Department of the Army at Fort Rucker,

Alabama. I am the principal author of a FM1-1 Army Aviation Operations, and either wrote or contributed to many other military publications during the formation of Army Aviation.

Simultaneously, I was writing my first novel, and on the sale of my third novel, resigned from government service and moved to the shores of Mobile Bay, where I have lived since.

My first book for children was written for G. P. Putnam's Sons at the insistence of Mrs. Alice Doughtie, then Supervisor of the Choctawhatchee (Alabama) Regional Library. The book, *The Wonders of Astronomy*, received the Author's Award of the New Jersey Association of Teachers of English, which I found very satisfying, for I had never been able to pass high school English when a student in New Jersey.

Since my first children's book, I've devoted about forty percent of my output to books for young people, generally for high school age. My most recent "young adult" book was *A Member of the Family*.

My wife and I have three children: Patricia Butterworth Black, was a reporter on the Birmingham (Alabama) *News* until she married James T. Black, who writes about travel for *Southern Living* magazine. The Blacks eight months ago presented us with our first grandchild, Emma Christine.

William E. Butterworth IV, who is twenty-two, began a journalistic career on the Dallas *Morning News,* and at this writing is Associate Editor of *Houston City* magazine. He shares a bachelor apartment with John S. Butterworth, eighteen, who is taking a year off before beginning college.

All three Butterworth children are graduates of the Marietta Johnson School, Fairhope, which is generally recognized to be one of the first progressive schools, i.e., one of the first to recognize that children are individuals who cannot be put into molds. I am a member of the Board of Directors, and my wife teaches a class in calligraphy.

The only philosophical observations I have to make vis-à-vis writing for young people are that young people are considerably brighter than they are normally given credit for being, and that they loathe being "written down to." A fan letter from a youngster (one not written at the suggestion of a teacher) is probably the nicest thing connected with the publishing business.

Among W. E. Butterworth's many books for adults are a series of books written with Richard Hooker: *M*A*S*H* Goes to Paris,* etc. He is a member of the American Legion, the U.S. Armor Association, and the National Rifle Association. He lives in Fairhope, Alabama.

In 1982, Butterworth was the first living member inducted into the Alabama Academy of Distinguished Authors. *Steve Bellamy* was on the 1969 Child Study Association list. *Orders to Vietnam* was a Junior Literary Guild selection, and *Leroy and the Old Man* was named a Best Book for Young Adults by the American Library Association in 1980.

SELECTED WORKS: The Wonders of Astronomy, 1964; Stock Car Racer, 1966; Orders to Vietnam: A Novel of Helicopter Warfare, 1968; Steve Bellamy, 1969; Stop and Search, 1969; My Father's Quite a Guy, 1972; Skyjacked!, 1972; Wheels and Pistons, 1972; Race Car Team, 1973; Black Gold: The Story of Oil, 1975; Careers in the Services, 1976; The Air Freight Mystery, 1978; Under the Influence, 1979; Leroy and the Old Man, 1980; Slaughter by Auto, 1980; Flunking Out, 1981; Hot Wire, 1982; A Member of the Family, 1982.

ABOUT: (as William Edmund Butterworth III) Contempory Authors (First Revision), Vol. 2; (New Revision Series), Vol. 2; Something About the Author, Vol. 5; Ward, Martha E. and Dorothy A. Marquardt. Authors of Books for Young People, 2nd edition (Supplement); Who's Who in the South and Southwest, 1975–1976.

LARRY CALLEN

LARRY CALLEN

April 3, 1927–

AUTHOR OF *Dashiel and the Night,* etc.

Autobiographical sketch of Lawrence Willard Callen Jr.:

I ENTERED the field of children's books through the side door.

I've spent my entire adult life in jobs that require writing of some sort in newspapers and magazines, speech writing, radio and television news writing. I have also been writing stories since I was a child, all aimed at adult readers, all rather heavily told, most focused on solving one or another moral or social problem.

When I approached fifty years of age, having acquired a wife and four children, assorted tropical fish, and a cat named Casey, I enrolled in a class in children's literature, hoping to learn something about what children read. It turned out to be a class in writing for children, and I began cranking out short stories joyfully, funny ones.

That writing class did several nice things for me. First, it channeled me into writing children's stories. I had never considered this before. Second, because of my teacher's encouragement, I began producing stories on a regular basis. A lot of these stories were written on a bus while I commuted from home to work. I squeezed in about two extra hours of writing a day that way. Third, I tried my hand at humor for the first time and learned I could do it well. That's always a good feeling.

In the stories I've written so far, I've drawn heavily on my boyhood, not on incident, but on what I remember of the south Louisiana locale I grew up in, on the people I knew, and on their values.

It's important that I convey my enthusiasm for writing to you. I like sitting before my typewriter (frequently I use a tape recorder to develop a story line) and asking myself questions about what will or should happen next (What if this happens? What if that happens?). I like confronting one character with another and watching tender feelings flow or sparks fly. I enjoy it immensely when I have sudden insight into the solution to a problem. Sometimes I explode with laughter. Sometimes I softly cry.

Of course, there are the other times when all of the ideas are bad, and the tragedy is that I don't know it at the moment. As a result, I do a lot of rewriting. No book of mine has ever been published before five or six rewrites. When an editor sends a book back for rewriting, at first there is ego-searing pain. But I quickly dry my tears and get to work. I know it will be a better book after the rewrite.

The two greatest pleasures of my first fifty years have been, first, my family (which came late—I was past thirty when I married, and almost forty when our first child arrived); and second, the writing of stories for kids of all ages. What's nice about it is that these are pleasures that will grow more intense during the next fifty years.

Larry Callen was born in New Orleans and married Willa Carmouche, a teacher and learning disabilities diagnostician, in 1958. He received a B.S. degree in Journalism in 1957 at the Florida State University in Tallahassee and has also studied at several Louisiana universities, doing some postgraduate work in social science at Louisiana State University, Baton Rouge. He has worked at the U.S. Department of Labor and at the Louisiana Department of Labor and has been a free-lance writer since 1979.

The Deadly Mandrake was selected to appear on *School Library Journal's* recommended book list, "Best of the Best 1966–1978" (December 1979).

SELECTED WORKS: Pinch, 1976; The Deadly Mandrake, 1978; Sorrow's Song, 1979; Muskrat War, 1980; Dashiel and the Night, 1981.

ABOUT: (as Lawrence Willard Callen Jr.) Contemporary Authors, Vol. 73–76; Something About the Author, Vol. 19.

TONY CHEN

January 3, 1929–

ILLUSTRATOR OF *Honshi,* etc.

Autobiographical sketch of Anthony Young Chen:

WHEN I WAS about eight years old, my uncle gave me a watercolor set, and to my surprise and everybody else's, my watercolors were better than my uncle's. At ten I attended the Chinese public school in Kingston, Jamaica, where I studied the art of Chinese calligraphy and drawing.

At about this time I developed a close friendship with a crippled schoolmate who could not participate in sports, so we both spent time together drawing. In high school I took up art in an extra-curricular class. My teacher advised me not to become an artist because I'd starve to death. I replied, "O.K., I'll starve to death."

Animals figure a lot in my work, due to my compulsive, bittersweet fascination with them. When I was a small child I used to get up early in the morning to watch the horses go to the beach for a bath. I once got too close, and one of the horses stepped on my little toe. I used to spend summer vacations at my grandmother's country home; there were pigs, goats, and cows everywhere. The first time I rode a donkey bareback, I was so sore I could not sit properly for a whole week. The donkey also dumped me on a rock pile.

But my worst experience with animals was yet to come. I used to raise goldfish in an outdoor fountain. A friend traded a pair of snow-white bunnies for six fish. In a year or so I had lots and lots of bunnies—"Too many," said my mother. But I said, "They are so cute." One day I came home to a very sumptuous meal of curried "chicken." After dinner I went out to feed my rabbits and cried, "Michelangelo is gone! Where is he? Oh, Mom! Was that really chicken I just ate?" Later on, I also lost a duck I had won in a raffle, when it flew away over the horizon.

These experiences were all forgotten, however, when one day I climbed a tree in my yard and all of a sudden I was aware of a presence. I turned around and saw that it was a Streamer-Tail Jamaican Doctor Bird sipping nectar from the flowers. It was a revelation of creation. The sunlight glistened on its feathers like so many emeralds and rubies. I marveled at the magnificent creature casually sipping flowers so close to me; then he was gone. It all came together then: the sunlight, the plant, the fauna, the people—the whole magic, the wonder, the glory of our little planet—earth.

I like very much being an illustrator. The work that I do for my own enjoyment is no different from what I do for books and other commercial enterprises.

In addition to the pleasure of having my artwork honored with awards, I am pleased to have had one of my poems, "A Question," included in an anthology of American poetry, *Timeless Voyages,* opposite a poem by Carl Sandburg.

———

Tony Chen was born in Kingston, Jamaica, where he spent his childhood. He came to the United States in 1949 and attended the Art Career School from 1949 to 1951. He graduated from Pratt Institute in 1955. Tony Chen married Pura De Castro in 1957 and they have two sons, who were born in 1958 and 1959.

After several jobs as a graphic designer and illustrator, Chen became assistant art director at *Newsweek* from 1961 to 1971. From 1971 to 1972, he was an Art Instructor at Nassau Community College on Long Island, New York. Since that time, Chen has illustrated over fifty books for adults and for children. His first children's book, *Too Many Crackers,* was published in 1962.

Chen has had many exhibitions of his work and has received a number of honors for both his original artwork and his book illustrations.

Over the years Chen has received many Awards of Merit from the Society of Illustrators, and was given the society's Award for Excellence in 1973. He also received the Creativity Award in 1972 from *Art Direction Magazine.*

Honshi was included in the American Institute of Graphic Arts children's book show in 1973/74, and was also in the Children's Book Showcase in 1973. *Run, Zebra, Run* also won the A.I.G.A. award in 1972.

SELECTED WORKS ILLUSTRATED: Tales From Old China, by Isabelle Chang, 1969; Honshi, by Aline Glasgow, 1972; About Owls, by May Garelick, 1975; Once We Went on a Picnic, by Aileen Fisher, 1975; Little Rystu, adapted by Mirra Ginsburg, 1978; In the Land of Small Dragon, told by Dang Manh Kha to Ann Nolan Clark, 1979; The Riddle of the Drum, translated and retold by Verna Aardema, 1979.

SELECTED WORKS WRITTEN AND ILLUSTRATED: Run, Zebra, Run, 1972.

ABOUT: Contemporary Authors (First Revision), Vol. 37–40; Kingman, Lee and others, comps. Illustrators of Children's Books: 1967–1976; The International Authors and Writers Who's Who, 1982; Mayor, Hyatt. Contemporary American Illustrators of Children's Books; Pitz, Henry C. 200 Years of American Illustration; Something About the Author, Vol. 6; Who's Who in American Art, 1978; Who's Who in the East, 1974; The Writers Directory 1982–84; American Artist May 1972.

ALICE CHILDRESS

October 12, 1920–

AUTHOR OF *A Hero Ain't Nothin' But a Sandwich,* etc.

ALICE CHILDRESS

Biographical sketch of Alice Childress:

ALICE CHILDRESS was born in Charlestown, South Carolina, and grew up and attended public schools in Harlem. She is proud of her Harlem roots and announced at a writer's conference at Fisk University in 1966: "All I know of generosity and kindness and love I learned in Harlem." In Harlem, she went to black church programs at which concert artists and readers appeared. Her first memory of a theatrical experience is hearing an actress recite scenes from Shakespeare. As Childress remarked: "A lot of Shakespeare is done in the Negro community. We are more identified with his flamboyancy than with a more restricted kind of theatre." The first role she remembers playing, at an early age, was Titania in *A Midsummer Night's Dream.* Her first stage appearances were in junior high school theatricals and later in amateur presentations by groups such as the Urban League Players and the Negro Youth Theatre.

Childress was one of the original members of the American Negro Theatre and worked there as an actress, member of the technical crew, and director for twelve years. She came to playwrighting via acting and directing in the late 1940s. While acting and writing, Childress worked in a variety of odd jobs, such as apprentice machinist, photo-negative retoucher, governess, salesperson, and insurance agent.

Trouble in Mind (1955) was critically acclaimed in an Off-Broadway production and won a 1956 Obie Award. It was Childress's first play to be produced outside Harlem.

In 1957, Childress won a grant from the John Golden Fund for Playwrights, and in 1966 her play, *Wedding Band,* opened in Ann Arbor, Michigan.

Between 1966 and 1968, Childress was at the Radcliffe Institute for Independent Study on a Harvard appointment. In 1969, her play *Wine in the Wilderness* was produced for television by WGBH in Boston, and in the 1972–73 season, *Wedding Band* was presented by Joseph Papp at the Public Theatre in New York, directed by Papp and Childress and starring Eartha Kitt.

Childress's works portray the complexity of relationships between blacks and whites and the various ways blacks survive in contemporary American society. She exhibits a strong theatrical sense in both her drama and in her fiction. She claims to have gotten her dramatic bent from her grandmother, a theatrical storyteller, and from the influences of the Bible, Shakespeare, and the poet Paul Laurence Dunbar.

In 1973, Childress published her first novel for young readers, *A Hero Ain't Nothin' But a Sandwich,* the portrayal of a young urban heroin addict. Enormously controversial, it was the first book banned in a Savannah, Georgia, school library since *The Catcher in the Rye.* The critics, however, were almost unanimous in their strong praise. Ed Bullins, writing in the *New York Times,* called the book a "brilliant study of a 13-year-old black heroin user" that "reaffirms the belief that excellent writing is alive and thriving in some black corners of America." John T. Gillespie, in his *More Juniorplots: A Guide for Teachers and Librarians* wrote: "Alice Childress's experience as playwright and actress is revealed in the brilliant characterization and dialogue in *Hero.* . . . *Hero* is not just a family of blacks and their problems; it deals with themes and experiences that are universal, such as rejection, love, the importance of family ties, poverty, and the problems of growing old." Miguel Ortiz, in *The Lion and the Unicorn,* wrote, "Alice Childress, in successfully portraying the complexity of character, has been able to show the effect of economic class and historical antecedent on the people she writes about." *A Hero Ain't Nothin' But a Sandwich* was nominated for a 1974 National Book Award. It was selected as a Notable Book by the American Library Association and won the 1974 Woodward School (Brooklyn, New York) Annual Book Award. It also won a 1975 Lewis Carroll Shelf Award and appeared on the *School Library Journal* "Best of the Best 1966–1978" list (December 1979). It was made into a movie, for which Childress wrote the screenplay.

In 1975, Childress published *When the Rattlesnake Sounds,* a one-act play for young readers about one summer in the life of Harriet Tubman. Mary M. Burns, writing in the *Horn Book,* called it " . . . a poignant celebration of courage, a beautifully crafted work."

Rainbow Jordan, a novel for young readers, is a portrait of three women: fourteen-year-old Rainbow, her unreliable mother, and the older woman who cares for Rainbow when her mother periodically leaves. Anne Tyler, writing in the *New York Times Book Review,* wrote that Rainbow is "a heartbreakingly sturdy character, and *Rainbow Jordan* is a beautiful book." It was named a Best Book for Young Adults in 1981 by the American Library Association and a Notable Children's Trade Book in the Field of Social Studies by a joint committee of the National Council for the Social Studies and the Children's Book Council, in 1981.

Many of Childress's plays have been anthologized and she is the author of a num-

ber of stories, articles, and plays that have appeared in *Negro Digest, Freedomways, Essence, Masses and Mainstream,* and *Black World.* She wrote a novel for adults in 1979, *A Short Walk,* and she is the editor of *The Black Scene,* a collection of fifteen scenes from works by black playwrights. She has lectured at numerous universities, for theater groups, and at public schools, and is well-known for her community volunteer work. She has also traveled around the world, observing life and art in such places as Africa, China, and Russia.

Childress has won many awards and honors, including an achievement award from the National Association for Negro Business and Professional Women's Clubs in 1975; the Virgin Islands Film Festival Award for Best Screenplay in 1977 for *A Hero Ain't Nothin' But a Sandwich*; and the Paul Robeson Award for Outstanding Contributions to the Performing Arts. She was elected to the Filmmakers Hall of Fame in 1977.

Childress is a member of P.E.N., the Harlem Writers Guild, the New Dramatists, the American Federation of Television and Radio Artists, the Society of Choreographers and Stage Directors, the Dramatists Guild, and the Authors League of Actors Equity.

Alice Childress is married to a musician and has a daughter, Jean Lee. She lives in New York City.

SELECTED WORKS: A Hero Ain't Nothin' But a Sandwich, 1973; When the Rattlesnake Sounds, 1975; Let's Hear It for the Queen, 1976; Rainbow Jordan, 1981.

ABOUT: Abramson, Doris E. Negro Playwrights in the American Theatre: 1925–1959; Contemporary Authors, Vol. 45–48; (New Revision Series), Vol. 3; Page, James A., comp. Selected Black American Authors: An Illustrated Bio-Bibliography; Rush, Theressa Gunnels and others, comps. Black American Writers Past and Present: A Biographical and Bibliographical Dictionary; Shockley, Ann Allen and Sue P. Chandler, comps. Living Black American Authors: A Biographical Directory; Something About the Author, Vol. 7; Vinson, James, ed. Contemporary Dramatists; Ward, Martha E. and Dorothy A. Marquardt. Authors of Books for Young People, 2nd edition (Supplement); Who's Who Among Black Americans, 1980–1981; Who's Who in America, 1982–1983; Who's Who of American Women, 1974–1975; The Writers Directory 1982–84.

MATT CHRISTOPHER

August 16, 1917–

AUTHOR OF *The Year Mom Won the Pennant,* etc.

Autobiographical sketch of Matthew F. Christopher, who also uses the pseudonym "Fredric Martin":

A QUESTION that is asked of me more than any other is: why did I become a writer?

The answer is simple: because I wanted to. It wasn't easy. It hasn't been, nor will it ever be. I still have difficulty coming up with new ideas, putting words in correct sequence without my editors making changes now and then, and constructing plots that seem great to me at the time, but not so great to the person behind the editorial desk. Yet I write on, because there is a nagging sensation gnawing at me if I don't.

Sometimes, as I think back, I've wondered myself why I chose a career that I happen to be able to love and make a living at. I'm the oldest of nine children—seven boys and two girls—none of whom, except me, care very much about reading, let alone writing. I was born on August 16, 1917, in Bath, Pennsylvania, of immigrant parents, neither of whom went beyond the fourth or fifth grade in school. When I was eight years old my family moved to upstate New York, near Ithaca, where I spent most of my life. My childhood consisted of going to school and playing games such as Duck on the Rock, Lost Turkey, and baseball. We had no books in our house, so I read very little. And until we kids could afford to buy baseball gloves and bats, we played with tennis balls, and used broom handles for bats. But baseball became my favorite sport, and eventually, at the age of nineteen, I signed a contract to play professional baseball for Smiths Falls, Ontario, Canada, in the Canadian-American League. But my pro career was short-lived; after less than two months I was given an unconditional release. So I returned home, continued to play semi-pro baseball, married (the former Catherine M. Krupa), worked (in various jobs, but I was the longest with the National Cash Register Company in Ithaca, New York), and raised a family of four children, three boys and a girl (Martin, Pamela, Dale, and Duane—in that order).

During all this time I wrote short stories, articles, and, now and then, poetry. I was fourteen when I started, and eighteen when I won a prize in the *Writer's Digest* short-short story writing contest. I was eager to make writing my career, regardless of how long it would take me. I began to sell stories to both adult and kid magazines—sports stories, pulp detective stories, and science fiction, and in 1967 to 1972, I wrote a comic strip (The Chuck White series) for *Treasure Chest Magazine.* (The magazine went defunct.) But sports was my forte: besides baseball, I played football, basketball, and soccer. After about eighty magazine sales I wrote an adult mystery novel, *Look for the Body,* for which I received the fat sum of $150, minus the ten percent agent's fee. Then, over a Thanksgiving weekend, I wrote *The Lucky Baseball Bat,* and sold it on my own to Little, Brown and Company, which has published nearly all of my books since then. Not only sports books, but adventure books, and mysteries (under my pen name, Fredric Martin) as well.

Now I'm into motor sports. *Dirt Bike Racer* was published in 1979, and *Drag Strip Racer* in 1982. They were sports I had never dreamed I would write about. But they were growing sports, and I thought I would like to try my hand at them. I had fun going to the races, talking with the participants, taking pictures, and learning all I could about the sports so that I'd be able to convey the excitement of them onto paper. It is research such as this that helps make my job enjoyable, which is a good thing, because writing is getting harder for me to do.

But perseverance pays off. In 1982 my first mystery, *The Return of the Headless Horseman*, was published; it's not a long book, but no one but me really knows how difficult it was to put those manuscript pages together, to make the book worthy enough for the editor to tell me that she "loved it," the sweetest words an author can hear.

SELECTED WORKS: The Year Mom Won the Pennant, 1968; Face-Off, 1972; Jinx Glove, 1974; The Submarine Pitch, 1976; Football Fugitive, 1976; The Twenty-One Mile Swim, 1979; Dirt Bike Racer, 1979; Wild Pitch, 1980; Run, Billy, Run, 1980; The Return of the Headless Horseman, 1982.

SELECTED WORKS AS FREDERIC MARTIN: The Mystery at Monkey Run, 1966; The Mystery Under Fugitive House, 1967.

ABOUT: Contemporary Authors (First Revision), Vol. 2; (New Revision Series), Vol. 5; The International Authors and Writers Who's Who, 8th edition; Hopkins, Lee Bennett. More Books by More People: Interviews with Sixty-five Authors of Books for Children; Something About the Author, Vol. 2; Ward, Martha E. and Dorothy A. Marquardt. Authors of Books for Young People, 2nd edition; The Writers Directory 1982–84.

PATRICIA CLAPP

June 9, 1912–

AUTHOR OF *Constance: A Story of Early Plymouth,* etc.

Autobiographical sketch of Patricia Clapp:

I AM sometimes asked what made me "decide to become an author." I can only reply that I never did decide to. I don't think anyone does. It happens to you. If you are the sort of person who is happiest putting words on paper, if writing a letter is a joy and not a chore, if you make lists of everything—you are basically a writer. A day may come when it occurs to you that someone might put your words into print, and if the idea bears fruit, you're hooked. But never, never have I heard of anyone leaping from the bathtub shouting "Eureka! I have decided to become an author!"

I have been putting words on paper as long as I can remember. I have a notebook started when I was eight years old (spelled "eaght"), in which I wrote poetry, blithely rhyming such words as "eight" (or "eaght") and "Cape." The Cape was Cape Cod, where I spent all the long summers with my beloved grandparents until I was sixteen.

I was born in Boston, and Cape Cod is my first and happiest memory. Even now I can instantly recall the dry, salty scent of pine trees and ocean air, the warm oozing of a tarred road under bare feet, the smell of Fels Naphtha soap shaved into my grandmother's wash barrel, the endless meadows of buttercups and Queen Anne's lace—I have it all forever, the way it was. I know that if I went back now nothing would be the same, so I don't. You can't go home again.

Home, since I was sevenish, has been New Jersey. I have also lived briefly in California, which I do not care for because I like four distinct seasons in my year, and in England, which I love and often revisit.

I was educated, more or less, in a girls' private school, where I was a whiz at English, not too bad at languages, and a dud

at everything else. I was thoroughly grown before I discovered that history, which I had loathed for so many school years, was nothing more than what people had done. Since people fascinate me, this came as a great revelation, and all but two of my books are historical novels.

I studied for a year and a half at Columbia School of Journalism and wrote a great deal of poetry, some of which was printed in poetry magazines that paid in copies, with which I showered my mother. On two wonderful occasions the *New York Times* bought poems and sent me into happy delirium.

I left Columbia to get married and in due course produced three children. I also became deeply involved in a community theater, where I still spend the majority of my time. When I was asked to direct my daughters' Girl Scout troop play I searched the library for material, found nothing I liked, and wrote my own. Someone talked me into submitting the result to a publisher and it was bought for the munificent sum of $25. I settled down to concentrated playwriting and told my husband he could retire and I would manage everything. Fortunately he didn't.

Some years later the first book, *Constance,* came as an accident when I tried to put the story of a Mayflower ancestor into play form. When it didn't work I found myself writing a book that stunned me by becoming a runner-up for the National Book Award. I didn't even know what the National Book Award was.

Now, forty-odd plays, six books and ten grandchildren later, I know I will never get rich from writing, but I also know it is the most satisfying hobby I could find. If I can be said to have a career, it is theater. The writing is for fun. I write when I feel like it, am under no pressures, and have no commitments. After a few hours at the typewriter I feel relaxed, cleansed, and triumphant. The fact that I will spend another few hours *rewriting* doesn't bother me at all.

Currently I lead three lives. As Patricia Clapp (which is what I was born) I write books, plays, some poetry, various bits and pieces, and answer hundreds and hundreds of letters from readers of all ages. Under my married name I work enthusiastically at administration and directing in that community theater. As the mother and grandmother of a large family I listen often, assist whenever possible, and advise only when asked. I can think of no happier way to live.

———

Constance, in addition to being a finalist in the National Book Awards in 1969, won a Lewis Carroll Shelf Award that year.

Some of Patricia Clapp's many plays can be found in anthologies, such as *100 Plays for Children* (A. S. Burack, ed., 1970), *Fifty Plays for Holidays* (Sylvia E. Kamerman, ed., 1969), and *Fifty Plays for Junior Actors* (Sylvia E. Kamerman, ed., 1966).

She has also had poetry and articles published in magazines, including *Yankee.*

SELECTED WORKS: Constance: A Story of Early Plymouth, 1968; Jane-Emily, 1969; Dr. Elizabeth: The Story of the First Woman Doctor, 1974; I'm Deborah Sampson: A Soldier in the War of the Revolution, 1977; Witches' Children, 1982.

ABOUT: Contemporary Authors, (First Revision), Vol. 25–28; Kirkpatrick, D. L., Twentieth-Century Children's Writers; Something About the Author, Vol. 4; The Writers Directory 1982–84.

BRUCE CLEMENTS

November 25, 1931–

AUTHOR OF *I Tell a Lie Every So Often,* etc.

Autobiographical sketch of Bruce Clements:

I WAS BORN in 1931 in New York City, and I started writing plays with a friend of mine when I was fifteen. Our idea was to start a radio station that would broadcast a one-hour play every night. We thought we'd write half of them, use old plays for the other half, and get our friends and other people to act in them. It was a great idea, but we found out that it was impossible to produce a play every other day.

My friend's name was Hank, and instead of going on as a writer he became an engineer and started his own business, which is still going on. I kept on wanting to be a writer, mostly because I wanted to be famous and rich. I had the idea that there was a world of grown-ups out there somewhere— interesting and happy people—actors and painters and novelists and reporters and concert pianists, who made great art and had a lot of fun with each other and got pointed at on the street and could buy almost anything they wanted.

I found out later that that *heaven of successful artists* doesn't exist, but I still like the ambition to join it. I still have it. Writing is fun some of the time and absorbing a lot of the time, but it is also very hard work and full of little defeats, and the dream of joining the magic circle of happiness and fame is one of the things that keeps me scribbling.

So now I'm fifty-two and I've written five novels and a biography, and together with Hanna Clements a book about drug addiction. I have three grown-up daughters, and they tell me I should keep on, so I guess I will. (Maybe they think I'm famous.)

———

Bruce Clements received a B.A. from Columbia University in 1954. He earned a B.D. degree from Union Theological Seminary in 1956 and an M.A. in 1962 from the State University of New York at Albany. He was married in 1954. A minister of the United Church of Christ, he has been both a pastor and a college teacher. He is now Professor of English and chairman of the department at Eastern Connecticut State University in Willimantic.

Coming Home to a Place You've Never Been Before is the story of a halfway house, which Clements says is very like Perception House in Willimantic, Connecticut, of which he was once a director. *From Ice Set Free* is the story of Clements' father-in-law, Otto Kiep, a German lawyer and diplomat who tried to speak out against Hitler. *I Tell a Lie Every So Often* was a finalist for a National Book Award in 1975 and also appeared on the *School Library Journal* "Best of the Best 1966–1978" list (December 1979).

SELECTED WORKS: Two Against the Tide, 1967; The Face of Abraham Candle, 1969; From Ice Set Free: The Story of Otto Kiep, 1972; I Tell a Lie Every So Often, 1974; Prison Window, Jerusalem Blue, 1977; Anywhere Else But Here, 1980.

SELECTED WORKS WRITTEN WITH HANNA CLEMENTS: Coming Home to a Place You've Never Been Before, 1975.

ABOUT: Contemporary Authors, Vol. 53–56; (New Revision Series), Vol. 5; Something About the Author, Vol. 27; Ward, Martha E. and Dorothy A. Marquardt. Authors of Books for Young People, 2nd edition (Supplement).

LUCILLE CLIFTON

LUCILLE CLIFTON

June 27, 1936–

AUTHOR OF *Some of the Days of Everett Anderson,* etc.

Biographical sketch of Lucille Sayles Clifton:

LUCILLE CLIFTON was born in Depew, New York, a small town outside of Buffalo where her father worked in the steel mills and her mother worked in a laundry. When she was growing up, her father, Samuel L. Sayles Sr., would tell her stories about her ancestors, beginning with her great-great-grandmother, Caroline, "born of Dahomey people in 1822," who was captured and brought as a slave to New Orleans. Lucille Clifton celebrates her ancestor's spirit in *Generations,* a memoir of five generations of Sayles and a eulogy to her father, who died of emphysema in 1969.

From her mother, Clifton learned to express herself in poetry. Thelma Moore Sayles suffered from epilepsy, but managed to put her feelings into poems, which she read aloud to her four children.

At age sixteen Clifton won a full scholarship to Howard University, where she majored in drama. She remembers feeling homesick and out of place at the cosmopolitan college. After two years, she left. In *Generations,* she explained why:

. . . Lost my scholarship because I didn't study. . . . And so I came home to a disappointed and confused Mama and a Daddy who was furious and defensive and sad.

"Feet of clay," he said to me. "My idol got feet of clay. God sent you to college to show me that you got feet of clay."

"Daddy," I argued with him, "I don't need that stuff, I'm going to write poems. I can do what I want to do! I'm from Dahomey women!"

From Howard University, she went to Fredonia State Teachers College near Buffalo. There, she joined a small group of blacks who read and performed plays and she began to find her voice as a writer. One member of the group was novelist Ishmael Reed, who showed her poems to Langston Hughes, who selected a few for his anthology *Poetry of the Negro, 1746–1970.*

Another important member of the play group was Fred Clifton, an artist, writer, and educator, then teaching philosophy at the University of Buffalo. Lucille Sayles married Fred Clifton in 1958 and they have six children: Sidney, Fredrica, Channing, Gillian, Graham, and Alexia.

In 1969, Lucille Clifton's poetry began to gain recognition. The YW-YMHA Poetry

Center in New York City honored her with the Discovery Award. In the same year, her first book of poems, *Good Times,* was published. It was chosen as one of the ten best books of the year by the *New York Times.*

In 1970 her first poetry book for children was published, *Some of the Days of Everett Anderson.* Clifton uses her prose to counteract stereotypes and to help black children to be proud of their heritage. In *The Black BC's,* for example, she praises the ways in which black people and their culture have enriched American life.

In a 1976 *Ms.* magazine interview, Clifton said that her children help with her writing. Their experiences are the basis of much of her work, but in a larger sense, she explained, "They keep you aware of life. And you have to stay aware of life, keep growing to write." She added, "They also keep me sane. I did this reading at the Library of Congress once. It was a great honor. Next day, I was ironing and I said, 'What is this great poet doing ironing?' The kids laughed, said, 'Are you crazy?' and I came back to earth."

Lucille Clifton has been the recipient of National Endowment for the Arts grants in 1969, 1970, and 1972 and was made poet laureate of the State of Maryland from 1979 to 1982. She has been a poet-in-residence at Coppin State College, Baltimore, Maryland, and a visiting writer at Columbia University School of the Arts, New York City.

Presently the poet lives in a house in Baltimore, Maryland, with her family. Between verses, she enjoys acting, reading, and people watching.

SELECTED WORKS: Some of the Days of Everett Anderson, 1970; The Black BC's, 1970; Everett Anderson's Christmas Coming, 1972; Good, Says Jerome, 1973; All Us Come Cross the Water, 1973; Don't You Remember?, 1973; The Boy Who Didn't Believe in Spring, 1973; Everett Anderson's Year, 1974; The Times They Used to Be, 1974; My Brother Fine With Me, 1975; Everett Anderson's Friend, 1976; Three Wishes, 1976; Amifika, 1977; Everett Anderson's 1-2-3, 1977; Everett Anderson's Nine Month Long, 1978; The Lucky Stone, 1979.

ABOUT: Clifton, Lucille. Generations, 1976; Contemporary Authors, Vol. 49–52; (New Revision Series), Vol. 2; Kirkpatrick, D. L., ed. Twentieth-Century Children's Writers; Page, James A., comp. Selected Black American Authors: An Illustrated Bio-Bibliography; Something About the Author, Vol. 20; Who's Who Among Black Americans, 3rd edition; The Writers Directory 1982–84; Ms. October 1976.

VICKI COBB

August 19, 1938–

AUTHOR OF *Science Experiments You Can Eat,* etc.

Autobiographical sketch of Vicki Cobb:

WHEN I WAS a little girl, more than anything else, I loved to make stuff. I made all kinds of things. I cooked, and made doll clothes, and drew pictures, and wrote poems. Once, when I was eight, I made a papier-mâché puppet in school. It was a man's head and he was bald like my father. I pasted short lengths of black yarn in a fringe for his hair and eyebrows. One night a mouse came and ate off his nose. My teacher was worried about my reaction to the destruction of my work but even then I knew that the work was not all that important. What was important was my ability to produce that work, or another even better. And no one could destroy *that.*

When I was older and had to choose an academic area, I was drawn to science. The orderliness of the universe was beautiful to me. I was constantly told that science was not for girls, and I was pushed toward the humanities. Nevertheless, I majored in zoology at Barnard College and had a minor in chemistry. Upon graduating I worked as a lab technician and found that lab work was definitely *not* for me. I loved the big ideas of science, not the day-to-day drudgery of ordinary research. So I went back to school and got a master's degree in high school science teaching.

Teaching was fun and challenging but a rat race. How I wished for the time to work

Vicki Cobb

up a lesson so I could present the big ideas of science in such a way that they could make a lasting impression! When I left teaching, right before my first son was born, I got my chance to do just that. I figured that if I could talk about science, I could write science; besides, I needed to make money. So I started looking for assignments to write scientific materials. I wrote teacher's guides and filmstrips and designed curricula, and I wrote children's science books for series where my title was one of many and no one noticed. I learned to write during this period. (It wasn't true that if I could talk about something I could automatically write well about it. It took time to learn to write.)

Finally, *Science Experiments You Can Eat* was published in 1972. That was the first book that expressed the creative part of me. It pulled together many of my experiences and interests. It was the first book that I wrote for the child I used to be . . . the little girl who was always looking for a project to do.

These days I am lucky to write only the books I want to write. I try to give my readers the thrill of discovery that comes from doing things. Science should be creative ac-

tivity, just like art. The challenge in science is to create ways of uncovering nature's secrets. Although there is only one nature to be discovered, there are as many ways of discovering it as there are imaginations. I also want to convey to my readers that it's okay to fail and make mistakes—science does not evolve full-blown and perfect, as it is often presented. Waste is always present in any creative process. Good artists, writers, and scientists throw out more than they keep.

I am always looking for the opportunity to do something new. I like to think of myself as a collector of experiences. My collection makes me feel rich.

―――――

Vicki Cobb was born in New York City and grew up in Tarrytown, New York. As a teenager, she studied art at the Art Students' League of New York and Columbia's School of Painting and Sculpture. She attended the University of Wisconsin from 1954 to 1957 and graduated from Barnard College in 1958. She received her M.A. from Columbia Teacher's College in 1960 and was married the same year.

Cobb taught science in high school in Rye, New York, from 1961 to 1964. She wrote for and appeared on a syndicated television show for children, "The Science Game," and has been a writer for ABC's "Good Morning, America" show. She writes a column, "Cobb's Corner on Science," for *Instructor* magazine and is a member of the Authors Guild. Cobb lives in Mamaroneck, New York with her two sons.

Both *More Science Experiments You Can Eat* and *How to Really Fool Yourself* were named Children's Choices by the joint committee of the International Reading Association and the Children's Book Council, in 1980 and 1982 respectively. The latter was also named a Notable Book of 1981 by the American Library Association. Both *Supersuits,* in 1975, and *Lots of Rot,* in 1981, were named Outstanding Science Trade Books for Children by the joint committee of the National Science Teachers Association and the C.B.C. *Bet You Can't!* won a New York Academy of Science Children's Science Book Award in 1980.

SELECTED WORKS: Science Experiments You Can Eat, 1972; Arts and Crafts You Can Eat, 1974; Supersuits, 1975; Magic . . . Naturally!: Science Entertainments and Amusements, 1976; More Science Experiments You Can Eat, 1979; Bet You Can't!, 1980; How to Really Fool Yourself: Illusions for All Your Senses, 1981; Lots of Rot, 1981; The Secret Life of School Supplies, 1981; The Secret Life of Hardware, 1982; Gobs of Goo, 1983; The Monsters Who Died: A Mystery About Dinosaurs, 1983;

ABOUT: Contemporary Authors (First Revision), Vol. 33–36; Something About the Author, Vol. 8; Ward, Martha E. and Dorothy A. Marquardt. Authors of Books for Young People, 2nd edition (Supplement); The Writers Directory 1982–84.

Barbara Cohen

BARBARA COHEN

March 15, 1932–

AUTHOR OF *The Carp in the Bathtub,* etc.

Biographical sketch of Barbara Cohen:

BARBARA COHEN writes, "When I was a kid, I was rather a creep. I was overweight, I was plain, I was messy, my nose was always in a book." Her father died when she was nine years old, and her mother ran a small hotel and restaurant on the outskirts of a New Jersey town. She had no neighbors, as the hotel was situated near a busy highway, and, in her words, in the town where her Jewish family lived, "ethnic, racial and religious prejudices did not lie deep beneath the affable surface."

Yet Barbara Cohen had happy memories of her childhood, of her "loving, wise and liberating" mother, of her loving relationship with her brother and sister, of the varied and interesting range of employees and guests at the inn, and of summers spent with grandparents at the beach. She had a "limitless" supply of books in local libraries.

When she was a child, she told people that she wanted to be a writer when she grew up; she wrote sporadically in grade school, and, later, in high school. She attended Barnard College for her B.A. degree and earned her M.A. from Rutgers University in 1957. Married by this time to Gene Cohen, she taught high school English in public schools in Tenafly, Somerville, and Hillsborough, New Jersey. She has three daughters, Leah, Sarah, and Becky, and was active in her community and in Jewish life in her town. "I didn't have much time for writing," she recalls, "except for a weekly newspaper column that my stepfather asked me to do, and for which I am now very grateful. It enabled me, all those years, to keep my pen dipped in ink." The column, "Books and Things," was published in New Jersey newspapers, including the *Somerville Messenger Gazette.*

When she began to get ideas for fiction, she started writing stories, and decided to leave the teaching job she loved to become a full-time writer. Except for the weekly column she wrote, all her writing has been for children and young adults. "I didn't intend it that way," she writes, "but that's how it's turned out. I think it happened because in some way my mind is stuck at thirteen." She writes of her own experiences as well as things she's heard of.

"I never know what thing outside of me is going to connect with something inside of me and get me started on a book or story. The moment when these connections occur are the most exciting in my life."

Cohen calls herself a "committed Jew" and states that she writes out of her own experience. The specific people in her fiction, she says, "happen to be Jewish, because I am." Several of her novels are set in a small country inn like the one where she grew up. Among her books are retellings of Bible stories, like *I Am Joseph,* and Jewish legends, such as *Yussel's Prayer.*

Barbara Cohen has received many awards and honors for her writing. She received the 1981 Sydney Taylor Body of Work Award from the Association of Jewish Libraries. She won two National Jewish Book Awards in 1983, for *King of the Seventh Grade* and for *Yussel's Prayer. Yussel's Prayer* was named a Children's Choice Book by the joint committee of the International Reading Association and the Children's Book Council, and was also named an American Library Association Notable Book in 1981.

Also named ALA Notable Books were *Seven Daughters and Seven Sons* and *Gooseberries to Oranges* in 1982, *Thank You, Jackie Robinson* in 1974, and *I am Joseph* in 1980. *Unicorns in the Rain* was designated an ALA Best Book for Young Adults in 1980.

Barbara Cohen is a member of the National Education Association, the Authors Guild, Hadassah, and the League of Women Voters. She lives in Somerville, New Jersey.

SELECTED WORKS WRITTEN: The Carp in the Bathtub, 1972; Thank You, Jackie Robinson, 1974; Bitter Herbs and Honey, 1976; The Innkeeper's Daughter, 1979; Unicorns in the Rain, 1980; Queen for a Day, 1981; Gooseberries to Oranges, 1982; King of the Seventh Grade, 1982; Molly's Pilgrim,1983.

SELECTED WORKS WRITTEN WITH BAHIJA LOVEJOY: Seven Daughters and Seven Sons, 1982.

SELECTED WORKS RETOLD: The Binding of Isaac, 1978; I Am Joseph, 1980; Yussel's Prayer: A Yom Kippur Story, 1981.

ABOUT: Contemporary Authors, Vol. 53–56; (New Revision Series), Vol. 4; Something About the Author, Vol. 10; Ward, Martha E. and Dorothy A. Marquardt. Authors of Books for Young People, 2nd edition (Supplement).

MIRIAM COHEN

October 14, 1926–

AUTHOR OF *Lost in the Museum,* etc.

Autobiographical sketch of Miriam Cohen:

I NEVER THOUGHT of being a writer until my three sons went to school. Their vulnerability as they ran off each morning filled me with a desire to "show" what was happening to them and the other little kids in their class. So the little gang of kids in all my books are made up, but have some parts of each of my boys.

A few of their teachers were "mean." A few were very, very kind and good. In my stories I always make the teacher wise and kind. And I try not to let her meddle too much with the children's business. That is, the kids first try to solve their difficulties alone, and have a life and thoughts of their own, without adult dictation. But she is always at the edge of the picture watching that no one is hurtful to anybody else. And she steps back in when it's time. ("She" makes me think I should have a man teacher in a story, because men teachers of small children give something very special.)

I was born in Brooklyn many years ago, and now I have moved back just a few blocks from there. This same "child," now approaching grandma-time, thinks and thinks about what it's like to have lived so long, and seen this same Prospect Park as an infant in a pram. It is fascinating—time lost and time regained! (Artists and writers it seems to me, can go outside of time and not lose it.)

Which brings me to what I'm reading:

Miriam Cohen

Marcel Proust for the last six months. (I can't bear to be finished with it.) And Katherine Paterson, whom I love, and Scott O'Dell's *Island of the Blue Dolphins,* which I study every year, and Madeleine L'Engle's *Summer of the Great Grandmother,* which is quite fine, and Minarik's *Little Bear,* and *Frog and Toad,* by Lobel, which I always love and need to study.

———

Miriam Cohen has lived in Afghanistan, where one of her sons was born, in Brazil, and in Greeenwich Village, New York City, where she paid four dollars a month for an apartment in the 1940s.

Three of her books were Junior Literary Guild selections, *First Grade Takes a Test, Jim Meets the Thing,* and *See You Tomorrow, Charles.* All three books were illustrated by Lillian Hoban.

SELECTED WORKS: Will I Have A Friend?, 1967; Lost in the Museum, 1979; First Grade Takes a Test, 1980; No Good in Art, 1980; Jim Meets the Thing, 1981; See You Tomorrow, Charles, 1983.

ABOUT: Something About the Author, Vol. 29.

JOANNA COLE

August 11, 1944–

AUTHOR OF *A Horse's Body,* etc.

Biographical sketch of Joanna Cole:

JOANNA COLE was born in Newark, New Jersey, and grew up in nearby East Orange. She attended the University of Massachusetts and Indiana University before graduating from the City College of New York with a B.A. in psychology. She took some graduate education courses, and spent a year as a librarian in a Brooklyn elementary school. Later, she became a letters correspondent at *Newsweek,* and then a senior editor for Doubleday Books for Young Readers.

During her year as an elementary librarian, Cole rediscovered her interest in children's books and remembered her childhood fascination with science, which she described recently: "my favorite subjects in school were science and writing, and in science I could combine both. I loved to do science experiments and write them up as reports. My science teacher in elementary school encouraged this, and my favorite books as a child were from this library.

"I was also interested in the plants and animals I found in my backyard. It was a small yard, actually, but I remember it as a place of wonderful variety. Even now, after so many years, I can take a mental trip around the place and imagine the cool ferns under the hedge, the shiny poison ivy near the rambling roses, the mulberry tree near the fence—and the insects. Much of my childhood was spent watching insects—ants, praying mantises, crickets, wasps, bees."

As an editor, she had an interest in good writing. Her own series of science books for children combine her interests in children's books, science, and clear explication, resulting in widely read titles.

Booklist commented that *A Chick Hatches* "has predicted children's questions with logical thoroughness, yet there's never a wasted word." Her other titles cover a wide

Joanna Cole

range of subjects from dinosaurs to cockroaches to fish. *Booklist* said that *A Fish Hatches* "spark[s] a sense of awe about the complex birth process and a new understanding about the lives of underwater creatures."

Her most well-known series, the "Body" books, was done in collaboration with photograher Jerome Wexler who was able to match Cole's explicit text with equally clear photographs. Cole realized in the course of researching and writing earlier books that her own main interest was in how the parts of an animal's body function to achieve what is required by nature, for example, how does the position of a cat's eyes help it in hunting? *A Frog's Body, A Horse's Body,* and *A Cat's Body* were characterized by comments such as, "the unity of word and illustration typifies the clarity and harmony to be seen here," from *Booklist,* and from the *Horn Book,* "sensible, straightforward, comprehensive."

In addition to enthusiastic reviews, Cole's books have received a number of honors. *A Horse's Body* and *A Snake's Body* were both named Outstanding Science Trade Books for children by the joint committee of the National Science Teachers Association and the Children's Book Council in 1981, and both were designated American Library Association Notable Books. *A Snake's Body* was also named a Children's Choice Book of 1982 by the joint committee of the International Reading Association and the Children's Book Council and received an honorable mention in 1981 in the New York Academy of Sciences Children's Science Book Awards. Also named ALA Notables were *A Chick Hatches,* in 1976, and *A Frog's Body,* in 1980. Both *A Cat's Body* and *A Bird's Body* were Junior Literary Guild selections.

More recently, Joanna Cole has branched out from science with the Clown-Arounds series, and enjoys inventing the jokes that accompany their light story line. Also, her *Best-Loved Folktales of the World* is a selection of two hundred folk and fairy tales. She concentrated on making selections that were true to the oral traditions from which they derive, and on choosing tales that are favorites in the cultures from which they come. Cole comments on the book jacket that "The folktales have always been part of my life, first as a child and now as an adult when they are even more important to me for the wisdom they have to offer."

She is married to Philip Cole, a psychotherapist. They live in New York City with their daughter Rachel.

SELECTED WORKS: A Chick Hatches, 1976; The Saber-Toothed Tiger and Other Ice Age Mammals, 1977; A Fish Hatches, 1978; Find the Hidden Insect, 1979; A Frog's Body, 1980; A Horse's Body, 1981; A Snake's Body, 1981; Best-Loved Folktales of the World, 1982; A Bird's Body, 1982; A Cat's Body, 1982; The Clown-Arounds Have a Party, 1982; Cars and How They Go, 1983.

CHRISTOPHER COLLIER

January 29, 1930–

AUTHOR, WITH JAMES LINCOLN COLLIER, OF *My Brother Sam Is Dead,* etc.

Autobiographical sketch of Christopher Collier:

I THINK that everyone who reads will agree that most history textbooks are boring. When I was teaching junior high school I began to think that there must be a better way to teach American History. History is terribly important to know if you want to live the kind of life where you make plans and carry them out. Every day you use history. You used your own personal history and your own memory of it just to get to school today. You had to remember the directions to walk in, or the bus route, or something like that. You used your own personal memory of the past to do it. When you study history you have the advantage of the memory of thousands of other people; you can make plans on the basis of what they have done—what they have tried to do and failed, and tried to do and succeeded. You can choose which course of action best fits what you want to do. Without a knowledge of history, you will never have anything to go on but your own very limited experience.

That is why I write books. Most of the writing I do helps other historians learn about the past. But grown-ups are very hard to teach new things to, so I suspect that the writing I do for kids really is more effective. I write for kids with my brother because he knows how to write very exciting stories. I research all the historical material and give him a true story with all the detail. Then we make up some fictional characters and he writes the true story around those fictional characters. In that way we are able to write books that tell about the real historical past and at the same time are very exciting stories full of interesting characters.

The books we write together take place in parts of the United States with which we are familiar—New England and New York, and mostly Connecticut, where we grew up. I write about the Revolutionary Era because that is what I have been studying for the past twenty-five years. Imagine studying American History for that long and still loving it. I'll tell you a secret, too; when I was in school I even liked my history textbooks. They never bored me; but I can understand how they bore other people. Biology books bored me, but I knew kids who loved biology.

I published my first article when I was in fourth grade. It was about how to raise chickens for eggs—which I was doing at the time. My father was a part-time writer. He wrote about cowboys, mostly. In your library you may have books by him. He wrote biographies of Kit Carson, Annie Oakley, and Buffalo Bill, among other people. I never wanted to be a writer, though, because it is a very hard way to earn money. Teaching is just as much fun, and you earn a lot more money. Now I have the best of both worlds. I still teach, but I manage to find time to write all sorts of things, too. I even write for lawyers to help them win cases. But they don't always win.

For fun, I keep up a house that was built in 1790 and has five fireplaces. I cut a lot of firewood. My wife, Bonnie, is a figure skater, and she has been teaching me to ice dance for the past five years. I am really klutzy, but I have passed several dance tests. I have a son who also skates. He plays hockey, figure skates, and roller skates. He also writes stories, though in 1982 he is only in second grade. I have two other children who are grown. *My Brother Sam Is Dead* is dedicated to them. *Jump Ship To Freedom* is dedicated to my young son. You can look in the front of those books to see what their names are.

————

Christopher Collier attended Clark University where he earned his B.A. and he received his M.A. and Ph.D. from Columbia University. He has taught school in Connecticut and at Teachers College, Columbia University. He is currently Professor of American History at the University of Bridgeport in Connecticut.

He was nominated for a Pulitzer Prize for a book for adults, *Roger Sherman's Connecticut: Yankee Politics and the American Revolution.*

My Brother Sam Is Dead, published in 1974, gave readers a realistic view of the Revolutionary War on the eve of the U.S. Bicentennial in 1976. It was a Newbery Honor Book in 1975 and was designated a Notable Book by the American Library Association. It was also nominated for a National Book Award in 1975. *Jump Ship to Freedom* was named a Notable Trade Book in the Field of Social Studies in 1981 by a joint committee of the National Council for the Social Studies and the Children's Book Council. *War Comes to Willy Freeman* is a companion book to the novel.

SELECTED WORKS WITH JAMES LINCOLN COLLIER: My Brother Sam Is Dead, 1974; The Bloody Country, 1977; The Winter Hero, 1978; Jump Ship to Freedom, 1981; War Comes to Willy Freeman, 1983.

ABOUT: Contemporary Authors (First Revision), Vol. 33-36; Directory of American Scholars, 1978, Vol. 1; Something About the Author, Vol. 16; Ward, Martha E. and Dorothy A. Marquardt. Authors of Books for Young People, 2nd edition (Supplement); Who's Who in the East, 1975; Language Arts March 1978.

JAMES LINCOLN COLLIER

June 27, 1928–

AUTHOR, WITH CHRISTOPHER COLLIER, OF *My Brother Sam Is Dead,* etc.

Autobiographical sketch of James Lincoln Collier, who also uses the pseudonym "Charles Williams":

I COME FROM a family of writers. My father, Edmund Collier, wrote adventure fiction and a half dozen children's books. My uncle, Slater Brown, was a novelist who figures in E. E. Cummings' story of their war adventure, "The Enormous Room." My cousin, Gwilym Brown, was for twenty years a staff writer with *Sports Illustrated.* My brother-in-law, James Buechler, writes short fiction and has been twice represented in the O. Henry Prize collection. An aunt, Susan Jenkins Brown, was an editor of such authors as Katherine Anne Porter, and published a book about her friendship with Hart Crane. My brother is a historian, an author of a number of scholarly works, and my collaborator on a half dozen historical novels for children. Two other cousins have had magazine articles published; my eldest son, a musician, has published in specialized magazines, and my other son is currently contemplating a career in journalism.

Going back into the past, my great-grandmother was courted by the Thoreau brothers, Henry and John. Further back there was Anne Bradstreet, generally accounted America's first poet. Further back still was a man named Morton, who wrote a publicity tract on the Plymouth Colony known today as "Mort's Relation."

I thus became a writer the way other young people go into the family business. It never occurred to me that I couldn't write; it was what people did, and it has been what I have done since I became an adult.

I worked first for six years as a magazine editor, writing in my spare time. In 1958 I quit to work free-lance. Since then I have published some six hundred magazine articles for dozens of periodicals, ranging from

JAMES LINCOLN COLLIER

Playboy and *Esquire,* to the *New York Times Magazine* and the *Village Voice.* I have published a half dozen books for adults, the most recent being *The Making of Jazz,* which was nominated for an American Book Award, was named to the *London Observer's* Books of the Year List for 1979, and has been published in English, French, German, and Russian editions.

I have also published twenty-three children's books, five in collaboration with my brother, Christopher Collier. These have been published in seven languages, and have won, among them, the Child Study Association Book Award, a Newbery Honor Medal, a Jane Addams Peace Prize, and a National Book Award nomination. Many of them have appeared on the ALA Notable Book List, and others on the New York Public Library's recommended book list.

I grew up, inevitably, surrounded by writers, artists, and intellectuals, and felt myself a part of the upper Bohemian mentality. But my forebears were New Englanders, and I was raised to an old morality that stressed hard work and the joys of accomplishment. Undoubtedly this background helped to give me the self-discipline a writer needs. Writing is never easy; but I continue to take satisfaction in any well-made thing, whether it is a bookcase, an apple pie, or a children's book. I am very leery of the term "artist." I think of myself as a professional, a craftsman, and I believe that if there is anything such as art, it is the residue of craft.

———

James Lincoln Collier graduated from Hamilton College in 1950 and served in the infantry during the Korean War. He is divorced and has two children. A professional trombonist, Collier writes fiction and nonfiction on the subject of music, and his book, *Rock Star,* won an award from the Child Study Children's Book Committee at Bank Street College.

Published in 1974, *My Brother Sam Is Dead* presents a compelling and realistic story of the Revolutionary War. It was a Newbery Honor Book in 1975 and was designated a Notable Book by the American Library Association as well as being nominated for a National Book Award in 1975. *Jump Ship to Freedom* was named a Notable Trade Book in the Field of Social Studies in 1981 by a joint committee of the National Council for the Social Studies and the Children's Book Council. *War Comes to Willy Freeman* is a companion book to the novel.

SELECTED WORKS: The Teddy Bear Habit, 1967; Rock Star, 1970; Inside Jazz, 1973; Give Dad My Best, 1976; Making Music for Money, 1976; The Making of Jazz: A Comprehensive History,1978.

SELECTED WORKS WITH CHRISTOPHER COLLIER: My Brother Sam Is Dead, 1974; The Bloody Country, 1977; The Winter Hero, 1978; Jump Ship to Freedom, 1981; War Comes to Willy Freeman, 1983.

ABOUT: Children's Literature Review, Vol. 3; Contemporary Authors (First Revision), Vol. 9–10; (New Revision Series), Vol. 4; Something About the Author, Vol. 8; Language Arts March 1978; New York Times Book Review November 28, 1965.

ELLEN CONFORD

March 20, 1942–

AUTHOR OF *Dear Lovey Hart: I Am Desperate,* etc.

Autobiographical sketch of Ellen Conford:

I DISCOVERED by accident that I could write. When I was in the third grade we had a weekly homework assignment for spelling. We would be given ten vocabulary words, and we would have to take each word and write it in a separate sentence. One day, while I was doing my spelling homework, I discovered that I'd made the last word of the second sentence rhyme with the last word of the first sentence. I thought that sounded pretty good, so I made the last word of the fourth sentence rhyme with the last word of the third. It still sounded good—and I wrote the rest of my spelling sentences the same way. When I was finished, I read the whole assignment out loud and said, "I think I wrote a poem."

When my teacher read my homework the next day, and called me up to the front of the room to read it to the whole class, I knew I'd done *something* good. From that time on, I wrote. I wrote my first book for kids by accident, too. I went to the library one day to take out some books to read to my son, who was four at the time. I couldn't find anything appealing that day, and went home frustrated, irritated, and empty-handed. I told my husband I could write a better book than anything I'd seen in the children's section that day. He said, "I'm sure you could. Why don't you?"

That night I wrote my first book: *Impossible, Possum.* It was published in 1971, and I've been writing for kids ever since. Now I'm concentrating on writing for the middle reader, and the teenage reader.

I was born in 1942 in New York, and grew up in Queens and on Long Island. In high school I worked on the newspaper and the yearbook, and was editor of our humor magazine. I went to Hofstra University, where I met my husband, David. He is now

a college professor. We have a son, Michael, who is in college studying to be a musician.

We live with an Old English sheepdog named Emma, and two cats, Priscilla and Children's Room. (Children's Room was found under the card catalogue, in the children's room of our local library. People always ask me "Then why don't you call her 'Card Catalogue?'" and I tell them that 'Card Catalogue' is a silly name for a cat.)

I think I turned out to be a writer for two reasons. The first is because writing was the one thing I felt I did well. Ever since I wrote those spelling poems in third grade, my friends and teachers not only praised my writing, but simply assumed that I was going to be an author when I grew up. So I assumed I would, too.

The second reason is because I read so much as a child. I still do, but when I was in elementary school I read eight books a week, every week. I'm sure I learned to write by reading what other people had written, because no one ever taught me to write—I've never taken any courses in it at all. And because reading was so enjoyable for me, writing just seemed to be a natural offshoot of all the hours spent curled up with all those books.

———

Several of Ellen Conford's humorous and popular books have been Literary Guild selections, including *Impossible, Possum* (illustrated by Rosemary Wells), *Dreams of Victory* (illustrated by Gail Rockwell), and *Felicia the Critic* (illustrated by Arvis Stewart). She has had her poems and stories published in magazines such as *Teen* and *Reader's Digest* and she has reviewed books for the *New York Times.*

SELECTED WORKS: Impossible, Possum, 1971; Dreams of Victory, 1973; Felicia the Critic, 1973; Me and the Terrible Two, 1974; Dear Lovey Hart: I Am Desperate, 1975; The Luck of Pokey Bloom, 1975; And This Is Laura, 1977; We Interrupt This Semester for an Important Bulletin, 1979; To All My Fans, with Love from Sylvie, 1982.

ABOUT: Contemporary Authors (First Revision), Vol. 33–36; Something About the Author, Vol. 6; Ward, Martha E. and Dorothy A. Marquardt. Authors of Books for Young People, 2nd edition (Supplement); The Writers Directory 1982–84; Elementary English September 1974.

PATRICIA COOMBS

July 23, 1926–

AUTHOR AND ILLUSTRATOR OF *Dorrie and the Blue Witch, etc.*

Autobiographical sketch of Patricia Coombs:

I WAS BORN in Los Angeles, California, the youngest of three children. For many years the family moved annually, so my first birthday was in Honolulu, my second in San Francisco, my third in Boston, my fourth in New York, my fifth in St. Louis. Contrary to expectations, and thinking to be unrooted at any moment, we remained in St. Louis for nine years.

I cannot remember a time when reading and drawing did not totally engross me. There is a suspicion that I read the labels on everything in the delivery room. I read anything and everything within reach. When forcibly stopped from reading ("you'll ruin

your eyes"), I drew pictures. Sent outdoors to play, I created fantasies, complete with an imaginary friend. Forty years later that experience became the story of *Lisa and the Grompet.*

When my brother and sister left for college, I wrote letters to them, and in so doing discovered the power of writing: I could write things that made my brother and sister LAUGH. Heady power for a nine year old! From then on, I was hooked.

Eventually I ended up at the University of Washington in Seattle. Theodore Roethke came there to teach poetry, and he was a truly inspiring teacher. Through my last years of undergraduate and graduate study I worked with him writing poetry while doing graduate work in seventeeth-century English literature, planning to teach after graduation.

Marriage, two children, and a house in Connecticut changed my teaching plans, though I continued to write, and sometimes publish, poetry. When our two daughters began to read by themselves, my own early fascination with books and illustrations was reborn. Our local library at the time was very, very small and the children could take out only three books at a time. They read them in the car going home, while eating the groceries.

When the inevitable colds, chicken pox, and mumps came along, the lack of reading material became critical. So I started making up a story for them, and drawing pictures. It was called *Mr. Feeters and the Blue Witch.* It went on and on. It must have been several hundred pages long by the time it ground to a halt. I wrote others. I wrote stories they could read on their own, with lots of pictures.

A novelist who was in our area for a job interview was caught by a blizzard and stayed over with us. Because of the blizzard, the house was littered with stories and drawings. The novelist liked them. "I have an agent," he said, "who has just started handling children's stories. . . . " Then a friend who owned the town bookshop remarked one day that there were virtually no stories just for girls. They had to read books that had boys as the heroes and doers of deeds.

At that point, I began really looking at children's books, especially those our two daughters read and reread. They liked books that were funny. They were fond of witches, and at that time the only witches were in folk tales too difficult for them to read by themselves. I had always loved witches, too, and in a witch story *anything* can happen, and their wardrobes never go out of style—a great advantage to an amateur artist.

Out of all this, the first Dorrie story evolved. She's a small witch dealing with all the familiar domestic problems children face: a messy room, bossy adults who are too busy with nonessentials.

I am still surprised that I am doing what I do. It wasn't planned, and when I wrote the first story, I certainly never guessed it would turn into a series. Almost every day there are letters from children in the mailbox, and that is one great joy in this most joyful occupation. One child wrote: "I've read every book that you've made. I've read them thousands of times. Please keep making them."

The *New York Times* named *Mouse Café* one of the Best Illustrated Books of the Year in 1972. Two of the Dorrie books, *Dorrie and the Blue Witch* and *Dorrie and the Weather Box,* were Junior Literary Guild selections.

Patricia Coombs has had poetry published in *Partisan Review* and *Poetry.*

SELECTED WORKS WRITTEN AND ILLUSTRATED: Dorrie's Magic, 1962; Dorrie and the Blue Witch, 1964; Dorrie and the Weather Box, 1966; Lisa and the Grompet, 1970; Mouse Café, 1972; The Magic Pot, 1977; Tilabel, 1978; Dorie and the Witches' Camp, 1983.

SELECTED WORKS ILLUSTRATED: Lobo, by Gladys Y. Cretan, 1969; Lobo and Brewster, by Gladys Y. Cretan, 1971.

ABOUT: Contemporary Authors (First Revision), Vol. 1; (New Revision Series), Vol. 4; Kingman, Lee and others, comps. Illustrators of Children's Books: 1957–1966; Kingman, Lee and others, comps. Illustrators of Children's Books 1967–1976; Something About the Author, Vol. 3; Ward, Martha E. and Dorothy A. Marquardt. Illustrators of Books for Young People, 2nd edition; The Writers Directory, 1982–84.

BARBARA CORCORAN

April 12, 1911–

AUTHOR OF *A Dance to Still Music,* etc.

Autobiographical sketch of Barbara Corcoran, who also writes under the pen names of "Gail Hamilton" and "Paige Dixon":

I WAS BORN in Hamilton, Massachusetts, where I lived for the first thirty years of my life, with time out for college, winter months in New York, etc. I graduated from Wellesley College in 1933, and much later and far from home I got an M.A. at the University of Montana in 1955. I am single.

After college I worked in summer theaters and spent a lot of time writing plays, a few of which got produced. During the war I worked a year for the Navy as an electronics inspector, and nearly a year for the

Army Signal Corps as a cryptanalytic aide in Arlington, Virginia. When the war was over, I was a copywriter for a while, and then moved to Los Angeles, where I managed the West Coast office of Celebrity Service for eight years.

I came to Montana in 1953 and stayed two years, working as a copywriter at a radio station and later getting my M.A. Then as now the Montana job market was not flourishing, so I went back to Los Angeles, and then to Santa Barbara as a radio copywriter.

I began to teach college students at the University of Kentucky Northern Center, and later at the University of Colorado for five years, and Palomar Junior College near San Diego for four years.

In 1967 I published my first children's book, *Sam,* for Atheneum. Before that, I had sold a lot of adult fiction to *Redbook, Woman's Day,* and other magazines. After *Sam,* I sold several more books to Atheneum, and in 1969 I decided to take the plunge and write full time. As they say, I've never looked back.

I sometimes write under the pen name of Paige Dixon (the latest of those is *Walk My Way*) and occasionally under the name of Gail Hamilton. The real Gail Hamilton was a well-known nineteenth-century writer from my hometown.

In the last three years I have also written eleven romances for Ballantine Books.

———

In 1972 *Sasha, My Friend* won the William Allen White Children's Book Award. *The Long Journey* was selected as a Child Study Association Children's Book of the Year in 1970. Barbara Corcoran travels extensively, and writes that "three people have to visit three times as many places as one person," referring to her two pseudonyms. She has visited or lived in Denmark, Finland, Sweden, Hungary, Russia, England, and Hawaii.

SELECTED WORKS: Sam, 1967; Sasha, My Friend, 1969; The Long Journey, 1970; A Dance to Still Music, 1974; The Winds of Time, 1974; The Clown, 1975; Hey, That's My Soul You're Stomping On, 1978; "Me And You and a Dog Named Blue," 1979; Rising Damp, 1980.

SELECTED WORKS AS GAIL HAMILTON: A Candle to the Devil, 1975; Titania's Lodestone, 1975; Love Comes to Eunice K. O'Herlihy, 1977.

SELECTED WORKS AS PAIGE DIXON: Promises to Keep, 1974; May I Cross Your Golden River?, 1975; Pimm's Cup for Everybody, 1976; The Search for Charlie, 1976; Skipper, 1979; Walk My Way, 1980.

SELECTED WORKS AS: BARBARA CORCORAN WITH JEANNE DIXON AND BRADFORD ANGIER: The Ghost of Spirit Run, 1968.

SELECTED WORKS AS BARBARA CORCORAN WITH BRADFORD ANGIER: A Star to the North, 1970; Ask for Love, and They Give You Rice Pudding, 1977.

ABOUT: Contemporary Authors (First Revision), Vol. 23–24; Something About the Author, Vol. 3; Ward, Martha E. and Dorothy A. Marquardt. Authors of Books for Young People, 2nd edition (Supplement); The Writers Directory 1982–84.

ROBERT CORMIER

January 17, 1925–

AUTHOR OF *The Chocolate War,* etc.

Cormier: *COR me ay*

Biographical sketch of Robert Edmund Cormier:

ROBERT CORMIER was born in Leominster, Massachusetts, where he and his wife still make their home. He attended Fitchburg State College for a year and began his writing career at radio station WTAG in Worcester in 1946. In 1948 he moved into print journalism, first as a reporter with the *Worcester Telegram and Gazette,* and then at the *Fitchburg Sentinel* as a reporter and wire editor. He left this paper in 1966, and moved into freelance writing, both journalism and fiction. Cormier has received three awards for his journalism, two top prizes for newswriting from the Associated Press in New England, and an award for the best newspaper column from K.R. Thomson Newspapers, Inc. Fitchburg State College named him Doctor of Letters in 1977.

Robert Cormier published his first novel, for adults, in 1960. *Now and at the Hour* was followed by two other adult books: *A Little Raw on Monday Mornings* in 1963, and *Take Me Where the Good Times Are* in 1965. While these were well received, it was in 1974, with his publication of a novel for teenagers called *The Chocolate War,* that

Cormier found himself the target of often hostile attention. *The Chocolate War* is about Jerry, a parochial school student who refuses to sell chocolates for the school's fund drive. For this he is ostracized and harassed by students and faculty alike, and finally he is savagely beaten and left unconscious, at the close of the book.

The crude language, violence, cynicism, and particularly the undeniably dismal ending of the novel left many critics horrified. "I am disturbed by this book because, in spite of being brilliantly structured and skillfully written, it presents a distorted view of reality and a feeling of absolute hopelessness that is unhealthy," wrote Norma Bagnall in the American Library Association's *Top of the News.* A spirited defense of the book was provided in a rebuttal by Janet Polacheck: "If we give young adults only those books described by Norma Bagnall as desirable, which would give students adults worth emulating, show goodness and honor being rewarded, detail situations where hope is proved right, I suggest that *that* would present a warped view of the world. Young adults must learn that if they are going to stand firm for something, there will be times of absolute aloneness." *The Chocolate War* was named a best book of the year in 1974 by the *New York Times* and a Best Book for Young Adults by the American Library Association, and was chosen for the *School Library Journal* "Best of the Best 1966–1978" list (December, 1979). It also won a Lewis Carroll Shelf Award in 1979.

I Am the Cheese is a different kind of book, marked by psychological torture rather than physical brutality. Like *The Chocolate War,* it has a dismal ending, suggesting the incipient death of the youthful, maddened protagonist. It was named both a Notable Book for children and a Best Book for Young Adults by the ALA. A movie version of *I Am the Cheese* was released in 1983.

Cormier combined physical and mental anguish in *After the First Death,* in which a father sacrifices his son in the name of patriotism. While many have denounced Cormier's themes and apparent cynicism, even his detractors have admitted that he is a skillful writer. "When I read [*After the First Death*] I was appalled by the author's abuse of his considerable power to involve impressionable young readers," wrote Sister Avila in *School Library Journal*. In the same periodical Judith Rosenfeld urged "the very skillful author Robert Cormier to offer his readers another theme, if he has one." It was also named a Best Book for Young Adults by the ALA.

Cormier's latest novel, *The Bumblebee Flies Anyway,* concerns advances and ethics in medicine as it tells the story of a sixteen-year old boy who is treated with mind-altering drugs in an experimental hospital for the terminally ill.

According to Donald Gallo, Robert Cormier the man is very different from what readers might expect. He wrote in the *ALAN Review* that "the first time readers of his recent novels meet Robert Cormier they are amazed to find him so soft-spoken, so friendly, so personable, so generous, so honest. . . . This unsentimental novelist seems quite sentimental as a person."

In addition to his novels, Robert Cormier has also written many short stories that have appeared in various magazines. Nine of these are found in *Eight Plus One*, a collection for young adult readers that was named a Notable Children's Trade Book in the Field of Social Studies by the joint committee of the National Council for the Social Studies and the Children's Book Council. These stories, according to Cormier's introduction, derive their impetus from his experiences with raising his four children, particularly when they were teenagers. He was struck by the similarity between their experiences and the ones he had as an adolescent. "I began to write a series of short stories, translating the emotions of both the present and the past—and finding they were the same, actually—into stories dealing with family relationships, fathers and mothers, daughters and sons." It is a

collection of quite tender stories in which the author hopes his readers "will meet that other Robert Cormier."

SELECTED WORKS: The Chocolate War, 1974; I Am the Cheese, 1977; After the First Death, 1979; Eight Plus One, 1980; The Bumblebee Flies Anyway, 1983.

ABOUT: Contemporary Authors (First Revision), Vol. 3; (New Revision Series), Vol. 5; Something About the Author, Vol. 10; ALAN Review, Fall 1981; English Journal September 1977.

RUTH CRAFT

August 30, 1935–

AUTHOR OF *The Winter Bear*, etc.

Autobiographical sketch of Ruth Craft:

WHEN I HEARD that *The Winter Bear* was to be published in America I experienced a tremendous sense of satisfaction. American books meant more to me as a child than English ones. My father was a librarian and my childhood coincided with his development of the National Service Library of New Zealand. Great treats were brought home for me to wonder over, and books like *The Rooster Crows, Paddle to the Sea, The Little House, Davy's Day, Rabbit Hill,* and *Caddie Woodlawn* formed the cornerstone of my appreciation of literature. So the idea that my books might be allowed a little elbow room in the excellent American tradition of books for children was an immensely appealing one.

The two picture books I'm happiest with are *The Winter Bear* and *Carrie Hepple's Garden.* They're both explorations of very ordinary incidents—going for a walk on a winter's day, sneaking into an old lady's garden—and what I've tried to do in both cases is to make the 'ordinary' quality very tangible by using a rhythmic structure for the words. I can't say it's poetry, but it has to be read aloud. I also deliberately choose a mixed vocabulary. Some of it is down to earth—some a bit more complex. The text

Ruth Craft

has to stand in its own right and be sure of itself, but the real challenge lies in creating something that is going to make the artist reach for a pen or brush with enthusiasm. If I can feel that the words inspire a picture rather than direct it, then I feel I'm doing my job.

I like to explore and celebrate the natural world, and the children in my books are from the country or the suburbs. I didn't have an urban childhood, and attempts by me to write stories with city backgrounds have so far lacked conviction. I write for the under fives in the certain knowledge that they are the most discriminating of audiences, and I love the way they can take over a book as a firm and comfortingly familiar old friend.

———

The Winter Bear was Ruth Craft's first picture book. Illustrated by Erik Blegvad, it was a Junior Literary Guild selection and was chosen to be in the Children's Book Council's Children's Book Showcase.

Ruth Craft was born in New Zealand and went to England in her late teens to pursue a career in the theater. She turned to writing in her early twenties and worked as an

advertising copywriter and free-lance writer for radio. She married Michael Craft and raised four sons while working as a free-lance scriptwriter and consultant to children's television programs, notably the BBC's daily program for preschoolers, *Playschool*. She began writing picture-book texts and went back to school in her early forties to complete a Bachelor's degree in English Literature.

She lives in Cambridge, England, and works in schools as a visiting writer.

SELECTED WORKS: The Winter Bear, 1975; Pieter Brueghel's The Fair, 1976; The King's Collection, 1979; Carrie Hepple's Garden, 1979.

ABOUT: Ward, Martha E. and Dorothy A. Marquardt. Authors of Books for Young People, 2nd edition (Supplement).

DONALD CREWS

AUTHOR AND ILLUSTRATOR OF *Freight Train,* etc.

Autobiographical sketch of Donald Crews:

I WAS BORN in Newark, New Jersey. I attended the public schools there. My first special art training came in Arts High School, a specialized school with training in music or art with admission by competitive examination. Drawing and sketching had long been a part of my life. My older brother and my sisters, one older and one younger, were all involved in art-related projects. Our interest probably came from my mother, who was an accomplished craftswoman and dressmaker.

Three years of further art education followed high school at the Cooper Union School for the Advancement of Science and Art in New York City. After two years of work experience came two years of military service. I was stationed in Germany for eighteen months and was joined there by Ann Jonas, with whom I attended Cooper Union. We were married and our daughter, Nina, was born there.

We Read A to Z, my first book, was designed in Germany toward the end of my service to add depth to my design portfolio. It was published several years later, more through good fortune than persistence, by Harper & Row. Back in the U.S., Amy, our second daughter, was born. *Ten Black Dots* followed *We Read A to Z* as a companion numbers primer. Assignments to illustrate manuscripts of others followed. Many years passed before I once again tested my abilities with a complete project. *Freight Train* turned out to be a very fortunate return to the ranks of author/illustrator. *Freight Train* came from remembrances of the times we spent traveling south to my grandparents' farm in Florida for summer vacations. The trip there was filled with passing freight trains pulled by steam locomotives. Hours of every day were filled with watching and counting the trains as they passed quite near the front porch in Cotttondale. I dedicated *Freight Train* to this memory. The popularity of *Freight Train* and the Caldecott Honor Award it received in 1979 helped focus my time and energies more toward being a picture-book artist. *Truck,* my next book, was similarly honored with popularity and a Caldecott Honor designation.

The success of both of these books afforded me the opportunity to travel and meet the children, teachers, librarians, and parents who bought and used my books. I found that they had been making use of my books from the beginning. Up until these face-to-face meetings, the indicators were more abstract. Very clearly, the subjects of the books I worked on were important to a great many people. The concepts, ideas, and images I created were exciting to many more people than I would ever have dreamed.

Having to talk about the things I did has had a positive effect on the things I've done since. I approach the things I do now with a new sense of seriousness, reflecting the seriousness of the people who view my particular way of interpreting reality. I don't begin any new project without thinking about this audience; they don't inhibit me; they inspire me.

———

In addition to having two of his books named Caldecott Honor Books—*Freight Train* in 1979 and *Truck* in 1981—Crews has won many awards and honors for his work.

Freight Train was an American Library Association Notable Book, was chosen for the *School Library Journal* "Best of the Best 1966–1978" list (December 1979), and was a Junior Literary Guild selection, as were *Blue Sea, Truck,* and *Carousel.*

Talking Stone, Truck, and *Carousel* were also named Notable Books, and *Light* was a Book-of-the-Month Club alternate. In 1979, the American Institute of Graphic Arts Children's Book Show exhibited two books, *Rain* and *Freight Train,* and Crews' art has appeared in *Graphis* magazine.

Crews has used unusual and innovative techniques in the making of his picture books. The artwork in *Harbor* is full-color collage, which is photographed; and in *Carousel,* he deliberately moved the camera while photographing four pieces of full-color artwork, in order to portray the carousel's movement.

SELECTED WORKS WRITTEN AND ILLUSTRATED: We Read A to Z, 1967; Freight Train, 1968; Ten Black Dots, 1968; Truck, 1980; Light, 1981; Harbor, 1982; Carousel, 1982; Parade, 1983.

SELECTED WORKS ILLUSTRATED: Eclipse: Darkness in Daytime, by Franklyn M. Branley, 1973; Rain, by Robert Kalan, 1978; Blue Sea, by Robert Kalan, 1979; The Talking Stone: An Anthology of Native American Tales and Legends, edited by Dorothy deWit, 1979.

ABOUT: Kingman, Lee and others, comps. Illustrators of Children's Books: 1967–1976; Something About the Author, Vol. 30; Ward, Martha E. and Dorothy A. Marquardt. Illustrators of Books for Young People; Graphis No. 155, 1971/2.

RICHARD CUFFARI

March 2, 1925–October 10, 1978

ILLUSTRATOR OF *The Perilous Gard,* etc.

Biographical sketch of Richard Cuffari by Ellen Cuffari-Arana:

RICHARD CUFFARI was born in Brooklyn, where he lived and worked until his death in 1978. He was an avid student of history as well as art history, and his book illustrations demonstrate a profound understanding of the heritage he was part of. He has said "I have always been fascinated by things historical; events, personalities, how people lived and how they looked. I believe that the study of these things helps provide insight into the present." As a result, he has amassed an impressive research library and was greatly concerned with accuracy in his illustrations.

He was raised in Flatbush during the Depression by immigrant parents, both of whom worked. As the only sibling of a retarded brother, he spent much of his free time caring for him, and developed a deep sense of responsibility at an early age. Receiving little artistic encouragement from his family, he persisted in drawing and painting. One of his early memories was of receiving a gift of oil paints from a favorite uncle, then a wild extravagance. He showed artistic precocity as well as being an outstanding student at Madison High School, where he won numerous awards for his artwork.

Upon graduation, he was called into service for the U.S. Army from 1943 to 1946, and was decorated for service in Europe. After the Second World War he continued his education at Pratt Institute until 1949. While there, he met and fell in love with Phyllis Klie, who was to become his wife. An exceptional artist herself, Phyllis was a strong influence on his work. They were married in 1950, when Cuffari began working at a commerical art studio. The first of four children was born the following year. In 1966, after an unsatisfying stint as a partner in his own company, he decided to begin freelancing as a children's book illustrator, and his first book, *The Wind in the Willows,* was highly successful. His interest in children as well as the opportunity to influence their interest in books was an exciting challenge. Concentrating on books for older children, he used simplicity of line in his pictures, and his use of pen-and-ink and wash is distinctive and often imitated. Cuffari was also an accomplished painter and had gallery exhibitions in New York.

In all, Richard Cuffari illustrated nearly two hundred books in eleven years, receiving numerous awards including two Citations of Merit from the New York Society of Illustrators, in 1969 and 1970; Citations from the American Institute of Graphic Arts in 1973 and 1974; and the Christopher Award in 1973. His work has also been represented in the Children's Book Showcase in 1974 and 1975.

Richard Cuffari's illustrations are a permanent part of the Kerlan Collection at the University of Minnesota and the de Grummond Collection at the University of Southern Mississippi, among others. His illustrations were included in the U.S. Information Agency's Graphic Arts-U.S.A. Exhibit in Russia. His credentials also include Instructor of Book Illustration at the Parsons School of Design in New York City.

The Endless Pavement appeared in an American Institute of Graphic Arts show in 1973. Among his books are many that have been Junior Literary Guild selections, including: *Nothing Is Impossible, The Golden Coyote, Ride the Crooked Wind,* and *The Endless Pavement.*

In one of Richard Cuffari's final books, *Balder and the Mistletoe,* colleague James Giblin wrote this tribute: "An admirer of good writing, Mr. Cuffari concentrated on illustrating novels and longer non-fiction books, although he was well aware that the lion's share of critical attention went to the illustrators of picture books for young children. Still, he had the satisfaction of doing the pictures for books by some of today's finest writers for children and young people.

"His work is bound to linger in the memories of the children who see it. And it will serve as a touchstone and inspiration for future artists who, like Richard Cuffari, want to devote their best efforts to book illustration."

SELECTED WORKS ILLUSTRATED: The Wind in the Willows, by Kenneth Grahame, 1966; Nothing Is Impossible: The Story of Beatrix Potter, by Dorothy Aldis, 1969; The Far Side of Evil, by Sylvia Louise Engdahl, 1971; Jackie Robinson, by Kenneth Rudeen, 1971; The Link Boys, by Constance Fecher, 1971; This Is a Recording, by Barbara Corcoran, 1971; Water for the Dinosaurs and You, by Roma Gans, 1972; The Endless Pavement, by Jacqueline Jackson and William Perlmutter, 1973; Ride the Crooked Wind, by Dale Fife, 1973 The Winged Colt of Casa Mia, by Betsey Byars, 1973; Escape from the Evil Prophecy, by Lee Kingman, 1974; The Perilous Gard, by Elizabeth Marie Pope, 1974; Sycamore Year, by Mildred Lee, 1974; Bee, by Peter Z. Cohen, 1975; Ruffles and Drums, by Betty Cavanna, 1975; The TV Kid, by Betsy Byars, 1976; The Ups and Down of Marvin, by Barbara Shook Hazen, 1976; Zenas and the Shaving Mill, by F. N. Monjo, 1976; "I'm Vinny, I'm Me," by Bianca Bradbury, 1977; Leave Well Enough Alone, by Rosemary Wells, 1977.

ABOUT: Kingman, Lee and others, comps. Illustrators of Children's Books: 1967–1976; Something About the Author, Vol. 6; Vol. 25; Ward, Martha E. and Dorothy A. Marquardt. Illustrators of Books for Young People; Who's Who in American Art, 1982; School Library Journal December 1978.

BETTY SUE CUMMINGS

July 12, 1918–

AUTHOR OF *Hew Against the Grain,* Etc.

Autobiographical sketch of Betty Sue Cummings:

THE DAY may come when I can take the fact that I am a writer for granted. Anything is possible. At this point I wake in the morning with the marvel of it, and I go to sleep at night with tomorrow's writing pushing me. When I retired from teaching in 1973, I freed myself for a ten-year internship in writing, during which time I must have some kind of success. Success had to be more than a friendly letter from an editor.

It could be that setting a time limit on achieving success made me work harder than I had before, or maybe forced my thinking in the right direction. It worked almost at once. My first children's story sold to a good market; my first adult story won a writer's conference award; my second adult story did not sell, but it attracted the

attention of a magazine editor who published my next story. My first young adult book was accepted by a good publisher. Now four books have been published. It seems strange to me, beyond my wildest hopes.

This is not to suggest that everything I have written has succeeded. Not at all. Two books and several short stories are out looking for a home.

There have been many benefits, one of the best is that I have learned that writers, editors, agents, and critics are warm-blooded creatures, too. They are downright human.

I grew up in Big Stone Gap, Virginia, in a big family, mostly boys, all of whom fought for first shot at new books and magazines. We read the newspaper together on the living room rug on our knees and elbows with our posteriors high. At that time I believe I acquired a distorted view of the wonderfulness of writers.

I graduated from Longwood College with a B.S. in 1939; I taught English in various places; I served in the U.S. Coast Guard (SPARS) during World War Two; I received an M.A. degree in English from the University of Washington in 1949; I taught

again; I received guidance certification from Stetson University; I left the classroom for a counselor's office.

During all those years I fooled around with writing occasionally. It now occurs to me that it's not smart to fool around with writing. You've got to marry it.

———

Hew Against the Grain was a finalist for the 1978 National Book Awards, and *Now, Ameriky* was named a Notable Children's Trade Book in the Field of Social Studies by a joint committee of the National Council for the Social Studies and the Children's Book Council.

SELECTED WORKS: Hew Against the Grain, 1977; Let a River Be, 1978; Now, Ameriky, 1979; Turtle, 1981.

ABOUT: Contemporary Authors, Vol. 73–76; Something About the Author, Vol. 15.

PAULA DANZIGER

August 18, 1944–

AUTHOR OF *The Cat Ate My Gymsuit,* etc.

Biographical sketch of Paula Danziger:

PAULA DANZIGER was born in Washington, D.C. and grew up in various towns including Arlington, Virginia, and Metuchen, New Jersey. She always loved books and knew from the time she was in second grade that she wanted to be a writer. An early and strong influence on her life and work was the poet John Ciardi. She graduated from college with a degree in English and later earned an M.A. in reading. Danziger spent many years teaching and counseling students in junior high, high school, and college, and her books are concerned with such adolescent issues as social and family relationships, personal development, obesity, and first love.

Although the critical reception to her books has been at times mixed—they have

Paula Danziger

been accused of lacking depth or fresh insight—their immense popularity affirms teenagers' appreciation of Danziger's portrayals of some of the more difficult aspects of growing up. Danziger's first book, *The Cat Ate My Gymsuit*, in which Marcy, a teenage girl, emerges from struggling with a weight problem and a controversy over her favorite teacher with greater self-confidence, was hailed by the *Journal of Reading* as "a thoroughly enjoyable, tightly written, funny/sad tale of an unglamorous but plucky girl who is imaginative, believable, and worthy of emulation." It was named a Children's Choice book of 1980 by a joint committee of the International Reading Association and the Children's Book Council.

The Pistachio Prescription, in which thirteen-year-old Cassie learns that liking herself is the answer to her problems, and not the pistachio nuts she nervously pops, was highly praised by Zena Sutherland in the *Bulletin of the Center for Children's Books*: " . . . this is unusually well done; the characterization and dialogue are strong, the relationships depicted with perception, and the writing style vigorous." It was a Junior Literary Guild selection and was named a

Children's Choice book for 1979 by the I.R.A. and the C.B.C. joint committee.

In *Can You Sue Your Parents for Malpractice?*, fourteen-year-old Lauren decides that between her parents, her two sisters, and school she has no rights at all, and poses the question that may well become a watchword for teens in the 1980s. Jane Langton, writing in the *New York Times*, called it " . . . clever and funny. The chapters rush by in a catapulting present tense. Adolescent and preadolescent girls, and even chubby children who might otherwise be reading *Winnie-the-Pooh*, will giggle and pass it from hand to hand." It was named a Children's Choice book for 1980, by the I.R.A. and the C.B.C. joint committee.

In *There's a Bat in Bunk Five*, the sequel to *The Cat Ate My Gymsuit*, a slimmer, more confident Marcy returns in triumph as a counselor in Ms. Finney's creative arts camp. Barbara Elleman, writing in *Booklist*, said, "Danziger's ability to create believable, funny dialogue and to capture the feelings and thoughts of a 14-year-old is highly evident. . . . Readers will be captivated by the natural flow and breezy style." It, too, was a Children's Choice book, for 1981.

The Divorce Express, in which fourteen-year-old Phoebe experiences the problems of divorce and joint custody as she commutes between her parents' homes on a bus she calls the Divorce Express, was acclaimed by *Booklist*: "Danziger's light style, laced with humor will . . . attract readers, both ardent and reluctant."

In 1982, Danziger was named Read-a-Thon Author of the Year by the National Multiple Sclerosis Society. In the past, she has logged as many as 50,000 miles touring the country speaking to parents, children, educators, and librarians about her writing, but more recently she has managed to stay closer to her two homes in New York City and Woodstock, New York, taking acting lessons and playing lots of video games. She said of her writing, "Most important to me is that writing allows me to use my sense of humor and sense of perspective. I hope that my books continue to help me grow and to help others grow."

SELECTED WORKS: The Cat Ate My Gymsuit, 1974; The Pistachio Prescription, 1978; Can You Sue Your Parents for Malpractice?, 1979; There's a Bat in Bunk Five, 1980; The Divorce Express, 1982.

ABOUT: Something About the Author, Vol. 30.

ANDREW DAVIES

September 20, 1936–

AUTHOR OF *Conrad's War*, etc.

Biographical sketch of Andrew Wynford Davies:

BORN IN Cardiff, Wales, Andrew Davies graduated with honors from the University College, London, in 1957. He began work as a teacher in London and married a fellow teacher, Diana Hentley. He has since managed two careers, creating a long list of writing credits in various fields in addition to his teaching. He currently works as a lecturer in teacher training at the University of Warwick.

The main focus of Davies's career has been as a dramatist. He wrote a dozen radio plays before branching out into television. He had immediate success with his first television play, which the BBC purchased for the prestigious Wednesday Play series. It was five years, however, before he sold another play, and he supplemented his teaching by writing comic material for children's television programs.

Since that time, Davies has written numerous television plays. His titles include *Grace* in 1974, *The Imp of the Perverse* in 1975, *The Signal Man* in 1976, and *Happy in War* in 1977. His best known television work is the highly respected trilogy on Eleanor Marx, the story of the daughter of Karl Marx. In addition to the plays, Davies also wrote two longer running BBC series, "The Legend of King Arthur," from which

he adapted a British children's book of the same name, and "To Serve Them All My Days."

He went from television plays into work expressly written for live theater. The idea occurred to him after hearing of the stage adaption of one of his radio plays. Among his stage plays are *Filthy Fryer, Going Bust, Brainwashing with the Boys* and his most successful, *Rose. Rose,* a critically acclaimed play starring actress Glenda Jackson, played in both London's West End and on Broadway in New York.

His first attempt in the field of children's books was a novel, *The Fantastic Feats of Doctor Boox.* His second novel, *Conrad's War,* received enthusiastic response. It won the Guardian Award in 1979 and the 1980 Boston Globe-Horn Book Award when it was published in the U.S. Conrad and his book are totally original, described by one reviewer as a combination of Monty Python, Joseph Heller's *Catch-22,* and the young adult novels of Daniel Manus Pinkwater.

Conrad is a fingersnapping, frenetic, frustrated, always-thinking devotee of World War II. His father, "The Great Writer" (which is, curiously, the title Andrew Davies's family uses to describe him) is, to Conrad's mind, an impossibly preoccupied, fuzzy-headed mess of a father. Yet when Conrad's world and the world of the Second World War fantastically meld together, his father is the one who comes along on the journey.

Davies states that he wrote the book, in spite of an aversion to novels, to please himself and his young son Bill, who shares some of Conrad's characteristics. The book is intended, in Davies's mind, as an antidote to the unrealistic portrayal of the relationship between fathers and sons in the "well meaning" books he had encountered. A reviewer of *Rose* commended Davies for being "a marvel at writing dialogue," and this skill helps lift Conrad above the ordinary. Instead of glorifying war and war games, the book lets Conrad understand the reality behind them. Didacticism never rears its ugly head; Conrad, in the end, remains true to his character.

In addition to his son, Davies has one daughter, who raged against the fate of sisters in her father's work. To please her, he wrote *Marmalade and Rufus*. Marmalade is as incorrigible and eccentrically lovable as Conrad. She has a hat-wearing male chauvinist donkey named Rufus to deal with instead of World War II.

Mr. Davies claims he is now committed to children's books.

SELECTED WORKS: The Fantastic Feats of Dr. Boox, 1973; Conrad's War, 1980; Marmalade and Rufus, 1983.

ABOUT: Contemporary Authors, Vol. 105; The International Authors and Writers Who's Who, 1982; Something About the Author, Vol. 27.

T. DEGENS

T. DEGENS

AUTHOR OF *Transport 7-41-R,* etc.

Biographical sketch of T. Degens:

T. DEGENS was born in what is now East Germany and, like many of her contemporaries, has used her memories of the Nazi regime along with her adult perceptions to create compelling children's books.

After university study in biology at Bonn, in 1956, Degens emigrated to the United States and has lived most of the time on Cape Cod in the town of Falmouth, Massachusetts. She returned to Germany in order to study psychology at the University of Hamburg, eventually hoping to work with the mentally handicapped.

Degens' first novel for children, *Transport 7-41-R,* draws upon her East German background. At the end of World War II, the thirteen-year-old heroine, toughened by the horrors she has witnessed during the war, and bitter at her father's abuse and her family's rejection of her, travels from the Russian-occupied zone to Cologne, held by the British. Wanting nothing more than to be left alone with her new-found freedom, she nonetheless becomes involved in a macabre plot to aid an old gentleman in bringing his dead wife's corpse home to be buried in Cologne.

The book reflects the author's interest in psychology, painting vivid psychological portraits of the characters in the crowded transport. Critic Mary M. Burns wrote in the *Horn Book*: "A powerful and unforgettable novel, taut and dramatic, which succeeds both as a suspense-filled adventure tale and as an evocative study of the psychological and emotional effects of war on its most innocent victims—children."

Transport 7-41-R won the 1975 International Reading Association Award and a Boston Globe-Horn Book Award in 1975. It was named a Best Book for Young Adults by the American Library Association in 1974 and appeared on the *School Library Journal* "Best of the Best 1966–1978" list (December 1979).

The Game on Thatcher Island, her next book, is set in America. It intensifies the psychological element present in *Transport 7-41-R*. The "game" is a sadistic war game in which the older, strong children prey on the younger ones. In exploring the reasons for their actions, Degens presents a study of one boy's discovery of the darker side of his nature and of human nature in general. *Friends* also concerns the acting out of a war game, this time using the Vietnam war as the basis for a mock battle.

In *The Visit,* the story moves back and forth between the days of Hitler's Youth Corps and contemporary times, when a young girl discovers the diary of her long-dead aunt. With growing horror the girl learns that her other aunt, the beloved Sylvia, may have had a hand in the diarist's death. The book, a psychological study, examines Aunt Sylvia's possible dual nature as well as the legacy of Hitler's time and what meaning it carries to the next generation.

Married and with three children, T. Degens, an enthusiastic camper and hiker, hopes one day to hike the entire length of the Appalachian Trail.

SELECTED WORKS: Transport 7-41-R, 1974; The Game on Thatcher Island, 1977; Friends, 1981; The Visit, 1982.

DIANE DE GROAT

May 24, 1947–

ILLUSTRATOR OF *Little Rabbit's Loose Tooth,* etc.

Biographical sketch of Diane L. de Groat:

DIANE DE GROAT was born in Newton, New Jersey, and grew up in Belleville, New Jersey. She was interested in art from the time she was a child, and started art lessons at age seven with the same teacher who was instructing her grandmother in painting. She drew and painted throughout her school years in New Jersey and spent the summer of 1964 at the New York Phoenix School of Design. Next, she attended the Pratt Institute, taking courses in photography, illustration, and life drawing, which

provided the foundation for the work she does today.

After graduating from Pratt with a B.F.A. in 1969, she began her career in the art department of a New York publishing house, first as a designer and eventually as the art director of their Basic Reading program. Among her responsibilities was assigning artwork to free-lance illustrators, and during the three years she spent there she began doing some of the illustrations herself. By 1971, when she left to become a full-time free-lance illustrator, she had a portfolio of published artwork. Other publishers began to use her work, and her career as an illustrator was launched.

De Groat works in two distinct styles: fantasy, done in pencil, charcoal, and watercolor, which she uses mainly for picture books; and a less whimsical, more stylized realism, done in charcoal or watercolor, more suited to illustrations in novels for older children. In order to achieve a greater realistic sense, she often uses live models (including herself, her husband, and her daughter) and photographs from magazines and newspapers.

Publishers Weekly described the illustrations for *Animal Fact/Animal Fable* as "appealing and colorful pictures in an outstanding book." In a review of *Mr. Tamarin's Trees, Booklist* commented on the "zest and spark provided by de Groat's pen-and-ink drawings, brightened with spots of colored pencil at just the right places." Diane de Groat's work has been exhibited at the Art Directors Club of New Jersey in 1977, the Art Directors Club of New York in 1974, the American Institute of Graphic Arts in 1974 and 1977, and the Society of Illustrators in 1972 and 1975. It has also appeared in *Print* and *Art Direction* magazines. *Little Rabbit's Loose Tooth* won the California Young Reader Medal in 1978.

De Groat lives in Yonkers, New York, with her husband and daughter.

SELECTED WORKS WRITTEN AND ILLUSTRATED: Alligator's Toothache, 1977.

SELECTED WORKS ILLUSTRATED: Luke Was There, by Eleanor Clymer, 1973; Little Rabbit's Loose Tooth, by Lucy Bate, 1975; A Book for Jodan, by Marcia Newfield, 1975; Bubba and Babba, by Maria Polushkin, 1976; Mr. Tamarin's Trees, by Kathryn Ernst, 1976; Animal Fact/Animal Fable, by Seymour Simon, 1979; Don't Be Mad, Ivy, by Christine McDonnell, 1981; Who Needs a Bear?, by Barbara Dillon, 1981; Toad Food and Measle Soup, by Christine McDonnell, 1982; The Toad Intruder, by Lynn Luderer, 1982; The Ewoks Join the Fight, by Bonnie Bogart, 1983.

ABOUT: Kingman, Lee and others, comps. Illustrators of Children's Books: 1967–1976; Who's Who in American Art, 1982; New York Times (Westchester section) August 29, 1982.

JUDY DELTON

May 6, 1931–

AUTHOR OF *Kitty in the Middle*, etc.

Autobiographical sketch of Judy Delton:

I WAS BORN on May 6, 1931, in St. Paul, Minnesota, and have lived here most of my life. I attended the College of St. Catherine and taught in parochial schools and worked in offices and never wrote anything more than a note to the milkman until 1971,

Judy Delton

when I found I had to support my four children by myself. Everyone, especially my mother, waited for me to get a safe, secure job teaching or digging ditches, but I didn't. I began to write. Bad poetry and insipid essays. But I had no criteria and plunged innocently into a narcissistic world where I was enamored with my own words. Before long I learned more about writing (from reading good fiction), and after that initial loss of innocence it never was as much fun again. It started to be work and it started to be professional and it started to be better.

Since that time I have published twenty-six books, four of them novels. I detest reading nonfiction except autobiographies and letters. I read E. B. White, Ann Tyler, Shirley Jackson, Flannery O'Connor, and Agatha Christie over and over again.

My own books seem to relive my childhood over and over again. In the Kitty books, I am Kitty. In the Brimhall books, I am Brimhall. Even in the adult novel I am writing now, I am Tess. And of course parts of Tess are Kitty, Brimhall, Bear, and Duck. I write fiction to discover. I find out all kinds of things I never knew; things tumble out of my typewriter, like the fact that my grandfather didn't like me. I never knew that till Kitty told me. Writing is the cheapest, finest therapy there is.

The Kitty books are about growing up Catholic in the 1940s, and so is my novel (with the complications and ramifications of marriage in the 1950s), but in *Only Jody* I've branched out and stolen my son's life as well. Now I'm sneaking into my daughter's childhood and fastening it onto paper.

I'm especially pleased (when I'm not jealous) that two of my daughters are publishing books of their own. Jina's book, *Two Blocks Down*, was written when she was fifteen and getting bad marks in English in high school. It has given her lots of credibility very young. Julie wrote *Uncle Nikos* after returning from a year spent in Greece.

Along with writing, I also lecture around the country at colleges, workshops, seminars, and afternoon tea parties. I enjoy this especially because writing fiction is a solitary occupation with limited contacts. It isn't taken seriously—I know my mother is still waiting for me to get a "real" job. But talking to people who are interested in writing makes it real and convinces me (when I'm dubious) that it's a bona fide profession. For five years I taught writing for publication in colleges in the area. After I said everything I had to say in that genre, over and over again, I quit.

While I don't have any "hobbies," things I enjoy on a daily basis are my children and their interests, my standard poodle (Etienne), my reading and writing, some films, and mostly, my lake home in northern Wisconsin.

Two Good Friends was an American Library Association Notable Book and a Junior Literary Guild selection. Also selected by the Junior Literary Guild were *Three Friends Find Spring* and *Brimhall Turns to Magic*.

Judy Delton has also contributed several hundred fiction and nonfiction pieces to magazines such as *Saturday Review* and *The Instructor*.

SELECTED WORKS: Two Good Friends, 1974; Rabbit Finds a Way, 1975; Two Is Company, 1976; Three Friends Find Spring, 1977; Brimhall Comes to Stay, 1978; Brimhall Turns to Magic, 1979; Kitty in the Middle, 1979; Kitty in the Summer, 1980; My Mother Lost Her Job Today, 1980; Here's Jody, 1982.

ABOUT: Contemporary Authors, Vol. 57–60; Something About the Author, Vol. 14; Ward, Martha E. and Dorothy A. Marquardt. Authors of Books for Young People, 2nd edition (Supplement).

TOMIE DePAOLA

September 15, 1934–

AUTHOR AND ILLUSTRATOR OF *Strega Nona,* etc.

Autobiographical sketch of Thomas Anthony dePaola:

WHEN I WAS very very young, before I had even started to go to school, I promised myself a lot of things.

One was that when I grew up, I would never tell children like myself things that weren't all true.

Another was that when I grew up, I would be an artist and draw pictures, especially for books. I promised myself that I would write stories, too!

That was a long long time ago, over forty years ago, and I can smile and say truthfully that I kept those promises to myself. (Some of the other promises I didn't keep. I didn't marry my baby sitter or become a movie star . . . yet!)

Being an artist was easy. I just sat down and drew pictures—all over the place. By second grade, I was considered the "best artist" by my teachers and classmates. I guess I saw things differently than most of my school friends, than most of my family and relatives. I saw with my eyes like everyone else but I also saw "inside" with "inner eyes." My mother told me that was *imagination*.

But "being an artist" was only a small part of it. I had to learn a great deal about art.

Tomie dePaola: *tommy de POW la*

I had to learn how to draw well—to learn that the hand and eyes can be trained and taught so that the hand can put down on paper what the eyes can see (and that includes the "inner eyes" too!).

I had to learn about different kinds of paints and papers, pastels and pencils, brushes and pens. To learn all of this, I went to an art school called Pratt Institute. It was like a college only we had art course after art course all day long, all week long. It was wonderful and I was very happy.

After four years of studying I was ready to graduate and one of my favorite teachers said, "OK, now comes the hard part. You are a good student and I know you are an artist, but you have to go out there and get recognized."

It was not easy becoming a "recognized artist." It meant I had to get other people to say, "Yes, you are an artist and I would like you to draw some pictures for me." I showed my drawings to many people, especially those who were in charge of choosing artists to draw pictures for books for children. I showed them my drawings for six years! Finally, I was given a book to illustrate. That was almost twenty years ago and since then, I've drawn pictures for over 100 books.

It's nice to be a "recognized artist."

The other promise I spoke of is an important one for me. I never want to tell children things that aren't all true. I try to keep this promise in my stories, especially stories that are based on experiences in my own life—stories such as *Nana Upstairs and Nana Downstairs; Watch Out for the Chicken Feet in Your Soup; Oliver Button Is a Sissy;* and *Now One Foot, Now the Other.*

But what about make-believe stories? Things happen in them that you might say aren't "all true," like Big Anthony having to eat all the pasta in *Strega Nona.*

Well, things like that can really happen "inside" (like the inner eye), in the IMAGINATION. I like to call those things "what if-things."

What if there was a little old lady named Strega Nona who lived in a little Italian village a long time ago and what if she had a magic pasta pot and what if a boy who didn't pay attention came to work for her and tried to make the magic pot work? What would happen?

I have to find the "answer" inside my imagination. And if I look and listen carefully to my imagination, the "answer" will be the true one.

Now that I've told you about some promises I made to myself a long time ago, I'm going to make another promise. I promise that I will try to do more books for children, both stories and pictures, that you will all enjoy.

———

Tomie dePaola received his B.F.A. from Pratt Institute in New York City and his M.F.A. from the California College of Arts and Crafts in Oakland in 1969. In 1970 he earned a doctoral equivalency at Lone Mountain College in San Francisco. Since 1956, he has been a professional artist and designer, a painter and muralist, and an author/illustrator and illustrator of children's books. He has taught art at Lone Mountain College, at Chamberlayne Junior College in Boston, and at New England College in

Henniker, New Hampshire, and was Artist-in-Residence at New England College from 1978–79.

Currently dePaola is a member of the Advisory Board of the Children's Radio Theatre of Washington, D.C. and he is on the Board of Directors of the Society of Children's Book Writers of Los Angeles.

He has illustrated over one hundred books for children and written almost forty of those. He is working on an autobiographical book to be published by Addison-Wesley.

The many awards and honors dePaola's books have received include a Caldecott Honor Book Award in 1976 for *Strega Nona,* which was also an American Library Association Notable Book and won several prizes in Japan.

Also designated ALA Notable Books were *Charlie Needs a Cloak, Helga's Dowry, The Quicksand Book, Big Anthony and the Magic Ring, Fin M'Coul, The Friendly Beasts, Francis: The Poor Man of Assisi,* and *Giorgio's Village.* The Kerlan Award was presented to Tomie dePaola in 1981, and in 1983 he received the Regina Medal.

The Quicksand Book won a Garden State (New Jersey) Children's Book Award in 1980, and many of his books have been International Reading Association/Children's Book Council "Children's Choices," and have been named "Children's Books of the Year" in their year of publication by the Child Study Association Children's Book Committee.

DePaola's work has been exhibited in many group and one-man shows, and several, like *Helga's Dowry,* have been included in American Institute of Graphic Arts Book Shows. Most of his original artwork and manuscript materials can be found in the Kerlan Children's Literature Research Collection at the University of Minnesota in Minneapolis.

SELECTED WORKS WRITTEN AND ILLUSTRATED: The Journey of the Kiss, 1970; Nana Upstairs and Nana Downstairs, 1973; Charlie Needs a Cloak, 1974; Watch Out for the Chicken Feet in Your Soup, 1974; Strega Nona (reteller), 1975; When Everyone Was Fast Asleep, 1976; Helga's Dowry: A Troll Love Story, 1977; The Quicksand Book, 1977; The Clown of God, 1978; Big Anthony and the Magic Ring, 1979; Oliver Button Is a Sissy, 1979; The Legend of Old Befana: An Italian Christmas Story (reteller), 1980; Fin M'Coul: The Giant of Knockmany Hill (reteller), 1981; The Friendly Beasts: An Old English Christmas Carol, 1981; Now One Foot, Now the Other, 1981; Francis: The Poor Man of Assisi, 1982; Giorgio's Village, 1982.

SELECTED WORKS ILLUSTRATED: Finders Keepers, Losers Weepers, by Joan M. Lexau, 1967; The Rocking Chair Ghost, by Mary C. Jane, 1969; This Is the Ambulance Leaving the Zoo, by Norma Farber, 1975; Beat the Drum, Independence Day Has Come, selected by Lee Bennett Hopkins, 1977; The Triumphs of Fuzzy Fogtop, by Anne Rose, 1980; The Good Giants and the Bad Pukwudgies, by Jean Fritz, 1982.

ABOUT: Contemporary Authors, Vol. 49–52; (New Revision Series), Vol. 2; Kingman, Lee and others, comps. Illustrators of Children's Books: 1957–1966; Kingman, Lee and others, comps. Illustrators of Children's Books: 1967–1976; Something About the Author, Vol. 11; Ward, Martha E. and Dorothy A. Marquardt. Illustrators of Books for Young People; Who's Who in American Art, 1978; Publishers Weekly July 19, 1976; Language Arts March 1979.

DONNA DIAMOND

October 19, 1950–

ILLUSTRATOR OF *Bridge to Terabithia,* etc.

Autobiographical sketch of Donna Diamond:

I REMEMBER always wanting to be an artist. My two sisters and I were encouraged by our parents to pursue our interests in the arts. We were born and raised in New York City and were given lots of lessons. As children we studied dance and music and I took art classes at the Museum of Modern Art, as well. My sister Judy grew up to be a dancer/choreographer and my sister Susan, a musicologist. I attended the High School of Music and Art and went on to Boston University School of Fine and Applied Art where I received a degree in sculpture. I have always been attracted to children's books and when I returned to New York City after college, sculpture turned to print-making and illustration.

I think that one of the things the traditional training I received tried to do was to develop the critic in the student. When you are drawing and it is going well, you do not have to be a critic. But when you are drawing and it is going badly, you need to stop and say, "What's wrong?" Then you lean on the critical faculties your training has developed.

I think that my favorite children's book is *Alice's Adventures in Wonderland.* I have a cabinet photograph of Sir John Tenniel above my drawing board. When I look at Tenniel's other work, it is very dry. But the drawings for *Alice* seem to explode with invention. Something happened between Tenniel and the story, a rapport took place that made the illustrations for *Alice* quite special. I think that illustrating children's literature offers an artist the challenge of doing a pas de deux with the material. This challenge to the imagination as well as craft is a great pleasure to me. I find it is also very hard. However, the attempt to dance pictorially with a story is the most compelling work I can think of doing.

———

Donna Diamond has also attended the School of Visual Arts for a printmaking workshop and the Tanglewood Summer Art Program. She is divorced and lives in Boston.

Books that Diamond has illustrated have won many awards. *Bridge to Terabithia* won the 1978 Newbery Medal and a 1978 Lewis Carroll Shelf Award. *Mustard* won the 1983 Irma Simonton Black Award. *A Transfigured Hart* was a 1975 Golden Kite Honor Book and was named a Children's Choice book for 1976 by the joint committee of the International Reading Association and the Children's Book Council.

The Boy Who Sang the Birds was exhibited in the 1976 American Institute of Graphic Arts show. Three books that Diamond illus-

trated were named Notable Books by the American Library Association: *Beat the Turtle Drum,* in 1976; *The Dark Princess,* in 1978; and *A Gift for Mama, in 1981.*

SELECTED WORKS RETOLD AND ILLUSTRATED: The Seven Ravens: A Grimm's Fairy Tale, by the Grimm Brothers, 1979; Swan Lake, 1980; The Breman Town Musicians: A Grimm's Fairy Tale, by the Grimm Brothers, 1981; The Pied Piper of Hamelin, 1981.

SELECTED WORKS ILLUSTRATED: The Transfigured Hart, by Jane Yolen, 1975; Beat the Turtle Drum, by Constance Greene, 1976; The Boy Who Sang the Birds, by John Weston, 1976; Red Hart Magic, by Andre Norton, 1976; Anne's Spring, by Daniel Curley, 1977; Bridge to Terabithia, by Katherine Paterson, 1977; The Dark Princess, By Richard Kennedy, 1978; The Dream Book, by Olga Litowinsky and Bebe Willoughby, 1978; Are You Sad, Mama? by Elizabeth Winthrop, 1979; A Gift for Mama, by Esther Hautzig, 1981; The Crystal Child, by Barbara Wersba, 1982; Mustard, by Charlotte Graeber, 1982.

ABOUT: Kingman, Lee and others, comps. Illustrators of Children's Books: 1967–1976; Something About the Author, Vol. 30.

DIANE DILLON

March 13, 1933–

and

LEO DILLON

March 2, 1933–

ILLUSTRATORS OF *Ashanti to Zulu,* etc.

Autobiographical sketch of Leo and Diane Dillon:

WE BELIEVE in magic. To sit down with a blank piece of paper and see scenes and characters take form . . . it *is* magic. There's a voice inside guiding, saying "no, that's not right . . . change that line . . . add a bit here . . . take away there. . . ."

Children accept these things. As adults, we lose the faith. The best things come

when we let go and accept the guidance from that voice. Maybe that's why we love doing children's books . . . knowing that they (the children) will understand the zany logic and eagerly accept the impossible.

We came to children's books after many years of adult book jackets, album covers, and advertising art, and found a freedom we didn't know before. When doing a book or record cover, everything must be summed up in one picture. In a children's book there are pages and pages to build an idea—to add nuances and visual comments.

There are many levels of recognition and understanding. A book can be read again and again with new discoveries: expressions and details that were missed the first time will be discovered the second or third or fourth time.

It has been a form of magic in working together as one artist, and we created a third artist. What takes form on paper is a surprise to both of us and something neither of us would have come up with individually.

We met at Parsons School of Design and competed with each other until we joined

forces. It didn't come easy, this working together. Two egos and one piece of paper are a dangerous combination!

Now, when we sit down and talk about what we're going to do, we let the ideas fly until one triggers excitement in both of us. From that point on, it's an adventure.

One of the greatest gifts, we think, is to love what you are doing. And we do. We don't work for children; we work for the child in each of us. Children are little people, as complicated and mysterious as any adult. Unfortunately, too many adults feel that things must be simplified for children. We try not to fall into that trap. We must please ourselves first, and if we've been honest with ourselves and have worked with love, the reader—child or adult— will know that.

Our reward is the respect of our peers, the joy of children, and the freedom we take in listening to our own drummer.

———

Leo and Diane Dillon have won the Caldecott Medal twice, in 1976 for *Why Mosquitoes Buzz in People's Ears,* and in 1977 for *Ashanti to Zulu: African Traditions. Why Mosquitoes Buzz in People's Ears,* written by Verna Aardema, also received a Brooklyn Art Books for Children citation in 1977. The illustrators have also received the Hamilton King Award for excellence in illustration from the Society of Illustrators in New York, and the Hugo Award for science fiction and fantasy art.

Ashanti to Zulu was also named an American Library Association Notable Book, a Boston Globe-Horn Book Honor Book, and a *New York Times* Best Illustrated Book of the Year 1976. *Song of the Boat,* too, was a 1976 Boston Globe-Horn Book Honor Book, in 1976. *Who's in Rabbit's House?* was a Notable Book and also received a Lewis Carroll Shelf Award for 1978.

Appearing in the Children's Book Council's Showcase collection were *Whirlwind Is a Ghost Dancing* (in 1975) and *Behind the Back of the Mountain* (in 1974). The latter was also included in the 1973/74 American Institute of Graphic Arts Show, as was *The Third Gift; Ashanti to Zulu* was in the 1976 show.

Leo Dillon was born in Brooklyn, and Diane Dillon in Glendale, California. She studied at Los Angeles City College and at Skidmore College. Both attended American Institute of Graphic Arts workshops, the Parsons School of Design, and the School of Visual Arts.

The Dillons have a teenage son, Lee.

SELECTED WORKS ILLUSTRATED: Hakon of Rogen's Saga, by Erik Christian Haugaard, 1963; The Ring in the Prairie: A Shawnee Legend, by John Bierhorst (editor), 1970; The Untold Tale, by Erik Christian Haugaard, 1971; Behind the Back of the Mountain: Black Folktales from Southern Africa, by Verna Aardema, 1973; The Third Gift, by Jan Carew, 1974; Whirlwind Is a Ghost Dancing, by Natalia Belting, 1974; The Hundred Penny Box, by Sharon Bell Mathis, 1975; Song of the Boat, by Lorenz Graham, 1975; Why Mosquitoes Buzz in People's Ears, by Verna Aardema, 1975; Ashanti to Zulu: African Traditions, by Margaret W. Musgrove, 1976; Who's in Rabbit's House?: A Masai Tale, by Verna Aardema, 1977; Children of the Sun, by Jan Carew, 1980.

ABOUT: Kingman, Lee and others, comps. Illustrators of Children's Books: 1967–1976; Pitz, Henry C. 200 Years of American Illustration; Preiss, Byron, ed. The Art of Leo and Diane Dillon; Something About the Author, Vol. 15; Graphis No. 156, 1979; Horn Book August 1976, August 1977; School Library Journal March 1977.

JOHN DONOVAN

1928–

AUTHOR OF *I'll Get There. It Better Be Worth the Trip,* etc.

Biographical sketch of John Donovan:

SINCE 1967, John Donovan has been the executive director of the Children's Book Council, a nonprofit association of publishers concerned with the promotion of children's books and reading. Prior to this appointment, he was employed at St. Martin's Press, in charge of rights, promotion, and advertising. Holding a law degree from the University of Virginia, Donovan has also worked as an examiner at the U.S. Copyright Office, and as an English teacher.

Donovan's first novel, *I'll Get There. It Better Be Worth the Trip,* is generally regarded as the first young adult novel to have as a major aspect of its story a homosexual relationship between two young teens. Davy and Altschuler are very close friends, and on a couple of occasions this closeness turns into sexual intimacy. While many critics praised this frankness, others believed it would do more harm than good. Martha Bacon, writing in *The Atlantic Monthly,* felt that "a book focused on a love affair between schoolfellows . . . would not meet the needs of the initiated and might arouse in the unconcerned unnecessary interest or alarm or both." British critic David Rees, writing in *Children's Literature in Education,* believed the book would reinforce negative prejudice toward homosexuals and increase the insecurity of young homosexuals themselves. But both Lavinia Russ in *Publishers Weekly* and Zena Sutherland in the *Bulletin of the Center for Children's Books* noted that the book really was not about homosexuality at all; instead, the interlude was simply another step toward maturity. In any case, *I'll Get There. It Better Be Worth the Trip* felled a long-standing taboo, and young adult novels with homosexual characters and relationships are now common in the genre.

Donovan's second novel, *Wild in the World,* also became the focus of controversy, as many reviewers questioned whether this story about death, desolation, and a close, sensual relationship between a boy and a wolf was at all suitable for young people. June Jordan, writing in the *New York Times Book Review,* asked, "Do kids accept such an 'adult' view of things? Do they need such guidance into gloom?"; but in the same issue, young adult novelist Barbara Wersba wrote that *Wild in the World* "is more suited to contemporary children than

almost any kind of literature I can think of."
The book was included in the *School Library Journal* "Best of the Best 1966–1978" list (December, 1979), and was a finalist for the 1972 National Book Award.

Donovan's latest novel for young adults, *Family,* was an unqualified critical success. Turning from the examination of human relationships, in this novel Donovan wrote of another species: apes. Sasha finds out that he and the other apes are about to be subjected to dangerous laboratory experimentation, so he leads his "family" out into the wilderness. Jean Mercier, writing in *Publishers Weekly,* felt that *Family* had "the impact of a Greek tragedy."

In addition to his young adult novels, Donovan has written two books for younger readers, *The Little Orange Book* and *Good Old James,* and a play for adults, *Riverside Drive,* which was produced in New York in 1964.

SELECTED WORKS: The Little Orange Book, 1961; I'll Get There. It Better Be Worth the Trip, 1969; Wild in the World, 1971; Remove Protective Coating a Little at a Time, 1973; Good Old James, 1974; Family, 1976.

ABOUT: Contemporary Authors, Vol. 97–100; Kirkpatrick, D. L., ed. Twentieth-Century Children's Writers; Something About the Author, Vol. 29; Publishers Weekly January 2, 1967.

ANNE OPHELIA DOWDEN

September 17, 1907–

ILLUSTRATOR OF *Shakespeare's Flowers,* etc.

Biographical sketch of Anne Ophelia Todd Dowden, who also writes under the pen name "Anne Ophelia Todd":

ANNE OPHELIA TODD was born in Denver, Colorado, but she grew up in the foothills of the Rocky Mountains, where her father was on the faculty of the University of Colorado in Boulder. As a child she developed a keen interest in collecting and drawing living things and a determination to become an artist, but it did not for many years occur to her to combine the two.

After attending the University of Colorado for a year, she went east to study painting and illustration at the Carnegie Institute of Technology in Pittsburgh. She graduated in 1930 at the height of the Depression and, intent on illustrating books, headed even farther east to New York. She made the rounds of the publishers, but to earn a living she took a job teaching at the Pratt Institute in Brooklyn. To her surprise, she discovered that pedagogy suited her and, in 1935, she moved from Pratt to Manhattanville College in Purchase, New York, where she served as chairperson of the art department for more than twenty years.

During her tenure at Pratt, she continued to study at the Art Students League and the Beaux Arts Institute of Design. Though not a muralist herself, she became associated at Beaux Arts with a group of artists who designed and executed a mural for the Chicago World's Fair. This group later dubbed itself the American Design Group, and its members went on to design wallpapers and drapery fabrics with great success for fifteen years.

Though in all this time the scientific study of plants never entered into her work, she often sketched plants for fabric design, and nature provided her with a hobby. In 1934, she married Raymond Baxter Dowden, head of the art department at the Cooper Union School of Art and Architecture. On summer vacations she and her husband drove all over the United States, painting, drawing, and observing as they went.

While on a sabbatical from Manhattanville, Dowden created a series of paintings of edible wild plants, which she hoped to have published. In 1952, *Life* magazine used nine of the paintings. Three more illustrated articles for *Life* followed in 1955 and 1957. Her career in botanical illustration was launched. Dowden gave up teaching and textile design to concentrate on botanical painting. One of her paintings appeared on the cover of *House Beautiful*. Then she researched, wrote and illustrated two articles for *Natural History* magazine. In 1961, her first book was published.

Since then, she has illustrated fourteen more books, seven of which she also wrote. Her work has reaped many honors: *Look at a Flower, The Blossom on the Bough, The Golden Circle* (by Hal Borland) and *The Lore and Legends of Flowers* (by Robert L. Crowell) were named Notable Children's Books by the American Library Association in their years of publication; *Look at a Flower* was included on the ALA list "Notable Children's Books 1940–1970." *The Blossom on the Bough* (in 1976) was a Children's Book Council Showcase selection, as was *Wild Green Things in the City* (in 1973), which was also included in the 1973 American Institute of Graphic Arts exhibit. Three of the books she illustrated were named outstanding Science Trade Books for Children by a joint committee of the National Science Teachers Association and the Children's Book Council: *Wild Green Things in the City* in 1972, *The Blossom on the Bough* in 1975, and *The Golden Circle* in 1977.

Her paintings have been exhibited in several museums, galleries, and libraries, in-cluding the Metropolitan Museum of Art, the Carnegie Institute, and the Whitney Museum of American Art, and the Frame House Gallery has issued a series of her botanical paintings as limited edition prints. Dowden was one of two artists chosen to represent American botanical art of the twentieth century in *Botanical Illustration* by Ronald King, former secretary of the Royal Botanical Gardens in Kew, England.

For most of her paintings, Dowden uses the medium of transparent watercolor, which is well-suited to the delicacy of her subjects. She has evolved what she terms as "probably the world's slowest working method." Working from living plants in natural light, she makes literal and detailed research paintings, to which she later refers when repainting the plants in whatever arrangement is demanded by the project at hand. "I find that photographs don't give me the information that I want. You want to know how a stamen attaches—there's a shadow over it. Or you can't see of two leaves whether they're opposite each other on the stem or staggered." Her research paintings now number in the hundreds and constitute a valuable reference file for future projects; Dowden refuses to part with a single one.

Her insistence on working only from living plants often requires extensive long-range planning and organization, beginning in the winter months with a list of species, their blooming dates, and where they can be found. If the plants cannot be seen in the New York botanic gardens or a nearby state, Dowden relies on friends and collectors all over the country to send her specimens, or allow her to visit when the blooms are ready. Of this research, she says, "Synchronizing my schedule with that of nature and my friends requires a lot of phone calls and voluminous correspondence; the file of letters in preparation for a book is often bulkier than the manuscript itself." In the course of her work, Dowden has also had to learn botany, which she has studied diligently though informally.

Now widowed, Anne Ophelia Dowden divides her time between her apartment in New York City and a house in Hanover, New Hampshire.

SELECTED WORKS WRITTEN AND ILLUSTRATED: Look at a Flower, 1963; The Secret Life of the Flowers, 1964; Wild Green Things in the City: A Book of Weeds, 1972; The Blossom on the Bough: A Book of Trees, 1975; State Flowers, 1978; This Noble Harvest: A Chronicle of Herbs, 1979.

SELECTED WORKS ILLUSTRATED: Shakespeare's Flowers, by Jessica Kerr, 1969; The Golden Circle: A Book of Months, by Hal Borland, 1977; Wildflowers and the Stories Behind Their Names, by Phyllis S. Busch, 1977; The Lore and Legends of Flowers, by Robert L. Crowell, 1982.

ABOUT: Contemporary Authors (First Revision), Vol. 11–12; (New Revision Series), Vol. 3; Kingman, Lee and others, comps. Illustrators of Children's Books: 1967–1976; Something About the Author, Vol. 7; Ward, Martha E. and Dorothy A. Marquardt. Authors of Books for Young People, 2nd edition; Who's Who in American Art, 1982; The Writers Directory 1982–84; The Lion and the Unicorn Vol. 6, 1983.

Lois Duncan

"LOIS DUNCAN"

April 28, 1934–

AUTHOR OF *Summer of Fear,* etc.

Autobiographical sketch of Lois Steinmetz Arquette, who writes under the pen names of "Lois Duncan" and "Lois Kerry":

I CAN'T remember a time when I didn't think of myself as a writer. It was my one hope for glory, as there was nothing else I was any good at. A fat, shy child with braces and glasses, I started submitting stories to magazines when I was ten, and at thirteen I made my first sale. It was the most incredible moment of my life. I continued to write for young people's publications, particularly for *Seventeen,* during my teen years, and wrote my first novel when I was twenty. It was the winner of the "Seventeenth Summer Literary Award."

This early success wasn't due to literary genius, but to the fact that I was the same age as my readers. They related to the subject matter, and my adolescent agonies mirrored their own. Many of the stories and poems I had published during those years are included in my autobiography, *Chapters.* Strung together, they are as good as a diary. Whenever anything terrible, wonderful, or thought-provoking happened to me, I rushed home and wrote a story about it.

I grew up in Sarasota, Florida, the daughter of magazine photographers Joseph and Lois Steinmetz, and married when I was nineteen. That was a mistake. Nine years later, I was divorced and faced for the first time the challenge of supporting not only myself but three children. With no college degree or job training behind me, my alternatives were limited; I wrote for the women's magazines, the confessionals, religious publications, and juveniles; for advertising agencies, newspapers, and greeting-card manufacturers—anyone and everyone who was willing to pay for material. Those weren't easy years, but they were valuable to me. By the time I remarried, happily, and was able to shift the role of "family provider" onto broader shoulders, I found

I didn't *want* to. Writing was by then a way of life for me, and I had made the joyful discovery that it was possible to have a full-time career doing something I loved.

My husband, Don Arquette, is an electrical engineer, and we make our home in Albuquerque, New Mexico, in a big brick house in the shadow of the Sandia Mountains. We have five children—my first three (whom Don adopted) and the two younger ones we produced together. Although the books I write for young people are primarily fiction, I continue to draw upon the people and situations I'm familiar with, just as I did in my early years. My daughter Kerry is "Bambi" in *Daughters of Eve,* and my son Brett is the mischievous "Brendon" in *A Gift of Magic.* My youngest two, Don Jr. and Kate, are "Neal" and "Megan" in *Stranger with My Face,* and most of my books are laid either here in the Southwest or by the ocean that was such an important part of my childhood.

I write in a number of assorted areas. I do nonfiction for women's magazines (including "Can This Marriage Be Saved?" features for *Ladies' Home Journal*)—personal experience pieces, verse, humor and devotionals—and I'm the author of twenty-seven books. These include romances, poetry, a biography, a historical novel, mysteries, and adventure. My most recent and most successful books have been psychological suspense novels for teenagers, and these are what I enjoy writing most. It's like a game. You develop a group of interesting characters, set them in a situation, make something startling happen, and watch to see what they *do.* Each day is a new adventure. I can hardly wait to get to the typewriter.

————

Lois Duncan was born in Philadelphia and graduated from the University of New Mexico. She is a member of the National League of American Pen Women and has been an instructor in Journalism at the University of New Mexico.

Summer of Fear won the 1978 Dorothy Canfield Fisher Award. *Ransom,* in 1966, and *They Never Came Home,* in 1968, were nominated for Edgar Allan Poe Awards by the Mystery Writers of America. *Stranger with My Face* was named a Best Book for Young Adults in 1981 by the American Library Association. Three of her books have been Junior Literary Guild selections: *Silly Mother,* which was illustrated by Suzanne Larsen, *Summer of Fear,* and *They Never Came Home.* Her Seventeenth Summer Literary Award was presented for *Debutante Hill.*

Duncan's *Summer of Fear* was adapted for television as "Strangers in Our House." Her books have been published in many countries, including Holland, Portugal, Norway, Denmark, and Brazil.

SELECTED WORKS: Debutante Hill, 1958; The Littlest One in the Family, 1959; The Middle Sister, 1960; Game of Danger, 1962; Silly Mother, 1961; Ransom (retitled Five Were Missing, 1972), 1966; Point of Violence, 1966; They Never Came Home, 1968; I Know What You Did Last Summer, 1973; Down a Dark Hall, 1974; Summer of Fear, 1976; A Gift of Magic, 1977; Killing Mr. Griffin, 1978; Daughters of Eve, 1979; Stranger with My Face, 1981; Chapters: My Growth as a Writer, 1982.

SELECTED WORKS AS LOIS KERRY: Love Song for Joyce, 1958; A Promise for Joyce, 1959.

ABOUT: Contemporary Authors (First Revision), Vol. 3; (New Revision Series) Vol. 2; Duncan, Lois. Chapters: My Growth as a Writer; Something About the Author, Vol. 1; Ward, Martha E. and Dorothy A. Marquardt. Authors of Books for Young People, 2nd edition; The Writers Directory 1982–84; Writer's Digest December 1957; December 1959; May 1962.

ELLA THORP ELLIS

July 14, 1928–

AUTHOR OF *Roam the Wild Country,* etc.

Autobiographical sketch of Ella Thorp Ellis:

I'VE ALWAYS BEEN a drifter who yearns

ELLA THORP ELLIS

to live in one place. I was born in Los Angeles and we kept moving north along the beaches of California. We were poor, I had polio, and my parents couldn't get along. One or the other took care of me when they could and left me with friends when they couldn't. Two years were spent with an uncle who was a painter, two years in a writers' commune, and some time with a country doctor's family in the beach town where four of my novels are set.

Much of my writing comes out of this varied childhood. You could say that living in seven families provided a large cast of characters, understanding, a well-honed intuition, and a basis for comparison. I was a lucky kid. Everyone I ever lived with was kind and most were loving. Still, always starting over (crossing that schoolyard on the first day of school where everyone else already has friends) made me so adaptable that for years I worried about lacking character. I was forever choosing someone I'd rather be in a story and then reading everything that author wrote to see if he or she had anyone even better to offer. They often did. I looked for heroines who yelled back.

Some stories come directly out of my life. For example, *Celebrate the Morning* comes

from living with my mother when she was committed to a mental hospital and from combining the best traits of two boy friends. *Sleepwalker's Moon* comes out of trying to be born again into a foster family and from my first real love.

Some stories are harder to pin down. They filter through the conflicts of sons (*Riptide*) or a brother (*Where the Road Ends*) or even a hero (the poet-grandfather in *Hugo and the Princess Nena*). Even so, these stories soon get down to writing about what I know firsthand.

So far, I'm still trying to stay in one place. I married an engineer (who later became an economist), and we moved a dozen times and had three sons the first five years we were together. Eventually we bought a home for the boys. Then we promptly went to Argentina for two years. Out of the ranch life there and our oldest son's love for horses I wrote *Roam the Wild Country,* the story of a horse drive.

Nothing in *my* childhood had prepared me for PTA meetings, casseroles, changing diapers, or even aging. I took to day dreaming a planet where I could sensibly eliminate these pains in the neck. It was a comfort. Later, a fight between a niece and a nephew sparked the story of an irreconcilably incompatible step-brother and step-sister set on my planet of *Hallelujah*. Of course, characters never remain the people who spark them. If they are worth the two or three years of writing and rewriting my books take, they'll mutiny early and do and say and think and feel in ways I certainly never expected. This is what makes writing an addiction and characters such good company. They come alive, like Pinocchio.

I've always thought that getting tuberculosis as a teenager and having nothing to do but read eighteen hours a day was what made me a writer. I discovered that what I like to read are adventure stories that don't leave people out, that deal with how people feel about each other and what they do about it. Some writers I started reading then and still enjoy rereading are Carson

McCullers, Scott Fitzgerald, Willa Cather, and Anton Chekhov.

I took a course or two in college wherever we lived and have a B.A. in English from the University of California at Los Angeles and an M.A. in English from San Francisco State University, where I later taught. We are again temporarily in Argentina, where I'm writing about a boy and about his brother who was killed in a war.

———

Ella Thorp Ellis was married in 1949. Since 1972 she has been teaching courses in writing novels, biographies, and books for children. Starting in 1977 she has taught short story and short drama courses for junior and high school English teachers in the Education Department of the University of California and has been a lecturer on the short story, drama, and poetry in the Creative Writing Department of San Francisco State University. She is a member of the Sierra Club, the California Writers' Club, the American Civil Liberties Union, and the Audubon Society. *Celebrate the Morning* was a Junior Literary Guild selection, and *Roam the Wild Country* was on the American Library Association's "Notable Children's Books 1940–1970" list.

SELECTED WORKS: Roam the Wild Country, 1967; Riptide, 1969; Celebrate the Morning, 1972; Where the Road Ends, 1974; Hallelujah, 1976; Sleepwalker's Moon, 1980; Hugo and the Princess Nena, 1983.

ABOUT: Contemporary Authors, Vol. 49–52; (New Revision Series), Vol. 2; The International Authors and Writers Who's Who, 1982; Something About the Author, Vol. 7; Ward, Martha E. and Dorothy A. Marquardt. Authors of Books for Young People, 2nd edition (Supplement); Who's Who of American Women, 1979–1980; The Writers Directory 1982–84.

JEANNETTE EYERLY

June 7, 1908–

AUTHOR OF *Escape from Nowhere,* etc.

Jeannette Eyerly

Autobiographical sketch of Jeannette Hyde Eyerly, who also uses the joint pseudonym "Jeannette Griffith":

I RECEIVED my first byline in the children's column of a local newspaper when I was eight years old and have been writing ever since.

Ideas for my books usually come from conversations with young people, something I have observed first-hand or read about in a magazine or newspaper. Usually, an idea will be a combination of all three. I often visit schools to talk about books and writing, and I receive many letters—all of which I answer personally—from my readers. In this way, I can keep up with young people's current concerns and problems, most of which will eventually work their way into my novels.

Librarians and teachers of adolescent literature have said—and I believe myself to be—I am a pioneer in the subjects I write about. My book, *Drop-Out,* published in 1963 and still being avidly read, was the first young adult novel that dealt with a real social problem. Subsequent novels have dealt with other difficult and sensitive topics: unwed parenthood (*A Girl Like Me, He's My Baby Now*); drug abuse (*Escape from*

Nowhere); runaways (*See Dave Run*); suicide (*The Girl Inside*); abortion (*Bonnie Jo, Go Home*); the problems faced by children of alcoholic parents (*The World of Ellen March, The Phaedra Complex*); the search for identity (*Radigan Cares*).

If I Loved You Wednesday, the story of a seventeen-year-old boy's first encounter with love in the form of his substitute English teacher, is in a lighter vein, as are my two suspense novels (*Good-bye to Budapest, The Leonardo Touch*) and a romance (*More Than a Summer Love*).

But always, I want my books to be "about something," and I want them to have a "point." Most of all, I want them to be readable. In other words, I want them to be the kind of novel *I* like to read. The question, "Will the reader turn the page?" is always at the top of my mind. And readers *do* turn the page. Literally hundreds of young people have written to tell me that *Drop-Out* was the first book they ever read all the way through.

I was graduated from the State University of Iowa with majors in English and Journalism. After graduation I began contributing articles and fiction to major national magazines, and in 1962, at the insistence of my daughters, wrote my first young adult novel. It was accepted and published that year.

My major interests are art collecting, bird watching, gardening, cooking (bread-making in particular), conservation, mental health, and reading. I also enjoy taping books for the blind so they, too, can read.

Throughout my adult life I have been active in several organizations concerned with mental health and work with the blind. My book for younger children, *The Seeing Summer,* published in 1981, is the story of a friendship between a blind child and a sighted child. In May, 1980, I received the National Federation of the Blind's Jernigan-Altig Award "in recognition of dedicated service to the blind of Iowa and the nation," and in July of that same year I received the Polk County Mental Health Cen-

ter's Award for my role as one of the founders of the Center for fourteen years' service to it. I have also served on the Board of Directors and as President of the Des Moines Child Guidance Center, on the board of the Iowa Commission for the Blind and on the Acquisition Committee for the Des Moines Art Center.

My husband, Frank, the longtime Managing Editor of *The Des Moines Register & Tribune,* is the kind of helpmate every author should have.Our two daughters are Jane, an author in her own right, who is married to an artist and teacher, and Susan, a potter, who is married to a corporation executive.

We have always had a dog. The present inhabitant is a lovable, gentlemanly, seventy-eight-pound Airedale named Titon.

———

Jeannette Eyerly has been a lecturer, Publicity Director of the Des Moines Public Library, and a teacher of creative writing. She is a member of the American Association of University Women, the League of Women Voters, and the Authors Guild. She has collaborated with Valeria Winkler Griffith to write under the pseudonym "Jeannette Griffith."

Escape from Nowhere won the 1970 Christopher Award, and *He's My Baby Now* was made into a TV special called "School-Boy Father."

Jeannette Eyerly's novels have been published in many countries, including Denmark, England, Finland, and Germany.

SELECTED WORKS: More than a Summer Love, 1962; Drop-Out, 1963; The World of Ellen March, 1964; A Girl Like Me, 1966; The Girl Inside, 1968; Escape from Nowhere, 1969; Radigan Cares, 1970; The Phaedra Complex, 1971; Bonnie Jo, Go Home, 1972; Goodbye to Budapest, 1974; The Leonardo Touch, 1976; He's My Baby Now, 1977; See Dave Run, 1974; If I Loved You Wednesday, 1980; The Seeing Summer, 1981.

ABOUT: Contemporary Authors, (First Revision), Vol. 4; (New Revision Series), Vol. 4; Foremost Women in Communications, 1970; Something About the

Author, Vol. 4; Ward, Martha E. and Dorothy A. Marquardt. Authors of Books for Young People, 2nd edition (Supplement); Who's Who in America, 1980; Who's Who of American Women, 1982.

NORMA FARBER

August 6, 1909–

AUTHOR OF *As I Was Crossing Boston Common*, etc.

Autobiographical sketch of Norma Farber:

NOT UNTIL I turned grandmother did it occur to me to write for children.

Even as a small child I'd written what I intended to be serious, mature verse. My Class Poem, on graduation from Girls' Latin School, was a solemn, grandiloquent piece in Spenserian stanzas. And throughout the raising of two sons and two daughters I continued writing "adult" poems, hundreds and hundreds of them.

Grandchildren changed all that. For the last twenty years I've been quite as eager to "reach" youngsters as to communicate with my own aging peers.

For I've discovered that certain stories I'd like to tell, certain moods I want to share, certain problems I need to explore, require the fresh ear and attention of a child encouraging me. Which is to say here's an author who writes for children because they fulfill, in some wondrous way, the intent of her books. They complete the purpose of her writing by accepting and confirming it.

I practice my profession of writing in a high-rise apartment overlooking the Charles River on its way to Boston Harbor. Though I have traveled widely, and lived for long periods abroad, I now like best of all to stay home on my Cloud Fifteen, with its east and north and west exposures. (If I crane my neck southward from my terrace I can see Blue Hill rising rotund and bluish in the fourth quadrant.) Thus, I have at hand splendid sunrises and moonrises, and sunsets and moonsets as well. The world of

Cambridge lies at my feet, its dwellings reduced almost to dollhouse size. I look *down* on trees, and on the shadows of trees. From this vantage I can see how tree-shadows on the street refuse to be run over by cars or trucks or buses, but rather rise up and over the most threatening hood and chassis. It's fresh way of seeing. Children like to visit me and look down and around with me. They enjoy the far places brought close up through my binoculars. They laugh at how my prism *crazies* the view. We blow bubbles together.

I shouldn't forget to mention that for many years I was a concert singer, with a wide range of interest in music old and new, traditional and avant-garde. I've been told the influence of music on my work is noticeable. Not surprisingly, then, certain of my poems have caught the attention of composers. A recent record of twenty-four song-settings of my lyrics bears witness, I guess, to the musical character—tone-color, meter, counter point—of my poetry.

And I should admit that I can be tempted, even in my seventies, to undertake new and difficult assignments. I welcome a challenge, a *dare*! Love to try something I've never tried before, especially if it seems to be 'way beyond me.

After all, what've I got to lose?

Or so I rationalize a project I lately submitted myself to, when my Unicorn-Dutton editor said, "Norma, I wish you'd write a novel."

But so late in the day?

Well, I've done the thing, and I think it has succeeded. The book's been categorized as "young adult"—with a content and style engaging adult readership as well.

Next try: a *wholly adult* fiction.

As I Was Crossing Boston Common, illustrated by Arnold Lobel, was in the Children's Book Showcase in 1975 and was nominated for a National Book Award in 1976.

Norma Farber received her B.S. from Wellesley College and her M.A. from Radcliffe College. She has four children and seven grandchildren. Her poetry for adults has been published in *The Horn Book Magazine, The Nation, The New Republic, The New Yorker,* and *Poetry.*

Mercy Short is not poetry, but a fictionalized account of the troubled seventeenth year of Puritan Mercy Short who, suffering from fits and hallucinations after her release from captivity by Indians, came under the care of Cotton Mather.

SELECTED WORKS: Did You Know It Was the Narwhale?, 1967; As I Was Crossing Boston Common, 1975; Six Impossible Things Before Breakfast, 1977; A Ship in a Storm on the Way to Tarshish, 1977; How the Left-Behind Beasts Built Ararat, 1978; Never Say Ugh to a Bug, 1979; Small Wonders, 1979; There Goes Feathertop!, 1979; Mercy Short: A Winter Journal, North Boston, 1692–93, 1982.

ABOUT: Contemporary Authors, Vol. 102; Ward, Martha E. and Dorothy A. Marquardt. Authors of Books for Young People, 2nd edition (Supplement).

CAROL FARLEY

December 20, 1936–

AUTHOR OF *The Garden Is Doing Fine,* etc.

Autobiographical sketch of Carol Farley, who also uses the psuedonym "Carol McDole":

WRITING fiction is my way of trying to make sense of a crazy world. I like to write for young people because they seem less crazy than the adults I know. They're more open and honest, more willing to listen and think, more able to feel real emotion. Very old people often are this way, too, and so I use them as characters in my books. I think the very old and the very young are special—I like to think my work might appeal to both groups.

When I was a child I was shy, lonely, homely, and frightened. Books were my gateway to other worlds. Immersed in pages of print, I could become anybody, could live anywhere, do anything at all. To me opening the covers of a book was like standing before a magic cave shouting, "Open Sesame!" I was always certain that a treasure was waiting inside. Authors were wizards, magicians, gods.

I was stunned when I finally discovered—much later than I care to admit—that authors were plain people. So plain, in fact, that even *I* could become one. I proceeded to write.

By the time I was in tenth grade, I had written dozens of novels in torn and worn spiral notebooks. In my real world, my father, my best friend, and a stepbrother had died, two wars had been fought, and the nuclear age had begun, but in my stories the characters were royal princes and princesses who lived perfect lives in blissful peace. Just as I escaped reality by reading, I escaped it by writing. But my stories were worthless. An author who writes simply to avoid reality writes trash.

As I grew older, I finally realized that a writer must write about what he or she knows and cares about—only then can a reader get caught up in a fictional world that has real meaning. Since I learned that lesson, I have tried to share what I know with the people who read my books. I know that life can be difficult, and can end without warning; but I also know that life can be marvelous, filled with laughter and miracles. Most of life is a mystery, and we can only wonder about all the questions we can't answer. I like to think my books make readers wonder.

I was born in Michigan, and since I know that area best, I often use it as a setting in my work. In the past twenty-five years, I have moved twenty times, living and traveling in many states and countries, but my childhood home is still the most vivid setting in my memory, and what I did then remains the most clear. As my own four children were growing up, I used some of their ideas, too, relating them to my own long-ago ideas, for I feel that children of all times and places have very similar thoughts.

Now that I'm living in Michigan again, I like to work with young writers in schools. In Young Author Conferences today, I'm meeting the people who will write the books of the future. Hurrah for young readers and writers!

_____

In 1975, *The Garden Is Doing Fine,* a novel about a beloved father dying of cancer, was the winner of the Golden Kite Award presented by the Society of Children's Book Writers. It also received the "Best Book of the Year" citation by the Child Study Children's Book Committee at Bank Street College and was a Junior Literary Guild selection. *Loosen Your Ears,* short stories about a poor but humorous Michigan farm family, won a Friends of American Writers Award in 1978. Carol Farley received a teacher's certificate from Western Michigan University in 1956 and has taught school and worked in a library. She is a member of the Authors Guild. A number of her books have been published in Japan, Denmark, Germany, Sweden, and the Netherlands.

SELECTED WORKS: Mystery of the Fog Man, 1966; Mystery in the Ravine, 1967; Sergeant Finney's Family, 1969; The Bunch on McKellahan Street, 1971; The Garden Is Doing Fine, 1975; Loosen Your Ears, 1977; Settle Your Fidgets, 1977; Ms. Isabelle Cornell, Herself, 1980; Twilight Waves, 1981.

SELECTED WORKS AS CAROL McDOLE: Yekapo of Zopo Land, 1958.

ABOUT: The International Author's and Writer's Who's Who, 1977; Something About the Author, Vol. 4; Ward, Martha E. and Dorothy A. Marquardt. Authors of Books for Young People, 2nd edition (Supplement); The Writers Directory 1982–84; (as Carol McDole) Contemporary Authors (First Revision), Vol. 21–22.

JOHN D. FITZGERALD

1907–

AUTHOR OF *The Great Brain,* etc.

Biographical sketch of John Dennis Fitzgerald:

JOHN DENNIS FITZGERALD was born in Utah, the son of a Catholic father and a Mormon mother. *The Great Brain* and all its sequels are reminiscences of his childhood with his older brother Tom. In fact, there were four children, Sweyn Dennis, Tom Dennis, John Dennis, and Katie, as well as

JOHN D. FITZGERALD

an adopted brother, Earnie. All the boys carried Dennis as a middle name thanks to an Irish ancestor named Dennis who betrayed six cousins to the English in a rebellion; the traitor's father decreed that all male Fitzgeralds must bear the middle name Dennis to remind them of the cowardice of his son. Fitzgerald's father owned a newspaper, *The Advocate*. John D. Fitzgerald was also a journalist, a foreign correspondent, a short story writer, a bank auditor, and a jazz drummer.

Before turning his hand to children's books, he wrote three adult autobiographies, including *Papa Married a Mormon*, which was a best seller. *Papa* . . . was not intended as a children's book, but it includes some accounts of life in the Fitzgerald house that are amusing to younger readers. Besides the three memoirs, he wrote two books for professional writers and one of historical fiction for young people. He was forced to give up short story writing as a full-time occupation when it would no longer support him; the fact that he wasn't earning enough was made clear when he and his wife had pancakes with no syrup for Thanksgiving dinner one year. That's when he became a bank auditor. He

did not write again professionally until his wife gave him a typewriter for Christmas in hopes that he would record all his anecdotes about Tom's great brain.

All of Fitzgerald's accounts of growing up in Utah Territory around the turn of the century are suffused with warmth and humor. The *Great Brain* books are extremely popular with readers. According to a review in the *New York Times Book Review*, "Tom would be enough to send most younger brothers stuttering off to the psychiatrist. But not J. D. The plucky youth is a willing Watson to his brother's Holmes, a Tonto to his Lone Ranger." A movie was made of *The Great Brain* in 1978.

Fitzgerald's one foray into historical fiction, *Brave Buffalo Fighter,* is loosely based on the diary of Susan Parker as her family journeyed west to Fort Laramie. It is unclear how much the diary was fictionalized, "but the result is an absorbing description of an eventful trip," according to *Booklist*. Fitzgerald currently lives in Titusville, Florida, with his wife.

SELECTED WORKS: The Great Brain, 1967; More Adventures of the Great Brain, 1969; Me and My Little Brain, 1971; The Great Brain at the Academy, 1972; The Great Brain Reforms, 1973; The Return of the Great Brain, 1974; The Great Brain Does It Again, 1975.

ABOUT: Contemporary Authors, Vol. 93–96; Something About the Author, Vol. 20; Ward, Martha E. and Dorothy A. Marquardt. Authors of Books for Young People, 2nd edition (Supplement).

PAUL FLEISCHMAN

September 5, 1952–

AUTHOR OF *Graven Images,* etc.

Autobiographical sketch of Paul Taylor Fleischman:

IF ONLY I could write music I'd give up writing books in an instant. I'd compose operas—by the dozen! String trios. Quartets. Barcarolles, bagatelles, choral fantasias . . .

Paul Fleischman

As it happens, I haven't the talent for writing music. Which leaves books. Which isn't such a bad second choice. I've always felt that the sound of words is as important as their sense, and composing a sentence gives me the same satisfaction that I imagine writing music would. There's the rhythm to tinker with, the shape of the sentence, the harmony of the sounds involved. Figuring out the sense of a story can be difficult, but I spend far more of my time dealing with the sound: juggling phrases, calculating accents, searching for a two-syllable word starting with an *s* . . .

It was through my father, Sid Fleischman, that I first learned the importance of the sound of a story. He writes children's books as well, and when he'd finished a chapter he'd gather the family together and read it to us aloud. As well as being a good writer, he's an excellent reader. The sense of beginning communicated by the rhythm of an opening sentence, the feeling of closing inherent in a chapter's last line were unmistakable. His books brim with the pleasures to be found in the sounds of speech: dialect, forgotten turns of phrase, wonderful names for characters.

Then there was the influence of music it-

self. In the eleventh grade I suddenly developed a craving for classical music. With the help of the local library's record collection (for which I shall always be grateful) I set off on the trail of Bach, Beethoven, and Brahms, and am still in hot pursuit of new music to enjoy. From music, as much as from reading, I've learned to shape a phrase, a paragraph, a chapter, a book. In some cases the content of the music I've listened to has affected my writing as well. The gloomy outer stories in *Graven Images* were written while I was absorbed with the dark, ominous music of Benjamin Britten's *Peter Grimes* and *Billy Budd*. I only hope that my recent infatuation with Italian opera won't result in some improbable plotting on my part.

Like sound, atmosphere is important to me. Many of my stories are set in colonial times. Like my father, I'm attracted to the past. From him I learned the joys of research: digging up old names, old words, old facts about how people dressed, what they ate, how they worked. I haunt used bookstores in search of such information. You never know what you'll stumble onto in a book. I was researching a story on sealing when I came upon a picture of a binnacle boy—which led me to the first tale in *Graven Images*. *Path of the Pale Horse* grew out of a description of an epidemic I chanced to read about in a book on early American doctors. When I'm in between books, as now, I usually take off several weeks or months to read randomly—books about lighthouses, puppet troupes, superstitions, papermaking—in hopes of coming upon something of just that sort, something that might light my way to my next book.

———

Paul Fleischman was born in Monterey, California, and grew up in Santa Monica. He attended the University of California at Berkeley for two years and was graduated from the University of New Mexico in Albuquerque in 1977. He was married in 1978. Fleischman worked in libraries and bookstores and does free-lance editorial work for publishing companies. He has also worked in a bagel bakery and has been a gardener. He and his wife live in Albuquerque, New Mexico, and he owns three dogs.

Graven Images, which was illustrated by Andrew Glass, was a 1983 Newbery Honor Book. *The Half-a-Moon Inn* won a Commonwealth Club of California Award in 1980.

Selected Works: The Birthday Tree, 1979; The Half-a-Moon Inn, 1980; Graven Images, 1982; The Animal Hedge, 1983; Finzel the Farsighted, 1983; Path of the Pale Horse, 1983.

IAN FLEMING

IAN FLEMING

May 28, 1908–August 12, 1964

Author of *Chitty Chitty Bang Bang,* etc.

Biographical sketch of Ian Lancaster Fleming:

IAN FLEMING was born in London, one of four sons of Evelyn Beatrice Fleming, who was reputed to have been one of the most beautiful women in England, and Valentine Fleming. His father, who was at one time a Conservative Member of Parliament, was killed in the Battle of the Somme in 1916, and his obituary in the *London Times* was written by Winston S. Churchill.

Fleming was educated at Eton, England's most exclusive school, and Sandhurst, the military college. He earned his commission at Sandhurst, but feeling that tanks and trucks were a step down from horses and sabers, and not wanting to be a "glorified garagehand," he gave up his commission before beginning service in the British Army. Instead, he decided to pursue a diplomatic career, and attended the Universities of Munich and Geneva to further his education in French and German. On returning to London, he didn't do well enough on the Foreign Office entrance exam (scoring seventh when there were only five vacancies), so he embarked on a career in journalism instead.

From 1929 to 1933, Fleming was the Moscow correspondent for Reuter's Ltd., where he had the most exciting time of his life. "It was in Reuter's that I learned to write fast and, above all, to be accurate, because in Reuter's if you weren't accurate you were fired, and that was the end of that." In 1933, he was offered the post of Assistant General Manager for Reuter's in the Far East. Instead, he joined Cull & Company in London as a banker and in 1935 he became a stockbroker with the firm of Rowe & Pitman's.

In 1939, Fleming returned to Moscow, officially as a reporter for the *Times* but unofficially as a representative for the Foreign Office. At the outbreak of war, he was given a Navy commission, with the rank of Commander (special duties) in the Royal Naval Volunteer Reserve, and made personal assistant to Admiral J. H. Godfrey, Director of Naval Intelligence.

Although most of Fleming's work with Naval Intelligence remains secret, his experiences no doubt provided the basis for the creation of the character who made him famous, James Bond, Agent 007. Although Fleming claimed to have no literary aspirations, and that he only wrote for the money, the Bond books have been astonishingly popular, have been translated into many languages, and have been made into a highly successful series of films.

Chitty Chitty Bang Bang is an oddity compared to the Bond books. It was published in 1964, and is Fleming's one and only children's book. A fantasy and a parody of detective stories, it is the story of an English family that becomes involved with a group of French smugglers. Their magic car can fly or become a boat, and it rescues them from danger. Eric Moon, writing in *Library Journal*, praised Fleming's "narrative magic" and "brilliant imagination," and *Booklist* said, "the inventive, nonsensical story is divertingly told." The book enjoyed a posthumous success almost comparable to the 007 books. In 1968, it was made into a musical movie, starring Dick Van Dyke and Sally Ann Howes. The screenplay was written by Roald Dahl and Ken Hughes, directed by Hughes, and distributed by United Artists.

Fleming was married in 1953 to Anne Geraldine Charteris, and they had one son, Caspar. Besides his Bond-like love of golf, gambling, and fast cars, Fleming collected first editions and rare books, and published the bibliophilic magazine *The Book Collector*. His personal library was considered so important that Oxford's Bodleian Library housed it during the war. After the war, Fleming became Foreign Manager of *The Sunday Times* of London, and spent three months of each year in his home in Jamaica, "Goldeneye," writing one novel per year. Besides the Bond novels and *Chitty Chitty Bang Bang*, Fleming wrote a column for the *Sunday Times* under the pseudonym "Atticus," as well as a book of essays, *Thrilling Cities*, and *Ian Fleming Introduces Jamaica*, which is non-fiction.

Fleming died of a heart attack when he was fifty-six.

SELECTED WORKS: Chitty Chitty Bang Bang, 1964.

ABOUT: Contemporary Authors (First Revision), Vol. 7–8; Current Biography, 1964; Something About the Author, Vol. 9; Ward, Martha E. and Dorothy A. Marquardt. Authors of Books for Young People, 2nd edition; World Authors 1950–1970; Life August 10, 1962; New York Times August 13, 1964; New Yorker April 21, 1962; Playboy December 1964; Publishers Weekly August 24, 1964; Saturday Review May 26, 1962.

EDWARD FRASCINO

November 15, 1938–

ILLUSTRATOR OF *The Trumpet of the Swan*, etc.

Biographical sketch of Edward Frascino:

EDWARD FRASCINO was born in the Bronx early in the Great Depression. When he was ten, his family moved to Yonkers. Frascino's career as a cartoonist began with the comic strips he drew as a young boy. He continued his involvement with art by studying at the Parsons School of Design. After art school, Frascino describes his career as "floundering." "I would show my work to art directors," said Frascino, "but they were always commenting: 'if you could only be more like. . . . ' That always seemed ridiculous to me. I couldn't see copying. I went with what was unique."

After serving in the Army in Korea from 1951 to 1953, Frascino designed greeting cards, worked as a draftsman for Remington Rand, and created ideas for a Madison Avenue advertising agency. Since 1965 he has been a free-lance cartoonist. His cartoons have appeared in *Punch, Saturday Review,* and the *New York Times Book Review.*

After many years of trying, Frascino became a cartoonist for *The New Yorker,* and his cartoons now appear regularly in that magazine. His *New Yorker* series on married couples has also been included in an adult humor collection *Avocado Is Not Your Color.*

Of the numerous books he illustrated for children, E. B. White's *The Trumpet of the Swan* is probably the best known. Frascino said he was assigned to the book because of

Frascino: *Fra SHEE no*

his reputation for working quickly. "E. B. White wanted the book to be on the spring list. They wanted Garth Williams, the illustrator of *Charlotte's Web* and *Stuart Little,* to do this book, too, but he was away. So I got it. I would have liked to have had more time on the book. I liked the change to a less cartoony style."

Becoming an author, Frascino said, "came about in a cliché sort of way. My editor and I used to tell each other stories. One day she said, 'You ought to write a book.' So I did." The book was *Eddie Spaghetti,* based on memories of Yonkers. The ten amusing episodes in the life of a skinny nine-year-old boy growing up in the early 1940s are somewhat biographical. Eddie Spaghetti and Edward Frascino are both Italian-Albanian-Americans who grew up with the funny papers. Frascino's second juvenile reader, *Eddie Spaghetti on the Home Front,* picks up where the first book left off and deals with its hero's feelings of inadequacy during World War II.

Edward Frascino currently lives in Manhattan with several cats. When he is not "doodling" for *The New Yorker* or working on ideas for a third novel, he likes to paint, sculpt, and watch old movies.

SELECTED WORKS WRITTEN: Eddie Spaghetti, 1978; Eddie Spaghetti on the Home Front, 1983.

SELECTED WORKS ILLUSTRATED: Say Something, by Mary Stolz, 1968; Dragons of the Queen, by Mary Stolz, 1969; The Trumpet of the Swan, by E. B. White, 1970; Gladys Told Me to Meet Her Here, by Marjorie Weinman Sharmat, 1970; The Little Mermaid, by Hans Christian Andersen, translated by Eva Le Galliene, 1971; A Hole, A Box, and a Stick, by Gladys Y. Cretan, 1972; Crystal Is the New Girl, by Shirley Gordon, 1976; Crystal Is My Friend, by Shirley Gordon, 1978; Me and the Bad Guys, by Shirley Gordon, 1980.

ABOUT: Kingman, Lee and others, comps. Illustrators of Childrens's Books: 1967–1976; Ward, Martha E. and Dorothy A. Marquardt. Illustrators of Books for Young People, 2nd edition.

DICK GACKENBACH

February 9, 1927–

AUTHOR AND ILLUSTRATOR OF *Hattie Rabbit,* etc.

Autobiographical sketch of Dick Gackenbach:

I WAS BORN in Allentown, in the heart of the Pennsylvania Dutch country. By the time I was four, the Great Depression was in full swing. But despite the hard times and lack of new shoes, my childhood was a happy one, due mainly to the tender loving care of my family. Love was about all they had to give then, and they gave generously. Toys were unaffordable, so we used our imagination to devise our fun and games. The fun, along with the love I received, and the values I learned during those difficult times, have been the source of many of my books.

By the time I was seventeen, the Depression was replaced by World War II. I enlisted in the Navy and was eventually stationed near San Francisco. For a boy from a small town, San Francisco was an eye-opener. I discovered art museums, concerts, and the theater. I even discovered that pot roast and roast beef were two different things. Then and there I decided I had to be an artist, and that I never wanted to live in a small town again.

After the war, thanks to the G.I. Bill, I went to art school. First, for a year at Abbott Art School, in Washington, D.C. Then on to New York City for two more years at Jameson Franklin School of Art. When school was over, I took a job at the main headquarters of the J. C. Penney Company in New York City. I remained there for nearly twenty-five years. When I resigned in 1972, I was Director of Creative Planning for the chain of nearly 2,000 department stores.

By then, I had developed an overwhelming desire to do something different with my life, to try a second career. And the small-town boy in me wanted to return to the country. Since I had never married, and

Gackenbach: *GOK in bok*

DICK GACKENBACH

had no dependents, I made up my mind to say goodbye to the big city, and to my job and security. I moved to the tiny and beautiful village of Washington Depot, Connecticut.

Once I was settled in Connecticut, I was still faced with the spectre of making a living. What, out of all things that were available, did I really want to do? That was an easy decision! I always had a passion for children's books, perhaps because I never had any when I was young. I would browse in bookstores for hours looking at books for young readers, and over the years I had collected quite a few. I not only wanted to, I felt I had to do children's books.

One of my first efforts was called *Claude the Dog*. It was accepted and published in 1974. The day I received the telephone call telling me the book was accepted must have been the happiest day of my life. That was over thirty books ago. It is difficult to tell adults, concerned with adult things, how wonderful it is to write and illustrate for children. It is difficult to convey the reward you feel when you meet young readers, and they, in their own way, let you know they have found the love you hope had gone into the pages of a book.

So after many years of searching, I am doing what I love to do. I'm living in the country, sharing my house with three dissolute dachshunds, and working for the finest people on earth—children.

———

Hattie Rabbit won the 1979 Garden State (New Jersey) Children's Book Award, and *Mother Rabbit's Son Tom* was designated a "Children's Choice" in 1978 by the International Reading Association and the Children's Book Council.

SELECTED WORKS WRITTEN AND ILLUSTRATED: Claude the Dog: A Christmas Story, 1974; Do You Love Me?, 1975; Hattie Rabbit, 1976; Hound and Bear, 1976; Mother Rabbit's Son Tom, 1977; The Pig Who Saw Everything, 1978; More from Hound and Bear, 1979; Harry and the Terrible Whatzit, 1978; A Bag Full of Pups, 1981; Mr. Wink and His Shadow, Ned, 1983.

SELECTED WORKS ILLUSTRATED: Is Milton Missing?, by Steven Kroll, 1975; What Is Papa Up to Now?, by Miriam Bourne, 1977; Rat's Christmas Party, by Jim Murphy, 1979; One, Two, Three—Ah-Choo!, by Marjorie N. Allen, 1980; Friday the 13th, by Steven Kroll, 1981.

ABOUT: Something About the Author, Vol. 30; Ward, Martha E. and Dorothy A. Marquardt. Authors of Books for Young People, 2nd edition (Supplement).

ROY A. GALLANT

April 17, 1924–

AUTHOR OF *Our Universe*, etc.

Autobiographical sketch of Roy Arthur Gallant:

THERE ARE few things in life I am certain about for more than an hour or two, or sometimes even a day or two. When I was seventeen years old I was certain about something for a whole year, then she walked out of my life for another man. Since then I have become cautious over what I choose to be certain about.

An exception to that statement is that I

Roy A. Gallant (signature)

am certain that I will continue to write for as long as I am able to. I'm in love with my work of science writing and would be lost without it. No matter what I may be writing at the moment—a book about fossils, a magazine article about the formation of limestone caves, or an occasional short story—I'm happy working out the problems of putting it all down so that others may learn something they did not know before. I often think that what I like best about writing is that I am educating people. I think that is important and I enjoy doing it, both in front of my word processor and in my college classroom. While I can reach only twenty or so students in my classroom, I reached 700,000 when I wrote my book *Our Universe* for the National Geographic Society.

I have been writing ever since I was about fourteen years old. I wrote lots of poetry when I went to Deering High School in Portland, Maine, where I was born. I enjoyed writing book reviews and just about anything else I was asked to write. During World War II, I gave up writing for a while and learned to navigate B–29s across the sky. I then went to Bowdoin College, where I majored in English and minored in philosophy and science. I then went to graduate

school at Columbia University in New York City. I studied journalism for a master's degree and then over the following years entered a doctoral program and eventually taught writing at Columbia.

In 1950 I got caught up in another war—the Korean War—and did military intelligence work in Tokyo for a year and a half. I have worked as a newspaper reporter, magazine editor, and book editor for companies including Fairchild Publications, Scholastic Publications, and Doubleday. From 1959 to 1963 I was Executive Editor of Aldus Books in London, England, where I worked with several well-known scholars, including Sir Julian Huxley, Dr. Carl Jung, Sir Fred Hoyle, Lord Bertrand Russell, and Lancelot Hogben. On my return to New York in 1963 I became editor-in-chief of The Natural History Press, owned jointly by Doubleday and The American Museum of Natural History. In our first year we published more than twenty-five books, and I started a young people's magazine called *Nature and Science.* During that time I taught science at a private school, the Hackley School in Tarrytown, New York. I also was on the faculty at the Hayden Planetarium in New York. Around 1966 I decided to return to writing full time. Since then I have written many science books, including textbooks for elementary school, high school, and college.

In the early 1970s I decided to return to Maine to live. I now have a large house on a lake near Rangeley, Maine. I spend part of my time teaching at the University of Southern Maine, in Portland, where I also am Director of the Southworth Planetarium. The rest of the time I continue to spend writing books and magazine articles for *Science–83* and *Omni.* I live alone with my English setter, Zu.

———

Roy Gallant is a member of P.E.N., the Authors Guild, and the American Association for the Advancement of Science, and is a Fellow of the Royal Astronomical Society. *Memory* was named an Outstanding Science Trade Book for Children in 1980 by the National Science Teachers Association. His *Exploring Chemistry* won the Boys' Clubs of America Junior Book Award in 1959, and *Exploring the Universe* won the Thomas Alva Edison Foundation National Mass Media Award in 1956.

SELECTED WORKS: Exploring Chemistry, 1958; The ABC's of Astronomy: An Illustrated Dictionary, 1962; Exploring the Moon, revised edition, 1966; Exploring the Universe, revised edition, 1968; Explorers of the Atom, 1973; Astrology: Sense or Nonsense?, 1974; How Life Began: Creation Versus Evolution, 1975; Beyond Earth: The Search for Extraterrestrial Life, 1977; Fires in the Sky, The Birth and Death of Stars, 1978; The Constellations: How they Came to Be, 1979; Earth's Changing Climate, 1979; (with Margaret Sedeen) National Geographic Picture Atlas of Our Universe, 1980; Memory: How It Works and How to Improve It, 1980; The Planets; Exploring the Solar System, 1982.

ABOUT: Contemporary Authors (First Revision), Vol. 7–8; (New Revision Series), Vol. 4; Something About the Author, Vol. 4; Ward, Martha E. and Dorothy A. Marquardt. Authors of Books for Young People, 2nd edition; The Writers Directory 1982–84.

STEPHEN GAMMELL

STEPHEN GAMMELL

February 10, 1943–

ILLUSTRATOR OF *Where the Buffaloes Begin,* etc.

Biographical sketch of Stephen Gammell:

STEPHEN GAMMELL was born in the Midwest and attended school in Des Moines, Iowa. He drew on memories of summers on his grandfather's farm in Iowa when writing and illustrating *Once Upon MacDonald's Farm.*

A self-taught artist, Gammell's favorite medium is pencil. In the early 1970s, while living in New York and doing editorial illustrations for various publications, Gammell went the rounds of the publishing companies with his portfolio. A young editor at G. P. Putnam's Sons asked him to illustrate his first book, *A Nutty Business,*

written by Ida Chittum. It was published in 1972, and since then Gammell has illustrated many books, some of which he has also written.

Stephen Gammell's lifelong interest in the American West has stood him in good stead in illustrating such books as *The Glory Horse* and *Alice Yazzie's Year,* both written by Ramona Maher. His careful research and affection for the subject are especially reflected in his drawings for *Where the Buffaloes Begin,* which were called "magnificent" by the *Horn Book.* The book was also a 1982 Caldecott Honor Book and was nominated for a 1982 American Book Award in the Children's Picture Book category.

Books that Stephen Gammell illustrated have won many other awards. *The Kelpie's Pearls* was on the American Library Association's "Notable Children's Books 1940–1970" list. *Meet the Vampire* was named a Children's Choice book of 1980 by the joint committee of the International Reading Association and the Children's Book Council.

Stonewall was named a 1979 ALA Notable Book and a *New York Times* Outstanding Book of the Year 1979. It was also a

Boston Globe-Horn Book Award Honor Book in 1980. *The Hawks of Chelney* was both an ALA Notable Book and a Best Book for Young Adults in 1978.

The watercolors for his first full-color book, *Wake Up, Bear . . . It's Christmas!,* which he also wrote, were done in his studio in Minneapolis. Well-received in the United States, the book was also published in France, Germany, England, Spain, and Italy. Mr. Gammell says he had no particular inspiration for the story—just an enjoyment of winter, Christmas, bears, and sleeping.

He and his wife, Linda, who is a professional photographer, enjoy camping out in the West and big breakfasts.

SELECTED WORKS WRITTEN AND ILLUSTRATED: Once Upon MacDonald's Farm, 1981; Wake Up, Bear . . . It's Christmas!, 1981; The Story of Mr. and Mrs. Vinegar, 1982; Git Along, Old Scudder, 1983.

SELECTED WORKS ILLUSTRATED: A Nutty Business, by Ida Chittum, 1972; The Glory Horse, by Ramona Maher, 1975; The Kelpie's Pearls, by Mollie Hunter, 1976; Alice Yazzie's Year, by Ramona Maher, 1977; A Furl of Fairy Wind, by Mollie Hunter, 1977; The Hawks of Chelney, by Adrienne Jones, 1978; Meet the Vampire, by Georgess McHargue, 1979; Stonewall, by Jean Fritz, 1979; And Then the Mouse, by Malcolm Hall, 1980; Blackbird Singing, by Eve Bunting, 1980; Scary Stories to Tell in the Dark, compiled by Alvin Schwartz, 1981; Where the Buffaloes Begin, by Olaf Baker, 1981; The Best Way to Ripton, by Maggie S. Davis, 1982; The Old Banjo, by Dennis Haseley, 1983.

ROMA GANS

February 22, 1894–

AUTHOR OF *When Birds Change Their Feathers,* etc.

Autobiographical sketch of Roma Gans:

I WAS BORN in St. Cloud, Minnesota, the second child of ten lucky children. We grew up within walking distance of lakes, ponds, and the Mississippi River.

Each season was welcomed with certain activities, but spring, seemed best to me.

That's when I'd wander through woods and prairies to spot wild flowers. I knew every violet patch and trillium spot.

The return of the birds was a family affair. A robin came spring after spring to build in the same tree. Also a blue jay that used strips of colored cloth we'd put out for the nest. But the real thrill was to catch a glimpse of the scarlet tanager on my favorite walk in the woods.

Later, as a teacher of math, I encouraged students to become bird watchers and flower "viewers" not "pickers."

I mentioned before that I am one of ten *lucky* children. We were especially lucky because both my mother and father were active readers. We had three daily newspapers, Sunday comic strips, and books! A common experience occurred when my father, in reading a newspaper, would look up and say "Here's something you'll be interested in" to one or more of us present. Then he would read some news item of a new discovery or how-to idea. Reading, to all of us, naturally became read-to-find-out. I can still see my brother and me hunched up in a chair reading *The Last Days of Pompeii.*

My teaching career began in 1917 after a two-year normal school course. In 1923 I entered Teachers College, Columbia, to get my B.S. and ultimately my Ph.D. from Columbia in 1940. I began teaching at Teachers College in 1929 and continued there until my retirement in 1959.

Each class, each student, was a privileged experience. Long before the Supreme Court decision to integrate schools, our Teachers College classes were integrated. I learned much from the black teachers of the South who became creative in spite of a great dearth of teaching materials.

One day, in a discussion of the need for better written informational materials for young readers, I voiced this need strongly. Dr. Franklyn M. Branley, who later became the leader of education at Hayden Planetarium in New York City, was present. He came to me and said, "Why don't you and I start writing such books?" And that's how the Let's-Read-and-Find-Out Series began.

My new home in the woods in my retirement had given me the chance to attract and feed birds. How surprised I was to discover how much they ate. I seemed to fill the feeders "every hour on the hour." That inspired me to write my first book, *Birds Eat and Eat and Eat,* which has enjoyed a continuing life.

While teaching at Teachers College, I always kept contact with young children by visiting schools and talking to groups about their reading. These contacts gave me insight into what makes youngsters tick and continue to add to my second career, writing for young readers.

———

The successful and widely used Let's-Read-and-Find-Out Science Book Series was co-edited by Roma Gans and Franklyn M. Branley, and Roma Gans wrote some of the books. Gans has also written many books for adults on reading, including *Common Sense in Teaching Reading: A Practical Guide* (1963).

In addition to teaching in New York and in Minnesota, Missouri, and Wisconsin, Roma Gans is co-founder and Chairman of New York City's Citizen Committee for Children. She is now Professor Emeritus of Childhood Education at Teachers College, Columbia.

SELECTED WORKS: Birds Eat and Eat and Eat, 1963; Birds at Night, 1968; Hummingbirds in the Garden, 1969; Bird Talk, 1971; Water for Dinosaurs and You, 1972; Caves, 1977; When Birds Change Their Feathers, 1980.

ABOUT: Bader, Barbara. American Picturebooks from Noah's Ark to the Beast Within; Contemporary Authors, Vol. 77–80; Ward, Martha E. and Dorothy A. Marquardt. Authors of Books for Young People, 2nd edition (Supplement); Language Arts October 1980.

JACK GANTOS

July 2, 1951–

AUTHOR OF *Rotten Ralph,* etc.

Autobiographical sketch of John Bryan Gantos, Jr.:

I HAD NO intention of writing picture books for children. As a child I don't recall reading them and as an adult I hardly knew they existed. When I visit my friends, or strangers, I'm always shown their favorite books from childhood. "Don't you remember these," they say, certain that I will. When I don't express recognition they're usually surprised. To me it is no surprise that as an adult I do things that I had no love or deep exposure to as a child. It's silly to expect a child to know his future. There are many myths as to what a children's book writer is: perhaps a socially retarded adult, a dreamer who lives in a pink bubble, a moral pervert. I don't care if writers are all of the above as long as they write great fiction for children. Another attitude that I'm constantly confronted with is, "How can you write for children when you don't have any?" I reply that I don't know any, either. I never read a story to a child before rewriting it or submitting it to a publisher. Everyone must remember that I once was a child. I remember my childhood and write to please it.

Jack Gantos

The best critical information I have is that the books that are my favorites are the ones children like best—and those are the books that excite them to act out and behave as my characters behave. My favorite character is *Rotten Ralph*. He is a rotten cat who does rotten things to his owner, Sarah, and others. My biggest thrill is when I watch a child read this book and then instantly become rotten! Once I saw several children looking through a shop window at a *Rotten Ralph* display. As I passed by they began to slap the window and shout, "Rotten Ralph! Rotten Ralph! Rotten Ralph!" I thought they might charge into the store, stick out their tongues at the owner and grab the book and run off. Now what a compliment that would be to me! One time I went into a school and, dressed as Rotten Ralph, read the book to a class of second graders. On one page Rotten Ralph paints all the walls in the house when his owner is away. "Who's gonna go home and draw on their walls!" I asked. "I am," they shouted back. "You promise?" I asked. "Yes!" they promised. All the while the teachers, who were stationed in the back of the room, were waving their arms at me and screwing up their faces in disapproving

expressions. Those children were making plans. They were influenced by a book that was written for them.

I began writing for children when I met my illustrator, Nicole Rubel. She had illustrated a book without words and when I saw it I asked permission to write the story. We started that way. I then wrote *Rotten Ralph,* which she illustrated, and since then have continued to write for children. At present I teach creative writing at Emerson College in Boston. I am finishing an adult novel, which I hope to publish this year.

———

Jack Gantos was born in Mount Pleasant, Pennsylvania and received his B.F.A. from Emerson College in Boston, in 1976. *Rotten Ralph* was selected for the *School Library Journal* "Best of the Best 1966–1978" list (December 1979).

SELECTED WORKS: Rotten Ralph, 1976; Sleepy Ronald, 1976; Fair-Weather Friends, 1977; Aunt Bernice, 1978; Worse Than Rotten Ralph, 1978; Greedy Greeny, 1979; The Perfect Pal, 1979; The Werewolf Family, 1980.

ABOUT: (as John Bryan Gantos Jr.) Contemporary Authors, Vol. 65–68; Something About the Author, Vol. 20; Ward, Martha E. and Dorothy A. Marquardt. Authors of Books for Young People, 2nd edition (Supplement).

JANE GARDAM

July 11, 1928–

AUTHOR OF *Bilgewater,* etc.

Autobiographical sketch of Jane Gardam:

I WAS BORN in Yorkshire, England, by the cold North Sea, but I spent three months of every year on my grandparents' farm in the English Lake District—Arthur Ransome, Beatrix Potter country. When I was seventeen I went to college in London, did research there afterwards, became a journalist, got married, and had three children. I have lived in London now for thirty

Jane Gardam

years—but I go 'home' as much as possible—and we have a little house at the head of one of the English dales. When I go back I begin to speak with a Northern accent. Everybody knows me and remembers my family and is interested in my children as though they were country children. They even like my London lawyer husband who is what they call a foreigner. All my children's books have been about the North, but not because I yearn for the past or for my childhood. Probably because the people up there seem to talk more, and better, and have more dramatic lives than in towns or in the South. And the weather's exciting.

I wrote about girls first—a five-year-old, then a twelve-year-old, then a sixteen-year-old, then a younger teenager who ends up middle-aged. Lucy, Jessica, Athene, Marigold. I like Jessica (*A Long Way From Verona*) best, but I'm glad she's not my daughter. Too exhausting. I'd have got no books written. Then I wrote two First Readers, *Bridget and William* and *Horse,* because so many late readers have said to me, 'Why should all reading books be so young?' Then I got tired of girls and wrote *The Hollow Land,* which is mainly about a town boy and a country boy who are friends all their

lives. They go on being friends until 1999, when the book ends. I enjoyed putting a toe into the future. The illustrations in this book are all of our house in the country and the places and people round about, even our kitchen furniture.

I never write about people I know but I never write about people I don't know—i.e., have not experienced in some way. My characters have bits of many people in them, but, if they work, all the bits have to be swirled up together like in an electric mixer and come out transformed: like the oil and eggs in mayonnaise.

I didn't try to publish anything until I was nearly forty. I am glad. What I wrote earlier was very heavy and laboured and earnest and boring. I didn't work at all for very long after I was married. I meant to. I left my desk at the newspaper to have my first son and intended to be back in three weeks. But it was fifteen years before I took the typewriter out of its case again. I had three children who were always getting ill or doing something sensational at the wrong moment. My husband became a Queen's Counsel and being his wife became almost a job in itself. We have travelled to and worked in Hong Kong, Singapore, the West Indies, Indonesia, and Bangladesh as well as in Europe. I didn't try to write until the third child was at school all day—not on principle (I think they'd have quite liked me out of the way), but because I couldn't concentrate. My son Timothy is now a producer at BBC Television; my daughter Kit is doing research in Mediaeval History and spends her time crawling about cathedral floors with a measuring tape; my son Tom, when not climbing 500-foot rock faces on the end of a rope, is still at school. For four years he went to an American school in London—he was a late reader and we were told that Americans took dyslexia seriously. You do—he was reading in a month. So we have a lot to thank America for. My American publisher, Susan Hirschman of Greenwillow, invited me to America in 1979 and we went to California and the East Coast and to Madison [Wisconsin] in the middle. Meeting readers from far away is one of the great amazements. One of the big prizes. Just seeing America itself, and this year as a guest of the Adelaide Arts Festival, Australia, are the most unexpected and wonderful prizes of all.

I don't write for children only but for everyone. It makes me sad that those who read my 'children's books' have never heard of my 'adult books'—and vice versa. My favourite author is Dickens—with a dozen others thundering at his heels.

There is no book, however, I would not put down to go to the theatre. When I am old I want to live in a rabbit-hole house under London's Waterloo Bridge and then I can totter out each night to a play not five minutes from home. Of course I'll pick the book up again as soon as I get back. I hope I may even be writing it.

———

Jane Gardam received a B.A. degree from Bedford College, London University, in 1949. She was married in 1952 and worked at the *Weldons Ladies Journal* from 1952 to 1953 and at *Time and Tide* from 1953 to 1955. She received the David Higham Prize for fiction in 1975 and the Winifred Holtby Memorial Prize for fiction in 1976 and is a Fellow of the Royal Society of Literature. Her books for adults include *The Pineapple Bay Hotel, God on the Rocks, and The Bridgeport Letters.*

Gardam's books for children have won several awards. Both *A Long Way From Verona* and *The Hollow Land* were named Notable Books by the American Library Association, in 1972 and 1982 respectively. *The Hollow Land* also won the Whitbread Award. *Bilgewater* was on the *School Library Journal* "Best of the Best 1966–1978" list (December 1979), and *The Summer After the Funeral* was a Boston Globe-Horn Honor Book for 1974.

SELECTED WORKS: A Few Fair Days, 1972; A Long Way From Verona, 1972; The Summer After the Funeral, 1973; Bilgewater, 1977; Bridget and William, 1981; The Hollow Land, 1982.

ABOUT: Blishen, Edward, ed. The Thorny Paradise: Writers on Writing for Children; Contemporary Authors, Vol. 49–52; (New Revision Series), Vol. 2; Kirkpatrick, D.L. Twentieth-Century Children's Writers; Something About the Author, Vol. 28; Ward, Martha E. and Dorothy A. Marquardt. Authors of Books for Young People, 2nd edition (Supplement); The Writers Directory 1982–84.

NANCY GARDEN

May 15, 1938–

AUTHOR OF *Annie on My Mind,* etc.

Autobiographical sketch of Nancy Garden:

WHEN I WAS about sixteen, I had a terrible argument with my English teacher; she wanted me to be a writer, and I wanted to be an actress. For a while, I thought I'd won, for I spent a number of years in theater as an actress, lighting designer, and jill-of-all-trades. But in the long run, my English teacher won, and I'm very glad she did. I should have realized she would, too, for I'd written for pleasure throughout my childhood and continued to do so as an adult no matter what other kind of job I had. That's one of the wonderful things about writing: that you can do it just about any place and almost any time, even in snatched moments, without having to depend on other people to help.

One of the very first things I wrote outside of school, when I was about eight, was a poem about the noises an old-fashioned steam radiator makes. In the poem, I explained to my little brother that the sounds that frightened him at night came from the radiator instead of from horrible monsters or robbers. In reality, though, I didn't have a little brother, and it was I who was afraid of the noises. That's another wonderful thing about writing: it can help you feel better about things that frighten or trouble you.

I suppose one reason why I always liked writing is that my parents read to me a lot when I was growing up. Our house was full

Tim Morse

of books; so was the house of my favorite aunt. During family parties at her house, I used to escape from the grown-ups as soon as I could and go up to the second floor landing, where the children's books were, and read and read and read. Sometimes I pretended to be the characters from my favorite books, and I made up and acted out new stories for them, either alone or with other kids.

My family moved a lot when I was little, and I suppose another reason why I read and wrote so much was that I was always changing schools and having to make new friends, which I didn't do easily. I think that's also one reason why places are often almost as important as people to me when I write.

I think some of the people who read autobiographical sketches of writers are people who would like to become writers themselves. Sometimes young writers ask me what special kind of education they should have to prepare them for their future profession. I think any kind of education is fine, including the eduation you get outside of school, from just living. The important things to do are read as much as you can, write as much as you can, and notice and

remember as much as you can about people, your surroundings, and your own feelings and thoughts.

And also remember that even though, like most writers, you will probably have to work at other jobs along the way, you can always write too, for as long as it's important enough to you, you will be able to find the time.

———

Nancy Garden was born in Boston, Massachusetts. She earned a B.F.A. degree from Columbia University in 1961 and an M.A. in 1962. She has been contributing editor to *Junior Scholastic* magazine and *American Observer* magazine. She was also an editor at the Houghton Mifflin Company of Boston. She now lives in Massachusetts.

What Happened in Marston was made into an ABC After School Special in 1981, under the title "The Color of Friendship." *Annie on My Mind* was named a Best Book for Young Adults by the American Library Association in 1982, and *Fours Crossing* was a Book-of-the-Month Club selection and has been nominated for the 1983–1984 William Allen White Award.

SELECTED WORKS: Berlin: City Split in Two, 1971; What Happened in Marston, 1971; The Loners, 1972; Vampires, 1973; Werewolves, 1973; Witches, 1975; Fours Crossing, 1981; Annie on My Mind, 1982; Watersmeet, 1983.

ABOUT: Contemporary Authors (First Revision), Vol. 33–36; Something About the Author, Vol. 12; Ward, Martha E. and Dorothy A. Marquardt. Authors of Books for Young People, 2nd edition (Supplement); The Writers Directory 1982–84.

JOHN GARDNER

July 21, 1933– September 14, 1982

AUTHOR OF *Dragon, Dragon and Other Tales*, etc.

Biographical sketch of John Champlin Gardner Jr.:

© Joel Gardner

JOHN GARDNER

JOHN GARDNER was born in Batavia, New York. His father, a farmer and "memorizer of poetry and scripture," and his mother, an English teacher (once his father's high-school teacher), were great influences on Gardner's literary career and education. Besides giving public readings of poetry, Shakespeare, and the Bible, they were known all over western New York as singers and performers.

At the age of seven, Gardner started writing poetry, and he always claimed that this early verse was much better than the poetry he wrote later in his life. He also wrote thrillers, reading them at night, a chapter at a time, to his cousins on the farm. Throughout his career, he wrote for oral effect: "You don't have to understand words," he said. "Language is texture."

Gardner wrote that as a child he was influenced by his favorite authors: God, Dickens, and Disney. Dickens and Disney both created what he called "wonderful cartoon images, [and] told stories as direct as fairy tales. . . . " "God," he said in the *New York Times Book Review,* is "an extremely uneven writer, but when He's good, nobody can touch Him."

Gardner attended De Pauw University from 1951 to 1953, and then went on to graduate with a B.A. from Washington University in St. Louis. He had started off studying the sciences, but moved quickly into literature. For postgraduate studies he went to the State University of Iowa on a fellowship, earning his M.A. and Ph.D. degrees in classical and medieval literature. He had intended to study in the Writers' Workshop, but ended up in medieval studies instead. This became his life-long specialty, and he went on to write a biography of Chaucer and studies of the Gawain poet, as well as translations of Old and Middle English poetry.

After receiving his doctorate, Gardner went to Oberlin College in Ohio to teach from 1958 to 1959. He also taught at California State University, San Francisco State University, Southern Illinois University, the University of Detroit, Northwestern University, and Bennington College. In 1978, he founded the creative writing program at the State University of New York at Binghamton, as well as founding and editing *MSS* magazine, a forum for new writers (publishing such writers as Joyce Carol Oates, William Stafford, and John Hawkes, when they were still unknown). He also headed the Bread Loaf Writer's Conference at Middlebury College for several summers.

In 1953, Gardner married Joan Louise Patterson, and they had two children, Joel and Lucy. They were divorced after nearly twenty-five years of marriage. He then married L. M. Rosenberg, who became co-editor of *MSS*.

John Gardner wrote three books of contemporary fairy tales and one book of poems for children. Like all three story books, *Dragon, Dragon* contains four humorous, offbeat stories in mythic settings. In the title story, a dragon makes mischief: he "robbed graves and put frogs in people's drinking water and tore the last chapters out of novels. . . . " Jonathan Yardley, writing in the *New York Times,* wrote that Gardner's writing established "the premise that the young reader is sophisticated enough to appreciate the funny cruelty of tearing out the last chapters of novels" and that "the writer is not condescending to him." Yardley also wrote that Gardner was "a respecter of tradition so in each tale he points a moral." But he does so "with a twist. Happy endings are reached, but through human rather than heroic means." He compares Gardner's humor to Woody Allen's. *Kirkus* calls *Dragon, Dragon* a "fanciful collection . . . written with ingenuity and wry humor." *Saturday Review* called *Gudgekin the Thistle Girl* "eerie, inventive, funny," and the book was a Junior Literary Guild selection. The stories in *The King of the Hummingbirds* were called "surprising and hilarious" by *Publishers Weekly* and "witty, wacky fun" by the *New York Times Book Review.*

A Child's Bestiary is a collection of over sixty humorous verses about animals, which "virtually beg to be memorized," according to *Publishers Weekly. Kirkus* called them "sly, sparkling fun," and Ann A. Flowers, writing in the *Horn Book,* wrote that the "humorous and wryly sophisticated" poems were "in the tradition of Hilaire Belloc and Ogden Nash."

In addition to his children's books and his work in medieval studies, Gardner wrote criticism (*On Moral Fiction*), poetry (*Jason and Medeia*), librettos for two operas, short stories (*The King's Indian and Other Fireside Tales*), and novels. *Grendel* was named one of 1971's best fiction books by *Time* and *Newsweek,* and *October Light* was named one of ten best books in 1976 by *Time* and the *New York Times,* as well as winning an award, in 1977, from the National Book Critics Circle. He also wrote a book on writing, *On Becoming a Novelist,* which was published in 1983.

Gardner died at the age of forty-nine when his motorcycle crashed. He was separated from his wife at the time and was living in Susquehanna, Pennsylvania.

SELECTED WORKS: Dragon, Dragon and Other Tales, 1975; Gudgekin the Thistle Girl and Other Tales, 1976; (with Lucy Gardner and Eugene Rudzewicz) A Child's Bestiary, 1977; The King of the Hummingbirds and Other Tales, 1977.

ABOUT: Contemporary Authors, Vol. 65–68; Current Biography Yearbook, 1978; 1982; Ward, Martha E. and Dorothy A. Marquardt. Authors of Books for Young People, 2nd edition (Supplement); Who's Who in America, 1982–1983; The Writers Directory 1982–84; Christian Science Monitor June 24, 1980; Detroit Free Press March 23, 1975; New York Times Book Review January 30, 1983; Newsday September 15, 1982; Washington Post July 25, 1982.

EVE GARNETT

AUTHOR AND ILLUSTRATOR OF *The Family from One End Street and Some of Their Adventures,* etc.

Biographical sketch of Eve C. R. Garnett:

EVE GARNETT was born in Worcestershire, England. She was educated at the Convent and at West Bank School in Devon and at the Alice Ottley School in Worcester. She studied art at the Chelsea Polytechnic School of Art in London and at the Royal Academy School of Art, where she received a five-year studentship. Although she was ill and could only attend the school for two years, she won both the Creswick Prize and a Silver Medal for her landscape painting.

Garnett had a distinguished career as an artist. She completed forty feet of murals for Children's House in Bow, London, and had exhibitions at Le Fevre Gallery and the New English Art Club in London. In 1939 her work was exhibited at the Tate Gallery.

Garnett wrote in 1938 to the editor of *Junior Bookshelf,* a quarterly review of children's literature, that when she was still a child, she began to take an interest in the poor. "To my neo-Georgian nursery there descended from the Edwardian one of my elder sisters, who in their turn received them from a Victorian establishment, a series of tales about 'The Poor' with which the parents of the 'Eighties had sought to beguile and improve the leisure of their offspring. While my contemporaries were enjoying *Peter Pan* or *The Wind in the Willows,* I was absorbing these dramatic biographies; the life story of *Lost Gyp* and her bare-footed brother who, in the intervals of searching mortuaries and coffin shops for his sister, would endeavour to make a living selling damp fusees [matches] in the blinding rain outside the Mansion House; or the fortunes of Little Meg (her red frock in pawn) eternally shivering outside a gin palace awaiting Father."

As a young artist, Garnett sketched children in London's East End slums. She says that in showing an interest in these children she exercised her curiosity ("not the usual tepid curiosity of maturity—but the vital and dynamic curiosity of the child carried into adult life") for her fellow man. Her drawings of these children were the basis of a commission to illustrate *The London Child* by Evelyn Sharp in 1927. Later, in 1938, she published another book for adults about children, *"Is It Well with the Child?,"* which included a foreword by Walter de la Mare.

What Garnett saw in the London slums became the inspiration for her books about the Ruggles family, a poor, but cheerful and loving working-class family to whom an unexpected expense could be a disaster. The first book about the Ruggles, *The Family from One End Street,* was rejected by eight publishers, and Garnett was told that it was unsuitable for children. However, it was published in England in 1937 and won the Carnegie Medal in 1938.

Garnett was a pioneer in portraying a realistic view of poverty in children's literature. She wrote to *Junior Bookshelf* that once people are interested in the way people live, "they are usually concerned . . . and it seems to me that like many other useful things, this interest is best begun in the nursery." Garnett says of the tales about the poor that her sister told her in her childhood, "I see no reason why the modern child should not be presented with something on the same lines but in a less morbid and more humorous vein. . . . What *The Family from One End Street* is, its readers

must decide. 'The excellence of every art depends upon the complete fulfillment of its purpose,' and the poor—may I repeat it?—are with us always."

In addition to her careers as artist and writer of children's books, Eve Garnett has written radio scripts and has been a broadcaster for the BBC, the Australian National Broadcasting Corporation, and the New Zealand Broadcasting Company in the 1950s. She is a member of the Society of Authors and of P.E.N., and lives in Lewes, Sussex, England.

SELECTED WORKS WRITTEN AND ILLUSTRATED: The Family from One End Street and Some of Their Adventures, 1939; Further Adventures of the Family from One End Street, 1956; Holiday at the Dew Drop Inn: A One End Street Story, 1962.

SELECTED WORKS ILLUSTRATED: A Child's Garden of Verses, by Robert Louis Stevenson, 1948.

ABOUT: The Author's and Writer's Who's Who, 6th edition; Contemporary Authors (First Revision), Vol. 4; (New Revision Series), Vol. 2; Doyle, Brian, ed. Who's Who of Children's Literature; The International Authors and Writers Who's Who, 1982; Kingman, Lee and others, comps. Illustrators of Children's Books: 1956–1966; Kirkpatrick, D. L., ed. Twentieth-Century Children's Writers; Mahony, Bertha E. and others, comps. Illustrators of Children's Books: 1744-1945; Something About the Author, Vol. 3; Viguers, Ruth Hill and others, comps. Illustrators of Children's Books: 1946–1956; Ward, Martha E. and Dorothy A. Marquardt. Authors of Books for Young People, 2nd edition; The Writers Directory 1982–84.

PATRICIA LEE GAUCH

January 3, 1934–

AUTHOR OF *This Time, Tempe Wick?,* etc.

Autobiographical sketch of Patricia Lee Gauch:

I ADMIT that I was an only child, but I never stayed curled up in a window seat writing precocious pieces in a hidden journal. I don't even remember writing anything creative in school, though I might have. "Ants in her pants," my father used to say. "Her

Gauch: *GOUCH*

Patricia Lee Gauch

motor's always running," my Aunt Irene used to say. I had so much energy that inside school what I remember best is jiggling; outside of school I played. Paper dolls, lead soldiers, "dress-up." I was a superb first baseman (. . . well, I hustled, anyway), loved roller skating over our bumpy sidewalks, and helped set up the annual Hampton Road basement talent show. (I ran the lights and sang; I suspect I ran the lights better than I sang.) So, I played, pretended, ran everywhere, and I laughed a lot—which always ended in an uncontrollable floor-rolling bout of hiccups. I liked living.

Maybe that was what led me into newspaper work. I didn't like high school much, for all the usual traumatic reasons, but when I walked into the basement office of the Miami *Student,* the Miami University college newspaper, I knew I was home. The people were curious, energetic, and slightly crazy. Red-headed, temperamental Mike Kelly; moody, talented Bob Gates; feisty Tabby Tabor. I loved their individuality, and I loved interviewing people, discovering stories (including the one about old Fisher Hall being haunted), making up pages.

At the Louisville *Courier-Journal,* where

I went after graduation from Miami, I was the youngest reporter, so I got the assignments no one else wanted, like the one covering a 38-mile Girl Scout hike to Abraham Lincoln's birthplace. I also filled a lot of glue pots and sharpened 8,573 number-two pencils. 9,824? Anyway, somewhere between the hiking blisters, glue pots, and number-two pencils, I decided I wanted to be a writer. At least I was nosy and determined.

I think the Michigan Lakes have been important in my life. I grew up two blocks from Lake St. Clair, camped at Lake Michigan, hiked up Lake Huron, went turtle-hunting in more tiny lakes than I can name. (We never kept the turtles long.) More than once I nearly went down in storms when my family crossed the Georgian Bay in our tiny thirty-foot boat. I'll get to those stories some day, but I wrote my first book in the middle of a summer night at our Lake Huron farmhouse. *Grandpa and Me* it was called, and it was about a boy, a grandfather, and the lake.

A lot has happened to me since newspaper days. When my daughters, Sarah and Chris, reached school age, I went back to Manhattanville College for my education degree and joined the Jean Fritz Children's Writers Workshop at the same time. My son John was born the evening of my last Shakespeare class, just months before my first book was accepted. My husband Ron has turned out to be my best critic, but John's getting better every day. His motor's always running, too. In the mid-seventies I started teaching creative writing at a very special school: Gill-St. Bernard's in Gladstone, New Jersey. It's a school where I can take my senior high students off into the world to write. And I do. We write about Cape May's porch swings, the elevators at Gucci's, the umbrella hot-dog stands by the New York Public Library. I guess you could say my motor's still running, too.

For subjects, usually a real person or real event will suggest a book to me. I thought of *Morelli's Game,* for example, after biking with twenty teenagers on the towpath to Washington, but when I turned the incident into fiction, I narrowed the number to five and set them off on a mysterious journey. These five—Peter, Partini, Thad, Chris, and Jerry—were crazy characters, too, but usually a reader can suspect that I am after more than character or even action in a book. I'm after an idea. In *Morelli,* the clue is Tolkien.

When I hear from kids, or from other people I respect, that they liked a book, I am pleased, but alone in my house I get discouraged, too. Plenty of times. Maybe that's why I go on writing. I've still got that reporter's nose for a story anyway, but I am convinced each time that I can write the next book better. For sure, I will follow an idea anywhere, into a picture book, easy-to-read, novel—even into an adult book. The idea comes first.

———

Patricia Lee Gauch was born in Detroit, Michigan. She has three children and is working on a doctorate in English Literature at Drew University. She lives in New Jersey.

This Time, Tempe Wick?, illustrated by Margot Tomes, was named a Notable Children's Trade Book in the Field of Social Studies by a joint committee of the National Council for the Social Studies and the Children's Book Council.

SELECTED WORKS: Aaron and the Green Mountain Boys, 1972; Christina Katerina and the First Annual Grand Ballet, 1973; The Time, Tempe Wick?, 1974; Once Upon a Dinkelsbühl, 1977; On To Widecombe Fair, 1978; Kate Alone, 1980; Morelli's Game, 1981; Night Talks, 1983.

ABOUT: Contemporary Authors, Vol. 57–60.

PATRICIA REILLY GIFF

April 26, 1935–

AUTHOR OF *Fourth-Grade Celebrity*, etc.

Patricia Reilly Giff

Autobiographical sketch of Patricia Reilly Giff:

WHILE the rest of the kids were playing hide-and-seek, I sat under the cherry tree, reading. On winter evenings, I shared an armchair with my father while he read *Hiawatha* and *Evangeline* to me. I read the stories of my mother's childhood, and every book in our little library in St. Albans.

I wanted to write. Always.

But the people who wrote were dead . . .or important, far away and inaccessible. And who was I to dream about writing something like *Little Women* or *The Secret Garden,* or *Jane Eyre?*

In college, I studied Keats, and Poe, and Pope, and Dryden and, overcome by their genius, switched from English to business, and then to history, where I listened to a marvelous man named Mullee spin tales about the past. I fell into teaching because my beloved dean, who had no idea that I wanted to write, saw that it was a good place for me.

I taught for almost twenty years before I wrote a story. I was married and had three children. I had a Master's in history, a Professional Diploma in reading. I had started doctoral studies.

Then suddenly I was forty. I hadn't written a story; I hadn't even tried.

By this time I had worked with so many children who had terrible problems that I wanted to say things that would make them laugh. I wanted to tell them that they were special. That we all are. Maybe I didn't have to be a Milton or a Longfellow to do that.

I began. Early on dark cold mornings, fortified by innumerable cups of hot tea, I worked at it. It was hard. It was really so hard. But then I began to feel the joy of it, learning as I wrote, laughing . . .

It's still hard. But I can't stop now. I'm still getting up early, still trying to learn, still laughing.

I wish I had started sooner.

Patricia Reilly Giff is a reading consultant. She has a B.A. from Marymount College and an M.A. from St. John's University. She has been a school teacher. She is a member of the Society of Children's Book Writers and lives in Elmont and Harvard, New York. Her husband is a detective.

Most of Giff's books are humorous books for middle grade readers, including two books about Casey Valentine, *Fourth-Grade Celebrity* and *The Girl Who Knew It All*. She has also written two picture books, *Today Was a Terrible Day* and *Next Year I'll Be Special*. *The Gift of the Pirate Queen* was a Junior Literary Guild selection.

SELECTED WORKS: Fourth-Grade Celebrity, 1979; The Girl Who Knew It All, 1979; Left-Handed Shortstop, 1980; Next Year I'll Be Special, 1980; Today Was a Terrible Day, 1980; Have You Seen Hyacinth Macaw?, 1981; The Winter Worm Business, 1981; The Gift of the Pirate Queen, 1982; Loretta P. Sweeny, Where Are You?, 1983.

ABOUT: Contemporary Authors, Vol. 101.

NIKKI GIOVANNI

June 7, 1943–

AUTHOR OF *Spin a Soft Black Song,* etc.

Autobiographical sketch of Yolande Cornelia Giovanni Jr.:

I NEVER trusted people who said they always wanted to be something, as in "I always wanted to be a writer since I was ten years old" or something. It seemed to me to show a poverty of opportunity or imagination. Life is an interesting experience, and I would identify only the fact that we should remain open to and with our responses in order to contribute effectively to the process. I do, however, like writing; and as long as I feel I can make a valid contribution in this area, I will continue to try.

Writing is the art of maturation. The older you get, the better you will write. Not only because of the craft aspect of writing, but also because of the gained insight. One isn't born with insight, one obtains it. And that is the existential proposition.

I was born in Knoxville, Tennessee, a small, quiet town in the Smokey Mountains. It's grown considerably now, but it still lends itself to reflection. The mountains cause you to raise your eyes upward and ponder the heavens. They help to create a larger vision. You are small but not alone. I was graduated from Fisk University in

Nashville, Tennessee, taking a major in History. I do love the historical process. The past is not always exactly instructive, but the clues to the human dilemma (Are we civilized or not?) do reside there. It is the past that shows us progress; it is the future that gives us hope.

I am a poet. Poets are not special people, we only function in a special profession. So do doctors or lawyers or teachers or most people. We are not different; what we do is different. Once we understand that variations of birth as to country, race, gender, and age are just that—different—then we all will have achieved a poetic vision. I think that's the ultimate task of my profession. To show us how unique and yet how similiar we are. This is not something I can achieve alone; it is a process we all work on. We live. I hope that my poetry is instructive with that process; that my poems help us to understand life's joys and pains. The purpose of a poem is to help the reader and writer look at other people as if we know them. I hope I contribute to that vision. That mankind can do better. That we can love.

———

Nikki Giovanni also attended the University of Pennsylvania and the Columbia University School of the Arts. She is a well-known poet for adults, a writer, and lecturer who led a demonstration in the 1960s that restored the campus chapter of the Student Nonviolent Coordinating Committee at Fisk University. She has taught Black Studies and English and was awarded several Honorary Doctorates, in Humanities (Wilberforce University) and in Literature (Smith College, among others). The Harlem Cultural Council, the Ford Foundation, and the National Endowment for the Arts have all awarded her grants.

Mademoiselle magazine named her a woman of the year in 1971, and the *Ladies' Home Journal* gave her a Woman of the Year Youth Leadership Award in 1972.

Some of her books for adults are *Black*

Feeling Black Talk/Black Judgment, 1970; *Re: Creation,* 1970; *Gemini* (essays), 1971; *My House,* 1972; and *Cotton Candy On a Rainy Day,* 1978. Giovanni has made six recordings of her poetry, some with jazz or gospel music as accompaniment.

She is currently an editorial consultant for *Encore American and Worldwide News* magazine, and writes a column, "The Root of the Matter," for it. She is a member of the National Association of Negro Women.

Nikki Giovanni has one son, Thomas.

SELECTED WORKS: Spin a Soft Black Song, 1971; Ego Tripping and Other Poems for Young Readers, 1974; Vacation Time: Poems for Children, 1980.

ABOUT: Biography News, Vol. 2; Contemporary Authors (First Revision), Vol. 29–32; Contemporary Poets, 2nd edition; Current Biography Yearbook, 1973; A Directory of American Poets, 1975; The Ebony Success Library, Vol. 1; Kirkpatrick, D. L. Twentieth-Century Children's Writers; Myers, Robin, comp. and ed. A Dictionary of Literature in the English Language: From 1940 to 1970; Shockley, Ann Allen and Sue P. Chandler. Living Black American Authors: A Biographical Directory; Something About the Author, Vol. 24; Ward, Martha E. and Dorothy A. Marquardt. Authors of Books for Young People, 2nd edition (Supplement); Who's Who Among Black Americans, 2nd edition; Who's Who in America, 1982; The Writers Directory 1982–84; Christian Science Monitor June 4, 1970; Publishers Weekly November 13, 1972; Time April 6, 1970; January 17, 1972.

DIANE GOODE

September 14, 1949–

ILLUSTRATOR OF *When I Was Young in the Mountains,* etc.

Autobiographical sketch of Diane Capuozzo Goode:

I WAS BORN in Brooklyn, New York and grew up in the suburbs. My father is of Neopolitan descent and my mother is French. Our family is widespread but emotionally close.

When I was an infant I made my first trip to Corsica, my mother's home, and thereaf-

is a constant reminder of who my audience really is.

Illustrating is a great privilege and a pleasure. I give it all I've got. If I fall short, it is not from lack of trying. Fortunately, the amount of work involved in each book almost insures continued growth and improvement. If practice does not make perfect, at least it makes better, and my aim is to keep improving.

———

Diane Goode taught in New York City public high schools in 1972 and 1973 and taught book illustration at the University of California at Los Angeles from 1976 to 1978. She has illustrated twenty-four record album covers and had her work exhibited at the Metropolitan Museum of Art in 1982.

When I Was Young in the Mountains was a 1983 Caldecott Honor Book and an American Book Awards nominee in the hardcover picture book category. Goode received an award in 1975 from the Southern California Council on Literature for Children and Young People for *The Selchie's Seed* and *Little Pieces of the West Wind,* and one in 1979 for *The Dream Eater. Tattercoats* was named a Notable Book in 1976 by the American Library Association. *The Good-Hearted Youngest Brother* was named a Notable Children's Trade Book in the Field of Social Studies by the joint committee of the National Council for the Social Studies and the Children's Book Council in 1981.

ter spent many happy summers. We traveled abroad often as a family and my early exposure to the great museums of Europe had a profound effect on me. To say I was in awe of the old masters would be an understatement.

As children, my brother and I were seldom permitted to watch television and so I developed an early reading habit. I was a very serious child. I took pleasure in drawing for as long as I can remember.

I received my B.A. in Fine Arts in 1972 from Queens College, where I also met my future husband David. I took a year off to attend les Beaux-Arts in Aix-en-Provence, where I gained more from the cafés and pastry shops than I did from the studios. I resolved then to make illustration my profession.

In 1973 I married David and we moved to Los Angeles. Curiously enough, it was after this move that I had my first job illustrating a picture book for a New York press. I learned color separation over the telephone. I had no knowledge of commercial art. I was lucky to have a patient publisher and a very supportive husband.

Our son, Peter, was born in 1978 and his presence has added much to my work. He

SELECTED WORKS ILLUSTRATED: Little Pieces of the West Wind, by Christian Garrison, 1975; The Selchie's Seed, by Shulamith Oppenheim, 1975; Tattercoats: An Old English Tale, by Flora Annie Steele, 1976; Beauty and the Beast, by Madame LePrince de Beaumont, 1978; The Dream Eater, by Christian Garrison, 1978; The Good-Hearted Youngest Brother, retold and translated by Emoke de Papp Severo, 1981; The Unicorn and the Plow, by Louise Moeri, 1982; When I Was Young in the Mountains, by Cynthia Rylant, 1982; Peter Pan, by J. M. Barrie, 1983.

ABOUT: Kingman, Lee and others, comps. Illustrators of Children's Books: 1967–1976; Something About the Author, Vol. 15.

BETTE GREENE

June 28, 1934–

AUTHOR OF *Summer of My German Soldier,* etc.

Autobiographical sketch of Bette Greene:

I GREW UP in a small, dusty, Arkansas town surrounded by endless miles of cotton-fields during those super-patriotic days of World War II. My parents owned a country store that sold everything from nails to Easter bonnets to Hershey Bars. Actually they didn't sell Hershey Bars because all sugar products were so rationed that we rarely saw a candy bar, much less a brand-name candy bar. The explanation we kids were invariably given was that all candy (ditto cigarettes) was being sent to our fighting men. Sometimes I wonder if those brave American soldiers who managed to survive Nazi bullets were equally successful surviving both tooth decay and lung cancer.

Even way back then, I thought about becoming a writer, but I didn't think it was realistic. The three reasons why not, more or less in this order, were: 1) in a world where everything was going on, I was living in a place where almost nothing was going on; 2) I was a bad student; and 3) an even worse speller.

In spite of my academic nonperformance, it was my third grade teacher, Miss Ada Norsworthy, who, more than anybody else, allowed me to believe that just maybe and in spite of everything I just might be able to be a writer after all. It was something that she wrote in the autograph book that nobody, not even I, has laid eyes upon for more than a third of a century. Even so, I'll never forget what she wrote there: "I believe that you can be a comedienne, if that is your wish."

Although I'm not sure that I figured out then and there the great similarities between the comedienne and the novelist, I knew, for sure, that Miss Norsworthy was saying that I had talent. Maybe I read too much into Miss Norsworthy's words, but I

also thought that the words meant that I was special. Incredible as that seemed, cause what I felt was common. I felt that I was as common as dirt. I guess it's fair to say that when I began believing in myself, I was merely following my teacher's lead.

Because it was no more cool to thank a teacher then as it is to thank a teacher now, I never did. Never once uttered a single appreciative word to Miss Norsworthy or any other teacher who, in some way or other, helped me out. And that's one thing I regret.

Some of the things I don't regret are: marrying the man I married, having the children I have, and leading the life I lead. Although my roots, my memories are all of Arkansas, I live with my husband, a Boston doctor who specializes in diseases of the nervous system, in a big old house in Brookline, Massachusetts.

During the summer months, we take trips in our boat, *The Philip Hall,* to places like Cape Cod and Nantucket Island. Donald, my husband, and Jordan, my son, like to skipper the boat, which is fine with me because I like to work on my tan, read, talk, and watch the flight pattern of the sea gulls.

Although I have attended seven schools of

Bette: *BET tee*

higher learning, including Columbia University, Harvard, Alliance Francaise in Paris, the University of Alabama, and Memphis State University, I don't have a degree. I'm always working on educating me, but apparently not in ways that lead to a college degree. Fortunately for me, having or not having "a college education" is no more or less helpful to a novelist than freckles.

————

Bette Greene's first novel, *Summer of My German Soldier,* is the story of a twelve-year-old Southern Jewish girl who hides an escaped German prisoner of war in the 1940s. It was a popular and critical success, winning the Golden Kite Award of the Society of Children's Book Writers in 1973. It was nominated for a National Book Award in 1974 and named an American Library Association Notable Book. Both that novel and her next book, *Philip Hall Likes Me. I Reckon Maybe.,* were recognized by the *New York Times* as Outstanding Books of the Year in the years of their publication. *Philip Hall Likes Me. I Reckon Maybe.* was a Newbery Honor Book for 1975 and a Junior Literary Guild selection. It was also named an ALA Notable Book.

Morning Is a Long Time Coming is a sequel to *Summer of My German Soldier,* for which Greene wrote a screenplay; it was made into a prime-time TV movie and was first shown in 1978.

Bette Greene is a member of P.E.N. and the Authors Guild. She has two children.

SELECTED WORKS: Summer of My German Soldier, 1973; Philip Hall Likes Me. I Reckon Maybe., 1974; Morning Is a Long Time Coming, 1978; Get On Out of Here, Philip Hall, 1981; Them That Glitter and Them That Don't, 1983.

ABOUT: Children's Literature Review, Vol. 2; Contemporary Authors, Vol. 53–56; (New Revision Series), Vol. 4; Kirkpatrick, D. L. Twentieth-Century Children's Writers; Something About the Author, Vol. 8; Ward, Martha E. and Dorothy A. Marquardt. Authors of Books for Young People, 2nd edition (Supplement); Who's Who in America, 1982; The Writers Directory 1982–84. Publishers Weekly August 27, 1973.

ELOISE GREENFIELD

May 17, 1929–

AUTHOR OF *She Come Bringing Me That Little Baby Girl,* etc.

Autobiographical sketch of Eloise Greenfield:

I DIDN'T LIKE to write when I was a child. I dreaded school writing assignments. Grammar and spelling were not the problem. Shyness was. I was too shy to put my thoughts and feelings on paper. It was hard to write a paragraph or a page without saying anything, but I used to try.

I was in my early twenties when I discovered the fascination of working with words. I had loved reading all of my life, and I believe now that during those years, I was storing up feelings and knowledge about the rhythms and sounds and meanings of words, until I was ready to write.

I was born in Parmele, North Carolina. When I was four months old, our family moved to Washington, D. C. It was a racially segregated city. The schools, the theaters, the restaurants. Salespeople in the downtown stores were often rude to us. Mama and Daddy explained that they were ignorant.

Music was (and still is) of extreme importance in my life. I took piano lessons, and I sang in the glee club at school. My first career ambition was to be an elementary school teacher who directed both the glee club and the plays. I was in fourth or fifth grade when that combination occurred to me. By the time I reached high school, I had forgotten it.

My second career ambition, to be a writer, didn't occur to me until years later, after I had married Bob Greenfield and was the mother of a young son, Steve. I was bored with my job as a clerk-typist, and one day, for a reason I can't remember, I began to write rhymes. It was fun. Then I wrote some songs and, in writing the lyrics, discovered my ambition. I wrote three stories and sent them to magazines as a test to see

Eloise: *EL oh ees*

Eloise Greenfield [signature]

er made me feel that I had to impress the world. I still follow my interests. In 1982, with musician Byron Morris, I produced *Honey, I Love,* a recording of poetry and jazz. Rehearsing the children for the record was almost like directing a play. Very close to my first ambition. I anticipate that, in time, I will get even closer.

———

whether I had any writing talent. They were all rejected, and I gave up the idea of being a writer.

By the time my daughter, Monica, was born, a few years later, I had realized my mistake. So I began to read everything I could find on the craft of writing and the techniques of marketing manuscripts. I practically lived at the library. After almost five years, I had my first publication—a poem, "To a Violin," on the editorial page of the *Hartford Times.*

It's not easy for writers to make space in their lives, in their heads, for writing. There are so many other things to do and to think about. Writers have to choose which of the important things are most important. For me, it's my family (my mother and I have written two books together) and my efforts against racism.

When I'm carrying a story around in my head, I feel as if I'm holding my head funny. Sometimes I want to explain to people on the street that I'm just trying to keep the words from spilling out until I get to a quiet place with pen and paper.

I discovered my love for writing by following my interests. For the freedom to do that, I am grateful to my parents. They nev-

Eloise Greenfield attended Miner Teacher's College in Washington, D.C. (now called the University of the District of Columbia), from 1946 to 1949. She has worked in the U.S. Patent Office and as a case control technician in the Work and Training Opportunity Center, from 1967 to 1968. She was Co-director of Adult Fiction at the District of Columbia Black Writer's Workshop from 1971 to 1973 and Director of Children's Literature in 1973 and 1974. She was writer-in-residence with the District of Columbia Commission on the Arts in 1973.

Greenfield has been a contributor to *Black World, Ebony, Jr.!, Ms., The Horn Book Magazine,* and the *Interracial Books for Children Bulletin.* Her books have ranged from picture books to biographies to *Honey, I Love,* which was her first book of children's poetry. The recording of *Honey, I Love* has been widely reviewed and always praised by reviewing publications, and the *Horn Book* calls it "a spirited performance and a joyous occasion."

Greenfield's books received many honors and awards. *Rosa Parks* won the 1974 Carter G. Woodson Award; *She Come Bringing Me That Little Baby Girl* won the 1974 Irma Simonton Black Award. *Paul Robeson* won the Jane Addams Children's Book Award in 1976, and *Africa Dream* won the 1978 Coretta Scott King Award. Both *Me and Neesie* and *Honey, I Love* were named Notable Books by the American Library Association, in 1975 and 1978 respectively. *Childtimes,* which she wrote with her mother, was illustrated by Jerry Pinkney and was included in the 1980 American Institute of Graphic Arts show.

SELECTED WORKS: Bubbles, 1972; Rosa Parks, 1973; Sister, 1974; She Come Bringing Me That Little Baby Girl, 1974; Me and Neesie, 1975; Paul Robeson, 1975; First Pink Light, 1976; Africa Dream, 1977, Mary McLeod Bethune, 1977; Honey I Love and Other Love Poems, 1978; Talk About a Family, 1978; (with Lessie Jones Little) Childtimes: A Three-Generation Memoir, 1979; Grandmama's Joy, 1980; Alesia, 1981.

ABOUT: Contemporary Authors, Vol. 49–52; (New Revision Series), Vol. 1; The International Authors and Writers Who's Who, 1982; Page, James A., comp. Selected Black American Authors: An Illustrated Bio-Bibliography; Rush, Theressa Gunnels and others. Black American Writers: Past and Present: A Biographical and Bibliographical Dictionary; Shockley, Ann Allen and Sue P. Chandler. Living Black American Authors: A Biographical Directory; Something About the Author, Vol. 19; Who's Who Among Black Americans, 1980–81; The Writers Directory 1982–84.

SHEILA GREENWALD

May 26, 1934–

AUTHOR AND ILLUSTRATOR OF *The Mariah Delaney Lending Library Disaster,* etc.

Autobiographical sketch of Sheila Ellen Green, who writes under the pen name of "Sheila Greenwald":

I WAS BORN in New York City, where I have lived all my life. I went to a mixture of public and private schools. The best was a progressive school where we played and were read to a lot (*Mary Poppins* and *Dr. Dolittle*); the worst a public elementary school where we were routinely beaten up. I tried to avoid getting beaten up by bribing the beaters with my personalized comic strips. I graduated from Music and Art High School, which was a wonderful place because we were all kids who had drawn comic strips to bribe beaters, and I went to Sarah Lawrence College. At Sarah Lawrence I majored in English, wrote plays, doodled, and got my B.A. After graduation in 1956 I put a bunch of the doodles together and took them up to *Harper's* magazine. I was given two articles to illustrate and sent over to Ursula Nordstrom, who was head of

children's books. She gave me a book of poetry to illustrate. For the next fourteen years I illustrated books (cookbooks, children's books, anthologies of humor) and magazine pieces. Also I got married to George Green, a heart surgeon, in 1960, and had two sons, Sam in 1962 and Ben in 1964. When Ben entered kindergarten I was encouraged by an editor, Ann Diven, to try to write my first children's book. It was so gratifying to do both words and pictures that I was eager to repeat the experience. By now I have done so twelve times. My next to last book, *Blissful Joy and the SATs,* has no illustrations at all.

I have always enjoyed satire—reading it, writing it, and drawing satirical sketches in pen and ink. My favorite authors are Jane Austen, Nancy Mitford, Evelyn Waugh, Joyce Cary, and Elizabeth Taylor (the novelist). I do not write autobiographically or confessionally. I would never use my children's lives in my work. I am very opinionated. I write about my points of view and the subjects on which I feel strongly, trying to soften them and, with luck, make them funny, the better to persuade. I invent characters, plots, and situations upon which to hang my diatribes. I write from a combination of imagination and observations. The fun for me is in the invention, the peopling of a world I have cooked up in my own head, not the recording of real events and heartfelt experiences. My last book has to do with a girl in her junior year of high school who has to deal with the S.A.T.'s [scholastic aptitude tests]. I think S.A.T.'s are dreadful, but that's hardly a novel. The job was to create a real girl having to go through the experience. Two of my books are literary satires. I had loved *Northanger Abbey* and *Cold Comfort Farm* when I was thirteen. I remembered what great fun it was to laugh at the books I loved to read. The habit of injecting humor between oneself and ungovernable emotion and chaos is a blessed one. The earlier it can be learned, the better.

I was very lucky growing up. I had a pair of remarkable parents, sensible, smart, humorous, and encouraging without ever butting in. I have had a terrific agent, Harriet Wasserman, and a fine editor in Melanie Kroupa. Altogether a mix of circumstances for which I am grateful.

———

Sheila Greenwald has illustrated over fifty-five books, fourteen of them for adults. *Give Us a Great Big Smile, Rosy Cole* was named a Notable Book of the American Library Association in 1981 and was a 1982 Children's Choice selection of the International Reading Association-Children's Book Council Joint Committee.

SELECTED WORKS WRITTEN AND ILLUSTRATED: Miss Amanda Snap, 1973; The Secret Museum, 1974; The Mariah Delany Lending Library Disaster, 1977; The Secret in Miranda's Closet, 1977; All the Way to Wits' End, 1979; It All Began With Jane Eyre: Or, the Secret Life of Franny Dillman, 1980; Give Us a Great Big Smile, Rosy Cole, 1981; Will the Real Gertrude Hollings Please Stand Up?, 1983.

SELECTED WORKS WRITTEN: Blissful Joy and the SATs: A Multiple Choice Romance, 1982.

SELECTED WORKS ILLUSTRATED: The Pink Motel, by Carol Ryrie Brink, 1959; The Boy Who Couldn't Make Up His Mind, by Hila Colman, 1965; Who'll Mind

Henry?, by Anne Mallett, 1965; The Pretender Princess, by Mary J. Roth, 1967; Mystery Cup, by Jean Bothwell, 1968.

ABOUT: Kingman, Lee and others, comps. Illustrators of Children's Books: 1957-1966; Ward, Martha E. and Dorothy A. Marquardt. Illustrators of Books for Young People, 2nd edition; (As Sheila Ellen Green) Contemporary Authors (First Revision), Vol. 4; (New Revision Series), Vol. 2; Foremost Women in Communications, 1970; Something About the Author, Vol. 8.

ROSA GUY

September 1, 1928–

AUTHOR OF *The Friends,* etc.

Biographical sketch of Rosa Cuthbert Guy:

ROSA GUY was born in Trinidad, The West Indies, in 1928. The daughter of Henry and Audrey (Gonzales) Cuthbert, she was brought to the United States in 1932 and grew up in New York City's Harlem and attended New York University. She was married to the late Warner Guy and has one son, Warner.

Her writing career began with a one-act play, *Venetian Blinds,* for the American Negro Theatre in 1954. Her first novel, *Bird at My Window* in 1966 was reviewed by *Life* magazine, which praised the author as a new voice in black American fiction, moving the genre "out of the emotional ghetto into the territory of the pigmentless soul." Her characters, too, were cited as being "so saturated in humanity that their color soon becomes transparent."

This first work was followed by an anthology of black writing, *Children of Longing,* which she edited. Then came a trilogy of novels: *The Friends, Ruby,* and *Edith Jackson.* The initial two volumes concerned three young black women growing up in Harlem, two West Indians and one native-born American. The last book revolved around Edith, a seventeen-year-old Harlem orphan living as a foster child in Peekskill, New York, who dreams of getting

a factory job at 18, in order to make a home for three younger siblings.

The *Friends* trilogy won Rosa Guy three American Library Association citations as Best Books of the Year for Young Adults. *The Friends* was selected for the *School Library Journal* "Best of the Best 1966–1978" list (December, 1979) and named a *New York Times* Outstanding Book of the Year in 1976. It has been made required reading for university-bound students in England, and her novels have been published both in Scandinavia and Japan.

Rosa Guy has embarked on a second trilogy, this one about a black teenager Imamu (born John) Jones. In *The Disappearance,* the boy is on probation following his reluctant role in a Harlem robbery-murder, and he is living with a middle-class black family in Brooklyn. Though he begins to sense a new freedom of options, and even the possibility of personal success, Imamu elects to return to Harlem to care for his own alcoholic mother. *The Disappearance* was named a *New York Times* Outstanding Book of the Year in 1979. The second volume, *New Guys Around the Block,* finds Imamu repainting and repairing the dreary apartment he

shares with his mother, as well as gaining insight into the constricting and dangerous environment in which he has thus far managed barely to survive. A third volume, *Measure of Time,* is in the offing.

A founder and former president of the Harlem Writers Guild, Rosa Guy remains active in this organization, which is dedicated to helping young writers through a program of workshops and personal counseling. She has lectured widely at universities here and abroad and she also wrote articles for the *New York Times Magazine, Redbook, Cosmopolitan,* and *Freedomways.*

Guy said: "I am interested in the historical and cultural aspects of all peoples of African descent." She speaks both French and Creole and has visited Haiti as well as her birthplace, Trinidad, to study customs and language-links with Africa that were retained by blacks over the centuries.

Rosa Guy's book for younger children, *Mother Crocodile,* with illustrations by John Steptoe, won both an ALA Notable Book citation and the 1982 Coretta Scott King Award. Guy, who lives on New York's West Side, has two further works in progress: a biographical study, *Alexander Hamilton: The Enigma,* and a ninth novel dealing with a Trinidadian family in New York. For relaxation, she does research in African languages.

SELECTED WORKS: Bird at My Window, 1966; The Friends, 1973; Ruby, 1976; Edith Jackson, 1978; The Disappearance, 1979; Mother Crocodile: An Uncle Amadon Tale from Senegal, 1982; New Guys Around the Block, 1983.

ABOUT: Contemporary Authors (First Revision), Vol. 17–18; Kirkpatrick, D. L., ed. Twentieth-Century Children's Writers; Rush, Theressa Gunnels, and others. Black American Writers Past and Present: A Biographical and Bibliographical Dictionary; Something About the Author, Vol. 14; The Writers Directory 1982–84.

MICHAEL HAGUE

September 8, 1948–

ILLUSTRATOR OF *The Wind in the Willows,* etc.

Biographical sketch of Michael Hague:

BORN IN LOS ANGELES, Michael Hague decided at an early age to become an artist when he first saw the Mickey Mouse Club on television, and much of his early drawing experience came from copying Disney characters. He held to his interest in drawing until high school, when he was distracted for a time by baseball. He attended a junior college and then the Arts College of Design, from which he graduated with honors in Fine Arts in 1972. While at the Arts College, he met his wife Kathleen, now an author of children's books.

Upon graduation, unable to find a job teaching art, Hague worked for Hallmark Cards for a little over two years, and then for Green Tiger Press in Colorado. Throughout this period, he persistently submitted his portfolio to publishers in hopes of getting illustrating contracts. The first piece of Hague's art published as children's illustration was the cover of the December 1978 issue of *Cricket* magazine. After illustrating several calendars for publishers, he eventually broke into book illustration. *Demetrius and the Golden Goblet* is an example of his early book work. Since then, he has illustrated books by several well-known authors and editors, including Julia Cunningham, Jane Yolen, and Lee Bennett Hopkins. He generally works in watercolor and gouache, with ink outlines added last, but occasionally he uses pen and ink alone.

Hague is best known, however, for the children's classics he has interpreted. First was Kenneth Grahame's *The Wind in the Willows,* a book he has loved since his own childhood. Two previous editions were illustrated by two of his idols in children's illustration, Ernest Shepard and Arthur Rackham. He tried, he said, "to infuse [his] . . . illustrations with the same spirit that Kenneth Grahame's magic words convey." Since his edition of *The Wind in the Willows* appeared in 1980, he has produced *Michael Hague's Favorite Hans Christian Andersen Fairy Tales* and new editions of Frank Baum's *The Wizard of Oz* and Margery Williams' *The Velveteen Rabbit.*

Hague sees a particular relationship between handcrafted illustration and the fantasy world. He feels that skillfully crafted illustrations will help children develop their taste and imagination. "In a good illustration of a knight riding on a horse, the viewer will ride over the next hill with that knight, even though the artist hasn't illustrated what's over there." Hague's illustrations have been well received, earning comments such as Patricia Dooley's in *School Library Journal*: " . . . this is a classic as a classic ought to look . . . the [details] are all meticulously and tenderly rendered. These paintings are a joyous celebration of things English. . . . Most important of all, the illustrations wonderfully fulfill Grahame's nostalgic vision of life on the River Bank." *The Dream Weaver* was included in the 1980 American Institute of Graphic Arts Show.

Michael Hague lives in Colorado with his wife and two daughters.

SELECTED WORKS ILLUSTRATED: Demetrius and the Golden Goblet, by Eve Bunting, 1979; The Dream Weaver, by Jane Yolen, 1979; The Wind in the Willows, by Kenneth Grahame, 1980; The Unicorn and the Lake, by Marianna Mayer, 1982; The Wizard of Oz, by Frank Baum, 1982; The Velveteen Rabbit, by Margery Williams, 1983.

SELECTED WORKS COMPILED OR RETOLD AND ILLUSTRATED: (with Kathleen Hague) East of the Sun and West of the Moon, 1980; Michael Hague's Favourite Hans Christian Andersen Fairy Tales, 1981.

D. S. HALACY, JR.

May 16, 1919–

AUTHOR OF *Earth, Water, Wind and Sun: Our Energy Alternatives,* etc.

Halacy: *HAL a see*

Autobiographical sketch of Daniel Stephen Halacy, Jr., who also writes under the names Dan Halacy and Daniel S. Halacy:

I WROTE my first story while I was still in high school. It was about a trip to the moon, but it never traveled past my English teacher. Not until after serving in the Air Force in World War II did I write another short story. I sent this one to a magazine and they sent it right back. I wrote sixty-six more before one was published. And that one was a story for young readers, published in a Sunday School paper.

Since then, I have published hundreds of short stories, articles, and humorous pieces, as well as seventy-six books on a variety of subjects. I have seldom been a full-time writer and over the years have worked in aircraft and electronics firms, fought in the Korean War, taught English in colleges, and served in the Arizona Senate. I now work in the Solar Energy Research Institute in Golden, Colorado. Six of my books are about solar energy.

About a third of my writing is for young people. I wrote the text for *Charlie Brown's Encyclopedia of Energy,* published by Ran-

dom House in 1982. Just recently I interviewed a young soccer player and a young bike rider for *Boys' Life,* and have also written some aviation stories for that magazine. Many of my science books, and two science fiction books, were written for young people. So I guess I have never grown up myself. Most of my letters come from children, and I enjoy writing back to them.

My wife is named Beth, and she and I wrote the *Solar Cookery Book.* We have two daughters. Jessica is married and lives in Midland, Texas, with her husband Paul and sons Paul and Zachary. Big Paul flies an airplane for El Paso Natural Gas, and he and I build radio-controlled model airplanes. I was a navigator in the Air Force and have flown sailplanes for years. My longest flight was 326 miles, and now I am trying to fly to 31,000 feet here in Colorado to earn my "Diamond Altitude" and complete my Diamond Badge. Many of my stories and books are about flying, and my advice to people who want to write is to write about things that interest them. And also to read a lot. If you aren't a reader, you will probably not succeed as a writer.

Computers have always interested me, and I now write my books and articles on an Apple III with a word processor. Computers can do far more than I ever dreamed they would when I wrote *Computers: The Machines We Think With* back in 1962. I carry a pocket calculator with me all the time; it is solar powered, as is my watch.

One of my problems with writing is that it is hard to find time to do it. I work full-time in solar energy now because I believe in it. We have many friends and are active in church. Our daughter Deirdre is still at home, and we are involved in her college acting career. Beth and I enjoy hiking Colorado's mountains and jogging regularly in the foothills we live in. This summer part of our vacation will be spent hiking the Grand Canyon, and when we return to Colorado, Long's Peak is next on our list. But all these interests give me things to write about, of course. Now I had better get back to that new book on solar energy!

Daniel S. Halacy received his Asssociate of Arts degree from Phoenix College, where he later taught creative writing, and received his B.A. from Arizona State University in 1957. He was a first lieutenant in the U.S. Air Force.

SELECTED WORKS: Computers: The Machines We Think With, 1962; Century Twenty-One: Your Life in the Year 2001 and Beyond, 1968; Man and Memory: Breakthrough in the Science of the Human Mind, 1970; Solar Science Projects For a Cleaner Environment, 1974; With Wings as Eagles: The Story of Soaring, 1975; Survival in the World of Work, 1975; Earth, Water, Wind and Sun: Our Energy Alternatives, 1977.

SELECTED WORKS AS DAN HALACY: Nuclear Energy, 1978; (with Beth Halacy) The Solar Cookery Book, 1978.

ABOUT: Contemporary Authors (First Revision), Vol. 5–8; Ward, Martha E. and Dorothy A. Marquardt. Authors of Books for Young People, 2nd edition.

DONALD HALL

September 20, 1928–

AUTHOR OF *Ox-Cart Man,* etc.

Autobiographical sketch of Donald Andrew Hall Jr.:

I LIVE on the farm in New Hampshire where I spent all my summers as a boy. My great-grandfather moved here in 1865. He was a sheep farmer, and his youngest daughter was my grandmother Kate, who married Wesley Wells—the grandparents I visited for so many years. During the school-time of year I lived in Connecticut, where my mother read me poems from an early age. I remember the anthology *Silver Pennies,* and in particular a poem by Vachel Lindsay in which the moon was the north wind's cookie. In summer on the farm, my grandfather recited endlessly long poems that he had learned to speak at school and for the entertainments young adults put on for each other. As he milked cattle, or as we rode on the hayrack together, he would tell

me story-poems, sometimes comical and sometimes sad—and never-ending.

I decided early on that I wanted to be a writer, most especially a poet. I suppose I have published about sixty books, and only three of them are for young children. I have published seven or eight books of poems; I have published literary criticism, textbooks, biography, short stories, all sorts of things. For many years I was a Professor at the University of Michigan, where I taught English, and only in 1975 was I able to leave teaching and return to this place where I have always wanted to live. Now I write full-time, and make my living doing it.

When I had first returned here, my cousin Paul Fenton, in his early seventies then, told me the story of the Ox Cart Man. I made a poem out of the story, a little poem that was published in the *New Yorker.* When I was almost finished writing the poem, after about two years of working away at it, I had the notion that it (the anecdote) might make a story for young children. It did. When the Viking Press found Barbara Cooney to illustrate it, of course my story retold from my cousin's tale found its true enhancement.

I hope to write more for children. I published a book called *Andrew the Lion Farmer* (Franklin Watts), and another called *Riddle Rat* (Frederick Warne), but I don't feel that I discovered the way to use the language—in a book for small children—until I wrote *Ox-Cart Man*. Although the lines are not really verse, the economy of language is like the economy of poetry. The line of the story must be pure, and must carry itself along without visible strain. Each word must lend its muscle. And the rhythm by which the words attach themselves to each other, by which they roll and move, must be economical but forthright. In all these qualities, the language of the picture book resembles the language of the poem.

But the *story*. . . . You can work on the language, on the rhythm, as you would work on a poem. . . . But you always must find the story, or your cousin must tell it to you.

Donald Hall was born in Hamden, Connecticut. He graduated from Harvard in 1951; he received a B. Litt. from Oxford University on a Henry Fellowship and won the Newdigate Prize for Poetry. After a year at Stanford on a writing fellowship he returned to Harvard for three years as Junior Fellow in the Society of Fellows, 1954-1957, and then began teaching at the University of Michigan. In 1952 he married Kirby Thompson, and his son Andrew was born in 1954 and his daughter Philippa in 1959. In 1969 he was divorced, and in 1972 he married Jane Kenyon, also a poet, with whom he lives in New Hampshire.

Hall has written stories, articles, and plays, but is best known for his work in poetry; he has edited many anthologies and was poetry editor of the *Paris Review* from 1953 to 1962. His own poems have been published in the *Times Literary Supplement, Poetry, Atlantic,* and *Harper's.* He has given hundreds of poetry readings and has received two Guggenheim fellowships. He is a member of P.E.N., the Authors Guild, and the Modern Language Association.

Ox-Cart Man won the 1980 Caldecott Award; it was also on the *New York Times* list of Best Illustrated Children's Books of the Year 1979.

SELECTED WORKS: Andrew the Lion Farmer, 1959; Riddle Rat, 1977; Ox-Cart Man, 1979.

ABOUT: Benet, William Rose. The Reader's Encyclopedia, 2nd edition; Contemporary Authors (First Revision), Vol. 7–8; (New Revison Series), Vol. 2; Contemporary Poets, 2nd edition; Hall, Donald. String Too Short to Be Saved; Herzberg, Max J. The Reader's Encyclopedia of American Literature; The Oxford Companion to American Literature, 4th edition; The Penguin Companion to American Literature; Something About the Author, Vol. 23; Wakeman, John, ed. World Authors, 1950-1970; Ward, Martha E. and Dorothy A. Marquardt. Authors of Books for Young People, 2nd edition; Who's Who in America, 1980-1981; The Writers Directory 1982-84; New York Times Book Review December 11, 1966; Saturday Review February 18, 1956.

LYNN HALL

November 9, 1937–

AUTHOR OF *The Leaving,* etc.

Autobiographical sketch of Lynn Hall:

THE FUNNY THING about wish-fulfillment is that the enjoyment of it can go on long after the actual wishes are realities. At least it's been that way for me.

As a youngster growing up first in suburban Chicago and then in suburban Des Moines, all of my passions were aimed in two directions, dogs and horses. My family couldn't afford a horse, didn't really want a dog, and assumed that I was going through a stage. Wrong. My hunger for these animals went unfed except for the nourishment of *The Black Stallion* and *Misty of Chincoteaque* and *Lad: A Dog.* I was a voracious reader, but only in these areas, and had to be forced to read other kinds of books.

Oddly enough, the idea of writing for other youngsters the books that had gotten me through my own youth didn't occur to

me until I was in my mid-twenties and had developed enough self-esteem to entertain such a possibility. By then I had tried several other kinds of work, none of which fitted me very comfortably, and I had begun to grow desperate at my lack of progress toward my one big goal, a life in the country with a four-legged family.

When the idea finally struck, ignited by a bookstore display of a juvenile horse story by a local author, it was overwhelming in its rightness. Within three months I had written *The Shy Ones,* and within a year had managed to place it, by trial and rejection, with a publishing company that was to publish my next twenty-six books. Four years and a dozen books later I was on my way, out of the city and into an old brick farmhouse in the scenic hill country in northeast Iowa. Friends sometimes commented on my bravery at severing the steady paychecks and going to an area where jobs would be scarce if things didn't work out with the book-writing, but it didn't seem brave to me. It was escape from everything I hated and running open-armed toward everything I loved. In the

fourteen years since that day, I don't believe I have ever had a genuinely low mood, an amazing testimony to the fact that dreams do come true and that, if one chooses his dream carefully and attunes it to his deepest nature, there is such a thing as happy ever after.

Six years ago another dream came true: a lovely little stone cottage named Touchwood, which I designed and helped to build, doing well over half of the work myself. The sofas and window seats are covered with English Cocker Spaniels. The lawns are inhabited by Pasco Fino horses who eat rose bushes and roll in strawberry beds and carry me around the fields and woods in their unique floating gait. One is a filly I delivered myself, and trained; the other is an opinionated golden buckskin whose Spanish name aptly translates to "Son of a Small Gun." The big dreams have all come true for me, and yet one of my greatest pleasures is still diving into a thumping good horse story, either reading it or writing it.

Lynn Hall was born in Lombard, Illinois. She was married in 1960 but divorced in 1961. She has been a dog show handler and a veterinarian's assistant. She breeds and exhibits collies and is a member of the Collie Club of America, the Cedar Valley Collie Club, and the Dubuque Kennel Club.

The Leaving is about an eighteen-year-old girl who leaves her parents' Iowa farm to try an independent life, taking a job in Des Moines. The book won the 1981 Boston Globe-Horn Book Award for fiction and was named a 1980 Best Book for Young Adults by the American Library Association. The Mystery Writers of America awarded the 1980 Edgar Allan Poe Award to *The Whispered Horse* and both *Too Near the Sun* and *Gently Touch the Milkweed* were Junior Literary Guild selections.

SELECTED WORKS: The Shy Ones, 1967; Gently Touch the Milkweed, 1970; Too Near the Sun, 1970; A Horse Called Dragon, 1971; Flowers of Anger, 1976;

Sticks and Stones, 1977; The Whispered Horse, 1979; The Leaving, 1980; Tin Can Tucker, 1982. .

ABOUT: Contemporary Authors (First Revision), Vol. 21–24; Something About the Author, Vol. 2; Ward, Martha E. and Dorothy A. Marquardt. Authors of Books for Young People, 2nd edition (Supplement).

DEBORAH HAUTZIG

October 1, 1956–

AUTHOR OF *Second Star to the Right,* etc.

Biographical sketch of Deborah Hautzig:

DEBORAH HAUTZIG was born and raised on New York City's Upper West Side, which is the setting for most of her work. Her father is a musician and her mother is a writer. She was graduated from the Chapin School, studied fine arts at Carnegie Mellon Institute, and received a Bachelor of Arts degree from Sarah Lawrence College in 1978, the year her first children's book was published. *Hey, Dollface* was named a Best Book for Young Adults by the American Library Association. It is the story of Chloe and Val, both new girls at a private school in Manhattan. During a year bracketed by the deaths of Val's grandmother and Chloe's father, they become the best of friends, playing hooky, sleeping over at each other's house, painting pictures together, and struggling with sexual feelings—towards members of the opposite sex, and towards each other.

The following year saw the publication of *The Handsomest Father,* a book for beginning readers that deals with a little girl's apprehensions about Father's Day at her school. So convinced that she will be embarrassed by her father's appearance and behavior, she pretends to be sick on the special day. In the end, however, she decides that he is, after all, most definitely the handsomest father.

Hautzig says, "Books are kind of like children. You have a child and raise that child and think, 'Oh! Now I know how to raise a

DEBORAH HAUTZIG

child.' But then you have another child and you can't do it the same way because it's a *different child* ! That's how it is with novels. The 'next book' is always a brand-new challenge."

Deborah Hautzig's next "child" was another young adult novel, *Second Star to the Right.* In a *School Library Journal* review, Pamela D. Pollack wrote, "This is the least graphic and best book yet on the adolescent disease . . . anorexia nervosa. . . . It's a loving book, written with great care, about love gone wrong."

Second Star to the Right tells the story of fourteen-year-old Leslie, who slips from ordinary dieting into disaster as her anorectic behavior leads to hospitalization. Therapy eventually leads to recovery and self-knowledge. The book was a nominee for a 1982 American Book Award in the children's hardcover fiction category.

Deborah Hautzig worked for a number of New York City publishing firms. She lives in New York City, and when she isn't writing, loves to read and paint, and says, "I don't ever want to stop getting better as a writer. The minute you stop reaching, you're finished. I feel very good about the books I've written, and I look forward to the books I'm going to write."

SELECTED WORKS: Hey, Dollface, 1978; The Handsomest Father, 1979; Second Star from the Right, 1981.

SELECTED WORKS RETOLD: The Christmas Story, 1983.

ABOUT: Contemporary Authors, Vol. 89–92.

LILO HESS

1916–

AUTHOR AND PHOTOGRAPHER OF *Animals That Hide, Imitate, and Bluff,* etc.

Biographical sketch of Lilo Hess:

LILO HESS was born in a small town in Germany. She grew up in Berlin and attended finishing school in Switzerland. She later studied photography in Berlin and London. Her love of animals dates from her childhood, when she rescued a mangy stray dog that her parents would not allow her to keep; she used her own money for the veterinary bill. Throughout her childhood, she was always collecting and observing animals. She studied commercial photography at the Photographic School in Berlin, and won some prizes for animal pictures taken at the zoo, but it was not until she attended the Polytechnic School in London that she began to consider animal photography as a specialty. There she met a commercial photographer who gave her an assignment to take the animal photographs for a children's book on zoos; her career was decided. She said, "I succeeded in combining my profound and abiding interest in zoology with my special hobby of photography."

When Hess came to the United States in 1938, she worked as a volunteer at the American Museum of Natural History in New York City. In 1939, she worked for Frank Buck, a famous animal exhibitor, at the World's Fair, where he was making animal post cards and publicity photographs. Later she worked as a special assignment photographer at the Brooklyn Zoo.

Since then, she has frequently contribut-

ed articles to magazines in Europe and the United States. Her first children's book, *Odd Pets,* was published in 1951; in 1954, *Christine the Baby Chimp* appeared, illustrated with her own photographs. Since that time, she has published many more photographic essays on animals for children and is considered one of the foremost author-photographers of animal books for young people. Her style emphasizes documentation of how the animals live, rather than portraiture.

Because most of her animal subjects are found in the wild, she has had to win their confidence before they allow her to photograph their young. This has often meant observing closely as two or three generations of young foxes or raccoons were raised, which could take as long as three years. To write *The Remarkable Chameleon,* she imported some varieties of chameleons to observe firsthand the differences between them and those native to North America. She also consults with scientists and zoologists to be sure her text is correct. One of her goals in writing these books is to help young people realize how important it is to protect the animals around them.

Animals That Hide, Imitate, and Bluff was

named one of the Child Study Association's Books of the Year in 1970. All of her books are known for their quality of information and clarity of style, as well as their advocacy of animal welfare. The *New York Times Book Review* noted that *Monkeys and Apes Without Trees* is a "plea not to make pets of them but to leave them to the zoos where, with the development of more natural settings, we will be able to observe our closest relatives the way they really are. . . ." The belief that animals should be left as they are pervades all her books.

Lilo Hess is a member of the American Society of Magazine Photographers and of the Authors Guild. She currently divides her time between her home in Brooklyn, New York, and her farm in Pennsylvania, where she keeps many pets. She has had, at one time or another, ducks, dogs, cats, ponies, and a chinchilla.

SELECTED WORKS ILLUSTRATED: Odd Pets, by Dorothy Childs Hogner, 1951.

SELECTED WORKS WRITTEN AND ILLUSTRATED: Christine the Baby Chimp, 1954; The Misunderstood Skunk, 1968; The Remarkable Chameleon, 1968; Animals That Hide, Imitate, and Bluff, 1970; The Praying Mantis, Insect Cannibal, 1971; A Snail's Pace, 1974; Life Begins for Puppies, 1978; The Amazing Earthworm, 1979; Listen to Your Kitten Purr, 1980.

ABOUT: Bader, Barbara. American Picturebooks from Noah's Ark to the Beast Within; Contemporary Authors (First Revision), Vol. 33–36; Something About the Author, Vol. 4; Ward, Martha E. and Dorothy A. Marquardt. Authors of Books for Young People, 2nd edition (Supplement).

JAMAKE HIGHWATER

February 14, 1942–

AUTHOR OF *Anpao: An American Indian Odyssey,* etc.

Biographical sketch of Jamake Highwater, who also writes under the pseudonym "J Marks":

Jamake: *juh MAH kuh*

JAMAKE HIGHWATER, the son of a Blackfoot mother and a Cherokee father, was born in Glacier County, Montana, in 1942. His early years are remembered for a mother, whose "vivid teachings were my access to the Indian world," and a father whose career as a rodeo clown meant that the family was always on the move. The elder Highwater also found employment as a stuntman in movie Westerns—he "died hundreds of times for John Wayne"—but this new career was short-lived, and poverty resulted in the young Jamake being placed in an orphanage. When his father was killed in an automobile accident, Jamake was adopted by his father's best friend, a non-Indian. Jamake took on a new name, "J Marks," and spent his teenage years in California's San Fernando Valley.

Early in the 1960s he was instrumental in setting up the San Francisco Contemporary Theater, a group that toured the North American continent, coincidentally visiting Indian reservations and many of the sites of older American civilizations. These rekindled Highwater's interest in his own heritage, but his true awakening came with the Indian invasion of Alcatraz Island in 1969. He reverted to the name he had been given at birth and commenced work on his first "Indian" book: *Indian America: A Cultural and Travel Guide,* published in 1975.

Jamake Highwater produced three books in the next two years. *Song from the Earth,* which was a Literary Guild Alternate, is a study of American Indian painting that was selected for the 1979 Moscow International Book Fair by the Association of American Publishers. *Ritual of the Wind* deals with Native American ceremonies, music, and dances.

In 1977 his first novel, *Anpao: An American Indian Odyssey,* was published. It combines many diverse legends and stories, from the Creation to the coming of white men, in the tale of Anpao ("Dawn") and his contrary twin Oapna, who search for their parentage. *Anpao* was a 1978 Newbery Honor Book and a Boston Globe-Horn Book Award Honor Book.

Many Smokes; Many Moons: A Chronology of American Indian History Through Indian Art contains reproductions of art and artifacts from 35,000 B.C. to 1973, the date of the occupation of Wounded Knee. Short paragraphs of historical text give the American Indian point of view of historical and cultural events, and a *Publishers Weekly* review stated, "Sad to say, it includes an almost unbroken account of whites' betrayal of a conquered people." The book won the Jane Addams Children's Book Award in 1979 and was named a Notable Children's Trade Book in the Field of Social Studies by the joint committee of the National Council for the Social Studies and the Children's Book Council. *Moonsong Lullaby* was named a Notable Book by the American Library Association in 1981. Two subsequent novels were published: *Journey to the Sky,* which documented the rediscovery of the Maya civilization, and *The Sun, He Dies,* about the end of the Aztec empire.

On March 29, 1979, Highwater received an honor from his Native American people: "Ed Calf Robe, Elder of the Blood Reserve of Blackfeet Indians, a member of the Horns Society, and a descendant of the famous chief Calf Robe, conferred a new name upon me to honor my achievements on behalf of my people. It is a ceremony usually reserved for *minipoka,* 'favored children' of the Blackfeet Nations. My new name is Piitai Sahkomaapii, meaning 'Eagle Son.' This name-ceremony was the vindication of my mother's constant efforts to keep my heritage alive within me."

Jamake Highwater is a frequent contributor to many newspapers and magazines, including the *New York Times, Smithsonian, Saturday Review, Esquire, Horizon, After Dark,* and *Cosmopolitan.* For five years he was the classical music editor for the *Soho Weekly News.* He lectures extensively and has appeared on television. Jamake Highwater is a member of P.E.N. and the Authors Guild. He travels frequently, and makes his home in New York City.

SELECTED WORKS: Anpao: An American Indian Odyssey, 1977; Many Smokes, Many Moons: A Chronology of American Indian History Through Indian Art, 1978; Moonsong Lullaby, 1981; Eyes of Darkness, 1983.

ABOUT: Contemporary Authors, Vol. 65–68; Something About the Author, Vol. 30; Who's Who in America, 1982–1983; Who's Who in American Art, 1978.

MARILYN HIRSH

January 1, 1944–

AUTHOR AND ILLUSTRATOR OF *Deborah the Dybbuk: A Ghost Story,* etc.

Autobiographical sketch of Marilyn Joyce Hirsh:

I HAVE ALWAYS loved to draw and luckily was born to parents who believe that children should be encouraged. So when I was six, my mother took me to the Junior School of the Art Institute of Chicago, and I have been drawing ever since. Of course my mother expected a ladylike watercolorist or perhaps a high school art teacher. It was not expected that I consort with beatniks

(1950s), or hippies and foreigners (1960s) and go on to become somewhat eccentric myself. Still, my parents have supported my efforts to this day. This has not always been easy. As my father looked with horror upon my large combined Abstract-Expressionist and German-Expressionist paintings in my senior year at Carnegie-Mellon he was only somewhat consoled by the wise and prophetic words of Dean Rice, who said, "It's only a phase, Mr. Hirsh. Her work will be all the better for having gone through it."

Perhaps the most influential period in my life was the two years I spent in India with the Peace Corps after graduating from Carnegie-Mellon in 1965. That time (1966–1967) gave me a profound respect and love for the Indian people and their rich art and culture. Also, for me, India was the land of opportunity. Through a long series of lucky meetings I found my way to the Children's Book Trust in New Delhi, where its founder Mr. Shankar enthusiastically agreed to publish *The Elephants and the Mice* in 1967, and kept me on to do three more books.

When I returned to the United States in 1968 I had four published books. However, I found myself typecast as an Indian illus-trator. I kept telling editors and art directors that my art was Indian because I lived in India; and that if I had been in the Peace Corps in Peru or the Congo, my work would be influenced by those places. Still, I was told: "If we have anything Indian we'll call you!" Finally one editor said, "Why don't you submit an original story with illustrations? Then you will be considered on the basis of it and not told to wait until we have something Indian." This seemed very sensible. Not knowing what to write, I turned to that old but good saying, "Write what you know best." I remembered a story my grandmother had told me about my father getting lost when he was a baby in Hungary. *Where Is Yonkela?*, published by Crown, was my first book written and illustrated in America. It was very well received as a folk tale and a Jewish book. It soon became clear that there were very few nondidactic and well illustrated Jewish children's books. Since my father seems blessed with total recall about his childhood in Europe, I feel very close to the humor and vitality of the Eastern European ghettos that disappeared in World War II, and to the immigrant experience. Although only about half of my over thirty books have been of Jewish content, these seem to have made the greatest impact. I was very honored to win the First Annual Association of Jewish Libraries Sydney Taylor Body of Work Award for my contribution to Jewish children's literature in 1980.

Sometimes, however, I feel a little peculiar about my reputation as an author and illustrator of Jewish children's books. I am also completing a Ph.D. in Indian art history. My husband and I met when we were studying Indian art. Today he designs and imports Indian folk sculptures, painting, and decorative arts from India. So we are both very involved with India, although now I am typecast as a Jewish author/illustrator.

Although my two careers seem quite distinct on the surface, my art history training helps me when I am researching the costumes, architecture, and traditional art of a period for my books. The present work I am doing for Viking, *Joseph Who Loved the Sabbath,* is a Talmudic tale that takes place during the Babylonian exile in the sixth century B.C. So I am doing it in an ancient Near Eastern style. I find that it is very exciting to make a 2500-year-old style lively, and even humorous.

These days with all the cutbacks in school and library budgets, I'm finding it hard to make ends meet with my books. They are not very middle-of-the-road so they don't get into paperback very often. Therefore, I'm branching out into advertising illustration, but children's books are my first love and I hope to always be able to do them.

———

Marilyn Hirsh was born in Chicago. She studied painting and art educaton at Carnegie-Mellon Institute in Pittsburgh and received her M.A. at the New York University Institute of Fine Arts.

While in India, she taught English and art to children aged ten to thirteen. She also had a solo exhibition of her art in New Delhi and Bombay.

She teaches art history at the Cooper Union School for the Advancement of Science and Art in New York. She and her husband, James Harris, who was also in the Peace Corps, travel to India frequently.

Two books Hirsh illustrated have been named Junior Literary Guild selections: *The Elephants and the Mice: A Panchatantra Story,* which she also wrote, and *Wales' Tale* by Susan Saunders.

SELECTED WORKS WRITTEN AND ILLUSTRATED: Where Is Yonkela?, 1969; The Elephants and the Mice: A Panchatantra Story, 1970; The Pink Suit, 1970; Hannibal and His Thirty-Seven Elephants, 1977; Deborah the Dybbuk: A Ghost Story, 1978.

SELECTED WORKS ADAPTED AND ILLUSTRATED: How the World Got Its Color, 1972; Captain Jiri and the Rabbi Jacob, 1976; The Rabbi and the Twenty-Nine Witches, 1981.

SELECTED WORKS ILLUSTRATED: Mushy Eggs, by

Florence Adams, 1973; Wales' Tale, by Susan Saunders, 1980.

ABOUT: Contemporary Authors, Vol. 49–52; (New Revision Series), Vol. 1; Kingman, Lee and others, comps. Illustrators of Children's Books: 1967–1976; Something about the Author, Vol. 7; Ward, Martha E. and Dorothy A. Marquardt. Authors of Books for Young People, 2nd edition (Supplement); Wilson Library Bulletin October 1971.

ISABELLE HOLLAND

June 16, 1920–

AUTHOR OF *The Man Without a Face,* etc.

Biographical sketch of Isabelle Holland:

ISABELLE HOLLAND was born in Basel, Switzerland. By the time she was ten years old she had also lived in Guatemala City and northern England. Her father was a United States Foreign Service officer, and it was because of his job that the family moved so much. For Isabelle, the move to the rainy climate of northern England was a difficult adjustment after the sunny and festive atmosphere of Guatemala City. She attended private and boarding schools in England. Her mother frequently told her stories, which Isabelle later recognized as being from the Bible, history, mythology, and novels—rich sources that remained in the author's imagination through adulthood.

Holland started writing at an early age, and when whe was thirteen her first story, "Naughty Betty," won a contest in a comic magazine called *Tiger Tim.* Holland studied for two years at the University of Liverpool, but was sent home to the United States during World War II at the age of twenty. It was the first time she had lived in her own country. She completed her B.A. at Tulane University in New Orleans in 1942. Shortly thereafter, she moved to New York City and found her way into a career in publishing.

In New York Isabelle Holland worked for

Isabelle C. Holland

several magazines, including *McCall's.* Then, in 1956, she became publicity director of Crown Publishers, where she worked until 1960. At that time, she moved into the same position at J.B. Lippincott, where she remained until 1966. During the following year she was assistant to the publisher of *Harper's* and subsequently became publicity director of G.P. Putnam's from 1968 to 1969. After 1969, she turned her energies to writing full-time.

She has had short stories published in *Collier's* and *Country Gentleman,* and her first novel, for adults, *Cecily,* was published in 1967. Ruth Hill Viguers, writing in the *Horn Book,* described the book as "a beautifully polished gem of a novel," that concerns the relationship between an unhappy thirteen-year-old girl in an English boarding school and the beautiful, intelligent teacher who can hardly tolerate her. On the basis of the characterization of the girl Cecily, Holland was asked to write her first book for children. Since that time she has written over ten novels for children and young adults, and several adult novels as well.

Isabelle Holland's books for children and young adults have been well-received: Zena

Sutherland of *The Bulletin of the Center for Children's Books* has praised "the depth and polish of the writing style," and Ethel Heins of the *Horn Book* admired Holland's "storytelling skill, sensitivity, and psychological acumen." *Booklist* noted that she writes "with compassion and a sensitive understanding of human nature and its idiosyncracies."

The Man Without a Face, published in 1972, was widely discussed because of the controversial element of homosexuality in the book. But the attention drawn by the book was largely in praise of the sensitive, perceptive treatment of the relation between McLeod, an island recluse whose face has been badly scarred, and Charles, a fourteen-year-old boy who seeks out the man's help as a summer tutor. The book presents several themes that recur in Holland's work: among them, the complexity of relationships between individuals of different generations and the difficulty of making one's way through the grey areas of life and morality. In an article in the *Horn Book,* she wrote: "the total lie is always easy to combat. It stands out a mile and can be knocked down by almost anyone. It is when some degree of truth, however small, is blended into the distortion that people are seduced."

Another theme—a philosophy she claims to have acquired from her father—is that we are all responsible for our own lives and must learn to accept the consequences of our actions. In *The Man Without a Face,* McLeod says to Charles, "'Just don't expect to be free from the consequences of what you do, while you're doing what you want.'"

Zena Sutherland said that Holland "does not talk down to her readers." This point is borne out in all her writing. Critics have noted that Holland takes her characters and their problems seriously, no matter what their age. She writes especially sympathetically about the child or adolescent in isolation, and seems to throw her characters' problems into relief against a variety of backgrounds. Alan MacGowan, the twelve-year-old protagonist of *Alan and the Animal Kingdom,* has been called "as vulnerable and lonesome a child as has been portrayed in recent children's fiction." And *Of Love and Death and Other Journeys,* a story about a fifteen-year-old girl, was described by the *Horn Book* as "a moving study of a young girl's sudden confrontation with life's paradoxes. . . . joy and grief, love and anger, tragedy and comedy." The book was nominated for the National Book Award in 1976.

Animals often play an important role in her stories and not surprisingly, for Holland shares her New York City apartment with four cats. She writes every day, usually in the mornings. Holland says, "The main lessons I have learned about writing are 1) to keep writing no matter what, even when I'm discouraged, and 2) to write every day, if possible—even a small amount."

SELECTED WORKS: Amanda's Choice, 1970; The Man Without a Face, 1972; Heads You Win, Tails I Lose, 1973; Journey for Three, 1975; Of Love and Death and Other Journeys, 1975; Alan and the Animal Kingdom, 1977; Hitchhike, 1977; Dinah and the Green Fat Kingdom, 1978; Now Is Not Too Late, 1980; Perdita, 1983.

ABOUT: Contemporary Authors (First Revision), Vol. 21–22; The International Authors and Writers Who's Who, 1982; Kirkpatrick, D. L., ed. Twentieth-Century Children's Writers; Something About the Author, Vol. 8; Ward, Martha E. and Dorothy A. Marquardt. Authors of Books for Young People, 2nd edition (Supplement); The Writers Directory 1982–84; English Journal March 1977; Horn Book June 1973; April 1974; April 1980.

HELEN M. HOOVER

HELEN M. HOOVER

April 5, 1935–

AUTHOR OF *Another Heaven, Another Earth,* etc.

Autobiographical sketch of Helen M. Hoover:

I NEVER set out to write for children. It just happened that that was the kind of story I enjoyed writing, and children or young adults are the market for that sort of story now. But I've never deliberately thought, "Hey, a child will really like this touch." . . . One has to know the child and the touch.

My parents were great readers. So were their four children, either by choice or in self-defense. I don't really remember a time when I couldn't read or was not read to. I do recall that the reading texts in school came as a distinct shock. I couldn't believe I was being asked to waste my time with Dick and Jane after reading "The Relief of Lucknow" in the McGuffey's Fifth in our attic. It had always struck me as odd that few of our friends or neighbors had any books in their houses, while ours was overrun with reading material. I slowly decided that if people's first exposure to reading was Dick and Jane, it was probable that for the rest of their lives the very sight of a book might induce anxiety and the mad urge to cry "Run, Self! Run! Run!"

If I waited for inspiration, I'd get nothing done. Writing is a matter of discipline, of working at it each day, of thinking about it in the bathtub, or while reading or watching TV—but never when driving or cooking. (I once found a lost coffeepot in the freezer—absent-mindedly put there while I was plotting.) Some days it's fun to write; other days it's not. Halfway through each book I despair of ever finishing it, and when I do, I am always surprised and a bit puzzled as to how it all happened.

As to how much influence my parents had on my becoming a writer, I suppose being exposed to books, magazines, and reading as a way of life had a lot to do with it. But my two brothers and sister grew up with no literary ambitions. I had no urge to write as a child and suspect it is vaguely unhealthy for children who do. Writing is a solitary activity, much given to introspection.

As for basic information: I was born and raised in Ohio, attended two different colleges, but have no degree. I've lived in California and New York City and Virginia and enjoyed them all for different reasons. I've worked in everything from personnel to insurance bonding to food manufacturing to advertising to chemical consulting. All were interesting in their own way; all added to my education—sometimes in ways I would have rather avoided. I think Y. A. Tittle was the finest quarterback who ever played and Tebaldi the best soprano of the century. I like petunias—they are an honest, wholesome flower that gives a lot for a little work—and pastel winter sunsets. I like animals and people—except those people who feel the need to tell you how sensitive they are. My favorite authors range from Josephine Tey to Lewis Thomas, from Gabriel Garcia Marquez to Michael Bond. I'm very fond of Robert Graves and Richard Burton's *Arabian Nights* translation. I think one's regard for a book depends very much on the age you are when you read it. I read a lot of history and natural history, biographies and letters, since the best of fiction can only reflect the reality of its time. I do not care for message books, or problem books or books where the plot succeeds only because of the stupidity of the main character. I think most television intended for

children is greatly insulting to them; but no more so than that intended for adults. I do not think fantasy can be made into film; the camera distorts the mind's eye.

————

Helen M. Hoover attended college in New York City and in Los Angeles, and she now lives in Virginia, near Washington, D.C.

Hoover's manuscripts reside in the Kerlan Collection at the University of Minnesota. Her *Another Heaven, Another Earth* was named an American Library Association Best Book for Young Adults in 1981.

SELECTED WORKS: Children of Morrow, 1973; Treasures of Morrow, 1976; The Delikon, 1977; The Rains of Eridan, 1977; The Lost Star, 1979; Return to Earth: A Novel of the Future, 1980; This Time of Darkness, 1980; Another Heaven, Another Earth, 1981; The Bell Tree, 1982.

ABOUT: Language Arts April 1980; October 1982.

LEE BENNETT HOPKINS

April 13, 1938–

AUTHOR OF *Wonder Wheels*, etc.

Autobiographical sketch of Lee Bennett Hopkins:

BOOKS, unfortunately, were not a part of my childhood years. My reading was limited to movie magazines, comic books, and an occasional adult novel that my mother passed on to me. Developing a love of reading takes time. Time was something I did not have much of. As I was the oldest child in the family, most of my days and nights were spent working at odd jobs to help with the family budget.

I was born in Scranton, Pennsylvania. Most of my growing-up years, however, were spent in a housing project in Newark, New Jersey. I shared a small, crowded, four-room apartment with my mother, brother, and sister, while daring to strive to

become a teacher. In 1960 I reached that goal.

I taught elementary school in Fair Lawn, New Jersey, for the first six years of my professional life. It was then that I found out how truly important books are for children. I found poetry during my teaching years, too, and for the past twenty-three years, I have shared verse with children and educators throughout the country by speaking and by compiling anthologies. I strongly believe that poetry should flow freely in our children's lives; it should come as naturally as breathing, for nothing—*no thing*—can ring and rage through hearts and minds as does this body of literature.

For me, compiling anthologies of poetry is relaxing, exciting, almost therapeutic, and I enjoy working on them most when I'm exhausted from other work. But putting together an anthology isn't as easy as some people think; the most difficult task is to choose a theme. Once that's done, I begin gathering hundreds of poems from which I select about twenty to thirty, depending on the length of the collection. Therefore, delicate selections must be made in order to maintain a balance among the poets.

Writing is a curious profession. One thing leads to another. When the writing bug stings you, the bite never heals! That sting paved the way for three young adult novels, all of which are largely autobiographical. *Mama* is a love story about a wise, wonderful, very outrageous and outspoken working-class mother who steals to provide her two young sons with what she thinks are the "better things in life." *Mama and Her Boys* continues the plight of that gutsy mother. *Wonder Wheels* is a story of love and loss based upon something I experienced when I was sixteen years old.

I now live in a large duplex apartment in Westchester County, New York. I share land with raccoons and squirrels, and view breathtaking foliage. The commanding Hudson River can be seen from every window. All of this is quite a contrast to my childhood days spent in the city, on asphalt and cement sidewalks.

The plastic plants in *Mama* have been replaced by dozens of flowering orchids, eight-foot tall Dracenas, and a variety of long-named species, some of whose names I can't even pronounce! The roller skates in *Wonder Wheels* have given way to a car— an awesome machine that I have to have in order to buy even a bottle of ketchup!

Today, writing is my life and love. In addition to anthologies, novels, professional books, and articles, I write a feature column for *Instructor* magazine, called "Poetry Place," and another column for librarians, "Book Sharing," in *School Library Media Quarterly*. In short, I'm busy!

Writing is not an easy task. Sometimes it is downright hard and painful. But the accident occurred, the writing bug has stung, and the wound still hasn't healed. I hope it never, ever will.

Lee Bennett Hopkins graduated from Kean College, in Union, New Jersey in 1960 and received his M.S. from Bank Street College of Education in New York in 1964. He earned a Professional Diploma in Educational Supervision and Administration from

Hunter College in 1966 and received a Doctor of Laws degree from Kean College in 1980.

In addition to his work for children, Hopkins has written curriculum materials and professional texts such as *More Books By More People: Interviews with 65 Authors of Books for Children*. He has lectured on children's literature and has served as Senior Consultant to the Bank Street College of Education. He hosted a fifteen-part television series, *Zebra Wings,* on different styles of writing, from creative writing to advertising copy.

Hopkins has served as a literature consultant for several publishing companies. He has also been active in the National Council of Teachers of English, chairing the 1978 NCTE Poetry Award Committee. He is a member of the Authors League of America.

Wonder Wheels was an International Reading Association/Children's Book Council Joint Committee Children's Choice selection for 1980. *To Look at Any Thing* was included in the International Youth Library Choice Books of 1978 Exhibition in Munich, Germany. *Me!: A Book of Poems* was a Junior Literary Guild selection, and *Don't You Turn Back: Poems of Langston Hughes* was an American Library Association Notable Book for 1969.

SELECTED WORKS WRITTEN: Charlie's World: A Book of Poems, 1972; Mama: A Novel, 1977; Wonder Wheels: A Novel, 1979; Mama and Her Boys: A Novel, 1981.

SELECTED WORKS WRITTEN WITH MISHA ARENSTEIN: This Street's for Me, 1970.

SELECTED WORKS COMPILED: Don't You Turn Back: Poems of Langston Hughes, 1969; Me!: A Book of Poems, 1970; On Our Way: Poems of Pride and Love, 1974; Good Morning to You, Valentine, 1976; A-Haunting We Will Go, 1977; Beat the Drum: Independence Day Has Come, 1977; To Look at Any Thing, 1978; By Myself, 1980; Moments: Poems About the Seasons, 1980; Circus! Circus!, 1982; City!: A Book of Poems, 1982; The Sky Is Full of Song, 1983.

ABOUT: Contemporary Authors (First Revision), Vol. 25–28; Something About the Author, Vol. 3; Ward, Martha E. and Dorothy A. Marquardt. Authors of Books for Young People, 2nd edition (Supplement); Who's Who in the East, 1975–1976; The Writers Directory 1982–84; Language Arts November/ December 1978.

SHIRLEY HUGHES

July 16, 1927–

AUTHOR AND ILLUSTRATOR OF *George the Babysitter,* etc.

Autobiographical sketch of Shirley Hughes Vulliamy:

I DREW the pictures for other people's stories for a long time before trying to write my own. Like most illustrators, I started by learning to draw in an art school. But I think we differ from other artists by having a narrative turn of mind, with strong theatrical overtones. Designing a picture-book, after all, is like being a whole company of actors, producer, stage designer, and lighting manager, all in one. That's why it's so enjoyable.

I liked books a lot as a child, but mostly for the pictures. I doted on comics, too, and was also much given to bursting out from the sitting-room curtains expecting applause. But this was during the war, when the grown-ups were far too harrassed to pay much attention. There was very little entertainment on hand. One had to combat boredom by making things up; an ideal breeding ground for creative endeavour. I drew a lot, and wrote stories and plays on the backs of old envelopes.

Later, gripped by film fever, we bicycled through the blackout to an ancient flea-pit cinema on the sea-front. If the air-raid siren went you stayed in there while the projectionist played the programme over and over until the all-clear, a wonderful bonus. Plaster fell like snow from the ceiling as bombs dropped on nearby Liverpool, but we sat tight, oblivious and enthralled.

In my late teens, as an art student, I moved on to being stage-struck. I even took

Shirley Hughes

a vacation job as a dogsbody in a repertory theatre, painting scenery and mending tights. Much to the relief of the management, I eventually decided this wasn't for me. By this time I was at Oxford and other horizons were opening up.

Since then I've been completely involved with books. I think I've illustrated around two hundred. I started to write my own picture-books when my three children were very young, about the age to be read to. When I'm thinking up the idea for a book it floats about like an iceberg, mostly below the surface, for a long time before I start putting pencil to paper. As I think in pictures, the crucial bit is getting it into words. Onion-like, a good picture-book text should be smoothly rounded and simple, but it's the result of many layers of editing. The final test, if word and image work well together, is in the reading and re-reading, the nightly encores it gets from its young audience.

I'm always being pleasurably astonished, when I meet children in schools and libraries up and down the country, at what they can actually *do* with a picture-book, the way they can use stories like *Alfie Gets in First* and *Alfie's Feet,* for instance, or a wordless book like *Up and Up,* to reinforce their own experiences and feelings, or as a starting-point for their own writing and pictures.

When I started writing fiction for older children, *Here Comes Charlie Moon* and, more recently, *Charlie Moon and the Big Bonanza Bust-up,* the drawings got all over the page, spaced in with the narrative. I found myself chopping up bits of text and drawing round them, just as when I'm planning a picture-book. A lot of work and glue were expended. All highly entertaining, for me, at least. And for the reader too, I hope.

———

Shirley Hughes was born in Hoylake, near Liverpool, England. She was trained at Liverpool Art School and at the Ruskin School of Fine Art, Oxford, where she later became a visiting tutor in illustration. Married to John Vulliamy, an architect, in 1952, she has three children, two boys and a girl.

In addition to the great number of books Hughes has illustrated, she has written and illustrated a dozen picture books and two novels for older children. *David and Dog* (called *Dogger* in England) won the 1978 Kate Greenaway Medal as well as the Silver Slate Pencil in Holland in 1980. *George the Babysitter,* originally published in Britain as *Helpers,* won the 1976 Children's Rights Workshop Other Award and was also a runner-up for the 1976 Kate Greenaway Medal. Allan C. McLean's *Storm Over Skye,* which Hughes illustrated, was named an American Library Association Notable Book for the years 1940–1970. *Flutes and Cymbals* was commended for the Kate Greenaway Medal in 1968. *Alfie Gets in First* was named an ALA Notable Book for 1982. Her books have been published in Europe, Australia, and Japan.

SELECTED WORKS WRITTEN AND ILLUSTRATED: David and Dog, 1978; George the Babysitter, 1978; The Haunted House, 1978; Moving Molly, 1978; Up and Up, 1979; Alfie Gets in First, 1982; Alfie's Feet, 1983.

SELECTED WORKS ILLUSTRATED: Storm over Skye, by

Allan C. McLean, 1957; A Crown for a Queen, by Ursula Moray Williams, 1968; Flutes and Cymbals, by Leonard Clark, ed., 1969; The Family Tree, by Margaret Storey, 1973; the Phantom Carousel, and Other Ghostly Tales, by Ruth Ainsworth, 1978; The Trouble With Dragons, by Oliver G. Selfridge, 1978.

ABOUT: Contemporary Authors, Vol. 85–88; Kingman, Lee and others, comps. Illustrators of Children's Books: 1957–1966; Kingman, Lee and others, comps. Illustrators of Children's Books: 1967–1976; Kirkpatrick, D. L., ed. Twentieth-Century Children's Writers; Something About the Author, Vol. 16; The Writers Directory 1982–84.

RACHEL ISADORA

RACHEL ISADORA

AUTHOR AND ILLUSTRATOR OF *Ben's Trumpet*, etc.

Biographical sketch of Rachel Isadora:

BEFORE she was an artist, Rachel Isadora was a dancer. She started dancing at a very early age and performed professionally at eleven. She began professional training at the American School of Ballet on a Ford Foundation scholarship. Always struggling with her acute shyness, she preferred at first to observe in class and then to spend hours alone in the practice studio until she had mastered the lesson.

Faced with the high pressure of the ballet school, she began to draw for relaxation and release of emotion. Her drawing was her private exercise, entirely self-taught. Not even her supportive parents saw her work for many years.

At seventeen, she was offered a chance to dance with Balanchine's New York City Ballet. Suddenly, the pressure of seven years' preparation for this opportunity was too much, and she retreated to her room for three months. Several years later she tried dancing again, this time with the Boston Ballet Company, but was forced to retire due to a foot injury. The need for a new career gave her the courage to carry her random sketches in a paper bag to a New York publisher in hopes of a chance at illustrating. Luckily, she did not have to wait long

for an assignment. Her first book, *Max*, was published in 1976, and was named a Notable Book in that year by the American Library Association, a Classroom Choice of the International Reading Association in 1976, and a selection of the 1977 Children's Showcase.

In 1977, she married Robert Maiorano, a soloist with the New York City Ballet and an author of children's books, with whom she collaborated on several titles, including *Backstage* and *A Little Interlude*. The marriage ended in divorce.

More recently, she has also illustrated Elizabeth Shub's *Seeing Is Believing* and *The White Stallion*, which were both named Notable Books by the American Library Association, each in their years of publication. She is best known, however, for a solo effort, *Ben's Trumpet*, which was named a Caldecott Honor Book in 1979. It was also named a Boston Globe-Horn Book Honor Book in 1979, and the *New York Times* called it the "most original and surprising picture book of the season."

Isadora told *Publishers Weekly* that most of her main characters are "doing something on their own, by themselves . . . because *they* want to. And all of a sudden, it's not what peers think, not what the world around them thinks, but the joy of doing it *by themselves*"; this is the autobiographical aspect of her work, the memories of the loneliness of performing. She added, "I see the way a child sees. So I decided, I'll just draw it the way I see it, and the kids will see it their way."

Rachel Isadora currently lives in New York with her husband James Turner and their daughter Gillian Heather.

SELECTED WORKS: Max, 1976; Willaby, 1977; Ben's Trumpet, 1979; My Ballet Class, 1980; The Nutcracker (reteller), 1981; City Seen from A to Z, 1983.

SELECTED WORKS WITH ROBERT MAIORANO: Backstage, 1978; A Little Interlude, 1980.

SELECTED WORKS WITH ELIZABETH SHUB: Seeing Is Believing, 1979; The White Stallion, 1982.

ABOUT: New York Times Book Review March 1, 1981; Publishers Weekly February 27, 1981.

SULAMITH ISH-KISHOR

1896–June 23, 1977

AUTHOR OF *A Boy of Old Prague*, etc.

Biographical sketch of Sulamith Ish-Kishor:

SULAMITH ISH-KISHOR was born in London, England, in 1896. One of nine children, she moved with her family to the United States in 1909. She later attended Hunter College where she specialized in history and languages.

She began writing at the age of five, and by the time she was ten she had already had several poems published in literary magazines. During her prolific career, she wrote numerous books with Jewish themes and contributed articles on music, art, theater, and personalities to the *New York Times*, the *New York Herald-Tribune, The New Yorker, Saturday Review*, and *Menorah Journal*.

Most of her books are set in the past. *A Boy of Old Prague*, which won the Schwartz Juvenile Award from the National Jewish

SULAMITH ISH-KISHOR

Book Council in 1963, tells about Jewish ghetto life during the sixteenth century. This somber story is narrated by Tomas, a young Christian peasant, who is bound to a Jewish family as punishment for stealing. Tomas brings many misconceptions to his new household, but is soon drawn to the family, who show him a kindness he has never known. As the story unfolds, Tomas learns with horror that others do not share his compassion and understanding. The book was named an American Library Association Notable Book for the years 1940–1970.

Our Eddie, a 1970 Newbery Honor Book, is the story of a Jewish family living at the turn of the century and the conflicts between a tyrannical father and his resentful son, Eddie. *Our Eddie* won the Association of Jewish Libraries Children's Book Award in 1969, and it was also named an ALA Notable Book for the years 1940–1970.

The intensity of Ish-Kishor's books is matched by her thorough knowledge of her subjects. She was a master reteller of Hebrew legend. In *The Carpet of Solomon*, she created a dreamlike mood as she told the tale of King Solomon and his magic carpet. The book was included in the *School Li-*

brary Journal "Best of the Best 1966–1978" list (December, 1979).

The Master of the Miracle is based on the legend of the Golem, a man-like creature made out of clay. The story is told by an orphan boy, Gideon ben Israyel. Gideon is entrusted by the High Rabbi with the guidance of the Golem, but the boy makes one fateful mistake. As punishment for disobeying the holy command, Gideon is forbidden to die until the Jews return to Palestine and Jerusalem is rebuilt. Until then he had to watch over the charred remains of the Golem; legend says that Gideon lived for three centuries.

Sulamith Ish-Kishor died at home in New York City in 1977.

SUSAN JESCHKE

SELECTED WORKS: The Children's Story of the Bible, 1930; Children's History of Israel from the Creation to the Present Time (3 Volumes), 1930–33; Jews to Remember, 1941; American Promise: A History of Jews in the New World, 1947; A Boy of Old Prague, 1963; The Carpet of Solomon: A Hebrew Legend, 1966; Pathways Through the Jewish Holidays, 1967; Our Eddie, 1969; Drusilla: A Novel of the Emperor Hadrian, 1970; The Master of Miracle: A New Novel of the Golem, 1971.

ABOUT: Contemporary Authors, Vol. 69–72; 73–76; Kirkpatrick, D. L., ed. Twentieth-Century Children's Writers; Something About the Author, Vol. 17; Ward, Martha E. and Dorothy A. Marquardt. Authors of Books for Young People, 2nd edition; A. B. Bookman's Weekly September 5, 1977; New York Times June 25, 1977.

SUSAN JESCHKE

October 18, 1942–

AUTHOR AND ILLUSTRATOR OF *The Devil Did It,* etc.

Autobiographical sketch of Susan Jeschke:

I GREW UP in Cleveland Heights, Ohio. As a child, I never cared for school and spent most of my time daydreaming. What I liked to do besides daydreaming was to draw and read. I did all of these things well. Nothing else seemed important and I did nothing else particularly well, academically speaking.

My parents often read to me and gave me beautiful and excellent books. In about fourth grade I read my first Greek myth. The thrill of reading something meaningful for the first time on my own was boundless. A whole world opened up to me. It was my first clear introduction to love and death, passions (of all sorts), rewards, revenge—all of the important things about human beings.

My father often supplemented my information with juicy little tidbits about the gods. He was as devoted to the myths as I was, and he seemed to have known the gods personally. It was as if his old friends had become my new friends, and there was lots of gossip to share.

My parents also took me to films. I was addicted from the start. My earliest addictions were to Walt Disney Films, both the animated and nature films. To this day, films and books are two of my great pleasures and influences because they take me into worlds where I could otherwise never have access.

Towards the end of high school, I developed an interest in the theater and decided

I wanted to be an actress. After three years at the Goodman Theater in Chicago, I knew I did not want to be an actress. However, I didn't know what I could do. I moved to New York and after a long succession of not very satisfying jobs, took a course in illustration at the School of Visual Arts. From this course I assembled a portfolio. It wasn't long before I got my first illustration job and not long after that I met Miriam Chaikin, my editor and friend for the last ten years. It was Miriam who encouraged me to write a story, since at the time I was looking only for illustration work. My first story was *Firerose.*

For the first time in my life I was doing work that was relatively satisfying. The most satisfying thing about it was being able to control almost the whole show. In acting, I was one element being controlled by the vision of the director. Now, the characters, story, dialogue, sets, costumes, and gestures are all my creations.

The central characters of my stories are always people and animals. They remain for me the most fascinating to draw and I never tire of observing them.

The story itself is also important. I always want to write about something that I think is meaningful, in the same way that the Greek myths are meaningful. I suppose that I would like to be a modern mythologist. However, I often remind myself that it's a good thing the myths, Grimms' folktales, and Hans Christian Andersen's stories were written when they were, since none of the authors would get a job in today's market, which is dominated by prettiness, cuteness, and trivia.

Throughout my school years, the admonitions to "pay attention" and accusations of "not concentrating and daydreaming" left me with the feeling that perhaps something was wrong with me. Today, I smile at the irony of it. Little did my accusers know (or for that matter, did I know) that it would be through this very daydreaming and fantasizing that I would one day make my living.

———

Susan Jeschke studied at the Brooklyn Museum School as well as at Chicago's Goodman Theatre School and the School of Visual Arts in New York. She now lives in Brooklyn.

The Devil Did It won the 1976 Friends of American Writers Award. Two of her books have been named Notable Books by the American Library Association, *Firerose* in 1974 and *New Neighbors for Nora* in 1979.

SELECTED WORKS WRITTEN AND ILLUSTRATED: Firerose, 1974; The Devil Did It, 1975; Sidney, 1975; Rima and Zeppo, 1976; Angela and the Bear, 1979; Perfect the Pig, 1981.

SELECTED WORKS ILLUSTRATED: The Times They Used to Be, by Lucille Clifton, 1974; Busybody Nora, by Johanna Hurwitz, 1976; Outrageous Kasimir, by Achim Bröger, 1976; Nora and Mrs. Mind-Your-Own-Business, by Johanna Hurwitz, 1977; New Neighbors for Nora, by Johanna Hurwitz, 1979.

ABOUT: Contemporary Authors, Vol. 77–80; Kingman, Lee and others, comps. Illustrators of Children's Books: 1967–1976; Publishers Weekly February 27, 1978.

NORMA JOHNSTON

AUTHOR OF *The Keeping Days,* etc.

Biographical sketch of Norma Johnston, who also writes under the pen names "Elizabeth Bolton," "Catherine E. Chambers," "Pamela Dryden," "Lavinia Harris," and "Nicole St. John":

NORMA JOHNSTON was born in Ridgewood, New Jersey, the daughter of an engineer and a teacher who owned a boutique. Though an only child, she was surrounded by several generations of family during her growing-up years. Stories about family members and family enterprises were as much a part of her life as her own experiences. It was on these she drew when she began to write books.

She attended public schools in Ramsey, New Jersey, and Montclair State College (where she obtained a B.A. degree and a

Norma Johnston
(Nicole St. John)

teaching certificate for grades 7–12, in English). She also attended the American Theater Wing in New York City and did graduate work at Montclair State College and the London (England) campus of Ithaca College.

Of herself she says, "It is usually easy to write one's life as a chronological résumé of fact; it is not for me, because all my life I have lived in many different overlapping worlds. Only child, ahead of myself in school; too young there, while a "little old lady" at home; member of one crowd at church and another crowd in high school. Wrote my first book at twelve, which no one but an English teacher ever read; wrote my second at sixteen, which after a decade of revisions became my first one published. Teenage teacher of art and dramatics, disastrously; assistant to a buyer in a department store; part-time actress; secret writer. Buyer for mother's specialty shop; student at the American Theatre Wing; owner of own dress shop; published writer. Producer of summer theater; assistant in a New York fashion publication office; assistant to editor of a religious publishing house. Church youth advisor. Middle-aged "retread" col-

lege student. Teacher in junior high (about which the less said, the better, but out of which came books and lasting friendships). Director of Geneva Players, an ecumenical religious drama group that uses the stage as a second pulpit to disturb the status quo and draw people into a closer understanding of themselves, their neighbors, and their God. That last statement is a pretty good summation of why I write, as well.

"Who am I? A Victorian. A cat curled by the fire (but I'm allergic to cats). An herb garden. The color red. Old houses with low-ceilinged rooms, with a teakettle on the hearth and a fire burning bright. Long dresses, and crosses worn on chains. Candlelight. Shakespeare, mythology, John Donne. England in the summers."

Currently Norma Johnston spends most of her time writing; but writing is not all. With a group of friends she operates St. John Enterprises, an organization that does free-lance editing, ghost writing, and typing, and even sells herb mixtures for cooking. Her early books, published in the 1960s, include *The Wishing Star, The Wider Heart,* and *The Bridge Between.* These are teenage novels, the area in which she has done most of her subsequent writing.

In the early 1970s she began her Keeping Days series, a group of historical novels set largely between the turn of the century and the end of World War I, in which the characters are based on members of her own family. In *The Keeping Days,* the protagonist Tish has great plans to be a writer. Critic Mary M. Burns, writing in the *Horn Book,* said the book was reminiscent of *Little Women* and stated, "Nostalgic but not sentimental, flavored generously with romance, the novel captures the anxieties of adolescence with its naïveté and awareness." Of *Glory in the Flower,* which is also part of the Keeping Days series, *Library Journal* said that it offers "the interaction of many vivid characters of all ages and [traces] attractively serious Tish's growth from self-concern to mature consideration for others."

Johnston also began another group of

books, retelling the great Greek heroic myths. In her most recent books for young people she has moved away from historical novels, which nevertheless dealt with modern problems and indicated that these problems are not so modern as we think, to books set in the present day.

In addition to her novels for young adults, Norma Johnston has also written adult gothic novels, mystery series for several paperback houses and book clubs, and romances, many of these under pen names.

SELECTED WORKS: The Wishing Star, 1963; The Wider Heart, 1964; The Keeping Days, 1973; Glory in the Flower, 1974; Strangers Dark and Gold, 1975; A Striving After Wind, 1976; A Mustard Seed of Magic, 1977; The Sanctuary Tree, 1977; The Crucible Year, 1979; A Nice Girl Like You, 1980; Myself and I, 1981; The Days of the Dragon's Seed, 1982; Timewarp Summer, 1982; Gabriel's Girl, 1983.

ABOUT: Something About the Author, Vol. 29.

ADRIENNE JONES

July 28, 1915–

AUTHOR OF *So, Nothing Is Forever,* etc.

Autobiographical sketch of Adrienne Jones:

HOMETOWN. It doesn't matter how many years and miles separate a person from Hometown, its imprint lasts forever. My hometown is Atlanta, Georgia. My mother, my sister, and I left there when I was seven. My father remained in Atlanta. Those early years still cast their sunshine and shadow. They have formed my writing in good part. Maybe they are what made me *be* a writer. Let me tell you what I mean by that:

My family lived in Atlanta during the fall, winter, and spring. Summers were spent in the Blue Ridge Mountains where they reach down into north Georgia. Our vacation house there was called Cloudacres. It was at Cloudacres that my love of the mountains and the out-of-doors started. So, mountains, shore, sea, uplands all play a large part in the background of each of my novels.

Also, it was during the Cloudacres-Atlanta years that my sister, Doris, and I started our love affair with books. We were read to and we read. *Everything.* Books, magazines, encyclopedias, dictionaries, poetry, package labels, Sears Roebuck catalogs; and the funnies from that gem of newspapers, *The Atlanta Constitution.* Books were so exciting to me that I wanted to become a part of them, to make up the stories and to people them with all sorts of fascinating characters.

And we did a lot of talking in our family, too. The Word was used for just plain communication, or for humor, or affection, or love, or disagreement—mild or wild. When we fought, my sister and I, we weren't allowed to hit. There's no better way to sharpen the wit or expand the vocabulary than argument with an older, brighter sibling. "Argue yes, hit no!"—if Mother's ultimatum were a universal one, there would be no more wars!

Yes, the influence of Hometown, the mark of place, time, family, friends is permanent.

When Mother, Doris, and I moved to California, we lived in a Theosophical Society colony called Krotona. It was high on a hill overlooking Hollywood. We were thrilled when we found that Charlie Chaplin lived just down the road on our hill; Charlie Chaplin, the lovable little tramp of the silent films who could make you laugh and cry all at the same time.

It was a strange life at Krotona, but wonderful too. Still, those were lonely times for me. It is difficult for kids when a family breaks up. Yet frequently loneliness turns the mind inward and can feed the creative side. I began to write verses and simple short stories. A second-grade teacher praised them. I still remember her name—Miss McClatchy—and that she was dark-haired, pretty, smelled good, and had a velvet cheek when she hugged you. Her praise made me feel I was A Writer. From that time on I practiced my writing by turning out poems and articles for school newspapers and annuals, and later by constructing plays for me and my friends to act in.

Out of high school, I was ready to enter the University of California, but those were the years of the Great Depression. Money ran low for us. Doris and I had to scramble to find jobs so there would be food on the table and the house mortgage could be paid. No money or time for college. My English teacher at Beverly Hills High School cried when I told her, but life was too busy for me to mope. We continued to read voluminously, and took night school and university extension classes, so education continued, though we worked at any job we could find in that time of scarce jobs.

My love of the mountains had never faded. I joined the Sierra Club. Most of my friends there had as little money as I. But we went to the mountains anyway. As a member of the Sierra Club Ski Mountaineering and Rock Climbing Section, I took up skiing and climbing. Among the ascents I made was the sheer East Face Route on Mt. Whitney, then the highest mountain in the United States. I climbed it with a new friend, Dick Jones. We fell in love and were

married in 1939. We're still in love and still married!

In 1947 I started work on my first novel. By then we had a son, Gregory, and a daughter, Gwen. That first book's title was *Thunderbird Pass*, published in 1952. Its background was the High Sierra. My second novel was *Where Eagles Fly* (1957), the story of a boy and girl who try to climb a real High Sierra peak, Mt. Humphreys.

Life was very busy and exciting, with so much to do it was difficult to squeeze in the writing. But now at this present time I have had twelve books published: two mystery novels for adults co-authored with my sister; and ten of my own, five novels for boys and girls in the upper elementary school grades, and five for young adults. Another for young adults will be out in October of 1982, this one titled *Whistle Down a Dark Lane*. A sequel is well on the way to completion, with a working title, *A Matter Of Spunk*. If I move right along it may be ready for 1983!

————

Sail, Calypso!, So, Nothing Is Forever, The Hawks of Chelney, and *Another Place, Another Spring* were all named by the University of California at Irvine as outstanding books for young people. *Another Place, Another Spring* and *So, Nothing Is Forever* were both chosen in their year of publication for the Notable Book Award of the Southern California Council on Literature for Children and Young People. *The Hawks of Chelney* was an American Library Association Notable Book for 1979.

Jones travels to many states and overseas to talk to other writers, librarians, teachers, and young people about the craft of writing and the world of books and publishing. She has written a number of short stories for the Bank Street College of Education. Excerpts from her books have been used in various supplementary readers. Her books have also been published in England, Canada, Denmark, Germany, Holland, Italy, and Japan. Some of her writing has been used by the

Braille Institute in their publication, *Expectations,* for blind boys and girls.

Jones is a member of many organizations including the Authors Guild, the Society of Children's Book Writers, P.E.N., the American Civil Liberties Union, and the Southern California Council on Literature for Children and Young People.

SELECTED WORKS: Thunderbird Pass, 1952; Where Eagles Fly, 1957; Wild Voyageur: Story of a Canada Goose, 1966; Sail, Calypso!, 1968; Another Place, Another Spring, 1971; The Mural Master, 1974; So, Nothing Is Forever, 1974; The Hawks of Chelney, 1978; Whistle Down a Dark Lane, 1982; A Matter of Spunk, 1983.

ABOUT: Contemporary Authors (First Revision), Vol. 33–36; Something About the Author, Vol. 7; Who's Who of American Women, 1977–1978; The Writers Directory 1982–84.

Diana Wynne Jones.

DIANA WYNNE JONES

August 16, 1934–

AUTHOR OF *Charmed Life,* etc.

Autobiographical sketch of Diana Wynne Jones:

I DECIDED to be a writer when I was eight. I still don't know why, because I was always considered to be very bad at it at school, and my experiences of writers before that were all rather unpleasant. During World War II, when I was six, my younger sister and I were evacuated to a large house in the Lake District, which was once the house of the secretary of the writer John Ruskin, and also the house that figures in the books of Arthur Ransome. There was a paper shortage, so when I found a large stack of flower drawings in an attic, I settled down to rub these out—with an ink eraser—in order to draw on the paper myself. I was caught halfway down the pile. There was bad trouble. They proved to be original drawings by Ruskin (I shudder to think what they are worth now). I did not know Ruskin was dead; I thought it was very un-

generous of him. Arthur Ransome was worse. He lived in a houseboat on the nearby lake and objected to us playing on the shore opposite this boat. He came to complain. I saw him—a large bearded man with a face like thunder—and concluded that writers were very unpleasant people. This impression was confirmed by Beatrix Potter, who lived nearby. She hit my sister for swinging on her gate. Somehow this did not put me off writing—nothing could—but I think it did put me off writing anything like the things those three people wrote.

Three years after this, we moved to an isolated village in Essex. Here there were at least two self-confessed witches, a man who went mad at full moon, and many more extraordinary people. I have never put any of this in a book, because people would accuse me of making it all up, but it did serve to convince me that strange things were possible. The chief thing about that place, however, was that there were no books. We craved things to read. But my parents were very busy and also very mean (my father would have won a competition for meanness against any miser you care to name— he was World Class) and their solution to our craving was to buy all the books by Arthur Ransome—that man haunted my childhood—which they kept locked in a cupboard and doled out to us at the rate of one every Christmas. The rest of the year, I took to writing books myself, in dozens of old exercise books, which I used to read aloud to my sisters. These were probably very bad, but they did make me realise I was capable of getting a book finished. That is very important. Meanwhile, teachers at school kept scrawling SEE ME angrily in the margin of anything I wrote there. For one thing I wrote, I got into trouble from the Cookery Mistress as well as the English Mistress, because, she said, I was being insulting to food. I was. I was describing school meals as they deserved to be described.

After that there was a gap, in which I grew up and got married and had children of my own. I cannot describe how much my children taught me. I am more grateful to them than to anyone else. With them, I discovered all the books I had missed when I was a child, and also what makes a bad book for children. There were a lot of those about in those days. This encouraged me to get writing again, and I began doing all the sort of books I would like to have read as a child. Eight long years followed, in which these things kept coming back from publishers with letters enclosed to tell me that the children I wrote about were too naughty, and that my books were not polite enough about adults. Eventually, I decided to write one more book and, if that was not published, to give up writing. I do not know whether I would have done, because that one got published.

These days, I live in Bristol, which is my favourite city, and write most of the time, which is my favourite occupation, though I like music too, and telling fortunes (which I am creepily good at). I am owned by a strong-minded dog. But I never quite consider myself a real writer, because I get on quite well with children and people swing on our gate quite often. Everyone in the house helps themselves to my paper, whether I have written or drawn on it or not, and my pens too. I have to go and steal them all back when I feel a book coming on.

————

Diana Wynne Jones was born in London. She received a B.A. degree from St. Anne's College, Oxford, in 1956, the same year she married John A. Burrow. She has three sons.

Jones won the Guardian Award in 1978 for *Charmed Life,* and her *Homeward Bounders* was named a Best Book for Young Adults by the American Library Association in 1981. *Dogsbody* was an ALA Notable Book in 1977.

SELECTED WORKS: Witch's Business, 1974; The Ogre Downstairs, 1975; Cart and Cwidder, 1977; Dogsbody, 1977; Drowned Ammet, 1978; Power of Three, 1977; Charmed Life, 1978; The Magicians of Caprona, 1980; The Homeward Bounders, 1981.

ABOUT: The Author's and Writer's Who's Who, 6th edition; Contemporary Authors, Vol. 49–52; (New Revision Series), Vol. 4; The International Authors and Writers Who's Who, 1977; Kirkpatrick, D. L., ed. Twentieth-Century Children's Writers; Something About the Author, Vol. 9; The Writers Directory 1982–84.

JESSIE ORTON JONES

1886–

AUTHOR OF *Small Rain: Verses from the Bible,* etc.

Biographical sketch of Jessie Mae Orton Jones:

JESSIE ORTON JONES was born in Lacon, Illinois, the daughter of Thomas and Minnie Orton. After graduating from high school in 1909, Jessie Orton was given the choice of traveling around the world or going to college; she took the trip. In planning the journey, she met George Roberts Jones, a Harvard graduate working for American Express. When she returned home a year later, Jessie and George married.

They raised their three children (Eliza-

JESSIE ORTON JONES

beth, Annette, and Thomas) in Highland Park, Illinois. According to their eldest daughter, Elizabeth, "It was some household. Mother was a gifted pianist and Dad played violin and viola. Every single morning of our lives, they would play sonatas for an hour. One evening a week, Dad's string quartet met at our house. Everyone would come. We were the entertainment of the neighborhood."

The Joneses believed in an open-door policy. People from all walks of life gravitated to their home. While the children were growing up, three Bohemian girls worked for the family. They brought color to the home with their tales, songs, and dances drawn from their Eastern European heritage.

Jessie Jones was a deeply religious woman. When her children rebelled against Sunday School, she insisted on continuing religious classes in the home. "Mother would teach all six of us in Sunday school classes," says Elizabeth. "She believed in nonsectarian religion—the same God for everyone. She would take us to all places of worship: synagogues, temples, and churches."

During World War II, Jones taught nursery school and became interested in introducing children to the words of the Bible. She began collecting and editing verses from the Old Testament for young children. Her daughter Elizabeth was already well established as an illustrator, and together they created *Small Rain*. This collection of verses from the Bible was a Caldecott Honor Book in 1944. Elizabeth illustrated four of her mother's books. "It was a delight to work with Mother," said Elizabeth, "but it was pretty hectic. Mother wanted things done quickly. She was always very impatient with my perfectionism. She'd always say to me, 'Will you ever get done?'"

"Mother collected scrapbooks. We had an entire bookcase full of her collections that dated back to her courtship with Dad. She had a particular genius for the little things. One scrapbook even has the menu from her wedding. Another, called "They Came Up Our Walk," describes all the people who visited our Highland Park home. Someday I would like to try and publish that one."

The Bible was Jones's source in each of her five children's books. She describes her fondness for it in *Many Mansions*: "In the Bible, human words by some miracle bring the message of the spirit. They bring the untold truth, as God instructs the children of his own creating. Little words of man's invention carry to all creation the word of God."

Jessie Orton Jones lives in Wilmette, Illinois.

SELECTED WORKS SELECTED AND EDITED: Small Rain: Verses from the Bible, 1943; Secrets, 1945; A Little Child, 1946; Many Mansions, 1947; This Is the Way, 1951.

ABOUT: Chicago Schools Journal May 1951.

JEAN E. KARL

July 29, 1927–

AUTHOR OF *Beloved Benjamin Is Waiting,* etc.

Autobiographical sketch of Jean Edna Karl:

ALMOST my whole life has been involved with children's books. I was read to from the time I was a very small child. And as soon as I learned to read myself, I filled all of my spare time with books. Many of the things I read are long forgotten by everyone, including me. But I do remember my delight in some books that exist to bring pleasure. *Heidi, The Princess and Curdie, The Princess and the Goblins, Little Women, Swallows and Amazons, Caddie Woodlawn, The Good Master, Alice in Wonderland, The Secret Garden, Millions of Cats,* and many, many more.

Though I grew up in a city neighborhood, in Chicago, it was a neighborhood that was singularly scarce of girls most of the time. Only twice in my growing up years was there a girl near my age in the immediate neighborhood. There were plenty of boys, but I was a girl kind of girl. I liked dolls and playhouses and girl games, though I played my share of baseball, football, kick the can, and red rover. So when there were no girls near, I found girls and adventure and friends in books. One summer, to remedy the paucity of playmates, I was sent daily to a local day camp. I went, most of the time, but I hated it. I did not then, and still do not, like organized recreation.

Eventually I went to high school in Chicago and then to college in Ohio, where I took enough education to teach but came out resolved never to teach. Practice teaching had not been a pleasant experience. Perhaps if the circumstances of that practice teaching had been different, I would have lived a very different life and never come to write children's books. As it was, at the advice of the head of the English department at the college, I wrote to a number of publishers, looking for a job in book publishing. Neither of us knew how scarce such jobs were then and always are.

I was lucky. I lived in Chicago. And the Chicago publisher suggested that I come to see them. Most publishing aspirants wanted to go to New York. Eventually I got a job in the training department at Scott, Foresman in Chicago, as a junior editorial assistant. Later I was assigned to the reading department, where I worked on grade school readers—pre-primers through grade six. Dick and Jane and Spot and Tim and Sally! The woman I worked for, Zerna Sharp, had invented Dick and Jane and did not like to be reminded that I had learned to read with her brain children.

After some years at Scott, Foresman, I moved to New York to become the editor of children's books at Abingdon Press, and then five years later to start the children's book department at Atheneum Publishers. I have been there ever since. At Atheneum I have worked with such authors as Elaine Konigsburg, Zilpha Snyder, Robert C. O'Brien, Ursula Le Guin, Anne McCaffrey, Barbara Corcoran, and many more.

It was while I was at Atheneum that my own writing began. I wrote a great many speeches for various kinds of groups. And as examples of kinds of plots and styles of writing, I often wrote brief synopses of books—original ideas. These grew longer and longer until finally some speeches had completed stories in them. When someone asked me one day why I didn't do something with the science fiction story I had just read as part of a speech, it seemed so reasonable a suggestion, I wondered why I hadn't thought of it. So I wrote eight stories to go with the speech story, and that became *The Turning Place.* Since then I have written *Beloved Benjamin Is Waiting* and *But We Are Not of Earth,* both complete novels. And very slowly, because I have little time, I work at something tentatively called *Strange Tomorrow.*

I like reading children's books. I like editing children's books. And I like writing children's books. I hope I can go on for a long time doing all three.

———

Jean Karl received her B.A. degree from Mount Union College in Ohio in 1949 and a D. Litt in 1969. She wrote a book on children's literature, *From Childhood to Childhood: Children's Books and Their Creators,* in 1970, and has contributed articles to magazines, including *Publishers Weekly* and the *Wilson Library Bulletin.*

She is a Vice President of Atheneum Publishers. She was President of the Children's Book Council in 1965 and chaired the American Library Association/Children's Book Council Joint Committee from 1963 to 1965. Karl has been a trustee of Mount Union College since 1974 and is a member of the American Association of Publishers Freedom to Read Committee.

SELECTED WORKS: The Turning Place: Stories of a Future Past, 1976; Beloved Benjamin Is Waiting, 1978; But We Are Not of Earth, 1981.

ABOUT: Contemporary Authors (First Revision), Vol. 29–32; Foremost Women in Communications, 1970; Ward, Martha E. and Dorothy A. Marquardt. Authors of Books for Young People, 2nd edition (Supplement); Who's Who in America, 1980–1981; Who's Who in America Women, 1975–1976; Publishers Weekly July 18, 1977.

RICHARD KENNEDY

December 23, 1932–

AUTHOR OF *The Leprechaun's Story,* etc.

Autobiographical sketch of Jerome Richard Kennedy:

ALTHOUGH I was born in Missouri, I've lived in Oregon since I was three or so. The first words I remember being interested in were those on billboards I rode past on the trolley in Portland. I asked my mother to say the words out loud, and I suppose that's how I learned to read. Café, I remember, was a word that puzzled me and it was everywhere. Comic books came next, and I had drawers full of them. I never read children's books at all, and when I gave up comics I read nothing, even all the way through high school. But I was drawing pictures and cartoons, and I did have to write captions, and that was my first creative writing. My ambition was to be a *New Yorker* cartoonist. After four years in the service I entered college. My success with the cartoons was modest, and I wrote my first stories for the literary magazine, and found more satisfaction in that than in the cartoons.

So I wanted to be a writer then. Now we can skip fifteen years. I got married and we had two boys, and I worked at many different jobs, yet always I was writing something: poetry, journals, novels, sketches, journalistic pieces, and so forth, not having settled on what it was I could do best. Along about the time I was forty I went to the local library and checked out a bunch of children's books and was at once convinced that I could do as well, so I quickly did three or four and started sending them around. And Emilie McLeod at Atlantic accepted *The Parrot and the Thief.* Then it was easy, and since then (1974) I've had about fifteen more stories published. Currently I'm working on a novel for children, and also writing an English version of the songs in Brecht's *Threepenny Opera,* definitely not for kids. I think I'd like to write a musical if I could find a music man to work with.

I live alone in a small house by the beach and I work as a custodian at night and I misbehave like a pirate on the weekends. I find that life is best if you don't listen to the news or read the newspapers. I heard Mt. St. Helen's erupt 130 miles away, and there are other strange grumblings that I don't want to talk about. When the world comes to an end I hope to be asleep, or on vacation. Last night I went roller-skating, and right now I'm going to go get a hamburger and a beer, and God bless us, everyone.

richard kennedy

Born in Jefferson City, Missouri, Richard Kennedy graduated from Portland State University in 1958 with a B.S. degree. He did some graduate study at Oregon State University from 1964 to 1965. He served in the U.S. Air Force from 1951 to 1954 and has been a fifth-grade teacher in Oregon as well as an employee of an out-of-print book search service. He likes to read and to play the guitar. The novel he mentions working on is *The Boxcar at the Center of the Universe*.

Three of his books have been named American Library Association Notable Books: *The Blue Stone* in 1976, *The Dark Princess* in 1978, and *Song of the Horse* in 1981. The latter was also named a Children's Choice book in 1982 by a joint committee of the International Reading Association and the Children's Book Council. *The Leprechaun's Story*, which was illustrated by Marcia Sewall, was represented in the 1980 American Institute of Graphic Arts Book Show.

SELECTED WORKS: The Porcelain Man, 1976; Come Again in the Spring, 1976; The Blue Stone, 1976; Oliver Hyde's Dishcloth Concert, 1977; The Dark Princess, 1978; The Leprechaun's Story, 1979; Inside My Feet: The Story of a Giant, 1979; Song of the Horse, 1981; The Boxcar at the Center of the Universe, 1982.

ABOUT: Contemporary Authors, Vol. 57; Something About the Author, Vol. 22.

JACK KENT

March 10, 1920–

AUTHOR AND ILLUSTRATOR OF *Knee-High Nina*, etc.

Autobiographical sketch of John Wellington Kent:

ALL CHILDREN scribble. Most outgrow it. I never did. I scribbled in Burlington, Iowa, where I was born. I scribbled in Chicago, where I started school. I scribbled in towns all over the Central U.S., where I grew up. Dad was a traveling salesman who didn't like to leave his family. So he took us along—my mother, my sister, and me.

Whenever we found a town we liked better than the one we lived in, we moved. I went to a different school every semester . . . sometimes two or three. About halfway through high school I gave it up. I'm a high school drop-out and a self-taught artist, which explains a lot but excuses nothing.

I was in my teens when I started selling my scribbles to magazines as cartoons. A week after Pearl Harbor I volunteered to end the War. It took me four and a half years, after which I resumed my scribbling. In 1950 I started the comic strip *King Aroo*, which made me world-famous for blocks around.

In doing a comic strip, I was writing funny little stories and scribbling funny little pictures to illustrate them. I'm still doing

that. Now, however, my stories are printed in books, so I'm not a "cartoonist" anymore; I'm an "author/illustrator." There have been sixty-some-odd books since 1968, when I started doing them.

I enjoy what I'm doing. I hope the children the books are written for, and those who read the books to them, enjoy what I'm doing, too. I like to think that my little soufflés might instill an appetite for books in the wee folk and encourage them to sample weightier fare. Maybe they will learn to love books as I do.

The Kents are bibliomaniacs. We only buy books on the subjects in which we're interested, but we're interested in virtually everything. Our walls are bookshelves from floor to ceiling, making wallpaper unnecessary and picture-hanging well nigh impossible.

The nicest thing that ever happened to me was when a local newspaper subscribed to my comic strip and sent a reporter to in-

terview me. I married her and lived happily ever after. Our son, Jack Jr., is an architect in Houston.

I live and work in San Antonio in a house I designed. It's on the banks of the river, in a grove of huge pecan trees, just a mile and a half from the Alamo in the heart of town. The San Antonio River as it flows past us is a modest stream, having been born of springs just north of the city. My hometown is on the banks of the Mississippi. When visiting relatives ask where the San Antonio River is and I point it out to them, they say "That crick?!" But it's a pretty little river.

What with the river and the trees, it's as if we lived in the country. Our neighbors are squirrels and raccoons and opossums and fish and turtles and frogs and a wide variety of birds. With a wife like June to share it, surely Heaven must be something like this.

———

Jack Kent was a first lieutenant in the U.S. Army field artillery from 1941 to 1945.

King Aroo, his comic strip for the McClure Newspaper Syndicate, was published from 1950 to 1965. *Jack Kent's Happy-Ever-After Book* was named an outstanding picture book of the year 1976 by the *New York Times.* His cartoons have appeared in many magazines, from *Humpty Dumpty* to *Playboy.*

Kent's art was exhibited in the Contemporary Arts Museum in Houston, in 1975, and his work is part of the Kerlan Collection. He is a member of the National Cartoonists Society, the American Institute of Graphic Artists, the Authors Guild, and the Authors League of America.

SELECTED WORKS WRITTEN AND ILLUSTRATED: The Fat Cat, 1971; The Wizard of Wallaby Wallow, 1971; There's No Such Thing As a Dragon, 1975; Jack Kent's Happy-Ever-After Book, 1976; Floyd, The Tiniest Elephant, 1979; Knee-High Nina, 1980; The Scribble Monster, 1981.

SELECTED WORKS ILLUSTRATED: The Bremen-Town Musicians, by Ruth Gross, 1974; The Emperor's New Clothes, by Ruth Gross, 1977; No One Noticed Ralph, by Bonnie Bishop, 1979; *Laura's Story*, by Beatrice de Regniers, 1979.

ABOUT: Burke, W. J. and Will D. Howe. American Authors and Books: 1640 to the Present Day, 3rd edition; Kingman, Lee and others, comps. Illustrators of Children's Books: 1967–1976; Who's Who in America, 1974–1975; Who's Who in American Art, 1978; (as John Wellington Kent) Contemporary Authors, Vol. 85–88; Something About the Author, Vol. 24.

JUDITH KERR

June 14, 1923–

AUTHOR AND ILLUSTRATOR OF *When Hitler Stole Pink Rabbit,* etc.

Biographical sketch of Judith Anne Kerr:

JUDITH KERR was born to Jewish parents in Berlin, Germany, in 1923. Her father was a writer and drama critic and her mother a musician. Unlike many of his contemporaries, her father sensed the intent behind the Nazi's rhetoric and took his family into exile just before Hitler's rise to power in 1933. The family first journeyed to Switzerland, where they received word that the Nazis had confiscated all their possessions, including Judith's favorite toy, a stuffed pink rabbit—a loss that inspired the title of Kerr's best known book. In continually reduced circumstances, the family left Switzerland to live in France. Eventually, under the growing threat of invasion and unable to support themselves in France, the family emigrated to England.

During the Second World War, Judith Kerr worked as a secretary for the Red Cross by day and studied art at night. In 1945 she earned a scholarship to the Central School of Art in London and went on to teach art and work as a textile designer. Subsequently she worked as an editor and writer for BBC television. In 1954, she married a fellow writer, and they raised two children.

Her career as a children's book writer and illustrator began with her children. She

JUDITH KERR

wrote and illustrated stories to please her family, often beginning with ideas they had given her. Mog, the character of two of her picture books, is based on the family cat.

The successful novels *When Hitler Stole Pink Rabbit* and *The Other Way Round* were also, in a way, written for her children. Her husband encouraged Kerr to tell the story of her eventful childhood. Unsure of herself as a writer, Kerr decided to write the book so that her children, who were growing up so differently from the way she did, might know what her childhood was like. She wanted to fill out the bare bones of the facts with the story of her everyday life.

When Hitler Stole Pink Rabbit is the story of a girl, Anna, aware of the momentous changes and events around her, but also trying to get on with the business of school, friends, toys, and play and constantly finding them anew in each strange country she goes to.

The sequel, called *The Other Way Round,* continues the story of the Kerr family in England during the duration of the war. It tells of Anna's beginning studies as an art student and the growing gap between her parents, who remain refugees in an alien culture, and herself, who becomes assimilated into English life. *A Small Person Far Away* continues the story, and the *Horn Book* called it "introspective rather than suspenseful . . . an adult recalling childhood" to achieve understanding. *When Hitler Stole Pink Rabbit* was named a Notable Book by the American Library Association and appeared on the *School Library Journal* "Best of the Best 1966–1978" list (December 1979).

Judith Kerr lives in London with her husband, the writer Nigel Kneale.

SELECTED WORKS: The Tiger Who Came to Tea, 1968; Mog, the Forgetful Cat, 1972; When Hitler Stole Pink Rabbit, 1972; When Willy Went to the Wedding, 1973; The Other Way Round, 1975; Mog's Christmas, 1977; A Small Person Far Away, 1979.

ABOUT: (As Judith Anne Kerr) Contemporary Authors, Vol. 93–96; Kirkpatrick, D. L., ed. Twentieth-Century Children's Writers; Something About the Author, Vol. 24; Ward, Martha E. and Dorothy A. Marquardt. Authors of Books for Young People, 2nd edition (Supplement); The Writers Directory 1982–84.

Ethel Kessler

ETHEL KESSLER

January 7, 1922–

CO-AUTHOR OF *Big Red Bus,* etc.

Autobiographical sketch of Ethel Kessler:

WHEN OUR daughter Kim enrolled at the University at Madison in Wisconsin, she agonized about her choice of a major. "I'm so unsure about what I would like to do for the rest of my life," she said. As I reassured her that her indecision was natural, I reminded her that I had changed careers as I developed new skills and interests. Yet I enjoyed each one of my professions. I was employed first as a social worker, then as a teacher, and now as a writer of books for the preschool and primary-aged child.

I was born and grew up in Pittsburgh, Pennsylvania. As a child I dreamed of becoming a famous actress. I was plump and nonathletic, so books and the world of make-believe were my outlets. I performed regularly with first a children's and then a teenage theater group, playing a variety of roles from animal to Titania in *A Midsummer Night's Dream*. After attempting starvation as a method of slimming down my figure, I joined a modern dance class. The exercise did it, and it is still the way I manage to keep down the unwanted pounds.

Although Leonard and I lived just a few blocks apart, it wasn't until our college years that we discovered each other. After our marriage, we spent many summers working at children's camps. We began as counselors, and over the years moved on to surpervisory positions. Working at camp gave me practical experience with many new skills. I learned about outdoor camping and became interested in sports.

Although I did not realize it at the time, these summer experiences would lead me into teaching and writing. Homesick children were a breeze to handle compared with some of the complicated situations that developed among the staff. This was especially true of the kitchen staff, who worked long hours in close quarters. Once during a week of unrelenting rain, the entire kitchen staff walked out. Leonard and I took over the cooking until the new personnel were hired. We struggled with gigantic pots, and learned how difficult it was to cook oatmeal and eggs for two hundred and fifty hungry campers!

I received a B.A. from Carnegie Mellon in Pittsburgh and married Len when he returned from the army. After his graduation we decided that New York was the place for us. I worked at the Educational Alliance on the Lower East Side, developing recreational after-school and weekend programs for children. Len began to make the rounds, meeting people and experiencing the usual ups and downs of the young artist.

When our first child was born, Leonard and I discovered a need for books for infants and preschoolers. Margaret Lesser at Doubleday agreed with us. Len and I collaborated on *Plink, Plink, Crunch, Crunch, Kim and Me, The Big Red Bus, Peek-a-Boo, Do Baby Bears Sit in Chairs?,* and *The Day Daddy Stayed Home. Big Red Bus* was honored by the *New York Times* as one of the ten best illustrated books in 1957.

I continued my interest in early childhood education by taking courses during the evening at the Bank Street College of Education. When we purchased a home in New City, New York, I continued my studies and became certified to teach. When our youngest child, Kim, was in fourth grade, I decided that it was time to begin a teaching career.

I taught kindergarten for eleven years and first grade for several more. Now that I am writing again, I have the greatest admiration for Leonard's discipline. I frequently take breaks from my work to read, cook, and bake bread.

Leonard and I have collaborated on twenty-two books. Our latest books are *Grandpa Witch and the Magic Doobelator* and *Two, Four, Six, Eight.* It is difficult to remember who did what in the writing of our stories. We usually brainstorm ideas several times a week. We find it helpful to write a story outline before we go ahead on the writing. After the writing of a first draft, the hard work begins. We simplify and tighten the story, and write and rewrite.

Len and I share our job-related activities. Whoever has the time does research, answers letters from children, or completes the typing of a story. We also share the pleasure of visiting the art galleries and museums when we drive into New York City. In the summer I enjoy herb gardening, swimming, and playing tennis with Len. In the winter we love to walk at a fast pace for several miles.

———

Ethel Kessler received her B.A. degree in 1944. She married Leonard Kessler on January 23, 1946. *Big Red Bus,* which was illustrated by Ethel Kessler's co-writer and husband, was a *New York Times* Choice of Best Illustrated Children's Books of the Year in 1957. Both *Peek-A-Boo* and *The Big Mile Race* were Junior Literary Guild selections.

SELECTED WORKS WRITTEN WITH LEONARD KESSLER: Plink, Plink! Goes the Water in My Sink, 1954; Crunch, Crunch, 1955; Peek-A-Boo: A Child's First Book, 1956; Big Red Bus, 1957; Kim and Me, 1960; Do Baby Bears Sit in Chairs?, 1961; The Day Daddy Stayed Home, 1971; Our Tooth Story: A Tale of Twenty Teeth, 1972; Splish Splash, 1973; All for Fall, 1974; What Do You Play on a Summer's Day?, 1977; Two, Four, Six, Eight: A Book About Legs, 1980; Grandpa Witch and the Magic Doobelator, 1981.

LEONARD KESSLER

October 28, 1921–

AUTHOR AND ILLUSTRATOR OF *What's in a Line,* etc.

Autobiographical sketch of Leonard P. Kessler:

SINCE my college graduation, I have been self-employed. I have worked as a freelance illustrator since 1949, when I graduated from Carnegie Mellon University and moved to New York.

Leonard Kessler

I was born in Akron, Ohio, but my family moved to Pittsburgh, Pennsylvania, when I was an infant. At that time there was no smoke control in Pittsburgh, and I have vivid impressions of the smog and pollution that hid the sun. Another more significant experience was my first exposure to painting and drawing. I was only six years old when I visited our neighborhood community center. As I shyly peered through the window of the art school, fascinated by the students busily at work, the instructor invited me to come in and experiment. I attended the class devotedly after that, captivated by the opportunity to draw and paint. I still have several oil paintings, free and lively, from those early years in that engrossing environment.

My grandmother, who lived with us, was a great influence on me. She was a wise and gentle woman and I loved to spend time with her. She was an inveterate storyteller who fascinated me with stories of village life in Rumania. She encouraged me to read and write, and I began to write poems and stories. She was also a good cook and baker. My interest now in cooking is due to her influence.

During my teenage years, music preoccu-

pied most of my time. I played the clarinet and was a member of a number of jazz groups. I also loved to dance, and would travel all over the city to compete in the dance contests that were popular at that time.

I graduated from high school at the age of sixteen, the shortest boy in the class. The following year I added ten inches to my skinny frame, and met my future wife, Ethel.

My plans for college were interrupted by World War II. My art and musical background made me a perfect candidate for the infantry, where I served in five European campaigns. Part of that time I was an infantry scout, making reconnaissance sketches behind enemy lines. I earned the Purple Heart, the Bronze Star, and was promoted to staff sergeant.

When the war ended, Ethel and I were married, and I enrolled in Carnegie Mellon, from which I graduated with a degree in painting and design. After graduation, we moved to New York City, where Ethel had been hired as a social worker. I started making rounds and meeting people in the commercial art field.

My introduction into children's books was a happy coincidence. I had written some scripts about art for a prospective children's TV show. The program was cancelled, but an astute friend of mine thought that the scripts might make a good children's book. It became *What's in a Line?*, honored by the *New York Times* as one of the ten best children's books of 1951.

Since that first book, I have illustrated over one hundred and fifty books for other authors, collaborated with Ethel on two dozen more, and have illustrated my own stories. Among my most challenging assignments have been illustrating books for young readers about space and the planets. I wanted the pictures to be interesting and fun for the reader. At the same time, the manuscripts required that the detailed scientific material be accurate. For the research on the recently completed *Book of*

Saturn, I worked from photographs from the Jet Propulsion Labratory in California that were taken by the space probe, Voyager. For an earlier book, *A Book of Astronauts,* I visited the Kennedy Space Center.

Whenever I can, I include my real-life surroundings in my illustrations. Often I add small details that are not in the text, like a ladybug or an insect, to a picture book.

I began to write easy-to-read books, due to the encouragement of reading specialists. My approach to these books is to write a good story with action and interesting characters. Then as I rewrite, I discipline myself to trim away all the excess vocabulary.

Because of my interest in sports, I have written a number of sports books for the beginning reader. I have developed a family of animals in some of these books. Old Turtle, who likes to tell stories about baseball, is one of my favorite characters.

We live in New City, New York, now, where my studio faces the woods. I am a bird watcher and feed them summer and winter. From Ethel I learned their names, their songs, and their habits. We play tennis regularly and I enjoy both long and short distance running. I play music all the time as I work. One of the benefits of free-lance work has been that I could spend time with our children, Paul and Kim. They and their friends provided me with many ideas for stories when they were young. They are grown-up now, but writing for the school-age child will remain my major commitment. "Thank you, Grandmother."

Leonard Kessler received a B.F.A. degree from the Carnegie Institute of Technology in 1949. He married Ethel Kessler on January 23, 1946. Besides *What's in a Line,* three other books he has illustrated have been named *New York Times* Choice of Best Illustrated Children's Books of the Year: *Fast Is Not a Ladybug,* in 1953; *Heavy Is a Hippopotamus,* in 1954; and *Big Red Bus,* in 1957. *Peek-A-Boo* and *The Big Mile Race,*

both of which he wrote with Ethel Kessler, were Junior Literary Guild selections.

SELECTED WORKS WRITTEN AND ILLUSTRATED BY LEONARD KESSLER: What's in a Line, 1951; Here Comes the Strikeout, 1965; Last One in Is a Rotten Egg, 1969; Tale of Two Bicycles: Safety on Your Bike, 1971; On Your Mark, Get Set, Go, 1972; Who Tossed That Bat?: Safety on the Ballfield and Playground, 1973; The Forgetful Pirate, 1974; Riddles That Rhyme for Halloween Time, 1978; The Pirates' Adventure on Spooky Island, 1979; Hey Diddle Diddle, 1980; Super Bowl, 1980.

SELECTED WORKS WRITTEN WITH ETHEL KESSLER AND ILLUSTRATED BY LEONARD KESSLER: Big Red Bus, 1957; The Day Daddy Stayed Home, 1971; Our Tooth Story: A Tale of Twenty Teeth, 1972; Splish Splash, 1973; All for Fall, 1974; Two, Four, Six, Eight: A Book About Legs, 1980; Grandpa Witch and the Magic Doobelator, 1981.

SELECTED WORKS WRITTEN WITH ETHEL KESSLER: Plink, Plink! Goes the Water in My Sink, 1954; Crunch, Crunch, 1955; Peek-A-Boo: A Child's First Book, 1956; Kim and Me, 1960; Do Baby Bears Sit in Chairs?, 1961; What Do You Play on a Summer's Day?, 1977.

SELECTED WORKS ILLUSTRATED: Heavy Is a Hippopotamus, by Miriam Schlein, 1954; Fast Is Not a Ladybug, by Miriam Schlein, 1955; Sukkah and the Big Wind, by Lily Edelman, 1956; What Have I Got, by Mike McClintock, 1961; A Book of Astronauts for You, by Franklyn M. Branley, 1963; How to Play Better Baseball, by C. Paul Jackson, 1963; A Book of Planets for You, by Franklyn M. Branley, revised edition, 1966; Adventures with a Straw, by Harry Milgrom, 1967; Truck Drivers: What Do They Do, by Carla Greene, 1967; A Book of Mars for You, by Franklyn M. Branley, 1968; How to Play Better Basketball, by C. Paul Jackson, 1968; A Book of Outer Space for You, by Franklyn M. Branley, 1970; The Illustrated Baseball Dictionary for Young People, by Henry Walker, 1970; Homer the Hunter, by Richard J. Margolis, 1972; Too Many Rabbits, by Peggy Parish, 1974; The Age of Aquarius: You and Astrology, by Franklyn M. Branley, 1979; A Book of Saturn for You, by Franklyn M. Branley, 1983.

ABOUT: Bader, Barbara. American Picturebooks from Noah's Ark to the Beast Within; Contemporary Authors, Vol. 77–80; Kingman, Lee and others, comps. Illustrators of Children's Books: 1957–1966; 1967–1976; Something About the Author, Vol. 14; Viguers, Ruth Hill and others, comps. Illustrators of Children's Books: 1946–1956; Ward, Martha E. and Dorothy A. Marquardt. Authors of Books for Young People, 2nd edition.

DAVID KHERDIAN

December 17, 1931–

AUTHOR OF *The Road from Home: The Story of an Armenian Girl,* etc.

Autobiographical sketch of David Kherdian:

I HAVE become a children's book author quite by accident. It had its beginning nearly eleven years ago when I married Nonny Hogrogian. I couldn't even remember having read children's books when I was a boy, but when I found *The Five Chinese Brothers* in Nonny's library, I remembered that in fact I had read many many books as a youngster, and that they had nurtured my growing spirit and imagination.

I supposed, having married Nonny, I would do a children's book or two sooner or later, but I had no idea that it would one day take on the aspect of a career. I had been then—when we met—as I am still, a poet; but a poet cannot make a living in America, and so one day (after I left my job as editor of *Ararat* magazine, which preceded my job as poet-in-the-schools for the State of New Hampshire), it occurred to me that I might be able to edit an anthology of contemporary American poetry for children. I had seen the need for such a book when I taught in the schools, and the result was *Visions of America by the Poets of Our Time.* The book was successful (for an anthology) and so I was able to follow it with two others: *Settling America: The Ethnic Expression of Fourteen Contemporary Poets,* and *Traveling America with Today's Poets.*

I did five more anthologies before I stopped my editing career to begin writing *The Road from Home.* I still wasn't a children's book author, and I had no intention of becoming one—or not becoming one.

When I finished my mother's biography I didn't know where to send it. I thought perhaps it might be a good book for young girls, since the book ends with my mother still in her teens. After a great deal of deliberation, I decided to send it to a children's book department first, and, if they rejected it, to send it to an adult trade department. That it was accepted at once determined that I would become a children's book author, for a sequel followed, as did two novels about a couple of boys whose experiences were reminiscent of my own when I was their age. Since then I have written a novel and a fantasy, as well as two picture books in collaboration with Nonny, so, as the saying goes, I'm probably here to stay.

As to what a children's book author is or needs to be—or even would like to be—I have no clear idea. I discovered in writing *It Started with Old Man Bean* that if you write about childhood from the point of view of an adult looking back, you have an adult book, but if you write the same book from the point of view of the child himself, you have a children's book. I mean, one can pick and choose—or one cannot pick and choose, for I have just written my autobiography, and I have been told that it is not a children's book. So be it. It doesn't really matter to the writer, who is only a writer, first of this, then of that; now in poetry, then again in prose. What matters to him is the word, and how it is formed, and how it is made to sing—for himself and for all who come after, who find his song is also their own.

———

David Kherdian was born in Racine, Wisconsin, and received a B.S. degree in philosophy at the University of Wisconsin in 1960. He served in the U.S. Army, in 1952–1954. His first marriage ended in divorce.

In addition to the jobs he mentions, Kherdian has been the owner of a used book store, a literary consultant to Northwestern University in Illinois, the founder and editor of two small presses (Giligia Press, in California, now defunct, and Two Rivers Press, in Oregon) and an instructor in poetry at Fresno State College. He has also been writer and designer of the Santa Fe Theatre Company's program, and a translator and editor of poetry for adults. David Kherdian had ten books of poems published, and his poetry has appeared in magazines and anthologies.

The community in Racine where he grew up was composed of many Armenians who escaped or survived the Turkish massacres of the late 1800s and early 1900s. Nonny Hogrogian is also of Armenian descent, and they share an interest in the Armenian culture and have published many books reflecting their backgrounds.

Set in Turkey, *The Road from Home* is told in the first person from the point of view of the author's mother, who actually witnessed the death and destruction the book portrays, and who was forced to travel into Syria, losing most of her family to a cholera epidemic; she emigrated to the United States as a mail-order bride in 1924. The book won several major awards. It was named a 1980 Newbery Honor Book and was a nominee for an American Book Award in 1980. It received the Boston Globe-Horn Book Award for nonfiction in 1979 and the Jane Addams Children's Book Award for 1980. It also won a Lewis Carroll Shelf Award in 1979.

The Friends of American Writers gave their Juvenile Book Merit Award for 1982 to *Beyond Two Rivers;* it is a sequel to *It Started with Old Man Bean. Finding Home* is the sequel to *The Road from Home.*

Kherdian and his wife Nonny Hogrogian, whom he married in 1971, live in Aurora, Oregon.

SELECTED WORKS WRITTEN: Country, Cat: City, Cat, 1978; The Road from Home: The Story of an Armenian Girl, 1979; It Started with Old Man Bean, 1980; Beyond Two Rivers, 1981; Finding Home, 1981; The Song in the Walnut Grove, 1982; Right Now, 1983.

SELECTED WORKS EDITED: Visions of America By the Poets of Our Time, 1973; Settling America: The Ethnic Expression of Fourteen Contemporary Poets, 1974; Poems Here and Now, 1976; The Dog Writes on the Window with His Nose and Other Poems, 1977; If Dragon Flies Made Honey, 1977; Traveling America with Today's Poets, 1977; I Sing the Song of Myself: An Anthology of Autobiographical Poems, 1978.

ABOUT: Contemporary Authors (First Revision), Vol. 21–24; A Directory of American Poets, 1975; The International Authors and Writers Who's Who, 8th edition; Something About the Author, Vol. 16; The Writers Directory 1982–84.

NORMA KLEIN

May 13, 1938–

AUTHOR OF *Mom, the Wolf Man and Me,* etc.

Autobiographical sketch of Norma Klein:

I WAS BORN in New York City where I grew up and have lived all my life. I attended private progressive schools: The Dalton School from the age of three to thirteen and Elizabeth Irwin for high school. I attended Cornell for one year and then transferred to Barnard College, from which I graduated in 1960. I was a Russian major, mainly due to my love for the short stories of Anton Chekhov, and went on to receive my M.A. in Slavic languages from Columbia in 1963. I intended to go on for a doctorate, but, upon getting married in 1963 to Erwin

Norma Klein

Fleissner, I decided to devote myself full-time to writing, which I've done ever since.

I began publishing short stories for adults while in college. My first story was published in 1958 in the *Grecourt Review*. I devoted most of my time until the age of thirty as a short story writer and published about sixty in all, mainly in literary quarterlies. Several of these were anthologized.

My first children's book, *Mom, the Wolf Man and Me,* and my first adult book, *Love and Other Euphemisms,* a book of short stories, came out in the same year: 1972. I originally began writing novels in order to get a short story collection published, but now I find it a much more congenial literary form. I have always alternated between writing for adults and writing for children and hope to continue to do so. Usually I write two books a year, one for each age group. I compose on a much-loved IBM electric typewriter. I type ten pages a day, fifty pages a week, stopping work at noon or one o'clock. In the evening I pencil in some stylistic changes, but that's about all the revising I do, unless an editor requests further changes.

My parents were nonreligious Jews, politically left-wing, intellectual. My father was a Freudian psychoanalyst, my mother is a crackerjack tennis player and admirer of Virginia Woolf. My brother, Victor, who is sixteen months younger than me, is a social worker. My husband is a scientist; he does cancer research at Sloan Kettering. I have two daughters: Jenny, born in 1967, and Katie, born in 1970. They both say they want to be writers when they grow up. Jenny has already had several poems published and I've used her poems in my novels.

In addition to writing, which I love, I enjoy making collages, going to plays and movies, taking photographs, having lunch with friends, cooking, and playing tennis. I am extremely fond of: Mozart operas, doll houses, basset hounds, October, marzipan, Paul Klee, lilacs, and books, people, or movies that make me laugh.

I consider myself an ardent feminist and regard equal rights for women as the most important issue of the modern world. One of my favorite hobbies is reading; I read hundreds of novels a year. Among my favorite writers for young people are: Betty Miles, Judy Blume, Norma Fox Mazer, Beverly Cleary, and Deborah Hautzig. I like realistic novels about contemporary life told with directness and humor. My favorite adult authors are: Hilma Wolitzer, Alice Adams, Anne Tyler, Cynthia Propper Seaton, and Margaret Drabble. If I had to take the works of two authors to a desert island, I would pick Anton Chekhov and Jane Austen, but I hope never to be faced with such a decision.

———

Norma Klein graduated cum laude from Barnard College and was elected to Phi Beta Kappa.

She is the author of a novelization, *Sunshine: A Novel,* which was based on a movie script. Her very popular *Mom, the Wolf Man and Me* was one of the first books for children to deal with the subject of a single parent who has an affair. Her eleven-year-old daughter Brett is fully aware of what is happening and is fearful that her life with her mother will change. Klein's novels continue to explore nontraditional family situations and relationships.

Her short stories have appeared in the 1963 and 1968 editions of *Prize Stories: The O. Henry Awards* and in many magazines, including *Mademoiselle. Girls Can Be Anything* and *Dinosaur's Housewarming Party* were Junior Literary Guild selections. *Tomboy* is a sequel to *Confessions of an Only Child.*

SELECTED WORKS: Mom, the Wolf Man and Me, 1972; Girls Can Be Anything, 1973; It's Not What You Expect, 1973; Confessions of an Only Child, 1974; Dinosaur's Housewarming Party, 1974; Taking Sides, 1975; It's Okay If You Don't Love Me, 1977; Tomboy, 1978; Breaking Up, 1980.

ABOUT: Contemporary Authors (First Revision), Vol. 41-44; Kirkpatrick, D. L. Twentieth-Century Children's Writers; The International Authors and Writers Who's Who, 1977; Something About the Author, Vol. 7; Ward, Martha E. and Dorothy A. Marquardt. Authors of Books for Young People, 2nd edition (Supplement); The Writers Directory 1982-84.

ILSE KOEHN

August 6, 1929–

AUTHOR AND ILLUSTRATOR OF *Mischling, Second Degree: My Childhood in Nazi Germany,* etc.

Autobiographical sketch of Ilse Charlotte Koehn Van Zwienen:

FROM THE MOMENT I could hold a pencil and talk I have drawn pictures and told stories. When I was little, they were tales of ghosts, made up to scare my friends, though I often scared myself as well. I gave up ghost stories at the age of seven, when the world became more frightening than anything I could make up.

I was born in Berlin, Germany, to parents who loved laughter, music, and books. They called books friends and treasures or, on payday, when my father came home with yet another bulging briefcase of new (sec-

ond-hand) acquisitions, they were "jewels" he had found.

Books have been with me ever since. I rarely go anywhere without one. When I read I forget my surroundings. Standing in line, airport delays, even having to wait at the dentist's became bearable with a book.

I had good reason to want to escape into another, better world. Because of Hitler, my parents divorced. War was declared and after the first bombs fell on Berlin, school children were sent to rural areas.

Along with my classmates, I spent the four long years to the end of the war in evacuation camps. During those years of homesickness and boredom in camp there was demand for pictures and stories—not of ghosts and scary things; my friends wanted happy families. I created hundreds, complete with distant cousins, aunts, uncles, and pets. Writing texts for evenings of entertainment exempted me from kitchen duty and uniform marches, as did the newspaper I wrote, from Op-Ed page to ads.

I got back to Berlin in time for the heaviest air raids and the arrival of the Russians. The experiences of those years eventually became *Mischling, Second Degree: My Childhood in Nazi Germany.*

After the war my parents remarried and opened a flower shop. I went back to high school and then, secretly, took the entrance exam at the art academy. After I was accepted I told my parents. They were not pleased, because they had wanted me in the store—a secure future, as they saw it. I won the battle, but . . . for the following years I rose at four A.M. and took a train (an hour's ride) to the wholesale flower market in town. I went home to deliver my purchases, turned around and took a train back to town (an hour's ride) to attend art school. Late in the afternoon, another hour on the train to get back home in time to help in the store. I got a lot of reading done on those train rides.

I earned money for my tuition, materials, carfare, and clothing only partially in my parents' store. I also tutored (English), decorated windows, and worked at industrial fairs—which led to exhibition graphics.

These were difficult but happy years of learning from the best, most dedicated teachers. The work paid off. It was a great joy to see one of my posters all over town and articles and drawings in print. Exhibition graphics too were great fun, despite (or because) it meant often working thirty, or forty hours at a stretch to be ready for the opening.

When I worked in the American pavillion at the Brussels World Fair, I had the good fortune to meet the great artist Saul Steinberg. It was one of my duties to see that he had everything he needed (including sandwiches).

I arrived in New York, my dream town, on the first commercial Pan Am jet and was lucky to get a job with the J. Walter Thompson agency. Later, I also worked as art director at Campbell Downe. Then I decided to free-lance, the best decision I ever made, because John Van Zwienen, then art director at Dell, offered me the design of a book jacket, and after he liked what I had done (as he tells it), his hand in marriage.

I have become an American citizen, sailor, gardener, and football fan. John and I have become VanZee Associates, partners in our own design firm. John has written and had published four novels and has finished his fifth. I am working on my third. Had I listened to my parents none of these wonderful things would have happened.

———

Ilse Koehn attended Hochschuele Fuer Bildende Kuenste from 1948 to 1954. She came to the U.S. in 1958 and was naturalized as a U.S. citizen in 1976.

Mischling, Second Degree won a 1978 Boston Globe-Horn Book Award and was a finalist for the 1978 National Book Award. It was named a Best Book for Young Adults by the American Library Association in 1977 and a Jane Addams Award Honor Book in 1978. "Mischling" means a part Jewish heritage.

Tilla, Koehn's second book, is about a girl who is forced to leave Berlin after her family is killed in an air raid. It was named a Best Book for Young Adults by the American Library Association in 1981.

SELECTED WORKS WRITTEN: Mischling, Second Degree: My Childhood in Nazi Germany, 1977; Tilla, 1981.

SELECTED WORKS ILLUSTRATED: The Science of Ourselves: Adventures in Experimental Psychology, by William N. McBain and R. C. Johnson, 1962; the Liverpool Cats, by Sylvia Sherry, 1969; Looking for a Place, by Richard Margolis, 1969.

ABOUT: New Yorker May 1, 1978; Publishers Weekly November 21, 1977; (as Ilse Charlotte Koehn Van Zwienen) Contemporary Authors, Vol. 85–88; Something About the Author, Vol. 28.

JILL KREMENTZ

February 19, 1940–

AUTHOR OF *How It Feels When a Parent Dies,* etc.

Biographical sketch of Jill Krementz:

JILL KREMENTZ was born in New York

Krementz: *KREM entz*

JILL KREMENTZ

City and grew up in Morristown, New Jersey. After boarding school, she studied art for a year at Drew University, and at the age of nineteen she moved to New York. She began as a secretary at *Harper's Bazaar,* then became an editorial assistant at *Glamour.* In 1961 she took a year off and went around the world. Back in New York, she joined *Show* magazine as a reporter and columnist; it was at this time that she started taking pictures. When *Show* folded she was hired by the *New York Herald Tribune.* At twenty-four she was their youngest full-time photographer ever and the first woman staff photographer on any New York newspaper since World War II. At the paper she covered everything—fashion shows, fires, football games, the Harlem riots, and Churchill's funeral. "It was the most wonderful job in the world," said Krementz. "I couldn't believe I was actually being paid to do what I loved most." Her mentor at the *Herald Tribune* was Ira Rosenberg. "He taught me everything—the meaning of craftsmanship, how to think on my feet, and how to go the extra mile for a good picture. But more than anything else, he taught me that even if I got a page one picture, that today's paper was already yester-

day's, and I better concentrate on the next assignment."

In 1965 Krementz left the *Tribune* to spend a year as a free-lance photographer in Vietnam, photographing, not the combat, but the effects of the war on people. Out of this experience came her first book of photographs, *The Face of Vietnam,* in 1968, with a text by Dean Brelis.

In 1969 she published her first documentary for children, *Sweet Pea,* using as text the words of a ten-year-old black girl growing up in the South. Jane Langton, writing in the *Boston Globe,* said: "The reviewer is tempted to say something outrageous: if every white family in America owned this book it might be an end to prejudice."

As a free-lance photographer, Krementz has made writers her specialty since 1970. Her pictures of people like James Baldwin, Tennessee Williams, Eudora Welty, E. B. White, and hundreds of others appear in magazines and on book jackets. She had an exhibition in New York in 1975, "Famous Writers and Other Personalities," and has published two books of these portraits, the most recent in 1980. Her work has been exhibited at the Delaware Art Museum, the Madison Art Center, and Brentano's Gallery in New York, among other places. Her work is also included in the permanent photography collections of the Museum of Modern Art and the Library of Congress. In 1978 she was commissioned to take the official portraits of four members of the U.S. Cabinet, and in 1979 she was awarded a Doctor of Humane Letters From Caldwell College in New Jersey.

In 1975, Krementz started writing for children. Her first, *A Very Young Dancer,* is a photographic essay about a dedicated ten-year-old ballet student, with a casually conversational text in the girl's own words. *New York Times* critic Clive Barnes called it "the best ballet book ever written for children." It became the first of Krementz's "Very Young" series; a rider, a gymnast, a skater, and a circus flyer followed.

Krementz spent about a year following

each performer with her camera and note-book, immersing herself in the young person's world, recording the rigorous workouts, performances, and competitions. The "Very Young" series has been published in England, Germany, and Israel, and has become so well known that it even inspired a parody in 1979, *A Very Young Housewife,* by Del Tremens.

A Very Young Dancer won the Garden State Children's Book Award in 1979 and appeared in the American Institute of Graphic Arts show in 1977. *Rider* and *Circus Flyer* were both named Notable Books by the American Library Association, in 1977 and 1979 respectively.

In 1981 Krementz broke new ground with *How It Feels When a Parent Dies,* in which eighteen children of various ages speak about their experiences and feelings on the loss of a parent. This was followed by *How It Feels to Be Adopted,* and she is now working on *How It Feels When Your Parents Divorce.*

The "How It Feels" books have been praised by critics, psychologists, librarians, teachers, and young people. *When a Parent Dies* was named a Notable Book and a Best Book for Young Adults in 1981 by the ALA. It was named a Children's Choice book in 1982 by the joint committee of the International Reading Association and the Children's Book Council, and an Outstanding Science Trade Book for Children in 1981 by a joint committee of the National Science Teachers Association and the C.B.C.

Krementz met her husband, the writer Kurt Vonnegut, when she photographed him in 1970. They were married in 1979 and live in New York with their daughter, Lily.

SELECTED WORKS: Sweet Pea: A Black Girl Growing Up in the Rural South, 1969; A Very Young Dancer, 1976; A Very Young Rider, 1977; A Very Young Gymnast, 1978; A Very Young Skater, 1979; A Very Young Circus Flyer, 1979; How It Feels When a Parent Dies, 1981; How It Feels to Be Adopted, 1982.

ABOUT: Contemporary Authors (First Revision), Vol. 41–44; Something About the Author, Vol. 17; Who's Who in America, 1982–1983; Who's Who of American Women, 1974–1975; Boston Sunday Globe December 28, 1969; Camera 35, May 1975; Christian Science Monitor April 26, 1979; Detroit Free Press December 25, 1974; Mademoiselle March 1968; Miami Herald April 4, 1975; Modern Photography January 1976; New York Daily News March 29, 1974; New York Times June 19, 1981; November 14, 1982; New York Times Book Review December 26, 1976; New York Magazine July 28, 1975; Popular Photography April 1975; Saturday Review February 17, 1968; Wall Street Journal May 12, 1976.

STEVEN KROLL

August 11, 1941–

AUTHOR OF *Friday the 13th,* etc.

Autobiographical sketch of Steven Kroll:

I WAS BORN in New York City and grew up there, reading, dreaming, playing stickball, and hanging out at the Optimo candy store on 78th and Broadway on Manhattan's Upper West Side. For reasons I can't quite identify, the books I loved first were Albert Payson Terhune's dog stories and Walter Farley's black stallion series, but it wasn't too long before I went on to *The Adventures of Huckleberry Finn, The Great Gatsby,* and *The Catcher in the Rye.* Those three novels are still among my favorites. They taught me the importance of a strong narrative voice in fiction. Their voices weren't so different from what I was overhearing at the Optimo, but I wouldn't make that connection for years.

Until I was thirteen, it never occurred to me I might become a writer. In the sixth grade at Hunter College Elementary School, I wrote the customary "autobiography," and my teacher said she would introduce me to a journalist friend when I grew up. But that was reporting. That was nonfiction. That wasn't making up stories and making them live. The people who did that were gods. I could never hope to be one of them.

At thirteen all of that changed. I was taking a walk along Central Park West. It was

Transatlantic Review, and a book reviewer for several magazines. Back in New York three years later, I got a job as an acquiring editor of adult trade books at Holt, Rinehart and Winston. It wasn't until 1969, after three and a half years at Holt, that I was able to abandon the safety of my title and salary, move to Maine, and commit myself to writing—and eventually writing for children—full-time.

Even then the dream didn't come true, at least not for a while. My first book—a children's book, *Is Milton Missing?*—didn't come out until 1975, and at that point, I was back in New York, wondering if I hadn't made a terrible mistake.

Perhaps it's because of my long struggle that so much of my work seems to be about things going wrong and people trying to find themselves.

dark and raining, and suddenly I noticed, as if for the first time, that the streets were shimmering like glass in the light from the streetlamps. I ran home and began a story: "The world is made of glass, layer upon layer of glass, like the glass in the doors of the West End Plaza Hotel. . . . "

The story was very short and not very good, but I had felt that indescribable need to create, to put it all down on paper, and I would have that need with me ever after.

What I didn't have was confidence. I edited the McBurney School literary magazine and contributed a couple of stories of my own when we were short of material, but by the time I'd finished my first year at Harvard—and had seen the competition—I'd decided to become an editor. That way I would have something to do with books, but would not have to risk writing them. My advisor believed in me and said, "Write!" Instead, during my junior and senior years, I became a faculty aide at the Harvard University Press.

More years of evasion followed. Graduating from Harvard with an A.B. degree in 1962, I went to London and became a reader at the publishing house of Chatto and Windus Ltd., an associate editor of

In 1964 Steven Kroll married Edite Niedringhaus, a children's book editor. He was an English instructor at the University of Maine, in 1970 and 1971, and he now writes book reviews for many publications, including the *New York Times Book Review,* the *Village Voice,* and the *Times Literary Supplement.* He enjoys playing tennis and squash, and walking in New York City.

Is Milton Missing? was a Junior Literary Guild selection, and *If I Could Be My Grandmother* was designated an International Reading Association Children's Choice of 1977.

SELECTED WORKS: Is Milton Missing?, 1975; The Tyrannosaurus Game, 1976; That Makes Me Mad!, 1976; If I Could Be My Grandmother, 1977; Sleepy Ida and Other Nonsense Poems, 1977; Santa's Crash-Bang Christmas, 1977; Space Cats, 1979; Friday the 13th, 1981; One Tough Turkey: A Thanksgiving Story, 1982.

ABOUT: Contemporary Authors, Vol. 65-68; Something About the Author, Vol. 19; Ward, Martha E. and Dorothy A. Marquardt. Authors of Books for Young People, 2nd edition (Supplement).

HARRY KULLMAN

February 22, 1919– March, 1982

AUTHOR OF *The Battle Horse,* etc.

Biographical sketch of Harry Kullman by the co-translator of *The Battle Horse,* George Blecher:

WHEN HE WAS 29, Harry Kullman witnessed from his Stockholm apartment window an event that was to shape the course of his writing career. It was a street riot, an ugly confrontation between police and teenagers, and it served as inspiration for his first important book, *Den svarta fläcken* ("The Black Spot," 1949), which was hailed as a landmark in Swedish realism and which later became compulsory reading in Swedish schools. The book tells the story of Barbro, a young woman who is swept up into the illegal activities of a street gang. Torn between the excitement of the gang and her nagging conscience, she goes along with the group until it attempts a serious burglary—only then does she break ranks. What distinguishes the book—and is generally regarded as characteristic of all of Kullman's work—is his refusal to take sides; his wish to present Barbro's inner conflict as honestly as possible, not to preach to his audience.

One of Sweden's outstanding post-war children's book writers, Kullman was born in the south of Sweden, but moved when he was ten to Söder, the working-class district of Stockholm, where several of his novels are set. After graduating with an economics degree and working for a time in advertising, he began to produce a steady stream of young people's novels; by the time of his death in 1982, he had published nineteen books for teenagers and four for adults. During his lifetime, he earned virtually every award Sweden could offer a children's book writer: the Nils Holgersson Plaque (1955), a life-time grant from the Swedish government (1968), and the Astrid Lindgren Prize (1970); he was also a runner-up for the Hans Christian Andersen Medal of

HARRY KULLMAN

the International Board on Books for Young People (1980).

Kullman's work falls into three basic categories: historical fantasies; books about the American West, a region he loved and visited many times; and his studies of teenagers in the Stockholm of his youth. It is especially in these latter books where his imagination and his respect for young people's characters become most evident; the issues his young protagonists confront are always serious and complex ones. In *Gardårnas krig* ("War of the Back Yards," 1959), for example, the young hero must decide whether it is right to coerce his friends into joining his gang; and in *De rödas upprör* ("Red Revolt," 1968), an immensely popular book that was later adapted for Swedish television, the central character confronts the problem of whether to follow a charismatic young socialist whose ideals he shares but whose methods he questions.

Although many of Kullman's books have been published all over the world, only *Stridshästen* (published as *The Battle Horse,* 1981) is in print in the United States. In this novel Kullman creates a jousting match in the backyards of Stockholm where rich and poor kids act out a drama of conflict. The conflicts are not easily resolved, no one is completely good or evil, and the resolution, the death of the title character, is tragic and painful; yet the final effect is guardedly hopeful, and the reader comes away with a sense that teenagers are not less complex than adults.

The book received several prestigious honors in America: it appeared on the 1981 American Library Association's Best Books for Young Adults and Notable Books lists; it was named a Children's Choice book for 1982 by the joint committee of the International Reading Association and the Children's Book Council; and it received the 1982 Mildred L. Batchelder Award from the American Library Association as the best children's and young people's book in translation. The Association cited the book as "a memorable story that has depth and momentum as well as drama."

In addition to being adapted and serialized on Swedish National Radio, *The Battle Horse* has also become a successful musical in Sweden and is presently being adapted for film.

SELECTED WORKS: The Battle Horse, translated from Swedish by George Blecher and Lone Thygesen-Blecher, 1981.

ABOUT: Contemporary Authors, Vol. 93–96.

WILLIAM KURELEK

March 3, 1927– November 3, 1977

AUTHOR AND ILLUSTRATOR OF *A Prairie Boy's Winter*, etc.

Biographical sketch of William Kurelek:

BORN IN Alberta, Canada, William Kurelek was raised initially on the grain farm settled by his Ukrainian immigrant father. His family later moved to a dairy farm in Manitoba, where Kurelek stayed until he attended high school in Winnipeg at age sixteen.

After high school, he attended the Uni-

WILLIAM KURELEK

versity of Manitoba, receiving his B.A. in 1949. He worked in the summer of 1946 as a lumberjack at a camp in Ontario to earn his college fees and to prove to his father and to himself that he could live independently. He returned to lumberjacking for a year in 1951 to earn enough to study painting in Britain. While in Britain, however, he was hospitalized for four years in an English psychiatric hospital, where he was treated for depression. There, he discovered a deep religious faith that sustained him the rest of his life. In 1962, he married Jean Andrews; they have four children, Catherine, Stephen, Barbara, and Thomas.

His paintings are generally realistic depictions of Canadian prairie scenes and of his memories of his childhood in Ukrainian farming communities. His works reflect his Catholic faith, especially "The Maze" and "The Passion of Saint Matthew" series, which are now exhibited in the Niagara Falls Gallery and Art Museum. His paintings are also included in the collections of Queen Elizabeth II of England, the Museum of Modern Art in New York, and the National Gallery of Canada, among others. His work has been exhibited in over twenty-five one-man shows, and, in 1967, the Na-

Kurelek: *coo REH lek*

tional Film Board of Canada made a documentary film of his life and work, *Kurelek.*

Kurelek is especially well known for his children's books, which are reminiscences of his own pioneer childhood during the Depression; they have won many awards, and foreign editions have been issued in Great Britain, France, Germany, and Holland. *A Prairie Boy's Winter* details in twenty paintings and rich text the chores and entertainments of life on a dairy farm in the 1930s. It was named one of the nine Best Illustrated Books of 1973 by the *New York Times,* a Children's Book Council Showcase Book of 1974, a Best Illustrated Book of 1974 by the Canadian Association of Children's Librarians, and one of the four best children's books of 1973–74 chosen by all three American Institute of Graphic Arts juries (children, booksellers, and designers).

Its sequel, *A Prairie Boy's Summer,* is equally glorious in its representation of the swimming hole, haying, and softball. It was named a *New York Times* Outstanding Book in 1975, a Canadian Association of Children's Librarians Best Illustrated Book of 1976, a C.A.C.L. Best Book of the Year Runner-up in 1976, a Childen's Book Council Showcase Book in 1976, and an Imperial Order of the Daughters of the Empire Best Book of the Year in 1976.

Lumberjack provides a pictorial record of the old way of cutting wood for paper pulp, before modern machines; the twenty-five paintings depict life in the camps winter and summer, mosquitoes and all. It was named a *New York Times* Best Illustrated Book in 1974 and a Children's Book Council Showcase Book in 1975, and was designated a book of the year 1974 by the American Institute of Graphic Arts.

A Northern Nativity retells the Christmas story as it might have happened elsewhere, with Kurelek's own faith shining through. The paintings are, in fact, remembered dreams from his twelfth Christmas.

Kurelek has also published several books of paintings for adults, including *Kurelek's Country* and *The Passion of Christ According*

to Saint Matthew. He died on November 3, 1977, in Toronto.

SELECTED WORKS WRITTEN AND ILLUSTRATED: A Prairie Boy's Winter, 1973; Lumberjack, 1974; A Prairie Boy's Summer, 1975; A Northern Nativity, 1976.

ABOUT: Contemporary Authors Vol. 49–52; (New Revision Series), Vol. 3; Kingman, Lee and others, comps. Illustrators of Children's Books: 1967–1976; Something About the Author, Vol. 8; Vol. 27; Ward, Martha E. and Dorothy A. Marquardt. Authors of Books for Young People, 2nd edition (Supplement); Who's Who in American Art, 1978; The Writers Directory 1980–1982; Graphis No. 200, 1979.

JANE LANGTON

December 30, 1922–

AUTHOR OF *The Boyhood of Grace Jones,* etc.

Autobiographical sketch of Jane Gillson Langton:

I HAVE ALWAYS been good. It has plagued me all my life. I wish I could remember being bad, because my kind of goodness is often tarnished with insincerity and resentment. My older brother sometimes set an example by getting in trouble on purpose, and my little sister was sometimes naughty because she was too small to know any better—but there I was in the middle, excessively anxious to please.

But I have been lucky too, and happy most of the time. It was fun to be a child. I admired my father and mother. My father was a geologist. We three children were born in Boston, where he was studying at M.I.T. Then we all went to Wilmington, Delaware, when he started working for the DuPont Company. I didn't like Delaware much, feeling loyal to Boston (it was part of being good). I remember keeping my seat in the auditorium while everybody else stood up to sing "Oh, Our Delaware!" As a matter of fact, looking back on it, I feel proud. Surely that was a naughty thing to do. And I did a few other bad things, too,

Jane Langton

now that I think of it, shining exceptions to my timid reputation for goodness. Once I had a fight with Lawrence Hotchkiss, and knocked him down, because I hit him before he was ready to start fighting. But it didn't help. Before long I had won a gold ring for being generally harmless.

The best thing in Wilmington was the children's room in the public library. It was dark and cool, with a map of fairyland under a piece of glass on a long table. And the best thing about the library was the books of Arthur Ransome, right opposite the door, right *there* on the shelf. I can imagine no pleasure as keen as bringing home a new one, throwing myself down on the rug and beginning to read. I wanted to be like the jaunty tomboy heroine, Nancy Blackett, in the worst way. I can remember how it hurt, my longing to be a boy. When my Girl Scout troop went to Annapolis, I suffered painful yearnings, knowing I could never be a midshipman myself.

I didn't take any interest in writing until I was in college, when one of my freshman teachers encouraged me to major in English Composition. But my next teacher called one of my essays "a horrid murky fen of words and balderdash." Of course she was probably right, but I was discouraged. I majored in astronomy instead. It was a silly choice, since I have no talent for anything but irrational things like writing and drawing. But it led me straight to a husband, because I met Bill Langton when we were assigned as lab partners in a course called the Physics of Light. The choosing of partners was done alphabetically. Fortunately there were no Joneses between Gillson and Langton.

I was delighted and surprised to be getting married, because I thought I never would, since I didn't know how to dance or play bridge. A few years later we were settled down for good in Lincoln, Massachusetts, raising sons. Our fourth house in Lincoln is on the Walden Pond Road. It has too much peeling paint, too many cracks through which the wind whistles, too much grass, and too many weedy flower beds. But we have a fine view, and we like it here.

I am still sadly well-behaved, on the whole. Where, I wonder, is the fire and spark of rebellion? Perhaps when I am old I will rant and rage.

———

Jane Langton attended Wellesley College, 1940-1942, and received her B.S. in astronomy from the University of Michigan in 1944. She received master's degrees in the history of art from the University of Michigan in 1945 and from Radcliffe College in 1948. She is a member of Phi Beta Kappa. In the late 1950s she attended the Boston Museum of Art, taking a course in book design, and the book she made was developed into her first novel, *The Majesty of Grace*. Langton has written a trilogy of fantasies for children, consisting of *The Diamond in the Window, The Swing in the Summerhouse,* and *The Astonishing Stereoscope*. She says that they are her favorite works, and they are set in a real house in Concord, Massachusetts. *The Fledgling* was a 1981 Newbery Medal Honor Book and was nominated for a 1982 American Book Award in the paperback children's fiction category. She also writes suspense novels for adults.

Langton teaches writing for children at the Simmons College in Boston. She has worked on educational programs in the natural sciences for WGBH-TV in Boston, and she reviews children's books for the *New York Times Book Review*.

SELECTED WORKS: The Majesty of Grace, 1961 (retitled Her Majesty, Grace Jones, 1974); The Diamond in the Window, 1962; The Swing in the Summerhouse, 1967; The Astonishing Stereoscope, 1971; The Boyhood of Grace Jones, 1972; Paper Chains, 1977; The Fledgling, 1980.

ABOUT: Contemporary Authors (First Revision), Vol. 4; (New Revision Series), Vol. 1; Foremost Women in Communications, 1970; Kirkpatrick, D. L. Twentieth-Century Children's Writers; Something About the Author, Vol 3; Ward, Martha E. and Dorothy A. Marquardt. Authors of Books for Young People, 2nd edition; The Writers Directory 1982-84.

JOE LASKER

June 26, 1919–

AUTHOR AND ILLUSTRATOR OF *Merry Ever After: The Story of Two Medieval Weddings,* etc.

Biographical sketch of Joseph Leon Lasker:

JOE LASKER was born and raised in Brooklyn, New York, and won his first art prize at the age of eight. He graduated from the Cooper Union Art School in New York City in 1939 and served in the army in World War II from 1941 to 1945. He resumed painting immediately upon his return, and was awarded Edward Austin Abbey Mural Painting Fellowships in 1947 and 1948. His murals from that period hang in the post offices in Calumet, Michigan and Millbury, Massachusetts and in the Henry Street Settlement Playhouse in New York City. From 1947 to 1948 he taught art at the College of the City of New York, and in 1948, he married Mildred Jaspen, a teacher. They have three children, David,

Laura, and Evan. During 1948 Lasker went to Mexico to study at the Escuela Universitaria de Bellas Artes. In 1950, he was the subject of a profile in *Life* magazine as one of the young artists doing the best painting in the country. In 1950 and 1951, he won *Prix de Rome* fellowships. Between 1952 and 1953, he was a visiting associate professor of painting at the University of Illinois, and the following year he was awarded a Guggenheim Fellowship. His oil paintings are part of many permanent collections of art museums and universities.

Lasker began working on children's books in 1963 as the illustrator of *The Way Mothers Are*. He illustrated many books written by other people until 1972, when for the first time he wrote as well as illustrated, *Mothers Can Do Anything*. When his next book, *Merry Ever After: The Story of Two Medieval Weddings,* was published in 1976, it was an immediate critical and popular success. In the book, a noble wedding and a peasant wedding are illustrated with detailed paintings, recreating the lively world and manners of medieval Europe. Lasker said of it, "My love for the great masters of medieval and early Renaissance art—their paintings and illuminated manuscripts—led me to do this book. My research revealed to me a great many social conventions and conditions that surprised me. I wanted to share my discoveries with others, and I hope readers will be inspired, as I was, to look at these distant people and their magnificent art more closely and with greater understanding." *Merry Ever After* was chosen as an American Library Association Notable Book and a Classroom Choice of the International Reading Association, and it received an art books for children citation from the Brooklyn Museum and the Brooklyn Public Library. The *New York Times* named it both an Outstanding Book of the Year 1976 and a Choice of Best Illustrated Children's Book of the Year 1976. It was also an Alternate Selection of the Book-of-the-Month Club and has been translated into nine languages.

In 1979, Lasker illustrated *The Boy Who Loved Music,* a book written by his son, David. The collaboration also resulted in an ALA Notable Book Citation in 1980.

Joe Lasker said in *Contemporary Authors,* "Painting is my first love. I illustrate and write to support my habit and family." His studio is in his home in Norwalk, Connecticut.

SELECTED WORKS WRITTEN AND ILLUSTRATED: Mothers Can Do Anything, 1972; He's My Brother, 1974; Tales of a Seadog Family, 1974; Merry Ever After: The Story of Two Medieval Weddings, 1976; Nick Joins in, 1980; The Do Something Day, 1982; The Great Alexander the Great, 1983.

SELECTED WORKS ILLUSTRATED: The Way Mothers Are, by Miriam Schlein, 1963; Boxes, by Jean M. Craig, 1964; Benjy's Bird, by Norma Simon, 1965; When Grandpa Wore Knickers, by Fern Brown and Andree Grabe, 1966; My House, by Miriam Schlein, 1971; Night Lights, by Joel Rothman, 1972; Juju-Sheep and the Python Moonstone, by Miriam Schlein, 1973; Howie Helps Himself, by Joan Fassler, 1974; Rabbit Finds a Way, by Judy Delton, 1975; The Boy Who Loved Music, by David Lasker, 1979; The Cobweb Christmas, by Shirley Climo, 1982.

ABOUT: Contemporary Authors, Vol. 49–52; (New Revision Series), Vol. 1; Goodrich, Lloyd and Bauer, John. American Art of Our Century; Hills, Patricia and Tarbell, Roberta. The Figurative Tradition; Kingman, Lee and others, comps. Illustrators of Children's Books: 1957–1966; 1967–1976; Something About the Author, Vol. 9; Ward, Martha E. and Dorothy A. Marquardt. Illustrators of Books for Young People, 2nd edition; Who's Who in America, 1982–1983; Who's Who in American Art, 1982; Life March 20, 1950; Parade September 1, 1963.

SONIA LEVITIN

August 18, 1934–

AUTHOR OF *Journey to America,* etc.

Autobiographical sketch of Sonia Levitin, who also writes under the pen name "Sonia Wolff:"

I WAS BORN in Berlin, Germany, in 1934, the beginning of very hard times for Jews, and this fact had great bearing on my life. When I was only three my family fled from Germany. Many of our relatives were killed in the holocaust. This experience has influenced me in many ways. It has made me hate war and all threats to freedom and human dignity. It has helped me to understand how difficult it is for people to leave the familiar and head out for the unknown. It has made me value courage as a personal trait, freedom as a universal goal, and love as a necessity for survival. My first book, *Journey to America,* reflects my early experiences.

Since childhood I have loved books, and when I was eleven I decided to become a writer. I also loved animals. I was always picking up strays—cats, rabbits, dogs, and even a duck. Some of my happiest childhood times were spent with these pets. I would spend an entire afternoon training my dog and going roller-skating along the streets of Los Angeles, where I grew up. I also enjoyed playing the piano, painting, and reading, hobbies that still fill my leisure time along with tennis, jogging, and hiking.

In college I met my future husband, Lloyd. We have now been married for twenty-seven years and have a son, Dan, who is twenty-three, and a nineteen-year-

Sonia Levitin

old daughter, Shari. We have so much fun together. We like to travel and discuss new ideas. Lloyd encourages me with my writing. It was he who suggested, after I had already graduated from college and was teaching, that I return to school. I did go back and studied writing with Walter Van Tilburg Clark, a wonderful writer and teacher.

At first I wrote stories and articles. A number of them were published in magazines. It was twelve years before my first book was published. After that, I had found my niche. I wrote fourteen children's books in the next ten years. Several of them won awards.

I never write with any particular audience in mind. I write what I am feeling, what I am excited about. When I am composing at the typewriter I feel like an actor playing all the parts in a stage play. I become completely entranced—that is on a good day. On bad days I struggle to write a single page.

While I am writing, my pets are usually nearby. Presently we have only one German Shepherd and one cat. I'm sure our menagerie will grow again.

Last year I published my first adult novel,

and I plan to continue in this field, as well as writing more children's books. Writing is very hard work. It is also the best work in the world. Through writing I feel in touch with the world, and I also get to know myself better.

———

Sonia Levitin attended the University of California at Berkeley from 1952 to 1954 and received her B.S. degree from the University of Pennsylvania in 1956. She also attended San Francisco State University as a graduate student.

She was married in 1953. She has been a junior high school teacher, an adult education teacher in Americanization, history, and writing, and writer-in-residence at the Palos Verdes School District. She is a member of P.E.N. and the Society of Children's Book Writers, and founded the Moraga Historical Society with her husband. She has published articles in *Smithsonian Magazine, Ingenue, The Writer,* and *Scholastic.*

Journey to America won the National Jewish Book Award for 1970 and was named an American Library Association Notable Book in 1970; it was also a Junior Literary Guild selection. *Who Owns the Moon?* was also an ALA Notable Book, in 1973. *Roanoke: A Novel of the Lost Colony* was nominated for the Dorothy Canfield Fisher Award.

The No-Return Trail, a Junior Literary Guild selection, won a Lewis Carroll Shelf Award and the Western Writers of America Golden Spur Award in 1978. The Southern California Council on Literature for Children and Young People named *The Mark of Conte* a Notable Book of Fiction in 1977 and honored Levitin for her Distinguished Contribution to the Field of Children's Literature, for the body of her work, in 1981.

SELECTED WORKS: Journey to America, 1970; Rita the Weekend Rat, 1971; Roanoke: A Novel of the Lost Colony, 1973; Who Owns the Moon?, 1973; Jason and the Money Tree, 1974; The Mark of Conte, 1976; Beyond Another Door, 1977; The No-Return Trail, 1978; The Year of Sweet Senior Insanity, 1982.

ABOUT: Contemporary Authors (First Revision), Vol. 29–32; Something About the Author, Vol. 4; Ward, Martha E. and Dorothy A. Marquardt. Authors of Books for Young People, 2nd edition (Supplement).

MYRON LEVOY

AUTHOR OF *Alan and Naomi,* etc.

Biographical sketch of Myron Levoy:

BORN IN New York City, Myron Levoy, in addition to writing for children and adults, has worked as a chemical engineer in the fields of heat transfer and space propulsion. He holds an M.Sc. from Purdue University. One of the scientific projects he was involved in was the design of a manned space flight to Mars, which, as Levoy says, "obviously never got off the ground."

Levoy's first two books for children were published in 1972: *Penny Tunes and Princesses,* illustrated by the late Ezra Jack Keats, and *The Witch of Fourth Street,* illustrated by Gabriel Lisowski. The latter, a collection of stories about an immigrant neighborhood of New York City "many years ago," has proven to be a continuing favorite among children. It was a featured title on cable television's READIT children's book discussion program in 1983, and appeared in the 1973 Children's Book Showcase exhibit. Ethel Heins wrote in the *Horn Book* that these "tales and characters are highly original, sometimes humorous, sometimes poignant, and often profound." Writing in *Washington Post Book World,* Natalie Babbitt called *The Witch of Fourth Street* "a first book for children by a first-rate writer."

Levoy's next book, *Alan and Naomi,* also concerned an immigrant: Naomi, a shell-shocked, mentally disturbed young refugee from World War II France. Alan is an American Jewish boy who tries to help Naomi come back to reality, to make her realize the Nazis will never come for her and her family again. Critics praised Levoy's sensitive and realistic handling of a difficult sub-ject. As Milton Meltzer wrote in the *New York Times,* "This is no easy success story, for in the end [Alan's] work is destroyed by the cruelty of an anti-Semitic boy. This is a fine example of honest, compassionate writing about personal responsibility." *Alan and Naomi* was an American Book Award finalist in the paperback fiction category and an Honor Book for the Boston Globe-Horn Book Award. Popular in Germany, *Alan and Naomi* has also been awarded four prizes in Europe, including the Buxtehuder Bulle Award in West Germany, since its translation into Dutch and German.

Levoy's latest book, *Shadow Like a Leopard,* also takes place in New York City, but it is a contemporary novel about the friendship between Ramon, a young street tough, and a wheelchair-bound old man, a painter. It was named a Best Book for Young Adults by the American Library Association in 1981.

In addition to his books for children and young adults, Myron Levoy has written poetry and short stories for such magazines as *Massachusetts Review* and *Antioch Review.* Several of his plays have been produced in experimental and Off Broadway theaters in New York, and he has written an adult novel, *A Necktie in Greenwich Village.* The father of two grown children, Levoy now lives in Rockaway, New Jersey, with his wife, a junior high school teacher. He plans to continue writing in both juvenile and adult areas, but is no longer working as an engineer, "unless it creeps into my fiction."

SELECTED WORKS: Penny Tunes and Princesses, 1972; The Witch of Fourth Street and Other Stories, 1972; Alan and Naomi, 1977; A Shadow Like a Leopard, 1981.

ABOUT: Contemporary Authors, Vol. 93-96; Ward, Martha E. and Dorothy A. Marquardt. Authors of Books for Young People, 2nd edition (Supplement).

ELIZABETH LEVY

April 4, 1942–

AUTHOR OF *Lizzie Lies a Lot,* etc.

Elizabeth a. Levy

Autobiographical sketch of Elizabeth Levy:

ODDLY ENOUGH, my first published
work was a lie. When I was in the third
grade, a newspaper printed my poem,
"When I grow up/ I want to be a nurse all
dressed in white." I didn't want to be a
nurse. If I wanted to be anything, I wanted
to be a writer, but the idea of being a writer
seemed a fantasy. I grew up without any
concrete ambitions, but with an entire card
catalog of fantasies. Even though I enjoyed
school and took great pleasure in writing
short stories, it never occurred to me to
write for a living.

I was born on April 4, 1942, and I grew
up at a time when little girls were not asked
what they wanted to be. It was assumed
that we would be wives and mothers, and
that work would not be important. I would
like to think of myself as a feminist before
her time, a little rebel like Jackie in *Nice Little Girls*. I wasn't. But my characters can be.
I hate to confess that in the first draft of my
mystery, *Something Queer Is Going On,* the
lead character was male. Then I said to myself, "just because it's an inquisitive, active
character, why should it be a boy?" and
Gwen started to tap her braces.

After graduating from Pembroke College
in 1964, I came to New York and became
a researcher for ABC news. The job paid
very little, but it was a lot of fun. Unfortunately, they made it quite clear that "girls"
were not supposed to become reporters, and
after a while, I found the work less and less
satisfying.

I started writing professionally quite by
accident. I met someone who published
readers, the collection of stories sold to
schools to teach kids to read. He asked me
if I wanted to try to write a children's story
using a limited number of words. He
bought my story, and I began writing more
and more. Eventually I decided to see if I
could support myself on my writing. Looking back, I can see that was a key, if crazy,
decision. Once writing became my only
means of support, I had to take it seriously
and take myself more seriously.

I write for a wide variety of ages and
write both fiction and nonfiction. One of
the great joys of my work is that I can
switch from novels like *Lizzie Lies a Lot* and
Come Out Smiling to mysteries and adventure series like the *Something Queer* books,
Running Out of Time, or *Jody and Jake* series. The books I write reflect the kinds of
books I like to read. I read a tremendous
number of mysteries and thrillers, inter-
spersed with occasional books of weightier
concern.

In reading about authors, I'm always impressed when they talk about losing themselves in their work, shutting off the phone,
and closing the door to family and friends.
I lose myself in everything but my writing.
Even paying bills can seem like a treat.
When writing I act like a person whose
chair was bought at an auction from a fun
house, one that pinches you whenever you
sit down. I pace and stare out of the window
and rarely lose myself for more than a paragraph. Since I actually love to write, I'm
hard put to explain why it is so difficult to
stay in my chair, I only know it is. I usually
start writing early in the morning and end
around two in the afternoon. I tend to work

from Monday to Friday, and only occasionally work on weekends.

When I write for children, I am really writing about things that seem funny or interesting to me now. I don't think writing a good book for children is different from writing one for adults. The emotions we have as children are as complex as those we have as adults.

I think about my own childhood a lot, and when I write about a certain age, I have very vivid memories of what it felt like then. I think that memories from childhood are like dreams. It's not important to remember all of them, but what you do remember is important.

———

Born in Buffalo, New York, Elizabeth Levy attended Pembroke College, graduating in 1964. She received her M.A.T. degree from Columbia University in 1968 and taught social studies. She has worked at Macmillan Publishing Company, Inc., in New York as well as at the New York Public Library, where she was a writer in the public relations department. She is a member of the Authors League of America and the Mystery Writers of America. She has also written several plays, produced in small theaters in New York in 1976 and 1977.

Her *Something Queer at the Ballpark* was a Junior Literary Guild selection, and *Before You Were Three* was an alternate selection of the Book-of-the-Month Club. *Struggle and Lose, Struggle and Win* was named an Outstanding Book of the Year by the *New York Times* in 1977.

SELECTED WORKS: Something Queer Is Going On, 1973; Nice Little Girls, 1974; Something Queer at the Ballpark, 1975; Lizzie Lies a Lot, 1976; Struggle and Lose, Struggle and Win: The United Mineworkers Union (with Tad Richards), 1977; Before You Were Three: How You Began to Walk, Talk, Explore, and Have Feelings (with Robie H. Harris), 1977; Frankenstein Moved in on the Fourth Floor, 1979; The Tryouts, 1979; Politicians for the People: Six Who Stand for Change, (with Mara Miller), 1980; Running Out of Time, 1980; Come Out Smiling, 1981; Something Queer at the Haunted School, 1982; Dracula Is a Pain in the Neck, 1983; The Shadow Nose, 1983.

ABOUT: Contemporary Authors, Vol. 77-80; Ward, Martha E. and Dorothy A. Marquardt. Authors of Books for Young People, 2nd edition (Supplement).

JOAN LINGARD

AUTHOR OF *The Twelfth of July,* etc.

Autobiographical sketch of Joan Lingard:

I WAS BORN in Edinburgh, Scotland, of a Scottish mother and English father, but at the age of two went to live in Belfast where I stayed until I was eighteen, so all my formative years were spent in that city. This is reflected in my writing. I would say, in fact, that it is reflected in my life also, for the experiences, sights, sounds, and smells of childhood are so intense that they stay with one forever afterwards.

As a child I was crazy about books. I could never get enough to read. My own life seemed too limited; I wanted to cross frontiers, live in the country, at the sea, in the city, climb the Himalayas, track down smugglers, go up the Amazon in pursuit of Colonel Fawcett. One way to do it was through books. When I read, I inhabited different worlds, lived inside different skins.

One day when I had nothing new to read and had read everything in the house at least six times over, my mother, fed up no doubt by the sound of my complaining, turned to me and said, "Why don't you write your own books?" I went away and thought about it and it didn't seem like such a bad idea, so I got lined, foolscap paper, filled my fountain pen with green ink (terribly suitable for a writer, I considered), and began. I wrote about a girl called Gail who did track down smugglers, in Cornwall, in the South-West of England. I had never been to Cornwall then. When I finished I copied the whole thing out again in a exercise book, made a wrapper, illustrated it, wrote the blurb, and on the back put BOOKS BY JOAN LINGARD and underneath wrote my first title, *Gail*. At the bottom I

Joan Lingard

printed PUBLISHED BY LINGARD AND CO. My career as a writer had gotten under way. I was eleven years old. From then on I had only one ambition, as regards a career anyway.

All the books that I wrote as a child were set in places that I had never visited. I didn't write a word about Belfast. Dull dreary old Belfast. What could happen there that would be interesting or exciting enough to make a book out of? It was only when I came into my twenties that I realised that I would write convincingly when I knew the backgrounds and people well.

I published six adult novels before writing my first children's one, *The Twelfth Day of July,* about a Protestant girl called Sadie and a Catholic boy called Kevin. Subsequently I wrote another four books about them, going with them through seven crucial years of their lives. Letters talking about Sadie and Kevin come to me from all over the world.

I live now in Edinburgh with my Canadian husband, who lectures in architecture at Edinburgh University, and my youngest daughter Jenny, who is seventeen. My other daughters Bridget (nineteen) and Kersten (twenty) are students in England. I contin-

ue to write novels for both adults and young people, as well as plays for television. A serial in eighteen episodes based on a quartet of my books about a Glasgow girl called Maggie is currently showing on BBC TV. I like travelling very much and I still enjoy reading other people's books.

———

Joan Lingard attended Bloomfield Collegiate School in Belfast and at the age of eighteen returned to her birthplace, Edinburgh, to train as a teacher. She received a General Certificate of Education from Moray House Training College and taught school from 1953 to 1961.

Lingard has adapted her "Maggie quartet" (*The Clearance, The Resettling, The Pilgrimage,* and *The Reunion*) into a television series, first shown in England by the BBC in 1981.

The File on Fraulein Berg is called by the author her most biographical novel so far, though the events did not occur exactly as they were in the book; but there was a teacher at her school who was followed by some girls who suspected her of being a Nazi.

Strangers in the House was a Junior Literary Guild selection.

SELECTED WORKS: The Twelfth Day of July, 1972; Across the Barricades, 1973; Into Exile, 1973; The Clearance, 1974; A Proper Place, 1975; The Resettling, 1976; Hostages to Fortune, 1977; The Pilgrimage, 1977; The Reunion, 1978; The File on Fraulein Berg, 1980; Strangers in the House, 1983.

ABOUT: The Author's and Writer's Who's Who, 1971; Contemporary Authors (First Revision), Vol. 41–44; Kirkpatrick, D. L. Twentieth-Century Children's Writers; Something About the Author, Vol. 8; Ward, Martha E. and Dorothy A. Marquardt. Authors of Books for Young People, 2nd edition (Supplement); The Writers Directory 1982–84.

ROBERT LIPSYTE

January 16, 1938–

AUTHOR OF *The Contender,* etc.

Autobiographical sketch of Robert Lipsyte:

I WAS BORN in New York City. Both my parents were teachers and the house overflowed with books. Because I was very fat until I was fourteen, I spent most of my free time reading or writing; I'd decided early to become a writer because a writer could hide behind a typewriter and control the universe.

The three writers who had the greatest impact on my growing up were Richard Halliburton, John Steinbeck, and J. D. Salinger. Halliburton, author of *The Royal Road to Romance* among other travel books, introduced me to the author as hero; first, you swim the roiling croc-infested waters, then you write about it. *Cannery Row* was the first Steinbeck novel I read, and then I read and reread every other one. His compassion for people, his sense of place, and his love for nature overwhelmed me. Although I never tried to emulate his style or subjects, he was my early role model as a writer. I read Salinger's *The Catcher in the Rye* when I was fourteen. It was a portable support group. Here was a character, intelligent, sensitive, real, who was crazier than I was. But only by degree. And he was

speaking directly to me. Later, I would come to appreciate Salinger as the quintessential dedicated, driven artist of my time.

After I was graduated from Columbia College in 1957, I decided to attend graduate school in California, where I would seek my fortune as a writer. I even sent my dorm deposit. But I never made it. I had taken a job as copy boy in the sports department of the *New York Times*. I planned to stay only for the summer. I hadn't planned to fall in love with journalism. The summer lasted fourteen years.

I arrived at an exciting time; the sports boom had just begun. In the next fourteen years I traveled around the world, covered every major sport and every major event, won a number of prizes and eventually became an internationally syndicated sports columnist.

In 1965, in Las Vegas to cover a prizefight, I heard an old boxing manager tell about three flights of dark, twisting steps that led up to his gym. Haunted by the image, I wrote my first novel for young people, *The Contender,* which won the Child Study Children's Book Committee at Bank Street College Award for 1967. The pleasure of writing that book and the wonderful response from readers were important factors in my leaving daily journalism in 1971 to devote myself to writing books.

Since then, I've written a number of adult books, movie and television scripts, radio commentaries, and even some more newspaper columns, but the novel for and about adolescents has become the heart and soul of my work.

One Fat Summer, whose hero, Bobby Marks, lost fifty pounds one summer, as I did, was the first novel of my fifties trilogy. The others were *Summer Rules,* published in 1981, and *The Summerboy,* published in 1982. *Jock and Jill,* published the same year, draws heavily on my sports background, as does the nonfiction *Free to Be Muhammad Ali.*

I'm married to the novelist Marjorie Lipsyte, whom I met while we both worked at the *Times*. We have two children and we live in northern New Jersey.

———

Robert Lipsyte received his M.S. degree from the Columbia School of Journalism in 1959. He has written five books for adults, including *Nigger,* which he wrote with Dick Gregory in 1964. He is now a commentator for National Public Radio. In 1966 he received the Mike Berger Award for distinguished reporting.

In addition to the Child Study award, *The Contender* was named a Notable Book by the American Library Association in 1967 and a Notable Book for the years 1940–1970. *One Fat Summer* was named an ALA Best Book for Young Adults in 1977 and an Outstanding Children's Book of the year 1977 by the *New York Times*.

SELECTED WORKS: The Contender, 1967; One Fat Summer, 1977; Free to Be Muhammad Ali, 1978; Summer Rules, 1981; Jock and Jill, 1982; The Summerboy, 1982.

ABOUT: Contemporary Authors (First Revision), Vol. 17–20; Something About the Author, Vol. 5; Ward, Martha E. and Dorothy A. Marquardt. Authors of Books for Young People, 2nd edition (Supplement).

LOIS LOWRY

March 20, 1937–

AUTHOR OF *A Summer to Die,* etc.

Autobiographical sketch of Lois Lowry:

I WAS BORN in 1937, in Honolulu, Hawaii. Occasionally that prompts someone to say, "Gee, you don't look Hawaiian." That is the kind of person I drift away from at cocktail parties.

My father was a career army officer, so like all army brats I had no real home, but moved from place to place during my growing-up years. I went through junior high school in Tokyo (and gee, I don't look Japanese, either), and still remember a few

phrases in that language, which I spoke fairly well at age twelve. I remember things like "Where is the bathroom" and "My left leg hurts," which will come in handy if I am ever in an accident in Yokohama, at least if the accident leaves me with a sprained knee and a bruised kidney.

I went to Brown University at seventeen to major in writing, and left there at nineteen to get married, this being the fifties when romance and domesticity took precedence over literacy.

The marriage did not last, but the four children—now grown—did, and their escapades during childhood and adolesence have provided me with enough material to write books for young people for countless years to come. I began writing when they were kids, after going back to get my college degree, so there were a number of years when there was a well-worn path between the typewriter and the washing machine. The first money I ever earned went to hire a housekeeper, and whenever I am asked if there was any one person who influenced my career, I make a short speech of tribute to a Czechoslovakian woman named Marga, who for years dealt with my children's lost sneakers and vacuumed around a soporific Newfoundland dog.

Now the dog has gone to the Great Kennel in the Sky, and the kids: Alix, Grey, Kristin, and Ben, are scattered here and there around the United States. Another speech of tribute goes to Bell Telephone, which allows offspring to call Mom collect, and to Hallmark Cards, which invented Mother's Day to remind them to do so.

I live now in Boston, on Beacon Hill, in an apartment that overlooks the Charles River and the buildings of M.I.T. and Harvard. My apartment houses the requisite furniture and an inordinate number of books; a 1908 diploma from a School of Embalming, which I found at an antique shop once; paintings by artist friends; and all the records Billie Holiday ever made. Hanging from my dining room ceiling is a piece of tumbleweed sent to me by young fans in Idaho, and on top of a lamp in my study is a hat, decorated with all the titles of my books, given to me by the seventh graders in Boylston, Massachusetts. My bed is covered with a patchwork quilt made by my great-great grandmother.

I hate writing autobiography, except when I can disguise it, as I have in a couple of books, as fiction. I wish I could have hired Woody Allen to write this.

———

Lois Lowry finished her B.A. degree in 1972 at the University of Maine, where she also did some graduate study. She is a photographer who specializes in photographing children, and a writer of textbooks like *Black American Literature* (1973) and *Literature of the American Revolution* (1974). She has had articles published in magazines including *Redbook, Yankee,* and *Downeast.*

Her first novel, *A Summer to Die,* is an unsentimental story of a thirteen-year-old girl who loves and resents her older sister, and who learns that the sister is dying. It won the International Reading Association Children's Book Award for 1978, and was placed on the *School Library Journal* "Best of the Best 1966-1978" list (December 1979).

Four of Lowry's books have been named American Library Association Notable Books, each in their year of publication: *A Summer to Die, Autumn Street, Anastasia Krupnik,* and *Anastasia Again!* In 1983, *Anastasia Again!* was nominated for an American Book Award in the paperback children's fiction category.

SELECTED WORKS: A Summer to Die, 1977; Find a Stranger, Say Good-bye, 1978; Anastasia Krupnik, 1979; Autumn Street, 1980; Anastasia Again!, 1981; The One Hundredth Thing About Caroline, 1983; Taking Care of Terrific, 1983.

ABOUT: Contemporary Authors, Vol. 69-72; Something About the Author, Vol. 23; Ward, Martha E. and Dorothy A. Marquardt. Authors of Books for Young People, 2nd edition (Supplement).

DAVID MACAULAY

December 2, 1946–

AUTHOR AND ILLUSTRATOR OF *Cathedral,* etc.

Biographical sketch of David Alexander Macaulay:

DAVID MACAULAY was born in Burton-on-Trent, England. As a young boy, living in Lancashire, he was fascinated with simple technology. Out of cigar boxes, string, and tape, he constructed elevators; out of yarn, intricate systems of moving cable cars. At a very early age, he became interested in the way things worked and how objects were constructed. He was eleven when his parents moved from England to Bloomfield, New Jersey, and he found himself having to adjust from a lyrical English childhood to life in a fast-paced American city.

During this period of change, he began to draw seriously. So exciting did he find this process that he undertook undergraduate education at the Rhode Island School of Design (RISD), eventually receiving a bachelor's degree in architecture in 1969 and spending his fifth year of study in the Euro-

DAVID MACAULAY

pean Honors Program in Rome, Herculaneum, and Pompeii. After a short period of time working for an interior designer, as a junior high school teacher, and as a teacher at RISD, he began to experiment with creating books on his own. One of his first ideas for a book, depicting a gargoyle beauty pageant, was submitted to an editor who was impressed by the picture of a gargoyle against the Notre Dame Cathedral. This led to discussions about cathedrals and architecture, and soon Macaulay was off to Amiens, France, to make sketches for his first book, *Cathedral.*

Since then he has created a series of books on various architectural subjects—the construction of a Roman city (*City*), the erection of the monuments to the pharaohs (*Pyramid*), the building of medieval fortresses (*Castle*), and the evolution of the architecture of nineteenth-century New England mills (*Mill*). As the trip to France indicates, a great deal of work precedes all of Macaulay's books. Initially, he reads widely from all available sources, then spends much time traveling to photograph details that he will later draw. For *Pyramid,* he climbed the Great Pyramid at Cheops to get a sense of the vistas from various points

on the Pyramid's side. He spent weeks climbing down manholes to record material for *Underground,* and hours with experts in demolition firms to gather accurate information for *Unbuilding.*

David Macaulay's work defies definition by standard categories—fiction or nonfiction, for children or adults. Of his two books published for adults in the late 1970s, *Motel of the Mysteries* and *Great Moments in Architecture, Motel* has become a favorite in junior and senior high schools; of his books published for children, *Underground* is a standard work for many architectural firms, and *Cathedral* and *Castle* are used as college texts. The books are basically informational in nature, since he wants to show the evolution of a typical structure, but the text is always fictional. His technique of using the invented or imagined to present accurate information is most dramatically realized in *Unbuilding,* in which Macaulay depicts the step-by-step demolition of the Empire State Building in the year 1989. So realistic is the treatment and so believable the text that the publisher received letters stating that the date of demolition was a typographical error and should be changed in the next edition.

Although David Macaulay admires the work of Maurice Sendak, Milton Glaser, and G. B. Piranesi and his architectural fantasies, his work is clearly his own. He has developed a unique approach to what can be communicated in a book, one that has won him worldwide recognition. *Cathedral* was awarded the German Jugenbuchpreis and the Dutch Silver Slate Pencil Award. It was a 1974 Caldecott Honor Book and a *New York Times* Choice of Best Illustrated Children's Books of the Year 1973. It was included in the 1974 Children's Book Showcase and the American Institute of Graphic Arts 1973–1974 exhibit. *City* was also included in the 1975 Children's Book Showcase.

Pyramid won a 1975 Christopher Medal and was named an Outstanding Children's Book of the Year 1975 by the *New York*

Times. It was also a Boston Globe-Horn Book Award Honor Book in 1976. *Underground* was named a *New York Times* Outstanding Children's Book of the Year 1976 and appeared on the *School Library Journal* "Best of the Best 1966–1978" list (December 1979). *Castle* was a 1978 Caldecott Honor Book and was a Boston Globe-Horn Book Award Honor Book in 1978. It also received honorable mention in the New York Academy of Sciences Children's Science Book Awards in 1977. *Unbuilding* won honorable mention in 1980 from the New York Academy of Sciences Awards and was named a *New York Times* Choice of Best Illustrated Children's Books of the Year 1980. Many of Macaulay's books have been named Notable Books by the American Library Association: *Cathedral* in 1973, *City* in 1974, *Pyramid* in 1975, *Underground* in 1976, and *Castle* in 1977.

David Macaulay was awarded the Washington Children's Book Guild Nonfiction Award in 1977 and has been chosen as the United States nominee for a Hans Christian Andersen Award. In 1977, the American Institute of Architects presented him with their medal for his contribution as "an outstanding illustrator and recorder of architectural accomplishment." *Time Magazine* said, "What he draws . . . he draws better than any other pen-and-ink illustrator in the world."

Macaulay lives in Providence, Rhode Island, with his wife, whom he married in 1978. He has a daughter from his first marriage.

SELECTED WORKS WRITTEN AND ILLUSTRATED: Cathedral: The Story of Its Construction, 1973; City: A Story of Roman Planning and Construction, 1974; Pyramid, 1975; Underground, 1976; Castle, 1977; Unbuilding, 1980; Mill, 1983.

SELECTED WORKS ILLUSTRATED: Help! Let Me Out!, by David Lord Porter, 1982.

ABOUT: Contemporary Authors, Vol. 53–56; (New Revision Series), Vol. 5; Kingman, Lee and others, comps. Illustrators of Children's Books: 1967–1976; Pitz, Henry C. 200 Years of American Illustration; Something About the Author, Vol. 27; Ward, Martha E. and Dorothy A. Marquardt. Authors of Books for Young People, 2nd edition (Supplement); Who's Who in America, 1982–1983; Who's Who in American Art, 1980; The Writers Directory 1982–84; Abitare May 1977; Art Express May–June 1981; Children's Literature in Education Spring 1977; Language Arts April 1982; New York Magazine December 16, 1974; Print February 1982; Publishers Weekly April 10, 1978; Top of the News April 1974.

JAN MARK

June 22, 1943–

AUTHOR OF *Thunder and Lightnings,* etc.

Autobiographical sketch of Jan Mark:

MY EVERY childhood experience was accompanied by a simultaneous translation into third-person narrative. I immediately turned the most trivial event into a story, often while it was still taking place, and as I had learned to write at the age of four, I was fortunate in that by the time I was old enough to make up stories, I could also write quickly enough to enjoy putting them down on paper. I was not discriminating about my use of the medium. I wrote plays, poems, short stories, novellas, quite arbitrarily, but with an eye to the future; one day, I thought, I would certainly publish *something,* preferably while I was still at school, to the amazement of all who knew me. I was hell-bent on being a prodigy. The same idea occurred to me at art school. I wrote fragments of a novel. So did everyone else. We were all writing the same novel and nobody's effort, to my knowledge, ever got into print or even as far as the last page. After this, during which time I gained a diploma in stone carving—of no subsequent use whatsoever except as background material for *The Ennead*—I taught Art and English for six years in a secondary school. (I recently met someone who gave up banking and became a teacher because he thought it would give him time to write: deluded fool.) I had little energy to spare for either writing or reading during those six years, an

academic desert, in retrospect; what a pleasing paradox. However, I did write two plays for the students, and thereby learned a valuable lesson in technique of which I was quite unaware at the time and which became apparent only recently. Our kids were overwhelming personalities, able to project a powerful presence across the footlights, possessed of carrying voices and with an impressive vocabulary of verbal and facial expression, but in no way could they be described as actors. It was no use writing dialogue and expecting them to interpret it. I had to write lines that approximated as nearly as possible the way in which they actually spoke. I thus learned, unknowingly, to develop an ear for spoken English and to transcribe it, producing that curious hybrid known as realistic dialogue. Written and spoken English being two separate and distinct languages, there is no such thing as realistic dialogue in narrative prose, but the ability to make people think that they are reading it is a craft, if not a confidence trick, and nothing flatters me more than to be told that I have mastered it. The other requisite for our plays was the inclusion of at least one fight, preferably one fight in each act, so that the cast could act naturally.

By now I had a husband and a two-year-old daughter. We left the South of England where we had all three been born, and moved to East Anglia, settling in an isolated village near the Norfolk coast and, although we did not notice it until the day after purchase was completed, on the flight path of the nearest air base, into which flew the BAC Lightning jet interceptor/fighter, with thunderous regularity. Shortly afterwards my son was born and about that time I noticed an advertisement in the *Guardian* newspaper for a competition to find a new children's novel, with a twentieth-century setting, by a previously unpublished author. Now over thirty, I wrote *Thunder and Lightings,* my first book, at last, and it won the competition. I still turn cold when I think how nearly it might not have happened. The competition might have been advertised a year earlier. I might not have been a *Guardian* reader. I might have been working, with no time to write. I might not have been living in a place where my subject matter was passing overhead at predictable intervals. I might have given up before it was finished—I very nearly did, many times; but for once I was in the right place at the right time, doing the right thing. The book that I wrote was the right book. I have been writing professionally ever since.

———

Jan Mark was born in Welwyn, England. She received her college degree from the Canterbury College of Art in 1965.

Thunder and Lightnings won the Carnegie Medal in 1976 as well as the Penguin/*Guardian* Award, in 1975. It was named a Notable Book by the American Library Association.

The Ennead was on the 1978 list of Notable Children's Trade Books in the Field of Social Studies, which were selected by a joint committee of the National Council for the Social Studies and the Children's Book Council.

SELECTED WORKS: The Ennead, 1978; Thunder and

Lightnings, 1979; Under the Autumn Garden, 1979; Divide and Rule, 1980; Nothing to Be Afraid Of, 1982.

ABOUT: Contemporary Authors, Vol. 93-96; Something About the Author, Vol. 22; The Writers Directory 1982-84.

HARRY MAZER

May 31, 1925–

AUTHOR OF *Snowbound,* etc.

Autobiographical sketch of Harry Mazer:

WHEN I WAS growing up I knew no writers. My parents didn't write. My father read, but there were few books in the house. There were no writers or professionals anywhere in my family among my cousins, aunts, and uncles. They were immigrants, Polish and Russian Jews, first-generation Americans. One uncle was a housepainter, another peddled candy and cigarettes, another had a clothing store. My father worked in a factory making dresses. On my mother's side one aunt ran a chicken farm, another was a secretary, and my mother, like my father, worked in a dress factory.

I feel—I've always felt—that I write and speak with difficulty. I am a writer not because this is something I do well—an inborn talent—but perhaps for the opposite reason, because I do it so poorly. Whatever I've done as a writer I've done despite the feeling that I have no natural talent. I've never felt articulate or fluent, rarely felt that flow of language that marks the writer.

Become a writer? I could hardly dream of it. I was a reader. As a boy my plan was to read my way through the library, starting with the letter *A*. My father thought I was ruining my eyes reading so much. As for my friends, they were mostly interested in science. One was going to be an electrical engineer, another a chemist, a third a dentist. I said I'd be a scientist and went to the Bronx High School of Science.

For many years I didn't write (I don't count school writing). I was young. I

HARRY MAZER

dreamed of making the world a better place. I met Norma Fox. She loved books, she was beautiful, and she wrote. (Did I know then that she would help me turn to writing?) For a time, our interest in each other, the family, the children, and work filled our lives. I was a husband, a father, a provider. I worked as a longshoreman, a railroad worker, a welder, an iron worker— even an English teacher. But more and more I was dissatisfied with the work I did.

"What do you really want to do?" Norma asked me one day. "If you could do exactly what you wanted?"

"Be a writer?" I smiled because the idea was so absurd. Write? What had I ever written? What did I have to write about? And who was going to support us and our three kids, while I learned?

But something changed that day. We talked late into the night, earnestly, practically. It wasn't just me. Norma wanted to write seriously, too. If we didn't let ourselves get discouraged, didn't set ourselves impossible goals, if we wrote a little each day, then in time, maybe we would be writers.

When we first began to write, our desks were jammed into a converted back porch bedroom next to the kitchen. Our children—there were three and then four—slept in the main part of the house. For one year we got up at three in the morning and worked at our desks, back to back, so crowded our chairs touched. In the winter we wrapped our legs in blankets to keep out the cold. At seven when we heard the kids stirring, Norma went out to make breakfast and I went to work in the factory where I was a welder.

I always wanted to write a survival story, loved them ever since I'd read *Robinson Crusoe* as a boy. I had a folder of articles about plane crashes, people floating in the ocean, trapped in desolate places, buried alive.

On one level all my stories beginning with *Guy Lenny* and *Snowbound* are survival stories. I am a survivor, have the survivor's mentality. Maybe because I'm Jewish . . . grew up during the Depression . . . the Second World War . . . maybe because I was shot down during World War II. (My book *The Last Mission* is based on that experience.) Survivors take nothing for granted, expect the worst, persist. . . . It's an uncertain world. We all live in the shadow of a holocaust so vast it's beyond our powers to comprehend. There is no end to uncertainty, especially for the young. What if? . . . What will I do? . . . Will I be ready? I write my stories with the hope that they have something to say to young readers about the qualities needed to live today, indeed, to live in any time.

———

Harry Mazer and his wife, the children's book author Norma Fox Mazer, live in upstate New York, in the country outside of Syracuse. Before his work was published, he worked as a bus driver and assembled springs at an automobile manufacturing plant at Green Island, New York, as well as the other work he mentions. When not at his desk, and depending on the season, he enjoys playing racquetball, gardening, or sailing in Canada.

Snowbound was made into an After School Special for television in 1978. It was published in Germany, France, and Finland. *The Solid Gold Kid* was named a Children's Choice book of 1974 by a joint committee of the International Reading Association and the Children's Book Council. *The Last Mission* was named an Outstanding Book of the Year 1979 by the *New York Times* and a Best Children's Book of the Year 1979 by the *New York Times Book Review*.

The Island Keeper was a Junior Literary Guild selection. Four of Mazer's books have been named Best Books for Young Adults by the American Library Association: *The Solid Gold Kid* (which he wrote with Norma Fox Mazer) in 1974, *The War on Villa Street* in 1978, *The Last Mission* in 1979, and *I Love You, Stupid!* in 1981.

SELECTED WORKS: Guy Lenny, 1972; Snowbound, 1973; The Dollar Man, 1974; (with Norma Fox Mazer) The Solid Gold Kid, 1974; The War on Villa Street, 1978; The Last Mission, 1979; The Island Keeper, 1981; I Love You, Stupid!, 1981.

ABOUT: Contemporary Authors, Vol. 97–100.

NORMA FOX MAZER

May 15, 1931–

AUTHOR OF *A Figure of Speech*, etc.

Autobiographical sketch of Norma Fox Mazer:

I GREW UP, the middle of three sisters, in a small town in the foothills of the Adirondack Mountains. My father drove a bread truck, my mother worked as a saleslady. My maternal grandparents, Jewish immigrants from Poland, started a bakery which, later on, one of my uncles took over. A vivid childhood memory: walking home from the bakery in the cold blue dusk eating a hot roll. The kindergarten I attended had a fishpond; I had taught myself to read and my first grade teacher loved me. In return for these epiphanies, I loved school.

Norma Fox Mazer

I played marbles with the boys, read everything possible between covers, and longed for my mother to be more like Marmie in *Little Women* and for myself to have "adventures."

Rhubarb grew wild alongside a garage, and we ate the red stems raw, puckering our lips. I got pennies now and then for the candy store and walked past a shabby bike repair shop every day on my way to school. Winter meant galoshes, King of the Hill of snow, and nostrils fragile as glass from twenty-below-zero temperatures. I ice-skated behind my school, but my ankles always collapsed.

I took violin lessons and drew screeches from the strings. For several weeks I toted home a bass fiddle far larger than I. Next came clarinet lessons. My teacher went into the Army, promising that his successor would look up the pupils with "promise." I never took another music lesson. Playing a game of some sort that I had made up, a girlfriend said to me, "What an imagination!" For the first time I sensed that that part of me that created witches in bathroom doorknobs and monsters creeping up the stairs to catch me asleep might be an asset. After that I lived in something of a dream. I had decided I wanted to be a writer.

In junior and senior high, I gravitated to the school newspaper. My English compositions drew praise. Yet no one ever said to me, as I say now to any aspiring writer, *Write. Write letters. Keep a journal. Only write something every day. Don't ever write what you think you ought to write, but only what you feel, think, and observe for yourself.*

Despite my dreams I was practical. I thought of becoming a social worker or a teacher. What I did become, not too many years after leaving high school, was married and then a mother. I never stopped dreaming. *Someday, when I'm a writer. . . .* My progress from dreamer to writer is marked in my mind by the stages of my children's growth. I kept notes on my first daughter's babyhood; made clumsy attempts at short stories during my son's infancy; wrote long letters about all of them after my second daughter was born; knuckled down to writing an-hour-a-day-no-matter-what about the time she was two years old; and shortly after the birth of my third daughter became a full-time free-lance writer. I was hesitant, frightened, unsure. I lacked confidence and had only a deep abiding desire to do this thing. My husband took his plunge into free-lance writing at the same time, and together we supported each other and our family.

I read every day and I write every day— both seem as necessary to my well-being as food and sleep. The more I write, the more I understand that I will rarely, if ever, write well enough to please myself, and yet the more I love it and the more privileged I feel to do this as my daily work.

———

Norma Fox Mazer grew up in Glens Falls, New York. She went to school at both Antioch College and Syracuse University. She has four children, three girls and a boy.

When We First Met is a sequel to *A Figure of Speech*, which was nominated for a National Book Award in 1974. *Saturday, the*

Twelfth of October won a Lewis Carroll Shelf Award in 1975. *Dear Bill, Remember Me? and Other Stories* won a Christopher Award in 1976 and was named an Outstanding Book of the Year 1976 by the *New York Times* and a Best Book for Young Adults by the American Library Association.

Taking Terri Mueller, which was first published in paperback and subsequently came out in hardcover, won the 1981 Edgar Allan Poe Award for best juvenile mystery.

SELECTED WORKS: I, Trissy, 1971; A Figure of Speech, 1973; Saturday, the Twelfth of October, 1975; Dear Bill, Remember Me? and Other Stories, 1976; Up in Seth's Room, 1979; Taking Terri Mueller, 1981; When We First Met, 1982; Someone to Love, 1983.

SELECTED WORKS WRITTEN WITH HARRY MAZER: The Solid Gold Kid, 1977.

ABOUT: Contemporary Authors, Vol. 69–72; Something About the Author, Vol. 24.

ANNE McCAFFREY

April 1, 1926–

AUTHOR OF *Dragonsong,* etc.

Biographical sketch of Anne Inez McCaffrey:

ANNE McCAFFREY was born in Cambridge, Massachusetts, and grew up in Essex County, New Jersey, "a moody, obnoxious, egregious,willful, self-centered and lonely tomboy," as she remembers herself. Her parents nurtured their daughter's independent spirit and gave her "the stout conviction that, if one worked hard enough at anything, one would succeed. Consequently it never occurred to me that there was anything which I couldn't do if I tried hard enough." They also read to her. She particularly remembers her mother reading Kipling's animal stories and A. Merritt's "The Ship of Ishtar" to her and her brothers; and her father reading "The Midnight Ride of Paul Revere" while she was ill with measles. After graduating from Radcliffe College with honors in Slavic languages and literature, McCaffrey worked as a secretary, waitress, and short-order cook. She was a copywriter for Liberty Music Shops in New York City and for Helena Rubinstein. She directed theater and opera and worked in summer stock. In 1970 to 1971 she did graduate study in meteorology in Dublin. She also studied voice for nine years, and music plays an important role in many of her books.

In 1950 she married a public relations man, Wright Johnson, and they have three children, Alec, Todd, and Georgeanne, and grandchildren. After twenty years the marriage ended in divorce.

McCaffrey began writing the sort of stories she wanted to read "when new and marvelous adventures did not appear quickly enough to satisfy my voracious appetite." Her first published novel was *Restoree* in 1967. The next year *Dragonflight* was published, the first of her "Dragon" novels and stories, combining elements of science fiction and fantasy, and set on the planet Pern, where huge, flying, flame-throwing dragons are linked telepathically with their men and women dragonriders. *Dragonquest* (1971) and *The White Dragon*

(1978) followed; meanwhile her series for young adults appeared, beginning with *Dragonsong,* then followed by *Dragonsinger* and *Dragondrums.*

Besides writing the "Dragon" series, McCaffrey has also edited a cookbook of recipes supplied by science fiction writers and a collection of short stories, and she wrote many other science fiction novels and short stories. Her own favorite is *The Ship Who Sang,* about a severely handicapped young woman who is cybernetically linked to a spaceship so that her body becomes the ship.

McCaffrey won the E. S. Smith Memorial Award for Imaginative Fiction in 1976, and the Balrog Award for Outstanding Professional Achievement in 1980. The Dragon books have won her the greatest acclaim. In 1968 two of the stories that make up *Dragonflight* received top awards: a Hugo science fiction award for Best Novella went to "Weyr Search," and a Science Fiction Writers of America Nebula Award went to "Dragonrider." *Dragonsinger* was chosen by the American Library Association as a Best Book for Young Adults in 1977. *The White Dragon* won the Gandalf Award for Best Fantasy Novel of 1978 and the Ditmar Award for Best International Fiction. *Dragondrums* won the Balrog Award for Best Novel of 1979.

McCaffrey says that she champions dragons partly because "Dragons have always had a bad press." Many young people have told her that the episode they love best in *Dragonsong* is when the runaway girl, Menolly, first feeds and "impresses" the little fire-lizards and they nuzzle against her and become her pets. "Fire-lizards must be the interstellar equivalent of cats," McCaffrey says.

McCaffrey lives with four cats in a house called "Dragonhold," in Wicklow County, Ireland. She also has three dogs and a number of horses. Her daughter, Georgeanne, lives at home and works with her in their small stable.

Anne McCaffrey told the *Dallas News*

that she writes science fiction because "It's one of the few fields of fiction that gives you hope."

SELECTED WORKS: Dragonsong, 1976; Dragonsinger, 1977; Dragondrums, 1979.

ABOUT: Ash, Brian. Who's Who in Science Fiction; Contemporary Authors (First Revision), Vol. 25–28; The International Authors and Writers Who's Who, 1982; Nicholls, Peter, ed. The Science Fiction Encyclopedia; Reginald, R. Contemporary Science Fiction Authors, 1st edition; Reginald, R. Science Fiction and Fantasy Awards 1981; Smith, Curtis C., ed. Twentieth-Century Science-Fiction Writers; Something About the Author, Vol. 8; Who's Who in America, 1982–83; Who's Who of American Women, 1977–1978; The Writers Directory 1982–84; Dallas News March 25, 1967; Newsday April 11, 1969.

GERALD McDERMOTT

January 31, 1941–

ADAPTER AND ILLUSTRATOR OF *Arrow to the Sun: A Pueblo Indian Tale,* etc.

Biographical sketch of Gerald McDermott:

GERALD McDERMOTT was born and raised in Detroit, Michigan. He has studied art since the age of four when his parents, realizing that his drawing talent needed special attention, enrolled him in art classes at the Detroit Institute of Arts. In the *Horn Book,* he said of these early years: "Every Saturday, from early childhood through early adolescence, was spent in those halls. I virtually lived in the museum, drawing and painting and coming to know the works of that great collection. I've kept a brush in my hand ever since."

At age nine, McDermott began a brief career as a child radio actor in a local show that specialized in dramatizing folktales and legends. This early exposure to sound effects, music, timing, and working with professional actors proved to be invaluable when he became a filmmaker.

McDermott attended Cass Technical High School, a public school for artistically

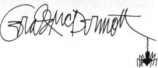

talented students in Detroit which specialized in design education firmly based on traditional Bauhaus principles. McDermott studied music and classical ballet as well. However, his interest in cinematography was so strong that he began to make films on his own time with his friends, since the school did not offer any film courses. He also took an after-school job designing backgrounds for a television animation studio.

In 1959, McDermott won a Scholastic Publications National Scholarship to Pratt Institute in New York. Again finding no film courses to take, he decided to take a year off (in 1962) to work as a graphic designer for Channel 13, New York's public television station. He designed the channel's distinctive owl symbol and pursued his interest in animation. The following fall he submitted the film work he had done at Channel 13 for credit at Pratt and returned there with special permission to work independently.

As an extracurricular project while he was at Pratt, McDermott made his first animated film. Called *The Stonecutter,* it was based on a traditional Japanese folktale, and was animated with silk-screen designs inspired by Japanese prints. Like all his

films that followed, *The Stonecutter* was created painstakingly by drawing six thousand frames in synchronization with prerecorded music and assigning one picture for each note. In both content and structure, *The Stonecutter* indicated the direction that all of McDermott's subsequent films would take.

McDermott says that Joseph Campbell, a Jungian mythologist and authority on the relationship between mythology and psychology, has had a great influence on his work.

The mythical stories that McDermott uses, although drawn from cultures as diverse as those of Japan, ancient Crete, and Africa, share a common theme. They deal with the universal idea of the hero quest, in which a hero encounters a supernatural force and wins a decisive victory, gaining the power to aid his fellow man in the process.

In the late 1960s, McDermott worked on several films but found little support for his artistic endeavors. He met and married the painter and author-illustrator of children's books, Beverly Brodsky. Just as they were moving to the south of France, McDermott came to the attention of a children's book editor at Viking Press who offered him a multibook contract to transfer his works from celluloid to paper. McDermott knew of no precedent for transforming a film into a picture book and took it upon himself to solve the technical problems involved. This led to a new career for him as an adapter and illustrator of folktales for childen. The McDermotts moved to France, where Gerald set to work transforming two of his films, *Anansi the Spider* and *The Magic Tree,* into picture books.

In 1970, McDermott's film *Anansi the Spider* won the Blue Ribbon at the American Film Festival and was called one of "the two most popular children's films produced in 1970" by *Wilson Library Bulletin.* In 1972, the book version of *Anansi the Spider* was published. It was named a Caldecott Honor Book and won a Lewis Carroll Shelf Award for 1973.

Arrow to the Sun: A Pueblo Indian Tale was published in 1974, and although several critics took exception to its style, most were enthusiastic, and it won the 1975 Caldecott Medal. In his acceptance speech, McDermott said, "It has been my experience that even the youngest children respond in a direct and receptive manner to the most stylized of images. I believe this quality is manifested in the magic and symbolism of their own paintings. . . . In a specific sense, in awarding the Caldecott Medal, you not only honor the artist for a singular achievement, but you also commission that artist to pierce the screen of convention. You challenge the individual to explore and experiment in future graphic work."

Arrow to the Sun was also chosen for the American Institute of Graphic Arts Book Show for 1973/74 and won the Brooklyn Art Books for Children Citation in 1977 from the Brooklyn Museum and the Brooklyn Public Library.

In addition to his literary honors, McDermott's film animation has brought him worldwide recognition. The Council on International Non-theatrical Events (CINE) has chosen five of his films to represent the United States in international festivals.

Gerald McDermott is now divorced. He lives and works in New Milford, Connecticut.

SELECTED WORKS ADAPTED AND ILLUSTRATED: Anansi the Spider: A Tale from the Ashanti, 1972; The Magic Tree: A Tale from the Congo, 1973; Arrow to the Sun: A Pueblo Indian Tale, 1974; The Stonecutter: A Japanese Folk Tale, 1975; The Voyage of Osiris: A Myth of Ancient Egypt, 1977; The Knight of the Lion, 1978; Papagayo the Mischief Maker, 1978; Sun Flight, 1980.

ABOUT: Contemporary Authors, Vol. 85–88; Kingman, Lee and others, comps. Illustrators of Children's Books: 1967–1976; Kingman, Lee, ed. The Illustrator's Notebook; Kingman, Lee, ed. Newbery and Caldecott Medal Books: 1966–1975; Something About the Author, Vol. 16; Ward, Martha E. and Dorothy A. Marquardt. Illustrators of Books for Young People; Who's Who in American Art, 1980; Horn Book April 1975; August 1975; School Library Journal November 1975; Print November/December 1973.

GEORGESS McHARGUE

June 7, 1941–

AUTHOR OF *The Impossible People,* etc.

Autobiographical sketch of Georgess McHargue, who also writes under the pen names Alice Elizabeth Chase and Margo Scegge Usher:

EVERY teacher, parent, or pediatrician knows me, or rather, knows the kid I was— the bookish one who was sick a lot, the tall one who detested basketball, the one who *liked* school, spouted polysyllables, and had a permanently skinned knee from falling (or being pushed) in the playground. In retrospect, it seems an oversight on Nature's part not to have provided me with horn-rimmed glasses.

I was born and raised in New York City, in a household I can only describe by coining the word bibliocentric. My parents did not play bridge, join clubs, or support causes; they read, and talked about what they read, and read some more. My mother preferred modern poetry and novels, with emphasis on *The New Yorker* writers. My father went in for English poetry before 1900, philosophy, Shakespeare, Plato, ancient history, psychology, and anthropology. As for myself, I can't remember when I couldn't read, although I know I skipped the first grade because I had already entered the halls of felicity.

My first efforts at fiction consisted of a long and melodramatic series of "autobiographical" adventures of the Wild West variety (derived from summers in my father's home state of Montana), which I narrated to a roomful of kindergarteners during "rest period" each school day. The tales were melodramatic because I was determined to hold the interest of my audience. They were long because I could seldom think of good endings. That problem still haunts me today.

I went to Radcliffe College, where, after a brief flirtation with microbiology, I perceived that it was my doom to be a general-

Georgess McHargue: *JOR jess mac HARG*

Georgess McHargue

ist, and majored in what might as well have been termed Ivory Towers (history and literature of the Renaissance). I would have made it comparative mythology, but at the time there was no such major for undergraduates.

I was already pursuing what is evidently going to be a lifelong interest in myth, folklore, fairy tales, legend, and the history of the occult, themes that seem to crop up in each of my books, whether I intend them to or not. My preoccupation with the subject dates not from a childhood love of the bizarre and magical, but from a force-feeding of world mythology in the sixth grade, when I was profoundly irritated by their arbitrary plots and absence of characterization. It was my father's inspiration, the next year, to point me toward his thirteen-volume set of Sir James Frazer's *The Golden Bough,* and there, in that world of rites, taboos, sacrifices, cosmic symbols, and astronomical cycles, I began to discern the "divinest sense" that lurks behind the "much madness" of those raped nymphs, devouring monsters, and shining heroes. For every book on mythology or folklore that I now write, I do the equivalent of the research for an M.A. thesis at least, and I consider myself unbelievably lucky to be paid for indulging a private intellectual

passion. I don't even have to write lesson plans or grade final examinations.

After college, I came to writing through publishing, having spent seven years as a children's book editor in New York. At present I live in Groton, Massachusetts with my husband Michael Roberts, who is an archaeologist. We have one daughter, three larcenous cats, one well-mannered border collie, and a garden of 130 varieties of ancient, old-fashioned, and modern roses. I wish to emphasize for those who have read my books on werewolves, vampires, and so forth, that the fact of our living next to a historic graveyard is purely coincidental.

Georgess McHargue was born in Norwalk, Connecticut. She received her B.A. degree from Radcliffe College in 1963 and was elected to Phi Beta Kappa. She has been an editor at Doubleday and Company, and has also worked at Golden Press. She is a member of the American Civil Liberties Union and the Wilderness Society.

In 1972 she received the Spring Festival Award from *Book World* for *The Impossible People. The Horseman's Word, The Wonderful Wings of Harold Harrabescu,* and *Facts, Frauds, and Phantasms* were Junior Literary Guild selections, and *Meet the Vampire* was on the list of the International Reading Association/Children's Book Council Children's Choices for 1980.

SELECTED WORKS: The Beasts of Never, 1968; The Baker and the Basilisk, 1970; The Wonderful Wings of Harold Harrabescu, 1971; Facts, Frauds, and Phantasms: A Survey of the Spiritual Movement, 1972; The Impossible People, 1972; The Mermaid and the Whale, 1973; Hot and Cold Running Cities (editor), 1974; Stoneflight, 1975; Funny Bananas: The Mystery in the Museum, 1976; Meet the Vampire, 1979; The Horseman's Word, 1981; The Turquoise Toad Mystery, 1982.

SELECTED WORKS AS ALICE ELIZABETH CHASE: Famous Artists of the Past, 1964; Famous Paintings: An Introduction to Art, 1964; Looking at Art, 1966.

ABOUT: Contemporary Authors (First Revision), Vol. 25–28; Something About the Author, Vol. 4;

Ward, Martha E. and Dorothy A. Marquardt. Authors of Books for Young People, 2nd edition (Supplement).

PATRICIA A. McKILLIP

February 29, 1948–

AUTHOR OF *The Riddle-Master of Hed,* etc.

Autobiographical sketch of Patricia Anne McKillip:

Patricia A McKillip

I WAS BORN in Salem, Oregon, the second of six kids. My father joined the Air Force later, and we traveled to various air bases in places like Arizona, Mississippi, California, England, and Germany, where I spent time switching grammar schools and helping keep track of my four younger brothers and sisters. My first efforts at storytelling began in the back seat of a station wagon, while we waited for our parents to finish shopping, and I told tales to wile away the boredom. I started writing seriously at fourteen. That was probably a reaction to being shy and highly imaginative in a very old country (England), feeling surrounded by myth and history and living across the street from a graveyard.

We finally settled for a good number of years in San Jose, California, where I went to high school and San Jose State University. Although I worked at the usual odd jobs during college, I had a feeling that I'd better get published before I graduated, because I never felt capable of holding down a nine-to-five job. So I got a Masters in English Literature and, upon graduating, was able to support myself by writing, which is largely what I've been doing ever since.

I never "chose" to write children's books—for the most part the characters I write about decide who the book will be written for. Some books surprise me, others don't. *The Forgotten Beasts of Eld* was probably the biggest surprise. I just moved my pen and watched a white-haired wizard tell her own story, without ever being exactly sure what she was going to do next. I wasn't even sure I liked her at the time, though I've grown to. The Riddle-Master trilogy was most carefully planned, in the sense that I knew the characters well, where they were going, and why. Precisely how they were going to get there, however, was at times as big a mystery to me as it was to them.

After moving several times, I'm now living in San Francisco, in a neighborhood full of Chinese bakeries, where I can hear the foghorns from the sea. San Francisco is not an easy city to write in—there are a thousand and one distractions—but I managed to finish my first adult novel, *Stepping from the Shadows,* here. (Which, predictably perhaps, is about a young girl growing up to become a writer.) I am also working on my first science fiction novel, which is like nothing I've ever tried to write before. Having no science background beyond high school, and only a polite acquaintance with the insides of my car, I'm finding it quite a challenge to figure out how a spacecraft 150 years from now gets itself off the ground. But I'm fascinated with the genre and all its potential for making us wonder at the simple fact that we exist on such a richly furnished planet.

Since somewhere along the line I forgot to get married, I'm living in a big flat with three friends (one of them twelve years old). I also live with seven cats (five of them kittens), an electric grand piano, a basement full of books, a pile of letters that seem to elude my best intentions, a sewing machine that also tends to elude my best intentions, and a brooding bust of H.P. Lovecraft (an award for ELD). When I'm not writing, I like listening to live music—anything from friends playing country rock to the San Francisco Opera. I also like skiing, traveling, chain-reading, and eating pork buns from all the bakeries that surround me.

———

Patricia McKillip received her B.A. from San Jose State University in 1971 and her M.A. in 1973.

Three of her books make up a trilogy: *The Riddle-Master of Hed, Heir of Sea and Fire,* and *Harpist in the Wind. The Forgotten Beast of Eld* was an American Library Association Notable Book for 1974, and won the World Fantasy Award for best novel in 1975. *The Throme of the Erril of Sherill* was included in the 1974 American Institute of Graphic Arts Children's Book Show and in the Children's Book Showcase.

SELECTED WORKS: The Throme of the Erril of Sherill, 1973; The Forgotten Beasts of Eld, 1974; The Night Gift, 1976; The Riddle-Master of Hed, 1976; Heir of Sea and Fire, 1977; Harpist in the Wind, 1979.

ABOUT: Contemporary Authors, Vol. 49-52; (First Revision Series), Vol. 4; Something About the Author, Vol. 30; Ward, Martha E. and Dorothy A. Marquardt. Authors of Books for Young People, 2nd edition (Supplement).

ROBIN McKINLEY

November 16, 1952–

AUTHOR OF *The Blue Sword,* etc.

Autobiographical sketch of Jennifer Carolyn Robin McKinley:

ONCE I LEARNED to read I disappeared into the world of books and have never really come out again. I was a Navy brat, and an only child at that, so I grew up feeling that books, which you could take with you when your father was reassigned halfway across the world, were more reliable friends than human beings, who stayed behind, or whose fathers got posted off in some other direction.

Writing has always been the other side of reading for me; why there are people who read but don't write puzzles me, and thus I can't answer that inevitable question about where I get my ideas. Somehow or other some of those pictures in my head that more responsible people call daydreams turn themselves into stories. (I remember as one of the discoveries that plunged me into adulthood the fact that some people did consider those pictures in one's head daydreams, and not source material for stories.) I'm not an organized writer; when a story wants out of my skull and onto paper, it lets me know: it keeps me awake at night, makes me forget to pay overdue bills, renders me incapable of holding rational conversation with old friends. I have learned some survival skills to get the bills paid before they turn off the electricity, but I can't complain. I love writing; it's exhausting and frustrating—it never goes down on paper as beautifully as I see it in my head—but it's also exhilarating and (except for proofreading for typos) never boring.

I don't know why what I write comes out fantasy; I was an English lit major in college and still want to grow up to be Joseph Conrad, but no matter what else I might yet find myself capable of, I would not wish to give up fantasy. I believe in embarrassing and tiresome things like heroism and honor and good and evil, and I think a good brisk wallop of black and white, such as is possible in the worlds of fantasy, is refreshing, and helps clear the head for coping with reality's shades of grey. My major literary preoccupation is with girls who do things.

I loved—and still love—the old-fashioned British Empire adventure novels by writers like P.C. Wren and A.W.W. Mason and H. Rider Haggard and especially Rudyard Kipling. But in their stories the boys go off and have adventures while the girls stay home and wring their hands. Thus, I write stories about girls who go off and have adventures too.

———

Robin McKinley was born in Warren, Ohio. After graduating from the Gould Academy in Bethel, Maine, she attended Dickinson College in Carlisle, Pennsylvania. She graduated summa cum laude and Phi Beta Kappa from Bowdoin College in Brunswick, Maine. She has had jobs in publishing and on a horse farm. McKinley says that "About the only irresistible attraction reality has ever exerted on me is in the shape of horses and riding." She presently lives in Staten Island, New York, and owns four thousand books.

The Blue Sword was a 1983 Newbery Honor Book and a Boston Globe-Horn Book Honor Book in 1978. Both *Beauty* and *The Blue Sword* were named Notable Books and Best Books for Young Adults by the American Library Association in their years of publication. McKinley plans two more books about the mythical kingdom Damar, which she created in *The Blue Sword*. A "prequel" is next, called *The Hero and the Crown*.

SELECTED WORKS: Beauty: A Retelling of the Story of Beauty and the Beast, 1978; The Door in the Hedge, 1981; The Blue Sword, 1982.

DAVID McPHAIL

June 30, 1940–

AUTHOR AND ILLUSTRATOR OF *Pig Pig Grows Up,* etc.

Autobiographical sketch of David Michael McPhail:

David McPhail

I WAS BORN in Newburyport, Massachusetts. My childhood was wonderful. My family was probably poor, but I didn't know it. I was surrounded by caring people. Besides my mother and father, there were two brothers, a sister, aunts, uncles, cousins, grandparents, and many friends.

I loved the fields and woods near my home. Much of my time was spent playing alone, imagining that I was Robin Hood.

Drawing has been a part of my life for as long as I can remember. I would draw on anything, with whatever I could find to draw with.

Books played a small, but significant role in my childhood, and I still have fond memories of the public library.

During my high school years, my ambitions changed with the seasons. In baseball season, I aspired to be a big league baseball player. Then during basketball season, I'd change my mind. I would be a basketball player. Unfortunately, I was never good enough at either sport, though I still enjoy playing.

After high school I went to art school for a year. Following that I spent six years working at a variety of low-paying jobs, and during that time I had dreams of being a rock-and-roll star. I had bought a guitar, learned a few chords, and joined a small combo. We toured the local nightclubs with our four-song repertoire but never made more than ten dollars for any single performance—hardly the big-time.

It was about that time that I decided to try art school again. So I spent the next three years at the school of the Museum of Fine Arts, Boston—making friends, attending parties, working odd jobs—and occasionally drawing.

During my third year at art school, my roommate showed some of my work to a young woman he was dating. This woman was an editor at a textbook publishing company. She offered me some work, and I took it. Thus an unillustrious illustrational career was launched.

My first trade book was published in 1971, and since then I've illustrated at least thirty books, many of which I also wrote.

I have four children—two sons (thirteen and eleven), and two daughters (nine and almost four).

I live in a small town in New Hampshire with my youngest daughter, her mother, one cat, one rabbit, and two horses.

I like warm sunshine, blue skies, soft sands, tall trees, the oceans, brooks, fields, dirt roads (but not in Spring, when they become *mud* roads), stone walls, books, nutmeg mousse, and dark beer.

I *don't like* snow, ice, bugs, cold weather, automobiles, guns, television, fast foods, and politicians.

All things considered, I enjoy my life somewhat.

———

Far from being "unillustrious," David McPhail's illustrations have appeared in a great range of popular books for children. His earlier work contains finely drawn pictures with lots of cross-hatching, and a typical recent picture book like *Pig Pig Grows Up* is done in watercolors with a great deal of open space on the double-page spreads. Two of his books have appeared in Ameri-can Institute of Graphic Arts shows, *Sailing to Cythera* in 1974 and *Grandfather's Cake* in 1980. *Pig Pig Grows Up* was named a Children's Choice book of 1980 by a joint committee of the International Reading Association and the Children's Book Council.

There is a children's bookstore in the Boston area named after McPhail's book *Henry Bear's Park*.

SELECTED WORKS WRITTEN AND ILLUSTRATED: In the Summer I Go Fishing, 1971; Bear's Toothache, 1972; Henry Bear's Park, 1976; The Train, 1977; Mistletoe, 1978; Grandfather's Cake, 1979; Pig Pig Grows Up, 1980; Great Cat, 1982; Pig Pig Rides, 1982.

SELECTED WORKS ILLUSTRATED: The Run Jump Run Book, by Robert Brooks, 1971; Sailing to Cythera and Other Anatole Stories, by Nancy Willard, 1974; The Bear's Bicycle, by Emilie McLeod, 1975; One Winter Night in August and Other Nonsense Jingles, by X. J. Kennedy, 1975; Stranger's Bread, by Nancy Willard, 1977; The Island of the Grass King: The Further Adventures of Anatole, by Nancy Willard, 1979.

ABOUT: Contemporary Authors, Vol. 85–88; Kingman, Lee and others, comps. Illustrators of Children's Books: 1967–1976; Ward, Martha E. and Dorothy A. Marquardt. Authors of Books for Young People (Supplement).

CAROLYN MEYER

June 8, 1935–

AUTHOR OF *C. C. Poindexter*, etc.

Autobiographical sketch of Carolyn Mae Meyer:

IN LEWISTOWN, Pennsylvania, where I was born, only child and only grandchild, I was the focus of all attention. What would this small bespectacled creature turn out to be?

A Writer. I knew that when, after learning to write my name, I began to write poetry and short stories. I would do it all my life. My proud, puzzled family smiled indulgently. I was bright but physically uncoordinated. Everybody played softball and roller-skated and climbed trees and skinned

Carolyn Meyer

the cat, and I sat inside and read and wrote and daydreamed, while my family worried. They wanted me to be normal.

I also wanted to be a Mother. I'm still surprised at how it's turned out—twenty books and three sons.

My teenage years were awful, and I remember exactly how awful they were and why, and that's why I like to write for teenagers. I even like having teenagers as relatives. But I had no idea then that that's what I would be writing about.

I graduated from Bucknell University in Pennsylvania with a major in English and a Phi Beta Kappa key to show how hard I had worked, and, because my father thought I should be able to earn a living, summer secretarial courses so that I could get a job that I hated. Soon I married, began a family, and tired of making beds and slipcovers and meatloaves, began to write again. By then I had developed the discipline I needed. My first sale was to a secretarial magazine: a little story printed in shorthand that none of my family could read, but my byline was clear, and that was good enough.

After a few years of magazine work, I decided to write a book for children. It was a

sewing book for little girls (because by then I had three little boys). Other how-to books followed, but my interest shifted from things to people. What's it like to grow up as an Eskimo in Alaska? To be a member of an Amish community in Pennsylvania? To be part of a rock-and-roll band? To live in a therapeutic community for teenagers with emotional problems? The question "What's it like . . . ?" carried over into fiction, too: What's it like to be a girl who's six-feet-one and still growing? What's it like to spend the summer on a remote island, isolated from all your friends?

In order to learn the answer to that basic question, "What's it like?", I've spent a lot of time in different places—in an Eskimo village near the Bering Sea, on an Amish farm, in a therapeutic community, in rock-and-roll clubs, on a small Caribbean island. Most recently I stayed for six weeks in Peru and Bolivia without quite knowing what the question was. It might be, "What's it like to grow up in a poor Andean village?" Or it might be a more personal question: "What's it like to find yourself completely cut off from your own culture?" I didn't know the question when I went to the West Indies either; it took five years for the finished book to emerge. It may take just as long to find out what I was asking in South America.

Although I began to write when I was in first or second grade, I didn't begin to publish professionally until 1963. I tried all kinds of things—fiction, nonfiction, short pieces, books—all in an attempt to find out what I'm good at, and learning that what I'm good at is subject to change. And *that* means trying things I'm not sure I can do and then accepting the disappointment if they don't work.

Since 1963 I've worried about running out of ideas, always terrified that after this project and the one I've planned to work on next, and the one after that, there would be no more. And then one day it happened, the thing I feared most: there were no new ideas. It was terrible, and it lasted a long time. Eventually I learned that I have to look in different places than I did before and to listen to different sounds.

Another novel for teenagers is coming along now, but after that, I don't know. I really don't. But now, having survived the thing that I feared most, I am no longer afraid of not knowing.

———

Carolyn Meyer graduated from Bucknell Cum Laude in 1957. She was married in 1960, but was divorced in 1973. She has taught children's literature at Bucknell as an Alpha Lambda Delta Lecturer. She wrote the "Cheers and Jeers" column for *McCalls* magazine from 1967 to 1968 and has also written for *Redbook, Family Circle,* and *Town & Country.*

Three of her books were Junior Literary Guild selections: *People Who Make Things, The Center,* and *Amish People. Amish People* was also an American Library Association Notable Book, as were *C.C. Poindexter* and *The Bread Book,* in their years of publication.

SELECTED WORKS: The Bread Book, 1971; People Who Make Things: How American Craftsmen Live and Work, 1974; Amish People: Plain Living in a Complex World, 1976; Eskimos: Growing Up in a Changing Society, 1977; C. C. Poindexter, 1978; The Center: From a Troubled Past to a New Life, 1979; Rock Band: Big Men in a Great Big Town, 1980; Eulalia's Island, 1982.

ABOUT: Contemporary Authors, Vol. 49-52; (New Revision Series), Vol. 2; Something About the Author, Vol. 9; Ward, Martha E. and Dorothy A. Marquardt. Authors of Books for Young People, 2nd edition (Supplement).

Mikolaycak

CHARLES MIKOLAYCAK

January 26, 1937–

ILLUSTRATOR OF *Shipwreck,* etc.

Autobiographical sketch of Charles Mikolaycak:

Mikolaycak: *mike o LAY chak*

I WAS BORN in Scranton, Pennsylvania on the 26th of January, 1937. My twin brother died after a few months. Remaining an only child, I soon discovered the joys and problems of being alone. When I was about six or seven years old, I began to draw. Those early efforts mostly reproduced in glorious color movie advertisements that I saw in newspapers. When I added color I was even more excited about seeing the films. I was very happy when I was allowed more than one movie a week. I experienced *The Corn Is Green, The Valley of Decision, The Yearling, How Green Is My Valley,* etc. as pictures before I realized they were available in words—as books. When I discovered the connection between movies and books, I became an avid reader. All those screen images swam in my head and were transformed when combined with words. About this time I made an unconscious decision to create books—those which combined words and pictures to tell a story.

During high school I decided to become an illustrator (but only after a brief flirtation with the idea of becoming a theatrical set designer). I enrolled in and graduated from Pratt Institute in Brooklyn, New York. I was drafted into the Army for two years and then I worked for fourteen years as a designer for Time-Life Books in New York City. During this time, I drew and illustrated children's books in the evenings and on weekends. I left Time-Life in 1976 to illustrate books full-time. I still live in New York City with my wife, Carole and two very nice cats, and illustrate exclusively for books. It is a most rewarding position. I very much enjoy re-creating the days of my boyhood as in *Peter and the Wolf,* discovering and knowing the richness of ancient worlds as when researching *I am Joseph* or having fun creating worlds of other places, as in the folktales from Middle Europe that I have illustrated. From films to theater to words. . . . I have found the perfect vehicle for myself—the picture book. I cast the rôles, dress the performers, design the sets, choose the moment to be illustrated and tell a story in visual terms. What an opportunity!

In 1958 and 1959, Charles Mikolaycak attended New York University for additional study. In 1970, he married Carole Kismaric, an author and picture editor.

His work is represented in both the Kerlan Collection at the University of Minnesota and the permanent collection of the International Youth Library in Munich, Germany. He has been a guest instructor at Syracuse University since 1976.

I Am Joseph and *How Wilka Went to Sea* were both named American Library Association Notable Books in their years of publication. Five of his books were represented in American Institute of Graphic Arts Book Shows: *Great Wolf and the Good Woodsman, Shipwreck, The Feast Day, The Tale of Tawny and Dingo,* and *The Twelve Clever Brothers and Other Fools. Shipwreck* was also in Children's Book Showcase in 1975 and *Peter and the Wolf* received a citation from the Society of Illustrators in 1983.

How the Hare Told the Truth About His Horse was included in the 1973 Biennial of Illustrations, Bratislava, and he received a

Gold Medal for art direction from the Society of Illustrators, in 1970.

SELECTED WORKS ADAPTED WITH CAROLE KISMARIC AND ILLUSTRATED: The Boy Who Tried to Cheat Death, 1971.

SELECTED WORKS ILLUSTRATED: Great Wolf and the Good Woodsman, by Helen Hoover, 1967; How the Hare Told the Truth About His Horse, by Barbara K. Walker, 1972; The Feast Day, by Edwin Fademan Jr., 1973; Shipwreck, by Vera G. Cumberlege, 1974; How Wilka Went to Sea and Other Tales from West of the Urals, by Mirra Ginsburg, trans. and ed., 1975; The Tall Man from Boston, by Marion L. Starkey, 1975; Three Wanderers from Wapping, by Norma Farber, 1978; The Tale of Tawny and Dingo, by William H. Armstrong, 1979; The Twelve Clever Brothers and Other Fools, by Mirra Ginsburg, comp. and adapt., 1979; I Am Joseph, by Barbara Cohen, 1980; The Nine Crying Dolls, by Anne Pellowski (reteller), 1980, Peter and the Wolf, by Sergei Prokofiev, 1982; The Highwayman, by Alfred Noyes, 1983.

ABOUT: Contemporary Authors, Vol. 61–64; Kingman, Lee and others, comps. Illustrators of Children's Books: 1967–1976; Something About the Author, Vol. 9; Ward, Martha E. and Dorothy A. Marquardt. Illustrators of Books for Young People, 2nd edition; Who's Who in the East, 1981; Language Arts October 1981.

BETTY MILES

May 16, 1928–

AUTHOR OF *The Real Me,* etc.

Autobiographical sketch of Betty Miles:

I LIVED ABROAD as a young child, and came back to this country at six. Of my first day in America I remember two things: the Statue of Liberty and Woolworth's. I thought America was amazing and wonderful, but I felt quite strange here. In some ways I still do, which is probably not a bad thing for a writer.

I went to elementary school in a suburb of St. Louis, Missouri. There was a pleasant library in that school—a huge room with tall windows—and a motherly librarian, Mrs. Moore, who let us read anything we wanted. I read *The Three Musketeers, Trea-*

Betty Miles

sure Island, The Good Master, Mr. Popper's Penguins, and whole sets of books about twins and dogs. In fifth grade I began to write for pleasure: poems, letters, articles for the school paper. By the time I was in high school, I knew I wanted to be a writer. I edited the high school newspaper, and later, at Antioch College, the newspaper there. During work periods at Antioch I wrote for the college news bureau, for a small-town paper, and for a sports weekly in New York City.

Before my last year of college, I married Matt Miles, who is now a social psychologist doing educational research. We came to New York City, where our three children—Sara, David, and Ellen—were born, and moved to suburban Rockland County in 1958. The children are grown now, but my husband and I still live in the same house. It is an old white house with a large yard, a front porch, and a messy basement. Some of the characters in my books live in homes surprisingly like it.

My first full-time job led directly to my present work: I became an assistant kindergarten teacher. Reading aloud to five-year-olds taught me a lot about children's books—and about children—and made me

want to try writing for children myself. I wrote my first book in 1955; it was published in 1958, after rejection by many publishers. That experience taught me persistence—a lesson I try to pass on to beginning writers today.

In the 1960s I worked part-time in the Publications Department of Bank Street College of Education, where I was an editor of The Bank Street Readers, one of the first multicultural reading series. At the same time, Knopf was publishing my picture books for young children. Most of these were really small essays, rather than stories. I seem to have a didactic streak—an irrepressible urge to *explain* things—like some of the mothers in the novels for older readers which I now write. The first of these, *The Real Me,* was published in 1974. You will find a lot of the real *me* in it and the other novels. I put my own feelings into my characters, and say things through them that I might be too shy to say in person. I enjoy speaking out through my books, and making connections with young readers. For me, the greatest reward of writing is being told that "you know just how I feel."

————

Betty Miles was born in Chicago. She received her B.A. degree from Antioch College in 1950. She has been a member of Feminists on Children's Media, and is now a member of the Authors League of America, and P.E.N. She has been a consultant to the Random House series, Beginner Books, and to the Children's Television Workshop. She frequently speaks to school children, teachers, librarians, and parents about books and writing.

Two of her books were named Notable Children's Trade Books in the Field of Social Studies by the National Council for the Social Studies: *All It Takes Is Practice,* in 1976, and *Maudie and Me and the Dirty Book,* in 1980. *Save the Earth!* was named an Outstanding Science Trade Book for Children by the National Science Teachers Association in 1974; it was also named an

International Reading Association Chil-
dren's Choice book in the same year. *The
Trouble with Thirteen* was a Children's Ch-
oice book in 1979. Other Children's
Choice books include *Maudie and Me* and
The Secret Life of the Underwear Champ.

SELECTED WORKS: A House for Everyone, 1958;
What Is the World?, 1958; Having a Friend, 1959; A
Day of Winter, 1961; The Real Me, 1974; Save the
Earth!: An Ecology Handbook for Kids, 1974; All It
Takes Is Practice, 1976; Just the Beginning, 1976;
Looking On, 1978; The Trouble with Thirteen, 1979;
Maudie and Me and the Dirty Book, 1980; The Secret
Life of the Underwear Champ, 1981; I Would If I
Could, 1982.

SELECTED WORKS WITH JOAN BLOS: Just Think, 1971.

ABOUT: Contemporary Authors (First Revision),
Vol. 3; (New Revision Series), Vol. 5; Foremost Wom-
en in Communications, 1970; Something About the
Author, Vol. 8; Ward, Martha E. and Dorothy A. Marquardt. Authors of Books for Young People, 2nd edition; The Writers Directory 1982–84.

FRANK MODELL

September 6, 1917–

AUTHOR AND ILLUSTRATOR OF   *Tooley!
Tooley!,* etc.

Biographical sketch of Frank Modell:

BORN IN Philadelphia, Pennsylvania,
Frank Modell says that he began to draw
"very early." Both of his parents encouraged his first scribbles, and in efforts to protect the wallpaper, window shades, and
other household surfaces from his son's eager artistic endeavors, Modell's father, who
was a traveling salesman, provided young
Frank with reams of hotel stationery to
draw on.

As a child Modell found the comic pages
of the evening newspaper fascinating. To
the delight of his schoolmates he began to
successfully copy comic strips such as Jiggs,
Maggie, Skippy, and Happy Hooligan, paying careful attention to the "direct, telling
lines" of the artwork. He also discovered the

book *How to Draw Cartoons* by Clare
Briggs—creator of "Mr. and Mrs."—in the
public library and considers that book to
have been his first real instruction in drawing.

After finishing high school Modell went
on to study art, painting, and design at the
Philadelphia College of Art and at the Philadelphia Graphic Club. He got a job at *The
New Yorker* magazine as an assistant in the
art department. In the 1950s Modell succeeded in getting some of his own cartoons
accepted by *The New Yorker,* and during
the next ten years he established himself as
a regular cartoonist for that magazine. His
work has also appeared in *Audubon* and
Playboy magazines. He does illustrations for
adult humor books as well, and in 1978 his
cartoons were published in a collection for
adults entitled *Stop Trying to Cheer Me Up.*
For television programs "Sesame Street"
and "The Electric Company" he created
humorous storyboards for animated films
illustrating the usage of certain words.

Not until 1979 did Modell try his hand at
creating books for children. Yet within a
few years he had written and illustrated
three successful picture books. They are
filled with cartoonlike illustrations—line

drawings with a pastel wash—and feature the two friends Marvin and Milton. According to Modell, the two boys very much resemble him and his friends when they were young. His "scrawly, expressive" drawing style has been likened to that of Whitney Darrow, and Modell says that the ideas for his books come from his own experiences and from "people, newspapers, everything."

Away from the drawing board he enjoys writing, photography, and investments. In the mid-1970s he took time off from his usual work to make a successful theatrical debut in a New York Public Theater production of "Marie and Bruce."

Frank Modell has exhibited his drawings, paintings, and sculptures in a number of one-man shows. The joint committee of the International Reading Association and the Children's Book Council named *One Zillion Valentines* a Children's Choice book; and *Toby in the Country, Toby in the City,* which Modell illustrated, was a 1982 Junior Literary Guild selection.

Modell presently lives in New York City, where he continues to draw, both in his home and office.

SELECTED WORKS WRITTEN AND ILLUSTRATED: Tooley! Tooley!, 1979; Seen Any Cats?, 1979; One Zillion Valentines, 1981.

SELECTED WORKS ILLUSTRATED: Toby in the Country, Toby in the City, by Maxine Zohn Bozzo, 1982.

LOUISE MOERI

November 30, 1924–

AUTHOR OF *How Rabbit Stole the Moon,* etc.

Autobiographical sketch of Louise Moeri:

SOMEONE asked me one day if I—or anyone else—would ever write the story of my life. I said I certainly hoped they didn't, because it would make a very dull book.

I was born in Klamath Falls, Oregon, on

Mrs Louise Moeri

November 30, 1924. My father was a mechanic when he could get work, and a farmer when he couldn't. Until I was grown and left home, we moved often, always in the hope of a better living, but never found ourselves in improved circumstances—only different ones. My mother was a housewife who was talented as a cook and seamstress; I remember that she had a lovely singing voice. My only brother died young, and I had no sisters.

Since nearly all the places I lived in as a child were big western ranches, I have to be called a country kid. I grew up with animals—cattle, horses, dogs, cats, chickens, pigs—and to this day I am really more comfortable with them than I am with people. It is my solemn contention that I can hold a lively "conversation" with a chicken, a friendly visit with a horse, an argument with a pig (they tend to be very one-way about things), and a time of comfort and healing with a dog or cat.

I learned to read easily in a one-room country schoolhouse and started writing poetry as a child. School was easy for me, and was often the best part of my life. Since I grew up during the Great Depression and in a family of limited resources, I faced the need for a good education early. My parents and I combined our efforts and I managed to get a B.A. degree from the University of California at Berkeley in 1946. Unfortunately I was unable to settle on a well-organized program and ended up with a hodge-podge of courses and no professional capacity of any kind.

I married later in 1946 and my husband, Edwin, and I have three wonderful children. (Incidentally—our name rhymes with the word "story." Isn't that lucky for me?) Our children are: Neal, Rodger, and Patricia. All are now married and there are three grandsons.

During the course of finding and losing several different jobs, I stumbled by accident into a part-time position with the Manteca Library. This led to eighteen years of service in that library and turned out to be a great blessing in my life. My scattered education turned out to be an asset after all when I did reference work, and the job threw me into the very spot where I needed to be—the world of books.

I had been writing sporadically all my life, but had been unable to find the exact kind of story that suited my talent. Meeting with children's books so late in life allowed me to bring perhaps a greater understanding and appreciation to the field, and opened up a way for me to take. I began to write children's stories and, after a long period, two were published in magazines, followed by *Star Mother's Youngest Child* in 1975. I have written four unpublished novels for adults and many more picture books and novels for children and young people.

Although my life has not been characterized by what others would call exciting adventures—I have never sailed around the world nor challenged the wilderness—I believe that the stresses and joys of an ordinary life have been such that I didn't need to go far afield to stretch my mind and discipline my soul.

I am a Christian, a Democrat, and overweight. I am proud of my accomplishments and sorry for my failures. I plan to keep on trying.

A Horse for X.Y.Z. was a Junior Literary Guild selection. Louise Moeri has had a story published in *Jack and Jill* magazine.

SELECTED WORKS: Star Mother's Youngest Child, 1975; How Rabbit Stole the Moon, 1977; A Horse for X.Y.Z., 1977; Save Queen of Sheba, 1981; First the Egg, 1982; The Unicorn and the Plow, 1982.

ABOUT: Contemporary Authors, Vol. 65-68; Something about the Author, Vol. 24.

NICHOLASA MOHR

November 1, 1935–

AUTHOR AND ILLUSTRATOR OF *Nilda,* etc.

Biographical sketch of Nicholasa Mohr:

NICHOLASA MOHR was born in New York. Daughter of Puerto Rican parents, Pedro and Nicholasa (Rivera) Golpe, she was raised in the Spanish neighborhoods of New York City.

Mohr was well-known as a graphic artist long before she gained recognition as a young adult novelist. Knowing at an early age that she wanted to be an artist, she worked her way through art schools—the Arts Students League, Brooklyn Museum Art School, and the Pratt Center for Contemporary Printmaking. Although her art career began as a fine arts painter, she is better known for eighteen years as a printmaker. In 1973 she decided to switch art forms again and turned to writing fiction.

Nilda, her first novel, won immediate praise. The young adult novel, set in Spanish Harlem in the early 1940s, traces a Puerto Rican girl's growth from childhood to adolescence. The autobiographical story tells how Nilda learns what it means to be poor and to belong to a scorned minority. *Nilda* has been cited for its social significance and its powerful literary style. It won the Jane Addams Children's Book Award for 1974 and was included in the *School Library Journal* "Best of the Best 1966–1978"

Nicholasa Mohr

list (December 1979). The book jacket, which she designed herself, received the Society of Illustrator's Citation of Merit.

Her second book, *El Bronx Remembered,* is a collection of short narratives about Puerto Rican immigrants living in the South Bronx between 1946 and 1956. It was a 1976 National Book Award finalist. Like *El Bronx,* her third book, *In Nueva York,* is a group of stories connected by setting and shared conflicts and emotions. In seven stories, Mohr explores the lives of Puerto Ricans from New York City's Lower East Side. She once said that her main concern in art and in writing is people. The *Horn Book* wrote that in *El Bronx Remembered,* "the short, Chekov-like narratives reveal universal emotions." Both *In Nueva York* and her most recently published book, *Felita,* have been named Notable Trade Books in the Field of Social Studies by the joint committee of the National Council for the Social Studies and the Children's Book Council. *Felita,* her first book for younger readers, describes the everyday experiences of a lively eight-year-old Puerto Rican girl, growing up in a loving family in a close-knit, urban community.

A selection from Nicholasa Mohr's work has been included in *Family in Harmony and Conflict,* edited by Peter Reinke. She has also contributed a number of short stories to *Children's Digest, Scholastic Magazine,* and *Nuestro,* a magazine where she is a member of the Board of Contributors.

Nicholasa Mohr wrote and co-produced programs for public television and radio with the Young Filmmakers Foundation, where she is a consultant and board member. She was the main writer and co-producer of *Aqui y Ahora* a series focusing on the cultural heritage of Caribbean Hispanic Americans in the Northeast United States, and a radio piece called "Inside the Monster," on the Latino Writers Symposium.

Nicholasa Mohr taught in art schools, lectured in Puerto Rican studies at the State University of New York at Stony Brook, and conducted numerous seminars and workshops on creative writing and literature. She was married in 1957 but is now single. She has two grown sons. She makes her home in Brooklyn, New York.

SELECTED WORKS WRITTEN AND ILLUSTRATED: Nilda, 1973; El Bronx Remembered: A Novella and Stories, 1975; In Nueva York, 1977; Felita, 1979.

ABOUT: Contemporary Authors, Vol. 49–52; (New Revision Series), Vol. 1; The International Authors and Writers Who's Who, 1977; Something About the Author, Vol. 8; Ward, Martha E. and Dorothy A. Marquardt. Authors of Books for Young People, 2nd edition (Supplement).

F. N. MONJO

August 28, 1924–October 9, 1978

AUTHOR OF *Poor Richard in France,* etc.

Biographical sketch of Ferdinand Nicolas Monjo III:

F. N. MONJO was born in Stamford, Connecticut in 1924. His father's family emigrated to the United States from Spain in 1850. Here they entered the merchant shipping business, organizing Arctic expeditions to trade with the Eskimos. His mother's family originally came from Mississippi, and Monjo often heard stories of his plantation forebears, particularly a great-grandmother who braved deprivation and Union gunboats to maintain the family land.

He remembered, "Hearing my two families discuss the past—often with considerable heat and color—made it clear to me that people like Grant and Lincoln certainly had been flesh and blood creatures. And if this was true, why then I could begin to imagine that perhaps even such remote creatures as Elizabeth of England or Caesar (or even Sir Edmund Andros) might once have been alive."

In addition to his love of history, as a child Monjo was deeply fond of music, never begrudging the time given to piano lessons or practice. Mozart was his favorite; this affection surfaced years later, in *Letters to Horseface, Being the Story of Wolfgang Amadeus Mozart's Journey to Italy, 1769–1770.*

Monjo graduated from Columbia University with a B.A. degree in 1946. While at Columbia, he had the opportunity to study with Lionel Trilling, Jacques Barzun, and Mark Van Doren. He was married in 1950 and became the father of four children.

After college, Monjo went into the publishing field, working for more than twenty years as an editor of children's books. He began at Golden Press and went from there to head the children's division at the American Heritage Press, where he initiated the American Heritage Junior Library, a series of factual histories for young adults that featured extensive research, historic pictures, and maps and documents.

Then he went to Harper and Row as a children's book editor. In 1968 his first book for children was published, *Indian Summer.* This story of how a pioneer mother and her children survive a marauding Indian attack, was well received critically but subsequently attacked on several fronts for presenting a negative image of American Indians. Monjo refuted the claims and went on to publish over twenty books for children, all of them historical or biographical fiction.

Almost all of Monjo's books, his "shirt sleeve miniatures" as he called them, have a young narrator telling of a specific historical episode or personage from the child's point of view, often using unusual or obscure information or events to get to the historical truth. Monjo believed that "most of the fun of history lay in the details most children's books seemed to omit." His books were meticulously researched, but Monjo tried through direct, simple, yet humorous storytelling to get the truth behind the dry facts of history.

In *The Drinking Gourd,* which appeared on the American Library Association's "Notable Books 1940–1970" list, he tells the story of the Underground Railroad through the eyes of a minister's son whose home is one stop on the way; and *The House on Stink Alley* tells the story of the Pilgrims before they set sail for the New World. *The One Bad Thing About Father* paints a portrait of Teddy Roosevelt through the eyes of his eight-year-old son Quentin, and Thomas Jefferson comes alive through the story of his nine-year-old granddaughter in *Grandpapa and Ellen Aroon.*

In 1974, Ferdinand Monjo was a finalist for a National Book Award for *Poor Richard in France,* a humorous, irreverent retelling of Benjamin Franklin's tenure as Ambassador to France during the American War of Revolution, from the point of view of Franklin's seven-year-old grandson.

The Secret of the Sachem's Tree was named an Outstanding Book of the Year 1972 by the *New York Times* and a Notable Children's Trade Book in the Field of Social Studies for the year 1972 by a joint committee of the National Council for the Social Studies and the Children's Book Council. It was also a Junior Literary Guild selection. Three of Monjo's books have been named Notable Books by the ALA: *The Drinking*

Gourd in 1970, *The Vicksburg Veteran* in 1971, and *Poor Richard in France* in 1973.

Ferdinand Monjo died in 1978 while serving as vice-president and editorial director of children's books at Coward, McCann and Geoghegan, where he had worked since 1969.

SELECTED WORKS: Indian Summer, 1968; The Drinking Gourd, 1969; The One Bad Thing About Father, 1970; Pirates in Panama, 1970; The Vicksburg Veteran, 1971; The Secret of the Sachem's Tree, 1972; Poor Richard in France, 1973; Me and Willie and Pa, 1973; Grandpapa and Ellen Aroon: Being an Account of Some of the Happy Times Spent Together by Thomas Jefferson and His Favorite Granddaughter, 1974; King George's Head Was Made of Lead, 1974; Letters to Horseface, Being the Story of Wolfgang Amadeus Mozart's Journey to Italy, 1769–1770, 1975; Gettysburg: Tad Lincoln's Story, 1976; The Porcelain Pagoda, 1976; Willie Jaspar's Golden Eagle, 1976; A Namesake for Nathan, 1976; Zenas and the Shaving Mill, 1976; The House on Stink Alley: A Story About the Pilgrims in Holland, 1977.

ABOUT: Contemporary Authors, Vol. 81–84; Kirkpatrick, D. L., ed. Twentieth-Century Children's Writers; Something About the Author, Vol. 16; Ward, Martha E. and Dorothy A. Marquardt. Authors of Books for Young People, 2nd edition (Supplement); The Writers Directory 1980–1982; Children's Literature in Education Winter 1978; Horn Book October 1975; School Library Journal November 1978; Publishers Weekly October 23, 1978.

ARLENE MOSEL

August 27, 1921–

AUTHOR OF *Tikki Tikki Tembo,* etc.

Autobiographical sketch of Arlene Tichy Mosel:

A MOTHER who constantly read fairy tales to me, a handsome father with a great sense of humor, and weekly trips to the library certainly sparked many interests.

I was born and raised in Cleveland Heights, Ohio. As a kindergartener I was too shy to go down the slide, so a doctor recommended dancing lessons. These lessons continued for ten years, eventually leading

Arlene Mosel (signature)

to performances with the Metropolitan Opera when the company appeared in Cleveland.

I graduated from Ohio Wesleyan University, and in 1942 married an Army officer and lived in Baltimore, Maryland. After frequent trips to Enoch Pratt Free Library, I became a member of the children's staff. On returning to Ohio after World War II, I worked in the children's department of the Cleveland Heights Public Library and attended Western Reserve University's School of Library Science. That was a beginning of a career: Shaker Heights Public Library, 1960; Assistant Co-ordinator of Children's Services for Cuyahoga County Public Library, Cleveland, Ohio (1961–1967). In 1967 I joined the faculty of Case Western Reserve University as an Assistant Professor—later becoming an Associate Professor, and retiring Emeritus in 1981. While at the University I taught courses in Contemporary Children's Literature, History of Children's Literature, and Storytelling.

In 1960 the H.W. Wilson Company published my pamphlet, "Tell Me Another," a calendar of stories for the storyteller.

Tikki Tikki Tembo, illustrated by Blair

Mosel: *Mo ZEL*

Lent, was a story my mother told me, and a story that I told hundreds of children.

The Funny Little Woman, also illustrated by Blair Lent, was also a favorite in my library story hours.

I have been widowed twice and now live on a lovely acre in Aurora, Ohio, with a winter spot in South Florida. My career as a librarian must have been contagious, for I have two daughters who are librarians, a law librarian and a children's librarian; also, a twenty-year-old son, who is now working toward a Master's degree in environmental science. At present I enjoy plants and travel. Humorous mythology is now on my writing list.

———

Arlene Mosel's two books have won many distinguished awards. *Tikki Tikki Tembo* won the 1968 Boston Globe-Horn Book Award for picture books; it was an American Library Association Notable Book in 1968 and was also named an ALA Notable Book for the years 1940–1970.

The Funny Little Woman won the Caldecott Medal in 1973 and was a runner-up for the Hans Christian Andersen Award in 1973. It won the Little Archer Award from the University of Wisconsin in 1976 and was placed on the International Board on Books for Young People Honor List in 1974. The book was also included in the 1973 Children's Book Showcase and was named an ALA Notable Book in the same year.

SELECTED WORKS RETOLD: Tikki Tikki Tembo, 1968; The Funny Little Woman, 1973.

ABOUT: Bader, Barbara. American Picturebooks from Noah's Ark to the Beast Within; Contemporary Authors, Vol. 49–52; Something About the Author, Vol. 7; Ward, Martha E. and Dorothy A. Marquardt. Authors of Books for Young People, 2nd edition.

WALTER DEAN MYERS

August 12, 1937–

AUTHOR OF *Fast Sam, Cool Clyde, and Stuff,* etc.

Autobiographical sketch of Walter Dean Myers:

I'M NOT SURE how many people from Martinsburg, West Virginia, have published books. Martinsburg isn't very large and, at least during the time covered by my earliest years, just surviving occupied the time of most of its inhabitants. I'm from an absurdly large family and when an offer of informal adoption came to my father he accepted it. I was put on a Greyhound bound for New York and the Dean family, friends of my deceased mother.

Compared to Martinsburg I found Harlem a marvel, an exotic land with an inexhaustable supply of delights and surprises. Plus, with the Deans, I could stop thinking of hunger as a way of life.

I loved Harlem and my new parents. The tarred streets, the fire escapes upon which we sought relief from the heat, two-sewer stickball, Chinese handball; this was the stuff of dreams. I played basketball in Morningside Park and Riverside Church's gym. I attended plays for children at Teacher's College and listened to stories at the George Bruce branch of the public library. The church I belonged to, and in which I attended summer Bible School, became the home of the Dance Theater of Harlem.

I had to whitewash the walls in the back of the church twice; once when the minister caught me throwing orange peels on the sidewalk and once when an assistant minister caught a bunch of us trying to lynch another boy. His offense had been to stare at the sun longer than any of us, go temporarily blind, and thus garner more than his share of attention.

Sugar Ray Robinson boxed with us on those streets. Josephine Baker came to the church and sang for us. Langston Hughes

chased my brother a block because he had thrown a candy wrapper in the poet's tiny patch of garden.

Yet this was not the Harlem I saw portrayed in books. The people I knew as a child were not the kind that were being written about. What I wanted to do was to portray this vital community as one that is very special to a lot of people. I wanted to show the people I knew as being as richly endowed with those universal traits of love, humor, and ambition as any in the world. This, I hope, is what my books do. That space of earth was no ghetto, it was home. Those were not exotic stereotypes, those were my people. And I love them.

Once my foster parents, people who have worked hard all their lives and mostly with their hands, asked me exactly what it was that I was doing. I tried to explain how the story writing I was doing was more sophisticated and purposeful than the endless stream of stories and poems I had produced as a child. I saw that it was difficult for them to understand my making a better living than they had without ever leaving the house. The world had, indeed, changed. Later, I heard my mother saying to my father that it was nice what I did, that it kept me out of trouble and all, but it was a wonder that anyone would actually pay me for it.

And it is that.

———

Walter Dean Myers attended the City College of the City University of New York. He has worked in the New York State Department of Labor and Bobbs-Merrill publishing company as a senior trade editor. He has three children.

Fast Sam, Cool Clyde, and Stuff has as its protagonist an eighteen-year-old boy who looks back five years to the day his family moved to Harlem. Black English used in the book lends authenticity to the novel.

Where Does the Day Go? received the Interracial Council Award for Children's Books in 1968, and *The Young Landlords* won the 1980 Coretta Scott King Award. *The Legend of Tarik* was named a Best Book for Young Adults for 1981 by the American Library Association. Myers' stories have been represented in several anthologies, such as *What We Must See: Young Black Storytellers,* edited by Orle Coombs; and he has contributed articles and stories to magazines, including *Black Creation* and *Black World.*

SELECTED WORKS: Where Does the Day Go?, 1969; Fast Sam, Cool Clyde, and Stuff, 1975; It Ain't All for Nothin', 1978; The Young Landlords, 1979; Hoops, 1981; The Legend of Tarik, 1981; Won't Know Till I Get There, 1982; Tales of a Dead King, 1983.

ABOUT: Contemporary Authors (First Revision), Vol. 33-36; Page, James A., comp. Selected Black American Authors: An Illustrated Bio-Bibliography; Rush, Theressa Gunnels and others. Black American Writers Past and Present: A Biographical and Bibliographical Dictionary; Shockley, Ann Allen and Sue P. Chandler. Living Black American Authors: A Biographical Directory; Who's Who in America, 1976-1977; Ward, Martha E. and Dorothy A. Marquardt. Authors of Books for Young People, 2nd edition (Supplement).

PHYLLIS REYNOLDS NAYLOR

January 4, 1933–

AUTHOR OF *Witch's Sister,* etc.

Autobiographical sketch of Phyllis Reynolds Naylor:

I CAN NEVER understand why people who have not seen me for a while ask if I am still writing. They might as well ask if I am still breathing. Writing is something I have been doing all my life. Even before I could put words down on paper, I was making up stories. There is no other job, I'm sure, that I would enjoy as much, for in my books I can be anyone I please—old or young, boy or girl. I can do wildly exciting things I would never dream of doing in real life, and can experience sorrows and terrors that I have always been curious about.

I was born in Anderson, Indiana, in 1933, right in the middle of the Great Depression. We didn't have a lot of toys, so we spent our time sliding down grassy hills on pieces of cardboard, building houses out of packing crates, snitching small pieces of ice off the back of the ice truck, and climbing around boxcars in the railroad yard. But my favorite pastime was writing. Since we weren't allowed to use good white paper, I got mine from the wastebasket, rescuing those sheets that had printing on only one side. I would staple them together and then begin my story, the words at the top, the picture at the bottom. The "book" was only as long as the number of pages I had found.

When I was sixteen, I had a story actually published in a church magazine, and from then on, began to write more and more each year. By the time I entered college, studying to be a clinical psychologist, I was able to pay a large share of my tuition by writing and selling stories. When I got my bachelor's degree, however, I decided I wanted to write more than anything else in the world, so I gave up plans to go on to graduate school and began writing full-time. Three years later my first book was published, and I have written over forty more since then.

I like to do all kinds of books, and usually work on two at a time—one for adults, one for young people. Perhaps I will work on a very serious book in the morning and a funny one in the afternoon. I particularly like writing books about realistic problems, books that are both sad and funny, but I have also done two trilogies of a different sort—a terrifying one about witchcraft (*Witch's Sister, Witch Water,* and *The Witch Herself*), and a trilogy about ghosts and gypsies (*Shadows on the Wall, Faces in the Water,* and *Footprints at the Window*). My favorite is *A String of Chances,* about a sixteen-year-old girl named Evie Hutchins who, during a summer that shakes her faith in her deepest beliefs, is finally able to look at both herself and her family with a new perspective.

There are two sons and a husband in my own family, and they all enjoy reading and criticizing my books. They often crop up in my stories—a mannerism here, a problem there, the shape of a chin, perhaps. . . . Of course you would never recognize them, for all of my characters are made up of little bits and pieces of many different people.

When I'm not writing I enjoy doing things with my family—going to the theater, swimming at the ocean, exploring someplace new. What I can do that my family can't is sing sixteenth-century madrigals and play the dulcimer. What some of them can do that I can't is ski, solve chess problems, understand French, and play a five-piece drum set.

Before she received her B.A. degree from American University in Washington, D.C., Phyllis Reynolds Naylor held several jobs, working in the Montgomery County Education Association offices in Rockville, Maryland and as editorial assistant with the *National Education Association Journal* in 1959 and 1960. She is a member of the Authors League of America and the Washington, D.C. Children's Book Guild. She has contributed about two thousand short stories and articles to magazines.

How I Came to Be a Writer was the 1978 recipient of the Golden Kite Award for nonfiction from the Society of Children's Book Writers.

SELECTED WORKS: Witch's Sister, 1975; Witch Water, 1977; The Witch Herself, 1978; How I Came To Be a Writer, 1978; How Lazy Can You Get?, 1979; Eddie, Incorporated, 1980; Shadows on the Wall, 1980; All Because I'm Older, 1981; Faces in the Water, 1981; Footprints at the Window, 1981; A String of Chances, 1982.

ABOUT: Contemporary Authors (First Revision), Vol. 21-24; The International Authors and Writers Who's Who, 1977; Naylor, Phyllis Reynolds. How I Came to Be a Writer; Something About the Author, Vol. 12; Ward, Martha E. and Dorothy A. Marquardt. Authors of Books for Young People, 2nd edition (Supplement); Who's Who of American Women, 1975-1976; The Writers Directory 1982-84.

JOHN NEY

May 3, 1923–

AUTHOR OF *Ox Under Pressure,* etc.

Autobiographical sketch of John Ney:

MY CONNECTION with children's books, rather tenuous at best, has now come to a halt, and I haven't published one in seven years. The three that were published were about Ox Olmstead, a very large boy from a very rich family in Palm Beach. They formed a series of sorts, taking Ox from the age of twelve in the first book to seventeen in the last.

I wrote the first, *Ox: The Story of a Kid at the Top,* to amuse my children, the traditional start. It was published in 1970 and the next two, *Ox Goes North* and *Ox Under Pressure,* followed in 1973 and 1976. All three circulated to a certain critical acclaim, and were published in paperback as well as hardback. *Ox Under Pressure* was a Book-of-the-Month Club Alternate and a National Book Award Nominee in 1977.

These details are only interesting because I had been under the impression, from having written and published some adult books, that relatively successful books in any field lead publishers to want more from the same source, to say nothing of the same characters. I was evidently wrong. The problem seemed to be, as my last editor told me, that Ox "grew out of his attractive weaknesses. He got stronger and more independent with each book until, in the last one, he doesn't need anybody. You have to understand that modern children's literature is all for the underdog—ethnically, emotionally, physically, whatever. You just can't make it with a kid who has nothing wrong with him."

Well, at least it was clear, and we understood each other. My choice was simple: write about underdogs or give up being published. I chose the latter. Actually, it was not a choice—I probably couldn't have written about underdogs well enough, anyhow.

It isn't, I should make clear, that I have anything against underdogs. In fact, Ox himself is an underdog in that he is out of place because he is so independent. (Truly independent children always have more problems than the rest.) It's just that I am irresistibly (and fatally) drawn to a nonfashionable sort of underdog.

I still write about those underdogs—or, more accurately, those outsiders—for my own amusement. I am also busy with business ventures, a number of grown children and grandchildren, and various sports. We live in the cattle country in Florida, far from the tourists, and usually go abroad in the summers.

In the adult book field, I am currently working on a book entitled *An Intelligent Woman's Guide to American Failure*. If the title seems too weighty, it will be changed. For the moment, though, it has to serve.

———

John Ney was born in St. Paul, Minnesota, and grew up in New York and St. Louis. In 1949, he moved to Italy, where he wrote movie scripts for the budding film industry there. He later lived in England, Italy, Switzerland, Austria, and several other European countries. He has also lived on the West Indian island of Jamaica and in Palm Beach, Florida, where the story of Ox takes place. Ney has been writing professionally for more than twenty years. In addition to his movie scripts, he has written nonfiction

books for adults, as well as the three Ox novels for children and young adults. Of Ney's juvenile hero, Mary M. Burns stated in a *Horn Book* review that "Ox may well become a Holden Caulfield for a new generation."

SELECTED WORKS: Ox: The Story of a Kid at the Top, 1970; Ox Goes North: More Trouble for the Kid at the Top, 1973; Ox Under Pressure, 1976.

ABOUT: Ward, Martha E. and Dorothy A. Marquardt. Authors of Books for Young People, 2nd edition (Supplement).

JOAN LOWERY NIXON

February 3, 1927–

AUTHOR OF *The Kidnapping of Christina Lattimore*, etc.

Autobiographical sketch of Joan Lowery Nixon:

WHEN I came home from a writers' conference and told my family that I had heard a good talk about writing for children and thought I might try it, I had a surprise. Our two older daughters, Kathy and Maureen, told me that if I were going to write for children I had to write a book, it had to be a mystery, and I had to put them in it!

It was quite a change from the magazine writing I had been doing for adults, but I did what they asked, and it turned out to be my first book for young people, *The Mystery of Hurricane Castle*. I enjoyed writing it so much I've been writing books for children ever since, and many of them have been mysteries. Mysteries, with all their real clues and fake clues and puzzles and twists and scary parts, are fun to plan and plot and write.

Each of our four children, Kathleen, Maureen, Joe, and Eileen, has been a character in a book; and I've used in other stories many of the things they did as they were growing up.

Places where I've lived or visited are of-

When I began writing for young people our own children were very young, with the youngest just a toddler. Now our first grandchild asks her mother to read her my books. Maybe someday our great-grandchildren will be reading them, too. I hope so.

———

After graduation from college in 1947, Joan Lowery Nixon was an elementary school teacher in Los Angeles, until 1950. In 1971 she became an instructor in creative writing at Midland College in Texas. She was also on the Summer Writers Conference Committee at the University of Houston and is a member of the Authors League of America and the Houston Writers' Workshop. She has been a columnist for the *Houston Post.*

Joan Lowery Nixon has won the Edgar Allan Poe Award from the Mystery Writers of America two years in a row: in 1979 for *The Kidnapping of Christina Lattimore* and in 1980 for *The Seance.*

Two of her books written with Hershell H. Nixon were named Outstanding Science Trade Books for Children by the National Science Teachers Association: *Volcanoes* in 1978 and *Glaciers* in 1980.

SELECTED WORKS WRITTEN: The Mystery of Hurricane Castle, 1964; The Alligator Under the Bed, 1971; The Secret Box Mystery, 1974; The Mysterious Prowler, 1976; Bigfoot Makes a Movie, 1979; The Kidnapping of Christina Lattimore, 1979; The Seance, 1980; Casey and the Great Idea, 1980; The April Fool Mystery, 1980; The Specter, 1982.

SELECTED WORKS WRITTEN WITH HERSHELL H. NIXON: Volcanoes: Nature's Fireworks, 1978; Glaciers: Nature's Frozen Rivers, 1980.

ABOUT: Contemporary Authors (First Revision), Vol. 9-12; Something About the Author, Vol. 8: Ward, Martha E. and Dorothy A. Marquardt. Authors of Books for Young People, 2nd edition (Supplement).

ten used as backgrounds in my stories. The two settings I like the most are the places I love the most: Los Angeles, California, and the whole big state of Texas.

I was born in Los Angeles and graduated from Hollywood High School and the University of Southern California, where I met my husband, Hershell Nixon. He's a geologist, and his work in finding oil and gas took us to Corpus Christi, Texas, in 1960. We've lived in Texas ever since.

I try to write every weekday morning from about 8:30 until noon. I save running errands, trips to the dentist, grocery shopping, and visiting friends for afternoons, because I'm a morning person and think better in the morning hours.

I used to compose my stories on a typewriter, but as I write I rewrite, making many changes; and the pages were so scribbled over by the time they came out of the typewriter, sometimes it was hard for me to figure out what I had written. Now I use a word processor, where I can see what I'm writing on a screen and make changes on that screen. While it prints what I have written I can be doing something else. While it printed the last novel I wrote I was watching a football game!

CHRISTINE NÖSTLINGER

1936–

AUTHOR OF *Fly Away Home,* etc.

Biographical sketch of Christine Nöstlinger:

CHRISTINE NÖSTLINGER was born in a working-class suburb of Vienna. Like so many children of her generation, her childhood was dominated and shaped by the events of World War II. Her family survived the Allied bombing of the city, enduring the lack of food, proper clothing, medicine, and even a home as the buildings of the city were destroyed.

As a young woman she attended art school, bent on a painting career. She interrupted her work to marry and have her first of two daughters, but she never returned to the art field. Nöstlinger began a new career as a journalist on one of Vienna's daily newspapers, work she continues to this day.

She then moved from newspaper writing to children's books. Her first novel to be published in the United States was the autobiographical *Fly Away Home,* which tells the story of a young girl, Christel, during the last part of the war, especially the difficult time of the Russian occupation. Completely true to the child's point of view, Nöstlinger mixes the horrible with the humorous, an attitude that has become a trademark of her work.

She has moved from the theme of the war to more contemporary settings in her later books, which remain, however, influenced by her childhood circumstances. *Girl Missing,* for example, is the story of a young girl's desperate search for her missing sister, who has run away from their broken home; yet it has been called a comic novel. *Marrying Off Mother* treats the subject of impending divorce, but comically, as the heroine decides to take upon herself the task of replacing Daddy.

Christine Nöstlinger has received numerous awards for her original work. In 1972 she was awarded the Friedrich-Bödecker Prize for her contribution to the field of

CHRISTINE NÖSTLINGER

children's literature and the following year was awarded the German State Children's Book Prize. The critically acclaimed *Luke and Angela* is the story of two friends, close since childhood, who have difficulty in coping with the changes brought on by young adulthood. It was named an American Library Association Notable Book for 1981. *Konrad,* her most openly humorous and satirical work, introduces a factory-produced, canned child—developed to provide the most perfectly behaved and obedient son— who is mistakenly delivered to the wrong family. The book, which chronicles the attempts of his new family to "normalize" Konrad, was awarded the 1977 Mildred L. Batchelder award. It was translated by Anthea Bell.

Nöstlinger has written over ten novels for young people. She lives in Vienna.

SELECTED WORKS: Fly Away Home, 1975; The Cucumber King, 1975; Fiery Frederica, 1975; Girl Missing, 1976; Konrad, 1976; Luke and Angela, 1981; Marrying Off Mother, 1982.

GRAHAM OAKLEY

August 27, 1919–

AUTHOR AND ILLUSTRATOR OF *The Church Mouse*, etc.

Biographical sketch of Graham Oakley:

GRAHAM OAKLEY was born in Shrewsbury, England, and grew up there and in Warrington. He attended Warrington Art School and then served in the British Army from 1945 to 1947. He worked as a scenic artist for several British repertory companies (1950–1955); as a designer's assistant at the Royal Opera House (1955–1957); in an advertising agency (1960–1962); and as a set designer for the BBC (1962–1977). His British television credits run the gamut from classics such as "How Green Was My Valley," "Nicholas Nickleby," and "Treasure Island" to two top-rated police shows, "Z-Cars," and "Softly, Softly."

Oakley was working as a free-lance illustrator of children's books when he began to envision Wortlethorpe, a small British country town caught between the past and the present, as the setting for a series of picture books for children. He said in a *Publishers Weekly* interview, "I was going to open with a high view on top of the town and a series of stories about each building starting with the church and moving on to the library and the town hall, but the first book . . . was so successful I never got to the library."

In each of the "Church Mice" stories, the endearing group of mice in the Anglican parish church in Wortlethorpe is threatened by the outside world in some way and must overcome the threat with the sometimes misguided help of their orange feline ally, Sampson, the church cat. Oakley said of their conflicts, "I try to think, 'How could a little creature get rid of a man?' The devices have to be contrived. I suppose what I'm trying to do is create a James Bond-type story on the mice level."

Oakley's first book, *The Church Mouse*, was an immediate popular and critical suc-

GRAHAM OAKLEY

cess. The *New York Times* raved: "Good for Graham Oakley! [the story] . . . is told with a lively touch of nonsense that children—of all ages—should find irresistible. It is an intelligent book, combining simplicity and sophistication, and it doesn't condescend. It is a well-integrated picture story, with a text almost as special as the art work." Across the ocean the *Times Literary Supplement* echoed the enthusiasm: "The text is richly interlarded with beautifully detailed illustrations showing the mice indulging in all manner of fascinating activities, from polishing brasses and staggering about with huge piles of confetti to rolling up a burglar in a carpet. Graham Oakley shows in this book how effectively words and pictures can be grafted together so that our understanding of the story depends on the combination of the two."

Seven more "Church Mice" stories have followed, each receiving critical acclaim. *New York Magazine* said in their review of *The Church Cat Abroad* (1973), "Oakley is an old-school storyteller who uses words and pictures to weave an up-to-date fantasy with countless realistic details to catch and hold attention." And *Publishers Weekly* wrote, "This British author-illustrator enchanted readers last year with *The Church Mouse.* Here are the further adventures of Sampson and friends in an even wilder, wittier book . . . a story and pictures that every member of the family should enjoy."

The Church Mice Adrift won particular critical praise. Jane Langton, writing in the *New York Times,* expressed her hope that "the brilliant author-artist will still be painting pictures when he is 99, like Titian, turning out new books about the church mice, cranking up from the bottomless well of his genius the same old Oakley bucket." And the *Bulletin of the Center for Children's Books* called it a "comic masterpiece." *The Church Mice Adrift* was nominated for a Kate Greenaway Medal in 1976 and was a *New York Times* Choice of Best Illustrated Children's Books of the Year 1977. In 1980, Oakley published *Graham Oakley's Magical Changes,* about which *Punch* said, "the mechanics alone . . . are enough to fascinate almost anyone old enough to turn the pages. . . . the drawings . . . have a surreal quality that gives them a wider appeal." It won a Special Citation from the Boston Globe-Horn Book Award Committee and was named a Notable Book by the American Library Association in 1980. *Church Mice in Action* was Highly Commended for the Kate Greenaway Medal in 1983.

Although he has been praised for the lack of anthropomorphism in his books, Oakley has mixed feelings on the subject: "I try not to let anything human creep into my portrayal of Sampson, to keep him looking like a cat at all times. He does just what a cat would do in any situation, when he is frightened, happy, puzzled. The church mice, on the other hand, are easy to anthropomorphize, and I think it's no great affront to nature to do so."

Graham Oakley lives in an eighteenth-century mill in Wiltshire, England. To date, he has illustrated over thirty books for children.

SELECTED WORKS WRITTEN AND ILLUSTRATED: The Church Mouse, 1972; The Church Cat Abroad, 1973; The Church Mice and the Moon, 1974; The Church

Mice Spread Their Wings, 1976; The Church Mice Adrift, 1977; The Church Mice at Bay, 1979; The Church Mice at Christmas, 1980; Graham Oakley's Magical Changes, 1980; Hetty and Harriet, 1981; Church Mice in Action, 1983.

SELECTED WORKS ILLUSTRATED: Dragon Hoard, by Tanith Lee, 1971.

ABOUT: Contemporary Authors, Vol. 106; Kingman, Lee and others, comps. Illustrators of Children's Books: 1967–1976; Something About the Author, Vol. 30; Publishers Weekly February 26, 1979.

NANCY WINSLOW PARKER

October 18, 1930–

AUTHOR AND ILLUSTRATOR OF *Poofy Loves Company,* etc.

Autobiographical sketch of Nancy Winslow Parker:

I WAS BORN in Maplewood, New Jersey in 1930, and grew up amid the swirling events of the Great Depression and the Roosevelt Administration. All children in Maplewood are weaned on the facts that Asher B. Durand, the great painter of the Hudson River School, was born there in the latter part of the eighteenth century; that the popular American novelist Agnes Sligh Turnbull made her home there; and that Teresa Wright left Maplewood for Hollywood and the stage. The conversation at the dinner table for the first eleven years of my life seems to have been devoted exclusively to FDR, Mrs. Roosevelt's trips, John L. Lewis, labor unions, and reminders to eat everything on my plate because the poor starving people in Europe had nothing. I used to silently wonder how we would get all our furniture on one truck and flee the town, just steps ahead of the Japanese soldiers; and having no subways to hide in like the Londoners, where we would go to escape German bombs.

I knew from the time I was born that I would grow up and be an artist, but had no idea that I would ever become a writer. My

Nancy Winslow Parker

favorite books were the *National Geographic,* of which my family had practically every issue. There were no stacks of children's books, but there were several hand-me-down books of my mother's, which were hopelessly Victorian and full of dull ink drawings of children in black stockings playing with hoops.

I survived the American public school system through the twelfth grade, which was by and large designed to suppress any creative energy in students. It is a miracle that so many artists (this includes music, dance, etc.) did survive and found instruction in larger cities and contribute to the cultural life of the United States today.

Mills College in California was nice enough to accept me as a freshman, and I spent some of the happiest years of my life on that delightful campus amid the eucalyptus, palm trees, acacia; and studied in Spanish style buildings with inspiring professors. I majored in art, and filled up the other requirements with English. I graduated with a B.A. degree and came to New York City to become rich and famous.

The next twenty-one years in New York were spent working in some of the giant corporations of America, and after toiling

in practically every department of these feudal systems, I left to devote full-time as an artist.

After a total of eighty-eight rejection slips from the publishers for a number of works, I published my first book in 1973, *The Man with the Take-Apart Head,* a story about a man who is always late for work. I see now that it was my parting shot at the time-clock and office drudgery. It was also my debut as a writer, something I never expected, but was forced to do so I could illustrate something.

Every book I write and illustrate is done in the spirit of fun. Many times I have wondered why the IRS forms were not written by happier people instead of sadistic beasts intent on reducing the reader to a heap of sobbing flesh.

During my lifetime so far I have lived with three fluffy white dogs and two cats. They have all enjoyed long wonderful lives and appear from time to time in most of my illustrations. *The Crocodile Under Louis Finneberg's Bed* has my little Bichon Frisé Mimi-Gladys throughout the illustrations, and *Poofy Loves Company* is about Poofy, a dog I bred, raised, and entered in all the dog shows for miles around. And what it's like to live the dog show life is explicitly documented in *The Spotted Dog: The Strange Tale of a Witch's Revenge.*

In New York City, Nancy Winslow Parker continued her education at the Art Students League in 1956 and 1957 and at the School of Visual Arts from 1966 to 1967. She worked in sales promotion and has been a graphic designer at Holt, Rinehart & Winston and an art director at Appleton-Century-Crofts.

In 1975 she was awarded a Jane Tinkham Broughton Fellowship in Writing for Children, at the Breadloaf Writers Conference at Middlebury College, Vermont.

She is a member of the Society of Illustrators as well as the Bichon Frisé Club of America.

She received two Christopher Awards: in 1976 for *Willy Bear*, and in 1981 for *My Mom Travels a Lot*, which was also named one of the ten best illustrated books of the year 1981 by the *New York Times*. *Willy Bear* was in the 1976 American Institute of Graphic Arts Book Show. *The President's Car* won an Honorable Mention from the New York Academy of Science Children's Science Book Awards in 1981, and *Oh, A-Hunting We Will Go* was a Junior Literary Guild selection. Two of Parker's books were named Notable Children's Trade Books in the Field of Social Studies by a joint committee of the Children's Book Council and the National Council for the Social Studies: *Goat in the Rug* in 1976 and *Warm as Wool* in 1976. *Poofy Loves Company* was designated an American Library Association Notable Book in 1980.

SELECTED WORKS WRITTEN AND ILLUSTRATED: The Man with the Take-Apart Head, 1974; The Party at the Old Farm, 1975; Love from Uncle Clyde, 1977; The Crocodile Under Louis Finneberg's Bed, 1978; The President's Cabinet, 1978; Poofy Loves Company, 1980; The Spotted Dog: The Strange Tale of a Witch's Revenge, 1980; The President's Car, 1981.

SELECTED WORKS ILLUSTRATED: Oh, A-Hunting We Will Go, by John Langstaff, ed., 1974; Warm as Wool, Cool as Cotton: Natural Fibers and Fabrics and How to Work With Them, by Carter Houck, 1975; The Goat in the Rug, by Charles L. Blood and Martin Link, 1976; Willy Bear, by Mildred Kantrowitz, 1976; My Mom Travels a Lot, by Caroline Feller Bauer, 1981.

ABOUT: Contemporary Authors, Vol. 49-52; (New Revision Series), Vol. 1; The International Authors and Writers Who's Who, 1977; Kingman, Lee and others, comps. Illustrators of Children's Books: 1967-1976; Something About the Author, Vol. 10; Ward, Martha E. and Dorothy A. Marquardt. Illustrators of Books for Young People, 2nd edition; Who's Who in American Art, 1978; The Writers Directory 1982-84.

FRANCINE PASCAL

May 13, 1938–

AUTHOR OF *Hangin' Out with Cici*, etc.

FRANCINE PASCAL

Biographical sketch of Francine Pascal:

FRANCINE PASCAL was born and raised in New York City. She has always wanted to be a writer, and after graduating from New York University, where she received a degree in journalism, her writing career began with humor and travel articles published in *Ladies' Home Journal* and *Cosmopolitan*. In the late 1960s, Pascal became interested in drama and wrote a soap opera and several television script adaptations. Then in 1968, she collaborated with John Pascal and Michael Stewart to write the script for the Broadway musical *George M!*. In 1973, Pascal wrote *The Strange Case of Patti Hearst*, which was for adults. She also wrote a novel for adults, *Save Johanna!*, which was published in 1981.

Hangin' Out with Cici, which was published in 1977, launched Pascal's new career in young adult fiction. Praised by critics for its humor and realism, the novel centers on fourteen-year-old Victoria, who gets a bump on the head and travels back in time to become friends with her own mother as a young girl. The story points up the painful conflicts of adolescence and the touching relationship of parent and teenager. *Hangin' Out with Cici* has become a favorite of teenage girls and has been listed in the New York Public Library's *Books for the Teenage* for six years running. It was also chosen to be aired on television as an ABC After School Special.

Her second novel for young adults, *My First Love and Other Disasters,* was named a Best Book for Young Adults by the American Library Association in 1980. In this novel, fifteen-year-old Vicky coaxes her parents into allowing her to take a summer job on Fire Island so that she can be near gorgeous Jim, her first love. *School Library Journal* praised Pascal's "delicate balance . . . between the explicit and the sensational." They added that "she writes about teen-age sex with candor and sensitivity."

The Hand-Me-Down Kid was published in 1980. Once again Pascal uses humor to portray contemporary characters, this time caught up in sibling rivalry. In a case of the survival of the youngest, eleven-year-old Ari Jacobs is the hand-me-down kid with a rather negative view of life; she is envious of her older brothers and sisters, not to mention their possessions. *Horn Book* noted that the novel "maintains a perspective on everything from training bras to older brothers and sisters and offers hand-me-down kids a believable example of assertiveness training." It, too, was made into an After School Special, entitled "My Mother Was Never a Kid."

Her most recent project is the creation of a twelve-book young adult paperback series called the Sweet Valley High Series. *Double Love by Kate William* is the first, and the following books will be published at one-month intervals.

Francine Pascal lives in Manhattan. Among her special interests are travel and reading. She is often invited to schools to speak on the subject of her books.

SELECTED WORKS: Hangin' Out with Cici, 1977; My First Love and Other Disasters, 1979; The Hand-Me-Down Kid, 1980.

KATHERINE PATERSON

October 31, 1932–

AUTHOR OF *Jacob Have I Loved,* etc.

Autobiographical sketch of Katherine Womeldorf Paterson:

I WAS BORN in the Jiangsu Province of China in the city of Qing Jiang, but my family's home where I spent my first four and a half years was in the nearby city of Hwaian. In the summer of 1937 we went to the mountains of Jiangxi for a vacation. While we were there war broke out between China and Japan, and although my father crossed through the combat zones to return to his work in Hwaian, my mother, brother, three sisters, and I never saw our home again.

Since that time I have lived in more than thirty homes in three countries. I am grateful that our four children have not had to live through war or enemy occupation or refugeeing or even much moving about, but I'm sure these early experiences shaped the person I became and helped me to write the kind of books I do.

Among the many frightening and lonely experiences of my childhood, there were, of course, some very happy events. I count in this number the books that I read or that were read to me. My mother read to us regularly, and because it opened up such a wonderful world, I taught myself to read before I entered school. Soon afterwards I began to write. I can't remember wanting to become a writer, but I loved stories and poems so much that it was only natural to try my hand at them. My first published work appeared in the Shanghai American School newspaper when I was seven years old.

> Pat. Pat. Pat.
> There is the cat.
> Where is the rat.
> Pat. Pat. Pat.

As you can see, there was plenty of room for improvement.

After college (where I majored in English

Katherine Paterson

literature and wrote a lot of term papers), I taught sixth grade in a rural Virginia school. Then I went back to school to study Bible and Christian Education before going to Japan in 1957. After I had studied the Japanese language for two years, I went to work on the island of Shikoku as an assistant for Christian Education to eleven country pastors, riding my small motorcycle from church to church.

I had planned to spend the rest of my life in Japan, but in 1961 I was given a fellowship for further study in Christian Education at Union Theological Seminary in New York City. There I met John Barstow Paterson, who was a Presbyterian pastor in Buffalo, New York. John and I were married in the summer of 1962. Before our children came along, I was a substitute teacher (the worst job I ever had), and then a teacher of English and Sacred Studies at a boys' prep school near Princeton, New Jersey.

My writing career began after our first son was born in 1964. Lin, our older daughter, was born in Hong Kong in 1962 and joined us when John, Jr. was six months old. David was born in 1966 soon after we moved to Takoma Park, Maryland. And Mary, who was born on an Apache reserva-

tion in Arizona, became a member of our family that same August.

Our children cannot remember a time when I was not writing, but for a long time only they and their father thought I was a writer. Although I had begun working seriously in 1964, it was nine years before my first novel was published. In 1977, after *The Master Puppeteer* won the National Book Award in Children's Literature, I heard myself proclaimed "an overnight success." My family and I knew that the "night" had lasted thirteen years.

But all those years when I couldn't sell my stories, I was learning how to write. I found that a writer must give her heart as well as her mind to her work. I learned to love the process of revising a book, going over and over it until I was sure that it was the best I could do. And I've never stopped reading. I'd still rather read than write, but I am very grateful to be able to do both.

———

Among Katherine Paterson's novels are three on feudal Japan: *The Sign of the Chrysanthemum, Of Nightingales That Weep,* and *The Master Puppeteer. The Great Gilly Hopkins* is about two foster children who may or may not last in the home of a new foster parent; *Bridge to Terabithia* concerns the death of one of two children who share a secret hiding place; and *Jacob Have I Loved* is the tale of a twin who is consumed with envy for and resentment of her sister.

Katherine Paterson won the Newbery Medal twice and has received many other major awards in children's literature. *The Master Puppeteer* won the National Book Award in 1977 and appeared on the *School Library Journal* "Best of the Best 1966–1978" list (December 1979). *Bridge to Terabithia* won the Newbery Medal in 1978 and a Lewis Carroll Shelf Award in the same year.

The Great Gilly Hopkins, which has been adapted for a television special, won the National Book Award in 1979 and was a 1979 Newbery Honor Book. The paperback edition was a finalist in the 1980 American Book Awards. It won a Christopher Award in 1978, the 1981 William Allen White Award, and the 1981 Garden State Children's Book Award. It also appeared on the *School Library Journal* "Best of the Best 1966–1978" list.

Jacob Have I Loved won the Newbery Medal in 1981 and was a finalist in the hardcover fiction category of the American Book Awards in 1980. It was also a finalist in the 1982 paperback category, as was *The Master Puppeteer.*

Katherine Paterson was the recipient of the 1983 Silver Medallion presented by the University of Southern Mississippi. *The Crane Wife,* translated by Paterson and illustrated by Suekichi Akaba, was named a 1981 Notable Book by the American Library Association.

She graduated from King College in 1954. She received her M.A. from the Presbyterian School of Christian Education in 1957, and her M.R.E. from Union Theological Seminary in 1962. Paterson wrote a book for adults on children's literature, *Gates of Excellence,* which was published in 1981.

SELECTED WORKS: The Sign of the Chrysanthemum, 1973; Of Nightingales That Weep, 1974; The Master Puppeteer, 1976; Bridge to Terabithia, 1977; The Great Gilly Hopkins, 1978; Angels and Other Strangers: Family Christmas Stories, 1979; Jacob Have I Loved, 1980; Rebels of the Heavenly Kingdom, 1983.

SELECTED WORKS TRANSLATED: The Crane Wife, by Sumiko Yagawa, 1981.

ABOUT: Contemporary Authors (First Revision), Vol. 21–24; Something About the Author, Vol. 13; Ward, Martha E. and Dorothy A. Marquardt. Authors of Books for Young People, 2nd edition (Supplement; see addenda).

RICHARD PECK

April 5, 1934–

AUTHOR OF *The Ghost Belonged to Me,* etc.

Autobiographical sketch of Richard Peck:

THERE ARE people who seem to have been born writing. There are others who come to writing later in life. I fall into this latter category, never having written a line of fiction until I was thirty-seven years old. But I was born listening—eavesdropping, if you like.

We lived in the middle of the Middlewest in a middle-sized town called Decatur, Illinois. In this wholesome setting well behind the line of battle during World War II, I dreamed for some reason of New York and London. I lay in front of the radio listening to "Manhattan Merry-go-round" and Edward R. Murrow. I read Richard Halliburton and *National Geographic* Magazine and longed for long-distance. Later, I studied at the University of London and became a writer in New York. You must be careful what you wish for; you're liable to get it.

When I outdistanced my past, I looked back at Decatur, Illinois, and began to hear its voices. The voice, for example, of my great-uncle, Miles Peck, an octogenarian rogue and journeyman carpenter who terrorized the town in his Model A Ford fitted out with a carpentry box where the rumble seat had been. At eighty-five he still had an eye for a pretty woman, a keen nose for scandal, and inconvenient memories of other people's pasts. He had married often but not seriously and was as free as I hoped adults were. Grown-ups dreaded him. I sopped up his every word. Then, when I thought him long dead, he marched forthrightly into a novel of mine called *The Ghost Belonged to Me* and took charge of it.

My father, his nephew, was no less colorful. I thought him the most popular man in town and he may have been. Possibly this fueled my plans for escape; I couldn't have competed with him. In a neighborhood where other fathers went whey-faced and white-collared off to offices in Plymouth sedans, mine roared away every morning in green coveralls astride a Harley-Davidson. He'd been born in the nineteenth century at the end of the Mark Twain tradition, hunting and fishing the Sangamon River bottoms. He ran a Phillips 66 gas station like a club. Elderly men less mobile than Uncle Miles hung out there and talked of old times. Large, twelve-year-old boys rolled their newspapers there, and while I was far too young to be hearing it, I learned vocabulary from them.

It was wartime, and that made the outside world dangerous and glamorous. There were three adults at our dinner table talking over my head. My father followed World War II from the perspective of World War I, in which he'd been badly wounded. He clenched his fist in rage at war and killing and Roosevelt. Later, I had to appear before him in an army uniform, and his fist clenched again, and his eyes were wet.

My mother was a dietician, struggling with wartime menus. My young, unmarried aunt volunteered her evenings as a nurses' aide and wrote cheering letters to servicemen she didn't know. At the dinner table, the smallest head, I learned viewpoint.

Later, too late to save me from only-child status, I acquired a small sister. She became the prototypical protagonist for any number of young adult novel heroines. I was the typical older child, she the typical younger. I conformed, she questioned. I recorded, she rebelled.

I fell easy prey to teachers. My mother had read to me and made me hungry for school and books. My teachers betrayed no interest in my ideas. They imposed the form and format of grammar and Latin—the symmetry of sentences and the shape of paragraphs. They knew that without the structure for sharing, ideas are nothing.

These were the people I came from, and the place. I thought it monotonous because I didn't know the narrowness of ghettos and the lockstep of suburbia. I dreamed secretly of being a writer and prepared soberly to be an English teacher.

From that first day in a classs room of my own, I heard the voices of the young, and found that I was no longer one of them. I'd never have become a writer without all this variety of voices, vocabulary, viewpoint. As an English teacher I learned things about the private life of the very young that their parents need never know. I learned that teaching is listening and that writing is compromise. I learned of problems I'd been spared as a kid, problems without solutions that require airing.

There are timely problems, even fashionable ones—of drugs and drink and divorce. But I learned of larger, timeless problems from my students that I wouldn't have evaluated in my own life. That being young in an old world is never easy. That the more freedom the young are given, the less they have. That to be over-praised is to be robbed of challenge. That your best friend and your worst enemy tend to be the same person.

I'd be a teacher yet if I'd been allowed to teach as I'd been taught. I went looking for another arena for communicating with the young, another corner to eavesdrop in. I found it in writing to and about young people coming of age. On a good day, a very good day, I receive a letter from some young reader in a town where I've never been, asking, "How do you know me? Do you live around here?" I try to.

———

Richard Peck attended the University of Exeter in England in 1954 and 1955 and received his B.A. degree from DePauw University in 1956. He earned his M.A. in 1959 from Southern Illinois University and also studied at Washington University, in 1960 and 1961. He has taught English in high school and college, has been a textbook editor, and was Assistant Director of the Council for Basic Education in Washington, D.C. from 1969 to 1970. His poetry has been published in anthologies and in magazines, including *Saturday Review*. He also writes on architecture for the *New York Times*.

Peck was named Illinois Writer of the Year by the Illinois Association of Teachers of English in 1977. *The Ghost Belonged to Me* won the Friends of American Writers Award in 1976 and *Are You in the House Alone?*, which is one of five of Peck's novels that have been made into television movies, won the 1977 Edgar Allan Poe Award. Both *Dreamland Lake* and *Father Figure* were included on the *School Library Journal* "Best of the Best 1966–1978" list (December 1979). *Close Enough to Touch* was a 1982 Dorothy Canfield Fisher Award nominee and was named a 1981 Best Book for Young Adults by the American Library Association. *Ghosts I Have Been* and *The Dreadful Future of Blossom Culp* are sequels to *The Ghost Belonged to Me*.

SELECTED WORKS: Don't Look and It Won't Hurt, 1972; Dreamland Lake, 1973; Through a Brief Darkness, 1973; Representing Super Doll, 1974; The Ghost Belonged to Me, 1975; Are You in the House Alone? 1976; Ghosts I Have Been, 1977; Father Figure, 1978; Secrets of the Shopping Mall, 1979; Close Enough to Touch, 1981; The Dreadful Future of Blossom Culp, 1983.

ABOUT: Contemporary Authors, Vol. 85–88; Kirkpatrick, D. L. Twentieth-Century Children's Writers; Something About the Author, Vol. 18; The Writers Directory 1982–84.

ROBERT NEWTON PECK

February 17, 1928–

AUTHOR OF *A Day No Pigs Would Die,* etc.

Biographical sketch of Robert Newton Peck III:

ROBERT NEWTON PECK was born in Vermont. The son of hardworking rural people, he was raised on a farm and worked as a lumberjack, in a papermill, killing hogs, and as an advertising executive before the publication of his first book in 1973. He also served as a machine-gunner in the U.S. Army 88th Infantry Division between 1945 and 1947. He received a B.A. degree from Rollins College in Winter Park, Florida, in 1953, and studied law at Cornell University.

A prolific writer of fiction for young people (Peck has written fifteen books in the last ten years), his work is rooted in the rural tradition of his boyhood. His first book, *A Day No Pigs Would Die,* concerns the rites of passage of a young boy growing up on a Vermont farm. The hard facts of farm life are realistically described in terse, vivid prose that has no room for sentimentality. In the book, the young hero is required to slaughter his own pet pig. Peck does not balk at the seemingly brutal necessities of a consumer world. "I can't con readers that bacon is made by DuPont out of soybeans," he says. "Killing hogs is honest work. My father did it. So did I. One time, at a cocktail party, I watched people ram goose liver into their maws and then announce how opposed they were to violence." This same violence, which is often gorily described, has had a mixed reception among reviewers, but overall, Peck has been praised for his down-to-earth, life-is-tough attitude. *A Day No Pigs Would Die* was named an American Library Association Best Book for Young Adults in 1973.

Soup (and five sequels, *Soup and Me, Soup for President, Soup's Drum, Soup on Wheels,* and *Soup in the Saddle*) draws heavily on a real-life character, Miss Kelly, who is a lov-

ROBERT NEWTON PECK

able but tough school teacher. She was one of the major influences in Peck's childhood, and he is unstinting in his praise of her and other teachers and their desire to get the children in their charge to read. "I was lucky. Miss Kelly . . . was my real-life teacher. One-room school, twenty to thirty kids spread among six grades, sons and daughters of mill workers, farmers, and timberjacks . . . most of our parents could neither read nor write."

Soup and Me was made into an ABC After School Special.

Motivating the young to read is a task of paramount importance to Peck. He believes that reading a chapter aloud whets the appetite so that the child will come back for more. In Peck's opinion, such "seed-sowing" unites the farmer with the educator. "Miss Kelly once told us . . . that teachers are akin to farmers. Because a farmer gets up and goes to his garden; but, she then added, she was more fortunate, as her garden came to her."

However, not all of Robert Newton Peck's books are directly based on personal experience. His fascination with the Colonial and Revolutionary periods of American history provided him with the setting for

three historical novels, *Hang for Treason, Fawn,* and *Rabbits and Redcoats.* In the first, a young boy struggles with individual loyalties to eventually reach manhood. This theme, coming-of-age, is a major component of all Peck's work.

Peck strives for verisimilitude and believability in his characters and their actions. In essence, he wishes readers to identify with the protagonists, whether they be Vermont farm boys or youngsters caught up in the turbulence of Colonial times. He believes that children are basically the same, no matter what age they live in. The believability of his work makes for strong storytelling, and can be traced back to a book that had a strong influence on the young Peck: *The Adventures of Tom Sawyer.*

Along with school teachers, Robert Newton Peck has a particular affection for librarians and, in fact, married one, Dorothy Houston, in 1978. (Fred Rogers, of *Mister Roger's Neighborhood,* was his best man.) They have two children, Christopher Haven and Ann Houston. In recent years, he has forsaken rural Vermont for Florida where, despite his prodigious output of books, he finds time to direct the annual Writers Conference at Rollins College. "It's not easy writing four books a year," he writes, "but it sure beats killing hogs."

SELECTED WORKS: A Day No Pigs Would Die, 1973; Millie's Boy, 1973; Soup, 1974; Soup and Me, 1975; Hang for Treason, 1976; Rabbits and Redcoats, 1976; Patooie, 1977; Trig, 1977; Soup for President, 1978; Clunie, 1979; Hub, 1979; Soup's Drum, 1980; Soup on Wheels, 1981; Banjo, 1982; Soup in the Saddle, 1983.

ABOUT: Contemporary Authors, Vol. 81–84; Kirkpatrick, D. L. ed. Twentieth-Century Children's Writers; Something About the Author, Vol. 21; Ward, Martha E. and Dorothy A. Marquardt. Authors of Books for Young People, 2nd edition (Supplement); The Writers Directory 1982–84.

ANNE PELLOWSKI

June 28, 1933–

AUTHOR OF *Stairstep Farm: Anna Rose's Story,* etc.

Autobiographical sketch of Anne Pellowski:

I WAS BORN on a farm in Wisconsin, and my older sisters and brothers probably reacted to my coming with a surprise not unlike the one I had on the morning of my youngest sister's birth. I describe this scene (of Virginia's arrival) in *Stairstep Farm* because it is one of my sharpest early memories. I can still feel the awful, tense moment of believing that my mother had given birth to a kitten instead of a baby. I first heard the name Brown Betty that January morning, when it evoked the vision of a rich, chocolate pudding; even now I continue to think of it that way, and only after a moment's pause do I remember that it is a nut-brown bread-and-apple crispness.

I was the sixth of nine children, but our oldest brother, Raymond, had died of polio before any of us, except Lawrence, was born. His blown-up photograph at age two, framed in a large oval of carved wood, hung on our living room wall next to a photograph (in a twin frame) of my parents in their wedding attire. His spiritual presence was very real to me, much like that of the guardian angels assigned to each of us, unseen but unmistakably there.

On the farms all around ours were Polish-American families similar to ours. When we went to town (Dodge or Arcadia) or to the city (Winona), it was to visit with relatives who were like us in background, or to shop in stores run by families obviously economically better off than we were, but who still gave greetings in the same Polish way we did. I was convinced that the world around me was made up exclusively of Polish-American Catholics.

I knew there were different people in the world, because I read about them, but they seemed far away, outside my sphere. It was a shock to discover that right in the towns and cities nearby there were families who could not understand Polish and who were Protestant and Jewish!

My grandfather on my mother's side was known as a good storyteller, but he died when I was a year old so I have no conscious memory of him. A maternal uncle told us stories, mostly of ghosts and devils, which we found thrillingly scary. But my favorite storyteller was my oldest sister, Angie, who told a cycle of stories about our dog, Pal. This must have occurred over a relatively short period of time, just before I learned to read. Angie remembers nothing of this, nor do my younger sisters. Sometimes I think: Did I dream it all? Yet those stories, and her manner of telling them, remain deeply in my memory.

By the time I was five my older sisters had taught me to read, and I became addicted to it from that moment on. I loved school because it gave me access to books.

I liked fairy tales and myths, but I loved best the stories of real persons, especially children, doing interesting and unusual things. My absolute favorite book until seventh grade was *The Good Master* by Kate Seredy.

Then, at age twelve, I discovered the

Betsy-Tacy books of Maud Hart Lovelace. All through my teens years I read the entire series at least once a year, not bothering to note that some of the first books in the series are for quite young children. Betsy Ray was one of the early inspirations for my determination to go off and see the world some day.

An earlier thrust toward this dream of visiting foreign places had been given by a grade school teacher, a Sister who had taught in the mission schools in China, and who kept us enthralled by her tales of strange happenings there. Later, in my first year of college, I read in French the biography of Marie Curie by her daughter, Eve, and that also gave me great impetus.

I got a good education in languages and literature at the College of Saint Teresa and as soon as I completed my B.A. I set out to see the world. Luckily, I had received a Fulbright Scholarship to the University of Munich, in Germany. While at the International Youth Library there, I determined to make my career in the field of international children's literature and storytelling, and that's what I have been doing ever since.

Ann Pellowski earned an M.S.L.S. at Columbia University in 1959, and did further graduate work at the University of Minnesota in 1955 and at the University of Munich in 1955 and 1956, and at the New School for Social Research in 1965. Her career as a children's librarian included positions as researcher, senior children's librarian, and storytelling and group work specialist in the Office of Children's Services of the New York Public Library. She was a researcher on children's literature at the International Youth Library in Munich, at the International Board on Books for Young People in Vienna, and at the Library of Congress. Pellowski was a member of the international jury of the Hans Christian Andersen Award, 1969–1970. She is an active member of the American Library Association and has served as consultant to the In-

ternational Relations Committee of the Association of Library Services to Children. She has lectured at the University of Maryland, the University of Wisconsin, and Columbia University, and has been Director of the Information Center on Children's Cultures for UNICEF since 1967.

Pellowski received the Grolier Award in 1979 and the Constance Lindsay Skinner Award in 1980. She wrote two books on children's literature, *The World of Children's Literature* in 1968, which is a reference book on the development of children's literature worldwide, and *The World of Storytelling,* in 1977.

SELECTED WORKS: The Nine Crying Dolls: A Story from Poland, 1980; Stairstep Farm: Anna Rose's Story, 1981; Willow Wind Farm: Betsy's Story, 1981; First Farm in the Valley: Anna's Story, 1982; Winding Valley Farm: Annie's Story, 1982.

ABOUT: Contemporary Authors (First Revision), Vol. 23–24; Lee, Joel M., ed. Who's Who in Library and Information Services; Something About the Author, Vol. 20; Ward, Martha E. and Dorothy A. Marquardt. Authors of Books for Young People, 2nd edition (Supplement); Who's Who of American Women, 1975–76.

RODNEY PEPPÉ

June 24, 1934–

AUTHOR AND ILLUSTRATOR OF *The House That Jack Built,* etc.

Autobiographical sketch of Rodney Peppé:

MY EARLY LIFE was spent in India, at the foothills of the Himalayas, on the Nepalese border. I grew up there with my twin brother before we came home to England in 1942 during the war to bombs and boarding school.

After completing a fairly conventional private education at St. Bede's School, Eastbourne, and St. Edward's School, Oxford, I went to Eastbourne Art School in 1951. This was interrupted but enlivened by two years' National Service in the Intelligence Corps.

Peppé: *PEP ee*

Most of my time was spent in Malaya—a beautiful country that I fell in love with at once.

On returning to England in 1955, I resumed my art studies at the Central School of Arts and Crafts in London and trained as an illustrator. But it was to advertising I turned for a living. I spent the next five years, first with S. H. Benson and then J. Walter Thompson, learning about print, packaging, press, and television, first as an art director and later as a television producer.

In 1960 I married Tatjana, an Estonian. The following year we had our first son Christen, who now, twenty years later, is studying American and Commonwealth Arts at Exeter University. In 1963 our second son, Jonathan, was born. He has become a talented artist currently studying at the Slade School of Fine Art, a part of London University.

I turned free-lance in 1965 and for the next seven years I worked as a design consultant from home, devoting three days a week to Ross Foods, a notable frozen food firm. The rest of the week and weekends I devoted to other graphic design work, but most importantly it allowed me to start producing my own picture books. In 1967 while convalescing from a bout of mumps I got the idea for my first picture book, *The Alphabet Book*. Like many illustrators I chose an ABC as a vehicle for my illustrations, unfettered by too much text.

Now, fifteen years and some twenty-five books later, I have learned to accompany my own illustrations with my own texts. Without question my most successful book, both artistically and commercially, is my latest: *The Mice Who Lived in a Shoe*. I am in no doubt as to the reason why. Some years ago I became interested in making toys and indeed have done a book, *Rodney Peppé's Moving Toys,* which gives plans and photographs on how to make them. I also made a little wooden articulated elephant that became the basis from which to draw my *Henry* books.

I used this method of making/writing/drawing for *The Mice Who Lived in a Shoe*. I built a shoe house model from which to draw, and as the model progressed, so did the pictures. I am currently working on a follow-up book featuring mice pirates who turn an old kettle into a pirate ship.

Making the transition from toy to book came, if not easily, joyfully, to me in my pop-up book *Run Rabbit, Run!* The wonders of paper engineering were put at my disposal by the pop-up wizards, Intervisual Communications of Los Angeles. It was a most exhilarating experience and one of the most enjoyable projects I have ever worked on.

My approach to picture books has always been intuitive rather than informed, though by now it has been tempered by a little knowledge—not least about myself. I still believe what I believed when I set out: that artists have something to offer children that teachers, librarians, psychologists, et al. can never produce—pictorial originality. If that can spark the child into making his own pictures in his own way . . . well, we've achieved something!

Selected Works Written and Illustrated: The Alphabet Book, 1968; Circus Numbers, 1969; The

House That Jack Built, 1970; Simple Simon, 1972; Three Little Pigs, 1980; Rodney Peppé's Moving Toys, 1981; The Mice Who Lived in a Shoe, 1982; Run Rabbit, Run!: A Pop-Up Book, 1982.

ABOUT: Contemporary Authors (First Revision), Vol. 33-36; The International Authors and Writers Who's Who, 1977; Kingman, Lee and others, comps. Illustrators of Children's Books: 1967–1976; Something About the Author, Vol. 4; The Writers Directory 1982-84.

STELLA PEVSNER

AUTHOR OF *A Smart Kid Like You,* etc.

Autobiographical sketch of Stella Pevsner:

ALTHOUGH I took studies in stride, to me, the best part of elementary grades was art projects, music, gym class (but only when we danced!) and "putting on plays."

In high school I was awash in activities ... Chorus, speech competition, drama, art events, and also school magazine assignments . . . which in my case was writing a humor column.

In college, I specialized in education and later taught two years, but I felt a failure because the students themselves were more interesting to me than the knowledge I was supposed to be dishing out.

One summer I moved to Chicago, worked at a bank (boring!) during the day and took art classes at night. Then, just to keep a friend company, I enrolled with her in an advertising class. Later, she became a reporter but I landed a job writing copy. From then on it was a series of jobs where I wrote everything from perfume and fashion ads to radio commercials. In my spare time I wrote for myself.

When marriage, and eventually four children, prompted a move to the suburbs, I still wrote . . . feature articles for newspapers, this and that for magazines, and reading texts for children.

One day one of my children remarked that since I seemed determined to write, it might profit the world more if I wrote a "funny book" for kids.

Considering this a challenge, I did indeed write what I hoped was a "funny book." Before it was published I had started on the next. One followed another, and soon I'll reach the place where I won't be able to count them on my fingers.

Anyone can guess my interests by reading a few of my books. Several have school plays worked into the story. There are bits about art fairs, antique doll collecting, cats (I've always adored them) and, of course, reading and writing. Travel is also mentioned because now, between books, I take off for foreign places.

People sometimes ask if I write about my own children. Well, partly. I may pick up on an incident, or a pattern of speech, or even a problem. Their friends often give me insights and I want to tell you, when you have four children you meet a lot of friends! I like being around the young (though not all the time) and seeing things from their angles. Lots of times they just break me up with the things they say and do.

It's strange, but when I'm writing from a young person's viewpoint I really become that person. I can even take exception to some of the grown-ups in the book, even though in *real life* I would probably share that adult's point of view. And then, after being a part of the protagonist's mind for several hours, I can glide back to being the parent without too much danger to my psyche . . . I hope.

As my children have grown older, the intended-for-age group of my books has become higher. When I talk with school children, I mention that I need to have a young kid around the house again and do they have a sister or a brother they could spare? The response is always overwhelming.

Stella Pevsner was born in Lincoln, Illinois and attended Illinois University.

A Smart Kid Like You was made into a television special, "Me and Dad's New Wife." It also won the Dorothy Canfield Fisher Award in 1977. *And You Give Me a Pain, Elaine* won the Golden Kite Award for fiction in 1978.

Pevsner's *Cute Is a Four-Letter Word* was named a Children's Classroom Choice book by the Joint Committee of the International Reading Association and the Children's Book Council in 1980. The National Council for the Social Studies named *Keep Stompin' Till the Music Stops* a Notable Children's Trade Book in the Field of Social Studies in 1976.

SELECTED WORKS: Call Me Heller, That's My Name, 1973; A Smart Kid Like You, 1975; Keep Stompin' Till the Music Stops, 1976; And You Give Me a Pain, Elaine, 1978; Cute Is a Four-Letter Word, 1980; I'll Always Remember You . . . Maybe, 1981.

ABOUT: Contemporary Authors, Vol. 57-60; Something About the Author, Vol. 8; Language Arts April 1979.

DANIEL MANUS PINKWATER

November 15, 1941–

AUTHOR AND ILLUSTRATOR OF *Lizard Music,* etc.

Biographical sketch of Daniel Manus Pinkwater, who also writes under the pseudonyms "Captain Duck," "Mike Lome," "Manus Pinkwater," and "Arthur Tress":

DANIEL MANUS PINKWATER was born in Memphis, Tennessee. He recalls being given a red pencil and a black pencil at the age of two, and when he was in elementary school, he won a story contest. He has vivid memories of moments in his childhood; he not only uses these memories in his writing, but he remembers more when he writes.

Pinkwater attended Bard College, where he earned his B.A. degree in 1964. For three years he studied sculpture with David Nyvall. He worked as a fine artist, has exhibited his prints, and later taught art to children.

He has lived in many places, including Chicago and Los Angeles, and now resides in upstate New York with his wife, author and illustrator Jill Miriam Pinkwater. They married in 1969, and ran a puppy training school together from 1974 to 1976. They collaborated on *Superpuppy,* which was based on the training of their two Malamute dogs. Pinkwater now writes books for children and young adults full-time.

Pinkwater says that he owns two rhinoceroses. He also says that he has a collection of false noses that may be the largest and most complete in the free world. Such statements are consistent with Pinkwater's brand of absurd and nonsensical stories for children and young adults.

When asked to write about himself, Daniel Manus Pinkwater responded with a letter from "Wally Wanamopo, Secretary to DMP," which reads, in part,

"Mr. Pinkwater has disappeared from the face of the earth—we hope this development is temporary.

"You may be interested to know that my

DOWN-YELL   MOW-NOOSZ   PEENK-WA-TAIRE

employer had just seated himself to begin work on the autobiographical sketch you requested when the unusual event took place. A very large object, apparently made of metal, descended from the night sky, and disappeared in the woods behind Mr. Pinkwater's house.

"Mr. Pinkwater went to investigate. He was observed entering the woods. A few minutes later the object, cylindrical in shape and about one hundred feet long, was seen rising into the air. This was observed by a number of reliable witnesses.

"Mr. Pinkwater was not seen again. There are any number of theories being put forth—but what I believe happened is that Mr. Pinkwater was abducted by extraterrestrial beings inside the cylinder.

"It is my hope that the beings will return Mr. Pinkwater. There is reason to believe this will happen—numerous accounts exist of people who have been kidnapped by "space men" and have been subsequently returned. I think this is likely to be the case with my employer, particularly if the space beings have a limited supply of food."

Subsequent letters from Pinkwater himself have verified that he is alive and well in upstate New York, and he has written a description of himself:

"Very fat. Medium height. Mostly bald. Likes television. Has owned several French automobiles, for which parts were seldom available. Likes sausage. Lives on a farm. Has a wife. Votes for fictional characters in elections. Finally quit smoking. Likes to write for kids because they are a more respectable audience than adults. Hates his own books. Expects to do better in the future."

Pinkwater's books range from picture books like *Roger's Umbrella*, to *Blue Moose* for middle-grade readers, to *The Last Guru* for older readers. *Booklist* calls *The Hoboken Chicken Emergency* "absurdity with perfect timing," and *Horn Book* calls *Lizard Music* "amusing and orignal," comparing the illustrations to those of M. C. Escher.

The Wuggie Norple Story was named a Children's Choice book for 1981 by a joint committee of the International Reading Association and the Children's Book Council. Pinkwater is a contributor to *Cricket* magazine and a member of the Authors Guild.

SELECTED WORKS WRITTEN AND ILLUSTRATED: Wingman, 1975; Lizard Music, 1976; The Hoboken Chicken Emergency, 1977; The Last Guru, 1978; Alan Mendelsohn, the Boy from Mars, 1979; Yobgorgle: Mystery Monster of Lake Ontario, 1979; The Magic Moscow, 1980; The Worms of Kukumlima, 1981; Young Adult Novel, 1982; I Was a Second-Grade Werewolf, 1983.

SELECTED WORKS WRITTEN AND ILLUSTRATED AS MANUS PINKWATER: The Terrible Roar, 1970; Magic Camera, 1974; Blue Moose, 1975; Wingman, 1975.

SELECTED WORKS WRITTEN: (with Jill Miriam Pinkwater) Superpuppy, 1977; The Wuggie Norple Story, 1981; Roger's Umbrella, 1982.

ABOUT: Contemporary Authors (First Revision), Vol. 29–32; The International Authors and Writers Who's Who, 1977; Something About the Author, Vol. 8; New York Times Book Review April 29, 1979; Publishers Weekly February 27, 1978; May 7, 1982; (as Manus Pinkwater) Graphis No. 155, 1971–72.

KIN PLATT

December 8, 1911–

AUTHOR OF *Chloris and the Creeps,* etc.

Biographical sketch of Kin Platt:

KIN PLATT was born in New York City. He started his career in quite another vocation from writing, when he went to work for the *Brooklyn Daily Eagle* as a theater caricaturist. After a stretch in the U.S. Army Air Transport Command, in China, Burma, and India, during which he received a Bronze Star, he returned to civilian life and drew two popular comic strips. "Mr. and Mrs." ran from 1947 to 1963 and "The Duke and the Duchess" ran for four years in the early 1950s. Both strips were carried by the New York Herald Tribune Syndicate. Platt continued to cover theater, in New York as the off-Broadway theater artist for the *Village Voice,* and in California for the Los Angeles *Times.*

He has also written comedy for radio, television, films and magazines, dividing his time between the East and West Coasts.

In 1961, in an attempt to combine the excitement, pace, and action of a comic book with the best literary style, Platt wrote his first novel, *The Blue Man,* a thriller for boys. Because it was a success, he continued to write for young people, producing books for various age groups and in different genres.

Platt wrote two easy-to-read books that feature Big Max, "the world's greatest detective," who may also be one of the world's smallest sleuths. Among the mysteries he has written for somewhat older readers is *Dracula Go Home* and the Sinbad Series. In 1967, Platt won the Mystery Writers of America Edgar Award for juvenile mystery writing, for *Sinbad and Me.*

Many of his novels deal with young people struggling to overcome backgrounds of emotional, intellectual, and economic deprivation. In *Chloris and the Freaks,* twelve-year-old Jenny tries to make some sense out of the bewildering behavior of the adults about her. *Chloris and the Creeps* won a Southern California Council on Literature for Children and Young People Award in 1974. *The Headman,* published in 1975, tells the story of Owen Kirby, who is sentenced to a rehabilitative camp for using a knife in a street fight. When released, he re-enters the tough street life in a relentless cycle of violence. Jack Forman, writing in *School Library Journal,* called the book "provocative and engrossing. . . . an especially good choice for the category of readers who need 'high interest, low reading level' material." *The Boy Who Could Make Himself Disappear* was adapted for a film entitled *Baxter* in 1973.

Platt is a prolific author, often having two books published in the same year. His books are often recognized as good high-interest/low vocabulary materials, likely to appeal to reluctant readers. A *School Library Journal* review of *The Ape Inside Me,* in which Eddie Hill struggles to control his violent temper, hailed it as "a book that may coax the lightly literate to . . . reading."

Platt lives in California and enjoys playing golf. He has one son, Christopher, and is very fond of English bulldogs.

SELECTED WORKS: The Blue Man, 1961; Big Max, 1965; Sinbad and Me, 1966; The Boy Who Could Make Himself Disappear, 1968; Hey, Dummy, 1971; Chloris and the Creeps, 1973; Chloris and the Freaks, 1975; Headman, 1975; Big Max in the Mystery of the Missing Moose, 1977; Chloris and the Weirdos, 1978; The Ape Inside Me, 1979; Dracula, Go Home, 1979; The Ghost of Hell's Fire Street, 1980; Brogg's Brain, 1981; Crocker, 1983.

ABOUT: Contemporary Authors (First Revision), Vol. 17–20; Something About the Author, Vol. 21; Ward, Martha E. and Dorothy A. Marquardt. Authors of Books for Young People, 2nd edition (Supplement); Who's Who in America, 1974–1975; Library Journal February 1, 1970.

ILSE PLUME

RETELLER AND ILLUSTRATOR OF *The Bremen-Town Musicians,* etc.

Autobiographical sketch of Ilse Plume:

MY PARENTS became aware of the budding artist in their midst sooner than I did. My first experience with paint was chewing it off the edge of my crib, as I was learning to stand. At first the disappearing paint was a mystery to everyone until the little, irregular chips along the rim were discovered to be toothmarks! Little did I know then that my life-long involvement with paint was just beginning, and would eventually become a continuing element in my diet!

After I managed the crawling stage I was quite happy to be left alone in a corner to redecorate walls and floors and any other surfaces which needed embellishing. Needless to say, this enterprise was frowned upon, so it was immediately agreed that I would be well-stocked with paper as well as with pencils and chalks from then on.

As an only child I was pretty much a loner and spent most of the time putting on plays (which I directed and starred in) for a rapt audience of dolls and stuffed bears as well as a motley assortment of nameless, indefinable creatures of varying sizes and shapes. When I wasn't talking to myself or enlarging my repertoire for my patient audience, I continued to draw and paint.

Around the same time that I started school, I also discovered coloring books, which opened up a whole new dimension for me. Sometimes I colored all the spaces within the lines, while at other times I discovered it was more fun to shade in the areas outside the lines and to decorate the margins as well. Years later I imaginatively embellished several margins in a few unbearably dull-looking books and was surprised that the teachers were less than pleased with my illuminating pastime. A book without pictures was . . . and continues to be . . . impossible!

My love affair with art continued and flourished as time went on, and most of my fondest recollections of elementary school deal with art class. I was the student most often selected to create bulletin boards or posters and to design programs for special events and school plays. Thus my life revolved around bulletin boards, and when I wasn't cutting and pasting autumn leaves and snowflakes and stars, I was probably drawing daffodils and tulips or painting beaches with children and mermaids and stars.

Since I proved to be an absolute klutz in sports, hated math with a passion, and daydreamed through most of my classes, it was a relief to find a niche for myself in art. That continued to be the focus of my existence during junior high and high school years. By the time college began I started off to class with an art smock and a drawing board instead of a math or biology text.

The years have flown by and I still find myself not quite grown up. I am, as usual, still drawing snowflakes and stars, but instead of decorating my school's bulletin board, I am able to share my magic with a wider audience now. I hope children everywhere will continue to share my dreams and I hope that when I am a hundred and ten I am still drawing stars for them and for me!

––––––

Ilse Plume, who is Latvian, was born in Dresden, Germany. Her family emigrated to the U.S. when she was about five years old, and she remembers sailing into New York harbor. She attended Drake University in Des Moines, Iowa, graduating in art and art education in 1968. She also earned an M.F.A. degree at Drake, in 1970. She did graduate work at the Santa Reparata Graphic Studio in Florence, Italy, in printmaking.

In 1971 and 1972 Plume taught design, lettering, and drawing at Iowa State University in Ames, and in 1973 and 1974 she was a research assistant in the art history department at the University of Iowa, where she did graduate work in art history. She was an art instructor at the Minneapolis College of Art and Design in 1974 and 1975, and taught art at the University of Wisconsin in Eau Claire. In 1978 and 1979, she lived in Florence, where she did the work for her first book.

The Bremen-Town Musicians was a 1981 Caldecott Honor Book, and Plume's work has been exhibited at the Justin Schiller Gallery in New York City.

Plume is divorced and has a daughter, Anne-Marie, who was born in 1964. She lives in Massachusetts.

SELECTED WORKS RETOLD AND ILLUSTRATED: The Bremen-Town Musicians, by the Brothers Grimm, 1980; The Story of Befana: An Italian Christmas Tale, 1981.

SELECTED WORKS ILLUSTRATED: The Velveteen Rabbit, or How Toys Become Real, by Margery Williams, 1983.

ELIZABETH MARIE POPE

May 1, 1917–

AUTHOR OF *The Perilous Gard,* etc.

Biographical sketch of Elizabeth Marie Pope:

ELIZABETH POPE was born in Washington, D.C., and grew up there and in Goshen, New York. She was graduated from Bryn Mawr College in 1940 and received her Ph.D. in English literature from Johns Hopkins University in 1944. That year she joined the faculty of Mills College in Oakland, California, and except for a brief stint as a Folger research fellow at the Folger Shakespeare Library in Washington, D.C. (1947–1948), she has remained at Mills ever since. Over the years she has risen through the ranks from instructor to her current position as the Lynn Townsend White Professor of English and Chairman of the Department.

Pope has written articles for scholarly publications such as *Shakespeare Survey* and the *Shakespeare Quarterly,* but she has also written for fun ever since she was a child. Her highly acclaimed first novel for young readers, *The Sherwood Ring,* was written for her younger sister who loved Orange County, New York and the eighteenth century, both of which figure prominently in the novel. *Saturday Review* called *The Sherwood Ring* "an unusual and utterly captivating book . . . a mystery, a ghost story, a tale of derring-do, drugged drinks and ciphers, as well as a modern romance aided and abetted by two pairs of eighteenth-century lovers . . . This has the excellence and

Elizabeth Marie Pope

Pope is a fellow of the Society for Values in Higher Education and a member of the American Association of University Professors, the Renaissance Society, the Mediaeval Society of America, and the Society for Creative Anachronism. Among her hobbies are reading mythology and cooking.

SELECTED WORKS: The Sherwood Ring, 1958; The Perilous Gard, 1974.

ABOUT: Contemporary Authors, Vol. 49–52; Directory of American Scholars, 1982–1983; Ward, Martha E. and Dorothy A. Marquardt. Authors of Books for Young People, 2nd edition (Supplement).

naturalness of fine English historical stories." The *Chicago Tribune* agreed: "Rich in mystery, romance, and historical lore. . . . The author, moving adroitly back and forth in time, creates an original and absorbing novel." *The Sherwood Ring* was selected as a Notable Book by the American Library Association in 1958 and appeared on the ALA list "Notable Children's Books 1940–1970."

Elizabethan England is one of Pope's special areas of interest, and she traveled to England to do research for the historical background of *The Perilous Gard,* her second novel for young readers. It is a tale of the sinister forces of pre-Druid magic that surround an Elizabethan castle and its inhabitants. Again, the critics' response was favorable. *Family Journal* called it "an unusual, hauntingly beautiful book . . . a masterpiece by Elizabeth Pope," and the *New York Times* wrote, "Miss Pope's strength is storytelling. . . . By treating the magic of her story with subtlety and intelligence Miss Pope illustrates how events may be shifted and shaped into myth." *The Perilous Gard* was selected as a 1975 Newbery Honor Book and was included in the 1974 Children's Book Showcase.

JACK PRELUTSKY

September 8, 1940–

AUTHOR OF *Nightmares: Poems to Trouble Your Sleep,* etc.

Biographical sketch of Jack Prelutsky:

JACK PRELUTSKY was born in Brooklyn and attended P.S. 33 and the High School of Music and Art in New York, graduating in 1958. He went to Hunter College at night; "basically bored," he took "whatever didn't require too much work." He says that he flunked seven languages—"eight if you count English." Prelutsky's translations of children's books from German and Swedish, however, belie his description of a lack of aptitude for languages.

Music has always been important to Prelutsky, and he states that opera was his first love. He wanted to be an opera singer, and had formal training and played the piano, but gave up the idea when he heard Pavarotti sing, he says. He has sung in the New Mexico Symphony Chorus and has also sung Gilbert & Sullivan in small opera companies.

Prelutsky was a folk singer in the late 1950s and early 1960s. He got started writing poetry for children in the early 1960s, when he was sent to see the juvenile editor at a New York publishing house. "I thought

Prelutsky: *pree LUT ski*

I was a brilliant young artist," he said, "and brought in poems about imaginary animals at first. She encouraged me to write about real animals instead, and the other poems were set aside."

Since then Prelutsky has written about thirty books of poetry. He once wrote about ninety poems in two months, which he calls "a wonderful creative stint. I wrote six poems in one day recently, and the better parts of two more, which is close to the most I've ever done in one day."

Prelutsky travels a great deal, spending two weeks a year in San Francisco, Los Angeles, Seattle, and Boston, and a month a year in New York City. He also spends four to five months a year visiting schools, where he tells stories to the accompaniment of his guitar. "I try to tell kids that poetry is not boring or a chore," he says. "It's not 'up there with the angels.' It is a natural continuation of everything else. It is one way a human being can tell another human being what's going on inside. Kids memorize pop songs; they don't think of that music as apart from what they do. Poetry is the music of language."

Prelutsky edited an anthology of poems, *The Random House Book of Poetry for Children,* which Arnold Lobel illustrated. He is also an avid collector of books of children's poetry, and owns several thousand volumes.

Nightmares, illustrated by Arnold Lobel, was in the American Institute of Graphic Arts book show, was chosen for the *School Library Journal* "Best of the Best 1966–1978" list (December 1979), and was named a Notable Book of 1976 by the American Library Association. Its sequel, *The Headless Horseman Rides Tonight,* was a *New York Times* Choice of the Best Illustrated Children's Book of the Year 1980.

The Mean Old Hyena was named a Children's Choice book by the joint committee of the International Reading Association and the Children's Book Council. *The Queen of Eene* was a Junior Literary Guild selection, as well as an ALA Notable Book for 1978, as was *The Snopp on the Sidewalk* in 1977. His works reside in the Kerlan Collection at the University of Minnesota.

When he isn't traveling, Jack Prelutsky lives in Albuquerque.

SELECTED WORKS: The Terrible Tiger, 1970; Circus, 1974; Nightmares: Poems to Trouble Your Sleep, 1976; It's Halloween, 1977; The Snopp on the Sidewalk and Other Poems, 1977; The Mean Old Hyena, 1978; The Queen of Eene, 1978; The Headless Horseman Rides Tonight: More Poems to Trouble Your Sleep, 1980; Rainy Rainy Saturday, 1980; Rolling Harvey Down the Hill, 1980; It's Christmas, 1981; It's Thanksgiving, 1982; The Sheriff of Rottenshot, 1982; It's Valentine's Day, 1983; Zoo Doings: Animal Poems, 1983.

SELECTED WORKS ADAPTED FROM THE SWEDISH: The Wild Baby, by Barbro Lindgren, 1981; The Wild Baby Goes to Sea, by Barbro Lindgren, 1983.

SELECTED WORKS EDITED: The Random House Book of Poetry for Children, 1983.

ABOUT: Contemporary Authors, Vol. 93–96; Something About the Author, Vol. 22; Ward, Martha E. and Dorothy A. Marquardt. Authors of Books for Young People, 2nd edition (Supplement).

BERNIECE RABE

January 11, 1928–

AUTHOR OF *Naomi,* etc.

Autobiographical sketch of Berniece Louise
  Rabe:

ALONG with Will Rogers, I'd like to say
I've never met a child nor young adult that
I didn't like . . . eventually. Sometimes it
meant that I had to get to know him or her
better. We all have goodness within us;
some of us are a little slow to reveal it, that's
all. I like my readers to know my characters
well enough to like very much in spite
of some very human faults they may have.

Most of my characters succeed in being
well liked and the reviews show it. Unfortunately for Little Adam in *The Orphans,* who
copied his beloved guardian and acted a bit
macho himself, I did not expose enough of
him for a couple of reviewers and he went
unliked. I wept for him, so I thought. (Actually it didn't bother Little Adam at all, he
knew who he was.) Then more mail came
in from children who had read deeper, understood and knew him well, so I felt much
better. You see, its not the character's fault,
but mine, if they go unliked.

Some young people have asked me to
make Rass from one novel and Naomi from
another get married. My reply is that I can't
really make these two love each other, but
on the other hand, if I helped them truly get
to know each other . . . well, maybe.
Stranger things than that have happened in
real life, maybe we could pull it off believably in fiction too. Writing believable, true-
to-life fiction is more difficult than reporting actual happenings, and more fun.

Some of my characters are patterned after real people, usually two or more people
I've known all blended together like butter
and sugar and chocolate to get fudge. I even
blend my pets. Clark Gable, Girlie's cat,
was a blend of a cat I had as a girl, and the
cat that now roams about our rambling
house.

I started writing children's books acci-

dentally when a writing instructor told me
to write about a good fight, and some of the
best fights I've witnessed came from children—water fights, word fights, you name
it. So the age I write for is solely determined
by whom, in my imagination, I see fighting.
My most recent book, *The Balancing Girl,* is
a picture book because I saw, in my mind,
my spunky granddaughter, who is a terrific
fighter, when she's not busy loving and giving, and she was only six years old at the
time. If any of you readers know of a good
fight, let me know, but do tell me everything you can about the person, whose side
you're on, for I want to like him or her as
much as you do.

———

Berniece Rabe grew up in a rural community during the Depression, in a family
of nineteen children. She uses that background in her book *Rass.* She was born in
Parma, Missouri and graduated from the
National College of Education in Evanston,
Illinois, in 1963. She was married in 1946
and did graduate study at Northern Illinois
University and at Roosevelt University.
Rabe was a model in 1945 and 1946 and, in
the 1960s, a teacher and tutor in special ed-

ucation. She has three grown sons and one daughter. She lives in Chicago and belongs to several small writers' groups.

The Girl Who Had No Name was the fiction winner of the Golden Kite Award in 1977. *Naomi* was included on the *School Library Journal* "Best of the Best 1966–1978" list (December 1979), and *The Balancing Girl* was named a Notable Book in 1981 by the American Library Association.

SELECTED WORKS: Rass, 1973; Naomi, 1975; The Girl Who Had No Name, 1977; The Orphans, 1978; Who's Afraid?, 1980; The Balancing Girl, 1980.

ABOUT: Contemporary Authors, Vol. 49–52; (New Revision Series), Vol. 1; Something About the Author, Vol. 7; The Writers Directory 1982–84.

MARY RAYNER

December 30, 1933–

AUTHOR AND ILLUSTRATOR OF *Mr. and Mrs. Pig's Evening Out,* etc.

Autobiographical sketch of Mary Yoma Rayner:

I WAS BORN in Mandalay, in Burma, and was brought up in that country and in India until I was eleven. I have never been back, but still hope to be one day. To some extent I still feel a foreigner in this country, although I am English—it is just that a dry, hot, dusty landscape under a blue sky feels to me right, the way the landscape should look, and anything else is like something off a picture postcard.

I was married for twenty-two years but am now divorced. I have three children and I used to try out my stories on them, but these days they are too grown-up. I always invent the stories first, and then illustrate them afterwards. When I make them up I know in my head what it all looks like, but it doesn't get drawn for a long time after that; I don't think, "that's something that would be good to draw," and then make up a story to fit.

I wrote one of my first stories when I was about eight. It was called "Conker, the Story of a Horse," and was crammed into a tiny fat book about four inches by three. I never stopped drawing horses; I used to draw all through class at school. It wasn't that I was particularly good at riding, it was all in my head, where I had whole stables of thoroughbreds at my beck and call, each with their own names and characteristics. I found a list of them the other day.

After I left school I went to St. Andrews University in Scotland where I took a degree in English, and I then worked in publishing. I stopped work when I had the children, but while the youngest was still quite small I went to Chelsea School of Art part-time to learn illustration. This meant that I used to be out every Monday evening, and my youngest son hated it so much that I made up the story for him about the worst babysitter in the world, a wolf who comes to a family of piglets. Later I illustrated it and it became *Mr. and Mrs. Pig's Evening Out.*

But that was not my first book. The first one to be published was *The Witch-Finder,* which was from an idea prompted by the prehistoric circle of standing stones at Avebury in Wiltshire; it took me a long time to get it to the right length and shape, and even now I can see lots of things wrong with it. However, maybe that is a hopeful sign; it must mean I've learned *something* since.

———

Both *Mr. and Mrs. Pig's Evening Out* and *Garth Pig and the Ice-Cream Lady* were named Notable Books by the American Library Association in their years of publication.

SELECTED WORKS WRITTEN AND ILLUSTRATED: Mr. and Mrs. Pig's Evening Out, 1976; The Witchfinder, 1976; Garth Pig and the Ice-Cream Lady, 1977; The Rain Cloud, 1980; Mrs. Pig's Bulk Buy, 1981.

ABOUT: Contemporary Authors, Vol. 69-72; Kingman, Lee and others, comps. Illustrators of Children's Books: 1967-1976; Something About the Author, Vol. 22.

DAVID REES

May 18, 1936–

AUTHOR OF *The Exeter Blitz*, etc.

Autobiographical sketch of David Bartlett Rees:

I WAS BORN in London, England, and lived there for the first thirty years of my life, but of my twenty-two published books only one, *Silence,* is set wholly in London. I moved to Exeter in Devon in 1968, and most of my stories are set in that city or the surrounding countryside; some of the best times of my childhood, the years 1943 to 1945, I lived in a remote farmhouse on the north coast of Devon as an evacuee, escaping from the London of Hitler's bombs, and moving back to that part of England was the fulfillment of a wish to return to a place where I had been very happy as a child. Since 1982 I have been living in San Francisco, California, a city I find as inspirational from a writing point of view as Exeter; it is my "second home."

David Rees

I had wanted to be an author for as long as I can remember, but I did not start my first novel until I was thirty-seven. Why the process took so long, I don't know, but once started it has proved impossible to stop. Since 1973 I have been writing two or three books a year. Ten years ago I read a book about the great rebellion in 1798 of the Irish against the British; my great-great-great-grandfather was one of the rebels. I had to write a novel about him, I decided, and I did so—in three weeks. It was called *The Green Bough of Liberty*. Nobody wanted to publish it, however; but it did finally appear in print some seven years later, after a multitude of alterations, and won the Other Award for 1980.

Some of my novels have a historical setting, some a contemporary background, and some are fantasies, but whatever the place or time, I am writing about myself and the years of my growing up, rearranging patterns so that the central character often chooses the course of action I did *not* take. *The Exeter Blitz,* which won the Carnegie Medal in 1978, is apparently concerned with the great air-raid that devastated the city of Exeter in 1942, but I am actually writing about my memories of the bombing of London, re-creating the fears and excitements of that period of my life, exorcising nightmares I suppose. *The Ferryman* is set in a cholera epidemic in Exeter in 1832, but underlying the writing is the fear that is probably common to all children of what happens if they lose their parents, either by death or the break-up of a marriage.

My most recently published novel, *The Estuary,* is for adults. What happens, I asked myself, to all those people I've created in children's books and young adult books *afterwards?* So I took some of the characters from *Quintin's Man, Storm Surge,* and *In the Tent* and wrote about their lives from the ages of twenty-one to twenty-five. I'm now writing about them, in a novel called *Flux,* when they're thirty.

What else? I went to the University of Cambridge, England, and graduated in English. I've been a teacher all my adult life, most recently at California State University, San José, but from September 1984 I shall be earning my living as a free-lance writer. I was married once, and I have two teenage sons who, I'm glad to say, are avid readers of books, including my own.

———

David Rees taught English to high school students from 1960 to 1968 in London and Ickenham, Middlesex. Since 1968 he taught college students, and was Senior Lecturer in English at St. Luke's College, Exeter, from 1968 to 1978. His sons were born in 1968 and 1970.

Rees writes criticism of children's literature and has had articles published in the *Times Literary Supplement, Children's Literature in Education, The Horn Book Magazine, School Librarian,* and *Top of the News.* His first book of criticism, *The Marble in the Water: Essays on Contemporary Writers of Fiction for Children and Young Adults,* was published in 1980, and he is working on a second one.

SELECTED WORKS: Quintin's Man, 1978; Risks, 1978;

The Exeter Blitz, 1980; The Night Before Christmas Eve, 1980; A Beacon for the Romans, 1981; Silence, 1981.

ABOUT: The International Authors and Writers Who's Who, 1982; The Writers Directory 1982–84.

JOHANNA REISS

April 4, 1932–

AUTHOR OF *The Upstairs Room,* etc.

Autobiographical sketch of Johanna de Leeuw Reiss:

IT IS a cold day in the year 1982. As I am looking out of my window—in New York City—I shake my head. How did I get here?

It's a far cry from where I grew up, in a very small town, in a country, small too, Holland. I came here twenty-seven years ago. My father thought it would be good for me to get away for a while. I thought so too. I had already applied at KLM Airlines for a position as stewardess to anywhere at all, but I was not tall enough to wait on people in planes.

As I stepped onto the boat that would bring me to America, I waved to my father and sisters. "Don't cry so," I comforted myself (in Dutch), "It's only for a year . . . ." That was in 1955. I knew so little about the U.S.A. . . . Is it true, I wondered, holding on to the railing and staring at the ocean below, that the entire country is populated by Indians, as I had read in a book?

I arrived in June. No one had ever told me that New York gets hot in the summer. I stood at the pier in a tweed suit, a turtleneck sweater, stockings and what-not. The temperature was hovering around a sweaty one hundred degrees. It didn't take me long to realize that Dutch summers and American ones have little in common. They are almost opposites, if you will. For several months I said little. I was afraid I'd make a mistake.

The first job I had was as a babysitter.

JOHANNA REISS

The girl was six and I had to take her to the beach every day. It scared me; I couldn't swim and was afraid to go after her when more than four inches covered her feet. "Soon out of water come now," I'd yell from the sand. Next I worked as a cheesecutter at a supermarket, where I had to open every carton of eggs to see which ones were cracked. Those had to be thrown out. I don't think that job exists any more. When I became more comfortable with English I got a job in a bank. Very often Americans have strange last names, I found out, with difficult spelling, which I had a hard time catching. Every time the phone rang and someone other than Smith, Brown, or Johnson asked after their balance, I felt as hot again as I felt the day I got off the boat.

I married an American, moved to Detroit, began to speak rapid English, had a baby, moved back to New York, and had another baby. I never thought of being a writer, until my children were seven and nine. It struck me how free they were—as free as you can be growing up in Manhattan—as compared to me, when I was their age. I wanted to write for them what my childhood had been like: in Holland, with the Second World War going, on, and the Germans wanting to kill the Jews. I hid in a tiny room and stayed there for close to three years, until that war was over.

Little did I realize that writing a book is a big job. Instead of taking two weeks as I had reassured myself before I began, it took three years. The result was *The Upstairs Room*. I was so shocked that I had written a book, and it did so well, that when my editor introduced me as, "She's the woman who wrote *The Upstairs Room*," I looked over my shoulder to get a look at an author. I was never going to write another book again, I promised myself. Never. It takes too long, it is too hard. Who needs it? Within a year I was at the desk again. I began to write a sequel to *The Upstairs Room*. That book is called *The Journey Back*. It took a very long time to finish that one too. Never again, I said once more. Who needs it? But who knows?

———

In Holland, when Johanna Reiss was ten, she and her younger sister Sini were hidden by a Christian couple, Johan and Dientje Oosterveld, so that the girls would not be sent to a concentration camp. *The Upstairs Room* describes the girls' frightening ordeal, and *The Journey Back* tells of the Reiss family's fate after the war. In addition to Johanna and Sini, the father and another sister, Rachel, survived.

After Reiss graduated from college, she taught elementary school for several years. In the U.S., where she is now a citizen, she teaches Dutch and writes in English.

The Upstairs Room was awarded the Buxtehuder Bulle, a German children's book award, in 1976, and Reiss and her two daughters traveled to Germany to accept the award. In the U.S., the book was named a Newbery Honor Book and won a Jane Addams Book Award in 1973. It also received the National Jewish Book Award in 1972 and was included on the *School Library Journal* "Best of the Best 1966–1978" list (December 1979).

SELECTED WORKS: The Upstairs Room, 1972; The Journey Back, 1976.

ABOUT: Contemporary Authors, Vol. 85–88; Kulkin, Mary-Ellen. Her Way: Biographies of Women for Young People; Something About the Author, Vol 18; Ward, Martha E. and Dorothy A. Marquardt. Authors of Books for Young People, 2nd edition (Supplement); Saturday Review June 12, 1976.

EVE RICE

February 2, 1951–

AUTHOR AND ILLUSTRATOR OF *What Sadie Sang,* etc.

Biographical sketch of Eve Hart Rice:

EVE HART RICE was born in New York City, the daughter of Henry Hart, a real estate broker, and Grace Hecker Rice, a former art instructor. In 1954 the family moved to Bedford, New York—where Eve Rice spent her childhood. While she was growing up, she was amply provided with crayons, pencils, and paper by her mother. Her earliest subjects included the family menagerie: three dogs, a cat, snakes, polliwogs, frogs, turtles, beetles, etc.

Rice attended an elementary school in Banksville, New York, that was so small it had only three teachers. She went on to larger school in neighboring Armonk, New York. While in high school, she began to think about making children's book illustration her career.

She majored in English history at Yale University, but a senior seminar in children's literature rekindled her interest in children's books. Following her graduation from Yale in 1972, Eve Rice illustrated her first book for children, *I Am Big, You Are Little.*

After graduate study at Yale, she went to live in New York City. In 1973, after a year's study at the New School for Social Research, she began to devote her full working time to children's books. She became as interested in text as she was in illus-

tration. Being able to do both, she felt, would make the work tighter than would be possible in a collaborative effort between artist and writer. Beginning with the publication of her first picture book, *Oh, Lewis!*, in 1975, Eve Rice has been a prolific writer and illustrator of picture books and easy-to-read books.

Her ideas for the books usually begin with words, and she tries to finish a text before adding illustrations. Although she has also written a novel for children, she most enjoys creating picture books for the very young, which provide "enormous scope and freedom for creativity" and also require a challenging amount of discipline. She prefers working with only two colors or with black alone.

Rice believes that there are many influences on her work. She attributes its almost homey, 1950s quality to the fact that she grew up with the classics and picture books of the 1950s by such artists as Wanda Gag, Marie Hall Ets, Hans Fischer, and Edward Ardizzone. She also mentions Georges Seurat, Diego Rivera, Stuart Davis, Georgia O'Keefe, and Mary Cassatt as painters whose work she particularly admires.

In 1978 Eve Rice married Timothy Mattison, a dermatologist, and during the spring of 1980 they moved back to Bedford, where they live in the house in which she grew up. Rice follows a full schedule of writing and illustrating, taking "the necessary time out to be a harried home owner, with all that entails." She works in a studio, which she describes as being "complete with requisite drawing table, light box, and hundreds and hundreds of picture books (and also, interesting toys, which I collect)." She manages to swim every day and travels to Manhattan once a week for a taste of "the city." Her numerous other interests include walking, biking, calligraphy, etching, and collecting wildflowers.

In addition to having seven of her titles chosen as Junior Literary Guild selections, Rice had three books named American Library Association Notable Books: *What Sadie Sang* in 1976, *Goodnight, Goodnight* in 1980, and *Benny Bakes a Cake* in 1981. In 1978 *Sam Who Never Forgets* was named a Children's Choice book by the joint committee of the International Reading Association and the Children's Book Council. *What Sadie Sang* was included in the 1977 Children's Book Showcase exhibit.

SELECTED WORKS ILLUSTRATED: I Am Big, You Are Little, by Helen Puner, 1973; Stories from a Snowy Mountain, by Carla Stevens 1976.

SELECTED WORKS WRITTEN AND ILLUSTRATED: Oh, Lewis!, 1974; New Blue Shoes, 1975; Mr. Brimble's Hobby and Other Stories, 1975; Ebbie, 1975; What Sadie Sang, 1976; Papa's Lemonade and Other Stories, 1976; Sam Who Never Forgets, 1977; The Remarkable Return of Winston Potter Crisply, 1978; Goodnight, Goodnight, 1980; Benny Bakes a Cake, 1981.

SELECTED WORKS ADAPTED AND ILLUSTRATED: Once in a Wood: Ten Tales from Aesop, 1979.

ABOUT: Contemporary Authors, Vol. 53–56; (New Revision Series), Vol. 4; Kingman, Lee and others, comps. Illustrators of Children's Books: 1967–1976; Ward, Martha E. and Dorothy A. Marquardt. Authors of Books for Young People, 2nd edition (Supplement).

ADRIENNE RICHARD

October 31, 1921–

AUTHOR OF *Wings*, etc.

Autobiographical sketch of Adrienne Richard:

MOST of my school years were spent in schools that valued creativity and fostered it in one form or another. For me it was writing. I've been writing since I was six and in the first grade. My initial work was a poem about the sun very much in the manner of Robert Louis Stevenson, who is still a literary hero of mine. My first story, in second grade, was about Jacob and his brothers—it was the many-colored coat that attracted me. I still love the old stories—the Biblical stories, myths, folktales—they are right at the heart of human experience. I wrote my first novel in fifth grade, and it had a historical setting in the ancient Greek city of Sparta—we were studying the Greeks at the time. Later I loved to write short sketches like "A Day in the Life of King Alfred's Court," with a ten-year-old page as the main character. These I created as I walked home from school turning vacant lots and silent houses into dark woods and battlefields, medieval towns, and castles. Books like *Otto of the Silver Hand* and *Durandal* and *Boy of the Lost Crusade* fed my particular fires. I don't remember any female main characters that excited me. Too passive, I suppose. Adventure was what nourished me.

I grew up in various places: around Chicago, in southern California, in New Mexico and Arizona—all very American places in their turbulent diversity, places demanding the adventurous spirit in both men and women, places where the present was more visible than the past, where long traditions had been left behind in other parts of the world.

My work springs from the thrill, the excitement of envisioning a certain time and place. What was it like to live then, there, in that way? In Montana at the time of the

Adrienne Richard

drought and the Great Depression, to be a boy growing up, becoming conscious of the world around him as it shrivels up economically, blows away on the dry winds? (*Pistol*) What is it like to be an Arab boy in Israel? An Israeli? A rebellious American kid there in these terrible times? (*The Accomplice*) Right now I am thrilled and excited about Civil War-period Pennsylvania—what was it like to be a little girl growing up then? What did she eat? How did she keep her long stockings up? How did they bury the dead in those days? What was stocked on the shelves in crossroads stores? I need to know everything.

I always do a great deal of research in libraries and other places, and I visit the region where my story takes place. For my book *Into the Road,* the contemporary story of two brothers touring New England on motorcycles, I attended every motorcycle event within two hundred miles, picking up all kinds of sensory data and little vignettes, innumerable things that gave me the feel of the multiple motorcycle worlds. There are wonderful sources in old books, in historical societies, in little museums, and collections. Then I play with that information, embodying it in living situations, giving it character and movement.

Essentially my work is about what it feels like to be a certain age in a certain time, to be involved in that time and place and to grow with it and out of it, prepared better for whatever comes next. Mainly I explore what it means to be an American. Those moments in history that strike me with greatest force are watershed moments, when everything is changing fast. This seems most American of all. The rapidity of change as it occurs over and over again in our history is characteristically American. For us nothing holds still very long. This vision of American life is thrilling and exciting and heartbreaking for me all at once, and these feelings move through my work as they do through my life.

I am married to a man from Montana and have three sons, to whom three of my four books are dedicated, and now two granddaughters, so I am going to do some serious thinking about adventurous women especially for them.

———

Adrienne Richard was born in Evanston, Illinois. She received her B.A. degree from the University of Chicago in 1943 and attended the Writers Workshop at the University of Iowa from 1948 to 1950. She also has done graduate work in English literature at Boston College.

She is editor of a national newsletter called *In Touch* for those interested in the psychology of C. G. Jung. She is co-owner of, and a laborer at, Stone Gate Vineyard in Westport, Massachusetts. She writes short stories and articles; her work has appeared in newspapers and in magazines like *Art in America, Better Homes & Gardens, Harper's,* and *Boys' Life.*

Richard also teaches small groups of adults and junior-high school aged children in journalism and creative writing; she has taught in public schools and was a guest instructor at Emmanuel College in Boston in 1982.

Wings was a finalist for the 1975 National Book Award. *Pistol* was named a Notable

Book by the American Library Association in 1969 and was later named an ALA Notable Book for the years 1940 through 1970. *Pistol* was also a runner-up for the Golden Spur Award of the Western Writers of America in 1970.

SELECTED WORKS: Pistol, 1969; The Accomplice, 1973; Wings, 1974; Into the Road, 1976.

ABOUT: Contemporary Authors, Vol. 29–32; Something About the Author, Vol. 5; Ward, Martha E. and Dorothy A. Marquardt. Authors of Books for Young People, 2nd edition (Supplement); The Writers Directory 1982–84.

WILLO DAVIS ROBERTS

May 29, 1928–

AUTHOR OF *The View from the Cherry Tree,* etc.

Autobiographical sketch of Willo Davis Roberts:

MY NAME is pronounced as if it had a *w* on the end of it, but please leave it off when you spell it. When I was a kid, they called me pussy willow and willow tree. It has made a good pen name, because nobody knows if "Willo" is a man's name or a woman's, and to some people that makes a difference. I never figured out why. If the writing is good, what difference could it possibly make whether it was done by a man or a woman?

I grew up in Michigan, and I won't specify a town because we moved a lot and there aren't many areas where we didn't spend at least a short time. The year I was in the fourth grade, I went to six different schools, and I didn't really learn very much. I never did completely memorize the multiplication tables. Luckily, someone invented pocket calculators, so I get by.

I began to write as soon as I could put the stories on paper; before that I just made them up and told them to my younger sisters. However, though I often wrote *about*

children, I never intended to write *for* them at all. *The View from the Cherry Tree* is about an eleven-year-old boy who sees a murder committed, and it was for adults, but it didn't sell that way. Eventually, with very few changes, it was published as a juvenile book, and it became so popular so quickly that my career was adjusted in that direction, a little bit.

Only five of the more than sixty books I've written so far are juveniles, but they produce about ninety-five per cent of my fan mail and, so far also, all the awards. I've enjoyed doing them, and also enjoyed the contacts with kids all over the country. Since *Don't Hurt Laurie!* just won an award in Australia, maybe I can say all over the world!

For many years, while my family was growing up, I wrote nights and held down a full-time job in the paramedical field during the days, and kept house in whatever fashion was possible at the time. Now my two sons and two daughters are grown-up and writing themselves, and the grandchildren are beginning to display active imaginations, too. Since my husband, David, retired, he has become a photographer/writer also, and we have an office built into our motorhome so that we can work as we travel. Traveling to research a book is one of the more rewarding aspects of our lives.

I am now writing a sixth juvenile book, a mystery titled *The Dangerous Summer,* which will be published by Atheneum, and I have contracts to produce during 1982 books through number sixty-four. I write full-time now and thoroughly enjoy my relationships with other professional writers. I organized and am currently regional vice-president of the Northwest Chapter of Mystery Writers of America; I belong to the Seattle Freelances and the Science Fiction Writers of America; I am an active participant in the Pacific Northwest Writers Conference, held annually in the Puget Sound area; and I lead a writers' workshop that meets twice a month to read and discuss manuscripts intended for publication. One of my biggest thrills is to be rewarded with an autographed book by someone I've coached or encouraged through the difficulties of finding a publisher.

Most of Roberts's books are mysteries, historical novels, and gothic novels for adults. Some of them draw on the world of nursing and hospital settings.

While most of her books for children are mysteries, *Don't Hurt Laurie!* is a realistic novel about an eleven-year-old girl whose mother frequently injures her; in the end the mother receives psychiatric help. The book was named a Notable Children's Trade Book in the Field of Social Studies in 1977 by a joint committee of the National Council for the Social Studies and the Children's Book Council. It also won the Young Hoosier Award in 1980.

The Girl with the Silver Eyes was a Junior Literary Guild selection.

SELECTED WORKS: The View from the Cherry Tree, 1975; Don't Hurt Laurie!, 1977; The Minden Curse, 1978; The Girl with the Silver Eyes, 1980; More Minden Curses, 1980; The Pet-Sitting Peril, 1983.

ABOUT: Contemporary Authors, Vol. 49-52; (New Revision Series), Vol. 3; Something About the Author, Vol. 21; The Writers Directory 1982-84.

BARBARA ROBINSON

October 24, 1927–

AUTHOR OF *The Best Christmas Pageant Ever,* etc.

Autobiographical sketch of Barbara Webb Robinson:

I GREW UP in a small Southern Ohio town, and began writing when I was in the fourth or fifth grade, as a hobby and for fun. I'm happy to say it's still fun today, probably because every book I write has to be a book that I also want very much to read. I'm like the reader who turns the page to see what happens next—except, of course, that the page is blank and I get to fill it up with whatever seems exciting, funny, scary, happy or sad . . . and with characters who become as real to me as my next-door neighbors—so real, in fact, that sometimes they just step in and show *me* 'what happens next.' Sometimes, too, the character I've had in mind changes as I get to know him better. Sometimes a minor character just won't stay in the background and takes over the whole story.

Obviously, I'm one of those writers whose story ideas spring more from people than from plot—the Fourth of July parade may pass right before my eyes, and I will miss the excitement of a runaway float because I'm watching, instead, a small child who has lost her balloon and dropped her ice cream cone at the very same moment.

Since characters—to come alive for a reader—need to be more than simply short or tall or dark or fair, it's necessary to get inside the skin of, let's say, Janet, in *Temporary Times, Temporary Places,* and to know everything about her, and especially to feel what she is feeling. Oddly enough (or maybe it's not so odd), my college education was in the field of theater, in which ac-

socks, borrowed sweat pants, car keys, scotch tape, light bulbs, and, all too often, somebody's contact lens.

My kids would say that all this is unimportant—that the really important thing about me is that I bake a terrific chocolate chip cookie.

———

Barbara Robinson was born in Portsmouth, Ohio, where she grew up. She received a B.A. degree from Allegheny College in Meadville, Pennsylvania, in 1948. Before her marriage to John Robinson in 1949 she worked as a librarian. She now lives in Berwyn, Pennsylvania.

Robinson is the author of about fifty short stories, which have appeared in magazines like *McCall's, Ladies' Home Journal,* and *Redbook.* She received a fellowship in Children's Literature to the Bread Loaf Writers' Conference in 1962. She was a lecturer on the short story at the Star Island Writer's Conference in 1964 and at the Philadelphia Writers' Conference in 1982.

Robinson wrote a play version of *The Best Christmas Pageant Ever,* which was first performed in Seattle by the Poncho Theatre. Plans for its publication are under way. The book won the Maud Hart Lovelace Award in 1982.

Across from Indian Shore was a Junior Literary Guild selection, and *Temporary Times, Temporary Places* was named a 1982 Notable Book by the American Library Association.

tors must do the very same thing with the characters they portray.

It's very hard for me to choose a favorite of my own books, because they are all so different from each other, and there is something special for me in every one—*Across from Indian Shore* and *Trace Through the Forest* are adventure stories about American Indians, which are a particular interest of mine; *The Fattest Bear in the First Grade* is my only book for very young children; *Temporary Times, Temporary Places* takes me home again, to summer in a small town . . . but I would have to put *The Best Christmas Pageant Ever* at the top of my list, for the best reason of all— boys and girls tell me that it is *their* favorite—and that's the most important thing to me.

Since leaving my small town—though writers never really leave the place where they grew up; it can always be found, one way or another, in most of our books—I've lived in Pittsburgh and New England and still go back to Cape Cod every summer— and live now in a suburb of Philadelphia with my husband and two daughters. I spend most of my nonwriting time in the pursuit of misplaced homework, missing

SELECTED WORKS: Across from Indian Shore, 1962; Trace Through the Forest, 1966; The Fattest Bear in the First Grade, 1969; The Best Christmas Pageant Ever, 1972; Temporary Times, Temporary Places, 1982.

ABOUT: Contemporary Authors (First Revision), Vol. 3; Something About the Author, Vol. 8; Ward, Martha E. and Dorothy A. Marquardt. Authors of Books for Young People, 2nd edition.

ANNE ROCKWELL

February 8, 1934–

and

HARLOW ROCKWELL

Author of *The Toolbox,* etc.

Biographical sketch of Anne F. and Harlow
Rockwell:

ANNE AND HARLOW ROCKWELL, together and separately, have created many
distinguished books for young readers.

Anne Rockwell was born in Memphis,
Tennessee, but lived in many different
parts of the United States while she was
growing up, including New Mexico, Arizona, Ohio, and New York. About the importance of books to her in her early years, she
wrote: "My closest friends were characters
in books and my best thoughts came from
them. . . . As I grew up, I wondered
whether I wanted to be an artist or writer,
for although drawing was what I did most
naturally, it was the tremendous power of
words to create people, places, and stories
that made me envy a good writer whenever
I read one."

Having spent several years of her childhood on an Indian reservation, where she
also went to school, she developed a special
interest in the American Indians. In New
Mexico and Arizona, she came to know Indians personally, and she began to draw
pictures of them. Outside of her own family, they were her first live models. Several
of her earliest books, such as *Paintbrush and
Peacepipe: The Story of George Catlin* and
The Dancing Stars: An Iroquois Legend reflect this abiding interest.

A mainly self taught artist, Anne Rockwell studied art at the Brooks Memorial
Gallery in Memphis and at the Palace of the
Governors in Santa Fe. Later, after coming
to New York, she studied sculpture at the
Sculpture Center and etching and engrav-
ing at the Pratt Graphic Arts Center.

ANNE ROCKWELL

HARLOW ROCKWELL

In the early 1950s Anne worked for the
production department of a publishing
house and in the art department of an advertising agency. She married Harlow
Rockwell in 1955, and after their first child
was born, she realized that what she really
wanted to do was make children's books.
Since that decision, she has written and illustrated many popular books for children

and illustrated many books written by others. The first book she illustrated was included in the American Institute of Graphic Arts selection of the Fifty Best Books of the Year. She has become best known as creator of picture books for young children. Her work reveals her wide range of interests and also her meticulous research. For instance, to research *The Wolf Who Had A Wonderful Dream: A French Folktale,* Rockwell spent a summer in Normandy, France, the book's setting, sketchbook in hand, drawing the farms, the manor houses, the people, and the countryside so that her illustrations would be accurate.

As her three children grew up, Anne became interested in their development of language skills. This interest led to her creation of her many Ready-to-Read books, carefully constructed stores and pictures designed to meet the need of the beginning reader. And she and her husband Harlow are the creators of early concept books, including *The Toolbox, Machines, Thruway,* and *The Supermarket,* and two realistic Ready-to-Read stories, *Blackout* and *Out to Sea.*

Harlow Rockwell has worked as an advertising agency art director, a free-lance magazine illustrator, a lettering man, a printmaker, a package designer, and a new products designer as well as an author and illustrator of children's books. Like Anne Rockwell, he is largely self-taught as an artist, though his education has included course work at the Albright-Knox Gallery in Buffalo, New York, and at the Pratt Institute in New York City. He won the Art Directors Club Gold Medal three times, and his prints, watercolors, and woodcuts have been exhibited at the Library of Congress Print Show and the Audubon Artists Annual. Many magazines, including *Good Housekeeping, McCall's,* and *Parents* have published his work. He has written two Ready-to-Read handbooks for early readers, *Look at This* and *I Did It,* and assorted other children's books, including the highly praised *My Doctor. My Kitchen* was named

a 1980 Notable Book by the American Library Association.

The books of Anne and Harlow Rockwell have received consistently complimentary reviews and many awards and honors over the years. The American Institute of Graphic Arts Children's Book Show 1973/74 included four of their books: *Games, Head to Toe, The Awful Mess,* and *Paul and Arthur and the Little Explorer.* The Children's Book Showcase included *Toad* in 1973, and *Befana* in 1975. *Albert B. Cub and Zebra: An Alphabet Story* was selected to be a Notable Children's Books of 1977 by the American Library Association; *Games* was also selected to be a Notable Children's Book by the ALA in 1973 and was named a *New York Times* Outstanding Children's Book of 1973 as well. *Poor Goose,* was selected as a Classroom Choice of 1977 by a joint committee of the International Reading Association and The Children's Book Council.

The Rockwells live with their three children in Old Greenwich, Connecticut, where much of their leisure time is spent painting, sculpting, and printmaking. The whole family loves to travel and has visited Europe often, especially France, where Anne and Harlow pursue their interest in Romanesque architecture. Harlow, who learned to sail as a child, enjoys sailing his catboat on Long Island Sound each summer. And Anne's greatest interests, outside of travel and art in all its forms, are designing and making needlework tapestries, mythology, reading, and French cooking.

Selected Works Written and Illustrated by Anne Rockwell: Temple on the Hill: The Building of the Parthenon, 1969; Paintbrush and Peace Pipe, 1971; The Dancing Stars: An Iroquois Legend, 1972; Paul and Arthur and the Little Explorer, 1972; Games (and How to Play Them), 1973; Befana: A Christmas Story, 1974; Albert B. Cub and Zebra: An Alphabet Storybook, 1977.

Selected Works Retold and Illustrated by Anne Rockwell: When the Drum Sang: An African Folktale, 1970; The Wolf Who Had a wonderful Dream: A French Folktale, 1973; Poor Goose: A French Folktale, 1976.

SELECTED WORKS SELECTED AND ILLUSTRATED BY
ANNE ROCKWELL: Savez-vous Planter les Choux? and
Other French Songs, 1969; El Toro Pinto and Other
Songs in Spanish, 1971; The Three Bears and Fifteen
Other Stories, 1975; Gray Goose and Gander and Oth-
er Mother Goose Rhymes, 1980.

SELECTED WORKS WRITTEN AND ILLUSTRATED BY
ANNE AND HARLOW ROCKWELL: The Toolbox, 1971;
Machines, 1972; Thruway, 1972; Toad, 1972; The Awful Mess, 1973; Head to Toe, 1973; The Supermarket,
1979; Blackout, 1979; Out to Sea, 1980; My Barber,
1981; Happy Birthday to Me, 1981; Can I help?, 1982;
Sick in Bed, 1982.

SELECTED WORKS WRITTEN AND ILLUSTRATED BY
HARLOW ROCKWELL: My Doctor, 1973; I Did It, 1974;
My Dentist, 1975; My Nursery School, 1976; Look at
This, 1978; My Kitchen, 1980.

ABOUT ANNE ROCKWELL: Contemporary Authors
(First Revision), Vol. 21–22; Kingman, Lee and others,
comps. Illustrators of Children's Books: 1967–1976;
Ward, Martha E. and Dorothy A. Marquardt. Illustrators of Books for Young People, 2nd edition.

ABOUT HARLOW ROCKWELL: Kingman, Lee and others, comps. Illustrators of Children's Books: 1967–
1976; Ward, Martha E. and Dorothy A. Marquardt. Illustrators of Books for Young People, 2nd edition.

THOMAS ROCKWELL

March 13, 1933–

AUTHOR OF *How to Eat Fried Worms,* etc.

Autobiographical sketch of Thomas Rockwell:

MY FATHER was an artist, my mother an
unpublished writer; my older brother became an artist, my younger brother, a
sculptor; I write children's books. As a child,
I read omnivorously: books, comic books
(which we used to read free all afternoon on
the steps of Howard's General Store on
Route 7), cereal boxes, the directions on
toothpaste tubes. My mother bought lots of
books for my brothers and me and often
read out loud to us, even after we had
learned to read to ourselves.

I grew up in rural Vermont, where we
moved when I was five from a wealthy suburb of New York City. I played marbles,
pick-up-sticks, "guns" (it was World War
II). I can still remember my delight when
I discovered one afternoon how to make not
just a *bang bang bang,* but a marvelously realistic *kzkzkzkzkzkzkz* machine-gun noise.
I hunted chipmunks in the stone walls and
later gray squirrels and deer, helped out on
a neighboring dairy farm, swam under the
covered bridge on the Battenkill River—
and after an agonizing afternoon perched
in the rafters of the bridge trying to get up
my nerve, I jumped. I was bored a lot in
school, worried a lot about tests, behaved almost too well, so that I was almost in danger
of becoming the teacher's pet and was concerned about the high marks I got. But
then, to my surprise, I became somehow the
leader of a recess gang in sixth grade. In my
freshman and sophomore years of high
school I went away to school but returned
home for my last two years, played basketball and baseball (Arlington Central School
was too small to have a football team), was
editor of the yearbook and valedictorian of
my class of twenty-three students—and suffered torments because of the speech I had
to make at graduation.

And so I went off to Princeton University,

left after two months with an ulcer, and then transferred to Bard College, where I majored in literature, writing poems for my senior project with the poet Theodore Weiss. In my senior year I married Gail Sudler, another artist. After graduation I worked for a gardening magazine in New York City and then moved to our present home beside a dairy farm outside Poughkeepsie, New York, so that I could help my father write his autobiography, *My Adventures as an Illustrator,* and a book about his work, *The Norman Rockwell Album* (1961). After that I wrote some short stories and floundered a little until, reading *The Oxford Book of Nursery Rhymes* to my son Barnaby (he's now twenty years old), I rediscovered my interest in children's books. In 1969 I published my first children's book, *Rackety-Bang and Other Verses,* illustrated by Gail. It received crushing reviews, the publisher declined my next book of verse, and so I wrote a novel for children, *Squawwwk!* (1972), also illustrated by Gail. Then came *Humpf!* (1971), *The Neon Motorcycle* (1973), *How to Eat Fried Worms* (1973), which has won ten awards, *The Portmanteau Book* (1974), with illustrations by Gail and our two children, our daughter Abigail having been born in 1967, *Hiding Out* (1974), *Tin Cans* (1975), *The Thief* (1977), illustrated by Gail, *How to Eat Fried Worms and Other Plays* (1980), which was written for Abigail, who has always liked acting, and *Hey, Lover Boy* (1981). Along the way, to keep food in the mouths of all of us and our various dogs and cats, a burro, a goose, three generations of ducks, and two unfortunate gerbils who were done in by our loving bloodthirsty cats, I have taught, sold second-hand books, worked for the War on Poverty, and tried sporadically and half-heartedly to write for television and advertising.

Looking back over so many years and now forward over I don't know how many or few gives one a queer feeling. But just as I still haven't stopped reading the directions on cereal boxes and toothpaste tubes, so I don't suppose I'll stop writing until I'm cut off right in the middle of a

———

In *How to Eat Fried Worms,* two boys bet another boy fifty dollars that he can't eat fifteen worms, one per day. They try devious tricks to keep him from eating the worms when it looks as though he may win. The book has been selected as an award-winner by groups of children in many states, among them Hawaii, Oklahoma, Iowa, Massachusetts, South Carolina, Missouri, Indiana, and California. In 1975, it also won the University of Wisconsin Golden Archer Award.

SELECTED WORKS: Rackety-Bang and Other Verses, 1969; Humpf!, 1971; Squawwwk!, 1972; How to Eat Fried Worms, 1973; The Neon Motorcycle, 1973; The Portmanteau Book, 1974; Hiding Out, 1974; Tin Cans, 1975; The Thief, 1977; How to Eat Fried Worms and Other Plays, 1980; Hey, Lover Boy, 1981.

ABOUT: Contemporary Authors (First Revision), Vol. 29-32, The International Authors and Writers Who's Who, 1977; Something About the Author, Vol. 7; The Writers Directory 1982-84.

MARY RODGERS

January 11, 1931–

AUTHOR OF *Freaky Friday,* etc.

Biographical sketch of Mary Rodgers Guettel:

MARY RODGERS was born in New York City, the daughter of composer Richard Rodgers and Dorothy Feiner, an interior decorator and author. She has been a composer, lyricist, playwright, novelist, columnist, and screenwriter.

She began her career by concentrating on music. She started writing songs at age sixteen, and when she was twenty, her first song, "Christmas Is Coming," was published. It was a children's song written with a fellow student at Wellesley College where Rodgers majored in music and from which she graduated in 1951.

Mary Rodgers [signature]

For a number of years she worked at Golden Records as a composer. She collaborated with many well-known lyricists, including Sammy Kahn, with whom she wrote the lyrics for "Ali Baba," which was recorded by Bing Crosby.

From 1957 to 1971 she was the script editor and assistant to the producer of the Leonard Bernstein New York Philharmonic Young People's Concerts. She has also written scripts for the Hunter College Little Orchestra Concerts.

Mary Rodgers is well known in the music world for her scores for the Broadway musicals "Once Upon a Mattress," "Hot Spot," and "The Mad Show." She has also composed numerous children's musicals: "Davy Jones Locker" performed with the Bil Baird Marionettes; "Three to Make Music," with her sister, Linda Rodgers Melnick; "Young Mark Twain," and "Pinocchio," another Bil Baird marionette production. She was also a contributing editor to the best-selling record and book *Free to Be . . . You and Me.*

In 1969, Harper and Row published *The Rotten Book,* her first book for children. The picture book, illustrated by Steven Kellogg, tells about a boy who imagines what it would be like to be absolutely rotten to everyone and everything. His reveries end when he realizes what the consequences would be. In *Freaky Friday* thirteen-year-old Annabel Andrews wakes up to discover that she has turned into her mother, and she goes through a day of disasters and revelations. As Annabel tries to cope unsuccessfully with cooking, laundry, budgeting, and such, she gains insight into her mother's problems as well as a new perspective on herself.

Rodgers wrote two sequels to *Freaky Friday. A Billion for Boris* tells what happens when Annabel and her boyfriend Boris discover a TV set that shows the next day's news. Boris tries to take advantage of their luck at the racetrack, but instead learns a costly lesson.

In *Summer Switch* Annabel's brother and father switch bodies. As Ape Face dreads a long summer at Camp Soonawissakit and Mr. Andrews faces an important meeting with his nasty new boss, father and son find themselves wishing they were in each other's shoes. Rodgers makes the transformation with hilarious results.

Her books have been highly praised for their engaging plots convincing characters, and snappy dialogue. *Freaky Friday* was an American Library Association Notable Book of 1972, and won a 1972 Christopher Award. *A Billion for Boris* won a 1974 Christopher Award and was also an ALA Notable Book, in the same year.

She also wrote the film script for *Freaky Friday,* a Walt Disney hit movie. Three years later she wrote the screenplay for another Disney movie, *The Devil and Max Devlin.*

Mary Rodgers is married to film executive Henry Guettel. They have five children and live in New York City.

SELECTED WORKS WRITTEN: The Rotten Book, 1969; Freaky Friday, 1972; A Billion for Boris, 1972; Summer Switch, 1982.

ABOUT: Contemporary Authors, Vol. 49–52 (New Revision Series), Vol. 8; The International Authors and Writers Who's Who, 1977; Kirkpatrick, D. L. ed. Twentieth-Century Children's Writers; Something

About the Author, Vol. 8; Ward, Martha E. and Dorothy A. Marquardt. Authors of Books for Young People, 2nd edition (Supplement); Who's Who in America, 1982–1983; Who's Who of American Women, 1975–1976; The Writers Directory 1982–84.

NICOLE RUBEL

April 29, 1953–

ILLUSTRATOR OF *Rotten Ralph,* etc.

Autobiographical sketch of Nicole Rubel:

IN THE DAYS of my birth, twins were uncommon. My sister Bonnie and I were born in an old World War II hospital in Miami Beach. My mother loves to tell the story of our birth because everyone in the hospital sent flowers to the woman who had twins.

A story my father likes to tell is about the time the police came to our door. The neighbors heard screams and crying from our house. When my poor tired father appeared at the door carrying two crying babies one in each arm the officer said he was sorry to bother and wished him luck.

My sister Bonnie and I tried to switch classes in the first grade. One day we got caught. I still feel guilty over what happened.

I played hookey from my class and my teacher came looking for me. She found Bonnie and spanked her in front of the class. In the meantime, I walked in. Our teacher was very surprised and sorry. We didn't try any more games for many years.

My art work has been described as brightly colored and bold. I must say that growing up in Miami had an everlasting influence on my sense of reality.

The first time I was asked to draw snow in school, I was very confused. I had never seen snow. I was used to drawing palm trees and beach scenes. Later I moved to New York and became used to snow and the changing of seasons.

My sense of color is not unusual for the surroundings that I grew up in. Directly

across the street from our house was a large group of strange and unusual Chinese styled houses painted in bright colors. On Sunday mornings I loved to sit under a palm tree while the air was still cool and draw from these buildings. Miami has beautiful flowering trees and bushes, which often show up in my illustrations.

When I was fourteen I stopped drawing and made papier-mâché monsters I painted them bright colors.

I continued on to ceramics and later silk screen. In my last year of art school at the Museum School of Fine Arts, I started working on a series of drawings about goldfish. I loved following one idea with another. This was my first step towards children's books. After I had started another series of ideas, I met Jack Gantos, who offered to give the pictures words. We worked on four in all and had a wonderful time. I had an awful cat at the time and I think the cat inspired Jack to write *Rotten Ralph. Rotten Ralph* was published in 1975 by Houghton Mifflin Company. After that Jack and I teamed up on many other books.

I still illustrate for writers, but I am now working on becoming a writer as well. After spending twenty-seven years as a visual artist, I am challenged by my new goal.

I was able to start by writing down my early experiences with my twin sister. I wrote about us in the guise of two kittens, *Sam and Violet*. Avon Books has now purchased six of these twin stories from me. I wrote and illustrated them. They are *Sam and Violet Are Twins, Sam and Violet Go Camping, Happy Birthday Sam and Violet, Merry Christmas Sam and Violet, The Sam and Violet Get Well Book,* and *Sam and Violet's Bedtime Story.*

I have dedicated all of these stories to my twin sister Bonnie.

———

Nicole Rubel received a joint B.S. degree in Art Education in 1975 from the Boston Museum School of Fine Arts and Tufts University. She has had several exhibitions of her work, including shows at the Boston Public Library in 1977 and at the Viewpoint Gallery in Newport, Rhode Island in 1977.

Rotten Ralph was on the *School Library Journal* "Best of the Best 1966–1978" list (December 1979) and was in the Children's Book Showcase of 1976. *Worse Than Rotten Ralph* was in the 1979 American Institute of Graphic Arts Show.

SELECTED WORKS WRITTEN AND ILLUSTRATED: Sam and Violet Are Twins, 1981; Sam and Violet Go Camping, 1981; Sam and Violet's Christmas Story, 1981; Sam and Violet's Birthday Book, 1982.

SELECTED WORKS ILLUSTRATED: Rotten Ralph, by Jack Gantos, 1976; Sleepy Ronald, by Jack Gantos, 1976; Fair-Weather Friends, by Jack Gantos, 1977; Aunt Bernice, by Jack Gantos, 1978; Worse Than Rotten Ralph, by Jack Gantos, 1978; The Perfect Pal, by Jack Gantos, 1979; The Werewolf Family, by Jack Gantos, 1980.

ABOUT: Something About the Author, Vol. 18; Kingman, Lee and others, comps. Illustrators of Children's Books: 1967–1976.

REYNOLD RUFFINS

See Jane Sarnoff and Reynold Ruffins

CHELI DURÁN RYAN

CHELI DURÁN RYAN

AUTHOR OF *Hildilid's Night,* etc.

Biographical sketch of Cheli Durán Ryan:

CHELI DURÁN RYAN was born in New York City, but her work and studies have taken her around the world. She graduated from Trinity College in Dublin, concentrating on English and Spanish literature, and went on to pursue her interest in Spanish at the University of Barcelona.

Returning to the United States, she worked as a children's book editor in New York City. She continued her interest in Spanish by translating Spanish poetry into English.

Her first children's book, published in 1974, was her most successful. *Hildilid's Night* was a finalist for the National Book Award and was a Caldecott Honor Book. The *Horn Book* called it a "true picture book" whose drawings "create patterns of eerie strength and humor that second the words." The story tells of an old woman's attempt to eliminate the night by variously trying to sweep it, cook it, tie it, shear it, singe it, and even tuck it into bed. Illustrated by Arnold Lobel, the book was included in the 1972 Children's Book Showcase and the American Institute of Graphic Arts Children's Book Show in 1972. It was also a finalist for the 1972 National Book Award.

Her second book, *Paz,* reflects the author's time spent in Spain and tells the story of Balthazar Paz, whose home straddles the Spanish and French borders.

Her knowledge of Spanish also led to her next book, *The Yellow Canary Whose Eye Is So Black.* Working this time as editor, she collected and translated a large group of poems from the Spanish-speaking countries of Latin America.

Cheli Durán, as she is now known, currently lives on the island of Crete.

SELECTED WORKS WRITTEN: Hildilid's Night, 1971; Paz, 1971.

SELECTED WORKS EDITED AND TRANSLATED: The Yellow Canary Whose Eye Is So Black, 1977.

ABOUT: Contemporary Authors, Vol. 102; Something About the Author, Vol. 20; Ward, Martha E. and Dorothy A. Marquardt. Authors of Books for Young People, 2nd edition (Supplement).

JANE SARNOFF

JANE SARNOFF

June 25, 1937–

and

REYNOLD RUFFINS

August 5, 1930–

REYNOLD RUFFINS

AUTHOR AND ILLUSTRATOR OF *A Great Bicycle Book,* etc.

Biographical sketch of Jane Sarnoff and Reynold Ruffins:

JANE SARNOFF and Reynold Ruffins were both born in New York City; Sarnoff in Brooklyn and Ruffins in Manhattan. Both of them have been pursuing their respective careers as writer and illustrator since childhood. Sarnoff started writing se-riously in the sixth grade when she was asked to make up a myth. Ruffins has been drawing, painting, sketching, and doodling for as long as he can remember.

After receiving her B.A. degree from Goucher College, in 1959, Jane Sarnoff worked at odd jobs as a waitress, market researcher, and writer of record-jacket copy. Then she took a job as a copywriter for

Sudler and Hennessey, a pharmaceutical advertising agency in New York. Following graduation from Cooper Union School of Art and Architecture in New York City in 1951, Ruffins worked in advertising as a designer and art director. He shared a studio with fellow Cooper Union artists Seymour Chwast, Milton Glaser, and Edward Sorel. These four were the early members of Push Pin Studios, which is credited with establishing lasting trends in the design field. They published a periodic promotion piece, *The Monthly Graphic*, which was a showcase of their talent. Later the name was changed to *The Push Pin Almanack*.

Sarnoff and Ruffins began working together in advertising and in creating games for adults. Their first book together was about bicycles. More than a dozen nonfiction books followed, on such subjects as chess, riddles, and superstitions.

Through every stage of a book's development, the collaborators discuss how each other's part can be improved. They work at making their nonfiction books entertaining as well as informational, choosing high-interest topics they hope will excite young readers. Sarnoff writes with tongue-in-cheek, and Ruffins contributes humorous illustrations. Even a serious book like *Words: A Book About the Origins of Everyday Words and Phrases* maintains a degree of light-heartedness.

When they are not working together, Sarnoff and Ruffins do free-lance work independent of one another. Sarnoff still does pharmaceutical writing and serves as an editorial consultant for a sport magazine. Ruffins does design and illustration for advertising and magazines. He also taught at the School of Visual Arts in New York City and at the Syracuse University College of Visual and Performing Arts. He has received awards from the Art Directors Club and the American Institute of Graphic Arts. Ruffins also won the Cooper Union Professional Achievement Award, and his children's books have been exhibited at the Bologna Children's Book Fair.

Words was named an American Library Association Notable Book of 1982. Three of their books have been named Children's Choices by the joint committee of the Children's Book Council and the International Reading Association: *The Code and Cipher Book*, in 1976; *The Monster Riddle Book*, in 1978; and *Words*, in 1983. Ruffins' *My Brother Never Feeds the Cat* was also a Children's Choice book, in 1980.

Reynold Ruffins' wife, Joan, is also an artist. They have four children—Todd, Lynn, Ben, and Seth—and many pets, including a boa constrictor. Reynold and Joan Ruffins live in New York City and spend summers sailing in Sag Harbor on Long Island.

Jane Sarnoff also lives in New York City. She has traveled through Japan, Hong Kong, Europe, and Mexico. When she is not working she likes to jog, read, and listen to music.

SELECTED WORKS WRITTEN BY JANE SARNOFF AND ILLUSTRATED BY REYNOLD RUFFINS: A Great Bicycle Book, revised edition, 1976; The Chess Book, 1973; What?: A Riddle Book, 1974; The Code and Cipher Book, 1975; The Monster Riddle Book, revised edition, 1978; I Know!: A Riddle Book, 1976; A Great Aquarium Book, 1977; Giants!: A Riddle Book, 1977; Take Warning!: A Book of Superstitions, 1978; Space: A Fact and Riddle Book, 1978; Light the Candles! Beat the Drums!: A Book of Holidays, 1979; If You Were Really Superstitious, 1980; That's Not Fair, 1980; Words: A Book About the Origins of Everyday Words and Phrases, 1981.

SELECTED WORKS WRITTEN AND ILLUSTRATED BY REYNOLD RUFFINS: My Brother Never Feeds the Cat, 1979.

ABOUT REYNOLD RUFFINS: Pitz, Henry C. 200 Years of American Illustration; Graphis No. 177, 1975.

ABOUT JANE SARNOFF: Contemporary Authors, Vol. 53–56; Something About the Author, Vol. 10; Ward, Martha E. and Dorothy A. Marquardt. Authors of Books for Young People, 2nd edition (Supplement).

HARRIET MAY SAVITZ

May 19, 1933–

AUTHOR OF *Run, Don't Walk*, etc.

Harriet May Savitz

Autobiographical sketch of Harriet May Savitz:

WHEN I BEGIN a book, I am the last one to know where it will end. It is as if I am embarking upon a strange new journey each time I set out on the adventurous path leading to the novel.

Somewhere during the process, I, who was the leader, become the follower, and my characters give the orders. "No," they say, "not in that direction . . . in this." I hear their voices while I tap on the typewriter keys. "You are not doing me justice." "I deserve a better outcome than that." "Who do you think you are, my writer friend, without us?"

At some point in the story, I feel the pulse, the actual breathing from within the pages, and I know the characters have come to life. I never know when that sensation will come, and it always takes me by surprise. But from that moment on, the characters have a will of their own.

Some writers rely on plot to take them through the novel. I cannot move off the first page without confidence in my characters. Most of the characters are drawn from real life. They are a blend of the people who come in and out of my life.

The next most important thing for me is background. Lately, my books have been set down at the seashore. I am a shore person, having gone there every summer of my life. There is nothing better than the feel of the sand on bare feet, the sound of waves beating against the jetty, the clapping of seagull's wings. Each time I go there, I discover a new face, a new sound, a new feeling.

I truly believe a writer can't stay in her room and expect stories to find her. I have to make them happen, or be a part of the happening that is already in progress. I go "out there" to see and feel it for myself. For *If You Can't Be the Sun, Be a Star,* I researched the background by spending days in a police station in a shore town. I also was involved in a neighborhood watch program. *Run, Don't Walk* was the culmination of fifteen years' involvement with the physically disabled; traveling with wheelchair sports teams, belonging to political groups that were trying to change the laws in this country, sharing some of the humiliation of being asked to leave restaurants. With the disabled, I was not able to get into restaurants; because of the disabled, I felt the separateness, the sectioning off, and realized the effect of a lack of bathroom facilities for the physically disabled. From all of that came anger, then determination, then *Run, Don't Walk.*

The people in my books are fighters because I am not. They have courage because I do not. They dare because I dare not. If I could sum up why I write for young people, it is because they honor truth and accept it. If I can encourage them to look outside themselves toward society and believe that they might change it, better it, leave their mark upon it, then the hours of isolation, frustration, doubt, and sometimes rejection, are worth it.

I often wonder how anyone anywhere manages to live without writing at least five hundred words a day.

Harriet May Savitz was born in Newark, New Jersey. She attended Upsala College and Rutgers University. She and her husband, who is a pharmacist, have two children and live in Plymouth Meeting, Pennsylvania.

Savitz is a member of several organizations that work for and with disabled people. She is a member of the League of American Pen Women and of the Philadelphia Children's Reading Round Table, which she co-founded. She has lectured at East Tennessee State University, at Villanova University, and at Mansfield State College, and spoke at the Mid-Atlantic Library Conference. She teaches writing at the Philadelphia Writer's Conference, gives workshops in writing novels, and has been guest lecturer of English Literature at the University of Pennsylvania. Her short stories have appeared in *Boy's Life* and *Scholastic Magazine,* and she has written articles for the *Philadelphia Inquirer,* the *Denver Post,* the Associated Press, and *Encyclopaedia Britannica.*

Fly, Wheels, Fly! was nominated for the Dorothy Canfield Fisher Award in 1971. *Run, Don't Walk* was nominated for a 1983–84 California Young Reader Medal, and was produced for ABC as an After School Special.

SELECTED WORKS: Fly, Wheels, Fly!, 1970; On the Move, 1973; The Lionhearted, 1975; Wheelchair Champions: A History of Wheelchair Sports, 1978; Run, Don't Walk, 1979; Wait Until Tomorrow, 1981; If You Can't Be the Sun, Be a Star, 1982.

ABOUT: Contemporary Authors (First Revision), Vol. 41–44; Something About the Author, Vol. 5; Ward, Martha E. and Dorothy A. Marquardt. Authors of Books for Young People, 2nd edition (Supplement); Who's Who of American Women, 1979–1980.

ELEANOR SCHICK

April 15, 1942–

AUTHOR AND ILLUSTRATOR OF *City in the Summer,* etc.

Biographical sketch of Eleanor Schick:

ELEANOR SCHICK has lived most of her life in the same place where she was born and raised, New York City. The daughter of a psychiatrist and a social worker, she chose a different route for herself. From the age of eight, she studied and worked to be a dancer. She had early success with this career, performing as a soloist with the Tamiris-Nagrin Dance Company while still in her teens. She went on from there to study with Martha Graham and with Alvin Ailey. She also performed as a soloist with the American Dance Festival and as a member of the Juilliard Dance Theatre.

While training as a dancer, Schick also studied to be a dance instructor. She lectured on dance and taught at Hofstra University, Bryn Mawr College, and Connecticut College.

In 1964, with the publication of *A Surprise in the Forest,* she began a new career as an illustrator and writer of children's books. Her earlier profession makes its appearance in *The Dancing School,* and she draws upon her New York City background for such books as *City in the Winter, City in the Summer* and *5A and 7B.* In *City in the Winter,* published in 1970, Jimmy spends a routine day with his grandmother, who cares for him while his mother is at work, and city life is reflected in every scene of their home and neighborhood. Critic Barbara Bader calls this glimpse into city life "representative of the new social and emotional climate" in children's books. Bader says that there is a "value" in showing the child's world: "To enter into other, different lives as real as one's own is a means of understanding; and of caring." Both *City in the Winter* and *City in the Summer* have been produced as filmstrips.

Among her many titles, Schick has written easy-to-read books such as *Summer at the Sea,* the story of a city family's escape to a summer house at the shore. She works primarily in black and white, but has branched out to color. She draws in a realistic style, though her earlier books tended to be stylized; all conform to what Schick calls her "personal" sense of realism.

She is married to an artist and has two children, David and Laura.

SELECTED WORKS WRITTEN AND ILLUSTRATED: A Surprise in the Forest, 1964; The Little School at Cottonwood Corners, 1965; I'm Going to the Ocean!, 1966; The Dancing School, 1966; 5A and 7B, 1967; City in the Summer, 1969; Making Friends, 1969; City in the Winter, 1970; Andy, 1971; City Green, 1974; City Sun, 1974; Neighborhood Knight, 1976; Rainy Sunday, 1981; Joey on His Own, 1982.

SELECTED WORKS ILLUSTRATED: Christmas in the Forest, by Jan Wahl, 1967.

SELECTED WORKS WRITTEN: Peter and Mr. Brandon, illustrated by Donald Carrick, 1973.

ABOUT: Bader, Barbara. American Picturebooks from Noah's Ark to the Beast Within; Contemporary Authors, Vol. 49–52; (New Revision Series), Vol. 4; The International Authors and Writers Who's Who, 1977; Kingman, Lee and others, comps. Illustrators of Children's Books: 1957–1966; 1967–1976; Something About the Author, Vol. 9; Ward, Martha E. and Dorothy A. Marquardt. Authors of Books for Young People, 2nd edition (Supplement).

ANN SCHLEE

ANN SCHLEE

May 26, 1934–

AUTHOR OF *Ask Me No Questions*, etc.

Biographical sketch of Ann Schlee:

THE DAUGHTER of Duncan and Nancy Cumming, Ann Schlee was born in Greenwich, Connecticut, and spent the first eleven years of her life in the United States with her American grandparents. At the end of World War II her father was stationed in Cairo, and Ann and her mother joined him there. She spent two years in Egypt and then sent to boarding school in England. During the holidays, she traveled a great deal and followed her parents to various parts of Africa, including a western province of the Sudan, Khartoum, and Ethiopia. In the mid-1950s, she studied English at Oxford and received her B.A.; she also taught for two years in an American school for girls. On July 27, 1957, Ann Cumming and D. N. R. Schlee were married. They have three daughters—Emily, Catherine, and Hannah—and a son named Duncan. The Schlees live outside of London.

Most of Ann Schlee's novels for children are based on historical fact. While traveling to different parts of the world, she was influenced by and drew ideas from places she visited. Her first book, *The Strangers,* is set in 1651 on the Scilly Isles, which she visited. She writes that the book "attempts to give a picture of the poverty and simplicity of the islanders' lives and was written out of affection for the place." Published in England in 1971, *The Strangers* had favorable reviews; it was then published in the United States in 1972. *The Consul's Daughter* and *The Guns of Darkness* soon followed. Perhaps one of the best known of Ann Schlee's works is *Ask Me No Questions.* A 1982 Boston Globe-Horn Book Award Honor Book, the novel takes place outside of London in the 1840s during a cholera epidemic. As in most of Schlee's writing, historical events are seen from a child's point of view. She is noted for clear writing and skillful characterization.

Ann Schlee wrote one novel for adults, *Rhine Journey,* published in 1981. It, too, has an historical background. A striking departure from her historical novels is *The Vandal,* a work of science fiction and the 1980 winner of England's prestigious Guardian Award. A review of *The Vandal* in the *Guardian* stated that "here, once more, her calm, civilized style cloaks that density of passion and fierce morality that is peculiarly her own."

SELECTED WORKS: The Strangers, 1972; The Consul's Daughter, 1972; The Guns of Darkness, 1974; The Vandal, 1981; Ask Me No Questions, 1982.

ABOUT: Contemporary Authors, Vol. 101; Kirkpatrick, D. L., ed. Twentieth-Century Children's Writers; The Writers Directory 1982–84.

ALVIN SCHWARTZ

April 25, 1927–

AUTHOR OF *Cross Your Fingers, Spit in Your Hat,* etc.

Autobiographical sketch of Alvin Schwartz:

I WAS BORN in Brooklyn, New York. I lived there with my parents and sister in a series of modest apartments during the years in which I grew up.

Actually my family was far larger than this. There were dozens of aunts, uncles, and cousins who lived within a mile or two of us. They were so lively and intriguing that, when I was eleven or twelve, I devoted my first piece of writing to them. It was a newspaper filled with the news and gossip of this extended family. Since my typewritten manuscript was the only copy, I rented it by the day to anyone who wanted to read it.

The elders in my family had immigrated from Hungary and Russia around the turn of the century, and they clung tenaciously to their old ways. As a result, I was affected by two cultures when I was growing up: the traditional beliefs and practices of my family and an American culture that had far less of an effect.

As my eighteenth birthday approached, I was in my second year at the City College of New York. But with World War II still in progress, I left school and enlisted in the U.S. Navy. When I was discharged two years later, I had decided that I wanted to be a newspaper reporter and a writer. I transferred to Colby College in Maine, then went on to the graduate school of journalism at Northwestern University.

After I finished at Northwestern, I found a job on a newspaper in Binghamton, New York. Five years later in 1955, I took the first of a series of jobs as a writer and editor in the New York area. By then I had married a teacher and home economist named Barbara Carmer and we had a brand-new son named John.

By 1960 our family had grown to four children. I had become communications director for a research organization in Princeton, New Jersey, and we moved there. But I soon found that I was not too happy in my work. I spent too much time in meetings and travel, and not enough as a writer.

In my spare time I managed to complete two non-fiction books for adults, and I was at work on a third, a travel book. It seemed to me that the time had come to make a full commitment to this work and take my chances as a free-lance writer. My wife agreed, but with four children to support, it was clear that we would have to accumulate a nest egg before I went out on my own.

On a Friday afternoon in October, 1963, I cleaned out my desk at work, got on my bicycle and rode home to begin my new career. I took over a bedroom in our house for my new office, but this proved to be too disruptive. So I moved to a tool shed in the backyard and worked there.

My first children's book did not appear until 1966. It was *The Night Workers,* an account of the people who work at night. It took only three months to complete, far less time than any of the books I have written since then.

The Night Workers was followed by a number of books for young people that explored contemporary life. These dealt with urban problems, labor unions and other subjects. I had covered such matters as a reporter, but now I had the time to explore them in greater depth and write about them with greater care.

In the early 1970s, I began to give my work a different emphasis. I continued to write occasional books on contemporary life, but I also began to write and compile books about American folklore, a part of the American culture I knew almost nothing about when I was growing up in the bosom of my extended family.

I had become particularly interested in folk humor, which was pervasive in this material. The wordplay, the use of hyperbole, and the colorful imagery in folk dialects fascinated me.

I decided to systematically explore the folkloric genres and devote books for young people to each. The first of these books was published in 1972. It was *A Twister of Twists, a Tangler of Tongues.* At this writing (1982), I have completed a dozen additional collections, each drawn from searches in archives and libraries and from the folklore collecting I have done with young people and others throughout the United States. Quite a bit more, however, remains to be done.

Three of Alvin Schwartz's books were named Notable Children's Trade Books in the Field of Social Studies by a joint committee of the Children's Book Council and the National Council for the Social Studies: *Cross Your Fingers* in 1974; *Whoppers* in 1975, and *Chin Music* in 1979. The International Reading Association/Children's Book Council Joint Committee named three of his books Children's Choices: *Whoppers* and *Cross Your Fingers* in 1975 and *Kickle Snifters* in 1977. *The Cat's Elbow* was named a 1982 Notable Book by the American Library Association.

Schwartz is a member of the American Folklore Society and the Authors Guild.

SELECTED WORKS: The Night Workers, 1966; A Twister of Twists, a Tangler of Tongues, 1972; Tomfoolery: Trickery and Foolery with Words, 1973; Witcracks: Jokes and Jests from American Folklore, 1973; Cross Your Fingers, Spit in Your Hat: Superstitions and Other Beliefs, 1974; Whoppers: Tall Tales and Other Lies, 1975; Kickle Snifters and Other Fearsome Critters, 1976; Chin Music: Tall Talk and Other Talk, 1979; Flapdoodle: Pure Nonsense from American Folklore, 1980; Ten Copycats in a Boat and Other Riddles, 1980; Busy Buzzing Bumblebees and Other Tongue Twisters, 1982; The Cat's Elbow and Other Secret Languages, 1982; There Is a Carrot in My Ear and Other Noodle Tales, 1982.

ABOUT: Contemporary Authors (First Revision), Vol. 13–16; Something About the Author, Vol. 4; Ward, Martha E. and Dorothy A. Marquardt. Authors of Books for Young People, 2nd edition (Supplement); Who's Who in the East, 1977–1978; Language Arts September 1977.

SANDRA SCOPPETTONE

June 1, 1936–

AUTHOR OF *Happy Endings Are All Alike,* etc.

Autobiographical sketch of Sandra Scoppettone:

HAVING TO write about myself is a nightmare to me. I have yet to write any autobio-

Scoppettone: *SCOP pet tone*

Sandra Scoppettone

graphical fiction although I keep threatening to do so. In other words I HATE doing this but am honored to be asked!

I was born in Morristown, New Jersey. I am an only child. I spent my formative years in South Orange, New Jersey, where I graduated from Columbia High School. I chose not to go to college. Instead, at eighteen, I moved to New York City, where I set out to be a writer. But for the first few years I didn't do much writing. I played. I was twenty-five before I published my first book, which was *Suzuki Beane*, illustrated by Louise Fitzhugh. After that I turned to writing plays for theater and television. I made some money writing for TV but none writing for the theater. As a woman it was almost impossible to get produced at that time. I also wrote some adult novels in my twenties . . . all four were rejected. It wasn't until 1973 that I sold my first Young Adult novel, called *Trying Hard to Hear You.*

Until the year before I wrote that book I was an active alcoholic, but I have been sober since that time. If I wasn't sober I couldn't have written any of the books I've published since 1973. I also write novels for

adults, but I'm better known for the books I write for young adults. This troubles me sometimes, but I'm grateful to receive the positive response to my YA's. I will continue writing for both audiences as long as I'm able to write. In the spring of 1982 my fourth YA book, *Long Time Between Kisses,* was published.

I live with Linda Crawford, who is also a novelist. We have a home in Greenport, New York and also in New York City. Three years ago we bought a loft in SoHo and had it built to our specifications. With us live two dogs, Tansy and Max, and three cats, Gilda, Putnam, and Vivian. If the names seem familiar it's because I've used them in my books.

My father was an influence on me as a writer. He wanted to write, but had to support his family and couldn't work at it as a writer must. He was extremely encouraging to me, as was my mother, and in fact they supported me financially during my first ten years in New York. Other influences have come from reading. I have always been a prolific reader and can attribute my interest in YA's to Paul Zindel and M. E. Kerr. But my favorite YA book is *I Am the Cheese* by Robert Cormier. My favorite adult writers are Beryl Bainbridge, Ann Tyler, and Sumner Locke Elliot. And, of course, Linda Crawford. I love English mysteries and I think Ruth Rendell is the best. My secret ambition is to write an English mystery under a pen name and see if I can sell it.

I am an avid movie- and theater-goer. I love to walk around New York City and hate to walk in the country. I adore libraries. My latest hobby is to play with my Atari: favorite games are Space Invaders and Asteroids. Computers fascinate me.

Most of the time I feel very lucky to be alive, as I am one of those people who has been granted a second chance at life. My priorities are to stay sober and help others to do so, and to become a better writer with each new book.

Both *Trying Hard to Hear You,* in 1974, and *Happy Endings Are All Alike,* in 1978, were named Best Books for Young Adults by the American Library Association.

The Late Great Me was made into a television special, first shown in 1979, and won an Emmy Award.

Scoppettone wrote the screenplay for the film *A Scarecrow in a Garden of Cucumbers,* which was released in 1972. She has also written for television: "A Little Bit Like Murder" was written for ABC's Wide World of Entertainment in 1973, and she wrote the shows *Where the Heart Is* and *Love of Life.*

SELECTED WORKS: Suzuki Beane, 1961; Bang Bang You're Dead, 1968; Trying Hard to Hear You, 1974; The Late Great Me, 1976; Happy Endings Are All Alike, 1978; Long Time Between Kisses, 1982.

ABOUT: Contemporary Authors (First Revision), Vol. 7-8; Something About the Author, Vol. 9; Ward, Martha E. and Dorothy A. Marquardt. Authors of Books for Young People, 2nd Edition (Supplement); Cosmopolitan April 1961.

Ouida Sebestyen

OUIDA SEBESTYEN

February 13, 1924–

AUTHOR OF *Words by Heart,* etc.

Autobiographical sketch of Ouida Sebestyen:

BOTH *Words by Heart* and *Far from Home* are set in Texas because I was born there and grew up in a little town called Vernon near the Oklahoma line. Unless I've lived in a place a long time, I'm afraid I'll write, "The sunflowers bloomed by the roadside," where they really don't. My third book, *IOU's,* is set in Colorado because Boulder has been my home for sixteen years and I'm beginning to think I know the country.

One of my favorite treats is criss-crossing the western states, poking around old forts and ghost towns, or retracing the Pony Express route. Actually I love to travel *anywhere.* The first place I ever traveled outside the United States was Iceland. I remember what grew by the roadside there because I got so hungry for green vegetables that I ate every dandelion I could find.

Since I was an only child and a bit shy and delicate, I was lucky to be surrounded by a lot of relatives, pets, books, and miles of history-filled space. Reading gave me so much joy that I hoped I would be able to pass it on someday by writing books of my own. I started in high school, and sent out my first novel when I was twenty. Back it came. So did the next three books I wrote. A few of my short stories appeared in magazines, encouraging me to keep trying. I stopped attending the University of Colorado to paint airplanes during World War II. Through years and years of odd jobs I thought of myself as A Writer, even when there was nothing to show for the efforts but four hundred rejection slips.

I married a Hungarian refugee and designed and helped to built a home in Marin County, California. When our son was born, we couldn't agree on a name for him. His father liked Hungarian ones that started off *Sziksz*— and I liked ones that sounded like cowboys. We finally went down a list I kept of possible hero-names and com-

Ouida Sebestyen: *WEE da Sa BEST yen*

promised on *Corbin,* but our differences of temperament were prophetic.

When I found myself divorced a few years later, Corbin and my recently widowed mother and I set up a three-generation household in Colorado. We decided I had to give writing one final chance in spite of the hardships it might involve. Luckily we didn't set a time limit, because for another twelve years my novels, plays, poems, articles, and true confessions were regularly rejected. Finally in near-desperation I sent a short story to the children's book editor at Atlantic Monthly Press, asking if it might have possibilities as a novel. Back came the loveliest word I had heard since I started writing thirty-five years before: *Yes.* When *Words by Heart* was accepted for publication six months later I felt like Cinderella when the slipper fit.

I drew upon the reminiscences and hardships of my parents and their families for the "feel" of that book, and upon my own (very young!) memories of the years around 1929 for *Far from Home.* I like doing the research that helps me create a believable little world for my characters. For *IOU's* I tried to remember what it had been like to live through being thirteen with my son and his friends. I don't write about real people, but of course each character has to be a facet of myself because he or she can only come alive through my own emotions and experiences. It's wonderful and frightening to write for young people, because they are asking for answers and examples and confirmation, and I want always to remind them of their specialness and nourish their idealism.

———

Words by Heart won the 1980 International Reading Association Children's Book Award and was a finalist in the hardcover fiction category of the American Book Awards in 1980. It was also named a Best Book for Young Adults and a Notable Book in 1979 by the American Library Association and a Best Book of the Year 1979 by the *New York Times.* In 1982 the paperback version won an American Book Award.

Far from Home was named an ALA Best Book for Young Adults in 1980.

SELECTED WORKS: Words by Heart, 1979; Far from Home, 1980; IOU's, 1982.

ABOUT: The Writers Directory 1982-84; English Journal October 1980; Publishers Weekly May 28, 1979.

MARCIA SEWALL

November 5, 1935–

ILLUSTRATOR OF *Come Again in the Spring,* etc.

Autobiographical sketch of Marcia Osgood Sewall:

PROVIDENCE, RHODE ISLAND was my birthplace and home through college. That old city with its characterful houses and interesting streets and alleys, with violets poking out from under forsythia bursting over fences, is a part of me.

The interests of my family have come together in my own desire to illustrate books. My father was full of good tales, particularly of Maine, and would love to entertain us with long humorous poems memorized, and anecdotes of people. My mother has always been artistic in so many different ways.

I appreciate how fortunate I was to attend schools where art and all creative endeavors were encouraged and respected. We designed costumes, danced in a school pageant, painted sets for plays and were offered "life drawing" classes at an early age.

I have a B.A. degree from Brown University and an M.Ed. from Tufts-Boston Museum School. Although I am not trained as a children's book illustrator, I have a deep interest in drawing and painting and have studied both. Since graduating from college, I have been involved with art and children, primarily teaching high school

Marcia Sewall

students. It is only within the last few years that I have become a full-time illustrator.

In my books, I spend much time trying to establish characters. They are vintage people whom I inherit from an author, focused upon for some period of their lives, each with a past that has given them their particular form and substance. How do they move? What do they wear? Where do they live? How do they look from three-quarter back view! Just who are they? A most difficult story I was given to illustrate became very enjoyable when I finally deciphered the quirk-filled personality of *Old Mrs. Brubeck.* She then moved about my drawing paper effortlessly, almost directing my pencil. If a book is for me to illustrate, then I immediately begin to imagine people and places and sometimes the materials I would like to use. While reading the manuscript for *Song of the Horse,* I saw vibrant black-and-white images and knew instantly that I wanted to use scratchboard as my medium to express this vivid impression.

It seemed as though it was a very long time that I carried my portfolio about without success. One year when I was teaching (and dreaming of illustrating), I put together a "dummy" book for a well-known folk-tale, never expecting that an editor would be interested in my work. Although it was never published, a career that I love began.

As I look out from my vantage point on a Boston cityscape, on my paper emerges a country squire or another gentle old horse.

———

Marcia Sewall received her B.A. degree in 1957 and her M.Ed. in 1958. She has also studied at the Rhode Island School of Design. She was a staff artist at the Children's Museum in Boston from 1961 to 1963 and taught art in Winchester, Massachusetts.

Two of the books she illustrated were exhibited in American Institute of Graphic Arts shows, *Come Again in the Spring* in 1976 and *The Leprechaun's Story* in 1979.

The *New York Times* has named several of her books Best Illustrated Books of the Year. These include *Come Again in the Spring* in 1976, *The Nutcrackers and the Sugar-Tongs* in 1978, *Stone Fox* in 1980, and *The Story of Old Mrs. Brubeck* in 1981.

Both *Little Things* and *The Song of the Horse* were named Notable Books by the American Library Association, in 1978 and 1981 respectively.

SELECTED WORKS: The Squire's Bride: A Norweigan Folk Tale, by P. C. Asbjørnsen and J. E. Moe, 1975; The Porcelain Man, by Richard Kennedy, 1976; Come Again in the Spring, by Richard Kennedy, 1976; The Nutcrackers and the Sugar-Tongs, by Edward Lear, 1978; Little Things, by Anne Laurin, 1978; The Birthday Tree, by Paul Fleischman, 1979; The Leprechaun's Story, by Richard Kennedy, 1979; Stone Fox, by John Reynolds Gardiner, 1980; The Song of the Horse, by Richard Kennedy, 1981; The Story of Old Mrs. Brubeck and How She Looked for Trouble and Where She Found Him, by Lore Segal, 1981; When I Was Little, by Lyn Littlefield Hoopes, 1983; Finzel the Farsighted, by Paul Fleischman, 1983.

ABOUT: Contemporary Authors, Vol. 45–48; Kingman, Lee and others, comps. Illustrators of Children's Books: 1967–1976; Graphis No. 200, 1979.

MARJORIE WEINMAN SHARMAT

November 12, 1928–

AUTHOR OF *Nate the Great,* etc.

Autobiographical sketch of Marjorie Weinman Sharmat:

I WAS BORN and grew up in Portland,
Maine, a city that I later used as the setting
for one of my novels, *A Visit with Rosalind.*
It was a cold and snowy childhood. I now
live in Arizona, where I suffer from a
chronic case of blizzard nostalgia.

I more or less read my way through my
childhood, and was perhaps the stereotypical future writer: introspective, nonathletic,
nearsighted, and shy. I started to write stories and poems when I was eight, and I also
"published" a newspaper, *The Snooper's
Gazette,* with a friend. We got most of our
news by spying on grown-ups for the detective agency that we were running concurrently. I continued to write through my
teenage years, but after I graduated from
high school I studied merchandising because I thought I could never become a
commercially published writer.

My first professionally published "work"
consisted of four words. It was a national
advertising slogan for the W. T. Grant
Company. A few years later, I sold my first
story (for adults) to a small magazine while
I was working at the Yale University Library. Then I sold an article about Yale to
another small magazine. The article became a part of the Yale Memorabilia Collection. My writing was now tied into the
tradition and dust of a great university.
There would be no stopping me! I sold a
greeting card verse. That marked the temporary end of my writing "career," but I
was $52.50 richer than when I started.

I married Mitchell Sharmat, and my interest in children's books began after the
birth of our sons. Finally, in 1967 my first
book, *Rex,* was published by Harper &
Row. Our sons are now grown and I write
full-time. I've written over sixty books and
they have been translated into eleven foreign languages.

This productivity has some drawbacks.
I've received my first "Are you still living?"
letter. This was from an earnest young fan,
and her query was politely and sincerely
put, which somehow made it worse. Why
didn't she pick on Isaac Asimov who, at last
count, had written 216 books?

Whatever success I've had is the result of
my family's love and encouragement in my
childhood and the help I've received from
my husband, who is a keen critic and sup-
plier of ideas. He has also entered the children's book field and has had several books
published. We've collaborated on two, *I Am
Not a Pest* and *The Day I Was Born.*

I've named many of my book characters
after my family, and readers will find the
names (and variations of them) of my parents, Anna and Nathan Weinman, my sister
Rosalind, my uncle Harry, my husband
Mitchell, our sons Craig and Andrew, and
our faithful dog Fritz Melvin. Perhaps the
most visible example is *Nate the Great,*
named after my father. I've also used the
names of real places in my books, such as *51
Sycamore Lane,* which is the title of my first
novel and was the address of our house
when we lived in Irvington, New York.

Parts of my real life are mirrored in my

books, sometimes subconsciously. But I guess it shows. A woman once rushed up to me at a convention and told me that I look just like my characters. She dashed off without revealing which characters inspired this marked resemblance. I was left wondering whether it was the mouse, the hippo, the wolf, the rat, the monster, etc. Now that I've written a young adult novel called *How to Meet a Gorgeous Guy,* I wish that lady would come back.

I love the atmosphere of writing, of being at the typewriter and not having to wash my face or be a social creature. I also like to draw, play the piano, sing, eat pizza, drink iced coffee, and solicit favorable comments about my work-in-progress from my dog.

———

Marjorie Weinman Sharmat graduated from Westbrook Junior College in Portland, Maine, in 1948. She has two sons.

Two of her books have been Junior Literary Guild selections: *Burton and Dudley* and *I'm Not Oscar's Friend Anymore.*

Many of her books have been named Children's Choice books by the International Reading Association/Children's Book Council Joint Committee: *Maggie Marmelstein for President,* in 1976; *Mooch the Messy,* in 1977; *Nate the Great and the Phony Clue,* in 1978; *Nate the Great and the Sticky Case,* in 1979; *A Big Fat Enormous Lie,* in 1979; *I Am Not a Pest,* in 1980; *Scarlet Monster Lives Here,* in 1980; and *The Day I Was Born,* in 1981. *Edgemont* was named a Notable Children's Trade Book in the Field of Social Studies in 1976 by a joint committee of the National Council for the Social Studies and the Children's Book Council.

Her *Square Pegs* is a novelization of the television show.

SELECTED WORKS: Rex, 1967; Getting Something on Maggie Marmelstein, 1971; Nate the Great, 1972; Burton and Dudley, 1975; I'm Not Oscar's Friend Anymore, 1975; Maggie Marmelstein for President, 1975; Nate the Great and the Lost List, 1975; Walter the Wolf, 1975; Mooch the Messy, 1976; The Lancelot Closes at Five, 1976; Edgemont, 1977; Nate the Great and the Phony Clue, 1977; A Big Fat Enormous Lie, 1978; Nate the Great and the Sticky Case, 1978; Scarlet Monster Lives Here, 1979; Square Pegs, 1982; How to Meet a Gorgeous Guy, 1983; I Saw Him First, 1983; Rich Mitch, 1983.

SELECTED WORKS WITH MITCHELL SHARMAT: I Am Not a Pest, 1979; The Day I Was Born, 1980.

ABOUT: Contemporary Authors (First Revision), Vol. 25–28; The International Authors and Writers Who's Who, 1977; Kirkpatrick, D. L. Twentieth-Century Children's Writers; Something About the Author, Vol. 4; Ward, Martha E. and Dorothy A. Marquardt. Authors of Books for Young People, 2nd edition (Supplement); The Writers Directory 1982–84.

ELIZABETH SHUB

TRANSLATOR, WITH ISAAC BASHEVIS SINGER, OF *Zlateh the Goat and Other Stories,* etc.

Autobiographical sketch of Elizabeth Shub:

AS IT HAPPENS, I was brought up in a family of writers and it was early decided that when I grew up I would be one, too. I wrote my first poem (it rhymed but was awful) when I was six, and by the time I was eleven I had quite a portfolio of "collected works." And then revolt set in. I was quite determined not to have anything to do with the literary field. When I was sixteen, I remember my father, smiling as if he knew better, agreeing to let me go to dramatic school, providing I went to college at night.

My father did know better, but I'm afraid my entry into the literary field took considerably longer than he had expected. I spent several years trying to be an actress and married very young, a journalist, needless to say.

Actually I think fate was in league with my father, for it was circumstance that forced me into my first literary job. World War II had started and my husband was drafted into the army. I was working in the theater, but earning very little, and I had to

Elizabeth Shub

have regular employment. My first job was with a publicity department where I "ghosted" speeches to be given at various fund-raising functions. I would have been fired had I not been rescued by a brilliant young woman, the daughter of friends of my parents, who conveniently was starting a new magazine called *This Month*. I became her associate editor. My forte was writing rhymed blurbs for various articles (a practice that lasted only two or three issues). I learned, however, that being a novice editor with a steady salary was perhaps more rewarding than being a struggling actress. After the war had ended, my husband was assigned to Berlin to work for the U.S. Military Government, and I joined him there. We were home again after two years, but it was not until a good many years later that I resumed my literary career. And again it was circumstance rather than inclination. I was divorced and needed work. I applied for a job at Harper & Row and as luck—or fate—would have it, the only opening was in the children's book department. I started as a free-lance reader and soon became an associate editor. I left Harper to work at Charles Scribner's Sons, and then went to Macmillan's children's book

department to work again with Susan Hirschman, who had started me in the children's book field four years before at Harper. Working with Susan Hirschman became a happy habit and I was delighted to have the opportunity to join her as senior editor when she left Macmillan to create Greenwillow Books at William Morrow & Company.

Oddly enough, my career as a translator started accidentally as well. I had known Nobel Prize winner Isaac Bashevis Singer since my childhood when he was a regular visitor at my parents' home, and so when I came to Harper, I urged him to write some children's stories. He agreed, and it seemed only natural that I should work with him on the translations. *Zlateh the Goat and Other Stories* was the first of the many Singer children's books that we translated together.

My first translation from the German was the Brothers Grimm's *The Twelve Dancing Princesses*. It was a favorite childhood story of mine, and with it began my fascination for translating the Grimms. I must admit, however, that it is more comfortable to sit with a live author who, if he must, can change the untranslatable than it is to commune with the dead. On the other hand, the challenge of finding the right wavelength on which to transmit the words of an author of another time has its own, somewhat mysterious, but gratifying reward.

Born in Vilna, Poland, Elizabeth Shub came to America as a baby. She studied English and German at the Brooklyn College of the City University of New York and attended the New York School of the Theater. She is a member of P.E.N.

Shub is on the 1982 Honor List of the International Board on Books for Young People for her translations of books by Nobel Prize winner Isaac Bashevis Singer, especially for *Zlateh the Goat*. That book and another of Singer's books she translated, *When Shlemiel Went to Warsaw and Other Stories,* were both Newbery Honor Books, in 1967 and 1968 respectively.

Two books Elizabeth Shub translated were American Library Association Notable Books in their years of publication: *About Wise Men and Simpletons,* and *Sir Ribbeck of Ribbeck of Havelland. The White Stallion* was also an ALA Notable Book.

SELECTED WORKS WRITTEN: Seeing Is Believing, 1979; The White Stallion, 1982.

SELECTED WORKS ADAPTED AND TRANSLATED: Clever Kate, by the Brothers Grimm, 1973.

SELECTED WORKS TRANSLATED: The Twelve Dancing Princesses, by the Brothers Grimm, 1966; Jorinda and Joringel, by the Brothers Grimm, 1968; Sir Ribbeck of Ribbeck of Havelland, by Theodor Fontane, 1969; The Thieves and the Raven, by Janosch, 1970; About Wise Men and Simpletons: Twelve Tales from Grimm, by the Brothers Grimm, 1971; The Adventures of Little Mouk, by Wilhelm Hauff, 1974; The Fisherman and His Wife, by the Brothers Grimm, 1978; The Bremen Town Musicians, by the Brothers Grimm, 1980.

SELECTED WORKS BY AND TRANSLATED WITH ISAAC BASHEVIS SINGER: Zlateh the Goat and Other Stories, 1966; When Shlemiel Went to Warsaw and Other Stories, 1968; Joseph and Koza, or the Sacrifice to the Vistula, 1970; The Fools of Chelm, 1973; Why Noah Chose the Dove, 1974.

ABOUT: Contemporary Authors (First Revision), Vol. 41–44; Something About the Author, Vol. 5; Ward, Martha E. and Dorothy A. Marquardt. Authors of Books for Young People, 2nd edition (Supplement).

DOROTHY E. SHUTTLESWORTH

October 10, 1907–

AUTHOR OF *Exploring Nature with Your Child,* etc.

Autobiographical sketch of Dorothy Edwards Shuttlesworth:

DURING school years (kindergarten through high school) in New Rochelle, New York, my greatest interest was the theater. The only indication of potential as a writer lay in getting good marks for written assignments and, on my own during the eighth grade, producing countless poems of

the absurd. Nearly all concerned animals—anything from pollywogs to chimpanzees. Today the notebook in which they were written still exists. Occasionally I re-read them, and wonder at the strangeness of it all as I come on something like "The Periwinkle's Sad Adventure"—an epic in its own way.

I delighted in school plays and dreamed of becoming a professional in the theater. However, during the spring I was graduated from high school, family tragedies, including the death of my father, made such hopes out of the question. Attempting to find a short-term job until life settled down, I was fortunate enough to find one at the American Museum of Natural History. It was a simple clerical operation, presumably to last until autumn. But shortly after it began, a museum official who knew I had been on the staff of my high school paper asked me to leave what I was doing to assist on the museum's *Natural History Magazine* because the "regular" there had left unexpectedly. I made the change happily, though little realizing it was to be the beginning of a fascinating career. Soon I came to know all members of the museum staff, including such luminaries as Margaret Mead and Roy Chapman Andrews, and learned to appreciate and share their interest in the natural world. The life stories of wild animals, including their struggles for survival as their habitats were destroyed, provided as much drama as formerly I had found in the theater.

I was asked to stay permanently with the magazine, and part of my work came to be re-wording scientific articles, making them more understandable for popular consumption. After several years of doing this, the museum agreed to my starting a magazine for children. And so *Junior Natural History Magazine* came into being. I was its editor for twelve years, during which time I married Melvin Shuttlesworth, a social studies teacher in East Orange, New Jersey. During the next few years our two children, Gregory and Lee Ann, were born, and while they were still young, I decided against commuting and carrying on my magazine work.

I had already written two books for young people, but at that time began one addressed to both parents and children. *Exploring Nature with Your Child* was an instant success, and from then on I had requests from various publishers to write books for them. To date thirty-nine have been published. A number have been named by a National Review Committee of Science Educators as outstanding science books of the year. In 1979 I was given an award by Rutgers University for a Distinguished Contribution to Children's Literature, in recognition of a "body of notable work." One book was cited by Keep America Beautiful for "distinguished public service."

Since my husband retired a few years ago, we have traveled to all parts of the world, including China. I am now working on a manuscript about the story behind the Great Wall.

———

In addition to the awards she mentions, Dorothy Shuttlesworth won an Eva L. Gor-

don Award from the American Nature Society in 1978. Her *Gerbils and Other Small Pets* was named a Child Study Association Book of the Year 1970, and *Zoos in the Making* was named a Notable Children's Trade Book in the Field of Social Studies by the joint committee of the National Council for the Social Studies and the Children's Book Council.

Dorothy Shuttlesworth was born in Brooklyn. She now lives in New Jersey.

SELECTED WORKS: Exploring Nature with Your Child, 1952; The Story of Cats, 1964; Animal Camouflage, 1966; The Story of Horses (revised edition), 1966; The Story of Rocks, 1966; Wildlife of Australia and New Zealand, 1967; Dodos and Dinosaurs, 1968; Gerbils and Other Small Pets, 1970; The Story of Monkeys, Great Apes, and Small Apes, 1972; Animals That Frighten People: Fact Versus Myth, 1973; To Find a Dinosaur, 1973; Wildlife of South America, 1974; The Hidden Magic of Seeds, 1976; How Wild Animals Fight, 1976; Zoos in the Making, 1977; Playful Animals, 1981.

SELECTED WORKS WRITTEN WITH GREGORY J. SHUTTLESWORTH: Farms for Today and Tomorrow: The Wonders of Food Production, 1979.

SELECTED WORKS WRITTEN WITH LEE ANN WILLIAMS: Disappearing Energy—Can We End the Crisis?, 1974; The Moon—Stepping Stone to Outer Space, 1977.

ABOUT: Contemporary Authors (First Revision), Vol. 1; (New Revision Series), Vol. 4; Foremost Women in Communications, 1970; Something About the Author, Vol. 3; Ward, Martha E. and Dorothy A. Marquardt. Authors of Books for Young People, 2nd edition.

ARANKA SIEGAL

June 10, 1930–

AUTHOR OF *Upon the Head of the Goat,* etc.

Autobiographical sketch of Aranka Siegal:

BORN in Beregszasz, Hungary, as the decade of the thirties opened, I was the fifth girl in the family. Early in my childhood my life was divided into two cultures—that

Franka Siegal

Eastern Carpathian city of 20,000 where my family lived, and the Ukrainian farming community of Komnyat where I'd spend the summer months on my grandfather's farm. Beregszasz had a single cinema, the circulating library was in the only book store on our side of town, and I well remember the day when the first public telephone booth was installed on Main Street, and I copied the phone number from the hardware store window to spend my filaérs harassing the sales clerks just to hear voices on that intriguing device. Men kissed ladies' hands in greeting, and class distinction was meticulously observed by either formal or familiar language usage. Gyar Street, where I lived, was lined on both sides with flowering chestnut trees, which were in front of the low brick and stucco homes, and the curbs were covered with blankets of portulaca.

By contrast, grandmother's house was typical Komnyat lime-washed mud brick with a thatched roof. Crude wagons were drawn by oxen on rutted dirt roads. The peasants dressed in homespun flax grown and pond-soaked on their own land. They farmed barefoot with handmade tools in fields ablaze with red poppies and blue

bachelor's buttons dotted profusely among the stalks of wheat. The forest provided welcome respite from their toil in the sun-drenched fields and was the source of firewood. For us children it was the target of forays after berries, hazelnuts, and mushrooms of every variety, and a place of lurking adventure and mystery. Susperstition and folklore competed with their catechism in governing their existence. Their social life centered around their heavily adorned and gilded Russian Orthodox Church and the periodic open-air harvest festivals.

My exposure to varied cultures intensified through the years. There soon began a pattern of being thrown together with people of many differing national origins in German concentration camps. In the pressure cookers of Auschwitz, Christianstadt, and Bergen-Belsen, astuteness and awareness in understanding people of different cultural background and makeup was necessary for coexistence. For existence itself. I had been deported before my fourteenth birthday, and after surviving the concentration camps, spent several years in Sweden following my liberation by the British First Army in April of 1945.

Arriving in America at age eighteen, I found mirrored in the microcosm of New York City the kaleidoscope of varied cultures that I had witnessed in my early growing years. I supported myself by modeling in the garment district and attended night school to learn English—my sixth language. I married an American and moved to Westchester, where I raised my daughter Rise and my son Joseph and continued my education with courses in the humanities at the local colleges. Feeling the need for a formal education more with every passing year—before I had the chance to finish my elementary school education the anti-Jewish measures prohibited me from attending public school—and yearning for a degree, I harbored my eventual self-expression through writing. Notes and passages would be written and tucked in a box for future reference. With Rise finishing at John Hopkins and Joseph off to the University of Virginia, I enrolled as a full-time matriculating student at Empire State College. My interest in the similarities and dissimilarities in people due to their cultures of origin deepened into the search for common denominators, which I found in the pursuit of social anthropology. Within three years I had my degree in that specialty, assisted by credits awarded for life experience.

The anthropological vignettes of Eastern Europe that comprised many of my term papers were soon adapted to radio and heard in a Saturday morning show on the radio station WHBI, of which I was host for a year. These in turn were the basis of *Upon the Head of the Goat*. Having derived some confidence as a storyteller, I sat down to write my first book. Pouring my heart out, and reliving my childhood, I was brought closer by these pages to my family, and I deepened my conviction about the importance of our cultural roots. Oddly enough, most of these segments of my childhood were sacrificed for the sake of brevity when it was decided to shorten the book to a length suitable for young adults to convey this part of history to the emerging generation.

Aranka Siegal's first book, *Upon the Head of the Goat,* is a powerful story of one family's struggle to survive and remain together during the increasing dangers to them before and during World War II. It was lauded by critics and won the 1981 Janusz Korczak Literary Competition, for being the best book for young readers that exemplifies selflessness and human dignity.

The book was also named a 1982 Newbery Honor Book and won the 1982 Boston Globe-Horn Book Award for nonfiction.

SELECTED WORKS: Upon the Head of the Goat: A Childhood in Hungary, 1939–1944, 1981.

SHEL SILVERSTEIN

1932–

AUTHOR AND ILLUSTRATOR OF *The Giving Tree,* etc.

Biographical sketch of Shelby Silverstein, who also writes under the pseudonym "Uncle Shelby":

SHEL SILVERSTEIN is a cartoonist, a playwright, a composer, and a singer and guitarist; and he is a most successful poet for children. *The Giving Tree* has sold over one and a half million copies and a French version, *L'Arbre Au Grand Coeur,* was published in 1973; *Where the Sidewalk Ends* has sold over a million copies; and *A Light in the Attic* was on the *New York Times* bestseller list for over a year. Silverstein illustrates his own books and has written two picture books for children. *Who Wants a Cheap Rhinoceros?* was first published in 1964 under the pseudonym "Uncle Shelby."

Silverstein was born in Chicago in 1932 and grew up in a small town in the Midwest. "When I was a kid—12, 14, around there—I would much rather have been a good baseball player or a hit with the girls," he said in an interview with *Publishers Weekly.* "But I couldn't play ball, I couldn't dance. . . . So, I started to draw and to write. I was also lucky that I didn't have anyone to copy, be impressed by. I had developed my own style, I was creating before I knew there was a Thurber, a Benchley, a Price and a Steinberg."

In the early 1950s he was a G.I. in Japan, doing cartoons for *Pacific Stars and Stripes.* He was first introduced to children's books by the author-illustrator Tomi Ungerer, who illustrated some of Silverstein's verses in a 1970 anthology compiled by William Cole, *Oh, How Silly!.*

In 1961 Lewis Nichols wrote in the *New York Times Book Review* about *Uncle Shelby's ABZ Book,* part of which first appeared in *Playboy:* "Uncle Shelby has a theory that children and elderly parties like to be treated as anyone else, not as children and elderly parents. Got the idea . . . [for the ABC Book] while standing on a street corner licking an ice-cream cone. Kid came along and looked at it wistfully. 'Very good,' remarked Uncle Shelby, 'Why don't you ask your mother to get you one?' Kid got a cone, Uncle Shelby got a dirty look—and a book."

In a 1978 interview in the *New York Times Book Review,* Silverstein commented on his books for children: "Happy endings, magic solutions in children's books create an alienation in the child who reads them. The child asks why don't I have this happiness thing you're telling me about, and comes to think when his joy stops that he has failed, that it won't come back."

In the *Publishers Weekly* interview, Silverstein said of his writing, "I have an ego, I have ideas, I want to be articulate, to communicate but in my own way. People who say they create only for themselves and don't care if they're published . . . I hate to hear talk like that. If it's good, it's too good not to share. That's the way I feel about my work." Of his own favorites, Silverstein names *Uncle Shelby's ABZ Book, A Giraffe and a Half,* and *Lafcadio, the Lion Who Shot Back;* "I think I like . . . [*Lafcadio*) the most," he said. *A Light in the Attic* was named an American Library Association Notable Book in 1981, and *The Missing Piece Meets the Big O* was named a Children's Choice book for 1982 by the joint committee of the Children's Book Council and the International Reading Association. *Sidewalk* was both an ALA Notable Book and an Outstanding Children's Book of the Year 1974, as designated by the *New York Times Book Review.*

Silverstein now lives in New York City, Chicago, Key West, and Sausalito, where he has a houseboat filled with a piano, a guitar, a saxophone, a trombone, and a camera. He says in *PW* that he's trying them all, "just to see if I can come up with anything."

SELECTED WORKS: Uncle Shelby's ABZ Book, 1961; Lafcadio, the Lion Who Shot Back, 1963; A Giraffe and a Half, 1964; The Giving Tree, 1964; Where the Sidewalk Ends: Poems and Drawings, 1974; The Missing Piece, 1976; A Light in the Attic, 1981; The Missing Piece Meets the Big O, 1981; Who Wants a Cheap Rhinoceros?, 1983.

ABOUT: Something About the Author, Vol. 27; Who's Who in America, 1980; New York Times September 24, 1961; April 30, 1978; Publishers Weekly February 24, 1975.

ALVIN SILVERSTEIN

December 30, 1933–

and

VIRGINIA B. SILVERSTEIN

April 3, 1937–

CO-AUTHORS OF *Guinea Pigs: All About Them,* etc.

Autobiographical sketches of Alvin Silverstein and Virginia Barbara Opshelor Silverstein, who also writes under the pseudonyms "Ralph Buxton" and "Richard Rhine":

WE'RE KNOWN as a writing team, and we've been doing things together ever since we first teamed up on a project in the chemistry lab in 1958, so it seems logical to make these autobiographical notes a joint project, too. But first a little "prehistory," to cover the half of our lives before we met.

Autobiographical sketch of Alvin Silverstein:

I was born in 1933, the youngest of four boys. My parents had emigrated to Brooklyn, New York, from Austria-Hungary (a part that is now Poland). Though they never had much education themselves, they placed great stress on hard work and education. I fit that mold perfectly, having a voracious interest in learning (as a child, I read encyclopedias in my spare time) and

a workaholic capacity for single-minded dedication. My passions weren't all for academic pursuits: during high school I was an avid basketball player, and in college I spent each day hitting tennis balls against a wall and volleying with any experienced player I could corner on the court; I ultimately made the college tennis team. I began a lifelong hobby of "science watching" practically as soon as I learned to read. My first love was astronomy, but I also was crazy about animals. (I was the type who brought home stray cats and raised pet mice.)

I received a B.A. degree from Brooklyn College, an M.S. from the University of Pennsylvania, and a Ph.D. from New York University. I actually started out in chemistry, although it was not my favorite subject, because I was interested in biochemistry, and that was taught in the Chemistry Department at Brooklyn College. I slid into biology somewhat by accident—a fortunate accident, since I am much happier in that field.

Autobiographical sketch of Virginia B. Silverstein:

I was born in 1937, an only child, in Phil-

adelphia, Pennsylvania. My parents were American born, but had the same stress on hard work and education and looked forward to fulfilling their own dreams through me. (Both had wanted to go to college but could not afford it.) I have always been a voracious reader. (When I was seven or eight, I used to total up my money saved in terms of how many Thornton Burgess animal books it would buy.) I was never able to indulge my liking for animals in real life, because my mother didn't care to have anything messier than a goldfish in the house. I fell in love with chemistry in high school but also had a gift for languages, and for a long time I was torn between the two fields. Although practicality won out and I majored in chemistry in college, I ultimately wound up combining that with languages as a translator of Russian scientific works.

We met at the University of Pennsylvania, when I was a senior and Al was a graduate student. We were working on research projects under the same supervisor. Taking mixed melting points together and watching invisible spots move slowly down the paper chromatograms ultimately led to marriage, in August of 1958. (He proposed after I stayed up till 6 a.m. typing his Master's thesis.)

The next years were busy ones. Al went to New York University at night for his Ph.D. and worked first as a junior high school science teacher (for one brief and painful semester) and then as a college teacher, which he loves. He's now a Professor of Biology and former chairman of the department at the College of Staten Island of the City University of New York. While Al was progressing up the academic ranks, I abandoned a brief and undistinguished career as an analytical chemist, taught myself Russian, and became a free-lance translator. I realized later that that was an idiotic thing to attempt, but it worked. I now translate close to two million words of Russian each year, mainly from scientific journals, but sometimes whole books. I am very embarrassed by the fact that I can't speak Russian (although, of course, I read it fluently) and keep vowing to learn, but I never seem to find the time.

We did find the time to have six children: Robert, Glenn, Carrie, Sharon, Laura, and Kevin. At the moment they all live with us on a hilly seventeen-acre farm in Hunterdon County, New Jersey, except for the eldest, who lives in New Brunswick but keeps threatening to move to California.

How did we get to be a writing team? Like most of the major shifts in our lives, that was somewhat of an accident. After Al finished his graduate studies, he had some time on his hands (you'd think a full-time job and a houseful of children would be enough!) and started writing a college textbook. While he was working on that, he happened to mention to a book salesman who had just become a literary agent that we had some ideas for children's books. The agent was encouraging, and we wrote *Life in the Universe*. That book was quickly signed up, and we plunged happily into children's science writing. Then followed twenty-three straight rejections. We would probably have given up if we hadn't already had a manuscript accepted. We kept on writing and submitting books, and by the time *Life in the Universe* was actually published (in 1967), we had four more contracts.

So far, we've written more than sixty published children's science books, as well as two college texts, a nonfiction book for adults, and a novel (actually, a series of three novels: a "family saga trilogy") that is out looking for a publisher now. The adult book, *Conquest of Death*, and the novels are based on an idea that has been an important part of our lives for many years: that scientists are making exciting discoveries that will some day make it possible to cure all diseases, turn back the clock of aging, and perhaps even conquer death. Then we would have what we've named *emortality*, a condition in which there is no more natural death, and people can stay young and healthy indefinitely.

Our children's books fall into several main groups: the *Systems of the Body* series and *Story of Your . . .* series. (We're now working on *Hand*.) Much of the material for these books was taken from Al's biology lectures, which he has always tried to make as lively and interesting as possible.

Our books on pet animals are the ones we most enjoy writing. We have raised mice, hamsters, gerbils, rabbits, guinea pigs, cats, and dogs, and we draw heavily on our own experiences in writing about them. So these books are more "personal" than some in which we act only as science reporters. We currently have five cats, a puppy, and two rabbits in residence. Our children contribute their experiences, too, and now our son Bob is taking photographs for us.

Our books on diseases have been very popular. Obviously they're not as much fun to write as books about animals or nature, but we think they can be helpful to many people. When we focus on a disease like cancer or diabetes, we try to explain as clearly and simply as possible what it is, what science and medicine are doing about it, and prospects for the future.

With our hobby of science watching, we keep up on what's happening at many frontiers of science. We've enjoyed surveying some of these fields in books like *Germfree Life, World of Bionics, The Genetics Explosion, Future Life: The Biotechnology Revolution*, and our newest book, *The Robots Are Here*.

Our nature books have also been fun to write. Our favorite is *Nature's Champions*, which tells about the "biggest," the "fastest," and so forth. In addition to the straight fact books, we've written two "life cycle stories." In one of them, *The Long Voyage*, we invented a radio tracking device to follow the migrations of the green turtle. The artist asked us for a reference he could use in drawing the device, and we told him there wasn't any—we had made it up. Then the next year we read an article about real-life biologists using just the kind of tracking device we had imagined.

One last footnote about our writing activities: For a couple of years in the early 1970s we were writing a column of children's stories called "Tales from Dr. A." It was syndicated by the Chicago Tribune-New York News Syndicate and at one time it appeared in more than two hundred newspapers. We loved writing the stories, and the syndication experience was fascinating. Alas, the column was slain by the paper shortage. We miss it.

In case you're wondering how to pronounce our name: In Brooklyn, where Al was raised, it's "Silver-*steen.*" In Philadelphia, where I come from, people say "Silver-*stine.*" We spent the first dozen years of our marriage in New York as the Silver-*steens.* When we moved to neutral territory, in New Jersey, we thought of changing over but found we were too used to it. So pronounce it whichever way you like—we'll answer to either.

————

Many of the Silversteins's books have appeared on lists of recommended science books for children. In one year, six of their books appeared on the annual American Association for the Advancement of Science's "101 Best Science Books" list. Three of their books were named Outstanding Science Trade Books for Children by the National Science Teachers Association: *Animal Invaders* in 1974, *Itch, Sniffle and Sneeze* in 1978, and *Nature's Champions* in 1980.

Potatoes received honorable mention in 1976 for the New York Academy of Science Children's Science Book Awards. In the same "All About Them" series, *Rabbits* was named a Notable Children's Trade Book in the Field of Social Studies by the joint committee of the National Council for the Social Studies and the Children's Book Council. *The Left-Hander's World* was a Junior Literary Guild selection.

Virginia B. Silverstein is a member of the Authors Guild and the American Translators Association. Alvin Silverstein belongs to the Authors Guild, the American Chemical Society, the American Association for the Advancement of Science, and the American Institute of Biological Sciences. He was national chairman of the National Collegiate Association for the Conquest of Cancer from 1968 to 1970, and chairman of the Foundation for Research Against Disease and Death from 1979 to 1982.

SELECTED WORKS: Life in the Universe, 1967; Germfree Life: A New Field in Biological Research, 1970; The Long Voyage, 1972; Rabbits: All About Them, 1973; Animal Invaders, 1974; Hamsters: All About Them, 1974; Gerbils: All About Them, 1976; Potatoes: All About Them, 1976; The Left-Hander's World, 1977; Cats: All About Them, 1978; Itch, Sniffle, and Sneeze, 1978; World of Bionics, 1979; The Genetics Explosion, 1980; Nature's Champions: The Biggest, the Fastest, the Best, 1980; Futurelife: The Biotechnology Revolution, 1982; The Robots Are Here, 1983.

ABOUT: Contemporary Authors, Vol. 49–52; (New Revision Series), Vol. 2; The International Authors and Writers Who's Who, 1982; Something About the Author, Vol. 8; Ward, Martha E. and Dorothy A. Marquardt. Authors of Books for Young People, 2nd edition (Supplement).

SEYMOUR SIMON

August 9, 1931–

AUTHOR OF *The Paper Airplane Book,* etc.

Autobiographical sketch of Seymour Simon:

TEACHING has been such a maligned activity that it is almost embarrassing to admit that I've been doing it almost all my life both in and out of classrooms. For over twenty years I taught children in intermediate and junior high school. The subjects ranged over almost every field of science and also included philosophy, poetry, history, and a great deal more. I taught science as a method of finding out about the world.

Many of the books I write are just extensions of my talking with the children in my classes. I try to write the way I talk. I'm always thinking about the effect of my sentences on kids if they were read aloud. I

have a simple (Simon) mind. If my writing isn't crystal clear to me, I'll keep rewriting until *I* understand what I'm trying to say.

My interest in science began when I was very young. I loved reading science fiction magazines. This inevitably led to an interest in astronomy and technology. I attended the Bronx High School of Science, a specialized secondary school in New York City for scientifically-minded youngsters. I also became a member and later president of the American Museum of Natural History's Junior Astronomy Club.

At C.C.N.Y. I pursued another interest of mine, animals and animal behavior. In graduate school (after the army), I took courses in all kinds of things ranging from science to psychology, literature, history, and philosophy. To this day, my reading and interests remain very eclectic.

To many adults, science is almost a dirty word. It brings back memories of dreary courses that were endured only because they were required. But for children, science is different. They don't know that they are supposed to be bored by spaceships and stars, by poisonous snakes and killer whales, by paper airplanes and mirrors, by earthquakes and optical illusions. Those are some of the topics that I've written about that are lumped together and casually dismissed with the term, "science books."

The books that I am now writing try to combine science with something kids will enjoy. For example, I am writing a series of books of fiction, *Einstein Anderson, Science Sleuth.* These feature the exploits of a young science genius and lover of bad puns who solves mysteries in ten episodes in each book. The reader gets a chance to solve the puzzle, and, I hope, gets a chance to learn something about science as well.

Other books such as *The Long View into Space, Strange Mysteries from Around the World, Body Sense, Body Nonsense,* and *Mirror Magic* all try to make science enjoyable and interesting. Even though I am no longer formally teaching in front of a class, I haven't really given up teaching, and I suppose that I never will, not for as long as I keep writing.

———

Seymour Simon was born and grew up in New York City. He attended both undergraduate and graduate schools at City College of the City University of New York and taught science and creative writing in the New York City system. He is now writing and editing full-time. He has written dozens of magazine articles and more than seventy-five books for children. More than thirty of them have been named Outstanding Science Trade Books for Children by the National Science Teachers Association. *The Paper Airplane Book* was included in the 1972 Children's Book Showcase of the Children's Book Council. *The Long View into Space* was included in the 1980 American Institute of Graphic Arts Book Show; *Mirror Magic* appeared in the 1981 Show, and *Strange Creatures* in the 1981 Show.

Simon and his wife, Joyce, a travel agent, have two sons, Robert Paul and Michael Alan. When he is not writing or talking to children Simon travels all over the world or enjoys his principal hobbies: tennis, reading, music, and dress.

SELECTED WORKS: Discovering What Earthworms Do, 1969; The Paper Airplane Book, 1971; The Rock-Hounds' Book, 1973; Pets in a Jar, 1975; The Optical Illusion Book, 1976; Look to the Night Sky: An Introduction to Star Watching, 1977; Killer Whales, 1978; Animal Fact/Animal Fable, 1979; Danger from Below: Earthquakes: Past, Present, and Future, 1979; The Long View into Space, 1979; The Secret Clocks: Time Senses of Living Things, 1979; Einstein Anderson, Science Sleuth, 1980; Mirror Magic, 1980; Strange Mysteries from Around the World, 1980; Body Sense, Body Nonsense, 1981; Poisonous Snakes, 1981; Einstein Anderson Goes to Bat, 1982; The Long Journey from Space, 1982.

ABOUT: Contemporary Authors (First Revision), Vol. 25–28; Something about the Author, Vol. 4; Ward, Martha E. and Dorothy A. Marquardt. Authors of Books for Young People, 2nd edition (Supplement); The Writers Directory 1982–84.

GLORIA SKURZYNSKI

GLORIA SKURZYNSKI

July 6, 1930–

AUTHOR OF *What Happened in Hamelin,* etc.

Autobiographical sketch of Gloria Joan Fl ister Skurzynski:

I DIDN'T BEGIN to write until the youngest of my five daughters started school. It simply had never occurred to me, before my thirty-sixth year, that I had any desire to be a writer. Since I'd had no training, and didn't know how to go about getting any, I went to the library and looked up "Writing" in the *Readers' Guide to Periodical Literature.* Perhaps if I'd known how long it would take me to acquire satisfactory writing skills, I would have been too intimidated to try. But with the innocence of ignorance, I began putting words on paper.

Of course, I'd been a devoted reader from the time I received my first library card, at the age of seven. That was in the small steelmaking town of Duquesne, Pennsylvania, inside a castle-like library building donated to the town by Andrew Carnegie. The building was torn down several years ago—even though by that time I was living in Utah, I mourned.

My first novel was composed on a typewriter, at the rate of ten to twelve pages a day. Now I write with a pen in a notebook, at a rate that translates to four or five typed pages daily, and these pages are revised over and over. This shows, I think, that a beginning author's confidence erodes as she learns what practiced authors know: worthwhile writing requires a great deal of time, a great deal of labor.

I have friends who remain normal people when they're working on a book, and I envy them because I do not. While I write a novel, I'm only half aware of what's happening in my family, my house, and the world. The rest of me is so involved with the lives of my characters that it requires conscious effort for me to return to reality.

As soon as the first draft of the novel is completed, I emerge from my basement garret, surprised and grateful that my friends are still friends after I've neglected them for half a year. Because the housework has been neglected, too, I busy myself washing windows and cleaning closets, but the book still tugs at me, like a toddler who won't put up with being ignored. When the book's demand for attention becomes too insistent, I dash back to my desk to rewrite a line, or a page.

Skurzynski: *skur ZIN ski*

It may sound as though I write only novels. That isn't so. In the ten years between the publication of my first book and the setting down of these words, I've written picture books, folk tales, middle-grade adventure stories, and young-adult nonfiction books. It was necessary for me to sample all kinds of writing to decide which I liked to do best, and that turned out to be novels, young-adult and middle-grade. This doesn't mean I won't write any of the other kinds of books if I get a good idea for one, but novels are my favorite reading and my favorite writing.

My daughters are grown women now. Serena is a doctor, Jan an electrical engineer, Joan a legal secretary, Alane a housewife and mother, Lauren a computer scientist. My husband Ed is an aerospace engineer, so we have a variety of professions in the family.

The greatest fringe benefit of my profession is the opportunity to meet other children's book authors at conferences. They're a warm and wonderful breed, because in order to write for children, an author must keep a childlike sense of wonder about the world and its people.

———

What Happened in Hamelin was a 1979 Christopher Award winner. *Manwolf* was named a 1981 Best Book for Young Adults by the American Library Association and a 1981 Notable Children's Trade Book in the Field of Social Studies by a joint committee of the National Council on the Social Studies and the Children's Book Council.

SELECTED WORKS: The Magic Pumpkin, 1971; The Poltergeist of Jason Morey, 1975; In a Bottle with a Cork on Top, 1976; Two Fools and a Faker, 1977; Martin by Himself, 1979; What Happened in Hamelin, 1979; Honest Andrew, 1980; Manwolf, 1981; Lost in the Devil's Desert, 1982; The Tempering, 1983.

ABOUT: Contemporary Authors (First Revision), Vol. 33–36; Something About the Author, Vol. 8.

WILLIAM SLEATOR

February 13, 1945–

AUTHOR OF *House of Stairs,* etc.

Autobiographical sketch of William (Warner) Sleator:

I GREW UP in a suburb of St. Louis, Missouri. My parents' house was full of books and music, so it was natural that I began writing and playing the piano when I was very young. I wrote my first story when I was about six. I typed it, which is true to form, since I can only think in front of the typewriter. Here's the story:

The Fat Cat

Once there was a fat cat. Boy, was she fat! Well, not *that* fat. But pretty fat.

I always wanted to be a writer and a musician. It still amazes me that it has actually come true.

I went to college at Harvard, where I was miserable. The attitude there was elitist-academic, rather than practical. I was forced to analyze and interpret works of art, and not allowed to learn how to create them myself, and I found it terribly frustrating. So I didn't study much and instead wrote music for student films and plays, and kept a voluminous journal, over a thousand typed pages long. Most of it is drivel, but it did help get me through those four years.

After college I spent a year in England, where I studied musical composition and played the piano for the Royal Ballet School. It was there that I had the experiences that led to my first novel, *Blackbriar.* The book is about an old and secluded stone cottage that was once a pesthouse, where people with contagious diseases were isolated. And, in fact, I spent a lot of time in a cottage exactly like the one in the book. It was in the middle of the woods, with only a dirt track leading to it, there was no electricity or indoor plumbing, and it really had been a pesthouse, for people with smallpox, who carved their names on the cellar door.

Sleator: *SLA ter*

William Sleator

I think it was the fact that I was describing real experiences that made my first stumbling effort as successful as it was. That, plus the tremendous amount of help I received from my editor, Ann Durell.

With each book I've written, my dependence upon reality has gradually diminished. As I have, ever so slowly, become more skilled at writing, I have been able to let my imagination go wilder, and get more of that down on paper. *The Green Futures of Tycho,* for example, does bear a slight tangential relationship to my own upbringing. But the real meat of the book—time travel and an attempted alien takeover of the earth—did not really happen to me.

One of the most difficult aspects of writing, for me, is the isolation. There is no way to do it without spending most of your time hard at work alone. And so I am very fortunate that I also work as rehearsal pianist for the Boston Ballet Company. This job gets me out into the world, working with other people, while still leaving me time to write. And I find the backstage, blood-sweat-and-tears aspects of ballet very exciting—a refreshing relief from the quiet, contemplative job of writing. But strangely enough, I can't write about ballet. I have hundreds of pages of fascinating material, but have been unable so far to shape it into a book.

Recently a friend and I bought a Victorian row house in an old section of Boston. I have a tiny little study, too small to contain many distractions, and that helps me to concentrate. I am working on several books, and keep trying to make my writing better—a never-ending struggle. I still consider myself one of the luckiest people in the world to be able to write for young people.

William Sleator has also written the musical score for an animated film, "Why the Sun and Moon Live in the Sky," in collaboration with Blair Lent, the artist who illustrated Elphinstone Dayrell's book of the same name.

In addition to receiving a Fellowhip at the Bread Loaf Writers' Conference in 1969, Sleator has won several awards for his books. *The Angry Moon,* which Blair Lent illustrated, was a 1971 Caldecott Honor Book. It was also an American Library Association Notable Book for the years 1940–1970, and was nominated for an American Book Award for best paperback picture book of 1981.

Of *The Green Futures of Tycho,* Pamela D. Pollack wrote in *School Library Journal,* "Sleator's expert blend of future and horror fiction is unusually stark, dark and intriguing; and the breakneck pace he sets never falters."

SELECTED WORKS: The Angry Moon, 1970; Blackbriar, 1972; Run, 1973; House of Stairs, 1974; Among the Dolls, 1975; Into the Dream, 1978; The Green Futures of Tycho, 1981; Fingers, 1983.

ABOUT: Contemporary Authors (First Revision), Vol. 29–32; Something About the Author, Vol. 3.

JAN SLEPIAN

January 2, 1921–

AUTHOR OF *The Alfred Summer,* etc.

Slepian: *SLEP ee an*

Autobiographical sketch of Janice B. Slepian:

IT SEEMS to me that what has shaped my life is largely chance, happenstance, sheer accident all the way—and I've been lucky all my life. For example, I'm a writer by chance. I didn't have my mind set on being one, nor did I write poems and stories as a schoolgirl. I thought I was going to be a clinical psychologist.

I'm a New Yorker, born in Manhattan in 1921 when the going was good, who moved to Brooklyn when my engineer father lost his money in the stock market crash. Five of us shared a tiny bedroom in a tenement near the beach at Brighton. When I left graduate school at the University of Washington in Seattle, I couldn't get a job as a psychologist, so when I was offered one as language therapist in Boston I grabbed it. That's maybe the luckiest thing that ever happened to me because it was there that I met my husband David when he crawled through my bedroom window by accident. We were married in Paris, and after a six-month stay we returned to New Jersey, where David worked as a mathematician and I as mother of three children full-time and speech therapist part-time.

The writer part happened when a colleague of mine suggested we collaborate on writing a series of newspaper articles about everyday speech problems for worried parents. To our surprise this worked out well, and so we became braver and wrote a series of picture books called the Listen-Hear series, still out there going strong. Perhaps I would still be writing books for young children with my partner Dr. Ann Seidler if I hadn't happened to take a class in children's literature at Berkeley a few years ago.

We, my family, have the great good fortune to live alternately in Hawaii and New Jersey. We were on our way to the Islands when we stopped for a semester at that campus in California where my husband was a guest lecturer. I thought the course was about picture books, but instead I was introduced to a marvelous new (to me) genre that just didn't exist when I was growing up and reading everything in sight: books for older readers, teenage novels, books published as children's books for pragmatic reasons, but which are really for readers between puberty and senescence. Well, by chance I was at loose ends professionally, emptied of ideas for more picture books and all fired up by the reading I had been doing for the course. I was ready to tackle a subject that had been in the back of my mind for ages but had never really had the nerve to write about. And now, because of the course, I knew the form. I had no intention in the world to write about handicaps, or what it was like to grow up with a handicapped person, or anything as high-minded as that. I just wanted to write as true a made-up story as I could about my brother Alfred, what he was like in his heyday when he was young.

To do this I had to go back in time, back to my childhood in Brooklyn when my passions were handball and books, and my hates were Brooklyn and my brother Alfred. I didn't know that those two parts of my early life that I wanted so earnestly to shake at one time, were so tenaciously lodged within me, waiting to get their side said.

The Alfred Summer was written as if dictated, so ready was it to be heard. That's a spooky and I think rare experience for a writer and I don't expect to have it again. *Lester's Turn* was needed because I wanted to find out more about some characters I had met in the first novel.

Now that both have been written, and I am ready to leave them behind, I marvel at the mystery and the irony of their existence. The books were grounded in an old family sorrow, and now all that has been turned around and is instead the source of a great satisfaction. My brother Alfred's blasted life may touch more people than my own because of the books. I shake my head and echo Alfie's friend Lester: "Sometimes life just knocks me out!"

Jan Slepian's first novel, *The Alfred Summer,* won high praise from critics. It is the story of a fourteen-year-old boy with cerebral palsy who befriends Alfred, a mentally retarded boy, and with two other children they attempt to build and launch a boat. *Lester's Turn* is a sequel to the novel.

The Alfred Summer was a Boston Globe-Horn Book Award Honor Book in 1981 and a finalist in the hardcover fiction category of the American Book Awards in 1981.

SELECTED WORKS: The Alfred Summer, 1980; Lester's Turn, 1981.

SELECTED WORKS WITH ANN SEIDLER: Alfie and the Dream Machine, 1964; The Best Invention of All, 1967; Bendemolena (retitled The Cat Who Wore a Pot on Her Head, 1981), 1967; The Hungry Thing, 1972.

ALFRED SLOTE

September 11, 1926–

AUTHOR OF *Hang Tough, Paul Mather,* etc.

Biographical sketch of Alfred Slote:

ALFRED SLOTE was born in Brooklyn, New York. While he was growing up, he loved to play sports, especially baseball. After serving in the U.S. Navy from 1944 to 1946, he returned to complete his B.A. at the University of Michigan in 1949. He won the Avery and Jules Hopwood Award in creative writing at the University of Michigan and was elected to Phi Beta Kappa. He received his M.A. there in 1950. In the same year, he studied at the University of Grenoble in Switzerland as a Fulbright Scholar in Comparative Literature. In 1951, he married Henrietta Howell (Hetsy), who was an editor and writer and is now Assistant to the Dean of the University of Michigan Law School. The Slotes have three children; John, a free-lance writer; Elizabeth, a sculptor and illustrator (she illustrated Slote's *Clone Catcher*); and Ben, a teacher, coach, and writer.

Slote began his career as an English instructor at Williams College in Williamstown, Massachusetts from 1953 to 1956. In 1956, he returned to live in Ann Arbor and work as a producer-writer and associate director at the University of Michigan Television Center, where in 1973, he was promoted to Executive Director. He wrote and produced a prize-winning series of children's television programs, "The Art of Storytelling," and other programs including "Science: Quest and Conquest," and "The Progress of Man."

He has been writing since college, though his first novel was not written until he went to Grenoble. He wrote three adult novels, two adult mysteries, and one book of non-fiction in addition to his many children's books. It took the encouragement of his older son and a children's librarian to convince him to write for children. His first books for children were a modern folktale and two collections, *The Moon in Fact and Fancy* and *Air in Fact and Fancy*.

He feels that his experience as a baseball player and coach enabled him to write his first sports titles, including *Hang Tough, Paul Mather* and *Jake. Hang Tough . . .* was translated into Spanish as *¡Coraje, Campeon! Jake* won the Friends of American Writers Award in 1971, and was later made into an ABC After School Special, "The Rag Tag Champs." Slote researched *The Hotshot*, a controlled-vocabulary hockey story, while accompanying his sons on high school hockey trips. *Love and Tennis* is another departure from baseball, his favorite subject.

More recently, Slote has turned to science fiction with *My Trip to Alpha I, C.O.L.A.R., My Robot Buddy, Omega Station*, and *Clone Catcher. My Robot Buddy, C.O.L.A.R.,* and *Omega Station* are all about the same character.

Slote writes every day, commenting that morning is his best time, though he knows that for others, "morning time" may be late at night. He gets his best ideas in hot showers, and says that he wishes he could move his Royal Standard typewriter into the shower. He also admits that he writes everything three times; the first time is just to find out what he's writing about. "I'm not a writer, but a rewriter." He tells kids that all writers started as readers, though not all readers will be writers. "Books help you see life from other points of view . . . [they]

extend humanness." In 1983, he commented "I'm a fifty-six-year-old writer with an eleven-year-old voice."

SELECTED WORKS: The Moon in Fact and Fancy, revised edition, 1967; Air in Fact and Fancy, 1968; Jake, 1971; Hang Tough, Paul Mather, 1973; My Robot Buddy, 1975; The Hotshot, 1977; My Trip to Alpha I, 1978; Love and Tennis, 1979; C.O.L.A.R., 1981; Clone Catcher, 1982; Omega Station, 1983.

ABOUT: Something About the Author, Vol. 8; Ward, Martha E. and Dorothy A. Marquardt. Authors of Books for Young People, 2nd edition (Supplement).

DORIS BUCHANAN SMITH

June 1, 1934–

AUTHOR OF *A Taste of Blackberries*, etc.

Autobiographical sketch of Doris Buchanan Smith:

FROM THE TIME I first learned to read and write, I loved to do both. Whenever a teacher asked us to write a story, many of my fellow students groaned. I, however, welcomed such assignments.

In sixth grade my teacher asked me if I'd thought about being a writer when I grew up. I was awe-struck. A writer? I didn't even know that was something you could be. I read constantly but had never thought about where books come from, that they are written by real, live human beings. The idea settled on me like an extra skin, an epi-epidermis, and fit exactly right.

From there to becoming a writer was a long journey. For many years I was afflicted with the idea that a writer wrote when the inspiration struck, when one of the Muses landed on the shoulder. During my school years I wrote occasionally, sometimes completing stories but often writing only fragments. Later I set about learning how one goes about being published. Still, I wrote only when the idea, the mood, and the time came together all at once.

Whenever I heard or read what "real" writers said about writing, I heard or saw

the words "discipline" and "work." Though I wanted to be an artist-of-words, I was very slow to realize that with every art there is a craft. In fact, the art cannot live without the craft. In writing, this means much more than grammar, spelling, and sentence structure. It means descriptions, dialogue, drama, and it means finding the exact right words to say these things, in new, fresh ways. Some ideas drift down, as from the air, but most float up from the midst of the work.

Finally, finally, I took on writing as my work, which meant regular chunks of time at the typewriter. Someone has called it, "The glue in the chair trick." Making myself learn to sit there was hard work. Making myself learn how to think things through to completion was hard work. As Snoopy, who writes from atop his doghouse, once said, "Good writing is hard work."

Finally, finally, a publisher was interested in my work. What's more, I was paid for it. What a heady feeling, to do what you love to do and earn your living at it! Life became magical. And I see that same magic in everyone who sees a vision and a direction and follows it. If you are a young person reading this, the best wish I can give

you is that you will search out and really work at developing your own interests and talents. You can be the person you dream of being. You can have a magical life. All it takes is vision, direction—and work. I'm fond of saying, "All it takes is work."

Though writing is fulfilling, I am filled with many other things, too. I had always wanted a large family and ended up with five children. For a seven-year period, we were a family for a number of other children, many of whom keep in touch. During those years I often had to struggle for the uninterrupted time to write. Now the children are grown and living on their own, and my time is my own. I do not get lonely. I am content indoors, working with clay or curled up with a book, or outdoors where I enjoy walking, bicycling, canoeing, stargazing, or just gazing. A certain amount of staring into space is important for a writer and, perhaps, for anyone. For part of the year I live on the coast of Georgia, where my children grew up, and in summer I live in a primitive cabin in the North Carolina mountains. I have good friends in both places and life is, indeed, magical.

————

Doris Buchanan Smith was born in Washington, D.C. She attended South Georgia College and was married in 1954; that marriage ended in divorce. In 1975 she had a fellowship at the Bread Loaf Writers' Conference. She is a member of the Audubon Society.

A Taste of Blackberries won several awards. In 1973 it won an award from the Child Study Children's Book Committee at Bank Street College. It was named a Notable Book of 1973 by the American Library Association and won a Kinderbook Award in Holland in 1977. *Kelly's Creek* was named a Notable Children's Trade Book in the Field of Social Studies in 1975 by the joint committee of the National Council for the Social Studies and the Children's Book Council.

SELECTED WORKS: A Taste of Blackberries, 1973; Kick a Stone Home, 1974; Tough Chauncey, 1974; Kelly's Creek, 1975; Up and Over, 1976; Dreams and Drummers, 1978; Salted Lemons, 1980; Last Was Lloyd, 1981; Moonshadow of Cherry Mountain, 1982; The First Hard Times, 1983.

ABOUT: Contemporary Authors, Vol. 69–72; Something About the Author, Vol. 28; Ward, Martha E. and Dorothy A. Marquardt. Authors of Books for Young People, 2nd edition (Supplement); The Writers Directory 1982–84.

WILLIAM JAY SMITH

April 22, 1918–

AUTHOR OF *Laughing Time, etc.*

Autobiographical sketch of William Jay Smith:

ANYONE who grows up in the professional Army is known as an "Army brat." The term was first used scornfully by the civilian population, which looked on the children of the military as rowdy and ill-mannered, but later it was adopted affectionately and proudly by Army officers and enlisted men and their families. I grew up as an Army brat, indelibly marked by my youthful associaton with my father's profession. As a corporal in the Sixth Infantry Band, my father was not transferred regularly from one post to another, and so, unlike many Army brats, I do not have a patchwork of memories of various posts scattered across the country and around the world, but a single vision of the twenty years spent in and around a particular one, Jefferson Barracks, just south of St. Louis, Missouri, then a post of major importance. I went there with my father, my mother, and my brother not long after World War I and left at the time of our entry into World War II. I have written in my book *Army Brat: A Memoir* about growing up in those years between the two wars—1921 to 1941.

Jefferson Barracks was the oldest permanent Army base west of the Mississippi. The woods of the reservation, situated on high bluffs above the river, were a child's paradise; we knew every inch of those acres, followed the fern-lined muddy streams to our swimming holes, fished for crawfish with strips of bacon fat, and on the banks built our tree houses and lean-tos of sassafras. We went to school in south St. Louis in World War I liberty trucks.

My father was a gambler and heavy drinker, and he supplemented his meager corporal's pay with bottlegging on the side. An elocution—or expression—teacher came to the post and enlisted me as one of her pupils. Through her I discovered poetry, which I loved at once. We never had many books in our house, but my parents, as Southerners, were great talkers and wonderful storytellers. I came to love the rhythm of their speech and tried to reproduce it when I began to write. I was encouraged in my writing by my teachers, and had a poem accepted by a national magazine when I was fourteen.

Jefferson Barracks had been founded as an outpost in the Indian Wars, and the discovery that I was part Indian myself (my mother claims descent from Moshulatubbee, Head of the Choctaw Nation) had a profound effect on my development. The knowledge that I had forebears on the outside of the garrison and in the enemy camp gave me strength to face the limiting aspects of military life. Except for a few brief trips to Louisiana and Arkansas to visit the families of my mother and father, the enclosed life of the Army garrison was all that I knew until I entered Washington University in St. Lewis on a scholarship in 1935. There I met a number of other beginning writers, among them the playwright Tennessee Williams (then Thomas Lanier Williams). We formed a little group and met regularly to discuss our work.

I majored in French at Washington University and with money saved from part-time jobs, went in the summer of 1938 to study in France. I joined the Navy during War II and served for two years as liaison officer on a French ship in the Atlantic and the Pacific. After the war I went to England as a Rhodes Scholar at Oxford, and later studied in Italy. I began to write poems for children when my elder son David was four years old and have continued since that time. Because I can remember well what my own boyhood was like, I have tried to capture that youthful spirit—both its joys and sorrows—in my poems.

Smith was born in Winnfield, Louisiana. He received his B.A. degree in 1939 and his M.A. in 1941. After the Second World War, he studied at Columbia University (1946 to 1947), Oxford (1947–1948), and the University of Florence (1948–1950).

His first marriage, from which he has two sons, ended in divorce. He later married again.

From 1962 to 1966 Smith reviewed poetry for *Harper's* magazine, and his critical essays were collected in *The Streaks of the Tulip* (1972). He translates poetry from the French, Italian, Spanish, Russian, Swedish, and Hungarian. From 1968 to 1970 he served as Consultant in Poetry to the Library of Congress and from 1970 to 1976 as

an Honorary Consultant in American Letters. At Columbia University, Smith was visiting professor of writing at the School of the Arts, Acting Chairman of its writing division from 1973 to 1975 and on the Executive board of the Translation Center there. He is also an editor of the journal *Translation* and Professor Emeritus of English from Hollins College where he was writer-in-residence in 1965 and 1966. He is a member of the Association of American Rhodes Scholars, the Authors Guild, and P.E.N. and has contributed poetry, reviews, and articles to *Harper's, Poetry, The Nation, The New Republic, The Horn Book Magazine, The Yale Review,* and *The New Yorker.* He is the author of seven volumes of poetry for adults, two of which were National Book Award finalists.

William Jay Smith's first book of children's poetry, *Laughing Times,* was published in 1955. His children's verse is often humorous and has been called "bright and strong" and "within the intellectual grasp of his readers" by Patrick Groff in *Twentieth-Century Children's Writers.* Smith wrote, in the *New York Times Book Review,* "Children's poems must not only have a lilt to them; they must be graphic. Children think in images, and their poet, to capture these images, must choose words that convey color and movement. Children's poems are never static but filled with action. Nouns and verbs predominate; adjectives are used sparingly. . . . Precision and concreteness are, of course, along with musicality, the chief demands on the children's poet."

SELECTED WORKS WRITTEN: Laughing Time, 1955; Boy Blue's Book of Beasts, 1957; Puptents and Pebbles: A Nonsense ABC, 1959; What Did I See?, 1962; My Little Book of Big and Little, 1963; Ho for a Hat!, 1964; If I Had A Boat, 1966; Mr. Smith and Other Nonsense, 1968; Around My Room and Other Poems, 1969; Grandmother Ostrich and Other Poems, 1969.

SELECTED WORKS TRANSLATED: Children of the Forest, by Elsa Beskow, 1970; The Pirate Book, by Lennart Hellsing, 1972; The Telephone, by Kornei Chukovsky, 1976.

JAMES STEVENSON

SELECTED WORKS EDITED: (with Louise Bogan) The Golden Journey: Poems for Young People, 1967; Poems from France, 1967; Poems from Italy, 1972; A Green Place: Modern Poems, 1982.

ABOUT: Contemporary Authors (First Revision), Vol. 5–8; Current Biography Yearbook, 1974; Directory of American Scholars, 7th edition; The International Authors and Writers Who's Who, 1977; Kirkpatrick, D. L. Twentieth-Century Children's Writers; Nemerov, Howard, ed. Poets on Poetry; The Penguin Companion to American Literature; Something About the Author, Vol. 2; Vinson, James, ed. Contemporary Poets, 2nd edition; Ward, Martha E. and Dorothy A. Marquardt. Authors of Books for Young People, 2nd edition (Supplement); Who's Who in America, 1982–83; World Authors 1950–1970; The Writers Directory 1982–84; Harper's January 1964; New York Times Book Review May 2, 1976; Partisan Review Winter 1967.

JAMES STEVENSON

1929–

AUTHOR AND ILLUSTRATOR OF *Could Be Worse!*, etc.

Biographical sketch of James Stevenson:

BORN IN NEW YORK CITY and raised in a number of small towns in New York, James Stevenson entered Yale in 1947 to earn a B.A. in English, intending to become a writer. However, his first success was not in writing but in illustration, as he began selling cartoon ideas to *The New Yorker* while still a student.

After graduation from Yale in 1951, a two-year stint in the U.S. Marines, and a two-year reporting job for *Life*, Stevenson returned to *The New Yorker*, taking a job in the art department and continuing to conceive cartoon ideas for other artists. He began drawing his own cartoons as well, and in 1963 a collection of his *New Yorker* cartoons, titled *Sorry, Lady, This Beach Is Private!* was published.

Even in his early apprenticeship in the art department of *The New Yorker*, Stevenson continued to pursue his desire to become a writer, and in 1960, he began reporting for

that magazine as well. In his spare time he wrote adult fiction, and he had three adult novels published.

Deciding that he did not enjoy writing full-length adult fiction, he began to illustrate picture-book texts for other authors and to write and illustrate his own. His first picture book, *The Bear Who Had No Place to Go*, was published in 1972. The new field proved a satisfying one, since in picture books he "found a way to tell a story without doing it just in sentences."

Stevenson says that although he wrote and drew from a young age, his work is not greatly shaped by books he read as a child. "I think that my experience and creative mind have been formed much more by movies and comic books," he said. "I like the idea of a story board and I like the idea of a movie and all the different angles from which things can be viewed." In several of his picture books—like *Monty, The Sea View Hotel*, and *"Could Be Worse!"*—his use of frames in a comic-strip-like format provides a variety of perspectives and an energetic pace.

Many of Stevenson's stories explore the value of friendship, as in *Howard*, in which a duck who misses the annual migration south spends the winter in New York City. When the flock flies north in the spring, Howard must choose between joining them and staying with his new-found city friends.

The elderly, too, have a prominent place in Stevenson's work, perhaps most memorably in the Grandfather in *"Could Be Worse!,"* who startles and delights his two grandchildren with a whopping tale of midnight adventure that shows them he has more life and imagination than they might have assumed.

Whatever the medium—pencil, charcoal, watercolor—Stevenson depicts his appealingly scruffy characters with the humor and expressiveness that have won him many fans and much acclaim. *"Could Be Worse!"* was on the *School Library Journal* "Best of the Best" 1966–1978" list (December 1979) and was a *New York Times* Outstanding Book of the Year. The American Library Association has also recognized Stevenson's work, selecting as Notable Books *The Sea View Hotel* (1978), *Fast Friends* (1979), *Say It* (1980), and *That Terrible Halloween Night* (1980). In addition, *Howard* was chosen a *New York Times* Best Illustrated Book of the Year in 1980, and *We Can't Sleep* won a 1982 Christopher Award. Three of Stevenson's books have been named Children's Choices by a joint committee of the International Reading Association and the Children's Book Council: *The Worst Person in the World* (1978), *That Terrible Halloween Night* (1980), and *The Night After Christmas* (1982). *Cully Cully and the Bear* is a Book-of-the-Month Club selection, and *What's Under My Bed?* is a Junior Literary Guild selection.

James Stevenson is married and has nine children. He makes his home in Niantic, Connecticut.

SELECTED WORKS WRITTEN AND ILLUSTRATED: The Bear Who Had No Place to Go, 1972; Wilfred the Rat, 1977; "Could Be Worse!," 1977; The Sea View Hotel, 1978; The Worst Person in the World, 1978; Fast Friends, 1979; Monty, 1979; Clams Can't Sing, 1980; Howard, 1980; That Terrible Halloween Night, 1980;

The Night After Christmas, 1981; The Wish Card Ran Out!, 1981; We Can't Sleep, 1982; The Great Big Especially Beautiful Easter Egg, 1983; What's Under My Bed?, 1983.

SELECTED WORKS ILLUSTRATED: Tony's Hard Work Day, by Alan Arkin, 1972; Good Old James, by John Donovan, 1975; Jack the Bum and Haunted House, by Janet Schulman, 1977; Jack the Bum and the UFO, by Janet Schulman, 1978; Say It!, by Charlotte Zolotow, 1980; Cully Cully and The Bear, by Wilson Gage, 1983.

ABOUT: Bader, Barbara. American Picturebooks from Noah's Ark to the Beast Within; Kingman, Lee and others, comps. Illustrators of Children's Books: 1967–1976; Ward, Martha E. and Dorothy A. Marquardt. Authors of Books for Young People, 2nd edition (Supplement).

ALFRED H. TAMARIN

May 31, 1913–August 19, 1980

CO-AUTHOR OF *Voyaging to Cathay: America in the China Trade,* etc.

Autobiographical sketch of Alfred H. Tamarin composed by Shirley Glubok from material Tamarin wrote shortly before his death:

MY INTEREST in history began in my school days in Hudson, New York. Even after I moved to New York City, to go to New York University and then into the motion picture business, I spent my spare time reading history books. And when my travels took me to remote corners of the globe I always had my cameras with me. I married Shirley Glubok, author of the well-known series of art books for children, in 1968, and began to photograph works of art for her books. We have written four books together. Our latest, *Olympic Games in Ancient Greece* and *The Mummy of Ramose: The Life and Death of an Ancient Egyptian Nobleman,* took us to Greece and to Egypt for our research.

Our work on *Ancient Indians of the Southwest* took us to Santa Fe, New Mexico, where Navajo and Pueblo Indians can be

seen walking about town and sitting with their art objects in front of the Governor's Palace. This led me to wonder about the Indians of the Eastern seaboard, and I visited all of the existing tribes on the Eastern seaboard for *We Have Not Vanished.*

It has always been one of those tantalizing mysteries . . . how things can happen in one place and how other people far away learn about them. A drum beats in distant forests; a lone runner moves silently through the shadows in the woods. Signals pass from one tribesman to another, or perhaps to the stranger in the land across the river or even farther off, on the other side of the mountain. So it has been, even now when news can fly to the moon and beyond with incredible speed. And so it was many years ago with the native Americans who morning after morning turned their eyes to the rising sun as it burned away the morning fog, clinging to the heavy waters of the sea.

What did those native Americans think of the Europeans when the curtains of mist drew apart to reveal the forlorn masts of sailing ships? What about the first contacts of the Indians with European settlers? I have spent the past four years in the library researching this theme, which is all important in our study of American history.

———

Alfred Tamarin was born in Hudson, New York. He received his B.A. degree from New York University in 1934 and did graduate work at Hunter College, at Columbia University, and at New York University. He had one grown daughter from a previous marriage.

Tamarin was Director of Advertising and Public Relations for the Theatre Guild in New York City from 1942 to 1945. He was also Vice President for Music and Recording at United Artists and Vice President of Inflight Motion Pictures. He lectured at the Metropolitan Museum of Art and at the Universities of Arizona and Kansas.

Tamarin was a member of the Authors League, the Archaeological Institute of America, and Phi Beta Kappa.

Voyaging to Cathay won the Boston Globe-Horn Book Award for best nonfiction book in 1976, was named an American Library Association Notable Book, and was also included in the American Institute of Graphic Arts Book Show.

SELECTED WORKS: Japan and the U.S.: The Early Encounters, 1791–1860, 1970; Fire Fighting in America, 1971, We Have Not Vanished: Eastern Indians of the U.S., 1974.

SELECTED WORKS EDITED: Benjamin Franklin: An Autobiographical Portrait, 1969.

SELECTED WORKS WRITTEN WITH SHIRLEY GLUBOK: Ancient Indians of the Southwest, 1975; Olympic Games in Ancient Greece, 1976; Voyaging to Cathay: Americans in the China Trade, 1976; The Mummy of Ramose: Life and Death of an Ancient Egyptian Nobleman, 1978.

ABOUT: Contemporary Authors (First Revision), Vol. 29–32; (New Revision Series), Vol. 4; Vol. 102; Hopkins, Lee Bennett. More Books by More People: Interviews with Sixty-Five Authors of Books for Children; Something About the Author, Vol. 13; The Writers Directory 1982–84; New York Times August 20, 1980.

VIRGINIA A. TASHJIAN

September 20, 1921–

AUTHOR OF *Once There Was and Was Not: Armenian Tales Retold,* etc.

Autobiographical sketch of Virginia A. Tashjian:

I BECAME a librarian because, as a child, I used to bite my nails! My greatest solace when I was growing up and hating the sight of my broken, ragged nails was to scurry to the Brockton Public Library every day after school and watch my favorite librarian's beautifully manicured fingers stamp, check, and gently handle my books over the desk. Somehow or other I came to believe that all librarians must be possessed of lovely nails; thus, I too, had to become a librarian in order to improve my own unsightly ones! The fact that I loved to read and read omnivorously, in fact, only made my goal an easier one to achieve.

And so, after graduating from Girls' Latin School of Boston, I became a librarian, majoring in children's work at Simmons College because children's books seemed so much more exciting and because I wanted to share with other children the joy and warm comfort I had enjoyed in children's libraries myself.

Storytelling is part and parcel of a children's librarian's training—or should be. But to tell the truth, I had been a story teller long before college days. As the oldest of a swarm of Armenian cousins who congregated frequently on Sundays at the homes of relatives, I was used to telling stories to the younger ones who dared not move from the storytelling circle under my eagle eye. I retold the Armenian folktales my mother used to tell to me and to my sister. I repeated the tales from ancient Armenia that my great-uncle told to us as we sat spellbound at his feet when he came to visit.

Later, when I became a children's librarian in Newton, Massachusetts, I often told those same stories again and again to the children who came to the library and who, now in turn, sat spellbound before me.

Virginia A. Tashjian

So it was that I decided to write down those stories for all children—and as a memorial to my sister who had enjoyed them with me and was gone now. I hoped that my son and my two nephews would love them, too, and would someday repeat them to their own children.

Storytelling, both oral and via my books, has brought me great joy, as has my teaching of children's literature in various Greater Boston colleges. To share the literature for children with prospective teachers and librarians who will, in turn, be in a position to inspire other children seems very worthwhile to me.

My major work for many years has been as Library Director of the Newton Free Library. But this has simply extended the audience for storytelling, book reviewing, and "literature-sharing" to include adults as well as children—and it has been so worthwhile! I don't bite my nails anymore, either! In fact, my nails today are long and manicured and really quite presentable.

————

Virginia A. Tashjian was born in Brockton, Massachusetts. After finishing junior high school there, she moved with her family to Boston and then later to Cambridge. She was graduated from the Girls' Latin School of Boston and then attended Simmons College, earning both a B.S. and, subsequently, an M.L.S. from that institution.

Before Tashjian was Newton Free Library's Director, she was a children's librarian there. In addition to the activities she mentions, she reviews books, gives lectures, and has a daily radio show on station WNTN of adult book reviews and library information. She also enjoys music, travel, and gardening.

Tashjian is also active in professional circles and, among other offices, has served as president of the Massachusetts Library Association and president of the New England Library Association. She is married to journalist James H. Tashjian; together they participate in the Armenian community in Watertown, Massachusetts, where they reside. They have one son.

SELECTED WORKS: Once There Was and Was Not: Armenian Tales Retold, 1966; Juba This and Juba That, 1969; The Miller King, 1971; Three Apples Fell from Heaven: Armenian Folktales Retold, 1971; With a Deep Sea Smile, 1974.

ABOUT: Contemporary Authors (First Revision), Vol. 29–32; Foremost Women in Communications, 1970; Something About the Author, Vol. 3; Ward, Martha E. and Dorothy A. Marquardt. Authors of Books for Young People, 2nd edition (Supplement); Who's Who of American Women, 1975–1976.

MILDRED D. TAYLOR

AUTHOR OF *Roll of Thunder, Hear My Cry,* etc.

Biographical sketch of Mildred Delois Taylor:

MILDRED D. TAYLOR was born in Jackson, Mississippi, but grew up in Toledo, Ohio. Though the high schools in Toledo were integrated, a system of grouping students by ability levels worked against black

MILDRED D. TAYLOR

children who had attended inferior neighborhood schools, and in many of her college preparatory classes, Mildred Taylor was the only black student. Taylor was a class officer, a member of the honor society, and an editor of the school newspaper—but she often found herself painfully embarrassed by the lackluster portrait of black people as presented in history class.

That history was not at all like the oral history she heard at home and during annual family trips to Mississippi, where, she said in her Newbery acceptance speech, "when we children had finished all the games we could think to play, we would join the adults, soon becoming enraptured by their talk, for it would often turn to . . . a history of black people told through stories."

"Those stories about the small and often dangerous triumphs of black people . . . about human pride and survival in a cruelly racist society were like nothing I read in the history books. . . . There were no black heroes or heroines in those books; no beautiful black ladies, no handsome black men; no people filled with pride, strength, or endurance. . . . [The books told] a history of a docile, subservient people happy with their fate who did little or nothing to shatter the chains that bound them, both before and after slavery. There was obviously a terrible contradiction between what the books said and what I had learned from my family."

After graduating from the University of Toledo, Taylor joined the Peace Corps and was sent to Ethiopia, where for two years she taught English and history.

On her return to the United States, Taylor recruited for the Peace Corps and taught in one of its training programs before enrolling in the University of Colorado's School of Journalism. After receiving her master's degree, she took a job as study skills coordinator in the Black Education Program she had helped to structure. She says, however, that during all the years she spent studying, traveling, and living in Africa and working with the black student movement, she found herself turning again and again to the stories she had heard in her childhood.

Taylor resigned her position and moved to Los Angeles, where she took a nondemanding eight-to-five job so she could devote her evenings to writing. Soon, however, she knew she "needed an outside social force, something in which I could also be creative but which would be people-oriented. . . . I decided to return to school to receive a degree in international training."

Before returning to the East coast for graduate study, "on a well-remembered day in late September a little girl named Cassie Logan suddenly appeared in my life. Cassie was a spunky eight-year-old, innocent, untouched by discrimination, full of pride, and greatly loved, and through her I discovered I now could tell one of the stories I had heard so often as a child. From that meeting came *Song of the Trees.*"

Taylor entered the story in the Council on Interracial Books for Children competition and won first prize in the African-American category. The winning manuscripts were sent to various publishers, several of which expressed interest in Mildred Taylor's story.

Song of the Trees was published, and was named a *New York Times* Outstanding Book of the Year 1975 and a 1976 Children's Book Showcase book. But Taylor could not give up Cassie and her three brothers. "Those four children make me laugh; they also make me cry, and I had to find a way of keeping them from fading into oblivion. In August, 1974, came the answer: I would write another book about the Logans, one in which I could detail the teachings of my own childhood as well as incorporate many of the stories I had heard about my family and others. . . . I would write *Roll of Thunder, Hear My Cry.*"

Taylor's efforts were rewarded: *Roll of Thunder, Hear My Cry* won the 1977 Newbery Medal and was a nominee for the 1977 National Book Award. It was a Boston Globe-Horn Book Award Honor Book in 1977 and was named a Notable Children's Trade Book in the Field of Social Studies by a joint committee of the National Council for the Social Studies and the Children's Book Council in 1976. In her acceptance speech, Taylor said, " . . . I will continue the Logans' story . . . for it is my hope that these four books, one of the first chronicles to mirror a black child's hopes and fears from childhood innocence to awareness to bitterness and disillusionment, will one day be instrumental in teaching children of all colors the tremendous influence that Cassie's generation—my father's generation— had in bringing about the great Civil Rights Movement of the fifties and sixties."

The third book about the Logans, *Let the Circle Be Unbroken,* was a 1981 American Library Association Best Book for Young Adults, a 1982 American Book Award nominee in the hardcover fiction category, and the winner of a Coretta Scott King Award in 1982.

Mildred Taylor lives in Colorado, where she is at work on a fourth book about the Logan family.

SELECTED WORKS: Song of the Trees, 1975; Roll of Thunder, Hear My Cry, 1976; Let the Circle Be Unbroken, 1981.

ABOUT: Contemporary Authors, Vol. 85–88; Cullinan, Beatrice. Literature and the Child; Page, James A., comp. Selected Black American Authors: An Illustrated Bio-Bibliography; Something About the Author, Vol. 15; Ward, Martha E. and Dorothy A. Marquardt. Authors of Books for Young People, 2nd edition (Supplement); Horn Book August 1977; Language Arts May 1981; School Library Journal March 1977.

SUSAN TERRIS

May 6, 1937–

AUTHOR OF *Plague of Frogs,* etc.

Autobiographical sketch of Susan Terris:

ALMOST EVERY DAY I sit down at my desk and do some writing, so why is it that I feel so much fear when it comes to writing about myself? That's a question I've been trying to answer for months as I've put off composing a biographical sketch for this collection. The answer, I think, is both easy and hard.

Most of my novels are, in one way or another, written about myself. But that is *fiction.* What that means is that a reader can decide for himself how much of what I say is true. It also means that, as the writer, I can usually deny any embarrassing material as being made up rather than true. Now, however, I am trapped because anything written below has to be the truth. Well, first things first, I'll start with the basic information that everyone always wants to know.

In St. Louis, Missouri, where I grew up, I was a tomboy as well as an avid reader and writer. After high school, I went to Wellesley College in Massachussets, where I earned my B.A. I also have a master's degree in English Literature from San Francisco State University. For over twenty years, I have lived in San Francisco with my husband David. Our three children—Dan, Michael, and Amy—visit often; but they are mostly in college, working, or both at the same time. In addition to writing, I do some lecturing, teaching of creative writing, and some book reviewing. When I am not working, I enjoy hiking, going to the-

ater, and reading. I'm a nineteenth-century novel buff who believes that rereading is the best way to get to know literature. My favorite authors—Charles Dickens, Jane Austen, Thomas Hardy, and George Eliot.

When I was a student at Wellesley, I had an English professor named Philip Booth. He was (and is) a rather well-known poet. Although he liked my work, he frequently told me that I was going to have to "broaden my vision" if I wanted to be a writer. Looking back, I think that was polite way of telling me that I was going to have to grow up. You see, the stories that I was writing then at age eighteen, nineteen, twenty, and twenty-one were about children and adolescence.

Now, many years later, I am still writing about the same subjects. An unkind person would say that I have never grown up. An understanding person, however, would see that I have never lost my fascination for the experiences of children and young adults. The years between ten and fourteen were of particular importance in my life. I remember them with great clarity. They were both difficult and exciting—full of suffering yet full of joy. Most of all, though, I remember the fear—fear of new people, new situations, and the fear of wondering how any person could ever have a safe life in such an unsafe world. One of the reasons, I suppose, I am still writing about these fears is that I am still feeling some of them.

I am also interested in turning points. I believe that the young teenage years are filled with turning points which, in many instances, profoundly affect what we do with the rest of our lives. In a world filled with doubt and pessimism, I am still an optimist. I believe that people are able to change the directions of their own lives, work their way through unhappiness.

Dear Phillip Booth—wherever you are:

I am still writing about children and teenagers. Why? Because I believe that sooner or later—but preferably between ten and fourteen—everyone has to turn around, take a stand, and say, "This is me. I am going to struggle. I am going to take risks. I am in contol of my own life, my own future. Look out world—here I come!"

Sincerely yours,
Susan Terris

Susan Terris was born in St. Louis. She was married in 1958 and received her B.A. degree in 1959 and her M.A. degree in 1966. From 1964 to 1968 she was a teacher, a tutor, and a school librarian. She now teaches a course in writing for children through the University of California extension in San Francisco. Terris has reviewed books for the *New York Times*. She is a member of the Authors Guild.

Wings and Roots was a Junior Literary Guild selection, and *Plague of Frogs* was named a *New York Times* Outstanding Children's Book of 1973.

SELECTED WORKS: The Upstairs Witch and the Downstairs Witch, 1970; The Drowning Boy, 1972; Plague of Frogs, 1973; Pickle, 1983; The Pencil Families, 1975; No Boys Allowed, 1976; The Chicken Pox Papers, 1976; Two P's in a Pod, 1977; Tucker and the Horse Thief, 1979; Stage Brat, 1980; No Scarlet Ribbons, 1981; Wings and Roots, 1982.

ABOUT: Contemporary Authors (First Revision), Vol. 29–32; The International Authors and Writers Who's Who, 1982; Something About the Author, Vol. 3; Ward, Martha E. and Dorothy A. Marquardt. Authors of Books for Young People, 2nd edition (Supplement); Who's Who of American Women, 1975–76; The Writers Directory 1982–84.

COLIN THIELE

November 16, 1920–

AUTHOR OF *The Blue Fin,* etc.

Autobiographical sketch of Colin (Milton) Thiele:

MY NAME causes a lot of trouble. Few people seem to be able to pronounce it. I try to help by suggesting that they should say TEE LEE, but this often adds to the confusion because then everyone thinks I am Chinese. In actual fact my grandparents migrated to South Australia from Germany about 130 years ago.

I grew up on a farm. When I was five I started going to a little bush school that consisted of one room, one teacher, and twenty children. My mother says that until my first day at school I spoke nothing but German; after that I spoke nothing but English. Whichever language I used, I'm certain that there weren't enough books for me to read.

The school library was a box in a corner with twenty or thirty dog-eared novels in it, and our possessions at home included a few German stories and a big black German Bible. By the time I was eleven I had read everything I could find and so I decided to write a few books of my own. I did this at night by the light of a candle, without my parents' knowledge, although they became suspicious when I kept singeing off my left eyebrow in the candle flame.

When my elementary school days ended I wanted to stay at home on the farm, but the Great Depression was so severe that there was no hope of that. So I kept on going to school, travelling further and further in search of places that offered a higher edu-

Thiele: *TEE LEE*

I am certain that stories can do much to enrich their lives.

———

Colin Thiele was born in Eudunda, South Australia. He married in 1947, and received his education diploma the same year. Thiele was Principal of Wattle Park Teachers College from 1965 to 1972, and its Director from 1973 to 1980. He also held the position of Director of Murray Park College of Advanced Education.

Thiele won prizes in various fields for his books: the Miles Memorial Poetry Prize in 1944, two first prizes in the Commonwealth Jubilee Literary Competitions in 1951, and the South Australia prize in the World Short Story Quest of 1952. He also received the Grace Leven Poetry Prize in 1961, and was awarded a Commonwealth Literary Fund Fellowship to write a biography.

Among his books for children, *Blue Fin* was named a 1970 Australian Book of the Year, an American Library Association Notable Book for 1974, a Hans Christian Andersen Honor Book in 1972, and a Children's Choice book of 1975 by the joint committee of the International Reading Association and the Children's Book Council. It was also made into a feature film in 1978 by the Southern Australia Film Corporation.

Storm Boy was named an Australian Children's Book of the Year in 1975 by the Children's Book Council of Australia. *Magpie Island,* published in Australia in 1974, and *The Valley Between,* published in Australia in 1981, were also named Children's Books of the Year, in 1975 and 1982 respectively.

Colin Thiele is a Fellow of the Australian College of Education and a Companion of the Order of Australia. He and his wife have two daughters, and live in Wattle Park, South Australia.

cation, until I finally attended the University of Adelaide and graduated as a teacher.

Apart from three or four years in the Royal Air Force of Australia during the Second World War, I then spent most of my life teaching in schools and colleges. At the same time I continued to write, so that by the time I retired in 1980 I had published over fifty books in many different fields— poetry, history, biography, education, prose fiction, the environment, and stories for children. Now I live the life of a full-time writer.

I like to write what I know. That is why most of my books are set in South Australia—on the coastline, the River Murray, the opal fields, the farms, the desert, and in the German communities where my ancestors settled. I think the spirit of a place is important, and I think a book should catch that spirit, even though it is often a question of trying to catch the uncatchable. A book should also reveal something about human beings, about the universal things that live in people from generation to generation: happiness and sadness, wisdom and folly, avarice and generosity, cruelty and compassion.

Having worked with children all my life,

SELECTED WORKS: Blue Fin, 1974; Fire in the Stone, 1974; February Dragon, 1976; Fight Against Albatross Two, 1976; The Hammerhead Light, 1977; The Shadow on the Hills, 1978; Storm Boy, 1978.

ABOUT: Contemporary Authors (First Revision), Vol. 29–32; Kirkpatrick, D. L., ed. Twentieth-Century Children's Writers; Something About the Author, Vol. 14; The Writers Directory 1982–84.

ALAN TIEGREEN

ALAN TIEGREEN

July 6, 1935–

ILLUSTRATOR OF *Ramona Quimby, Age 8,* etc.

Biographical sketch of Alan Tiegreen:

ALAN TIEGREEN was born in Boise, Idaho. Because his father's job with the government required the family to make frequent moves, he grew up in such varied places as Nebraska, Alabama, and Ohio.

Interested in both art and music from an early age, Alan Tiegreen says his interest in drawing prevailed because he "did not have enough patience to practice" his music. After receiving his degee from the University of Southern Mississippi in Hattiesburg in 1957, Tiegreen continued his studies at the Art Center College of Design in Los Angeles, earning the degree of Bachelor of Professional Arts in 1961.

He is now a teacher of painting, drawing, and illustration at Georgia State University's urban campus in Atlanta. Tiegreen and his wife Judy, who is also an art teacher, live in Decatur, and he is the father of three children, Christopher, Carl, and Karen. His hobbies are music and tennis.

Tiegreen's paintings have been exhibited at the Smithsonian Institution in Washington, D.C., the Knoxville World's Fair, and in New York City, Atlanta, and Los Angeles. He has been the recipient of several honors, including the National Drawing Exhibition Award and the Art Directors Club Award for Illustration.

Appreciating the freedom allowed illustrators of children's books, Tiegreen was delighted when a publisher of the Baptist Home Mission Board asked if he would be interested in illustrating a book for children. He enjoyed the experience and began to develop a portfolio. Then, author Robert Burch saw Tiegreen's work and suggested to his editor at Viking that Alan Tiegreen illustrate his next book. *Doodle and the Go-Cart* was the result. Since then Tiegreen has illustrated several books, among them the more recent "Ramona" books by Beverly Cleary.

Tiegreen says that Cleary's characters "are universally appealing. They embody my feelings when I was a child. I can relate to Ramona's feelings especially. Cleary has an empathy with children and she writes of them with humor and understanding."

All of the "Ramona" books that Tiegreen illustrated have won awards. *Ramona the Brave* was included on the *School Library Journal* "Best of the Best 1966–1978" list (December 1979) and was named a 1975 Children's Choice book by a joint committee of the International Reading Association and the Children's Book Council. *Ramona and Her Father* was a 1978 Newbery Honor Book and a Boston Globe-Horn Book Award Honor Book in 1978. It also won a 1980 Garden State Children's Book Award and was a 1977 Children's Choice book. *Ramona and Her Mother,* too, was a Chil-

Tiegreen: *TIE green*

dren's Choice book, in 1979, and was named a 1979 Notable Book by the American Library Association. *Ramona Quimby, Age 8* was a Newbery Honor Book in 1982.

Alan Tiegreen believes children's books "offer the cream of what's being done in visual communications these days, the place where writers and illustrators can express themselves almost without hindrance. It's the most creative art."

SELECTED WORKS ILLUSTRATED: Doodle and the Go-Cart, by Robert Burch, 1972; Ramona the Brave, by Beverly Cleary, 1975; Adam's Key, by Eleanor Lattimore, 1976; Ramona and Her Father, by Beverly Cleary, 1977; Silver Woven in My Hair, by Shirley R. Murphy, 1977; Ramona and Her Mother, by Beverly Cleary, 1979; The Good-Guy Cake, by Barbara Dillon, 1980; Ramona Quimby, Age 8, by Beverly Cleary, 1981.

MARGOT TOMES

MARGOT TOMES

August 10, 1917–

ILLUSTRATOR OF *And Then What Happened, Paul Revere?*, etc.

Autobiographical sketch of Margot Ladd Tomes:

DRAWING and painting are not easy for me. I haven't much aptitude for them, although they do interest me. It's surprising that I can earn my living doing it, and I'm particularly lucky to be doing both for children's books—something which, in a foggy way, I wanted to do when I was only thirteen. For years, though, I worked as a wallpaper and fabric designer, which was even harder, and I'm much happier now.

I like children's books now because I loved them as a child. The first six years of my life were rather like Heaven (I should think). I was born in my grandfather's house in Park Hill, Yonkers, New York. I don't remember that, but I do remember the January evening, seventeen months later, when my sister was born in the same house. I remember feeling safe and impor-

tant, with a golden light all around. I think I was even conscious of the cold darkness outside, making the house warm and radiant in comparison. It's my first conscious memory, and I have loved winter ever since. This impression of good luck persisted even through the calamities that beset me later—not the least of which was my turning ugly and disagreeable, when I was seven. I guess the second was a result of the first, but I certainly don't imagine it, because I heard people saying so. But it wasn't so bad, because I stayed in a cocoon, expecting (mistakenly) a radical change in the future.

We moved to Nassau County, Long Island, when I was two and a half—grandparents, parents, and some cousins. It was still quite rural then, and it was lovely. I didn't even have to go to school until the third grade when I was seven (that unlucky year). My mother taught me to read when I was four, she threw in some arithmetic and geography, and she could draw very charming pictures, besides. The afternoons were free.

But then sickness and death and separations changed everything. For a while I was a child insomniac, listening fearfully for ghosts, etc. I think many children go through feelings of dispossession. They feel misfortune, or even change, as a kind of disgrace. But I kept on reading a lot, and drawing sporadically, and remained in that protective isolation—which (the isolation) made me socially backward, and stupid in many ways. But I was good at schoolwork.

There isn't much more to say to explain my becoming a children's book illustrator. I went to Pratt Institute, which I detested. I had dreamed of the snowy campus of some college in New England, where I would major in English Literature. But I got to work with books at last, after all. By now, I have illustrated more than forty.

I live in New York City with a friend and three cats, in two apartments on the third floor of a brownstone, (and we're lucky to have them). So all's well that end's well. I realize this is obscure, but the whole subject is murky, and it's the nearest I can come to clarify it, at any rate in less than ten pages. And this is long enough.

———

Margot Tomes comes from an artistic family; she is related to Guy Pène du Bois, the painter; William Pène du Bois, the illustrator; and Raoul Pène du Bois, the theatrical designer. Her mother drew, and her sister is an artist.

Margot Tomes has received many honors and citations for her work, including the Society of Illustrators Certificate of Merit for her 1979 book, *Wanda Gág's The Sorcerer's Apprentice,* which is one of three of Gág's retellings of Grimm that Tomes has illustrated.

Many of her books that illustrate history have been named Notable Children's Trade Books in the Field of Social Studies by the joint committee of the National Council for the Social Studies and the Children's Book Council. These books include *Paul Revere, Ben Franklin, Phoebe and the General,* and *This Time, Tempe Wick?.* Both *Paul Revere* and *Christopher Columbus* were also named American Library Association Notable

Books. *Jack and the Wonder Beans* was named a *New York Times* Choice of the Best Illustrated Children's Book of the Year 1977, and *Little Sister and the Month Brothers* was in the 1977 Children's Book Showcase exhibit.

In 1983 two of the books she illustrated won American Book Awards: *Homesick* in the hardcover children's fiction category, and *Chimney Sweeps* in the children's nonfiction category. The latter was also named an ALA Notable Book in 1982.

Her work is housed in the Kerlan Collection of the University of Minnesota.

SELECTED WORKS ILLUSTRATED: And Then What Happened, Paul Revere, by Jean Fritz; This Time, Tempe Wick?, by Patricia Lee Gauch, 1974; Everything Under a Mushroom, by Ruth Krauss, 1974; King George's Head Was Made of Lead, by F. N. Monjo, 1974; Lysbet and the Fire Kittens, by Marietta Moskin, 1974; Becky and the Bear, by Dorothy Van Woerkom, 1975; Where Was Patrick Henry on the 29th of May?, by Jean Fritz, 1975; Little Sister and the Month Brothers, by Beatrice Schenk de Regniers, 1976; What's the Big Idea, Ben Franklin?, by Jean Fritz, 1976; Jack and the Wonder Beans, by James Still, 1977; Phoebe and the General, by Judith Berry Griffin, 1977; The Halloween Pumpkin Smasher, by Judith St. George, 1978; Wanda Gág's The Sorcerer's Apprentice, by the Brothers Grimm, 1979; Clever Gretchen, and Other Forgotten Folk Tales, by Alison Lurie, reteller, 1980; Sara Crewe, or What Happened at Miss Minchin's, by Frances Hodgson Burnett, 1981; Where Do You Think You're Going, Christopher Columbus?, by Jean Fritz, 1981; Chimney Sweeps, by James Cross Giblin, 1982; Homesick: My Own Story, by Jean Fritz, 1982; Wanda Gág's The Six Swans, by the Brothers Grimm, 1982.

ABOUT: Kingman, Lee and others, comps. Illustrators of Children's Books: 1957–1966; 1967–1976; Something About the Author, Vol. 27; Who's Who in American Art, 1980; Graphis No. 200, 1979.

WALLACE TRIPP

June 26, 1940–

COMPILER AND ILLUSTRATOR OF *A Great Big Ugly Man Came Up and Tied His Horse to Me: A Book of Nonsense Verse,* etc.

Biographical sketch of Wallace Whitney Tripp:

WALLACE TRIPP

WALLACE TRIPP was born in Boston, Massachusetts. He grew up in rural New Hampshire, where he attended a two-room elementary school, and later in suburban Westchester, New York. As a boy he enjoyed reading about and drawing American Indians, knights, airplanes, and animals. He studied graphic art at the Boston Museum School and received a bachelor's degree in Education from Keene State College in New Hampshire. He also did graduate study at the University of New Hampshire and taught English in the New Hampshire schools for three years before he began to try to become a full-time artist.

Tripp is married and has a son and a daughter, and for a year they all lived in a fifteenth-century gate house on a large estate in Devon, England. His travels in Devon and Cornwall reflected his continuing interest in the era of knighthood and he used the trip as background for *Sir Toby Jingle's Beastly Journey.*

Besides illustrating over forty books for children, he and his family operate a greeting card company, Pawprints, Inc., for which he does the artwork. In 1973, Tripp published *A Great Big Ugly Man Came Up*

and Tied His Horse to Me: A Book of Nonsense Verse, which became a critical and popular success. A reviewer in *School Library Journal* wrote, "A collection of 43 nonsense rhymes. . . . Bright ink and watercolor cartoons, full of little jokes and surprises, provoke laughter at both the familiar and unfamilar nonsense." A *Publishers Weekly* review said: "The illustrations are hilarious . . . this nonsense collection would be a treat for any child." *A Great Big Ugly Man* was named a Notable Book by the American Library Association in 1973. In 1976, Tripp published *Granfa' Grig Had a Pig and Other Rhymes Without Reason from Mother Goose.* The *Horn Book* called it a "lively, colorful book . . . always exuding an air of good humor." *Granfa' Grig* won the Boston Globe-Horn Book Award for illustration in 1977.

Tripp's art is of a humorous nature with emphasis on strong pen-and-ink technique and draftsmanship that give his human and animal characters uncommon vitality and expressiveness. His special interests are classical music, aviation history, English literature, history, art, and illustration. He especially admires illustrators like N. C. Wyeth, Ernest Shepard, Garth Williams, Bill Peet, Raymond Briggs, Richard Scarry, and Graham Oakley.

In 1981, he started his own publishing house—Sparhawk Books, Inc., in Jaffrey, New Hampshire—which published two books so far, including *The Bad Child's Book of Beasts* by Hilaire Belloc and illustrated by Tripp.

Tripp is a member of the Author's Guild. He lives in New Hampshire, in a former cooperage.

SELECTED WORKS COMPILED AND ILLUSTRATED: A Great Big Ugly Man Came Up and Tied His Horse to Me: A Book of Nonsense Verse, 1973; Granfa' Grig Had a Pig and Other Rhymes Without Reason from Mother Goose, 1976; Sir Toby Jingle's Beastly Journey, 1976.

SELECTED WORKS ILLUSTRATED: Rabbits Rafferty, by Gerald Dumas, 1968; Mrs. Fox, by John Erwin, 1969; The Baseball Bargain, by Scott Corbett, 1970; No

Flying in the House, by Betty Brock, 1970; Come Back, Amelia Bedelia, by Peggy Parish, 1971; Play Ball, Amelia Bedelia, by Peggy Parish, 1972; The Bad Child's Book of Beasts, by Hilaire Belloc, 1982.

ABOUT: Contemporary Authors, Vol. 106; Kingman, Lee and others, comps. Illustrators of Children's Books: 1967–1976; Ward, Martha E. and Dorothy A. Marquardt. Illustrators of Books for Young People, 2nd edition; Who's Who in American Art, 1978.

CHRIS VAN ALLSBURG

June 18, 1949–

AUTHOR AND ILLUSTRATOR OF *Jumanji*, etc.

Biographical sketch of Chris Van Allsburg:

CHRIS VAN ALLSBURG was born in Grand Rapids, Michigan, where his father ran a dairy. "Not the kind with cows," the illustrator said. "Our family dairy converted milk into ice cream." Although as a child he drew with facility for the entertainment of his friends, he gave up drawing when other skills, like ball playing, proved more socially useful and he entered the University of Michigan, intending to study law. However, he took a figure drawing course during his freshman year that renewed his interest in art. A course in sculpture followed, and after he graduated from Michigan with a B.F.A. degree, he went on to the Rhode Island School of Design (RISD) for a master's degree in sculpture.

Van Allsburg's work has been shown at the Whitney Museum of American Art and in the mid-1970s, his first one-man show in New York exhibited sculpture that bore a notable relationship to his children's book art of later years. "I always had a penchant for pieces in which something was happening," he said. Thus, one bronze sculpture showed the Titanic nose-diving beneath the waves; another a flying saucer careening into an observatory; a third an obelisk with its brickwork being blown apart during a windstorm.

A teacher of drawing at RISD since 1977,

CHRIS VAN ALLSBURG

Van Allsburg became a children's book illustrator at the urging of his wife Lisa, a fellow art student at Michigan and a grade-school teacher, and David Macaulay, the children's book author and illustrator and another faculty member at RISD. Van Allsburg was too unsure of his work to present it himself, so his wife took his portfolio around to publishers in Boston and New York. Its reception was instantly favorable.

His early books were executed in black and white. *The Garden of Abdul Gasazi* was done with carbon pencil; *Jumanji* with pencil and with Conte dust, a softer medium producing subtle grays; and *Ben's Dream* in black line on scratchboard. With *The Wreck of the Zephyr,* Van Allsburg turned to color; he used Rembrandt pastels, thick crayons, and pastel pencils. "For me, the joy of being an artist," he said in a *Publishers Weekly* interview, "is the challenge of solving particular technical problems. . . . Obviously, when you use color, whole new vistas open up."

Van Allsburg's books all contain elements of fantasy. In *Jumanji,* for example, two children playing a board game about the jungle face life-threatening dangers in their house when the characters in the game become real. The only solution to their predic- ament is to finish the game, as animals crowd around them in the room. Van Alls- burg is fascinated with the idea of the artist as magician, "I like to achieve impossible worlds," he said. Among the artists he most admires are Magritte, Balthus, and Hopper. Like the cinematic master of suspense, Al- fred Hitchcock, who appeared in cameo roles in all of his films, Van Allsburg has adopted the bull terrier Fritz, from *The Garden of Abdul Gasazi,* as his surrogate in all of his books: the dog is a pull toy in *Jumanji,* a portrait on the wall in *Ben's Dream,* and a dockside observer in *Zephyr.* He sees similarities between working as a fine artist and as a children's book creator: "It takes the same kind of intelligence, if you're a serious draftsman, to do a piece of pure illustration or a picture book." He notes in *Publishers Weekly* that book illus- tration endures. "It's like having a perma- nent art exhibition between book covers."

Chris Van Allsburg's books have won sev- eral major awards. His first book, *The Gar- den of Abdul Gasazi,* was a Caldecott Honor Book in 1980 and won the Boston Globe- Horn Book Award and the Irma Simonton Black Award in the same year. It was placed on the Honor List of the Internation- al Board on Books for Young People as well as the *New York Times* list of Best Illustrated Books of the Year 1979. His second book, *Jumanji,* won the 1982 Caldecott Medal, was a Boston Globe-Horn Book Award Honor Book in 1981, and won an American Book Award in 1982 in the original art cate- gory.

Van Allsburg lives in Providence, Rhode Island, in a house that his friend David Macaulay describes in the *Horn Book* as "a slightly Scandinavian-possibly-Bavarian woodman's cottage built just before 1920 by a neo-Victorian." He and his wife collect the sort of 1930s furnishings that abound in his picture books.

SELECTED WORKS: The Garden of Abdul Gasazi, 1979; Jumanji, 1981; Ben's Dream, 1982; The Wreck of the Zephyr, 1983.

ABOUT: Horn Book August 1982; Publishers Weekly April 8, 1983.

JEAN VAN LEEUWEN

December 26, 1937–

AUTHOR OF *Tales of Oliver Pig,* etc.

Autobiographical sketch of Jean Van Leeu- wen:

AS A CHILD, I loved to read. I could be found with a book in my hand at all times and in all places, including under the covers at night when I was supposed to be sleeping. I remember going through phases where I read all of one kind of book that I could get my hands on—mysteries, dog stories, horse stories, historical novels. It was during my horse period in sixth grade that I, perhaps inevitably, decided to write a book myself.

It was an imitation *Black Beauty,* and it was a dismal failure. I never got beyond Chapter Three. But it did teach me several valuable lessons. I learned that (1) it's hard to write about things you don't know any- thing about (I'd never been on a horse in my life.); (2) It helps to know where the story is going before you start writing it; and (3) writing is hard work.

This experience was unfortunate in that it discouraged me from writing for several years. I finished school and went on to col- lege, where I majored in journalism and planned to become a magazine editor. Somehow, though, I wound up working in the children's book department of a New York publisher. And once again, I felt the urge to write a book myself. I took an eve- ning course in writing for children, and eventually worked up the courage to sub- mit one of my stories to the editor for whom I worked. Amazingly, it was accepted.

For some years after that, I continued to work as a children's book editor, doing my own writing on the side. But after my two children were born, I left publishing, moved out of the city, and began devoting my time solely to writing.

Van Leeuwen: *van Loo en*

Jean Van Leeuwen

I have discovered that I enjoy writing for a variety of age groups, from preschool to teenage. And I also like moving from one kind of story to another—from human to animal characters, from humor to serious themes, from realism to pure fantasy. When I finish a book in which I've been absorbed in the very real problems of a girl growing up, it's a relief to switch to a light fantasy about mice living in a New York department store. And after I've imagined myself a mouse for awhile, I'm glad to get back to human size. The variety seems to nourish me, to recharge my batteries.

When I first began writing, I worried that I would run out of ideas, that my next book would be my last. But somehow that hasn't happened. In fact, I always seem to have two or three ideas beyond the book I'm currently working on. Having children has certainly helped. Just eavesdropping on one of their conversations with a friend while driving a car pool is sometimes enough to start a whole book incubating in my mind. At this point I find I have the opposite worry—I wonder if I'll ever be able to capture on paper all the ideas I have now.

———

Jean Van Leeuwen was born in Glen Ridge, New Jersey. She grew up in Rutherford, New Jersey, and was graduated from Syracuse University in 1959. From 1960 to 1973 she worked as a children's book editor in several New York publishing houses. Married to Bruce D. Gavril, a computer designer, in 1968, she has two children, David (born in 1972) and Elizabeth (born in 1973). She now lives in Chappaqua, New York.

Jean Van Leeuwen edited *A Time of Growing,* a collection of short stories concerning adolescent girls. She also wrote for older readers *It Seems Like This Road Goes On Forever,* which was named an American Library Association Best Book for Young Adults in 1979 and was also selected as a Notable Children's Trade Book in the Field of Social Studies by the joint committee of the National Council for the Social Studies and the Children's Book Council.

She has won several other awards and honors; *The Great Christmas Kidnaping Caper* won the 1978 William Allen White Award. *Tales of Oliver Pig* and *More Tales of Oliver Pig,* both illustrated by Arnold Lobel, were Junior Literary Guild selections, and *More Tales of Oliver Pig* and *Amanda Pig and Her Big Brother Oliver* were both named ALA Notable Books, in 1981 and 1982 respectively.

SELECTED WORKS EDITED: A Time of Growing, 1967.

SELECTED WORKS: One Day in Summer, 1969; The Great Cheese Conspiracy, 1969; I Was a 98-Pound Duckling, 1972; The Great Christmas Kidnaping Caper, 1975; Seems Like This Road Goes On Forever, 1979; Tales of Oliver Pig, 1979; More Tales of Oliver Pig, 1981; Amanda Pig and Her Big Brother Oliver, 1982; The Great Rescue Operation, 1982.

ABOUT: Contemporary Authors (First Revision), Vol. 25–28; Something About the Author, Vol. 6; Who's Who of American Women, 1975–1976.

DOROTHY VAN WOERKOM

June 26, 1924–

AUTHOR OF *Becky and the Bear,* etc.

Van Woerkum: *van WORK um*

Autobiographical sketch of Dorothy O. Van Woerkom:

I WAS BORN into the O'Brien clan in Buffalo, New York, where I lived with my parents for thirty-six years. This amazes me now, and is a tribute to my mother's firm belief that the neighbors "talked" about unmarried girls who left home. My younger sister used to say that to get away we'd either have to get mad or get married. We got mad often enough (and married once, but not till much later).

I remember playing out in the snow for a while at a time, and trying to pretend that I liked tobogganing, but mostly I remember wondering why we lived so far north. The steel mills had brought my mother's parents and my father up from Pennsylvania, and I resented that the south did not have at least the attraction of some steel mills.

I was about eight when, during a cold winter in the drafty four-room schoolhouse on Abbott Road, Sister Amabilis read us *Hans Brinker: or The Silver Skates*. Sitting at my carved-up, ink-stained desk, I determined to marry a Dutchman—and move to a warmer place.

The Sisters of Mercy taught me through high school. These were Depression years, and so I went directly on to business school, then to work as a secretary. I could read before I began first grade, learning from nursery rhymes in an insurance company booklet. I recall this small booklet as being in color, though now I wonder if this was my imagination, whether a free handout would have been in color in the early 1930s. Still, it was my favorite childhood "book," along with *Merry Murphy the Potato* and *Mrs. Wiggs of the Cabbage Patch*.

My first memory of actually having written was at age seven, when I wrote a series of dog stories. Songs and plays followed, and later came prizes and essays. My mother wasn't always pleased. I was constantly either reading or writing, and she was constantly chasing me outside to "play." We lived on a hill and I used to walk down the dirt road to the cemetery, where I sat on my grandfather's headstone under a large tree, and wrote. My first "notebook" was a book of wallpaper samples. My aunt used to acquire these and use the pages to make party baskets. She taught me how and gave me a book. I discovered immediately that, turned backside-to, the wallpaper presented lovely, clean blank sheets for writing.

When I was thirty-six I married John Van Woerkom, an Army Major and a widower with a young daughter. I had my Dutchman. In late summer of 1962 we were transferred to Houston, so I was now happily "south," where John eventually retired from service and where we still live. By 1969 my stepdaughter had grown up and left home and I needed something to do. My husband suggested writing—an astonishing idea, since no one had ever given me that kind of serious encouragement.

As a child I had loved folklore and could never find enough of it. I wanted to grow up and write lots of folktales for myself—and I'd write some fox-and-wolf stories in which the wolf did not get killed. Now these resolves came back to me, but first I took a course in adult nonfiction and with my fifth lesson began selling to adult magazines. After a couple of years I felt brave enough to try writing books. Of course I began with the retelling of folktales, and eventually wrote *Meat Pies and Sausages,* three stories of fox and wolf, in which the wolf did not get killed.

———

Two of Dorothy Van Woerkom's books have been named Junior Literary Guild selections, *Becky and the Bear* and *The Queen Who Couldn't Bake Gingerbread.* Van Woerkom is a member of the Authors Guild and the Mystery Writers of America.

SELECTED WORKS: Becky and the Bear, 1974; The Queen Who Couldn't Bake Gingerbread, 1975; Meat Pies and Sausages, 1976; The Rat, the Ox, and the Zodiac, 1976; Harry and Shellburt, 1977; When All the World Was Waiting, 1979; Pearl in the Egg, 1980; Something to Crow About, 1982.

ABOUT: Contemporary Authors, Vol. 57–60; Something About the Author, Vol. 21; Ward, Martha E. and Dorothy A. Marquardt. Authors of Books for Young People, 2nd edition (Supplement); Who's Who in America, 1980–1981.

CYNTHIA VOIGT

February 25, 1942–

AUTHOR OF *Dicey's Song,* etc.

Autobiographical sketch of Cynthia Voigt:

I LIKE TO think of myself as a New Englander even though that's not strictly true. The true part is based on facts: I was born in Boston, raised in Connecticut, educated in Massachusetts. The not-strictly part is also based on facts: I live in Maryland, while real New Englanders live in Maine—I have never even been to Maine; real New Englanders are taciturn types who seem pretty clear about what they think—I am talky a lot of the time (although I do have a taste for silence and solitude) and am never as sure of things as I would like to be.

Cynthia Voigt

In my life, I have three jobs, all of which I like. I have the job of wife-and-mother, where you build relationships that you hope will last all your life long. I have the job of teacher, where you think about really substantial books, like *Hamlet,* and think also about who the students are and how they can make themselves better at being what they are. I have the job of writer, which is one of the world's strangest occupations, full of contradictions, intensely interesting.

I always wanted to be a writer, always from the age of twelve. Even earlier than that, I always was a reader. I love a good story, and I love to meet interesting characters, and I like thinking. I discovered children's literature not when I was a child but when I first taught fifth grade. I wanted my students to write book reports so I went to the library to make up a list of books for them to read. I started with the letter A and read my way through to Z, Alexander to Zindel. As a reader, I was delighted and excited. As a writer, it was as if somebody had opened a window for me, to show me a whole new landscape.

That is the inner biography. The outer biography runs parallel: I went to Dana Hall School, Smith College, and then, for educaton courses, to St. Michael's College in Santa Fe—while I didn't always like being at

school I did always enjoy learning; I have
had a number of jobs, in my early employment years, child-care, waitress, secretary;
once I discovered teaching, that has been
my favorite employment and I have taught
every grade from second through twelfth
(except for third, I've never taught third
graders) as well as doing tutoring in remedi-
al reading. I have been a single woman, a
divorced woman head-of-household, a married woman—and there are good and bad
things about all of those states, as far as I can
tell, although on the whole I prefer marriage. My husband is a teacher of the classics, Greek, Latin, Ancient History. We
have two children, Jessica who is twelve and
Peter who is five. We live in Annapolis during the school year and go off to the Eastern
Shore for the summers, to get away and to
be by the water. We all like being by the
water, to swim in or paddle around, to travel over and pull crabs out of, to have it nearby and watch the way the tides rise and fall,
the way the colors on it change.

———

Cynthia Voigt's first novel in what she
calls the Crisfield stories is *Homecoming,*
which was nominated for an American
Book Award in 1982. The sequel, *Dicey's
Song,* won the 1983 Newbery Award. The
Crisfield books concern an enterprising
thirteen-year-old, Dicey, who must keep
her younger brothers and sister together after their emotionally disturbed mother (and
only parent) abandons them. A companion
book to the two, *A Solitary Blue,* has as its
protagonist a friend of Dicey Tillerman.

SELECTED WORKS: Homecoming, 1981; Dicey's Song,
1982; Tell Me If the Lovers Are Losers, 1982; The Cal-
lender Papers, 1983; A Solitary Blue, 1983.

ABOUT: Contemporary Authors, Vol. 106; Horn
Book August 1983.

JOHN C. WALLNER

February 3, 1945–

ILLUSTRATOR OF *Little Fox Goes to the
End of the World,* etc.

Autobiographical sketch of John Charles
Wallner:

IT'S RATHER difficult for me to write
about what it is I do. By the time the words
come down my arm and out the pen and on
to paper, they don't seem the same. Pictures
on the other hand, hold up a bit longer for
me. They seem to stand still and allow their
costumes to be changed, the trees can be
pruned. You're allowed to move pictures
about more and take a good straight look at
them.

The task for me is to listen to the words
of the author and find what those words
look like. How to make visible the author's
words and still have a bit of me in it. More
likely it becomes a third world altogether,
not totally mine and not totally the author's.

The journey to this world almost always
requires endless sheets of tracing paper and
countless faces going by. You find yourself
searching your own past for places that hold
secrets all their own. People you know start
to blend with animals, and suddenly there's
your hero: not quite a bear and not quite
the man that used to sell vegetables when
you were young, rather he's a bear that
somehow you've met before.

Now you've got to find him the proper
clothes and a circle of friends only such a
bear could have, and you must remain
within the words of the author and their reality.

If it works, though, it usually looks like a
nice place to visit, and that's the whole
point, isn't it?—giving children nice places
to go to and friends to meet.

There's really no need for me to say anymore. I've enjoyed this time with you and
now you must excuse me. I've got three
dragons that need attention to their wings
and a group of folks still offstage that are
anxious to be brought on for fittings and
make-up all their own.

John C. Wallner was born in St. Louis, Missouri. He received a B.F.A. degree from Washington University in St. Louis in 1968 and a M.F.A. degree from Pratt Institute in Brooklyn in 1970. He was married in 1971.

Wallner's work has been exhibited in the Maryhurst College Invitational for Graphics in 1969, the Albany Small Print Show in 1970, and the Society of Illustrators Annual Exhibits for several years, and other shows. His work is in the permanent collection of the Children's Book Museum in Australia. It has also appeared in the Audubon Society annual in 1971 and 1972, and in the Society of Graphic Artists Annual in 1972. In addition to illustrating books, Wallner taught children's book illustration at Fairfield University in Fairfield, Connecticut, from 1978 to 1979.

Wallner's books won many awards and honors. *The Terrible Thing That Happened at Our House* was named a Notable Book by the American Library Association in 1975, as was *Little Fox Goes to the End of the World*, which was also a Junior Literary Guild selection and which received the Friends of American Writers Illustration Award in 1976 as well as a Society of Illustrators Citation of Merit. *A January Fog Will Freeze a Hog* was named both an ALA Notable Book and an Outstanding Science Trade Book for Children by the joint committee of the National Science Teachers Association and the Children's Book Council. *Charlotte and Charles* won a Creativity Award from Art Director's Magazine in 1979.

Three of Wallner's books were exhibited in American Institute of Graphic Arts shows: *Little Fox* in 1977, *The Night Stella Hid the Stars* in 1978, and *Good Night Annie* in 1980. *Annie* was also a Book-of-the-Month Club selection. *A Perfect Nose for Ralph* was exhibited in the 1981 Bologna Book Fair.

SELECTED WORKS ILLUSTRATED: The Terrible Thing That Happened at Our House, by Marge Blaine, 1975; Little Fox Goes to the End of the World, by Ann Tompert, 1976; A January Fog Will Freeze a Hog, by Herbert Davies, 1977; Little Otter Remembers, by Ann Tompert, 1977; The Night Stella Hid the Stars, by Gail Radley, 1978; Charlotte and Charles, by Ann Tompert, 1979; Good Night to Annie, by Eve Merriam, 1980; A Perfect Nose for Ralph, by Jane Breskin Zalben, 1980; Tonight's the Night, by Jim Aylesworth, 1981; Uncle Gus's Birthday Cake, by Jan Wahl, 1981; Grandma's Secret Letter, by Maggie Davis, 1982; When the Dark Comes Dancing, by Nancy Larrick, compiler, 1983.

ABOUT: Something About the Author, Vol. 10; Kingman, Lee and others, comps. Illustrators of Children's Books: 1967–1976.

ROBERT WESTALL

October 7, 1929–

AUTHOR OF *The Machine Gunners,* etc.

Autobiographical sketch of Robert Atkinson Westall:

I HAD a happy childhood: I never realised how happy until I grew up and talked to other people. My happiness was based on my father. He was the foreman-engineer of

a gasworks. I remember when I was quite small, being sent with his lunch to the enormous smoking works—quite alarming til he was summoned out of the smoke, dirty-faced, cap black with grease, men working beside him asking him what to do about something. He never had to throw his weight about with the men—his authority was based on always knowing how to do things. The men had a way of saying, "we'll have to ask Bobby."

I never saw him scared or in a muddle. Even the night he went out in the middle of an air-raid to free a high conveyor-belt that had iced-up—a job that normally took four men, and that night he was alone. I could see on his face he thought it was impossible, and yet there was a spark in his eyes that said excitedly, "maybe, maybe."

He gave me, suddenly, amazing presents—a full-size model machine-gun he'd made himself, model ships. Even today, at eighty-one, he does amazing things. He sent me an antique, packed in polystyrene fastened together with two-inch screws, *and it worked.* Who else but my father would screw polystyrene together?

He appears in two of my books, *The Machine-Gunners* and *Fathom Five.* He's

read them, so he knows how I feel about him. I could never say it to his face. That makes me very happy.

I'm not really a writer, but a teacher who writes. This is good for me, because as a teacher I could never feed a kid lies. A teacher who lies is the very worst kind of monster. On the other hand, my hero is Socrates, who was executed for telling kids too much truth (I have no intention of being executed, but would be gratified to escape it by the narrowest possible margin). People create great structures of lies all the time, mainly because they're frightened. People who really blow such structures up are the greatest people in the world. Greatest of all was Jesus Christ—try reading a gospel as a picture of a guy blowing-up lie-structures—it's refreshing. It's only a pity that some people have since built new lie-structures on his words. Other heroes of mine are Martin Luther, Martin Luther King, Oliver Cromwell, and Ralph Nader.

The thing I'm proudest to have done, apart from books, is to design from scratch, and build, a three-foot model sailing catamaran that not only sailed, but sailed fast. To *use* the wind and water correctly, with shapes born in your own mind, is *something.* My father said he didn't think I had such craftsmanship in me.

My favourite animals are cats. I have six. They are thieves, they are the most awful killers, they jump on my head in the middle of the night, and I adore them all. I quite like dogs, but I find them too slavish, too desperate to be approved of. Call a cat to you, and it will sit and stare at you and damn your eyes. Then, when you've forgotten all about it, it will come and sit in your lap to please itself. *That's* a compliment. There are cats in most of my books, always heroes. I like cats because they're free.

I wrote my books for my son. He was very blunt about them. If my books are fast-paced and interesting, it's because my son told me all the crap-bits to cut out (mainly descriptions of things). As he grew older, he became very free, like the cats. He was very good with hurt birds and animals. He argued with the bosses on behalf of his mates. He talked to anybody—old people, tramps, priests. He's the hero of *The Devil on the Road*. When he was eighteen, he died on his motorbike, instantly. It was the way he'd have chosen to die. He didn't leave me a single crappy memory, so I count myself lucky, though it's harder to write books now he's gone.

Robert Westall was born in Tynemouth, Northumberland in England. He received his B. A. in fine art at Durham University in 1953 and received a diploma in 1957 from the Slade School, University of London. He served in the Royal Signals of the British Army from 1953 to 1955 and was married in 1958. He has taught art to children since 1957 and is Head of Art and Head of Careers at Sir John Deane's Grammar School in Chester. He is also an art and architecture critic and contributor to the *Guardian* and the Chester *Chronicle*.

The Machine Gunners won the 1975 Carnegie Medal and was a runner-up for the 1976 Guardian Award. It also received the Boston Glove-Horn Book Award for fiction in 1977 and was included on the *School Library Journal* "Best of the Best 1966–1978" list (December 1979). *Fathom Five* is the sequel to the book.

Devil on the Road was named an American Library Association Notable Book in 1979, and *The Wind Eye* was named an ALA Best Book for Young Adults in 1977.

Some of Westall's books, like *The Machine Gunners*, are realistic novels, and some, like *The Scarecrows*, have elements of the supernatural or fantasy. His latest book, *Break of Dark*, is a collection of his short stories.

SELECTED WORKS: The Machine Gunners, 1976; The Wind Eye, 1977; The Watch House, 1978; The Devil on the Road, 1979; Fathom Five, 1980; The Scarecrows, 1981; Break of Dark, 1982.

ABOUT: Contemporary Authors, Vol. 69–72; The International Authors and Writers Who's Who, 1982; Kirkpatrick, D. L., ed. Twentieth-Century Children's Writers; Something About the Author, Vol. 23; The Writers Directory 1982–84.

BRENDA WILKINSON

January 1, 1946–

AUTHOR OF *Ludell,* etc.

Biographical sketch of Brenda Wilkinson:

BRENDA WILKINSON was born in Moultrie, Georgia, but like the young heroine in her three "Ludell" novels, grew up in the small town of Waycross, Georgia. She was the second of eight children who "grew up not having all we wanted, but all we needed," with no television and with the Bible as just about the only book available. Wilkinson's mother had high expectations for her children, and Brenda knew she would leave Waycross after high school. She traveled north to stay with relatives, attended Hunter College in New York City, and soon had her first short story published in *We Be Word Sorcerers,* an anthology edited by Sonia Sanchez. Wilkinson said, "I started writing . . . out of a personal need. . . . I'm a product of the last of the southern segregated schools and I'm trying to rebuild them in print, so my younger sisters and brothers can see the joy we had in *our* schools, and in general give a picture of growing up during the fifties in Georgia."

She was discovered by the editors of Harper and Row while she was reading her poetry at a publication party of an anthology of black poets. In 1975 Harper and Row published her first novel, *Ludell*. It is the story of Ludell Wilson, a strong and adventurous black girl growing up in a small Georgia town in the mid–1950s. An unusually fine first book, *Ludell* continued a tradition of racial compassion and concern in black fiction. The critics praised it for its liveliness, warmth, and vivid atmosphere. *School Library Journal, Kirkus,* and *Booklist*

BRENDA WILKINSON

all gave it starred reviews. Addison Gayle, writing in *The Nation,* said: "Brenda Wilkinson's novel is a remarkable accomplishment and bears comparison with an earlier novel—[Richard Wright's] *Native Son.* Both [authors] write in the naturalistic idiom, though Wilkinson has the better eye for detail and is more proficient in handling dialogue. *Ludell* is alive with innocence, and it is highlighted by the love and care that each black person exhibits toward the other. *Ludell,* a novel of substance, suggests . . . that the black novel will return to an explication of the ethics and values which have assured black survival in this society." *Ludell* was included on the *School Library Journal* "Best of the Best, 1966–1978" list (December 1979) and was a nominee for a 1976 National Book Award.

In 1977 *Ludell and Willie* was published, a novel that continued the rich, warm story of Ludell Wilson into her teenage years— her first love and her emergence into adulthood. Again, Wilkinson won praise from critics. *School Library Journal* called *Ludell and Willie* "an appealing and upbeat novel . . . Ludell and Willie epitomize the buoyancy of young love and impart a contagious feeling of hope. Characters are developed

believably; their dialect (essential to the mood of the story) and interplay with one another and with the rigors of Black life in a small Georgia town before desegregation are portrayed with honesty, immediacy, warmth and humor." *Publishers Weekly* called it "A brilliant novel." *Ludell and Willie* was selected as one of the Outstanding Children's Books of the Year 1977 by the *New York Times,* and as a Best Book for Young Adults by the American Library Association in 1977.

In 1980, Wilkinson completed her trilogy with *Ludell's New York Time,* in which Ludell, now eighteen and still in love with— but miles away from—Willie, adjusts with difficulty to her new life in New York City. *Booklist* said of it, "[Ludell] radiates strength and purpose that set her sharply apart . . . readers of the earlier novels will feel fully comfortable with the by now familiar and forthright Ludell."

Wilkinson said of her Ludell books, "Having read so many books on urban experiences, I thought it about time someone told the story of rural black kids coming out of the pre-civil rights period." She likes to preserve the different voices and dialects of her childhood in her writing: "It's a way of saying to young people, 'You don't have to be exactly like everyone else.'"

Brenda Wilkinson is a member of the Authors Guild of the Authors League of America, P.E.N., and the Harlem Writers Guild. She is separated from her husband and lives in New York City with her two daughters, Lori and Kim.

SELECTED WORKS: Ludell, 1975; Ludell and Willie, 1977; Ludell's New York Time, 1980.

ABOUT: Contemporary Authors, Vol. 69–72; Something about the Author, Vol. 14; Black American Writers Past and Present.

NANCY WILLARD

June 26, 1936–

AUTHOR OF *A Visit to William Blake's Inn: Poems for Innocent and Experienced Travelers,* etc.

Biographical sketch of Nancy Willard:

NANCY WILLARD was born in Ann Arbor, Michigan. At the age of seven, she had her first poem published, and while still a child, she began creating miniature books. One of these, *A Child's Star,* which she wrote and illustrated while a high school senior, was published in the *Horn Book* in 1954. She wrote the *Horn Book* that at the time she created *A Child's Star* she had had no formal art training outside of high school classes, and that although she hoped to study art, her first love was writing. She had in fact already won several honors for her writing, including merit awards in the *Atlantic Monthly* Creative Writing Contest for high school students.

After receiving a B.A. in 1958 from the University of Michigan, where her father had taught, Willard went to Stanford University, where she earned an M.A. in medieval literature in 1960. She then returned to the University of Michigan and earned her Ph.D. in modern literature in 1963. While an undergraduate, she received five Jules and Avery Hopwood Awards in poetry and essays, and her doctoral dissertation on the poetry of Rainer Maria Rilke and William Carlos Williams was expanded and published in 1970 as *Testimony of the Invisible Man.*

Between 1966 and 1974, she wrote several volumes of poetry, including *Nineteen Masks for the Naked Poet* and *The Carpenter of the Sun,* and two collections of short stories, *The Lively Anatomy of God* and *Childhood of the Magician,* both for adults. Willard has received several awards for her poetry, among them the Devins Memorial Award in 1967, for *Skin of Grace,* the Creative Artists' Public Service Award, and a National Endowment for the Arts Award.

She was also the recipient of the O. Henry Award for best short story in 1970.

Her first book for children, *The Merry History of a Christmas Pie,* was published in 1974, followed shortly by *Sailing to Cythera and Other Anatole Stories,* illustrated by David McPhail, which won a 1977 Lewis Carroll Shelf Award and was the first of a trilogy of books. Her son, James Anatole, who was four at the time it was written, was the model for the hero. Willard then wrote several picture books and a novel, *The Highest Hit,* based on her own childhood. In 1975 *The Island of the Grass King: The Further Adventures of Anatole* was published; it was illustrated by David McPhail and won a 1979 Lewis Carroll Shelf Award. In 1981 two more picture books were published, *The Marzipan Moon* and *A Visit to William Blake's Inn: Poems for Innocent and Experienced Travelers,* which in 1982 became the first book of poetry to win the Newbery Medal. Illustrated by Alice and Martin Provensen, it was also a 1982 Caldecott Honor Book, the winner of the 1982 Boston Globe-Horn Book Award for Illustration, and a nominee for a 1982 American Book Award in the children's picture book category. It was also named a 1982 Children's Choice book by a joint committee of the International Reading Association and the Children's Book Council.

On writing, Nancy Willard said, "With children's books, as with adult books, writing is a matter of words and silence, of pounding the material into submission and letting go of it, of trying to finish so many pages a day while telling yourself you have all the time in the world. It's important to keep in mind the story you want to write. But it is even more important to forget it. . . . The writer not only gathers experience, he masters what is experienced.

"I believe that for most writers there are three kinds of stories. The first is the story which you choose to write and which you believe you understand. The second is the story which chooses you, and where it comes from you don't know, for the material seems to have been worked on out of your sight and hearing. The third is the story that starts out as the first kind and ends up as the second. What you know is changed into more than you know."

Besides being an author, Nancy Willard has studied art in Europe and Mexico. She is also interested in sewing and cooking, and in the making of crafts from soft sculptures to painted ceramics. Willard lives with her photographer husband and their son, who is an avid reader, in Poughkeepsie, New York, where she is a lecturer in the English department at Vassar. She has also been a visiting poet at Oberlin College and has taught at the Bread Loaf Writers Conference in Middlebury, Vermont.

SELECTED WORKS WRITTEN: The Merry History of a Christmas Pie: With a Delicious Description of a Christmas Soup, 1974; Sailing to Cythera and Other Anatole Stories, 1974; Simple Pictures Are Best, 1977; Stranger's Bread, 1977; The Highest Hit, 1978; The Island of the Grass King: The Further Adventures of Anatole, 1979; The Marzipan Moon, 1981; A Visit to William Blake's Inn: Poems for Innocent and Experienced Travelers, 1981; Uncle Terrible: More Adventures of Anatole, 1982.

SELECTED WORKS ILLUSTRATED: The Letter of John to James, by John Kater, 1981; Another Letter of John to James, by John Kater, 1982.

ABOUT: Burke, W. J. and Will D. Howe. American Authors and Books; Contemporary Authors, Vol. 89–92; Something About the Author, Vol. 30; Who's Who of American Women, 1977–1978; The Writers Directory 1982–84; Horn Book October 1980; August 1982.

VERA B. WILLIAMS

January 28, 1927–

AUTHOR AND ILLUSTRATOR OF *A Chair for My Mother*, etc.

Biographical sketch of Vera B. Williams

THOUGH she was born in 1927, Vera Williams did not publish her first children's book until 1975. She brought to this new career many years of experience as a poet, graphic designer, educator, and political organizer. (The last gave her the distinction of a month's detention in a federal penitentiary, the result of a peaceful demonstration at the Pentagon in 1981.)

Williams was born in California. She first discovered her artistic talent in 1933 at the Bronx House, a neighborhood center in New York City. There she acted, danced, and played baseball as well as created paintings. When Vera Williams was nine, one of her paintings, called "Yentas," was exhibited at a WPA show at the Museum of Modern Art. At the same time she also studied art with Florence Cane, who later included Vera, under the pseudonym "Linda," in her book *The Growth of the Child Through Art*.

After graduating from New York's High School of Music and Art (where she wrote and illustrated her first children's book), Williams attended the now-famous Black Mountain School in North Carolina. Black Mountain was an experimental institution where learning took place, often informally, as a community activity. Williams says "At Black Mountain, everything was education; hauling coal, discussing admissions, as well as analyzing Melville." She graduated in 1949 with a degree in graphic arts.

Vera B. Williams

After leaving Black Mountain, Vera Williams moved to Stony Point, New York, where she helped to found an "intentional community," the Gate Hill Cooperative; and an alternative school for children called the Collaberg School. Williams, her husband Paul (an architect), and their three children remained at Gate Hill until 1970, when she moved to Canada after a divorce.

Vera Williams has since explored a wide range of personal and political interests. She also undertook a 500-mile trip on the Yukon River, which later became the basis for her picture book, *Three Days on a River in a Red Canoe.* Much of her time has been devoted to the feminist and nuclear freeze movements. She believes that all her pursuits are part of the holistic development she learned at Black Mountain: "My avocations have always been the same as my vocations; art, parenting, teaching, food, nature, justice. *Three Days on a River* . . . isn't a social issue book but I feel that my devotion to a full life for women and to an unpolluted nature and to adventure for children are all in there somehow."

In 1982, *A Chair for My Mother,* written and illustrated by Vera Williams, was named a Caldecott Honor Book by the

American Library Association. The story about a girl named Rosa who saves her money to help buy a comfortable chair for her hard-working mother to rest in is based on an incident in Williams' life. What had been sad in fact—Vera's mother could only afford to buy a chair on the installment plan, and Vera did not understand why there was so little money for anything else—became a celebration in fiction when the jar full of small change is joyfully emptied to buy a beautiful chair. Williams says, "When I got the inspiration to make *A Chair for My Mother* I had the wonderful feeling that I now had the power, as a writer and an illustrator, to change the past into something I liked better and to make it as a kind of gift to my mother's memory."

In 1983, Williams followed *A Chair for My Mother* with another story about Rosa and her family, *Something Special for Me.* She intends a third book in the series, *Music, Music for Everyone,* to be published in 1984.

SELECTED WORKS WRITTEN AND ILLUSTRATED: It's a Gingerbread House: Bake It, Build It, Eat It!, 1978; The Great Watermelon Birthday, 1980; Three Days on a River in a Red Canoe, 1981; A Chair for My Mother, 1982; Something Special for Me, 1983.

SELECTED WORKS ILLUSTRATED: Hooray for Me!, by Remy Charlip and Lillian Moore, 1975; Ostrich Feathers, by Barbara Brenner, 1978.

PATRICIA WINDSOR

September 21, 1938–

AUTHOR OF *The Summer Before,* etc.

Autobiographical sketch of Patricia Windsor:

WHEN I WAS a child, I had two terrible habits: writing and reading. If I didn't have my nose stuck in a book, I was adding another title to the long list of novels I planned to write. By the time I was in high school, I had more than two hundred titles and I'd collected thirty-five rejection slips. I got

Patricia Windsor

into poetry then, read a lot of T. S. Eliot, kept a "stream-of-consciousness" journal and generally mooned around like an arty Bohemian.

I never thought of writing as a career. Instead, I wanted to be a dancer or actress (even though I was very shy). I went to college to study modern dance but when it came time to get a job, I found my writing skills more useful—as a magazine editor, copywriter, corporate news editor. I taught dance and kept thinking I'd write a great novel—someday.

I got married, had two children, and immersed myself in domesticity. I remained an avid reader. Herman Hesse, Edith Wharton, Janet Frame, Isaac Bashevis Singer—they went along with me to the playground and sandbox; I think these writers influenced me a great deal.

One day, somebody gave me something called a Young Adult novel. I'd never heard of such a thing. I expected it to read like Nancy Drew. What a surprise I got! Paul Zindel changed my mind. I decided to try a YA novel myself.

Using my high school journals and plenty of sad and happy memories, I wrote *The Summer Before*. It was published in 1973

and is still my best-selling book. A lot of me went into that book; maybe that's why it's so good (it has won three awards) and was so easy to write.

Since my first book, I've written five more YA's. I used a lot of my experiences in these books, but the writing process metamorphoses them into something quite different. I was born in New York City, grew up there, raised my children there, so you'll find New York in my books and stories. My son's temper tantrums gave me an idea for a book about a poltergeist and a haunted house. We were living in England at the time and the setting seemed perfect for *Home Is Where Your Feet Are Standing*. Memories of my grandfather and experience working for social service organizations helped form *Mad Martin*. My divorce became someone else's breakup in *Killing Time*.

I enjoy teaching people how to write as much as I do writing myself. I live in a one-hundred-year-old house (not haunted) and still have the same habits: writing and reading. Add to the list: skiing, horror movies, ghost stories, pizza, London, New York, and my dog (an Australian Shepherd).

I still plan hundreds of books I'll never have time to write. I'm both astonished and grateful that I can make a living doing something I love: making up stories!

———

Patricia Windsor attended Bennington College and Westchester Community College. In addition to the work she mentions, she also worked on the staff of *Mademoiselle* magazine. She is a member of P.E.N. and of the Authors Guild.

Her *Summer Before* was named a Best Book for Young Adults by the American Library Association in 1973 and has been translated into German and Norwegian. *Diving for Roses* was chosen as an Outstanding Children's Book of the Year 1976 by the *New York Times*. *Something's Waiting for You, Baker D.* has been published in Japan. Windsor's works reside in the Kerlan Collection at the University of Minnesota.

SELECTED WORKS: The Summer Before, 1973; Something's Waiting for You, Baker D., 1974; Home Is Where Your Feet Are Standing, 1975; Diving for Roses, 1976; Mad Martin, 1976; Killing Time, 1980.

ABOUT: Contemporary Authors, Vol. 49–52; (New Revision Series), Vol. 4; Something About the Author, Vol. 30; The Writers Directory 1982–84.

ELIZABETH WINTHROP

September 14, 1948–

AUTHOR OF *A Little Demonstration of Affection,* etc.

Autobiographical sketch of Elizabeth Winthrop Mahony:

I WAS BORN in Washington, D.C. in a big rambling house where I grew up with my five brothers. My father was a political columnist. I used to come home every day from school and hear the typewriter clacking away in his office, and I would think, now that sure looks like an easy job. My father tried to convince me that I was wrong, but it wasn't until I grew up and tried writing for a living that I realized how hard it really is to face that blank page in the typewriter every day.

I wrote my first story when I was twelve years old. Unfortunately, I left it on a bus, which upset me so much that I didn't write anything else for five years. My senior year in high school, I took a writing course and that started me off again.

I basically believe that writing is ten percent talent and ninety percent practice and perseverence. I try to write *something* every day even if it's just an entry in a journal or a letter to a friend.

I read constantly because I love it and also because books are a writer's road map. Sometimes I read a book twice, once for the sheer enjoyment of it and then again, to note how another writer might have handled a scene or a transition.

Some of my favorite authors are Charles Dickens, Anne Tyler, Rumer Godden, and Edith Wharton. Of all the elements in fiction, character is most important to me. I have to be able to see clearly where my people live, so I often use places that I know well. The farm in *Walking Away,* for example, was modeled after a house in Maryland where I spent summers as a child and where my brothers and I really did fish from inner tubes floating around in the pond and smoke cigarettes secretly (we thought) behind the haystack in the barn.

Balancing my two roles as a mother and a writer is the hardest thing I have ever tried to do. I spend the beginning of every day getting my children off to school, reminding them about show-and-tell day, finding sneakers under beds, and braiding hair. Then I march upstairs to my attic office where my characters are sitting around waiting for me to tell *them* what to do. It's exhausting to be in charge of so many people!

———

Elizabeth Winthrop graduated from Miss Porter's School in Farmington, Connecticut and went on to earn her B.A. from Sarah Lawrence College in 1970. She worked as an assistant editor in the children's book department at Harper and Row from 1971 to 1973, when she left to write full time. In 1970, she married Peter Mahony, an urban planner, and they have two children, Eliza and Andrew.

Winthrop has written books for all ages. Two of her teenage novels, *A Little Demonstration of Affection* and *Knock, Knock, Who's There?* were named Best Books for Young Adults by the American Library Association, in 1975 and 1978 respectively. *A Little Demonstration of Affection* was included on the American Library Association's list of young adult books published between 1960 and 1975, "The Best of the Best," as well as on the *School Library Journal* list, "Best of the Best 1966–1978" (December 1979).

SELECTED WORKS: Bunk Beds, 1972; Walking Away, 1973; A Little Demonstration of Affection, 1975; Knock, Knock, Who's There?, 1978; Journey to the Bright Kingdom, 1979; Are You Sad, Mama?, 1979; I Think He Likes Me, 1980; Marathon Miranda, 1979; Miranda in the Middle, 1980; Sloppy Kisses, 1980.

ABOUT: Contemporary Authors (First Revision), Vol. 41–44; Something About the Author, Vol. 8.

DAVID WISEMAN

January 13, 1916–

AUTHOR OF *Jeremy Visick,* etc.

Autobiographical sketch of David Wiseman:

I CANNOT help writing. Writing is both a release and an obsession. When anything stops me writing (the need to eat, say), I feel miserable. My wife puts up with this state, and—since she feels about gardening as I do about writing—she sympathises with me.

From where I work, in my study, I can look down onto the garden and see my wife digging. I ought to feel guilty, I suppose, but I don't.

I write every morning for about four hours—and spend the rest of the day (and night) thinking about writing.

Writing was always an important part of my school work. At Manchester Grammar School the writing of several essays a week seemed to be taken for granted, mostly on literary criticism or on historical subjects. I found myself enjoying most those rare occasions when the subject given to us appealed to the imagination. I still remember being set a topic, "The End of the World," and recall what I wrote. One day I shall expand it into a novel.

After school I studied history at Manchester University. I took part in every aspect of University life and enjoyed every moment. It was there I met Cicely, my wife-to-be.

My next years were taken up by service in H.M. [His Majesty's] Forces, in Basutoland and Bechuanal (now Lesotho and Botswana), and in Egypt and in Germany. After the war I worked for some years in adult education, being editor of *The Journal of Adult Education.*

In 1952 I turned to school teaching, and from then until 1975 worked, first as a teacher, then for sixteen years as principal of high schools, in Yorkshire and in Cornwall. In 1975 I became responsible for the In-Service Education of Teachers in Cornwall. At the beginning of 1978 I gave up this work to become a writer, yielding to my instincts at last!

Although I now live in Yorkshire, most of the last thirty years have been spent in Cornwall, that part of Britain famed for its association with King Arthur and with Tristan and Isolda. It is a land of charm and legend, but to me its most interesting stories are to be found in the lives of its miners— men, women, and children—who produced copper and tin for the world until the 1870s. It is from this experience that the story of *Jeremy Visick* arose. And the same background enters into an adult novel I am writing.

I regard myself as a professional writer, and am learning all the time. My second book, *Thimbles,* has a historical theme at its core, but, though I am fascinated by history and its puzzles, I write of other themes with equal pleasure.

At the end of the street where I lived as a boy there stood a large red-brick building. It was a branch of the Manchester Public Library. I remember how the books were arranged into children's and adults' sections, and how the library assistants allowed me, when I was ten, to borrow books from the adult shelves. I remember changing books every day, for I read at least one book a day. I thought books—and libraries— were things of magic, and I still do. I hope that I can add something to that magic.

I am still learning my trade. I have drawn on only the smallest part of my experience so far, so I am sure there are many more books to come. I only hope they will be as well liked as was *Jeremy Visick.* I was flattered by a review in the English paper, *The Guardian,* in which the reviewer described me as "a writer to watch." I felt like a young man at the beginning of a career. And that, in fact, is what I am, a young man at the beginning of his career, now drawing upon rich years of living.

My wife and I have four children who now live as far apart as Munich in Germany, Yorkshire in Britain, and Atlanta, Georgia, and White Plains, New York. Our eight grandchildren keep us happily in touch with the world of the child. Two of my books, to be published within the next couple of years, were written as birthday gifts for the two oldest grandchildren.

———

David Wiseman's three books for children all contain elements of fantasy. His first, *Jeremy Visick,* was named an American Library Association Notable Book for 1981 and a Children's Choice book for 1982 by the joint committee of the International Reading Association and the Children's Book Council. It was also named 1981 Notable Trade Book in the Field of Social Studies by the joint committee of the National Council for the Social Studies and the C.B.C. *Thimbles* was named an ALA Notable Book for 1982.

SELECTED WORKS: Jeremy Visick, 1981; Thimbles, 1982; Blowden and the Guardians, 1983.

BERNARD WOLF

February 26, 1930–

AUTHOR AND PHOTOGRAPHER OF *Anna's Silent World,* etc.

Autobiographical sketch of Bernard Wolf:

I WAS BORN in New York City. I was a professional singer at the age of eight, singing in choirs. When I was a little boy I used to pray before getting into bed every night. One of my prayers was, "Please, God, one day let me sing on the stage of the Metropolitan Opera Company." I kept up my singing through high school, when I sang for several years on Rainbow House, a weekly radio program for the Mutual Broadcasting System. Music was not my only interest as a child and as an adolescent; I had ability in many areas. Art was a very important part of my life; I spent practically all my free time at the Metropolitan Museum of Art or the Museum of Modern Art

Bernard Wolf

when I was a kid. The theater was also very important to me.

I attended the High School of Music and Art, where I had a genius of a teacher who inspired me. She taught me Spanish, and this gift, this knowledge of foreign languages—Spanish and French—has helped me in my work around the world.

When I was eighteen, after graduating from high school, I contracted pleurisy. I was shipped off to Denver to a TB sanitorium for a year. At first I regarded this as an adventure, and the stopover in Chicago turned out to be one of the most terrific days I've ever spent, because I spent the afternoon in the Chicago Opera House; I just blithely walked in, and there was the Chicago Symphony Orchestra in the midst of rehearsal. I took a seat in the front row, right behind the conductor's podium, and after a while, the conductor asked my advice: "How do you think it went?" I told him! He thanked me and shook my hand, and I caught my train.

Denver was nice: a quiet, sleepy town. I was much too restless to be flat on my back in bed all the time, and I was allowed to go off on furlough to see the surrounding countryside. I had been seriously involved

with photography since the age of sixteen, and I took pictures not only of scenery, but of the very, very young children who had fatal types of tuberculosis. To this day, they remain some of the most painful pictures I have ever taken. A year after I arrived, the director sent me home, fat as a horse from inactivity.

My first job after that was as interlocutor and M.C. for a marionette company that traveled through the South and Texas. I took photographs as I went. After that trip, I began taking pictures of dancers and performers at the 92nd Street YMHC. I missed being active in music, and at one point, on a voice scholarship to the Mannes College of Music in New York City, I studied with a wonderful old Italian man in the field of opera. I just did not have an operatic voice, however. I also spent a lot of time researching and playing folk music, and mastered the granddaddy of all keyboard instruments, the lute. The point is, in my twenties I was constantly in conflict with myself and tormented with trying to make a choice, selecting one thing to concentrate all my talent and energy and effort and time on. That was the hardest decision for me to make in my entire life.

There came a point when I decided I had to earn a living. I worked for some furniture manufacturers, and became an interior designer. I made an awful lot of money for my employers and got very little thanks or remuneration for it. Then I decided, well, this is it. If it kills me I'm going to work for myself and be my own boss, one way or another. If I starve, let it be; but I am never going to have any other human being stand over my back telling me how I should employ my time or talent.

I then started working independently as an interior designer. When I discovered that professional photographers were getting a lot of money taking pictures of interior design, I began photographing my own work, which led to more work in photography. Some of my pictures were published in *House Beautiful*. Then I began getting travel assignments, and to this day that really is my favorite kind of assignment. I have worked in Madeira, Athens, Ceylon, Singapore, Thailand, Hong Kong, Macau, and Japan. I just love doing travel photography, and I don't think there's anybody in the world who does it as well as I do. My work has been in *Travel and Camera, Camera 35, Fortune,* and *New York Magazine.*

I began doing books for children when I was in Ecuador, shooting an annual report. I had an idea about doing a book on an Indian boy somewhere in the Andes. I knew that children's books utilized photographs, but didn't think they did it very effectively. Kids are hep. They are too smart to look at life through rosy-tinted glasses. They watch television, see all kinds of stuff, hear all kinds of language; but in schools and at home they're not exposed to anything beyond their own little "piece of pie." I thought of doing a book on kids in other countries, with no nonsense, no exaggerating. The result was my first book, *The Little Weaver of Agato.* The story evolved by itself and that's how my books take shape. You're dealing with real people and real-life situations. It would be foolish to try to manipulate circumstances to your convenience, and sometimes virtually impossible. I have set up shots when an event had already taken place and I felt called upon to try to recreate a scene that was needed. I did it, and effectively, I think, because I told the people involved to relive and rethink the experience. It's always worked.

I try to take spontaneous pictures. I tell the subjects, "make believe I'm not here. I'm invisible." After a while, they forget about me.

I've had ten books published, one is in production, and I'm shooting another. I've had some fine editors, and I don't have any ego problems about suggestions from the designer and the editor. The working relationship should be a collaboration, like a marriage, with both partners wanting the book to look great, to be great. Far more than I think I would in working on adult books, I enjoy the freedom of expression in working on books for children.

———

Bernard Wolf was married in 1969 and lives in New York City with his wife and his son Michael, who was born in 1974. Michael and his mother are the subjects of *Michael and the Dentist.*

Connie's New Eyes was selected for the *School Library Journal* "Best of the Best 1966–1978" list (December 1979). In 1976 it was named a Notable Children's Trade Book in the Field of Social Studies by the joint committee of the National Council for the Social Studies and the Children's Book Council, as was *Adam Smith Goes to School,* in 1978.

Don't Feel Sorry for Paul was named a Children's Choice book for 1975 by a joint committee of the International Reading Association and the C.B.C. *Anna's Silent World* was named a Notable Book of 1977 by the American Library Association and an International Year of the Child Honor Book by the International Board on Books for Young People.

SELECTED WORKS: The Little Weaver of Agato: A Visit with an Indian Boy Living in the Andes Mountains of Ecuador, 1969; Tinker and the Medicine Man: The Story of a Navajo Boy of Monument Valley, 1973; Don't Feel Sorry for Paul, 1974; Connie's New Eyes, 1976; Anna's Silent World, 1977; Adam Smith Goes to School, 1978; In This Proud Land: The Story of a Mexican American Family, 1978; Michael and the Dentist, 1980; Firehouse, 1983.

HILMA WOLITZER

January 25, 1930–

AUTHOR OF *Introducing Shirley Braverman,* etc.

Autobiographical sketch of Hilma Wolitzer:

THE FIRST THING I ever had published was a poem about winter in *The Junior In-*

Wolitzer: *WAL let sir*

Thomas Victor

Hilma Wolitzer

spectors Club Journal, sponsored by the New York City Department of Sanitation. I was ten years old. My mother took me downtown to get a certificate and I remember that the streets were lined with garbage trucks. They made the occasion seem official, and I was thrilled. Despite this early success, and the fact that I was the kind of kid who read *everything*—the dictionary, my mother's home medical advisor, cereal boxes at breakfast, shampoo bottles in the bathtub—I was really a late bloomer. Aside from some adolescent poetry, the next thing I published was a short story in the old *Saturday Evening Post,* and I was thirty-five by then. This time I was hooked, and I've been writing ever since.

I don't know why I started writing when I did, but I'm very glad. It's brought many pleasures: travel for readings and teaching (including a trip to Alaska), wonderful new friends, and the joy of the work itself. I still read a great deal, but my selection is less arbitrary. Among the authors I admire most are Virginia Woolf, Nathanael West, E. B. White, George Eliot, and the poets Randall Jarrell and Elizabeth Bishop.

In my own writing I care most about the characters and about the use of language.

Characters I care about seem to find their own plots, and wake me in the middle of the night to tell their stories. When that happens the work goes very quickly, in a pretty regular flow. I agree with Flannery O'Connor (another favorite writer), who didn't feel that writing is a lonely occupation. It's the time directly after finishing a book that I feel somewhat bereft and lonely for the characters whose stories are finished. Writing a sequel is a temptation to which I've not yet succumbed.

Between novels I keep busy writing short stories, occasional poems, book reviews, and television scripts, and teaching fiction workshops at various universities.

When I switch from writing a novel for adults to one for younger readers, the main change is in the sensibility of the major character. There is no conscious effort on my part to simplify language or story, only to be faithful to what the protagonist might honestly think or feel. Letters from readers, and particularly those from children, who feel connected to the characters and their experience, are very gratifying.

I think that *all* experience, real or imagined, ordinary or extraordinary, is useful to a writer. Even when a novelist is not deliberately autobiographical, part of oneself is inevitable in the work. The real challenge, to my mind, is to imagine the lives of others, and to find a satisfying mix of truth and invention.

———

Hilma Wolitzer was born and raised in Brooklyn. She attended the Brooklyn Museum Art School, Brooklyn College, and the New School for Social Research. She was married in 1952 and has two children.

She has written novels for adults, such as *Hearts,* in 1980. Her short stories have appeared in *Esquire, Ms., New American Review, and The Saturday Evening Post.* She was on the staff of the Bread Loaf Writers Conference of Middlebury College from 1975 to 1982. She has been Visiting Lecturer in Fiction Writing at the University of

Iowa Writers Workshop in 1978 and 1979 and has also been Adjunct Professor at Columbia University, Hurst Professor at Washington University in St. Louis, and Distinguished Writer in Residence at Wichita State University in Kansas.

She was a Guggenheim Fellow (1976–1977) and a Bread Loaf Scholar in Fiction (1970) among other fellowships she has received. She received the American Academy and Institute of Arts and Letters Achievement in Literature Award in 1981. Hilma Wolitzer lives in a Long Island suburb. She is a member of P.E.N. and of the Authors Guild.

SELECTED WORKS: Introducing Shirley Braverman, 1975; Out of Love, 1976; Toby Lived Here, 1978.

ABOUT: Contemporary Authors, Vol. 65–68; The Writers Directory 1982–84; Publishers Weekly July 17, 1978.

Diane Wolkstein

DIANE WOLKSTEIN

November 11, 1942–

AUTHOR OF *The Magic Orange Tree and Other Haitian Folktales,* etc.

Autobiographical sketch of Diane Wolkstein:

WHEN I WAS seven and eight, I remember my mother used to sit on my bed at night and tell me funny stories about what Martin, my younger brother, said to his two-year-old sweetheart in the sandbox during the day. By nine and ten, I was reading my own stories and can remember lying on my bed looking out at the trees and leaves and the wind blowing the branches and wondering which was more wonderful—the movement of the trees or the life of the people in the stories I was reading. I remember the books that made me cry were the ones I liked the most.

Later when I was in college I went to foreign films on weekends and experienced the same amazement and delight at the beauty and emotion of many of the films. I also wanted to re-create for others the thrill of feeling alive, but I didn't know how I could or would do it.

After college I traveled to Europe and acted and taught English and studied pantomime in Paris. When I returned to the United States I taught fifth grade and my students called me "the gym teacher" because I told so many stories and played "games" with them most of the day. Each morning I would read them a chapter of *The Odyssey,* which made me look forward to going to school every day to find out what would happen next in the story.

In the summer of 1967 I got a job telling stories in the parks throughout New York City. I sang and danced and used pantomime and loved to make children laugh. I also liked to tell stories where the audience could join in. From that summer I understood that telling stories combined the many things I loved, and what I had wanted most to do: to feel and share with others the incredibleness of being alive.

Out of the stories I told came the books I began to write. Whichever stories children and adults would ask to hear again and again, those were the ones I decided to put into book form so that other children could also "hear" them. From the first time I told the story, "The Magic Orange Tree," children and adults asked and wondered at it. I submitted it to four different publishers, but they all said, "Forget it, it's too violent." To me, it was filled with life and hope. What can be more amazing than the birth of a tree? The sprouting, the forming of the branches, the blossoms, the fruit? I resubmitted the story to the first publisher, combining it with other stories I had heard when I traveled to Haiti; at last, the book, *The Magic Orange Tree and Other Haitian Folktales,* was published. In the book are not only folktales but also my adventures with my daughter Rachel in Haiti and the stories of my finding and listening to the Haitian folktales. In Haiti, stories are told in the evenings outside the houses, often under the full moon. The Haitian storyteller always begins her story with the word, *"cric?"* (pronounced "creek"), which means "ready for a story?" Sometimes I would listen to the storytellers; other times I would listen to the sounds of the Haitian night: Babies crying, frogs croaking, crickets, goats, roosters, dogs, donkeys crying out in turn, or all calling out at the same moment. Again, I was caught in amazement, going back and forth between the wonder of humans creating and the universe speaking.

Two of my stories, *White Wave* and *The Magic Wings,* also have this same connection between the human being and nature. In *White Wave,* a young man finds a white stone that turns into a shell and then into a goddess who speaks. In *The Magic Wings,* a young girl watches the first spring flowers pop up out of the earth. I especially like the end of *The Magic Wings* when the girl calls to the flowers, "It's spring," and they all call back to her.

Part of what's wonderful about stories is the excitement and suspense of not knowing what will happen next. I don't know either what will happen to me next in my life or what stories I will choose to tell or write. I do know one thing though. Tonight, at nine o'clock, my daughter Rachel will ask for a story, and I had better be ready. *Cric?*

———

Diane Wolkstein received her B.A. degree from Smith College in 1964 and an M.A. in childhood education from the Bank Street College of Education in 1967. She was married in 1969, and her daughter was born in 1971.

An internationally known storyteller, Diane Wolkstein received a George C. Marshall Memorial Fellowship from the American-Scandinavian Foundation to travel to Denmark, in 1969, to visit castles that Hans Christian Andersen stayed in and to see the landscapes of many of Andersen's story settings. She then toured twenty American cities in 1976 and 1977, telling stories to adults. She had a radio show on WNYC in New York and has been an instructor in storytelling at the Bank Street College of Education; she teaches mythology at the New School for Social Research in New York. Wolkstein is often a guest storyteller at storytelling festivals throughout the U.S. and gives workshops on the art of storytelling. She now directs the storytelling that takes place every Saturday morning, from May to September, at the Hans Christian Andersen statue in New York's Central Park, which has been going on for eighteen years. She has made four recordings of Hans Christian Andersen stories and has also recorded stories for Canadian Broadcasting Corporation radio and TV. Articles by Diane Wolkstein have appeared in *The Wilson Library Bulletin, School Library Journal, Children's Literature in Education,* and *Parabola.*

White Wave, which was illustrated by Ed Young, was included in the 1980 American Institute of Graphic Arts show and was named a Notable Book by the American Library Association. *The Red Lion* was in the 1977 A.I.G.A. show and was named a 1977 Notable Children's Trade Book in the Field of Social Studies by the joint committee of the National Council for the Social Studies and the Children's Book Council. Two of

Wolkstein's books were given honorable mention in the New York Academy of Sciences Children's Science Book Awards, *8,000 Stones* in 1973 and *The Magic Orange Tree* in 1978. *The Magic Orange Tree* was also an ALA Notable Book, in 1978.

SELECTED WORKS: 8,000 Stones, 1972; The Cool Ride in the Sky, 1973; Lazy Stories, 1976; Squirrel's Song: A Hopi Indian Tale, 1976; The Red Lion: A Persian Story, 1977; The Visit, 1977; The Magic Orange Tree and Other Haitian Folktales, 1978; White Wave: A Tao Tale from China, 1979; The Banza: A Haitian Story, 1981; The Magic Wings, 1983.

ABOUT: Contemporary Authors (First Revision), Vol. 37–40; Something About the Author, Vol. 7; Who's Who of American Women, 1975–1976.

VALERIE WORTH

October 29, 1933–

AUTHOR OF *Small Poems,* etc.

Autobiographical sketch of Valerie Worth Bahlke:

AS A CHILD, I preferred reading and writing to everything else, and I still feel much the same way. I was also greatly attracted to "smallness," perhaps because throughout grade school I myself was the smallest in my class. My favorite fairy tale was "Catskin," about the princess given three ball gowns—one like the sun, one like the moon, and one like the stars—packed up in a walnut shell; and the idea of such magnificence hidden inside so plain and tiny a thing not only fascinates me still, but also has served as a model for many of my poems.

My first home was in a college town blessed with acres of fields and gardens and woods, which I spent a lot of time exploring, either just looking at things or bringing them home to savor—stones, dead mice, flowers, feathers, globs of road tar, insects, bits of broken glass—even the most ordinary appearing to me wonderfully significant, or mysterious, or both. I have tried to reproduce this response in my poetry, as well as to continue observing the world as I did then; in fact, writing poetry has in itself helped me to remember and retain that way of seeing.

Meanwhile, I have lived in a number of different places, even for a year or so in India, and everywhere I have discovered new interests and experiences and phenomena to write about, whether in poetry or in fiction. Still, through all times and places and changes, I seem to have remained essentially the same person I was to begin with, and this is surely one reason why most of my books have been written for the young.

On the other hand, I have recently been writing more extensively about old age, perceiving in it much the same quality as in childhood, a kind of wisdom in isolation, as opposed to the greater responsibility and distraction of one's middle years; and I would hope, given the chance, to find at the end of my own lifetime my original vision intact and even brought full circle, completed as well as preserved.

———

Valerie Worth was born in Philadelphia. She was graduated from Swarthmore College in 1955 and attended schools in Tampa, Florida, and Bangalore, India. She was married in 1955, and her three children were born in 1958, 1964, and 1966. From 1956 to 1958, Worth worked in the promotion department of Yale University Press. She has lived in Chicago, New Haven, Fredericksburg, Virginia, and Middlebury, Vermont, and now lives in Clinton, New York.

Worth's poems have been published in a collection for adults, *The Crone's Book of Words* (1971), and anthologized in *New World Writing, No. 7* and in *Best Poems of 1961–1963*. They have been published in magazines such as *Harper's, Gnostica,* and *New Letters.*

Two of her books have been named Notable Books by the American Library Association, *More Small Poems* in 1976 and *Still More Small Poems* in 1978. Valerie Worth has written one novel for adults, and is working on her first novel for children.

SELECTED WORKS: Small Poems, 1972; More Small Poems, 1976; Still More Small Poems, 1978; Curlicues: The Fortunes of Two Pug Dogs, 1980.

ABOUT: Something About the Author, Vol. 8; (as Valerie Worth Bahlke) Contemporary Authors (First Revision), Vol. 41–44.

LAURENCE YEP

June 14, 1948–

AUTHOR OF *Dragonwings,* etc.

Biographical sketch of Laurence Michael Yep:

LAURENCE YEP was born in San Francisco, California, where his father and mother lived and ran a small grocery in a predominately black neighborhood. Attending parochial school in San Francisco's Chinatown, Laurence felt like an outsider because he spoke no Chinese.

In high school, when he first came face to face with white American culture, he also discovered science fiction, which

LAURENCE YEP

seemed to speak to him of his own experiences. Influenced by the genre, he began to write short stories, and at age eighteen, while a freshman at Marquette University, he became a published writer. He was paid a penny a word for a story.

Yep transferred to the University of California at Santa Cruz and later completed his education at the State University of New York in Buffalo, where he earned a doctorate in English in 1975.

When a friend at a major New York City publishing house encouraged him to try writing a science fiction novel for children, the result was *Sweetwater,* the story of Tyree, who is a descendant of the early colonists sent from Earth to inhabit the star Harmony. *Dragonwings* is the novel for which Yep is perhaps best known; published in 1975, it was a Newbery Honor Book. Its setting is early twentieth-century San Francisco. In this novel Yep has woven Chinese tradition and legend gracefully into a narrative based on a true story of Fong Joe Guey, who built and flew an airplane in the Oakland hills in 1909. The tale is told by Young Moon Shadow, who has left China to join his father Windrider in California, in order to share his dream of flying.

The *New York Times* called *Dragonwings* "an exquisitely written poem of praise to the courage and ingenuity of the Chinese-American people . . . a triumph."

Dragonwings was chosen a Notable Children's Book of 1975 by the American Library Association, was on the "Best of the Best 1966–1978" list of the *School Library Journal* (December 1979), won a Lewis Carroll Shelf Award in 1979, and earned for its author the International Reading Association's Children's Book Award. It also won the 1976 Carter G. Woodson Book Award.

Child of the Owl was published two years later. It is based on an entirely different Chinatown, the Chinatown of the 1960s. The main character is twelve-year-old Casey, a Chinese-American girl who has been raised outside of Chinatown. When her father is hospitalized, she goes to stay with her grandmother in Chinatown, where she faces her ethnic heritage for the first time. The reviews were again enthusiastic, and *Child of the Owl* won the 1977 Boston Globe-Horn Book Fiction Award and the Jane Addams Children's Book Award of 1978. An adult novel, *Seademons,* was also published in 1977.

Chinatown, also figured largely in Yep's next novel for children, *Sea Glass.* Twelve-year-old Craig Chin, whose family has recently moved to the suburbs, misses his old home.

In 1982, Yep made a successful departure from Chinese-American themes into the world of teenage romance, in *Kind Hearts and Gentle Monsters.* Published in the same year, *Dragon of the Lost Sea,* is a fantasy based on traditional Chinese legend.

Laurence Yep lives in Sunnyvale, California, not far from San Francisco. He continues to write for both children and adults.

SELECTED WORKS: Sweetwater, 1973; Dragonwings, 1975; Child of the Owl, 1977; Sea Glass, 1979; Dragon of the Lost Sea, 1982; Kind Hearts and Gentle Monsters, 1982.

ABOUT: Contemporary Authors, Vol. 49–52; (New Revision Series), Vol. 1; Something About the Author, Vol. 7; Who's Who in America, 1982–1983.

CAROL BEACH YORK

January 21, 1928–

AUTHOR OF *I Will Make You Disappear,* etc.

Autobiographical sketch of Carol Beach York:

I STARTED WRITING as soon as I learned to write, and long before I learned to spell. I was about seven years old. I wrote poems and short stories in spiral-bound notebooks I bought at the local Woolworth's store.

My mother was my only reader, but she was an enthusiastic reader, and she gave me much inspiration and encouragement in the years that followed. I finally did learn to spell (most words), and finally, with published books, I had more readers than my mother.

As an adult writer, I began with short stories. I think this is a good way to begin. If the stories are short enough, you can finish before you get discouraged and give up.

But as time went by and I began to write books, I found that I liked this longer form of writing by far the best. It's fun to roll a sheet of crisp white paper into the typewriter and type out CHAPTER FIVE. Wonderful things seem about to happen, just as you type the chapter number.

People often ask where I get the ideas for my books. In some cases I have of course gotten ideas from my own life and from people I've known. When my daughter Diana was growing up, I got ideas from the things she did. My book *The Blue Umbrella* is all about Diana.

But I've written quite a few mystery, suspense, and supernatural stories, and for those I have not been able to use my own experiences. My life has no mysteries, no supernatural events. For those stories I just sit and think. When my head starts to hurt, I have thought enough for that day!

I hope to go on writing stories for many years to come.

––––––

CAROL BEACH YORK

Carol Beach York was born in Chicago and attended Thornton Junior College. She married in 1947 and her daughter was born in 1956. She is now divorced.

York's first story appeared in *Seventeen* magazine, and her short stories and nonfiction articles have also been published in *Family Circle* and other magazines. She lives in Chicago.

SELECTED WORKS: Where Love Begins, 1963; The Doll in the Bake Shop, 1965; Until We Fall In Love Again, 1967; The Christmas Dolls, 1967; The Blue Umbrella, 1968; The Ten O'Clock Club, 1970; The Tree House Mystery, 1973; The Midnight Ghost, 1974; I Will Make You Disappear, 1974; Nothing Ever Happens Here, 1975; The Witch Lady Mystery, 1976; Beware of This Shop, 1977; Revenge of the Dolls, 1979; Remember Me When I Am Dead, 1980; The Look-Alike Girl, 1980.

ABOUT: Contemporary Authors (First Revision), Vol. 3; (New Revision Series), Vol. 6; Foremost Women in Communications, 1970; Something About the Author, Vol. 6; Ward, Martha E. and Dorothy A. Marquardt. Authors of Books for Young People, 2nd edition (Supplement).

JANE BRESKIN ZALBEN

April 21, 1950–

AUTHOR AND ILLUSTRATOR OF *Basil and Hillary,* etc.

Autobiographical sketch of Jane Breskin Zalben:

IT IS DIFFICULT to verbalize what I do because I go in my studio, work, and sometimes I think another experience takes place, one that is different from the ordinary tasks of day-to-day living. Some of my happiest moments are when I am alone in front of that piece of parchment with a brush as thin as a wisp of hair, or at the typewriter "living" with the characters I have created out of nothing, whether they are animals or people. What happens to those characters, their feelings, emotions, how they relate to each other on a very basic human level, psychologically, is what interests me most: *that* is the story, whether it is for two-year-olds or fifteen-year-olds. It is odd, the rift in my work, because I enjoy illustrating fantasy, and writing about reality, which is why I have decided to put on different "hats" at times and be an author, or an artist, or both.

I began as a graphic designer in publishing after I graduated from college with a degree in painting and etching. I soon realized, after doing paste-ups and type spacing on other people's books, I'd much rather spend time doing my own. But I did learn how to become a book designer, which has enabled me to have complete control over the entire look of my work. I enjoy being involved in every stage of the process, from the first time the idea comes to when the book is bound. It's like waiting out the pregnancy until the delivery.

Since I was able to hold a crayon in my hand, I have never stopped being an artist. Children's books is a means for a fine artist to earn somewhat of a living. I remembered feeling amazed and excited that someone would pay me to sit in a room and draw. When I reached the turning point of thirty,

Jane Breskin Zalben

I began to consider I might want to say more than I had been, given the space of a thirty-two-page picture book. This isn't to say that an awful lot of very simple, direct language, pacing and rhythm of a picture book underlies a larger meaning, the old saying "less is more," but somehow, I emotionally needed another format for themes of friendship, anger, closeness I had been expressing for the younger audience. The time was ripe for me to delve into my work in a different way, since I was at home with two very small children of my own. I was exposed to a whole other well of feelings to explore besides my own childhood; I could now experience both sides: the child and the parent.

I think what is nicest about being an adult and a writer is having the distance to look back at pain and laugh, to chuckle with remembering what it really felt like growing up. I always identify with the child because I do *remember*. Maybe that is why I do children's books. There is a sense of honesty and truth in devoting my time to young people. It is special to be able to see the world through their eyes, even if it is a glimmer, and a hell of a lot of fun. Often when I wonder what I am doing because I don't earn

the kind of money I would like to, I sit back and smile at my typewriter at a funny line, or stare at an intricate detail on the drawing board and say to myself, this is why: the pleasure I get. And all I can do is keep trying!

———

Jane Breskin Zalben was born in New York City, where she attended the High School of Music and Art, graduating in 1967. She received a B.A. degree in art from Queens College in 1971, and did graduate work in lithography at Pratt Graphics Center in 1971 and 1972. She married in 1969 and has two young boys.

Zalben has worked in four New York publishing houses, including Scribners, where she was art director. She is now on the faculty of the School of Visual Arts, teaching the illustration, design, and writing of children's books, and she is also a free-lance type designer. Her work has been exhibited at the Metropolitan Museum of Art and at the Justin Schiller Gallery in New York. *All in the Woodland Early* was included in the 1980 American Institute of Graphic Arts show.

SELECTED WORKS WRITTEN AND ILLUSTRATED: Cecilia's Older Brother, 1973; Basil and Hillary, 1975; Penny and the Captain, 1977; Norton's Nighttime, 1979; Will You Count the Stars Without Me? 1979; "Oh, Simple!," 1981; Porcupines' Christmas Blues, 1982.

SELECTED WORKS WRITTEN: A Perfect Nose for Ralph, 1980; Maybe It Will Rain Tomorrow, 1982.

SELECTED WORKS ILLUSTRATED: An Invitation to the Butterfly Ball: A Counting Rhyme, by Jane Yolen, 1976; Jabberwocky, by Lewis Carroll, 1977; All in the Woodland Early: An ABC, by Jane Yolen, 1979.

ABOUT: Contemporary Authors, Vol. 49–52; (New Revision Series), Vol. 4; Kingman, Lee and others, comps. Illustrators of Children's Books: 1967–1976; Something About the Author, Vol. 7; The Writers Directory 1982–84.

PAUL ZINDEL

May 15, 1936–

Author of *The Pigman,* etc.

Biographical sketch of Paul Zindel:

BORN IN Staten Island, New York City, Paul Zindel never really knew his father, a New York City policeman who abandoned his family. Zindel's mother struggled to bring up Paul and his older sister, working as a hot-dog vendor, a shipyard laborer, a hat-check girl, a dog-breeder. As a licensed practical nurse, she also boarded a series of dying patients.

In an interview in *Top of the News,* Zindel said, "I felt worthless as a child and dared to speak and act my true feelings only in fantasy and secret." The family moved on the average of once or twice a year; but, hard as it was, each new neighborhood offered a new background to Zindel. As a solitary imaginative child he made puppets, ghost shows, and cycloramas. He did not read—there were no books in his home—and today he claims he writes for the people who don't like to read.

In his junior year he contracted tuberculosis and spent a year and a half in a sanatorium, the only young person in a world of adults. It was from this experience, as well as from his mother's patients, that Zindel drew his novel's medically based incidents. He remembers himself at this time, and at some later times in his life, as "drab, loveless and desperate."

Majoring in chemistry at Wagner College, he earned a B.S. in 1958 and an M.S. in 1959. (Later, Wagner awarded him an honorary doctorate.) He also took courses in creative writing at Wagner, where one of his teachers was the playwright Edward Albee. After working briefly as a technical writer for a chemical company, he spent ten years as a high school chemistry teacher, writing in his spare time.

His play *The Effect of Gamma Rays on Man-in-the-Moon Marigolds,* about a tormented family, was first produced in Hous-

PAUL ZINDEL

ton in 1965, opened Off-Broadway in 1970, and moved to Broadway in 1971, winning for Zindel a host of drama awards, including the Obie in 1970 for the Best American Play, and the prestigious Pulitzer Prize in 1971. "It was breathtaking," Zindel said of winning the Pulitzer. "I was immediately whisked out to Hollywood to work with Paul Newman and Barbra Streisand. It was all very preposterous, exciting, and corrupt—and fun and damning and useful."

Meanwhile Charlotte Zolotow, an editor, saw a TV version of *Marigolds* in 1966 and urged Zindel to write for teenagers. His first young adult novel, *The Pigman,* is about two alienated teenagers who take advantage of an old man. It was extraordinarily successful, and has sold over a million copies. It is listed as one of the Notable Children's Books of 1940–1970 by the American Library Association and as one of their Best of the Best Books for Young Adults (1975).

My Darling, My Hamburger; I Never Loved Your Mind; Pardon Me, You're Stepping on my Eyeball; The Undertaker's Gone Bananas; and *The Pigman's Legacy* were all named Outstanding Children's Books of the Year by the *New York Times Book Review. The Effect of Gamma Rays, Pardon Me, Confessions*

Zindel: *zin DELL*

of a Teenage Baboon, and *The Pigman's Legacy* were chosen as Best Books for Young Adults by the ALA in their years of publication. *The Effect of Gamma Rays* was also named a Notable Book of 1971 by the ALA.

These novels have been called "cruelly truthful about the human condition" by the *Horn Book* and praised for the candor, sensitivity, and humor with which they treat contemporary teenage concerns. They have also been controversial for their "bizarre" situations, unsympathetic portrayal of adults, and dramatic treatment of teenage crises.

Zindel draws on his experiences as a high school teacher, when many of his students—"usually the trouble-makers"—spoke openly to him about their problems and acts of rebellion. Mainly, however, he writes about himself. "I love the underdog and sympathize with his struggle because that's what I was and am in many ways still," he said in *Top of the News.* In writing each novel he tries to solve a personal problem. "*Confessions of a Teenage Baboon* is a story so close to me that I almost had a nervous breakdown writing it. I pushed myself too close to the inner demons which drive me." The teenage protagonists in *Pardon Me* and in *The Undertaker's Gone Bananas* are also based on his own experience.

Zindel has worked to overcome the effects of his unhappy childhood. He told *Publishers Weekly,* "I learned to quit nursing old wounds, to take joy in hard work, but never to push myself into trying the impossible." He wants his books to tell kids that "life can be sort of fun, but it isn't easy."

He enjoys movies and television, psychiatry, and dream interpretation. "I like all fattening foods, especially Hunan cuisine and ice cream. I like swimming, and struggle with tennis. I like new experiences and inventions and teenagers who desperately need someone to confide in."

At the age of thirty-seven Zindel married Bonnie Hildebrand, and they live in Manhattan with their two children, David and Elizabeth.

SELECTED WORKS: The Pigman, 1968; My Darling, My Hamburger, 1969; I Never Loved Your Mind, 1970; Pardon Me, You're Stepping on My Eyeball, 1976; Confessions of a Teenage Baboon, 1977; The Undertaker's Gone Bananas, 1978; The Pigman's Legacy, 1980; (with Bonnie Zindel) A Star for the Latecomer, 1980; The Girl Who Wanted a Boy, 1981; (with Crescent Dragonwagon) To Take a Dare, 1982.

ABOUT: Contemporary Authors, Vol. 73–76; Current Biography Yearbook, 1973; Kirkpatrick, D. L., ed. Twentieth-Century Children's Writers; Something About the Author, Vol. 16; Vinson, James, ed. Contemporary Dramatists, 1st edition; Ward, Martha E. and Dorothy A. Marquardt. Authors of Books for Young People, 2nd edition; Who's Who in America, 1982–1983; The Writers Directory 1982–84; English Journal October 1977; New York Times July 26, 1970; Publishers Weekly December 5, 1977; Time May 17, 1971; Top of the News Winter 1978.

Authors and Illustrators Included in This Series

The following list indicates the volume in which each individual may be found:

J—THE JUNIOR BOOK OF AUTHORS, second edition (1951)

M—MORE JUNIOR AUTHORS (1963)

3—THIRD BOOK OF JUNIOR AUTHORS (1972)

4—FOURTH BOOK OF JUNIOR AUTHORS AND ILLUSTRATORS (1978)

5—FIFTH BOOK OF JUNIOR AUTHORS AND ILLUSTRATORS (1983)

Camp, Walter—**J**

"Campbell, Bruce." *See* Epstein, Samuel—**M**

Carigiet, Alois—**3**

Carle, Eric—**4**

Carlson, Natalie Savage—**M**

Carpenter, Frances—**M**

Carr, Harriett H.—**M**

Carr, Mary Jane—**J**

Carrick, Carol—**4**

Carrick, Donald—**4**

Carrick, Valery—**J**

Carroll, Latrobe—**M**

Carroll, Ruth—**M**

Carter, Helene—**M**

Casserley, Anne—**J**

Caudill, Rebecca—**M**

Cavanah, Frances—**M**

Cavanna, Betty (Elizabeth Headley)—**M**

Chalmers, Mary—**3**

"Chambers, Catherine E." *See* Johnston, Norma—**5**

"Chance, Stephen." *See* Turner, Philip—**4**

"Chapman, Walker." *See* Silverberg, Robert—**3**

Chappell, Warren—**3**

"Charles, Nicholas." *See* Kuskin, Karla—**3**

Charlip, Remy—**3**

Charlot, Jean—**M**

"Chase, Alice Elizabeth." *See* McHargue, Georgess—**5**

Chase, Mary Ellen—**4**

Chase, Richard—**M**

Chastain, Madye Lee—**M**

Chauncy, Nan—**3**

Chen, Tony (Anthony Young Chen)—**5**

Childress, Alice—**5**

Chipperfield, Joseph E.—**M**

Chönz, Selina—**4**

Chorao, Kay (Ann McKay Sproat Chorao)—**4**

Chrisman, Arthur Bowie—**J**

"Christopher, John" (Samuel Youd)—**4**

Christopher, Matt(hew F.) ("Fredric Martin")—**5**

Church, Richard—**M**

Church, Alfred J.—**J**

Chute, B. J.—**M**

Chute, Marchette—**M**

Chwast, Jacqueline—**4**

Chwast, Seymour—**4**

Ciardi, John—**3**

Clapp, Patricia—**5**

"Clare, Helen." *See* Clarke, Pauline—**3**

Clark, Ann Nolan—**J**

Clark, Mavis Thorpe (Mavis Thorpe Clark Latham)—**4**

Clarke, Arthur C.—**M**

Clarke, Pauline ("Helen Clare") —**3**

Cleary, Beverly—**M**

Cleaver, Bill—**4**

Cleaver, Elizabeth—**4**

Cleaver, Vera—**4**

Clements, Bruce—**5**

Clifton, Lucille (Sayles)—**5**

Clymer, Eleanor ("Elizabeth Kinsey")—**4**

Coatsworth, Elizabeth—**J**

Cobb, Vicki—**5**

Cober, Alan E.—**4**

Coblentz, Catherine Cate—**J**

Cockshut, Gillian Elise Avery. *See* Avery, Gillian—**4**

Coggins, Jack—**M**

Cohen, Barbara—**5**

Cohen, Miriam—**5**

Colby, Carroll B.—**M**

Cole, Joanna—**5**

Cole, William—**4**

Collier, Christopher—**5**

Collier, James Lincoln ("Charles Williams")—**5**

"Collodi, C." (Carlo Lorenzini) —**J**

Colman, Hila ("Teresa Crayder") —**3**

Colum, Padraic—**J**

Cone, Molly ("Caroline More") —**3**

Conford, Ellen—**5**

Conklin, Gladys—**4**

Conly, Robert Leslie. *See* "O'Brien, Robert C."—**4**

Conroy, Robert. *See* Goldston, Robert Conroy—**4**

"Cook, John Estes." *See* Baum, L. Frank—**3**

Coolidge, Olivia E.—**M**

Coombs, Patricia—**5**

Cooney, Barbara—**M**

Cooper, Elizabeth K.—**4**

Cooper, Susan (Susan Mary Cooper Grant)—**4**

Corbett, Scott—**4**

Corbin, William (William Corbin McGraw)—**M**

Corcoran, Barbara ("Page Dixon," "Gail Hamilton")—**5**

Cormack, Maribelle—**J**

Cormier, Robert (Edmund)—**5**

Cosgrave, John O'Hara, II—**M**

Cosgrove, Margaret—**4**

Cottrell, Leonard—**4**

Craft, Ruth—**5**

Craig, M. Jean—**4**

Craig, Margaret Maze—**M**

Craig, Mary Francis. *See* Shura, Mary Francis—**3**

Crane, Walter—**J**

Crawford, Phyllis—**J**

"Crayder, Teresa." *See* Colman, Hila—**3**

Credle, Ellis—**J**

Cresswell, Helen (Helen Cresswell Rowe)—**4**

Crew, Fleming H. *See* Gall, Alice Crew—**J**

Crew, Helén Coale—**J**

Crews, Donald—**5**

Crichlow, Ernest—**4**

Crossley-Holland, Kevin—**4**

Crowell, Pers—**M**

Crownfield, Gertrude—**J**

Crump, Irving—**J**

Ctvrtek, Václav—**4**

Cuffari, Richard—**5**

Cullen, Countée—**4**

Cummings, Betty Sue—**5**

Cunningham, Julia—**3**

Curry, Jane Louise—**4**

Dahl, Borghild—**3**

Dahl, Roald—**3**

Dalgliesh, Alice—**J**

Daly, Maureen—**M**

Daniel, Hawthorne—**J**

Danziger, Paula—**5**

Daringer, Helen Fern—**M**

Darling, Louis—**M**

Daugherty, James—**J**

d'Aulaire, Edgar & Ingri Parin. *See* Aulaire, Edgar & Ingri Parin d'—**J**

Davies, Andrew (Wynford)—**5**

Davis, Julia (Julia Davis Adams) —**J**

Davis, Lavinia R.—**J**

Davis, Mary Gould—**J**

Davis, Robert—**J**

de Angeli, Marguerite—**J**

de Brunhoff, Jean. *See* Brunhoff, Jean de—**J**

de Brunhoff, Laurent. *See* Brunhoff, Laurent de—**M**

Degens, T.—**5**

de Groat, Diane (L.)—**5**

de Jong, Dola—**M**

DeJong, Meindert—**M**

De La Mare, Walter—**J**

de Leeuw, Adèle—**J**

de Leeuw, Cateau. *See* de Leeuw, Adèle—**J**

del Rey, Lester—**3**

Delton, Judy—**5**

"Delving, Michael." *See* Williams, Jay—**4**

Dennis, Morgan—**M**

Dennis, Wesley—**M**

Denslow, W. W. (William Wallace Denslow)—**4**

dePaola, Tomie (Thomas Anthony dePaola—**5**

de Regniers, Beatrice Schenk —**M**

de Saint-Exupéry, Antoine. *See* Saint-Exupéry, Antoine de—**4**

de Treviño, Elizabeth Borton. *See* Treviño, Elizabeth Borton de—**3**

Deucher, Sybil—**M**

Deutsch, Babette—**M**

Dewey, Ariane—**4**

Diamond, Donna—**5**
Dickinson, Peter—**4**
Dickson, Marguerite—**M**
Dillon, Eilís (Eilís Dillon O'Cuilleanain)—**3**
Dillon, Leo and Diane—**5**
Ditmars, Raymond L.—**J**
Dix, Beulah Marie—**J**
"Dixon, Page." *See* Corcoran, Barbara—**5**
Doane, Pelagie—**M**
Dolbier, Maurice—**M**
Domanska, Janina (Janina Domanska Laskowski)—**3**
Donovan, John—**5**
"Douglas, James McM." *See* Butterworth, W. E.—**5**
Dowden, Anne Ophelia (Todd)—**5**
Drummond, V. H.—**3**
"Drummond, Walter," *See* Silverberg, Robert—**3**
"Dryden, Pamela." *See* Johnston, Norma—**5**
du Bois, William Pène—**J**
Duggan, Alfred—**4**
du Jardin, Rosamond—**M**
Dulac, Edmund—**J**
Duncan, Norman—**J**
"Duncan, Lois" (Lois Steinmetz Arquette)—**5**
Dunlop, Agnes Mary Robertson. *See* "Kyle, Elisabeth"—**M**
Du Soe, Robert C.—**M**
Duval, Colette. *See* "Vivier, Colette"—**4**
Duvoisin, Roger—**J**

Eager, Edward—**M**
Earle, Olive L.—**M**
Eastman, Charles A.—**J**
Eaton, Jeanette—**J**
Eberle, Irmengarde—**J**
Eckert, Allan W.—**4**
Eckert, Horst. *See* "Janosch"—**4**
Edmonds, Walter Dumaux—**M**
Ehrlich, Bettina. *See* "Bettina" —**M**
Eichenberg, Fritz—**M**
Eipper, Paul—**J**
Elkin, Benjamin—**4**
Ellis, Ella (Thorp)—**5**
Ellsberg, Commander Edward —**J**
Elting, Mary ("Campbell Tatham")—**M**
Emberley, Barbara—**3**
Emberley, Ed—**3**
Emery, Ann—**M**
Engdahl, Sylvia Louise—**4**
Enright, Elizabeth—**J**
Epstein, Beryl Williams—**M**
Epstein, Samuel ("Adam Allen," "Bruce Campbell")—**M**
Erdman, Loula Grace—**M**
Estes, Eleanor—**J**
Ets, Marie Hall—**J**

Evans, Eva Knox—**M**
"Every, Philip Cochrane." *See* Burnford, Sheila—**4**
Eyerly, Jeannette (Hyde) ("Jeannette Griffith")—**5**
Eyre, Katherine Wigmore—**M**

Fabre, Jean-Henri—**J**
"Fall, Thomas" (Donald Clifford Snow)—**4**
Falls, C. B.—**J**
Farber, Norma—**5**
Farjeon, Eleanor—**J**
Farley, Carol ("Carol McDole")—**5**
Farley, Walter—**J**
Farmer, Penelope (Penelope Farmer Mockridge)—**4**
Fatio, Louise—**M**
Faulkner, Nancy (Anne Irvin Faulkner)—**4**
Feagles, Anita MacRae—**4**
Feelings, Muriel—**4**
Feelings, Tom—**3**
Felsen, Gregor—**J**
Felton, Harold W.—**M**
Fenton, Carroll Lane—**M**
Fenton, Edward—**3**
Fenton, Mildred Adams—**M**
Ferris, Helen—**J**
Field, Rachel—**J**
Fife, Dale—**4**
Fillmore, Parker—**J**
Fischer, Hans Erich—**M**
Fischtrom, Harvey and Margot Zemach. *See* Zemach, Harve and Margot—**3**
Fisher, Aileen—**M**
Fisher, Leonard Everett—**3**
Fitch, Florence Mary—**M**
"Fitzgerald, Captain Hugh." *See* Baum, L. Frank—**3**
Fitzgerald, John D(ennis)—**5**
Fitzhardinge, Joan Margaret. *See* "Phipson, Joan"— **3**
Fitzhugh, Louise—**3**
Flack, Marjorie—**J**
Fleischman, Sid—**3**
Fleischman, Paul (Taylor)—**5**
Fleming, Ian (Lancaster)—**5**
Floethe, Richard—**M**
Floherty, John J.—**J**
Flora, James—**3**
Folon, Colette Portal. *See* Portal, Colette—**4**
Forberg, Ati (Beate Gropius Forberg)—**4**
Forbes, Esther—**M**
Forman, James—**3**
Fortnum, Peggy (Margaret Emily Noel Nuttall-Smith)—**4**
Foster, Genevieve—**J**
Foster, Marian Curtis. *See* "Mariana"—**3**
Franchere, Ruth—**4**

Fox, Paula (Paula Fox Greenberg)—**4**
François, André—**3**
"Françoise" (Françoise Seignobosc)—**M**
Franklin, George Cory—**M**
Franklin, Madeleine. *See* "L'Engle, Madeleine"—**M**
Frascino, Edward—**5**
Frasconi, Antonio—**3**
Fraser, Claud Lovat—**J**
Freeman, Don—**M**
Freeman, Ira Maximilian—**M**
Freeman, Lydia—**M**
Freeman, Mae Blacker—**M**
French, Allen—**J**
"French, Paul." *See* Asimov, Isaac—**3**
Freschet, Berniece—**4**
Friedman, Frieda—**M**
Friermood, Elisabeth Hamilton —**M**
"Friis, Babbis." *See* Friis-Baastad, Babbis—**3**
Friis-Baastad, Babbis ("Eleanor Babbis," "Babbis Friis")—**3**
Fritz, Jean—**3**
Froman, Robert—**4**
Frost, Frances—**M**
Fry, Rosalie K.—**3**
Fuchs, Erich—**4**
Fujikawa, Gyo—**4**
Fyleman, Rose—**J**

Gackenbach, Dick—**5**
Gaer, Joseph—**M**
Gág, Flavia—**M**
Gág, Wanda—**J**
"Gage, Wilson" (Mary Q. Steele)—**3**
Galdone, Paul—**3**
Gall, Alice Crew—**J**
Gallant, Roy A(rthur)—**5**
Galt, Tom—**M**
Gammell, Stephen—**5**
Gannett, Ruth Chrisman—**M**
Gannett, Ruth Stiles (Ruth Stiles Gannett Kahn)—**4**
Gans, Roma—**5**
Gantos, John (Bryan)—**5**
Gardam, Jane—**5**
Garden, Nancy—**5**
Gardner, John (Champlin)—**5**
Garfield, Leon—**4**
Garner, Alan—**3**
Garnett, Eve (C. R.)—**5**
Garrett, Randall. *See* Silverberg, Robert—**3**
Garst, Shannon—**J**
Gates, Doris—**J**
Gatti, Attilio—**J**
Gauch, Patricia Lee—**5**
Gay, Zhenya—**M**
Geisel, Theodor Seuss. *See* "Seuss, Dr."—**M**

Levoy, Myron—**5**
Levy, Elizabeth—**5**
Lewellen, John—**M**
Lewis, C. S.—**M**
Lewis, Elizabeth Foreman—**J**
Lewiton, Mina—**M**
Lexau, Joan M. ("Joan L. Nodset")—**4**
Ley, Willy—**3**
Lifton, Betty Jean—**3**
Linde, Gunnel—**4**
Linderman, Frank B.—**J**
Lindgren, Astrid—**M**
Lindman, Maj—**J**
Lindquist, Jennie D.—**M**
Lindquist, Willis—**M**
Lingard, Joan—**5**
Lionni, Leo—**3**
Lipkind, William—**M**
Lippincott, Joseph Wharton—**M**
Lipsyte, Robert—**5**
Little, Jean—**4**
Lively, Penelope—**4**
Livingston, Myra Cohn—**4**
Lobel, Anita—**3**
Lobel, Arnold—**3**
Löfgren, Ulf—**4**
Lofting, Hugh—**J**
Longstreth, T. Morris—**M**
Lord, Beman (Harold Beman Lord)—**4**
"Lord, Nancy." See Titus, Eve —**3**
Lorenzini, Carlo. See "Collodi, C."—**J**
Lorraine, Walter—**4**
Lovelace, Maud Hart—**J**
Low, Joseph—**3**
Lownsbery, Eloise—**J**
Lowry, Lois—**5**
Lubell, Cecil—**4**
Lubell, Winifred—**4**
Lucas, Jannette May—**J**

Macaulay, David (Alexander)—**5**
"MacDonald, Golden." See Brown, Margaret Wise—**J**
MacGregor, Ellen—**M**
Mack, Stan (Stanley Mack)—**4**
Mackay, Constance D'Arcy—**J**
MacKinstry, Elizabeth—**M**
Mahony, Elizabeth Winthrop. See Winthrop, Elizabeth—**5**
Mahy, Margaret—**4**
Maitland, Antony—**4**
Malcolmson, Anne—**M**
Malkus, Alida Sims—**J**
Malvern, Corinne. See Malvern, Gladys—**J**
Malvern, Gladys—**J**
Manning-Sanders, Ruth—**3**
Mare, Walter De La. See De La Mare, Walter—**J**
"Mariana" (Marian Curtis Foster)—**3**
Mark, Jan—**5**

Mars, W. T. (Witold TadeuszJosef Mars)—**4**
Marshak, I. A. See "Ilin, M."—**J**
Marshall, James—**4**
"Martin, Fredric." See Christopher, Matt—**5**
Martin, Patricia Miles. See "Miles, Miska"—**4**
Mason, Miriam E.—**M**
Masters, Kelly Ray. See "Ball, Zachary"—**4**
Mathis, Sharon Bell—**4**
Matsuno, Masako (Masako Matsuno Kobayashi—**4**
Mayer, Marianna—**4**
Mayer, Mercer—**4**
Mayne, William ("Dynely James")—**3**
Mays, Victor (Lewis Victor Mays)—**4**
Mazer, Harry—**5**
Mazer, Norma Fox—**5**
McCaffrey, Anne (Inez)—**5**
McCloskey, Robert—**J**
McClung, Robert M.—**M**
McCord, David—**3**
McCracken, Harold—**J**
McCrindle, Honor Morfydd Arundel. See Arundel, Honor—**4**
McCully, Emily Arnold—**4**
McDermott, Beverly Brodsky. See Brodsky, Beverly—**5**
McDermott, Gerald—**5**
"McDole, Carol." See Farley, Carol—**5**
"McDonald, Jamie." See Heide, Florence Parry—**4**
McGinley, Phyllis—**J**
McGovern, Ann (Ann Weinberger McGovern Scheiner)—**4**
McGraw, Eloise Jarvis—**M**
McGraw, William Corbin. See Corbin, William—**M**
McHargue, Georgess ("Alice Elizabeth Chase," "Margo Scegge Usher")—**5**
McIlwraith, Maureen Mollie Hunter McVeigh. See Hunter, Mollie—**3**
McKillip, Patricia A(nne)—**5**
McKinley, (Carolyn) Robin—**5**
McKown, Robin—**3**
McLean, Allan Campbell—**4**
McMeekin, Isabel McLennan —**M**
McNeely, Marian Hurd—**J**
McNeer, May—**J**
McNeill, Janet (Janet McNeill Alexander)—**4**
McPhail, David(Michael)—**5**
McPherson, Margaret—**4**
McSwigan, Marie—**M**
Meader, Stephen W.—**J**
Meadowcroft, Enid—**J**
Meaker, Marijane. See "Kerr, M. E."—**4**
Means, Florence Crannell—**J**

Medary, Marjorie—**J**
Mehdevi, Anne Sinclair—**4**
Meigs, Cornelia—**J**
Meltzer, Milton—**3**
Mendoza, George—**3**
Merriam, Eve—**3**
Merrill, Jean—**3**
"Metcalf, Suzanne." See Baum, L. Frank—**3**
Meyer, Carolyn (Mae)—**5**
Meyer, June Jordan. See Jordan, June—**4**
"Michael, Manfred." See Winterfeld, Henry—**3**
Miers, Earl Schenck—**3**
Mikolaycak, Charles—**5**
Miles, Betty—**5**
"Miles, Miska" (Patricia Miles Martin)—**4**
Milhous, Katherine—**J**
Miller, Elizabeth Cleveland—**J**
Miller, Mitchell—**4**
Milne, A. A.—**J**
Minarik, Else—**3**
"Minier, Nelson." See Stoutenburg, Adrien—**3**
Mizumura, Kazue—**3**
Mockridge, Penelope Farmer. See Farmer, Penelope—**4**
Modell, Frank—**5**
Moeri, Louise—**5**
Mohr, Nicholasa—**5**
Monjo, F. N. (Ferdinand Nicholas III)—**5**
Montgomery, Rutherford—**M**
Montresor, Beni—**3**
Monvel, Boutet de. See Boutet de Monvel—**J**
Moon, Carl—**J**
Moon, Grace—**J**
Moore, Anne Carroll—**J**
Moore, Lilian (Lilian Moore Reavin)—**4**
Moore, Patrick—**4**
Moray Williams, Ursula (Ursula Moray Williams John)—**4**
Mordvinoff, Nicolas—**M**
"More, Caroline." See Cone, Molly—**3**
Morey, Walt—**3**
Morgan, Alfred P.—**M**
Mosel, Arlene (Tichy)—**5**
Mowat, Farley—**3**
Munari, Bruno—**3**
Murphy, Robert W.—**4**
Myers, Walter Dean—**5**

Nash, Ogden (Frediric Ogden Nash)—**4**
Naylor, Phyllis Reynolds—**5**
Nesbit, E.—**M**
Ness, Evaline—**3**
Neville, Emily—**T**
Newberry, Clare—**J**
Newcomb, Covell—**J**

Newell, Crosby. *See* Bonsall, Crosby Newell—**3**
Newell, Hope—**M**
Ney, John—**5**
"Nic Leodhas, Sorche" (Leclaire Gowans Alger)—**3**
Nichols, Ruth—**4**
Nicolay, Helen—**J**
Nixon, Joan Lowery—**5**
"Nodset, Joan L." *See* Lexau, Joan M.—**4**
Nolan, Jeannette Covert—**J**
North, Sterling—**3**
Norton, Alice Mary. *See* "Norton, Andre"—**M**
"Norton, Andre" (Alice Mary Norton)—**M**
Norton, Mary—**3**
Nöstlinger, Christine—**5**
Nuttall-Smith, Margaret Emily Noel. *See* Fortnum, Peggy—**4**

Oakley, Graham—**5**
O'Brien, Jack—**M**
"O'Brien, Robert C." (Robert Leslie Conly)—**4**
O'Cuilleanain, Eilís Dillon. *See* Dillon, Eilís—**3**
O'Dell, Scott—**M**
Olcott, Frances Jenkins—**J**
Olcott, Virginia—**J**
Olsen, Ib Spang—**3**
O'Neill, Mary—**3**
Orgel, Doris—**4**
Ormondroyd, Edward—**3**
Orton, Helen Fuller—**J**
"Osborne, David." *See* Silverberg, Robert—**3**
"Otis, James" (James O. Kaler)—**J**
Ottley, Reginald—**4**
Oxenbury, Helen (Helen Oxenbury Burningham)—**3**
"Paisley, Tom." *See* Bethancourt, T. Ernesto—**5**

Palazzo, Tony—**3**
Paradis, Adrian A.—**M**
Parish, Peggy—**4**
Parker, Bertha M.—**M**
Parker, Dorothy D.—**4**
Parker, Edgar—**3**
Parker, Nancy Winslow—**5**
Parker, Robert Andrew—**4**
Parnall, Peter—**3**
Parrish, Maxfield—**J**
Parton, Ethel—**J**
Pascal, Francine—**5**
Patch, Edith M.—**J**
Paterson, Katherine (Womeldorf)—**5**
Paton Walsh, Jill (Gillian Bliss Paton Walsh)—**4**
Paull, Grace A.—**J**

Pearce, Philippa—**3**
Peare, Catherine Owens—**M**
Pease, Howard—**J**
Peck, Anne Merriman—**J**
Peck, Richard—**5**
Peck, Robert Newton (III)—**5**
Peet, Bill—**3**
Pellowski, Anne—**5**
Peppé, Rodney—**5**
Perkins, Lucy Fitch—**J**
Petersham, Maud—**J**
Petersham, Miska—**J**
Peterson, Hans—**4**
Petry, Ann—**3**
Pevsner, Stella—**5**
Peyton, K. M. (Kathleen Herald)—**3**
Phillips, Ethel Calvert—**J**
"Phipson, Joan" (Joan Margaret Fitzhardinge)—**3**
Piatti, Celestino—**3**
Picard, Barbara Leonie—**3**
Pienkowski, Jan—**4**
Pier, Arthur Stanwood—**J**
Pincus, Harriet—**4**
Pinkwater, Daniel Manus—**5**
"Piper, Watty." *See* Bragg, Mabel Caroline—**4**
Pitz, Henry C.—**M**
Platt, Kin—**5**
Plume, Ilse—**5**
Pogány, Willy—**J**
Politi, Leo—**3**
Polland, Madeleine—**3**
Poole, Lynn—**M**
Pope, Elizabeth Marie—**5**
Portal, Colette (Colette Portal Folon)—**4**
Porter, Sheena (Sheena Porter Lane)—**3**
Potter, Beatrix—**J**
Poulsson, Emilie—**J**
Prelutsky, Jack—**5**
Preussler, Otfried—**4**
Price, Christine—**M**
Price, Edith Ballinger—**J**
Pringle, Laurence—**4**
Proudfit, Isabel—**M**
Provensen, Alice—**3**
Provensen, Martin—**3**
Pyle, Katharine—**J**

Quackenbush, Robert—**4**
Quennell, Charles Henry Bourne—**M**
Quennell, Marjorie—**M**

Rabe, Berniece (Louise)—**5**
Rackham, Arthur—**J**
Rand, Anne (or Ann)—**3**
Rand, Paul—**3**
"Randall, Robert." *See* Silverberg, Robert—**3**

Rankin, Louise S.—**M**
Ransome, Arthur—**J**
Raphael, Elaine. *See* Bolognese, Don—**4**
Raskin, Ellen—**3**
Ravielli, Anthony—**3**
Rawlings, Marjorie Kinnan—**3**
Raynor, Mary (Yoma)—**5**
Reavin, Lilian Moore. *See* Moore, Lilian—**4**
Reed, Philip—**3**
Reed, W. Maxwell—**J**
Rees, David (Bartlett)—**5**
Reeves, James—**3**
Reiss, Johanna (de Leeuw)—**5**
Rendina, Laura Cooper—**M**
Renick, Marion—**M**
Rey, H. A.—**J**
Rey, Lester del. *See* del Rey, Lester—**3**
"Rhine, Richard." *See* Silverstein, Virginia B.—**5**
Ribbons, Ian (Harold Ian Ribbons)—**4**
Rice, Eve (Hart)—**5**
Richard, Adrienne—**5**
Richter, Hans Peter—**4**
Ringi, Kjell (Kjell Arne Sorensen-Ringi)—**4**
Robbins, Ruth—**3**
Roberts, Willo Davis—**5**
Robertson, Keith—**M**
Robinson, Barbara (Webb)—**5**
Robinson, Irene B.—**4**
Robinson, Mabel Louise—**J**
Robinson, Tom—**J**
Robinson, W. W.—**J**
Rockwell, Anne F.—**5**
Rockwell, Harlow—**5**
Rockwell, Thomas—**5**
Rodgers, Mary (Mary Rodgers Guettel)—**5**
Rojankovsky, Feodor—**J**
Rolt-Wheeler, Francis—**J**
Roos, Ann—**M**
Rose, Elizabeth—**3**
Rose, Gerald—**3**
Rounds, Glen—**J**
Rourke, Constance—**M**
Rowe, Dorothy—**J**
Rowe, Helen Cresswell. *See* Cresswell, Helen—**4**
Rubel, Nicole—**5**
Ruffins, Reynold. *See* Sarnoff, Jane and Reynold Ruffins—**5**
Rugh, Belle Dorman—**3**
Ryan, Cheli Durán—**5**

Sabin, Edwin L.—**J**
Sachs, Marilyn—**4**
Saint-Exupéry, Antoine de—**4**
Sánchez-Silva, José—**3**
Sandberg, Inger—**3**
Sandberg, Lasse—**3**
Sandburg, Helga—**3**

Thompson, George Selden. *See* Selden, George—4
Thompson, Kay—4
Thorne-Thomsen, Gudrun—J
Thurber, James—M
Tiegreen, Alan—5
Titus, Eve ("Nancy Lord")—3
Todd, Ruthven—M
Tolkien, J. R. R.—M
Tomes, Margot (Ladd)—5
Torrey, Marjorie—M
Tousey, Sanford—J
Townsend, John Rowe—4
Travers, Pamela—J
Trease, Geoffrey—M
Tredez, Alain. *See* "Trez, Alain"—3
Tredez, Denise. *See* "Trez, Denise"—3
Treece, Henry—M
Tresselt, Alvin—M
Treviño, Elizabeth Borton de (Elizabeth Borton)—3
"Trez, Alain" (Alain Tredez)—3
"Trez, Denise" (Denise Tredez)—3
Tripp, Wallace (Whitney)—5
Trnka, Jiri—3
Tudor, Tasha—J
Tunis, Edwin—M
Tunis, John R.—M
Turkle, Brinton—3
Turner, Philip ("Stephen Chance")—4
Turngren, Annette—M

Uchida, Yoshiko—M
Uden, Grant—4
Udry, Janice—3
Ullman, James Ramsey—4
"Uncle Shelby." *See* Silverstein, Shel—5
Ungerer, Tomi—3
Unnerstad, Edith—3
Unwin, Nora S.—M
Urmston, Mary—M
"Usher, Margo Scegge." *See* McHargue, Georgess—5

Valen, Felice Holman. *See* Holman, Felice—4
Van Allsburg, Chris—5
Vance, Marguerite—M
"Van Dyne, Edith." *See* Baum, L. Frank—3
van Iterson, S. R. *See* Iterson, S. R. van.—4
Van Leeuwen, Jean—5
van Stockum, Hilda—J
Van Woerkom, Dorothy (O.)—5
Van Zwienen, Ilse Koehn. *See* Koehn, Ilse—5

Venturo, Betty Lou Baker. *See* Baker, Betty—3
Verne, Jules—J
Vining, Elizabeth Gray. *See* Gray, Elizabeth Janet—J
Viorst, Judith—4
"Vivier, Colette" (Colette Duval)—4
Voight, Virginia Frances—M
Voigt, Cynthia—5
Vugteveen, Verna Aardema. *See* Aardema, Verna—5

Waber, Bernard—3
Wahl, Jan—3
Waldeck, Jo Besse McElveen—J
Waldeck, Theodore, J.—J
Walden, Amelia Elizabeth—M
Wallace, Dillon—J
Wallner, John C(harles)—5
Walsh, Gillian Paton. *See* Paton Walsh, Jill—4
Warburg, Sandol Stoddard. *See* Stoddard, Sandol—4
Ward, Lynd—F. *See also* McNeer, May—J
Watkins-Pitchford, Denys James. *See* "BB"—3
Watson, Clyde—4
Watson, Sally Lou—4
Watson, Wendy (Wendy McLeod Watson Harrah)—4
Weber, Lenora Mattingly—M
Weil, Lisl—4
Weisgard, Leonard—J
Weiss, Harvey—3
Wellman, Manly Wade—M
Wells, Rhea—J
Wells, Rosemary—4
Wersba, Barbara—3
Werstein, Irving—4
Werth, Kurt—M
Westall, Robert (Atkinson)—5
Wheeler, Francis Rolt-. *See* Rolt-Wheeler, Francis—J
Wheeler, Opal—M
White, Anne Hitchcock—4
White, Anne Terry—M
White, E. B.—M
White, Eliza Orne—J
White, Pura Belpré. *See* Belpré, Pura—4
White, Robb—J
Whitney, Elinor—J
Whitney, Phyllis A.—J
Wibberley, Leonard—M
Wier, Ester—3
Wiese, Kurt—J
Wikland, Ilon—4
Wilder, Laura Ingalls—J
Wildsmith, Brian—3
Wilkins, Mary Huiskamp Calhoun. *See* Calhoun, Mary—3
Wilkinson, Barry—4
Wilkinson, Brenda—5

Willard, Barbara—4
Willard, Nancy—5
"Williams, Charles." *See* Collier, James Lincoln—5
Williams, Garth—M
Williams, Jay ("Michael Delving")—4
"Williams, Patrick J." *See* Butterworth, W. E.—5
Williams, Ursula Moray. *See* Moray Williams, Ursula—4
Williams, Vera B.—5
Williamson, Joanne S.—3
Wilson, Barbara Ker. *See* Ker Wilson, Barbara—4
Windsor, Patricia—5
Winterfeld, Henry ("Manfred Michael")—3
Winthrop, Elizabeth (Elizabeth Winthrop Mahony)—5
Wiseman, David—5
Wojciechowska, Maia—3
Wolf, Bernard—5
"Wolff, Sonia." *See* Levitin, Sonia—5
Wolitzer, Hilma—5
Wolkstein, Diane—5
Wondriska, William—3
Wood, Esther—J
Wood, James Playsted—4
Woody, Regina J.—M
Woolley, Catherine ("Jane Thayer")—M
Worth, Kathryn—J
Worth, Valerie (Valerie Worth Bahlke)—5
Wortis, Avi. *See* Avi—5
Wrightson, Patricia (Alice Patricia Wrightson)—4
Wuorio, Eva-Lis—3
Wyeth, N. C.—J
Wyler, Rose. *See* Ames, Rose Wyler—3
Wyndham, Lee—M

Yamaguchi, Marianne—3
Yamaguchi, Tohr—3
Yashima, Taro—M
Yates, Elizabeth—J
Yates, Raymond F.—M
Yaukey, Grace S. *See* "Spencer, Cornelia"—J
Yep, Laurence (Michael)—5
"Ylla" (Camilla Koffler)—M
Yolen, Jane (Jane Yolen Stemple)—4
York, Carol Beach—5
Youd, Samuel. *See* "Christopher, John"—4
Young, Ed—3
Young, Ella—J

Zalben, Jane Breskin—5

J—The Junior Book of Authors; M—More Junior Authors; 3—Third Book of Junior Authors

Picture Credits

Eddie Andino, Jack Gantos; *Enrique Arana,* Richard Cuffari; *Arax-Serjan Studios,* Thomas Rockwell; *Chris Alexander,* Mary Rodgers; *Steve Altman,* Patricia Windsor; *American Audio Visual,* Bernard Wolf; *Jerry Bauer,* Malcolm Bosse, Jane Gardam; *Ann Bennett,* David Mc-Phail; *Stephen Blos,* Joan Blos; *Henry Bolan,* Steven Kroll; *Frank Bulfer,* Doris Buchanan Smith; *John S. Butterworth II,* W.E. Butterworth; *Frank Coleman,* Seymour Simon William Sleator; *Susan Coles,* Alvin and Virginia Silverstein; *Bob Collister,* Barbara Cohen; *R.E. Condit Studio,* Dorothy Shuttlesworth; *William Coupon,* Jamake Highwater; *Jacquelyn L. Craft,* Louise Moeri; *Nancy Crampton,* Sandra Scoppettone; *Daniels Studio,* Marion Dean Bauer; *Egon T. Degens,* T. Degens; *Charles J. Egita,* Lee Bennett Hopkins; *Elsevier-Dutton Publishing Co.,* Mildred Taylor; *Andrew Festa,* Katherine Paterson; *Carolyn Field,* Elizabeth Marie Pope; *Finkle Photography,* Robert Cormier; *Trude Fleisshmann,* "Sheila Greenwald"; *Ralph Gabriner,* Vera B. Williams; *Eddie Gantos,* John Gantos; © *Joel Gardner,* John Gardner; *Bob Greenfield,* Eloise Greenfield; *The Guardian,* Ann Schlee, Robert Westall; *Archie Hamilton,* Brenda Wilkinson; *Keith Hawkins,* Shirley Hughes; *Mary Anne Hazo,* David Kherdian; *Pat Hill,* Ben Bova; *Susan Hirshman,* Elizabeth Shub, James Stephenson; *Tana Hoban,* Gerald McDermott; *George Janoff,* Isabelle Holland; © *1983 Barbette Johnston,* Alice Bach; *Lee Junda,* Adrienne Richard; *Jim Kalett,* David Macaulay; *Ellen Kelliher;* Joe Lasker; *Lillian Kemp Photography,* Jane Langton; *David Langley,* Elizabeth Levy; *Peter Letts, United Kingdom,* Graham Oakley; *Tom Lipton,* Rachel Isadora; *Eleanor Macdonald,* Mary Rayner; *Peter Mahoney,* Elizabeth Winthrop; *Michael Metz,* Nancy Willard; *James McGowan,* Harriet May Savitz; *Matt Miles,* Betty Miles; *Elaine Miller,* Alvin Schwartz; *Tim Morse,* Nancy Garden; *Dan O'Connor,* Tomie dePaola; *Richard Olson,* Aranka Siegal; *Altman Pach Studio,* Helen M. Hoover; *Pach Brothers,* Sulamith Ish-Kishor; *Jeff Peters,* Paul Zindel; *Pictures by Pitcher,* Norma Johnston; *Ruth Putter,* Harry Mazer, Norma Fox Mazer; *Rosemary Ranch,* Avi; *M. Roberts,* Georgess McHargue; *Jack Rosen,* Jan and Stan Berenstain; *Lizzy Rockwell;* Harlow Rockwell; *Mark Ross,* Beverly Brodsky; *Anand Rupo,* Robert Lipsyte; *Joel Seligmann,* Vicki Cobb; *Andrew Sharmat,* Marjorie Weinman Sharmat; *Gigi Shendler,* Leonard Baskin; *Michael Topf,* Ellen Conford; *Sophie Valenti,* Margaret Tomes; *Thomas Victor,* Hilma Wolitzer; © *Kurt Vonnegut,* Jill Krementz; *Babette S. Whipple,* Norma Farber; *Nancy White,* Stella Pevsner; *David Wilkinson,* Ruth Craft; *Matthew Wysocki,* Ashley Bryan; *Kathy Yep,* Laurence Yep.